GLOBAL SHIFT

7TH EDITION

2015

For Valerie, with love

GLOBAL SHIFT

MAPPING THE CHANGING CONTOURS OF THE WORLD ECONOMY

PETER DICKEN | 7TH EDITION

THE GUILFORD PRESS
New York   London

Copyright © Peter Dicken 2015

Published in the United States of America by
The Guilford Press
A Division of Guilford Publications, Inc.
370 Seventh Avenue, Suite 1200, New York, NY 10001
www.guilford.com

Printed and bound in Great Britain by Ashford Colour Press

This book is printed on acid-free paper

Last digit is print number: 9   8   7   6   5   4   3   2   1

Library of Congress Cataloging-in-Publication Data

Dicken, Peter.
   Global shift: mapping the changing contours of the world economy/Peter Dicken. — Seventh
edition.
      pages cm
   Includes bibliographical references and index.
   ISBN 978-1-4625-1955-2 (pbk.)
1. Industries—History—20th century. 2. International economic relations. 3. International
business enterprises. 4. Economic policy. 5. Globalization—Economic aspects.
6. Technological innovations—Economic aspects. I. Title.
HD2321.D53 2015
338.09′051—dc23   2014029508

Praise for Global Shift

SEVENTH EDITION

"Given the rapid changes in the configuration of the global economy, *Global Shift, Seventh Edition*, will be welcomed by academicians and assigned in graduate and undergraduate classes. While retaining the strengths that have made prior editions much adopted around the world, the seventh edition has been updated to weave in such important new topics as the impact of the recent global financial crisis, the global smartphone infrastructure, climate change, corporate social responsibility, and national and international inequality. Readable case studies and excellent figures and graphs provide students with the empirical illustrations they need to understand the larger theoretical concepts. A remarkable update by the foremost economic geographer of globalization that should be on everyone's reading list."

—Martin Kenney, Department of Human Ecology,
University of California, Davis; Senior Project Director,
Berkeley Roundtable on the International Economy

"*Global Shift, Seventh Edition*, continues to be a key resource for understanding the complexity of the global economy and the ongoing, often contentious negotiations among nations, corporations and locales. In addition to clearly outlining larger institutional and structural processes, Dicken provides a wealth of detailed new empirical material to explain how the outcomes of the global economy manifest in specific contexts. The book's diverse concrete examples – such as the global production network of iPhones or corporate strategies to shield profits from taxation – are drawn directly from the headlines. An extremely valuable text for all courses on economic geography, globalization, international business and economics."

—Matthew Zook, Department of Geography, University of Kentucky

"Given the dizzying pace of change in the global economy, it's more important than ever to have a comprehensive point of reference to allow us to understand and map the transformations around us. *Global Shift, Seventh Edition*, is that book.

While continuing to add new material on countries, sectors and the policies that shape global industries, *Global Shift* also provides a solid analytical framework that helps the reader navigate the new terrain. And its great graphs, diagrams and charts are a visual delight. If you had to use just one book to convey globalization's promise and perils, this is the book I would recommend."

—Gary Gereffi, Department of Sociology and Center on Globalization, Governance and Competitiveness, Duke University

"Not just an update, the seventh edition of *Global Shift* offers compelling theoretical and empirical insights as it takes on the critical global political-economic processes and debates of our time. Dicken provides a welcome synthesis and interrogation of prevailing theories of the global economy and addresses such fraught issues as the 2008 financial crisis and the intensification of inequality. An amazing resource."

—Erica Schoenberger, Department of Geography and Environmental Engineering, The Johns Hopkins University

"*Global Shift* defines the gold standard in the field of globalization studies, which it has had a large hand in defining. The revised seventh edition continues to accomplish what no other book in the field does – it presents a grounded but broad view of globalization, judiciously assesses the key debates and recognizes (but never drowns in) complexity. *Global Shift* combines an authoritative voice with meticulous documentation and outstanding illustrations; it's the trusted source."

—Jamie Peck, Canada Research Chair in Urban and Regional Political Economy, University of British Columbia

"I used this text in my undergraduate Global Apparel Industry Dynamics class. It is a valuable text that explains the critical components and dynamics of the global economy in a straightforward and engaging style that is accessible to undergraduates as well as graduates. Dicken provides important historical perspectives on the evolution of the global economy while keeping abreast of recent developments. Key industries are examined in a relevant manner, adding an extra dimension to the work. *Global Shift* will equip any young graduate/executive with important insights into the global characteristics of business environments."

—Peter Kilduff, Professor and Chair, Department of Apparel Merchandising and Management, California State Polytechnic University, Pomona

"*Global Shift* has become the de facto textbook for middle- and upper-level courses in economic geography. Dicken synthesizes the economic, political and social complexities of globalization in highly accessible prose. The case studies of various industries contribute to a better understanding of the processes of globalization."

—Marc Vachon, Department of Geography, University of Winnipeg

SIXTH EDITION

"A magnificent achievement. Since the publication of the first edition of *Global Shift* in 1986, Peter Dicken has constructed in successive editions a phenomenal record of the changing geography of capital accumulation on a world scale. This wholly new sixth edition of 2011 is an essential companion for anyone concerned to understand the rapid geographical shifts occurring in the world's economic power relations in these stressful and troubled times."
—David Harvey, Distinguished Professor, CUNY Graduate Center, New York

"A masterful new edition of a masterful text. Once again, Peter Dicken is at the cutting edge of the analysis of economic globalization and global trends. *Global Shift* is the authoritative text on these issues."
—David Held, Co-Director, Centre for the Study of Global Governance, London School of Economics and Political Science

"*Global Shift, Sixth Edition*, continues to deconstruct globalization to show that distance (economic geography) still matters. Dicken uses insights from international business research to demonstrate that world business activity is more regional than global. Multinational enterprises are at the hub of global production networks and service delivery; they interact with governments and generally act as agents of economic development. In short, economic geography and international business are closely aligned in their approach to globalization."
—Alan Rugman, Henley Business School, University of Reading, UK

FIFTH EDITION

"A comprehensive, balanced, thorough, interdisciplinary review of one of the critical issues of our time. A 'must' for anyone interested in globalization."
—Stephen J. Kobrin, The Wharton School, University of Pennsylvania

"Impressive in the extent of empirical research, *Global Shift* successfully captures the historical continuities and basic changes marking the world economy. Peter Dicken's new edition is a vividly written guide to globalizing processes."
—James H. Mittelman, School of International Service, American University

"*Global Shift, Fifth Edition*, remains the benchmark for studies of the geography of globalization. In accessible prose, Dicken presents tightly argued propositions about the emerging economic landscape. The fields of international business, economic geography, international relations, and economic sociology can profitably use the book to communicate the fundamentals of globalization. Clear, effective, and engaging case studies are

ideal for classroom use. There is no other text with such a broad reach or appeal for anyone interested in understanding the contemporary international economy."
—Amy K. Glasmeier, Department of Geography,
The Pennsylvania State University

"*Global Shift* just keeps on getting better. There is no other source that gives you the full story on globalization in such a fluent and authoritative way. This book is not just recommended, but essential."
—Nigel Thrift, Vice-Chancellor, University of Warwick, UK

"With this edition of *Global Shift*, Dicken confirms his mastery as one of the preeminent authorities in the study of globalization. This careful and penetrating analysis of the complexities of a unifying world should prove a seminal text for students, scholars, and policymakers. If you wish to explore beyond 'flatland,' I can't recommend a better source."
—William E. Halal, Department of Management Science,
George Washington University

"The fifth edition of *Global Shift* remains at the top of the ever more crowded field of globalization texts. Peter Dicken is a master of weaving together new theoretical arguments, visually compelling charts and graphs, and insightful industry case studies. If you had to use just one book to convey globalization's promise and perils, this is the book I would recommend."
—Gary Gereffi, Department of Sociology and Center on Globalization,
Governance and Competitiveness, Duke University

FOURTH EDITION

"Dicken identifies states and transnational corporations as the two key actors in the multiple processes of restructuring and institutionalization that we usually call the global economy. In so doing, he has written a political economy of globalization and produced a far more comprehensive account than is typically the case in books about the global economy, most of which tend to confine the analysis to firms and markets."
—Saskia Sassen, Ralph Lewis Professor of Sociology, The University of Chicago

"In these uncertain times, it is reassuring to have Peter Dicken as our guide to the world economy. No other commentator has his eye equally attuned to both the big picture of global corporations and capital flows, and the fascinating stories of local places, people, and industries. In this new edition of *Global Shift*, Dicken shows us once again why he has become one of the most respected social scientists studying the world of global business and economy."
—Meric Gertler, Department of Geography, University of Toronto, Canada

"The book presents not only a thorough and balanced description and analysis of globalization, but also a nuanced explanation of the globalization–antiglobalization debates and provocative examination of the distributional consequences of globalization. I will certainly continue to use *Global Shift* in my graduate seminar. In fact, I am contemplating using it in my introductory economic geography course as well."

—Robin Leichenko in *Economic Geography*

"A solid 640-page text on the phenomena of globalization in the modern age … provides detailed case studies of crucial global industries, more than 200 updated figures and tables, and well serves to broaden and illustrate the critical points toward understanding the world's economic future. This is an ideal text for classroom instruction and recommended to the attention of non-specialist general readers with an interest in understanding the complexities of global economics."

—*Library Bookwatch*

"One of human geography's minuscule number of ambassadorial texts. The social sciences, the humanities, and international business studies will be much poorer when *Global Shift* ceases emerging as regularly as a Tissot watch keeps time."

— Kris Olds in *Progress in Human Geography*

THIRD EDITION

"*Global Shift* has become a landmark and a classic. It remains a popular text whose strength lies in its clear presentation and analysis of empirical data and in its focus on the production chain. This alone makes it a welcome corrective for the many speculative works on globalization based, as Dicken says, more 'on rhetoric and hype than on reality'."

—Paula Cerni in *Review of Radical Political Economics*

"By far the best and most readable account of the past three decades of economic globalization. Replete with maps, graphs, and tables, the book offers the clearest and most complete exposition of the scale and depth of the transformation currently affecting all societies."

—John O'Loughlin in *Lingua Franca*

"A first-rate and eminently readable work, with a unique blend of empirical and conceptual material and an analytical depth rarely achieved in textbooks. The third edition of *Global Shift* continues to be one of the most useful, interesting, and readable texts in the field of economic geography. I thoroughly recommend it both to students of geography and to readers in other disciplines who are interested in seeing what contemporary economic geography is really all about."

—John Holmes, Department of Geography,
Queen's University, Kingston, Ontario, Canada

Contents

List of Abbreviations

ABS	Advanced business services
AFTA	ASEAN Free Trade Agreement
ANCOM	Andean Common Market
APEC	Asia-Pacific Economic Cooperation forum
ASEAN	Association of South East Asian Nations
B2B	Business-to-business
B2C	Business-to-consumer
BAIC	Beijing Automotive Industrial Corporation
BIS	Bank for International Settlements
BRIC	Brazil, Russia, India, China
BSE	Bovine spongiform encephalopathy
CA	Controlled atmosphere
CAFTA	Central American Free Trade Agreement
CAP	Common Agricultural Policy (EU)
CARICOM	Caribbean Community
CCC	Clean Clothes Campaign
CFC	Chlorofluorocarbon
CIS	Commonwealth of Independent States
CIVETS	Colombia, Indonesia, Vietnam, Egypt, Turkey, South Africa
CKD	Completely Knocked Down
CME	Coordinated market economy
CMEA	Council for Mutual Economic Assistance
CRA	Contingency Reserve Arrangement (BRICs)
CSO	Civil society organization
CSR	Corporate social responsibility
CUSFTA	Canada–US Free Trade Agreement
DC	Distribution centre
ECB	European Central Bank
ECE	Eastern and Central Europe
EDB	Economic Development Board (Singapore)
EDI	Electronic Data Interchange
EEC	European Economic Community
EFTA	European Free Trade Association

EMU	European Monetary Union
EOI	Export-oriented industrialization
EPB	Economic Planning Board (South Korea)
EPC	Electronic product code
EPOS	Electronic point of sale
EPZ	Export processing zone
ETDZ	Economic and Technological Development Zone (China)
ETI	Ethical Trading Initiative
EU	European Union
FAW	First Auto Works
FCCC	Framework Convention on Climate Change
FDI	Foreign direct investment
FSB	Financial Stability Board
FTAA	Free Trade Area of the Americas
G7	Canada, France, Germany, Italy, Japan, UK, USA
G8	G7 plus Russia
G20	Argentina, Australia, Brazil, Canada, China, France, Germany, India, Indonesia, Italy, Japan, South Korea, Mexico, Russia, Saudi Arabia, South Africa, Turkey, UK, USA, EU
GATS	General Agreement on Trade in Services
GATT	General Agreement on Tariffs and Trade
GCC	Global commodity chain
GCSO	Global civil society organization
GDP	Gross domestic product
GFA	Global Framework Agreement
GHG	Greenhouse gas
GII	Global Innovation Index
GM	Genetic modification
GNC	Global network connectivity
GNH	Gross national happiness
GNI	Gross national income
GNP	Gross national product
GPN	Global production network
GSM	Global social movement
GSP	Generalized system of preferences
GVC	Global value chain
HVF	High-value food
IATA	International Air Transport Association
IC	Integrated circuit
ICAO	International Civil Aviation Organization
ICFTU	International Confederation of Free Trade Unions
ICSR	International corporate social responsibility
ICT	Information and communications technology

IFI	International financial institutions
ILO	International Labour Organization
IMF	International Monetary Fund
IMO	International Maritime Organization
IPCC	Intergovernmental Panel on Climate Change
ISI	Import-substituting industrialization
IT	Information technology
ITU	International Telecommunication Union
JIT	Just-in-time
JLR	Jaguar Land Rover
LAFTA	Latin American Free Trade Area
LAIA	Latin American Integration Association
LBL	Labour Behind the Label
LDC	Less developed country
LETS	Local exchange trading system
LME	Liberal market economy
LSP	Logistics services provider
MAI	Multinational Agreement on Investment
MBS	Mortgage-based securities
METI	Ministry for Economy, Trade and Industry (Japan)
MFA	Multi-Fibre Arrangement
MFN	Most-favoured nation
MINT	Mexico, Indonesia, Nigeria, Turkey
MIST	Mexico, Indonesia, South Korea, Turkey
MITI	Ministry of International Trade and Industry (Japan)
MNC	Multinational corporation
MPI	Multidimensional Poverty Index
MSW	Municipal solid waste
MVMA	Motor Vehicle Manufacturers' Association
NAFTA	North American Free Trade Agreement
NDB	New Development Bank (BRICs)
NEM	Non-equity modes of international production
NGO	Non-governmental organization
NIE	Newly Industrializing Economy
NOC	National Oil Company
NTB	Non-tariff barrier
OECD	Organization for Economic Cooperation and Development
OFC	Offshore financial centre
OICA	International Organization of Motor Vehicle Manufacturers
OPEC	Organization of the Petroleum Exporting Countries
OPT	Outward Processing Trade
PGST	Permanent global summertime
PLC	Product life cycle

ppm	Parts per million
PRC	People's Republic of China
PTA	Preferential trading arrangement
QE	Quantitative easing
R&D	Research and development
RFID	Radio frequency identification
RIA	Regional integration agreement
RTA	Regional trade agreement
SAIC	Shanghai Automotive Industrial Corporation
SEZ	Special Economic Zone (China)
SME	Small and medium-size enterprises
SOE	State-owned enterprise
SPM	Solid particulate matter
SSA	Sub-Saharan Africa
SUV	Sports utility vehicle
SWF	Sovereign wealth fund
TCC	Transnational capitalist class
TCS	Tata Consultancy Services
TEU	Treaty on European Union
TNC	Transnational corporation
TNI	Transnationality Index
TPP	Trans-Pacific Partnership
TRIMS	Trade-Related Investment Measures
TRIPS	Trade-Related Intellectual Property Rights
TTIP	Transatlantic Trade and Investment Partnership
UNCTAD	United Nations Conference on Trade and Development
UNEP	United Nations Environment Programme
VOIP	Voice Over Internet Protocol
WCN	World city network
WHO	World Health Organization
WTO	World Trade Organization
WWW	World Wide Web

Preface to the Seventh Edition

What began, more than 30 years ago, as a one-off attempt to make sense of the changing geographies of the world economy has evolved, rather unexpectedly, into a longitudinal global project. Each successive edition, appearing at roughly four- or five-year intervals, has come to constitute a temporal and spatial 'marker' of the empirical changes in the configuration of the global economy and of changing interpretations of, and attitudes towards, 'globalization' and its effects on people and places.

Such a longitudinal perspective emphasizes the dangers of making hasty judgements about immediate events and extrapolating them into the future. What may seem to be dramatic changes at one moment in time can turn out to be ephemeral perturbations when seen from a longer-term perspective. Indeed, underlying the turbulent surface of change there is a great deal of continuity: of slower moving processes. Like the tectonic processes that reshape the earth's physical crust, their build-up may take long periods of time before we become fully aware of the true magnitude of change. The plate tectonics of the global economic map, therefore, are just as difficult to predict, but also as potentially catastrophic, as those of the earth's physical map. It is this interplay between the short and the long term that makes a project like this so challenging.

The basic principles on which *Global Shift* is based derive from my deep belief that we need:

- an approach to globalization that is firmly *grounded* in the real world but which is not merely empirically descriptive;
- an approach that engages with the theoretical and ideological/political issues of globalization, drawing upon a wide range of literature and ideas;
- an approach that allows us to adopt a more considered perspective on how the immediate 'events of the moment' fit into the longer-term underlying processes of global economic change so that we are not swept away by instant predictions about the future;

- an approach that recognizes that globalization is a profoundly complex set of interlocking economic, political and social processes that operate in highly uneven ways over space and time and in ways that are not easily predictable but which have immense effects (both positive and negative) on people's lives.

With these principles in mind, the basic aim of this Seventh Edition, as of its six predecessors, is to provide a clear path through the dense thickets of what are large, often conflicting, often confusing, debates and arguments about globalization; to show how the global economy works and what its effects are. It tries to separate the reality from the hype; to provide a balanced, grounded – but emphatically not an uncritical – perspective on a topic often richer in rhetoric than reality.

What is new about the Seventh Edition? As in all the previous editions, I have set out to produce the most up-to-date and comprehensive account of economic–geographic globalization. Hence, all the empirical data have been fully updated using the latest available sources as of early 2014. (Of course, anybody who has worked on the global scale will appreciate that this inevitably means that the 'latest' data always lag behind what we would ideally like to have.) The illustrations, which form such an integral element of this book, are, for the first time, in full colour, which greatly enhances their effectiveness. Each is either completely new or has been redesigned. Every chapter has been completely revised and extensively rewritten not only to take into account new empirical developments, but also to incorporate new ideas on the shaping and reshaping of production, distribution and consumption in the global economy. There is specific discussion of some of the key issues that have come to the fore in recent years, including:

- the continuing impact of the 2008 global financial crisis, an issue that permeates all of the chapters to a greater or lesser degree;
- the growing controversy over the tax-avoiding strategies of transnational corporations and other aspects of corporate social responsibility within increasingly interconnected and shifting business networks;
- the continuing debates over economic governance institutions and policies at the global, regional and national scales in the spheres of finance, trade and the environment;
- the fundamental issues of employment, unemployment, inequality, poverty and development, both between and within developed and developing countries;
- the real relevance of the so-called BRICs (and other over-simplifying categorizations);
- the eurozone crisis and broader issues and conflicts within the EU.

One major structural change has been made for the Seventh Edition. The sectoral case studies that made up Part Three of previous editions have been moved to the end to become Part Four. The previous Part Four ('Winning and Losing in the Global Economy') becomes Part Three, to create a much more direct connection between the discussion of the *processes* of global shift (Part Two) and the *outcomes* of these processes. This change, I think, improves the coherence and flow of the argument – at least I hope so.

Otherwise, *Global Shift* continues to be both a *cross-disciplinary* and a *multilevel* book. It deliberately spans, and draws from, a wide range of academic disciplines, including business and management, development studies, economics, economic geography, political science and sociology. At the same time, the book is designed for use at different levels. On the one hand, my aim is to make the book accessible to readers without any prior specialist knowledge by ensuring that all key terms are clearly defined, by avoiding excessive jargon and by making extensive use of graphics. On the other hand, for the specialist reader, each chapter contains end-of-chapter notes that connect to the extremely extensive and up-to-date research bibliography. Through such means, the book should be useful to undergraduate and graduate students and researchers, as well as to policy makers and to people in business. Certainly my experience of the reception of previous editions suggests that this is so.

★★★

With each successive edition, my debt to friends, colleagues and users of the book has widened and deepened. Indeed, without a rich network of friends and colleagues from all round the world, a book like this simply could not exist. To all of them, I offer my sincere thanks and I hope they will forgive me for not mentioning them all by name. However, several people deserve special mention. First in line must be Nick Scarle, Senior Cartographer at the University of Manchester. Nick has been responsible for designing and producing all the illustrations for all seven editions. Always superb, they have simply got better and better. Indeed, this book could not exist as it does without Nick's creativity, commitment and enthusiasm. I am immensely grateful to him. Second, I continue to rely on – and to appreciate so very much – the stimulus and friendship of Neil Coe and Henry Yeung, forged through long collaboration on global production networks at the University of Manchester (though both are now at the National University of Singapore). They, together with Martin Hess, Roger Lee, Anders Malmberg, Liu Weidong, Jamie Peck, Adam Tickell, Kevin Ward and Ray Hudson, amongst many others, provide continuing support and friendship. I particularly want to thank the following colleagues for providing material and inputs for specific topics: Neil Coe (Chapters 3, 17), Martin Hess (Chapter 3), Mark Graham, Matt Zook and Martin Dodge (Chapter 4), Liu Weidong (Chapters 6, 10, 15), Gavin Bridge (Chapter 12), and James Faulconbridge (Chapter 16). Henry Yeung (NUS), David Inglis (Exeter University) and Richard Woodward (Hull University) have created invaluable guides to supplemental reading material for the website, while Fiona Moore (Royal Holloway University of London) has again done an excellent job in devising and producing the support materials for business and management users of the book. Of course, none of them bears responsibility for any errors or misinterpretations on my part.

I am, as ever, extremely grateful to the team at SAGE Publications in London. SAGE is a publisher for whom I am proud to write. In particular, my long-standing editor, Robert Rojek, is the most caring, encouraging and stimulating publisher and friend. Katherine Haw has, yet again, lavished enormous skill and care on creating a visually stimulating book. I would also like to thank Keri Dickens, Izzi Drury and Michael Ainsley for all their help and enthusiasm. Thanks, too, to Seymour Weingarten and the staff at The Guilford Press in New York, especially C. Deborah Laughton.

However, at the end of the day, as the saying goes, it all ultimately comes back to the people who matter to me most of all: my family. Michael, Sally, Jack and Harry in Switzerland, Christopher and Annika in Germany are all such great fun to be with. And then, above all, there is Valerie, who makes everything worthwhile and who (still) does so with so much love, humour and tolerance. This is for her.

Peter Dicken
Manchester, 2014

About the Companion Website

GLOBAL SHIFT, 7th edition, is supported by a companion website including a range of additional teaching and learning resources.

Visit the companion website to take advantage of online resources, including:

FOR STUDENTS
www.guilford.com/dickenGS7

Student notes including applied case studies, further reading and discussion questions

Glossary flashcards to help you review key terms

Selected readings across Geography, Sociology and Politics

FOR LECTURERS
www.guilford.com/dickenGS7-instructors

Lecturer notes offering suggestions for discussion questions, exercises, further reading and multimedia that you can incorporate into your teaching

PowerPoint slides that can be used in lectures or edited to fit your needs

Features of the Companion Website for Global Shift

On the companion website for *Global Shift* – **www.guilford.com/dickenGS7** – you will find resources for each chapter:

- **Questions** that test your understanding of the Applied Case Study and **Further Reading** for each chapter for **Business, Management** and **Organization Studies**
- Suggested **Further Reading** for each chapter for **Geography, Politics** and **Sociology**; with an explanation of why each reading is important and relevant
- A set of **interactive flashcards**, so you can always test your knowledge of key terms

In addition, there are Applied Case Studies for each chapter and video overviews by Peter Dicken of each section:

1 What in the World Is Going On?

- **Video**: Peter Dicken introduces the new, 7th edition of *Global Shift*: How do we understand the complexity of globalization?: five approaches
- An **Applied Case Study**: How globalized was the world between 1880 and 1914? What are the differences between then and now?

PART ONE: THE CHANGING CONTOURS OF THE GLOBAL ECONOMY

2 The Centre of Gravity Shifts: Transforming the Geographies of the Global Economy

- **Video**: Peter Dicken introduces Part One of the new, 7th edition of *Global Shift*: How the world is changing; patterns of trade, investment and production; the rise and fall of economies – all understood in the long-term context
- An **Applied Case Study**: How important is the free circulation of labour to the formation of global networks? **Hamada's 'Under the Silk Banner'**

PART TWO: PROCESSES OF GLOBAL SHIFT

3 Tangled Webs: Unravelling Complexity in the Global Economy

- **Video**: Peter Dicken introduces Part Two of the new, 7th edition of *Global Shift*: How is change produced, what are the underlying processes, who are the key actors and institutions, who has the power, how do they all interact?
- An **Applied Case Study**: How does a global civil society organization use global networks to promote and achieve its aims? **Oxfam**

4 Technological Change: 'Gales of Creative Destruction'

- An **Applied Case Study**: What can a transnational social democracy movement show about the development of global networks and the unevenness of power relations? **www.indymedia.org**

5 Transnational Corporations: The Primary 'Movers and Shapers' of the Global Economy

- An **Applied Case Study**: How many ways can a transnational corporation be transnational, how diverse can the strategies be to accomplish this end? **ZwoBank and BMW**

6 The State *Really Does* Matter

- An **Applied Case Study**: How does the state act globally outside of formal policy making and economic activity? **The Chinese diaspora**

PART THREE: WINNING AND LOSING IN THE GLOBAL ECONOMY

7 The Uneasy Relationship Between Transnational Corporations and States: Dynamics of Conflict and Collaboration

- **Video**: Peter Dicken introduces Part Three of the new, 7th edition of *Global Shift*: Winning and losing in the global economy, the complex relations between transnational corporations and states

- An **Applied Case Study**: How does a company develop a 'stateless' image, and yet continue to have relationships with states, particularly with its home country? **Deutsche Bank**

8 'Capturing Value' within Global Production Networks

- An **Applied Case Study**: How complex is the relationship for transnational corporations between global and local within global production networks? **McDonalds**

9 Destroying Value? Environmental Impacts of Global Production Networks

- An **Applied Case Study**: How does social identity – factors like gender, class and ethnic identity – relate to how individuals recycle? **Waste**

10 Winning and Losing: Where You Live Really Matters

- An **Applied Case Study**: Does the present period of globalization show the emergence of a transnational elite, or 'transnational capitalist class'? **German business people and diplomats in London**

11 Making the World a Better Place

- **Video**: Peter Dicken introduces Part Four of the new, 7th edition of *Global Shift*: Variation across sectors – the processes of globalization involve the same actors but differ from case to case, sector to sector
- An **Applied Case Study**: What are the ongoing arguments for and against micro-finance as a tool for alleviating global poverty? **Micro-finance**

PART FOUR: **THE PICTURE IN DIFFERENT SECTORS**

12 'Making Holes in the Ground': The Extractive Industries

- An **Applied Case Study**: Is taking materials out of the ground a neutral activity, or one which can be undertaken in more or less ethical ways? **Shell**

13 'We Are What We Eat': The Agro-food Industries

- An **Applied Case Study**: How are labels and narratives used by pro- and anti–genetic-modification factions to influence consumer choice? **GM foods**

14 'Fabric-ating Fashion': The Clothing Industries

- An **Applied Case Study**: How is an African exporter influenced, formally and informally, by global and local debates about gender, labour and centre–periphery relations? **Lesotho**

15 'Wheels of Change': The Automobile Industry

- An **Applied Case Study**: What advantages and disadvantages has the most recent period of globalization – since the 2008 global recession – brought? **General Motors**

16 'Making the World Go Round': Advanced Business Services

- An **Applied Case Study**: How do 'global cities' act as hubs of networks developed by transnational businesses, migrants, activists and others in global production networks? **London**

17 'Making the Connections, Moving the Goods': Logistics and Distribution Services

- An **Applied Case Study**: Is e-tailing a completely different and revolutionary development from conventional forms of retailing? **Amazon.com**

One

WHAT IN THE WORLD IS GOING ON?

5/2/2016

THE END OF THE WORLD AS WE KNEW IT?

During the past 50 years the world economy has been punctuated by a series of crises. Many of these turned out to be quite limited and short-lived in their impact, despite fears expressed at the time. Some, however, notably the oil-related recessions of 1973–9 and the East Asian financial collapse of 1997–8, were very large indeed, although neither of them came close to matching the deep world depression of the 1930s. And recovery eventually occurred. Meanwhile, during the last three decades of the twentieth century the *globalization* of the world economy developed and intensified in ways that were *qualitatively* very different from those of earlier periods. In the process, many of the things we used in our daily lives became derived from an increasingly complex geography of production, distribution and consumption, whose geographical scale became vastly more extensive and whose choreography became increasingly intricate. Most products, indeed, developed such a complex geography – with parts being made in different countries and then assembled somewhere else – that labels of origin began to lose their meaning. Overall, such globalization increasingly came to be seen by many as the 'natural order': an inevitable and inexorable process of *increasing geographical spread* and *increasing functional integration* between economic activities (Figure 1.1).

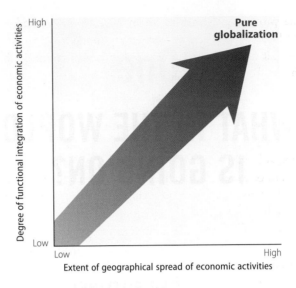

WHAT IN THE WO
IS GOING ON?

Figure 1.1   Globalization as inevitable trajectory

And then …

On 15 September 2008, the fourth largest US investment bank, Lehman Brothers, collapsed. It was an unprecedented event, heralding the biggest global economic crisis since the 1930s. And this crisis is still ongoing. The repercussions of the financial collapse that began with the disaster of the US 'sub-prime' mortgage market continue to be felt throughout the world, although to widely different degrees, as we will see throughout this book. Since 2008, for example, economic growth rates (production, trade, investment) have plummeted in most of the developed world, notably in parts of Europe but also in North America. In all these cases, job losses have been huge, and the fall in incomes of the majority of the population has been so serious as to place many more people and households on the margins of survival. At the same time, the incomes and wealth of the top 1 per cent have continued to increase even more astronomically, creating enormous social tensions and an upsurge of popular resistance in many countries. The most obvious recent example is the Occupy movement, which first emerged in late 2011 as 'Occupy Wall Street', using 'We are the 99%' as its rallying cry. In comparison, some developing countries – the so-called 'emerging markets' – have experienced relatively high growth rates, leading some observers to talk of the emergence of a 'two-speed world economy'. But that broad-brush picture, though valid in some respects, masks continuing and deep-seated issues of poverty and deprivation throughout the world. The notion that developing countries can somehow 'decouple' from the effects of financial crisis in developed countries is demonstrably far from the truth.

To individual citizens, wherever they live, the most obvious foci of concern are those directly affecting their daily activities: making a living, acquiring the necessities of life, providing the means for their children to sustain their future. In the industrialized countries, there is fear – very much intensified by the current financial crisis – that the dual (and connected forces) of technological change and global shifts in the location of economic activities are adversely transforming employment prospects. The continuing waves of concern about the outsourcing and offshoring of jobs, for example in the IT service industries (notably, though not exclusively, to India), or the more general fear that manufacturing jobs are being sucked into a newly emergent China or into other emerging economies, suddenly growing at breakneck speed, are only the most obvious examples of such fears. Such fears are often exacerbated by concerns about immigration, especially among lower-skilled workers who perceive, correctly or incorrectly, a double squeeze of jobs moving abroad and those at home being taken by immigrants on low wages. But the problems of the industrialized countries pale into insignificance when set against those of the very poorest countries. The development gap persists and, indeed, continues to widen alarmingly.

Hence, the world continues to struggle to cope with the economic, social and political fallout of the unravelling of the global financial system which occurred with such sudden, and largely unanticipated, force in 2007–8. The spectacular demise of Lehman was only one of many casualties. But its collapse was highly symbolic. Lehman was one of those institutions that epitomized the neo-liberal, free market ideology (sometimes known as the 'Washington Consensus') that had dominated the global economy for the previous half century. This was the ideology of so-called free and efficient markets: that the market knew best and that all hindrances to its efficient operation – especially by the state – were undesirable. But in 2008, all this was suddenly thrown into question. As one financial institution after another foundered, as governments took on the role of fire-fighters, and as several banks became, in effect, nationalized, the entire market-driven capitalist system seemed to be falling apart.

Question: does the economic turmoil that broke out in 2008 herald 'the end of the world as we knew it', 'the end of globalization'? Well, it all depends on what we mean by 'globalization': it is important to distinguish between two broad meanings of the term:[1]

- One is *empirical*. It refers to the actual *structural* changes that are occurring in the way the global economy is organized and integrated.
- The other is *ideological*. It refers to the neo-liberal, free market ideology of the 'globalization project'.

These two meanings are often confused. Of course, they are not separate but it is important to be aware of which meaning is being discussed.

It is too early to say whether the free market ideology has been irrevocably changed by the global financial crisis. Some think it has. Many more think it should be. Others believe that, once the dust finally settles, it will be business as usual. That may, or may not, be the case. But globalization, as we will see throughout this book, has never been the simple all-embracing phenomenon promulgated by the free market ideologists. We need to take a much more critical and analytical view of what is actually going on over the longer term; to move beyond the rhetoric, to seek the reality. That is one of the primary purposes of this book.

CONFLICTING PERSPECTIVES ON 'GLOBALIZATION'

Globalization is a concept (though not a term) whose roots go back at least to the nineteenth century, most notably in the ideas of Karl Marx. Indeed, in the light of the post-2008 crisis, many observers – even some who could by no stretch of the imagination be regarded as ideologically on the left – recognize that Marx's analysis of the development of global capitalism[2] was extremely acute and highly relevant to today's world. 'Globalization' as a term entered the popular imagination in a really big way only in the last four decades or so. Now it is everywhere. A perusal of Web-based search engines reveals millions of entries. Hardly a day goes by without its being invoked by politicians, by academics, by business or trade union leaders, by journalists, by commentators on radio and TV, by consumer and environmental groups, as well as by 'ordinary' individuals. Unfortunately, it has become not only one of the most used, but also one of the most *mis*used and one of the most *con*fused terms around today. As Susan Strange argued, it is, too often,

> a term … used by a lot of woolly thinkers who lump together all sorts of superficially converging trends … and call it globalization without trying to distinguish what is important from what is trivial, either in causes or in consequences.[3]

'Hyper-globalists' to the right and to the left

Probably the largest body of opinion – and one that spans the entire politico-ideological spectrum – consists of what might be called the *hyper-globalists*,[4] who argue that we live in a borderless world in which the 'national' is no longer relevant. In such a world, globalization is the new economic (as well as political and cultural) order. It is a world where nation-states are no longer significant actors or meaningful economic units and in which consumer tastes and cultures are homogenized and satisfied through the provision of standardized global products created by global corporations with no allegiance to place or community. Thus, the 'global' is claimed to be the *natural* order, an inevitable state of affairs, in which time–space has been compressed, the 'end of geography' has arrived and everywhere is becoming the same. In Friedman's terms, 'the world is flat'.[5]

This hyper-globalist view is the one shown in Figure 1.1. It is a myth. It does not – and is unlikely ever to – exist. Nevertheless, its rhetoric retains an extremely powerful influence on politicians, business leaders and many other interest groups. It is a world-view shared by many on both the political right and the political left. Where they differ is in their evaluation of the situation and in their policy positions:

- To the neo-liberals on the right – the *pro*-globalizers – globalization is an ideological project, one that, it is asserted, will bring the greatest benefit for the greatest number. Simply let free markets (whether in trade or finance) rule and all will be well. The 'rising tide' of globalization will 'lift all boats'; human material well-being will be enhanced. Although the neo-liberal pro-globalizers recognize that such a state of perfection has not yet been achieved, the major problem, in their view, it that there is too little, rather than too much, globalization.[6] Globalization is the *solution* to the world's economic problems and inequalities. This, then, is the global manifestation of the 'Washington Consensus' referred to earlier: the ideology of free and efficient markets regardless of national boundaries.

- To the hyper-globalizers of the left – the *anti*-globalizers – globalization is the *problem*, not the solution.[7] The very operation of those market forces claimed to be beneficent by the right are regarded as the crux of the problem: they are a malign and destructive force. Free markets, it is argued, inevitably create inequalities. By extension, the globalization of markets increases the scale and extent of such inequalities. Unregulated markets inevitably lead to a reduction in well-being for all but a small minority in the world, as well as creating massive environmental problems. Markets, therefore, *must* be regulated in the wider interest. To some anti-globalists, in fact, the only logical solution is a complete rejection of globalization processes and a return to the 'local'.

'Sceptical internationalists'

Although the notion of a global*ized* economic world has *become* widely accepted, some adopt a more *sceptical* position, arguing that the world economy was actually more open and more integrated in the half century prior to the First World War (1870–1913) than it is today.[8] The empirical evidence used to justify this position is *quantitative* and *aggregative*, based on national states as statistical units. Such data reveal a world in which trade, investment and, especially, population migration, flowed in increasingly large volumes between countries. Indeed, such levels of international trade and investment were not reached again (after the world depression of the 1930s and the Second World War) until the later decades of the twentieth century. In fact, international population migration has not returned to those earlier levels, at least in terms of the proportion of the world population involved in cross-border movement. On the basis of such quantitative evidence Hirst and Thompson argue that 'we do not have a fully globalized economy, we do have an international economy'.[9]

GROUNDING 'GLOBALIZATION': GEOGRAPHY REALLY DOES MATTER

Such national-level quantitative data need to be taken seriously. But they are only a part of the story. They do not tell us what kinds of *qualitative* changes have been occurring in the global economy. Most important have been the transformations in the *where* and the *how* of the material production, distribution and consumption of goods and services (including, in particular, finance). Old geographies of production, distribution and consumption are continuously being disrupted; new geographies of production, distribution and consumption are continuously being created. There has been a huge transformation in the *nature* and the *degree* of interconnection in the world economy and, especially, in the *speed* with which such connectivity occurs, involving both a *stretching* and an *intensification* of economic relationships. Without doubt, the world economy is a qualitatively different place from that of only 60 or 70 years ago, although it is not so much more open as *increasingly interconnected in significantly different ways*.

International economic integration before 1914 – and even until only a few decades ago – was essentially *shallow integration*, manifested largely through arm's-length trade in goods and services between independent firms and through international movements of portfolio capital and relatively simple direct investment. Today, we live in a world in which *deep integration*, organized primarily within and between geographically extensive and complex *global production networks (GPNs)*, and through a variety of mechanisms, is increasingly the norm.

Such qualitative changes are simply not captured in aggregative production, trade and investment data. For example, in the case of international trade, what matters are not so much changes in volume – although these are certainly important – as changes in its *composition*. There has been a huge increase in both *intra-industry* and *intra-firm* trade, both of which are clear indicators of more functionally fragmented and geographically dispersed production processes.[10] Above all, there have been dramatic changes in the operation of financial markets, with money moving electronically round the world at unprecedented speeds, generating enormous repercussions for national and local economies. We certainly do not need to be reminded of what that means.

The crucial diagnostic characteristic of a 'global economy', therefore, is *the qualitative transformation of economic relationships across geographical space*, not their mere quantitative geographical spread. This involves 'not a single, unified phenomenon, but a *syndrome* of processes and activities'.[11] There is not one 'driver' of such transformative processes – certainly not the technological determinism so central in much of the popular globalization literature. In other words,

> globalization is a … supercomplex series of multicentric, multiscalar, multitemporal, multiform and multicausal processes.[12]

It is because of such complexity that it is totally naive, for example, to try to explain uneven development in terms of a single causal mechanism called 'globalization':

> Establishing a link between globalization and inequality is fraught with difficulty, not only because of how globalization is defined and how inequality is measured, but also because the entanglements between globalization forces and 'domestic' trends are not that easy to separate out.[13]

Globalizing processes, therefore, are reflected in, and influenced by, multiple geographies, rather than a single global geography: the local and the global are, in effect, inseparable.[14] Although there are undoubtedly global*izing* forces at work, we do not have a fully global*ized* world. In fact, as Figure 1.2 shows, several tendencies can be identified, reflecting different combinations of geographical spread and functional integration or interconnection rather than the unidirectional trajectory shown in Figure 1.1:

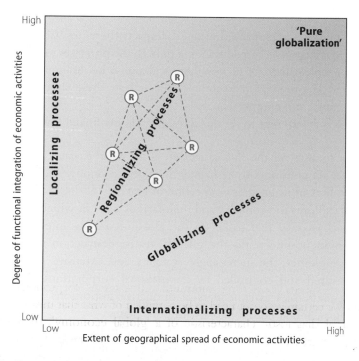

Figure 1.2 **Processes and scales of global economic transformation**

- *localizing* processes: geographically concentrated economic activities with varying degrees of functional integration;
- *internationalizing* processes: simple geographical spread of economic activities across national boundaries with low levels of functional integration;

- *globalizing* processes: both extensive geographical spread and a high degree of functional integration;
- *regionalizing* processes: the operation of 'globalizing' processes at a more geo-graphically limited (but supra-national) scale, ranging from the highly inte-grated and expanding EU to much smaller regional economic agreements.

Globalization, then, is not an inevitable end-state but, rather, a complex, indeter-minate set of *processes* operating very unevenly in both time and space. As a result of these processes, the nature and the degree of interconnection between different parts of the world are continuously in flux. A major task, therefore, is to challenge some of the more egregious *globalization myths*:

- The world is *not* flat (*contra* Friedman).
- The world is *not* borderless (*contra* Ohmae).
- Global corporations do *not* rule the world (*contra* Korten).
- Globalization is *not* always good (*contra* the neo-liberal hyper-globalizers).
- Globalization is *not* always bad (*contra* the anti-globalizers).

In trying to understand globalization and its impacts, therefore, we need to get real: to develop a *firmly grounded* understanding of both the processes involved and their impacts on people's lives. Of course, there will always be differences of diagnosis, prognosis and recommended treatment. But at least these should be based on sound conceptual and empirical analysis.

This book is an attempt to do this through a closely linked four-part structure:

- *Part One* focuses on the *shifting contours of the global economic map*: the 'global shifts' that are continuously reshaping the global economy and creating a pro-nounced shift in its geographical centre of gravity.
- *Part Two* explores the complex and multifarious ways in which the *actors, insti-tutions and processes* that make up the global economy interact to produce global production networks; the 'gales of creative destruction' set in motion by new technologies; the increasingly complex and extensive production net-works created and controlled by transnational corporations; the actions of states in their roles as containers of distinctive institutions and practices, as competitors, and as collaborators with other states.
- *Part Three* is concerned with *'winning' and 'losing'* in the global economy, on the *impact* of these processes *on people and places*: the uneasy relationships between TNCs and states, as each tries to exercise bargaining power over the other; the problems for national and local economies of capturing value in global pro-duction networks; the destruction of value through environmental degrada-tion; the staggeringly uneven contours of development; and, finally, the questions of how the world might be made a better place for all.
- *Part Four* presents six *sectoral case studies* to illustrate the diverse ways in which these processes actually operate in different contexts. The six cases have been

TNC = transnational corporation

carefully chosen to range across the entire spectrum of economic activities, from the basic/primary industries of mineral extraction and agro-food production, through such key global manufacturing industries as clothing and automobiles, to the advanced business, financial, logistical and distribution services that provide much of the 'lubrication' of the global economy. Precisely how production networks are configured and operate, precisely how TNCs, states, labour, consumers and CSOs are involved, precisely how they are subject to technological pressures, varies enormously between different kinds of economic activity.

5/2/2016

NOTES

1 See, for example, Chase-Dunn et al. (2000).
2 See Harvey (2011), Piketty (2014).
3 Strange (1995: 293).
4 A term introduced by Held and McGrew (2007: chapter 1). Jones (2010) provides a valuable survey of 'key thinkers' in the globalization literature. See also Cameron and Palan (2004).
5 Friedman (2005).
6 For an example of this position, see Friedman (1999, 2005). More nuanced writers within this general framework include Bhagwati (2004) and Wolf (2004).
7 See, for example, Greider (1997).
8 Hirst and Thompson (1992), Hirst et al. (2009).
9 Hirst and Thompson (1992: 394).
10 See Feenstra (1998), Gereffi (2005). A new initiative by the OECD and the WTO is attempting to capture this more fragmented nature of international trade by decomposing trade between countries according to the value added in each country. See OECD-WTO (2013).
11 Mittelman (2000: 4).
12 Jessop (2002: 113–14).
13 Amin (2004: 218).
14 See Massey (1994, 2005).

Want to know more about this chapter? Visit the companion website at **www.guilford.com/dickenGS7** for free access to author videos, suggested reading and practice questions to further enhance your study.

PART ONE

THE CHANGING CONTOURS OF THE GLOBAL ECONOMY

Two

THE CENTRE OF GRAVITY SHIFTS: TRANSFORMING THE GEOGRAPHIES OF THE GLOBAL ECONOMY

THE IMPORTANCE OF TAKING A LONG VIEW: THE IMPRINT OF PAST GEOGRAPHIES

Particularly at times of economic turbulence and uncertainty, it is all too easy to be dazzled by eye-catching forecasts about the changing shape of the global economy, especially potential winners and losers. Today, for example, we are presented with predictions of the rise of new 'miracle' economies: BRICs, MINTs, CIVETS, MISTs.[1] Such acronyms are seductive; people are always on the lookout for a catchy label, especially those responsible for them: notably investment bankers and business consultants. As we will see, some of these 'acronym economies' are more likely to be robust in the longer term than others. But we need to be careful in rushing to judgement, not least because of political uncertainties. After all, not so long ago, Yugoslavia was listed by the OECD as one of the world's 10 leading newly industrializing economies.

In fact, the global economic map is always in a state of 'becoming'. It is always, in one sense, 'new', but it is never finished. Old geographies of production, distribution and consumption are continuously being disrupted and new geographies are continuously being created. The new does not totally obliterate the old; what already exists constitutes the preconditions on which the new develops. Today's global economic map, therefore, is the outcome of a long period of evolution during which the structures and relationships of previous historical periods help to shape – though not to determine – the structures and relationships of subsequent periods. In that sense, we cannot fully understand the present without at least some understanding of the past. Indeed, traces of earlier economic maps – earlier patterns of geographical specialization or divisions of labour – continue to influence what is happening today.

There are continuing debates over when we can first identify a 'world' or a 'global' economy. To some, this appeared during what has been called the 'long sixteenth century' (1450 to 1640)[2] or with the 'eighteenth century transition to an industrial world'.[3] To others, the key period was the 1870s.[4] Regardless, 'by 1914 there was hardly a village or town anywhere on the globe whose prices were not influenced by distant foreign markets, whose infrastructure was not financed by foreign capital, whose engineering, manufacturing and even business skills were not imported from abroad, or whose labour markets were not influenced by the absence of those who had emigrated or by the presence of strangers who had immigrated. The economic connections were intimate …'[5]

Hence, over a period of 300 years or so, a *global division of labour* developed and intensified with industrialization, in which the newly industrialized economies of the West (led by the 'Atlantic' economies, notably the UK, some Western European countries, and later the USA) became increasingly dominant in a *core–periphery* configuration (Figure 2.1). Of course, over time, this structure became far more complex geographically. Some core economies declined to semi-peripheral status during the eighteenth century and new economies emerged, especially in the late nineteenth and early twentieth centuries. Figure 2.2 shows some of these dramatic changes,

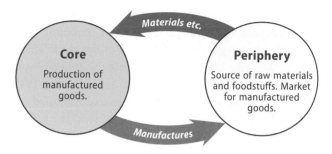

Figure 2.1   **A simple geographical division of labour: core and periphery in the global economy**

notably the steep decline of Asia and the emergence to unrivalled dominance of the USA, measured in terms of shares of global gross domestic product (GDP).

The broad contours of this core–periphery global economic map largely persisted until the outbreak of the Second World War in 1939. Manufacturing production remained strongly concentrated in the core: 71 per cent of world manufacturing production was concentrated in just four countries and almost 90 per cent in only eleven countries. Japan produced only 3.5 per cent of the world total. The group of core industrial countries sold two-thirds of its manufactured exports to the periphery and absorbed four-fifths of the periphery's primary products.[6] This long-established global division of labour was shattered by the Second World War, which destroyed most of the world's industrial capacity (outside North America). At the same time, new technologies were created and many existing industrial technologies were refined and improved.

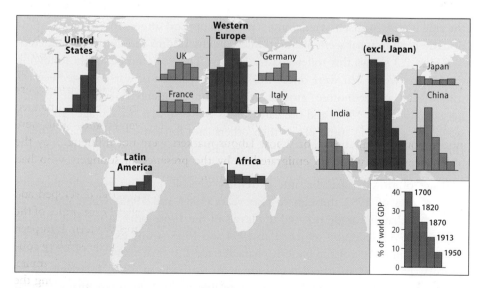

Figure 2.2   **Global shifts in GDP, 1700–1950**

Source: calculated from Maddison, 2001: Table B-20

The world economic system that emerged after 1945 reflected both the new geo-political realities of the post-war period and the harsh economic and social experiences of the 1930s. The major geopolitical division of the world after 1945 was that between the capitalist West (the USA and its allies) and the communist East (the Soviet Union and its allies). In the West the economic order built after 1945 reflected the domination of the USA. Alone of all the major industrial nations, the USA emerged from the war strengthened, rather than weakened: by 1950 the USA accounted for more than one-quarter of global GDP. It had both the economic and technological capacity and the political power to lead the way in building a new order, as, indeed, it did. The Soviet bloc drew clear boundaries around itself and its Eastern European satellites and created its own economic system (the CMEA – Council for Mutual Economic Assistance or Comecon) quite separate, at least initially, from the capitalist market economies of the West until its final break-up in 1989.

ROLLER-COASTERS AND INTERCONNECTIONS

Two particularly important features have characterized the global economy since 1950: the increased volatility of aggregate economic growth and the growing interconnectedness between different parts of the world.

The volatility of aggregate economic growth

The path of economic growth certainly does not run smooth. It is a real roller-coaster. Sometimes the ride is gentle, with just minor ups and downs; at other times, the ride is truly stomach-wrenching, with steep upward surges separated by vertiginous descents to what seem like bottomless depths. Booms and slumps are endemic.

Figure 2.3 shows this roller-coaster pattern. The years immediately following the Second World War were ones of basic reconstruction of war-damaged economies. Rates of economic growth reached unprecedented levels; the period between the early 1950s and the early 1970s was seen as a 'golden age'. In fact, it was more golden in some places than others, and for some people than others.[7] But then, in the early 1970s, the sky fell in. The long boom went bust; the 'golden age' became distinctly tarnished.

Rates of growth again became extremely variable, ranging from the negative growth rates of 1982 through to two years (1984 and 1988) when growth of world merchandise trade reached the levels of the 1960s once again. But then, in the early 1990s, recession returned. In 1994 and 1995, strong export growth reappeared. A similarly volatile pattern characterized the final years of the twentieth century. There was spectacular growth in world trade in 1997, followed by far slower growth in 1998 and 1999 (partly related to the East Asian financial crisis and to its contagious effects on other parts of the world). Then, once again, there

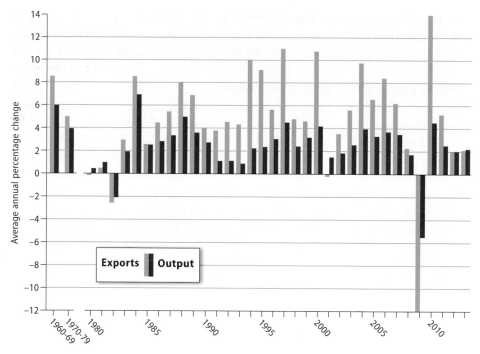

Figure 2.3 **The roller-coaster of world merchandise production and trade**

Source: calculated from WTO *International Trade Statistics*, various issues

was spectacular acceleration in world trade in 2000, followed by an equally spec-tacular bursting of the growth bubble, a problem certainly exacerbated (though not caused) by the 9/11 terrorist attacks on New York City and by the crisis in the IT (dotcom) sector of the so-called 'new' economy.

High growth rates returned once again. Then, in 2008, seemingly without warning, the deepest recession since the late 1920s suddenly occurred, triggered by the turmoil in the global financial system. In 2009, global exports *declined* by 12 per cent, in 2010 they recovered to grow by 14 per cent, in 2011 export growth was 5 per cent, in 2013 it had fallen again to around 2 per cent. The roller-coaster is back with a vengeance. Even short-term forecasts are proving very dif-ficult and frequently being revised.

Growing interconnectedness within the global economy

One major characteristic of global economic growth, therefore, is its inherent volatility. A second is the increasing *interconnectedness* of the global economy. Such interconnectedness has three major dimensions:

- trade has grown faster than output;
- foreign direct investment has grown faster than trade;
- serious structural imbalances in the world economy have emerged.

Trade has grown faster than output

Figure 2.3 shows that exports have grown much faster than output in virtually every year since 1960. In the second half of the twentieth century, world merchandise trade increased almost 20-fold while world merchandise production increased just over 6-fold. More and more production is now traded across national boundaries; countries are becoming more tightly interconnected through trade flows. This is reflected in the ratio of trade to GDP: the higher the figure, the greater the dependence on external trade. There is huge variation between countries in such trade integration. For example, international trade is bound to be more important for geographically small countries than for large ones, the result of a simple size effect (contrast, say, the USA with Singapore). However, in virtually all cases the importance of trade to national GDP has increased significantly, as Table 2.1 shows.

Table 2.1   **The increasing importance of trade for national economies (exports + imports as a percentage of GDP)**

	1960	1970	1985	1995	2000	2011
By income group						
High income	23.7	27.1	37.3	39.8	52.0	60.0
Middle income	–	–	–	55.9	55.0	64.0
Upper-middle income	34.3	36.4	41.8	51.4	55.0	64.0
Lower-middle income	–	–	–	58.7	53.0	63.0
Low income	–	34.6	41.8	60.5	45.0	67.0
By region						
East Asia and Pacific	20.1	18.6	35.7	58.3	62.0	70.0
China	9.3	5.2	24.0	40.4	44.0	58.0
India	12.5	8.2	15.0	27.7	27.0	54.0
Latin America and Caribbean	25.8	23.4	30.8	35.6	44.0	49.0
Sub-Saharan Africa	47.4	44.3	51.0	56.1	66.0	71.0
World	24.5	27.1	37.1	42.5	52.0	61.0

Source: based on Kaplinsky, 2004: Table 1; World Bank, 2013

Figure 2.4 maps the network of world merchandise trade. It shows the strong tendency for countries to trade strongly with their neighbours:

- Europe is the world's major trading region (39 per cent of the world total). Almost 70 per cent of that trade is intra-regional, that is between European countries themselves. Around 13 per cent of Europe's exports go to Asia and 7 per cent to North America.

- Asia is the second most significant trade region (29 per cent of the world total): 57 per cent of its trade is conducted internally while 12 per cent of its trade goes to Europe and 9 per cent to North America.
- North America (16 per cent of the world total) conducts around 38 per cent of its trade internally. Asia and Europe each account for 31 per cent of North America's trade and Europe for 16 per cent.

CIS - commonwealth of independent states

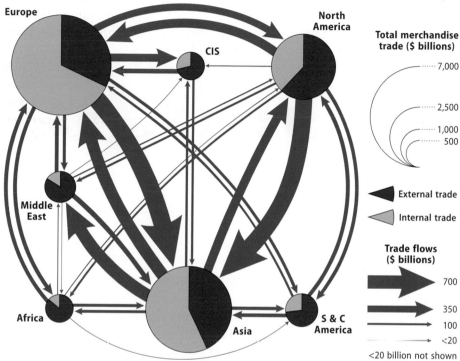

Figure 2.4   The network of world trade by region

Source: calculated from WTO, 2012: Table A2

FDI has grown faster than trade

A second indicator of growing interconnectedness is that the growth of foreign direct investment (FDI) has outpaced the growth of trade. 'Direct' investment is an investment by one firm in another, with the intention of gaining a degree of control over that firm's operations. 'Foreign' direct investment, therefore, is direct investment across national boundaries to buy a controlling investment in a domestic firm or to set up an affiliate. It differs from 'portfolio' investment, through which firms purchase stocks/shares in other companies purely for financial reasons.

Although FDI grew very rapidly during the first half of the twentieth century, such growth was nothing compared with its spectacular acceleration and spread after the

FDI

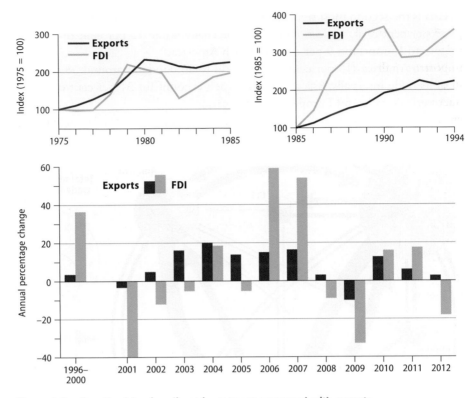

Figure 2.5   **Growth of foreign direct investment compared with exports**

Source: calculated from UNCTAD *World Investment Report*, various issues

end of the Second World War.[8] Figure 2.5 shows that during the 1970s and into the first half of the 1980s the trend lines of both FDI and exports ran more or less in parallel. Then, from 1985 the rates of growth of FDI and exports diverged rapidly. With some exceptions, FDI grew faster than trade, though with very wide fluctuations since the onset of the global financial crisis in 2008. Divergence in growth trends between FDI and trade is extremely significant: it suggests that the primary mechanism of interconnectedness within the global economy has shifted from trade to FDI.

However, these trends in the growth of FDI and trade are not independent of one another. The common element is the TNC. The number of TNCs has grown exponentially over the past three decades. In 2009, there were around 82,000 parent company TNCs controlling around 810,000 foreign affiliates.[9] TNCs account for at least two-thirds of world exports of goods and services, of which a significant share is intra-firm trade. In other words, it is trade within the boundaries of the firm – although across national boundaries – as transactions between different parts of the same firm. The 'ball park' estimate is that approximately one-third of total world trade is intra-firm, although that is probably an underestimate. One calculation is that 90 per cent of US exports and imports flow through a US [T]NC, with roughly 50 per cent of US trade flows occurring between affiliates of the same [T]NC.[10]

Unlike the kind of trade assumed in international trade theory – that trade takes place on an 'arm's-length' basis – intra-firm trade is not subject to external market prices but to the internal decisions of TNCs. Such trade has become even more important as the production networks of TNCs have become more complex and, in particular, as production circuits have become more fragmented and global. Such 'disintegration of production itself leads to more trade, as intermediate inputs cross borders several times during the manufacturing process'.[11] These are processes we will examine in detail in subsequent chapters.

A further measure of global integration, therefore, is the relative importance of inward and outward FDI to a country's economy, measured by its GDP. The relative importance of FDI to national economies has increased virtually across the board, a clear indication of increased interconnectedness within the global economy. In 2011, global FDI stocks were 30 per cent of world GDP (compared with only 10 per cent in the early 1990s).[12] But, as in the case of trade, the relative importance of FDI to national economies is highly variable. Table 2.2 shows this for a sample of countries. In virtually all cases, inward FDI has increased greatly in relative importance.

Structural imbalances in the world economy

The flexing and fluxing global economic map is the outcome of the major global shifts that have occurred over the past few decades. It is made up of complex

Table 2.2 Inward FDI as a share of GDP (%)

	1990	2012		1990	2012
Australia	24.8	39.0	Poland	0.2	47.3
Canada	19.4	35.9	Argentina	6.4	23.2
Denmark	6.8	47.3	Brazil	10.1	31.2
France	7.9	39.5	Chile	46.7	77.7
Germany	6.5	21.1	China	5.1	10.3
Ireland	78.8	113.9	Hong Kong, China	262.3	552.8
Italy	5.3	17.7	India	0.5	12.2
Japan	0.3	3.5	Indonesia	6.9	23.4
Netherlands	23.3	74.2	Korea	1.9	12.7
Spain	12.7	47.0	Malaysia	21.7	43.6
Sweden	5.2	71.7	Philippines	6.7	12.4
Switzerland	14.0	100.7	Singapore	78.5	252.3
UK	20.1	54.4	Taiwan	5.9	12.5
USA	9.4	26.2	Thailand	9.3	40.7
Czech Republic	2.5	69.6	Vietnam	3.8	51.6
Hungary	1.6	81.7			

Source: based on data in UNCTAD, 2013a: Web Table 7

interconnections, most notably those constituted through networks of trade and FDI. But such flows have created huge structural imbalances within the global economy. Figures 2.6 to 2.8 map the geography of trade surpluses and deficits in manufacturing, services and agriculture. The accumulated result of these three sets of trade balances creates a huge dilemma for the global economy: the potential instability created by the fact that some countries have huge trade and current account surpluses while others have enormous deficits:

> Countries with trade surpluses accumulated capital beyond their capacity to absorb it. Many ran large current account surpluses and accumulated record reserves. Countries with trade deficits financed their current account by increased borrowing abroad … China's current account surplus rose from 2 per cent of GDP in 2000 to an average of 10 per cent during 2005–07. The largest deficits were in high-income countries, with the US accounting for more than half the world's current account deficits. The US current account deficit increased from 4.3 per cent of GDP in 2000 to an average of 6 per cent in 2005–07 … As the global imbalances between savings and investment grew, countries with large deficits borrowed from countries with surpluses, while fast-growing exporters depended on expanding markets in deficit countries. China and other surplus economies accumulated record reserves … and sent capital overseas. The US and other deficit countries consumed more and financed their deficits by issuing more debt and equity.[13]

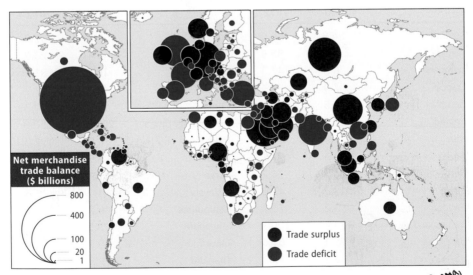

Figure 2.6   **The pattern of merchandise trade surpluses and deficits**
Source: calculated from WTO, 2012: Tables A6, A7

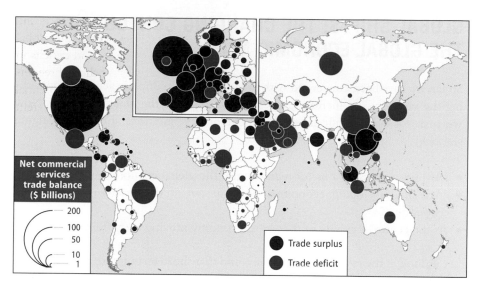

Figure 2.7 **The pattern of services trade surpluses and deficits**

Source: calculated from WTO, 2012: Tables A8, A9

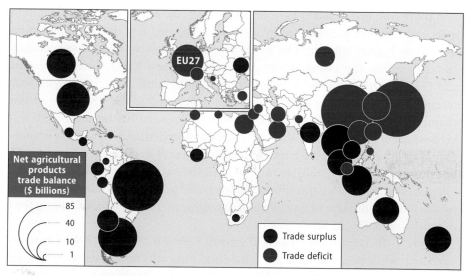

Figure 2.8 **The pattern of agricultural trade surpluses and deficits**

Source: calculated from WTO, 2012: Tables II.16, II.17

GLOBAL SHIFTS: THE CHANGING CONTOURS OF THE GLOBAL ECONOMIC MAP

So far, we have been concerned with broad trends in economic activity, emphasizing the volatility and increasing interconnectedness of the global economy. Now we turn to look specifically at a number of key questions about its changing *geography*:[14]

- Are we witnessing a major redrawing of the global economic map?
- Are the developing economies winning out at the expense of developed economies?
- Is the centre of gravity of the global economy moving away from west to east?

Let us look at the evidence, bearing in mind that short-term trends may not be an accurate predictor of long-term realities.

Continuing geographical concentration within the global economy – but a changing focus

Very substantial geographical shifts have undoubtedly occurred in the global economic map in the last few decades. At the broadest level, for example, the developing countries' share of global GDP, exports and inward FDI increased remarkably between 1990 and 2012, as Figure 2.9 shows. This is truly an epochal shift. However, by no means have all developing countries shared in the kinds of spectacular growth experienced by some over the past few decades. The figures tend to be heavily influenced by a few 'big hitters', notably China most recently and, before that, the so-called four Asian 'tigers' (Hong Kong, Korea, Singapore and Taiwan). Of course, the popular bets, at least by some financial analysts, have recently been on the 'acronym economies' mentioned at the beginning of this chapter: the BRICs, MINTs, CIVETS, MISTs. These, it has been claimed, will become the major players in a future world economy. Maybe they will. Certainly they have experienced rapid rates of economic growth in recent years, but it is far from clear that this is sustainable in every case. Indeed, in early 2014, the effects of US policy changes on its 'quantitative easing (QE)' policy led to increased pressure on the financial markets of several major emerging market economies, raising fears of serious capital flight from some of them.[15]

Figure 2.10 compares annual GDP growth between 2005 and 2012 for developed and developing countries as a whole and for a selection of individual countries. The contrasts are striking: GDP growth rates for developing countries were consistently very much higher than those for developed countries, in a few cases spectacularly so. But by 2013, there were clear signs of slowdown among many of these emerging market countries. Indeed, both the IMF and the OECD suggested in 2013 that 'momentum in the global economy is shifting away from emerging markets and back towards advanced economies after years in the doldrums'.[16] It is also important to stress that catching up is a slow process; that is why the contours of the global economy tend to change far more slowly than the short-term data often suggest. Once again, we need to beware of extrapolating short-term predictions into long-term certainties.

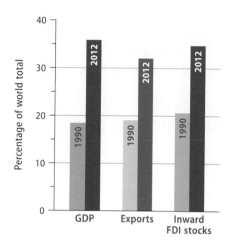

Figure 2.9   Developing countries' increasing shares of production, trade and foreign direct investment

Source: calculated from World Bank and UNCTAD data

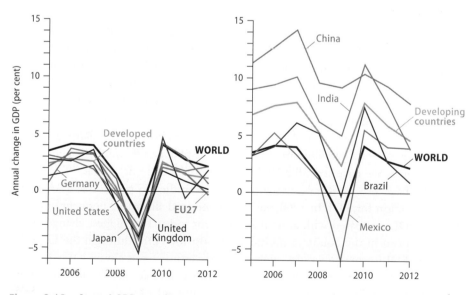

Figure 2.10   **Annual GDP growth rates**

Source: calculated from UNCTAD, 2013b: Table 1.1

In fact, the geographies of production, trade and FDI remain highly uneven and strongly concentrated. Around three-quarters of global manufacturing and services production, and around 90 per cent of world agricultural production, are concentrated in just 15 countries (Figures 2.13 to 2.15). Around one-fifth of world trade in goods, services and agriculture is generated by the two leading countries in each sector (Figures 2.16 to 2.18). The picture is similar in the case of FDI (Figure 2.19): more than 80 per cent of outward FDI stock originates from 15 countries. The leading two source countries – the USA and the UK – account for 30 per cent of the world total (Figure 2.20). Half of all the inward FDI in developing countries is concentrated in just five host countries; almost 30 per cent is concentrated in China and Hong Kong alone (Figure 2.21).

The USA still dominates the global economy – though less than it did

The USA has been the pre-eminent force in the global economy for almost 100 years, having displaced the original industrial leader, the UK, early in the twentieth century. However, its dominance has been much reduced as other competitors have emerged (see Figures 2.13 to 2.20). The USA has been overtaken as the world's leading manufacturing producer by China, although it is still the leading producer of commercial services (24 per cent). It remains the world's biggest foreign direct investor, the largest exporter of commercial services and agricultural products, and the third largest exporter of manufactured goods.

Between 1980 and 2003, US GDP grew at an annual average rate slightly above the world growth rate. But, as Figure 2.10 shows, its more recent growth has been weaker. Over the longer run, the deterioration in the US position is most apparent in the trade data, although trade is a smaller proportion of GDP in the USA than in all its major competitors, apart from Japan. Nevertheless, the US share of world merchandise exports has fallen from 17 per cent in 1963 to 8 per cent in 2011. At the same time, its share of merchandise imports has surged from less than 9 per cent to 12 per cent. Although US merchandise exports have grown at around 5 per cent a year, imports have grown at between 8 and 9 per cent a year. As a result, as we have seen, the USA has an enormous trade deficit.

There have also been very substantial changes in the US position as a source of, and destination for, FDI. In 1960, the USA generated almost 50 per cent of all the world's FDI, compared with around 20 per cent today. The biggest change, however, has been in the country's position as a host for FDI. Although the USA has attracted FDI for many decades, such inward investment was always a tiny fraction of the country's outward FDI. However, the USA has become significantly more important as an FDI destination. Inward and outward FDI are now much more balanced than in the past.

Europe is still a major player – but its performance is highly uneven

Europe, as a region, is the world's biggest trading area and the primary focus of global FDI. However, despite being the most politically integrated region in the world (see Chapter 6), the European economy is extremely diverse, experiencing variable rates of growth over the past two decades, as well as uneven rates of decline in the post-2008 recession. Between 2000 and 2007, the average annual rate of GDP growth in the core European countries was 2.3 per cent, significantly lower than the world average of 3.2 per cent and way behind those of East Asia and, indeed, of Eastern Europe. That differential widened in the post-2008 period (Figure 2.10).

Prior to 2008, the fastest growing Western European countries were the more 'peripheral' economies of Finland, Norway, Greece, Ireland and Spain. However, the last three, together with Portugal, were devastated by the 2008 recession and experienced severe contraction. The major difficulties facing Europe arise primarily from the wide economic divergences between member states in what is now a 28-state union. In particular, the massive strains experienced by many EU economies in the post-2008 recession – especially those of the weaker countries within the eurozone – pose problems that have no simple solutions.

Germany is by far the biggest European economy: the fourth largest manufacturing producer (after China, the USA and Japan), the second largest manufacturing exporter (recently overtaken by China), the third largest commercial services exporter and the third most important source of FDI.

Europe's second biggest economy, the UK, has experienced the greatest long-term relative decline insofar as it once dominated the world. It is now only the 10th-ranked manufacturing producer. However, it is still the world's second biggest source of FDI and second biggest exporter of commercial services.

There are considerable differences in trade performance between individual European countries. Whereas France, the UK, Spain and Italy have merchandise trade deficits, Germany, the Netherlands and Sweden have surpluses. In contrast, in commercial services the UK has a big trade surplus, France and Spain modest surpluses, while Germany has a substantial deficit.

Europe remains a major magnet for inward investment as well as the leading source of outward FDI.

Emergence of the 'transitional economies' of Eastern Europe and the Russian Federation

On 9 November 1989, the Berlin Wall came crashing down, making possible the reunification of West and East Germany. But this unforeseen event was of much broader significance. It represented both a concrete and a symbolic indicator of enormous geopolitical (and geoeconomic) change. The political collapse of the Soviet-led group of countries, and, indeed, of the Soviet Union itself, produced a group of so-called 'transitional economies': former command economies that transformed themselves into capitalist market economies. The process of transition, from a centrally planned economic system, with a heavy emphasis on basic manufacturing industries, to a capitalist market system, was painful and turbulent in many cases. The kinds of industries favoured in the centrally planned system were less viable in the context of a highly competitive global economy, as were the kinds of industrial organization themselves. In 1985, for example, the Soviet Union accounted for almost 10 per cent of world manufacturing output; by the mid-1990s, the share of the Russian Federation was around 1 per cent. Today, its share is 2.5 per cent. Nevertheless, Russia – identified as one of the BRICs – has become an increasingly significant presence in the global economy, especially in terms of its wealth of extractive resources, including oil and gas.

The transitional economies within Europe are a very diverse group. No fewer than 11 of them have become members of the EU and are therefore subject to both its opportunities and its constraints. These economies achieved impressive export performances during the 1990s. Poland, Hungary and the Czech Republic each had double-digit export growth while the Russian Federation and Slovenia grew at around 7–8 per cent per year. Such growth was underpinned largely by inward FDI, which grew substantially from the early 1990s, especially in the Czech Republic, Hungary, Poland and Slovakia. Much of this was driven by the shift of parts of firms' production networks from Western Europe to lower-cost Eastern European economies, as both the clothing and automobile industries demonstrate (see Chapters 14 and 15).[17] Between 2000 and 2007, the annual average growth rate of the leading Eastern European countries was 5.2 per cent, that of Russia was 6.6 per cent, on a par with, or even better than, some of the East Asian economies. However, the 2008 crisis created huge problems for these still rather fragile economies. Growth rates since then have been very low indeed, as has been the case in Europe as a whole as we have seen.

'Back to the future': the resurgence of Asia

By far the most significant global shift in the world economy during the past 50 years was a real 'back to the future' event: the *re*-emergence of Asia as the world's most dynamic economic region.[18] As Figure 2.2 shows, in 1700 Asia dominated the world economy: its share of global GDP was 62 per cent compared with the West's 23 per cent. But by 1950 those positions had been almost exactly reversed: the combined GDP of Western economies was almost 60 per cent; that of Asia (including Japan) was a mere 19 per cent. Much of this was due to the relative economic decline of China and India. In 1700, their combined share of global GDP was almost 50 per cent; by 1950, it had plummeted to less than 10 per cent. They had become totally peripheral. Today, the picture is so very different.

Although it often seems that the resurgence of Asia is just about China, it is, in fact, very much more than that. We can see it as a sequence of four developments:

- The rise of Japan after the Second World War.
- The rapid growth of what came to be called the 'four tigers': the newly industrializing economies of Hong Kong, Korea, Singapore and Taiwan. This was followed by the emergence of a second tier of East Asian developing economies, primarily Indonesia, Malaysia and Thailand.
- The (re-)emergence of China – the 'dragon' – as the increasingly dominant player in the global economy.
- The potential economic dynamism of India.

Japan

The world has become so obsessed with China that we tend to forget just how spectacular Japan's post-war economic growth really was. It is worth restating. Starting in the 1960s, Japan substantially transformed the global economy and laid the foundations for the subsequent development of other parts of East Asia. In the early 1960s, Japan ranked fifth in the world; by 1980 it had risen to second place. During the 1960s, Japan's rate of manufacturing growth averaged 13.6 per cent per year: two-and-a-half times greater than in the USA and four times greater than in the UK. The Japanese economy continued to grow at very high rates throughout the 1970s and most of the 1980s. Japan's share of world FDI grew from less than 1 per cent in 1960 to almost 12 per cent in 1990. As a result, 'Japan Inc.' came to be seen as the biggest threat facing both the USA and Europe, as a deluge of polemical, protectionist literature (especially in the USA) at the time demonstrated.

In the late 1980s, however, Japan's rapid growth rate fell as dramatically as it had risen in the 1960s, with the collapse of its so-called 'bubble economy'. Between 1990 and 2003, Japanese GDP grew at an annual average rate of only 1.2 per cent and its manufacturing sector by a mere 0.7 per cent. Merchandise exports, which had grown at almost 9 per cent a year between 1980 and 1990, grew at less than 3 per cent a year between 1990 and 2003. Growth was even lower between 2000 and 2007 (a mere 1.7 per cent). The US fear of the Japanese threat receded; the 'bash Japan' literature virtually disappeared. Nevertheless, Japan remains the world's third largest manufacturing economy and the second largest producer of commercial services. Japan's decline has been very much exaggerated.

The four tigers

At the same time as Japan was surging up the ranks of industrialized countries, a small group of East Asian developing countries also appeared on the scene as foci of manufacturing growth, especially in labour-intensive industries. The 'pioneers' were the so-called four 'tiger' economies of Hong Kong, Korea, Singapore and Taiwan. In terms of manufacturing production, for example,

- Korea's manufacturing sector grew at annual average rates of 18 per cent during the 1960s, 16 per cent during the 1970s, 13 per cent during the 1980s and 7 per cent during the 1990s (to 2003);

- Taiwan's manufacturing sector grew at rates of 16 per cent, 14 per cent, 8 per cent and 6 per cent respectively during the same periods.

Subsequently, Malaysia, Thailand and Indonesia also displayed extremely high rates of manufacturing growth.

In the global reorganization of manufacturing production and trade the increased importance of East Asia as an exporter of manufactures was unique in its magnitude. Seven East Asian NIEs (Korea, Hong Kong, Singapore, Taiwan, Indonesia, Malaysia, Thailand) increased their collective share of total world manufactured exports from a mere 1.5 per cent in 1963 to almost 20 per cent in 1999 (and remember that this period included the East Asian financial crisis of 1997–8, which had a devastating effect on most of the East Asian economies). By 2011, this share had declined to 13 per cent, largely as a result of the growth of China.

newly industrialized economies

So, it is in their role as exporters that the East Asian economies are especially significant. In some cases the transformation of their domestic economies was spectacular. For example, in 1980, less than 20 per cent of Malaysia's exports were of manufactures; by 1998 the figure was 79 per cent. In 1980 a mere 2 per cent of Indonesia's exports were of manufactures; in 1998 almost half was in that category. Others show a similar transformation. But they now face a very different competitive environment. Between 2000 and 2007, these economies grew at an annual average rate of 5.2 per cent; significantly above the world average, but far lower than in their 'golden age'.

China: rebirth of the dragon

Without question, the most recent, and the biggest, development within East Asia – indeed in the global economy as a whole – is the (re-)emergence of China. China has rather suddenly become a hugely significant presence in the global economy and 'China bashing' has replaced the 'Japan bashing' of an earlier period. Between 1980 and 2003, China's growth rate was the highest in the world, with annual average rates of well over 10 per cent. This remarkably high rate continued through to 2007. The 2008 global crisis inevitably had an effect and growth slackened, but it was still of the order of 9 per cent. Even in 2012, China's GDP grew by 7.8 per cent. Its average annual rate of growth of merchandise exports was 13 per cent in the 1980s and 14 per cent between 1990 and 2003. Exports as a share of China's GDP increased from 38 per cent in 2002 to over 50 per cent in 2012. As a result, China is now the world's largest manufacturing producer, the largest agricultural producer, the largest exporter of merchandise and the world's second largest importer (Figures 2.13 to 2.16). China has, indeed, become a 'mega-trader' (Figure 2.11).[19]

Figure 2.12 shows China's global trade networks in manufactures and fuels and mining products. The contrast between the two is striking. In the case of manufactures, exports dominate: China's main markets for its manufactures are other

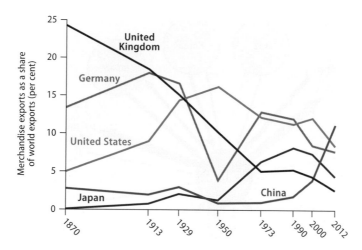

Figure 2.11   **The rise of China as a world 'mega-trader'**

Source: based on data in Subramaniam and Kessler, 2013: Table 2.2

parts of Asia (42 per cent), Europe (21 per cent) and North America (20 per cent). In the case of fuels and mining products, imports dominate: China's main sources for these commodities are Asia (33 per cent), the Middle East (22 per cent), Africa (13 per cent) and South and Central America (14 per cent).

The immense impact of China on the global economy over the past two decades has been especially significant in three major ways:[20]

- Through its effect on the *prices of commodities*. China is by far the world's biggest consumer of steel, aluminium, copper, zinc and nickel.
- Through its effect on the prices of manufactures, especially of labour-intensive products.
- Through its impact on capital flows, because of its accumulation of huge current account surpluses and foreign currency reserves.

Overall, then,

> the entry of China's massive labour force into the global economy may prove to be the most profound change for 50, and perhaps even for 100 years ... China's growth rate is not exceptional compared with previous or current emerging economies in Asia, but China is having a more dramatic effect on the world economy because of two factors: not only does it have a huge, cheap workforce, but its economy is also unusually open to trade. As a result, China's development is not just a powerful driver of global growth; its impact on other economies is also far more pervasive ... China's growing influence stretches much

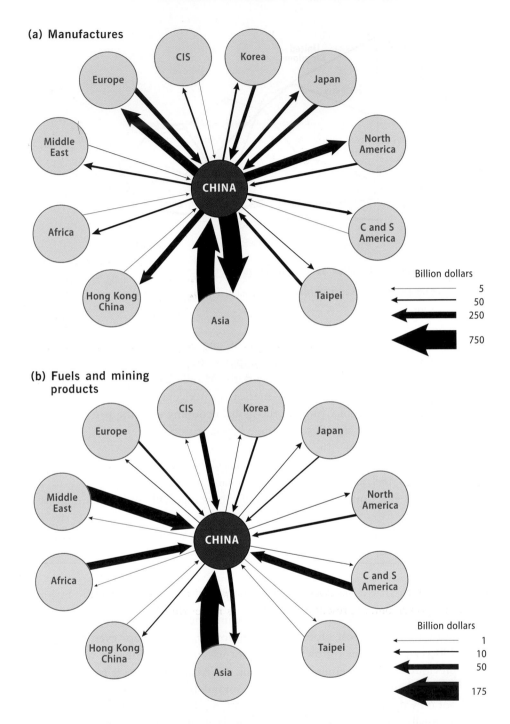

Figure 2.12   China's global trade network

Source: WTO, 2012: Table A22

deeper than its exports of cheap goods: it is revolutionising the relative prices of labour, capital, goods and assets in a way that has never happened so quickly before.[21]

Indian promise

Although most of the focus remains on China, recent attention has been drawn to the other very large Asian country (in population terms): India. Indeed, some commentators envisage a world economy that will increasingly be dominated by 'Chindia', defined by one writer as 'where the world's workshop meets its office',[22] an allusion to China's growth as a manufacturer and to India's growth in IT services. But beware the hype.

India has certainly shown spectacular growth in one specific type of economic activity: the outsourcing of IT services (software, data processing, call centres and the like). As such it has attracted huge publicity and a growing view that India could be 'the next China', given the size of its population and other advantages. That may be so. But, at present, the evidence is slender. India's GDP growth rate between 1980 and 2003, though well above the world average at between 5 and 6 per cent, was half that of China during the same period. Between 2000 and 2007, this difference lessened but remained significant. More recently, however, India's GDP growth has been only half that of China's.

India is the world's 11th largest manufacturing economy; China is number 1; India is not in the top 15 merchandise exporters, China is again number 1. Of course, it might be argued that India's strength lies in services rather than in manufacturing. Certainly it is true that the share of services in India's GDP is much higher than China's: 56 per cent compared with 42 per cent. Conversely, India has only 14 per cent of its GDP in manufacturing, compared with China's 30 per cent. Despite this, China generated one-third more commercial services exports than India in 2011. Unlike all the other fast-growing East Asian NIEs, India does not have a strong export base in manufactures. China's merchandise exports are six times larger than India's. Indeed, if India is ranked along with the leading NIEs of East Asia in terms of merchandise exports, India appears below Hong Kong, Korea, Singapore and Taiwan, despite being many times bigger than any of them. None of this is to suggest that India does not have the *potential* to become a really major economic power, but, at present, the evidence is rather thin.[23]

Latin America – unfulfilled potential

The Latin American and Caribbean region is once again facing a crisis of development. In 2005–6, growth rates lagged behind those of emerging economies in Africa, Asia and Eastern Europe and, except in certain pockets, indicators of social and human development were uninspiring and levels of inequality remained the highest in the world.[24]

Latin American countries are among the most resource-rich in the world. Several also have a long history of industrialization. Some, like Brazil and Mexico, are, in population terms, very large indeed. And yet most of the Latin American economies have not figured very prominently in the redrawing of the global economic map. Certainly, their modest economic performance contrasts sharply with that of East Asia. Within Latin America itself, there is huge diversity between individual economies. In general, however, few of them have 'punched their weight' as exporters. Over the past 20 years, their average export growth has been significantly lower than that of the East Asian economies.

Recently, as we saw earlier, the money has been on Brazil, as one of the BRICs. However, Brazil's GDP growth rate between 2000 and 2007 was by far the lowest of the four BRICs: half that of Russia, one-third that of China and less than half that of India. Its performance between 2008 and 2012 was rather stronger but, most recently, Brazil has been hit by the slowdown in commodity prices (especially by demand from China). Despite a long history of industrialization, and some undoubted successes (in automobiles, for example – see Chapter 15), Brazil's involvement in the world economy is mainly in primary commodities (agriculture, mining products). As such, it is highly vulnerable to fluctuations in commodity prices. Like India, Brazil has enormous economic potential but such potential is still far from being realized.

Mexico, on the other hand, has fared rather better, though very unevenly. Its very high export growth rate in the 1990s reflected its increasing integration with the USA through the North American Free Trade Agreement (see Chapter 6). However, Mexico's GDP growth between 2000 and 2007 was the lowest among the region's major economies (2.6 per cent, well below the world average as well). It seemed to be failing to take advantage of its preferential access (including its geographical proximity) to the USA. In particular, Mexico was being out-competed in the US market by China:

> Over half of Mexico's non-oil exports are under partial or direct threat from their Chinese counterparts. This 'threat' comprises all but a handful of Mexico's top 15 exports. What is more, recent changes indicate that Mexico's loss of export competitiveness to China may also be threatening the technological sophistication of its exports. Since 1994, Mexico has gained ground on China only in primary products ... Thus, Mexico is losing out in sectors abundant in unskilled labor where value-to-transport costs are cheap, but holding steady in assembly sectors where transport costs are more significant, and NAFTA's rules of origin serve as local content rules mandating that production stays in North America, such as lorries and autos.[25]

Recently, however, Mexico has performed much more strongly. Its competitiveness vis-à-vis China in the North American market has strengthened because of its advantageous geographical proximity (expressed in terms of time and cost of delivery). Between 2008 and 2012, Mexico's average annual GDP growth was 3.9 per cent compared with Brazil's 0.9 per cent.

The persistent peripheries

Alongside the areas of strong, though differential, economic growth in the global economy – the peaks as it were – are those parts of the world whose economic growth remains very limited. These are the 'persistent peripheries'. All of the maps shown at the end of this section tell more or less the same story: much of the continent of Africa, parts of Asia and parts of Latin America constitute the 'troughs' of the global economic map. Sub-Saharan Africa (SSA) is the largest single area of 'economic peripherality'. These are the parts of the world enmeshed in the deepest poverty and deprivation and whose existence poses one of the biggest social challenges of the twenty-first century.

But not all is gloom, by any means. Indeed, growth rates in many parts of Africa have risen substantially (albeit from very low base levels). According to the World Bank in 2013:

> The economic outlook for Sub-Saharan Africa is positive with growth rising to 5.3% in 2012 and 5.6% in 2013 ... African exports rebounded notably in the first quarter of 2012, growing at an annual pace of 32%, up from the −11% pace recorded in the last quarter of 2011. Growth has been widespread, with over a third of SSA countries posting six per cent or higher rates with another 40% growing between four to six per cent. Among fast-growing countries in 2011 were resource-rich countries such as Ghana, Mozambique and Nigeria.[26]

However, the continuation of such growth, especially for those peripheral countries heavily dependent on exporting commodities, is highly susceptible to external shocks. For example, there is no doubt that the insatiable demand by China for resources has driven recent growth in several African countries. Any major slowdown in Chinese growth, therefore, would have adverse effects. As always, there is the underlying danger of the 'resource curse' (see Chapter 10: p. 340).

THE CENTRE OF GRAVITY *HAS* SHIFTED

During the past six decades, the world economy has experienced enormous cyclical volatility, what we have described as the 'roller-coaster'. Underlying such cyclical trends, however, are deeper, longer-term *structural* changes, notably in the *geography* of the global economy, which has become increasingly *multi-polar*. New centres of production – new geographical divisions of labour – have emerged in parts of what had been, historically, the periphery and semi-periphery of the world economy. There have been big changes in the relative growth rates of different parts of the world. There has been a relative shift, in aggregate terms, from developed to developing economies although this should not be over-stated or, indeed, taken for granted. Many parts of the world remain, to a greater or lesser degree, disarticulated from the engines of economic growth.

Without doubt, the biggest single global shift reshaping the contours of the global economic map is the resurgence of East Asia to a position of global significance, commensurate with its importance before 'the West' overtook it in the nineteenth century. But this has not been a sudden event. As we have seen in this chapter, the resurgence of East Asia since the 1960s was manifested, initially, in the rise of Japan, whose spectacular growth across a whole range of manufacturing sectors transformed competitive relationships in the global economy. The relative decline of the Japanese economy in the 1990s was, however, counterbalanced by the spectacular (re-)emergence of China. At the same time, the original four 'tiger' economies continued to consolidate their strengths. The result is an *undoubted shift in the centre of gravity of the world economy*, a shift that seems now to be on solid foundations and not a mere passing phase.

But what of the future shape of the global economic map? It is always tempting ·to extrapolate recent trends. There is, of course, some logic in this. After all, there is a strong element of path dependency in human affairs. But it is not as simple as that. Path dependency does not mean determinacy. All paths have branching points: some go off in unexpected directions, others into dead-ends. Hence, it is almost impossible to identify with certainty which contemporary events and circumstances will have long-lasting effects. For example, when the East Asian financial crisis broke with such suddenness in 1997, the literature was full of prophecies of doom: the end of the East Asian 'miracle' had arrived. The future of the region was dire. Few would make those same predictions today. What of the outcome of the post-2008 financial crisis? Because we are still in the thick of it we cannot really see how the world will look in a few years' time.

Similarly, looking a little further back in time, who, from the standpoint of 1960, would have predicted that Japan would soon challenge the USA as an economic power and, in some respects, overtake it to the extent that, in the 1980s, doomsayers in the USA were lamenting the demise of their country as the world's leading economy? Japan bashing became a national pastime (and not only in the USA – there were outbreaks in Europe, too, especially in France). Who would have predicted that the Japanese economy itself would suddenly find itself deep in economic recession lasting for more than a decade and a half?

Who would have predicted that South Korea would become one of the world's most dynamic economies within the space of 20 years or so? After all, in 1960, South Korea was one of the poorest countries in the world, with a per capita income comparable with that of Ghana. Which observer in the early 1970s would have predicted that China would open up its economy and become, in a very short time, the most dynamic economy in the world? Or that the command economies of the Soviet Union and Eastern Europe would, by the end of the 1980s, begin to be transformed into capitalist market economies? Such examples should make us wary of prediction. But we do not learn. We are seduced, far too easily, by big numbers and by spectacular events. We focus too eagerly on the quantitative, rather than the qualitative, dimensions and processes of change.

This raises a much bigger question: will the tendency towards an increasingly highly interconnected and interdependent global economy intensify? Will the geographical centre of gravity continue to shift? Is 'globalization' an inexorable and unstoppable force? Not inevitably, as the period between 1919 and 1939 shows. During that time, the unprecedented openness of the world economy that had come into being in the period between 1870 and 1913 was largely reversed through the actions of states responding to recession through increased protectionism. It took several decades to return to a similar degree of openness, by which time the world was a very different place. Of course, the interconnections within the global economy are now much deeper – and faster – than in the past because of the ways in which the processes of production and distribution have been transformed. Primarily, this is because of the development of highly complex, geographically extensive, global production networks, which form the starting point of Part Two.

5/2/2016

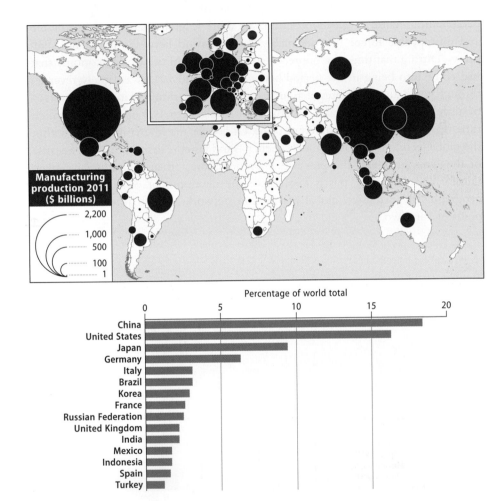

Figure 2.13   **The global map of manufacturing production**

Source: calculated from World Bank, *World Development Indicators*, 2013: Table 4.2

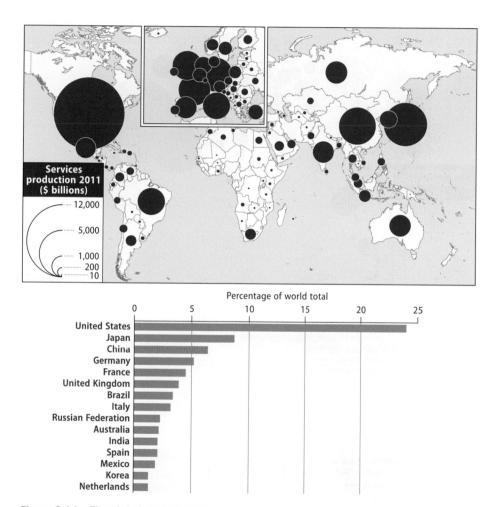

Figure 2.14   The global map of services production

Source: calculated from World Bank, *World Development Indicators*, 2013: Table 4.2

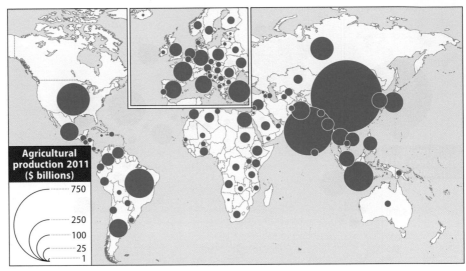

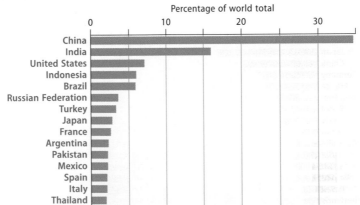

Figure 2.15   The global map of agricultural production

Source: calculated from World Bank, *World Development Indicators*, 2013: Table 4.2

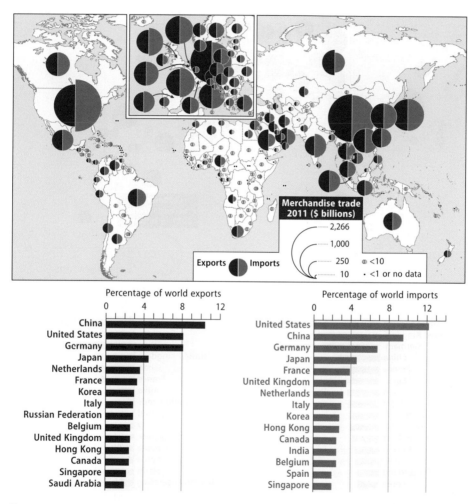

Figure 2.16   The global map of merchandise trade

Source: calculated from WTO, 2012: Tables A6, A7

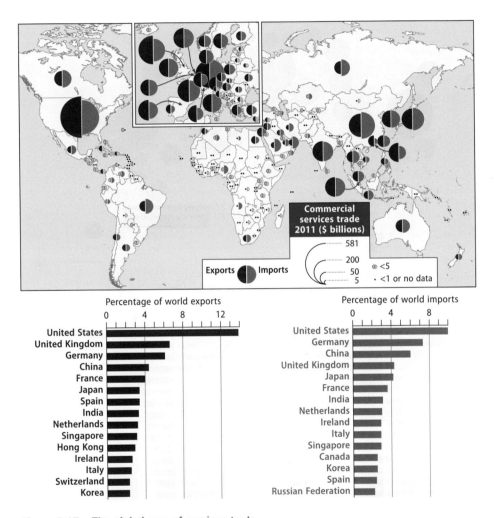

Figure 2.17   The global map of services trade

Source: calculated from WTO, 2012: Tables A6, A7

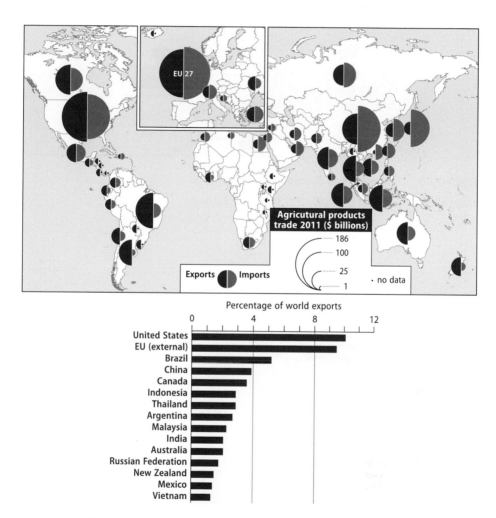

Figure 2.18   **The global map of agricultural trade**

Source: calculated from WTO, 2012: Tables II.16, II.17

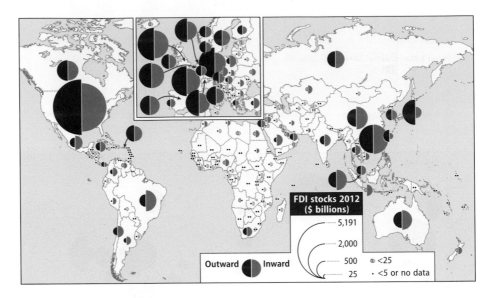

Figure 2.19   **The global map of inward and outward FDI**

Source: calculated from UNCTAD, 2013a: Annex Table 2

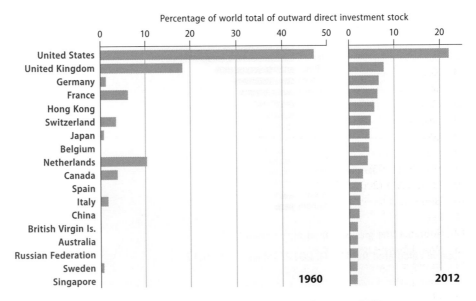

Figure 2.20   **Changing shares of leading source countries in outward FDI**

Source: calculated from UNCTAD, *World Investment Report*, various issues

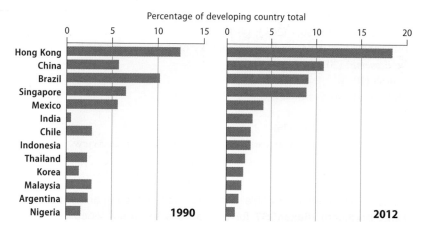

Figure 2.21 **Concentration of inward FDI in developing countries**

Source: calculated from UNCTAD, *World Investment Report*, various issues

NOTES

1   The acronym BRIC (Brazil, Russia, India, China) was introduced in 2001 by the chief economist of the US investment bank Goldman Sachs, Jim O'Neill. He also coined the acronym MIST (Mexico, Indonesia, South Korea, Turkey) in 2011. CIVETS (Colombia, Indonesia, Vietnam, Egypt, Turkey, South Africa) was introduced by the Economist Intelligence Unit in 2009. MINT is a slight variant on MIST, Nigeria replacing South Korea.

2   Wallerstein (1979).

3   Kozul-Wright (1995: 137).

4   See Bayly (2004), O'Rourke and Williamson (1999).

5   O'Rourke and Williamson (1999: 2).

6   League of Nations (1945).

7   Webber and Rigby (1996: 6).

8   Historical trends in FDI are discussed by Dunning and Lundan (2008) and Kozul-Wright (1995).

9   UNCTAD (2009: 17).

10   Blonigen (2006: 1).

11   Feenstra (1998: 34). See also Subramanian and Kessler (2013).

12   Subramanian and Kessler (2013: 7–8).

13   World Bank (2009a: 3).

14   In order to avoid breaking up the text, the detailed illustrations – Figures 2.13 to 2.21 – are gathered together at the end of the chapter.

15   *Observer* (2 February 2014).

16   *Financial Times* (4 September 2013).

17   Smith (2013).

18 Frank (1998) provides a long-run historical perspective.
19 Subramanian and Kessler (2013: 14–17).
20 Wolf (2008). See also Farooki and Kaplinsky (2012), Jacques (2012).
21 *The Economist* (20 July 2005).
22 Ramesh (2005).
23 See, for example, Saith (2008).
24 Phillips (2009: 231).
25 Gallagher et al. (2008: 1376).
26 World Bank, in 2013: www.worldbank.org/en/region/afr/overview.

Want to know more about this chapter? Visit the companion website at **www.guilford.com/dickenGS7** for free access to author videos, suggested reading and practice questions to further enhance your study.

PART TWO

PROCESSES OF GLOBAL SHIFT

Three

TANGLED WEBS: UNRAVELLING COMPLEXITY IN THE GLOBAL ECONOMY

5/5/2016

CHAPTER OUTLINE

CONNECTIONS, CONNECTIONS

In Chapter 2, we mapped the changing contours of the global economy, noting its immense geographical unevenness and temporal volatility. We now turn, in the four chapters of Part Two, to the *processes* of globalization; to an explanation of how such global shifts are produced. However, this is far easier said than done. There are, emphatically, no simple explanations of what are extremely complex and interrelated processes. So how and where do we start? What is a suitable point of entry?

The conventional unit of analysis of the global economy is the individual country. It is not difficult to see why this should be so. Virtually all the statistical data on production, trade, FDI, and the like are aggregated into national 'boxes'. However, such a level of statistical aggregation is less and less useful in light of the changes occurring in the *organization* of economic activities in today's far more complex world. Unfortunately, in empirical terms, we have to rely heavily on national-level data to explore the changing maps of production, trade and FDI. But, because national boundaries no longer 'contain' production processes as they once did, we need to find ways of getting below the national scale – to break out of the constraints of the 'national boxes' – in order to understand what is really going on in the world.

The key to opening up these boxes lies in the notion of *connectivity*. As we saw in Chapter 1, a diagnostic characteristic of contemporary globalization is that the component parts of the world economy are increasingly interconnected in qualitatively different ways from the past. Another way of saying this is that the world economy consists of *tangled webs of production circuits and networks that cut through, and across, all geographical scales*, including the bounded territory of the state. It is through an analysis of such networks – their participants, their interconnections, their power relationships – that we can begin to understand what is going on:

> The critical point about networks is that they involve *relational* thinking. What links people together across time and space? How are things and people connected and embedded economically, politically, and culturally? In what ways do goods and information and capital flow and why are they channelled down particular vertices and nodes? … Thinking in terms of networks forces us to theorize socioeconomic processes as intertwined and mutually constitutive.[1]

Figure 3.1 is based on such a network perspective. Its purpose is to provide both a structural perspective on globalization processes and outcomes and a sense of how the key 'actors' behave. In particular, it emphasizes the complex ways in which they are interconnected and governed through highly unequal *power* relationships. In fact, such a simplified diagram attempts the impossible: to capture and represent the multidimensionality of the global economy in just two dimensions. It is

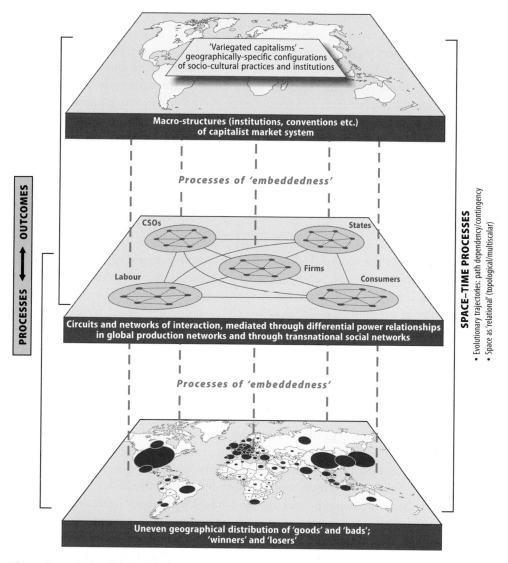

Figure 3.1 **A simplified analytical framework of the global economy**

Source: based on Dicken, 2004: Figure 2   CSO = civil society organization

an *idealized* representation of a world that is, in reality, infinitely more complex. Inevitably, it both grossly oversimplifies and distorts relationships and causalities. In particular, it is difficult not to imply a top-down set of processes whereas, in fact, we are dealing with a world of very complex, dynamically interconnected and simultaneous processes. So, the three layers in Figure 3.1 are not hierarchical 'top-down' levels but, rather, should be seen as three mutually interconnected 'slices'. Chapter 2 was concerned with the bottom slice: it mapped some of the *outcomes* of globalizing processes; others will be examined in Parts Three and Four.

We can cut into this highly interconnected system at many different points, according to our specific interest. But that necessitates understanding the relationships between the chosen 'slice' and the others. For example, the networks in the central slice of Figure 3.1 do not exist in isolation. They are simultaneously both deeply embedded in the broader institutional macro-structures of the global economy (the upper slice) and grounded in the prevailing geographical structures of the material world (the lower slice). Both history and geography matter. Previous structures and trajectories exert a powerful influence on present and future patterns and processes. As we saw in Chapter 2, the precise geographical configuration of the global economy at any one point in time constrains (though does not necessarily determine) future developments. It constitutes the context within which subsequent processes operate. The whole process is circuitous and highly path dependent.

In a similar vein, we must think of geographical scale in rather more nuanced ways than the conventional 'global–local' dichotomy allows. Figure 1.2 hinted at this. However, although terms like 'global', 'local', 'national' or 'regional' may be helpful, a network perspective forces us to think of geographical scale in a different way: as a *continuum*, rather than as a series of discrete 'boxes'. Instead of being thought of solely in *territorial* terms, then, scale can also be conceived in topological, that is *relational*, terms.[2] Networks may be seen as being 'more or less long and more or less connected'.[3] But this sharp distinction between a territorial and a topological view of geographical scale should not be pushed too far. A topological perspective is not, in itself, in conflict with the fact that, in terms of jurisdictional and regulatory practices, territorial scales of governance remain fundamental to the organization and operation of the global political economy and its constituent parts. *Bounded political spaces matter.* Some, like the nation-state, matter more than others (Chapter 6). In this sense, therefore, we have a very complex situation in which topologically defined networks (e.g. of TNCs, see Chapter 5) both 'interrupt' and are interrupted by political–territorial boundaries. What matters, however, is to think of territories not simply as 'bounded' spaces but, more importantly, as *interrelated* with a whole variety of other socially constructed scales of activity. Globalizing processes, therefore, can be thought of as an increasing *multiplication of scales* – local, national, regional, global – that overlap and interpenetrate in increasingly complex ways as the *relationship* between such scales changes.[4]

INSTITUTIONAL MACRO-STRUCTURES OF THE GLOBAL ECONOMY

The *major actors* in the global economy and the webs of *networked relationships* between them are enmeshed within the broader social, cultural, political and

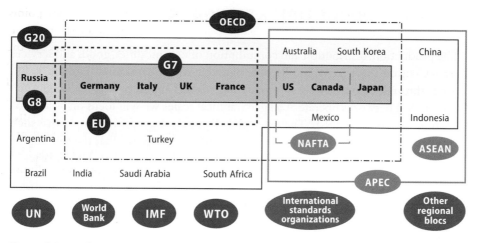

Figure 3.2   Major governance institutions in the global economy

Source: based in part on Cable, 1999: Figure 3.1

economic macro-structures of 'rules, procedures and conventions'.[5] The macro-structures of the contemporary global economy are essentially the institutions, conventions and rules of the capitalist market system. These are not naturally given but socially constructed – in their present form predominantly as a neo-liberal political–economic ideology, although the current crisis has raised big questions about this. Nevertheless, virtually the entire world economy has become a market economy.

Figure 3.2 maps the 'thickening web of multilateral agreements, global and regional institutions and regimes, and transgovernmental policy networks and summits'[6] that has developed. The IMF, the WTO and the World Bank, together with the various 'G' meetings (such as the G7, G8 and, more recently, the G20) and the many international standard-setting organizations are the most obvious manifestations of such global institutions, whose activities will be addressed at various points throughout the following chapters.

These global governance institutions are, themselves, only a part of the broader socio-cultural matrix of practices, rules and conventions that shape how the capitalist market economy works. The rules and conventions relate to, for example, private property, profit making, resource allocation on the basis of market signals, and the consequent commodification of production inputs (including labour). Such institutions and conventions continue to be manifested in *specific configurations* in specific places (notably within nation-states, but not only at that scale). In other words, they are *territorially embedded*. The geographies of capitalism in the global economy, therefore, are highly *variegated*.[7] 'Capitalism' is emphatically not the same everywhere.

GLOBAL PRODUCTION NETWORKS

The production, distribution and consumption of commodities, goods and services are set within this geographically differentiated, macro-structural framework and occur through complex webs of production circuits and networks. Although such circuits and networks operate at all geographical scales we will focus on *global* production networks (GPNs).[8] The term 'global' does not necessarily imply that such networks actually span the entire world but, rather, it suggests that they are highly geographically extensive and functionally integrated across national boundaries.

GPN

The 'core' of a GPN: transforming 'inputs' into 'outputs'

> The core of a GPN is the circuit of interconnected functions, operations and transactions through which a specific commodity, good or service is produced, distributed and consumed.

One point must be made absolutely clear: GPNs are emphatically *not* confined to physical commodities. Non-physical 'products', like financial services, for example, are just as much produced within a GPN as are the more obvious manufactured products.

Figure 3.3 identifies the major elements of a GPN: the four basic operations connected by a series of transactions between them. Inputs are transformed into 'products' that are distributed and consumed. But note that the processes are two-way. They form a *circuit*, rather than a chain. But there is much more to it than this, as Figure 3.3 shows:

- Each individual element in a production circuit depends upon inputs of technology, energy, services, logistics and finance. The whole circuit has to be coordinated, controlled and regulated.
- The individual elements within a production circuit may be disaggregated, both organizationally and geographically.

The dual role of services in GPNs

Services have a dual role in GPNs. On the one hand, services are produced within their own GPN. On the other hand, what are often called advanced business services (ABS) are fundamental to the operation of GPNs (see Chapter 16):

> Service functions are assuming a more pivotal role in the production process. At one level, this is a reflection of a continuing escalation in the complexity of the division of labour … At another, profitability increasingly depends not just on the manufacturing part of the production process, but on the knowledge aspects and service functions within which products are embedded: R&D, design, brand creation, advertising, finance packages, service package or upgrade packages are now the sources of profitability.[9]

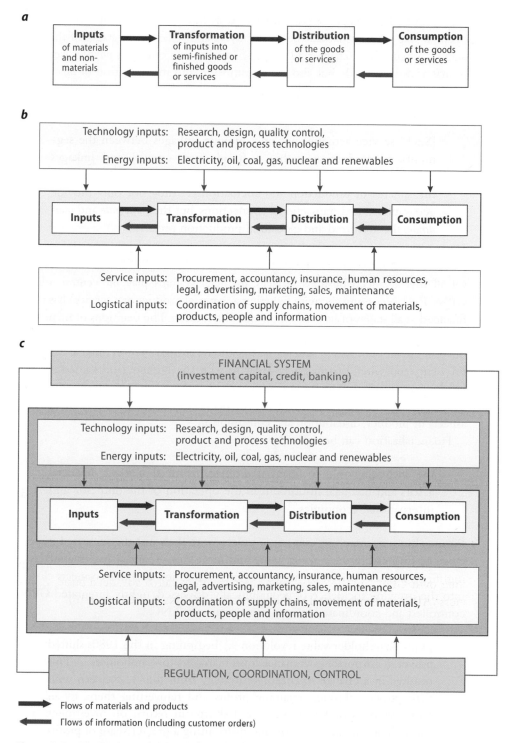

Figure 3.3 The basic components of a production circuit

An especially significant category of services within GPNs is that of *logistics*, whose essential role is to *intermediate* between buyers and sellers at all stages of the production circuit (see Chapter 17).[10] They involve not only the *physical movement* of materials and goods, but also the transmission and manipulation of *information* relating to such movements. They involve, above all, the organization and coordination of complex flows across increasingly extended geographical distances:

> [Such] service activities not only provide linkages between the segments of production within a [production circuit] and linkages between overlapping [production circuits], but they also bind together the spheres of production and circulation ... they not only provide geographical and transactional connections, but they *integrate* and *coordinate* the atomized and globalized production process.[11]

5|16|201 *Financialization*

Of all the advanced business services, financial systems play *the* central role in GPNs. Every economic activity (whether a material product or a service) has to be financed at all stages of its production and distribution. The decisions of financiers, therefore, exert an extraordinarily powerful influence, not only in *lubricating* production circuits, but also in actually *shaping* them through their evaluative decisions on what (and where) to invest in order to gain the highest (and sometimes the quickest) return. But there is more to finance than this. One of the most significant developments of recent years has been the pervasive *financialization* of virtually all aspects of product, distribution and consumption.[12]

Financialization can be defined as

> the increasing role of financial motives, financial markets, financial actors and financial institutions in the operation of the domestic and international economies.[13]

Financialization, therefore, consists of much more than just the increased importance of financial services firms. More and more non-financial (e.g. manufacturing) firms are now driven by motives of financialization and this connects closely into the growing incidence of geographically dispersed, tightly integrated GPNs controlled and coordinated by lead firms, primarily TNCs:

> [T]he shareholder value revolution ... beginning in the 1980s shifted power in corporate governance from managers to shareholders ... This resulted in a change in corporate strategy from the ... concern with firm growth, through retaining profits and reinvesting them, to an emphasis on shareholder value and short-run return on investment through downsizing the firm and distributing a greater share of profits back to shareholders ... traditionally non-financial firms became more

like financial holding companies, with a spectrum of financial services and financial investments swamping production in terms of their contribution to company revenues.

Largely coincidental with financialization in the 1980s was a growing tendency by firms to break up the process of producing goods and services and locate different parts in different locations depending on costs, markets, logistics or politics …

Financialization has encouraged a restructuring of production … And the rising ability of firms to disintegrate production vertically and internationally has allowed these firms to maintain cost mark-ups – and thus profits and shareholder value – even in a context of slower economic growth … global production strategies have helped to sustain financialization.[14]

In other words, financialization is an *all pervasive system of values* based on the overriding prioritization of an equity culture, in which 'shareholder value' and profitability have become central to *all* aspects of economic activity to the virtual exclusion of all other interests. It is a free market ideology in which regulation of financial markets is regarded with suspicion because it is seen to reduce market efficiency. The market is regarded as the most appropriate allocator of resources. The 2008 global financial crisis made nonsense of this claim. But what kind of future system will (or should) emerge is still unclear; this is an issue we will address in Chapter 11.

GPNs as arenas of contested relationships

Individual production circuits (Figure 3.3) are, themselves, *enmeshed in broader production networks of inter- and intra-firm relationships*, that is relationships between and inside firms. Such networks are, in reality, extremely complex structures with intricate links – horizontal, vertical, diagonal – forming multidimensional, multilayered lattices of economic activity. They vary considerably both within and between different economic sectors, as the case study chapters of Part Four demonstrate.

In particular, GPNs are not simply technical–economic mechanisms through which the production, distribution and consumption of commodities, goods and services occur. They are

> simultaneously economic and political phenomena … organizational fields in which actors struggle over the construction of economic relationships, governance structures, institutional rules and norms and discursive frames … GPNs thus exist within the 'transnational space' that is constituted and structured by transnational elites, institutions, ideologies.[15]

In fact, it is primarily the actions of, and the interactions between, the five actor-centred networks shown in Figure 3.4 – TNCs, states, labour, consumers, civil society organizations – that shape the changing geographical configuration of the global economy through their differential involvement in production circuits and networks. Let us look briefly at each of these five actors. Much more will be said about each of them in subsequent chapters.

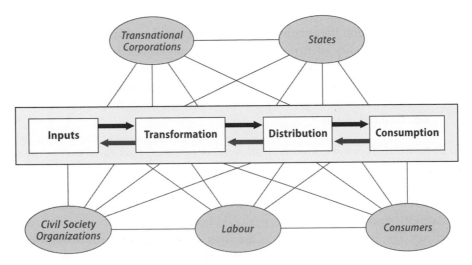

Figure 3.4   Major actor-centred networks in the global economy

Transnational corporations

In capitalist market economies, production networks are coordinated and regulated primarily by *business firms*, through the multifarious forms of intra- and inter-organizational relationships that constitute an economic system. As Figure 3.5 shows, economies are made up of many different types of business organization – transnational and domestic, large and small, public and private – in varying combinations and interrelationships. The firms in each of the segments shown in Figure 3.5 operate over widely varying geographical ranges and perform rather different roles in the economic system.

A major theme of this book, however, is that it is the *TNC* that plays the key role in coordinating *global* production networks and, therefore, in shaping the geoeconomy:

> TNCs are firms with the power to coordinate and control operations
> in more than one country, even if they do not own them.

In fact, TNCs often do own such assets but they are also, as we will see in Chapter 5 and in the case examples in Part Four, typically involved in intricate and multiple spiders' webs of non-equity modes of international production (NEMs) with other legally independent firms across the globe.[16]

Public Sector   **Private Sector**

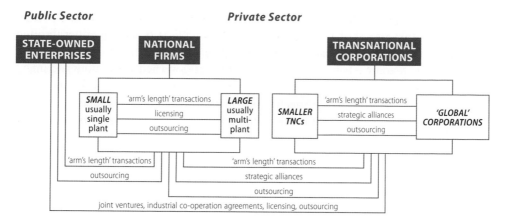

Figure 3.5   Types of firms in an economy

TNCs vary enormously in their size and geographical spread. However, their significance lies in three basic characteristics:

- their ability to coordinate and control various processes and transactions within GPNs, both within and between different countries;
- their potential ability to take advantage of geographical differences in the distribution of factors of production (e.g. natural resources, capital, labour) and in state policies (e.g. taxes, trade barriers, subsidies, etc.);
- their potential geographical flexibility – an ability to switch and to re-switch their resources and operations between locations at an international, or even a global, scale.

Hence, the changing geographies of the global economy are shaped by TNCs through their decisions to invest, not to invest, or to disinvest in particular geographical locations. It is shaped, too, by the resulting flows – of materials, components, finished products, technological and organizational expertise, finance – between their geographically dispersed operations. Although the relative importance of TNCs varies considerably – from sector to sector, from country to country, and between different parts of the same country – there are now very few parts of the world in which TNC influence, whether direct or indirect, is not important. In some cases, indeed, TNC influence on an area's economic fortunes can be overwhelming.

The nature of the coordination process within a TNC's production network depends, in part, on where the firm draws the boundary between those functions it *internalizes* (i.e. performs 'in-house') and those it *externalizes* (i.e. outsources to other firms). Theoretically, at one extreme, the whole TNC production network may be internalized within the firm as a *vertically integrated* system crossing national boundaries. In this case, the links consist of a series of *internalized transactions*, organized 'hierarchically' through the firm's internal organizational structure. At the other extreme, each function may be performed by separate firms, in which case the links consist of a series of *externalized transactions*, organized either through 'the market' or in collaboration with other firms in a kind of 'virtual' network.

This dichotomy – between externalized, market-governed transactions and internalized, hierarchically governed transactions – grossly simplifies the richness and diversity of the governance mechanisms in the contemporary economy. In fact, there is a *spectrum* of different forms of coordination, consisting of networks of interrelationships within and between firms. Such networks increasingly consist of a mix of intra-firm and inter-firm structures. These networks are dynamic and in a continuous state of flux; the boundary between internalization and externalization is continually shifting. They are also affected by the shifting *power relationships* between firms within a GPN. In some cases, one dominant actor calls all the shots; in other cases, power may be more widely dispersed with a greater degree of collaboration involved. Such variation in power relationships within GPNs has enormous implications for the places in which the GPN activities occur (see Chapter 8).

Territorial embeddedness of production networks: states as regulators in GPNs

Capital, it is often argued, has become 'hyper-mobile', freed from the 'tyranny of distance' and no longer tied to 'place'. In other words, economic activity has become 'deterritorialized' or 'disembedded'. Anything can be located anywhere and, if that does not work out, can be moved somewhere else with ease. But such seductive ideas are totally misleading. GPNs do not just float freely in a spaceless/placeless world. They exist within what the sociologist Manuel Castells calls a 'space of places' and a 'space of flows'.[17] Every component in a GPN – every firm, every economic function – is, quite literally, 'grounded' in specific locations. Such grounding is both physical (in the form of the built environment) and also less tangible (in the form of localized social relationships and in distinctive institutions and cultural practices).

Hence, the precise nature and articulation of firm-centred production networks are deeply influenced by the concrete socio-political, institutional and cultural contexts within which they are embedded, produced and reproduced:[18]

> We need to understand how global production networks are embedded within and constitute particular regimes of accumulation in national and macro-regional spaces, which are articulated with these regulatory and state regimes at different scales … there is a need to understand the state as constituted at different geographical scales and as an institutional and relational actor in the governance of global production arrangements.[19]

The *nation-state* continues to be the most important bounded territorial form in which production networks are embedded (Chapter 6). *All* the elements in a GPN are regulated within some kind of political structure, whose basic unit is the

national state, but which also includes such supranational institutions as the IMF
and the WTO, regional economic groupings such as the EU or the NAFTA, and
'local' states at the sub-national scale. The international institutions themselves,
of course, exist only because they are legitimized by national states. Sub-national
institutions are commonly subservient to the national level, although the situation
is more complex in federal political systems. As we will see in Chapter 6, the number of national states has grown markedly in the past 20 years.

All *global* production networks, by definition, have to operate within *multiscalar*
regulatory systems. They are, therefore, subject to a multiplicity of geographically
variable political, social and cultural influences. On the one hand, TNCs attempt
to take advantage of national differences in regulatory regimes while, on the other
hand, states attempt to minimize such 'regulatory arbitrage' and to 'manage' the
spaces in which GPNs operate. The result is a very complex situation in which
firms and states are engaged in various kinds of power play (Chapter 7): a triangular nexus of interactions comprising firm–firm, state–state and firm–state relationships (Figure 3.6). In other words, the geoeconomy is continuously being
structured and restructured not by the actions of either firms or states alone, but
by complex, dynamic, multiscalar interactions between the two sets of institutions.

Of course, TNCs and states are not the only actors involved in the operation of
GPNs. As Figure 3.1 shows, TNCs and states are continuously engaged in relationships with other major actors – labour, consumers, civil society organizations –
some of which also have strong territorial bases.

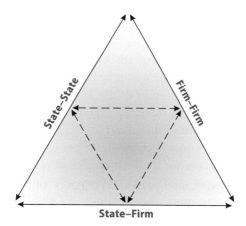

Figure 3.6   The triangular nexus of relationships between firms and states

Source: based on Stopford and Strange, 1991: Figure 1.6

Labour

In most conventional economic analyses, labour is treated as a commodity, a mere
'factor of production'. But such a dehumanized view overlooks the many and

varied ways in which labour (whether organized in labour unions or acting as individuals) influences how production networks operate.[20] Indeed, labour is absolutely *central* to production networks because people embody the knowledge and skills necessary for production to be carried out. *All* production of goods and services needs labour, either directly, in the form of workers, or indirectly, in the labour that is embodied in machinery and equipment. However, there are significant asymmetries in the relative power of labour and capital and these asymmetries have profound implications for how GPNs operate.

One of the most fundamental differences between labour and, especially, transnational capital (in the form of TNCs) is that, on balance, labour is more *place-bound* and generally far less geographically mobile than capital. Of course, the strength of labour's tie to place varies a great deal between different types of labour. On average, male workers are more mobile than female workers; skilled workers are more mobile than unskilled workers; professional white-collar workers are more mobile than blue-collar workers. Clearly, there are exceptions to such generalizations, as shown by the substantial waves of labour migration at different periods of history. Such migrant flows do not, however, contradict the basic point that labour is strongly differentiated geographically and deeply embedded in local communities in distinctive ways. As David Harvey points out, 'unlike other commodities, labour power has to go home every night'.[21]

This spatial asymmetry between capital and labour, though not the only issue, is fundamental in the context of *global* production networks. The dispersed nature of TNC operations and the tendency towards remoteness in corporate decision making make it very difficult for labour unions (which tend to be nationally based) to organize effectively to counter such issues as plant closure or retrenchment. In order to counteract the geographically extensive operations of TNCs, therefore, labour has to find ways of organizing across national boundaries. Although there have been some successful international labour union initiatives, their impact has been relatively limited.[22] Indeed, the proportion of the labour force organized into labour unions has been falling for a long time. For example, in the USA, the unionization rate has fallen from 20 per cent of the labour force in 1983 to around 12 per cent; across the EU, union membership declined by 15 per cent between 1993 and 2003 and is now around 20 per cent of the total employed population. Meanwhile, the effective global labour supply quadrupled between 1980 and 2005 as countries like China, in particular, became more integrated into the global economy.

Consumers

Production networks involve more than just 'production'; they are driven, ultimately, by the necessity, the willingness and the ability of customers to acquire and consume the products themselves, and to continue doing so (see Figure 3.3). Each of the case study chapters of Part Four shows how the nature of consumption varies according to the specific sector involved. Here, we need simply to emphasize some basic aspects of consumption processes.

First, we need to distinguish between the consumption of 'producer' goods or services (sometimes called 'intermediate' products because they are purchased by firms within a production circuit for further transformation) and 'consumer' goods ('final demand' goods: those purchased by individuals and households). In fact, the boundary between the two is often blurred. Second, consumption is very much more than merely the economic process of 'demand'. Obviously, it is greatly influenced by levels of income. But it is also a complex set of *social and cultural* processes, in which all kinds of personal motivations are involved. People buy (or aspire to buy) particular goods for a bewildering variety of reasons, ranging from the satisfaction of basic *needs* to ensure survival (food, shelter, clothing) through to ever more sophisticated *wants* (discretionary goods, such as fashionable clothing, particular kinds of car, exotic or organic foods, and the like).

Consumption, therefore, may be driven by the desire to acquire particular kinds of products (even specific varieties or brands) either because they are regarded as desirable in themselves or because they send out social messages signifying the particular lifestyles, attitudes, social positions or self-evaluations of the consumer. 'Positional' goods have become increasingly important. However, they lose their value as more and more people have access to them. New positional goods have to be sought:[23]

> 'The material object being sold is never enough' … Commodities meet both the functional and symbolic needs of consumers. Even commodities providing for the most mundane necessities of daily life must be imbued with symbolic qualities and culturally endowed meanings.[24]

It is, of course, precisely these *symbolic* qualities of consumption that the advertising, retailing and media industries attempt to manipulate. How far consumption is, or can be, manipulated in such ways is open to question. Some argue that consumption (and consumers) is becoming increasingly more important in the global economy than production (and producers). In Miller's view, the consumer has become the 'global dictator'.[25]

The bewildering proliferation of choice within many product areas is a direct reflection of producers' perceived need to meet the increasingly fragmented demands of consumers. The days when Henry Ford could dictate to his potential customers by telling them that they could have any colour Model T, as long as it was black, are long gone. Of course, in many cases the variety on offer is more apparent than real (heavily advertised 'newness' often being little more than superficial modification). But, in some cases, there is no doubt that consumer demands directly drive production circuits. It is also clear that the emergence of the Internet (Chapter 4) is transforming the abilities of consumers to make informed choices.

Hence, the idea that consumers are becoming more alike, that local tastes and preferences are being replaced by global consumer brands, needs to be treated with caution. The 'globalization of markets' identified by Levitt some 30 years ago[26] is not as clear as he claimed. In fact, other than in a superficial sense, Levitt has been proved wrong. Consumer diversity is the norm almost everywhere. Although there are some, mostly generation-related, mass markets, geographical variation in consumption patterns persists. Indeed, the experiences of many leading consumer product TNCs show that failure to be sensitive to local variations in tastes and preferences can be almost fatal.

Global civil society organizations

> Global social movements (GSMs) are networks that collaborate across borders to advance thematically similar agendas throughout the world and in doing so have become powerful actors in global governance.[27]

Insofar as both labour and consumers are often (though not always) relatively powerless compared with the TNCs that dominate GPNs, they need to *organize* to be effective. The problem is that such organization must be *trans*national, even global, to operate on the same playing field as TNCs. The Internet and the recent phenomenal growth of social media have been key enabling factors in the spread and development of *global* civil society organizations (GCSOs). Within the past 30 years, as Figures 3.7 and 3.8 show, there has been exponential growth in the number and diversity of GCSOs, ranging from the pre-1970 'old' social movements to

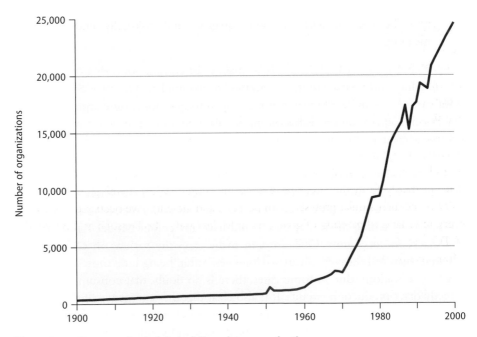

Figure 3.7   **The growth of global civil society organizations**

Source: based on Glasius et al., 2002: Figure 8.1

	'Old' social movements pre-1970	'New' social movements c. 1970s and 1980s	NGOs, think-tanks, commissions c. late 1980s and 1990s	Transnational civic networks c. late 1980s and 1990s	'New' nationalist and fundamentalist movements 1990s	'New' anti-capitalist movements c. late 1990s and 2000s
Issues	Redistribution, employment and welfare; self-determination and anti-colonialism	Human rights; peace; women; environment; third world solidarity	Human rights; development and poverty reduction; humanitarianism; conflict resolution	Women; dams; land mines; inter-national criminal court; global climate change	Identity politics	Solidarity with victims of global-ization; abolition or reform of global institutions
Forms of organization	Vertical, hierarchical	Loose, horizontal coalitions	Ranges from bureaucratic and corporate to small-scale and informal	Networks of NGOs, social movements and grass roots groups	Vertical and horizontal, charismatic leadership	Networks of NGOs, social movements and grass roots groups
Forms of action	Petition, demonstration, strike, lobbying	Use of media, direct action	Service provision; advocacy; expert knowledge; use of media	Parallel summits; use of media; use of local and expert knowledge; advocacy	Media, mass rallies, violence	Parallel summits; direct action; use of media; mobilization through internet
Relation to power	Capturing state power	Changing state/society relations	Influencing civil society, the state and international institutions	Pressure on states and international institutions	Capturing state power	Confrontation with states, international institutions and transnational corporations

Figure 3.8   **The diversity of global civil society organizations**

Source: based on Kaldor, 2003: Table 4.1

the 'new' social movements of the 1970s and 1980s, the NGOs and the transnational civic networks of the late 1980s and 1990s, the 'new' nationalist movements of the 1990s and the 'new' anti-capitalist movements of the late 1990s and 2000s.

GCSOs include the long-established NGO pressure groups such as Oxfam, Greenpeace, Friends of the Earth; more recent ones like Jubilee 2000 and its successors; organized labour unions like the AFL-CIO or the TUC; labour support organizations like Women Working Worldwide or the Maquila Solidarity Network; organizations focused primarily on TNCs and big corporations (like Corporate Watch or Global Exchange); anti-capitalist groups (like Attac, the Socialist Workers Party and, more recently, Occupy); and various anarchist groups. Widespread awareness of such groups dates primarily from the street protests at the Seattle WTO meeting in December 1999. Since then, similar protests (both peaceful and violent) have occurred at virtually every international meeting of government leaders and of bodies such as the IMF, the WTO, the World Bank, the G8 and the G20, as well as at environmental summits. Most recently, the post-2008 financial and economic crisis has

> given rise to transnational counter-movements aiming to challenge the consequences of crisis and the material impacts on the lives of those caught up in the events. From the Spanish *indignados* and the Greek *aganaktismenoi*, to the London August 2011 and the Occupy movements across Europe and beyond ... a movement has emerged

refusing to accept the consequences of crisis, which favour political and economic elites and an attempt to re-establish a neo-liberal, finance-driven status quo. *These new social movements are themselves linked, connected and inter-dependent.*[28]

Although the influence of GCSOs varies enormously, there is no doubt that, as important actors in the global system, they have become increasingly significant. In some GPNs, as we will see in Chapter 11 and in the case studies in Part Four, they are particularly prominent and are having a significant influence on corporate behaviour.

The unevenness of power relations within GPNs

GPNs are *contested* fields: each of the actors and institutions involved has their own agendas. The extent to which these agendas can be realized depends on the relative power configuration in specific situations. Significant variables in determining relative power are:

- control over key assets (such as capital, technology, knowledge, labour skills, natural resources, consumer markets);
- the spatial and territorial range and flexibility of each of the actors.

The two are not unconnected. Ability to control access to specific assets is a major bargaining strength. Where such assets are available virtually everywhere, then the power gradient is shallow or even non-existent. But where assets are 'localized', whether geographically, organizationally or even personally, then the power gradient may be very steep. However, actors able to tap into localized assets across geographical space have a significant advantage over those without such spatial flexibility. Power relationships within GPNs are highly *asymmetrical*.

But there is a further dimension. Each of the major actors in GPNs is involved in *both* cooperation and collaboration on the one hand *and* conflict and competition on the other. Such apparently paradoxical behaviour warns us against assuming that relationships between certain actors are always of one kind: for example, that those between TNCs, or between TNCs and states, or between TNCs and labour, or between TNCs and CSOs, are always conflictual or competitive. Or, conversely, that relationships between groups of workers or labour organizations are always cooperative (in the name of class solidarity). Not so. These various actor networks are imbued with an ever-changing mixture of both conflict and collaboration. Thus, although power relationships within GPNs are asymmetrical, they are not fixed.

So, for example, TNCs in the same industry are fierce competitors but also, invariably, enmeshed in a complex web of collaborative relationships (see Chapter 5). States compete in cut-throat fashion with other states to entice internationally mobile investment by TNCs (see Chapter 7) or to find ways to keep out certain types of imports while, at the same time, increasingly engaging in preferential trading arrangements, including bilateral and multilateral agreements, often within broader regional groupings (see Chapter 6). Labour unions in one country engage in competition with labour unions in other countries in the scramble for new jobs or to protect existing jobs while, at the same time, unions strive to create international alliances with unions in other countries, especially those involved in the geographically dispersed operations of major TNCs. They also increasingly attempt to negotiate international framework agreements with TNCs to protect workers' rights. GCSOs, likewise, are not immune from these conflicting actions. In the context of the anti–globalization protests, for example, GCSOs have developed collaborations across national boundaries but, at the same time, the goals and values of individual GCSOs are not always compatible, to say the least.

EVEN IN A GLOBALIZING WORLD, ECONOMIC ACTIVITIES ARE GEOGRAPHICALLY LOCALIZED

The view of the 'hyper–globalizers' (see Chapter 1) is that increasing *geographical dispersal* at a global scale is now the norm. But when we break free of the national statistical boxes in which most economic data are packaged, *geographical concentrations* of economic activity not only still exist, but are the normal state of affairs. If we could observe the earth from a very high altitude, particularly at night, what we would see are distinctive *clusters*, picked out by the lights, of localized agglomerations of people and activities. Such concentrations occur at different geographical scales, though the most prominent is, of course, the city. Figure 3.9 maps the world's major cities by population size. But size, in itself, is not everything. Most significant are those so-called global cities that contain huge concentrations of high-level financial and business services, corporate headquarters, etc. (see Chapters 5 and 16).

One of the most striking features of the global economic map, then, is the degree to which cities and localized clusters dominate. The world, very obviously, is very 'spiky'.[29] Why do such 'sticky places' continue to exist in 'slippery space'?[30] The answer lies in the complex and dynamic *processes of agglomeration*.

The bases of geographical clusters

Figure 3.10 identifies two idealized types of geographical cluster: *generalized* and *specialized*. Both are based on the notion of *externalities*, the positive 'spillovers' created when activities in a particular place are connected with one another, either directly (through specific transactions) or indirectly. Both are based on the idea that

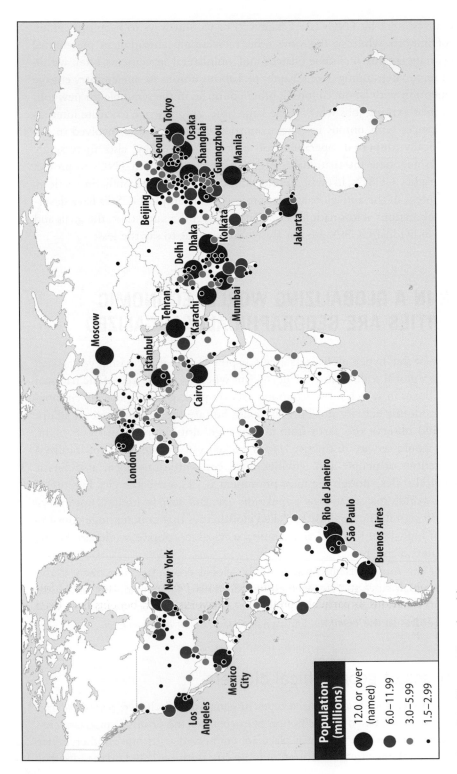

Figure 3.9 The world's major cities

Source: UN data

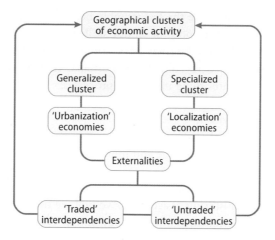

Figure 3.10   **The bases of geographical clusters**

the 'whole' (the cluster) is greater than the sum of the parts because of the benefits
that spatial proximity provides:

- *Generalized clusters* simply reflect the fact that human activities tend to agglom-
  erate to form urban areas. Hence, such benefits have traditionally been labelled
  urbanization economies. General clustering of activities creates the basis for sharing the costs of a whole range of services. Larger aggregate demand in, say, a
  large city encourages the emergence and growth of a variety of infrastructural,
  economic, social and cultural facilities that cannot be provided where their
  customers are geographically dispersed. The larger the city, the greater the
  variety of available facilities and vice versa.
- *Specialized clusters*, on the other hand, reflect the tendency for firms in the same,
  or closely related, economic activities to locate in the same places to form what
  are sometimes termed 'industrial districts' or 'industrial spaces'. The archetypal
  example is the industrial districts of Italy.[31] The bases of specialized clusters
  arise from the geographical proximity of firms performing different – but
  linked – functions in particular production networks. Such benefits have been
  called *localization economies*.

Geographical clusters facilitate two types of interdependency:

- *Traded interdependencies* are direct transactions between firms in a cluster (e.g.
  the supply of specialized inputs of intermediate products and services). In such
  circumstances, spatial proximity is a means of reducing transaction costs either
  through minimizing transportation costs or by reducing some of the uncertainties of customer–supplier relationships.

- *Untraded interdependencies* are the less tangible benefits, ranging from the development of an appropriate pool of labour skills to particular kinds of institutions (such as universities, business associations, government institutions and the like) to broader socio-cultural phenomena. In particular, geographical agglomeration facilitates three important processes:

  - face-to-face contact;
  - social and cultural interaction;
  - enhancement of knowledge and innovation.

Above all, it is the potential for *face-to-face contact* that is the single most important 'glue' in the localized clustering of activities. We will see this, especially, in Chapter 4, in the context of innovation and technology, and in Chapter 16, in the context of ABS, including finance. But it underlies the geographical concentration of *all* human activities. It is a key element of the human condition.

Advanced
Business
services

Why do clusters develop in the first place?

But why do clusters form in the first place? Why do they arise in one place rather than another? And how do they develop over time? These are difficult questions to answer. The reasons for the origins of specific geographical clusters are highly contingent and often shrouded in the mists of history. As Gunnar Myrdal pointed out:

> Within broad limits the power of attraction today of a center has its origin mainly in the historical accident that something once started there, and not in a number of other places where it could equally well or better have started, and that the start met with success.[32]

Once established, a cluster tends to grow through a process of *cumulative, self-reinforcing development* involving:

- attraction of linked activities;
- stimulation of entrepreneurship and innovation;
- deepening and widening of the local labour market;
- economic diversification;
- enrichment of the 'industrial atmosphere';
- 'thickening' of local institutions;
- intensification of the socio-cultural milieu;
- enhanced physical infrastructures.

The *cumulative* nature of these processes of localized economic development suggests that the process is *path dependent*. In other words, a place becomes 'locked into' a pattern that is strongly influenced by its particular history. This may be either a

source of continued strength or, if it embodies too much organizational or technological rigidity, a source of weakness. However, even for 'successful' clusters, such
path dependency does not imply the absolute inevitability of continued success.
Rigidity of local practices may reduce the capacity to adapt to external changes.
For example, the Italian industrial districts are being transformed: 'some of them
have entered a phase of decline, and some are losing their "district" features. Others
are reproducing themselves in another … form'.[33] More generally, cities rise and
fall – and some rise again if a new virtuous circle of development can be initiated.
Decline, like growth, can become locked in and often difficult to reverse.

NETWORKS OF NETWORKS

Rather than seeing the global economy as a system of interlinked national state-
focused economic units, we should think of it as the linking together of two sets
of networks:

- *organizational* (in the form of production circuits and networks);
- *geographical* (in the form of localized clusters of economic activity).

The major advantage of adopting such a *grounded network* approach to understanding the global economy is that it helps us to appreciate the interconnectedness
of economic activities across different geographical scales and within and across
territorially bounded spaces. The production of any commodity, whether it is a
manufactured product or a service, involves an intricate articulation of individual
activities and transactions across space and time. Such production networks – the
*nexus of interconnected functions and operations through which goods and services are pro-
duced and distributed* – have become both organizationally and geographically more
complex.

Global production networks not only integrate firms (and parts of firms) into
structures which blur traditional organizational boundaries (e.g. through the
development of diverse forms of equity and non-equity relationships), but also
integrate national and local economies (or parts of such economies) in ways which
have enormous implications for their economic development and well-being (see
Chapter 8). At the same time, the specific characteristics of national and local
economies influence and 'refract' the operation and form of larger-scale processes.
In that sense, 'geography matters' a lot.

The process is especially complex because, while states and local economies are
essentially territorially specific, production networks themselves are not.[34]
Production networks 'slice through' boundaries in highly differentiated ways,
influenced in part by regulatory and non-regulatory barriers and by local socio-
cultural conditions, to create structures that are *discontinuously territorial*. This has
major implications for the relative bargaining powers of the actors involved,

including labour, consumers and CSOs, as well as governments. *The geoeconomy, therefore, can be pictured as a geographically uneven, highly complex and dynamic web of production networks, economic spaces and places connected together through threads of flows.*

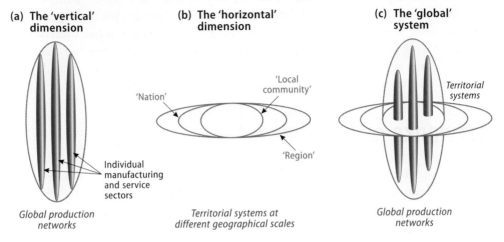

(a) The 'vertical' dimension

Individual manufacturing and service sectors

Global production networks

(b) The 'horizontal' dimension

'Nation'

'Local community'

'Region'

Territorial systems at different geographical scales

(c) The 'global' system

Territorial systems

Global production networks

Figure 3.11   **Interconnecting dimensions in a globalizing economy**

Source: based in part on Humbert, 1994: Figure 1

Figure 3.11 captures the major dimensions of these relationships. Individual production networks can be regarded as vertically organized structures configured across increasingly extensive geographical scales. Cutting across these vertical structures are the territorially defined political–economic systems at different geographical scales. It is at the points of intersection of these dimensions in 'real' geographical space where specific outcomes occur, where the problems of existing within a globalizing economy – whether as a business firm, a government, a local community or as an individual – have to be resolved.

NOTES

1   Mitchell (2000: 392; emphasis added).
2   Amin (2002).
3   Latour, quoted in Thrift (1996: 5).
4   See Swyngedouw (2000).
5   Martin (2000: 79). See also Berndt and Boeckler (2009), Lee (2007, 2009).
6   Held and McGrew (2007: 137).
7   Peck and Theodore (2007).
8   The GPN concept is explored in detail in a theme issue of the *Journal of Economic Geography* (vol. 8, 2008). See, in particular, Coe et al. (2008a), Coe (2011, 2014), Coe and Yeung (2015), Dicken et al. (2001), Henderson et al. (2002). The GPN perspective is closely related to, but broader than, that of global commodity chains (GCCs), initially pioneered by Gereffi (1994, 2005) and global value chains (GVCs) developed by Gereffi et al. (2005). See Bair (2009), Neilson and Pritchard (2009), Neilson et al.

(2014), UNCTAD (2011: chapter IV). The Global Value Chains Initiative based at Duke University is a comprehensive source of publications on GPNs and GVCs (www.globalvaluechains.org).

9   Daniels and Bryson (2002: 978). See also UNCTAD (2004), Flecker et al. (2013).

10 See also Coe (2014).

11 Rabach and Kim (1994: 123).

12 Dore (2008), Epstein (2005), Gibbon (2002), Lee et al. (2009), Milberg (2008), Milberg and Winkler (2010), Nölke et al. (2013).

13 Epstein (2005: 3).

14 Milberg (2008: 423, 424, 445).

15 Levy (2008: 948).

16 UNCTAD (2012: chapter IV).

17 Castells (1996).

18 Granovetter (1985) pioneered the concept of 'embeddedness' within the field of economic sociology. It has become a ubiquitous (though contested) term since then. See Hess (2004) for a discussion of the concept in a spatial/territorial context. Kelly (2013) and Neilson and Pritchard (2009) stress the need to reinsert place and institutions in these analyses.

19 Smith (2014: 10, 22).

20 See, for example, Carswell and De Neve (2013), Castree et al. (2004), Coe and Hess (2013), Cumbers et al. (2008), Herod (2001), Hudson (2001), Jones (2008), Peck (1996).

21 Cited in Peck (2000: 141).

22 Some examples are provided by Bieler et al. (2014), Cumbers et al. (2008), Cumbers and Routledge (2010), Evans (2010), Fichter et al. (2011), Herod (2001), Wills (1998, 2002).

23 Hirsch (1977).

24 Hudson (2005: 65).

25 Miller (1995: 1).

26 Levitt (1983).

27 Bennett (2013: 799).

28 Smith (2013: 4; emphasis added).

29 Florida (2005: 48).

30 Markusen (1996). 'Clustering' has become a hot topic in policy debates in virtually all parts of the world; see Martin and Sunley (2003), Porter (1990, 1998, 2000). However, the concept itself, as opposed to its policy connotations, has a very long history. See, for example, Amin and Thrift (1992), Bathelt et al. (2004), Krugman (1998), Malmberg (1999), Scott (1998, 2008), Storper (1995, 1997), Storper and Venables (2004).

31 For a recent discussion of Italian industrial districts and their changing fortunes see De Marchi and Grandinetti (2014).

32 Myrdal (1958: 26).

33 De Marchi and Grandinetti (2014: 82).

34 Dicken and Malmberg (2001).

Want to know more about this chapter? Visit the companion website at **www.guilford.com/dickenGS7** for free access to author videos, suggested reading and practice questions to further enhance your study.

Four

TECHNOLOGICAL CHANGE: 'GALES OF CREATIVE DESTRUCTION'

TECHNOLOGY AND ECONOMIC TRANSFORMATION

5|16|2016
(sw air
Aus → MDW)

Technological change is unquestionably one of the most important processes underlying the globalization of economic activity.[1] In Joseph Schumpeter's words, 'the fundamental impulse that sets and keeps the capitalist engine in motion comes from the new consumers' goods, the new methods of production or transportation, the new markets, the new forces of industrial organization that capitalist enterprise creates.[2] Schumpeter set technological change, specifically *innovation* – the creation and diffusion of new ways of doing things – at the very heart of the processes of economic growth and development. Technological change is unquestionably one of the most important processes underlying the globalization of economic activity. But a word of warning: technology, in itself, is *not* deterministic.

Technology is, essentially, an *enabling* or *facilitating* agent. It makes possible new structures, new organizational and geographical arrangements of economic activities, new products and new processes, while not making particular outcomes inevitable. Most importantly, technological change is a *socially and institutionally embedded process*:

> Specific choices within the frontier of technological possibilities are not the product of technological change; they are, rather, the product of those who make the choices within the frontier of possibilities. *Technology does not drive choice; choice drives technology.*[3]

The ways in which technologies are used – even their very creation – are conditioned by their social and their economic context. In the contemporary world this means primarily the values and motivations of capitalist business enterprises, operating within an intensely competitive system. Choices and uses of technologies are influenced by the drive for profit, capital accumulation and investment, increased market share, and so on.

PROCESSES OF TECHNOLOGICAL CHANGE: AN EVOLUTIONARY PERSPECTIVE

Technological change is a form of *learning* – by observing, by doing, by using – of how to solve specific problems in highly differentiated and volatile environments.

But it is much more than a narrowly 'technical' process. It is also about much more than just 'the new'; older technologies persist and often remain useful.[4] Technological change not only involves the *invention* of new things, or new ways of doing things, but also – more importantly – depends upon the transformation of inventions into usable *innovations*, and their subsequent *adoption and diffusion*. In the economic sphere, this is essentially an entrepreneurial process. In the long run, it is, essentially, an *evolutionary* process.[5]

Types of technological change

There are four broad types of technological change,[6] each of which is progressively more significant and far-reaching in its impact:

- *Incremental innovations*: small-scale, progressive modifications of existing products and processes, created through 'learning by doing' and 'learning by using'. Although individually small – and, therefore, often unnoticed – they accumulate, often over a very long period of time, to create highly significant changes.
- *Radical innovations*: discontinuous events that drastically change existing products or processes. A single radical innovation will not, on its own, have a widespread effect on the economic system; what is needed is a 'cluster' of such innovations.
- *Changes of technology system*: extensive changes in technology that impact upon several existing parts of the economy, as well as creating entirely new sectors. These are based on a combination of radical and incremental technological innovations, along with appropriate organizational innovations. Changes of technology system tend to be associated with the emergence of key generic technologies[7] (e.g. information technology, biotechnology, materials technology, energy technology, space technology, nanotechnology).
- *Changes in the techno-economic paradigm*: truly large-scale revolutionary changes embodied in new technology systems. These

> have such pervasive effects on the economy as a whole that *they change the 'style' of production and management throughout the system*. The introduction of electric power or steam power or the electronic computer are examples of such deep-going transformations. A change of this kind carries with it many clusters of radical and incremental innovations, and may eventually embody several new technology systems. *Not only does this fourth type of technological change lead to the emergence of a new range of products, services, systems and industries in its own right – it also affects directly or indirectly almost every other branch of the economy … the changes involved go beyond specific product or process technologies and affect the input cost structure and conditions of production and distribution throughout the system.*[8]

Trajectories of technological change

Large-scale technological changes take time. They do not occur overnight, not least because they require a suitable combination of social, organizational as well as technical conditions:[9]

> Radical individual innovations are usually introduced in a relatively primitive version and, once market acceptance is achieved, they are subjected to a series of incremental innovations following the changing rhythm of a logistic curve ... Changes generally occur slowly at first, while producers, designers, distributors and consumers engage in feedback learning processes; rapidly and intensively once a *dominant design* ... has become established in the market and slowly once again when maturity is reached and ... [the] ... law of diminishing returns to investment in innovation sets in.[10]

Figure 4.1 maps such an idealized trajectory.

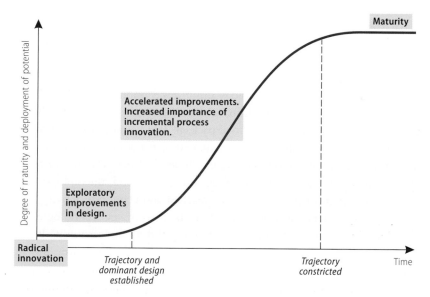

Figure 4.1 **Technological innovation: an idealized developmental trajectory**

Source: based on Perez, 2010: Figure 1

Technological revolutions and long waves

Central to such an evolutionary perspective is the idea that economic growth occurs in a series of cycles or 'waves'. The best-known version of this idea is the Kondratiev wave (K-wave), a long wave of roughly 50 years' duration.[11] In Figure 4.2, beginning in the late 1700s, four complete K-waves are identified. We are now well into

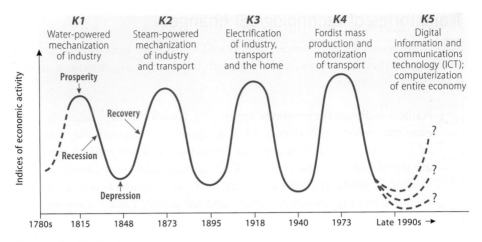

Figure 4.2   **Kondratiev long waves**

Source: based, in part, on Freeman and Louçã, 2001: Table II.1

a fifth, though precisely how far in, and what its precise trajectory will be, is not yet clear. Each wave can be divided into four phases: prosperity, recession, depression and recovery. Each wave tends to be associated with particularly significant techno-logical changes around which other innovations – in production, distribution and organization – swarm or cluster and ultimately spread through the economy.

Although such diffusion of technology stimulates economic growth and employ-ment, demographic, social, industrial, financial and demand conditions also have to be appropriate. In other words, it is the 'total package' that counts. At some point, how-ever, growth slackens: demand becomes saturated or firms' profits become squeezed through intensified competition. As a result, the level of new investment falls, firms strive to rationalize and restructure their operations, and unemployment rises. Eventually the trough of the wave will be reached and economic activity will turn up again. A new sequence will be initiated on the basis of key technologies – some of which may be based on innovations that emerged during recession itself – and of new investment opportunities. Although there is disagreement over the precise mechanisms and timing involved, each of the waves is generally associated with changes in the techno-economic paradigm, as one set of techno-economic practices is displaced by a new set. This is not a sudden process but one that occurs gradually and involves the ultimate 'crystallization' of a new paradigm.

As Figure 4.3 shows, the process involves much more than just technical change. Each phase is also associated with characteristic forms of economic organization, cooperation and competition. Each successive K-wave also has a *specific geography*, as technological leadership shifts over time, both in terms of lead nations (as the bottom row of Figure 4.3 makes clear) and at the micro-geographical scale. In effect, 'the locus of the leading-edge innovative industries has switched from region to region,

	K1	**K2**	**K3**	**K4**	**K5**
Main 'carrier' branches	Textiles; Textile chemicals; Textile machinery; Iron working/castings; Water power; Potteries.	Steam engines; Steamships; Machine tools; Iron and steel; Railway equipment.	Electrical engineering; Electrical machinery; Cable and wire; Heavy engineering/ armaments; Steel ships; Heavy chemicals; Synthetic dyestuffs.	Automobiles; Trucks; Tractors; Tanks; Aircraft; Consumer durables; Process plant; Synthetic materials; Petrochemicals.	Computers; Digital information technology; Internet; Software; Telecommunications; Optical fibres; Robotics; Ceramics; Nanotechnology; Biotechnology.
Core input and other key inputs	Iron; Raw cotton; Coal.	Iron; Coal.	Steel; Copper; Metal alloys.	Oil; Gas; Synthetic materials.	'Chips' (integrated circuits).
Transport and communications infrastructure	Trunk canals; Turnpike roads; Sailing ships.	Railways; Shipping.	Electricity supply and distribution.	Highways; Airports/airlines.	Digital networks; Satellites.
Organization of firms and forms of cooperation and competition	Factory systems. Individual entrepreneurs and small firms (<100 employees) competition. Partnership structure facilitates cooperation of technical innovators and financial managers. Local capital and individual wealth.	High-noon of small-firm competition, but larger firms now employing thousands rather than hundreds. As firms and markets grow, limited liability and joint stock company permit new pattern of investment, risk-taking and ownership.	Emergence of giant firms, cartels, trusts, mergers. Monopoly and oligopoly becomes typical. Regulation or state ownership of 'natural' monopolies and public utilities. Concentration of banking and 'finance-capital'. Emergence of specialized 'middle management' in large firms.	Mass production and consumption. 'Fordism'. Oligopolistic competition. Transnational corporations based on direct foreign investment and multi-plant locations. Competitive subcontracting on 'arm's length' basis or vertical integration. Increasing concentration, divisional-ization and hierarchical control. 'Techno-structure' in large corporations.	'Networks' of large and small firms based increasingly on computer networks and close co-operation in technology, quality control, training, investment planning and production planning ('just-in-time') etc.
Geographical focus: core country or countries	Britain.	Britain (spreading into Europe and USA).	USA and Germany forging ahead and overtaking Britain.	USA (with Germany at first competing for world leadership), later spreading to Europe.	USA (spreading to Europe and Asia).

Figure 4.3   **Key characteristics of successive K-waves**

Source: based, in part, on Freeman and Perez, 1988: Table 3.1; Freeman and Louçã, 2001: Table II.1; Perez, 2010: Table 1

from city to city'.[12] For example, 'Manchester was as much the cradle and the symbol of the Age of Steam as Silicon Valley has been for the microelectronics revolution'.[13]

Information and communications technologies: the digital world

> Information is what our world runs on: the blood and the fuel, the vital principle.[14]

K5 is associated primarily with *information and communications technology* (ICT) and, especially, with *digital* technologies:

> For the first time in history, information generation, processing and transmission have become the main commodities and sources of

productivity and power and not only a means of achieving better ways of doing things in the production process. New information technologies are not simply tools to be applied but processes to be developed.[15]

The 'new' telecommunications technologies are, in effect, 'the electronic highways of the informational age, equivalent to the role played by railway systems in the process of industrialization'.[16]

The current generation of information technologies has one very special characteristic, as Figure 4.4 shows. It is based upon the *convergence* of two initially distinct technologies: *communications technologies* (concerned with the transmission of information) and *computer technologies* (concerned with the processing of information). Both are now based on digital, rather than analogue, technologies. Digitization is, without doubt, the most pervasive and influential technological development of recent years. All kinds of information can now be stored in numerical (binary) form as electronic 'digits'. This means they can then be

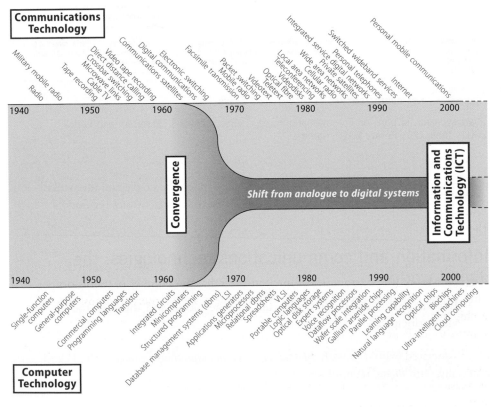

Figure 4.4   Information and communications technologies: a process of convergence

Source: based, in part, on Freeman, 1987: Figure 2

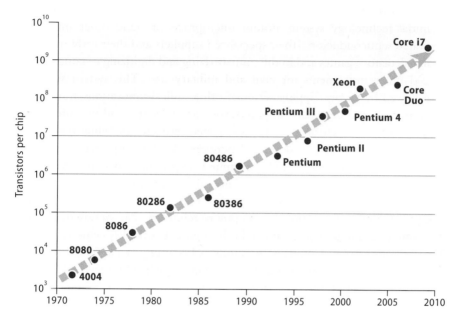

Figure 4.5 Exponential increase in the capacity of microprocessors

processed, manipulated and stored by computers, and transmitted anywhere in the world almost instantly. In particular, the remarkable, and very recent, growth of the Internet, of mobile telephony, together with big changes in electronic mass media and the rapid emergence of 'social media', are generating major global effects at all levels, including individuals, households, local communities, nation-states and, of course, business organizations, especially TNCs.

Each successive K-wave has been driven by a 'key input'. In the case of K5, as Figure 4.3 shows, this was the 'chip', the *integrated circuit (IC)* or *microprocessor*, which emerged in the USA in the late 1940s and early 1950s. Most important has been the process of *miniaturization*: the development of increasingly complex ICs of progressively smaller and smaller sizes. Figure 4.5 illustrates this stunning process of miniaturization. It reflects the so-called 'Moore's Law': the prediction by Gordon Moore (the co-founder of Intel) in 1965 that the number of transistors per chip would double every 18 months. In 1964, there were a mere 30 transistors on a chip. Intel's first commercial microprocessor produced in 1971 contained 3500 transistors; its Pentium 4 of the late 1990s contained 42 million. Today, Intel's Core i7 chip for the newest Mac and Windows PCs has 1.4 billion transistors on a surface area of 160 square millimetres. Such developments have made possible not only increasingly powerful computers, but also vast reductions in their cost and, therefore, in their increasingly ubiquitous use in all kinds of products and processes.

Perez summarizes the complex interconnected nature of the ICT revolution particularly well:

> The current information technology revolution ... opened up an initial technology system around microprocessors (and other integrated semiconductors), their specialized suppliers and their early uses in calculators, games and in the miniaturizing and digitizing of control and other instruments for civil and military uses. This system was followed by an overlapping series of other radical innovations, minicomputers and personal computers, software, telecoms and the internet, each of which opened up new system trajectories, while being strongly inter-related and inter-dependent. As they appeared, these systems interconnected and continued expanding together with intense feedback loops in both technologies and markets.[17]

As the power and sophistication of computer technology has increased, and as it has become increasingly widely available through networked systems, it is taking on the characteristics of a utility. Computing is becoming analogous to the electricity generating industry of the nineteenth century,[18] when businesses abandoned their own individual electricity generators to take advantage of the new electric grid system. Today they are beginning to move away from individual computer systems to networked systems provided through the Internet. An example of such new computers-as-utility systems is Google's global network of 'server farms':

> Designed to house tens of thousands of PCs, all wired together to work as a single supercomputer [these are] ... the information-processing equivalent of a nuclear power station, able to pump data and software into millions of homes and businesses ... No corporate computing system, not even those operated by big companies, can match the efficiency, speed and flexibility of plants such as Google's. One analyst estimates that Google can carry out a computing task for one-tenth of what it costs a typical company ... *Cheap and plentiful electricity shaped the world we live in today ... The transformation in the supply of computing promises to have equally sweeping consequences.*[19]

This development has become known as 'cloud computing': clusters of servers 'in the sky', as it were. However,

> its physical aspect could not be less cloudlike. Server farms proliferate in unmarked brick buildings and steel complexes, with smoked windows or no windows, miles of hollow floors, diesel generators, cooling towers, seven-foot intake fans, and aluminum chimney stacks. This hidden infrastructure grows in a symbiotic relationship with the electrical infrastructure it increasingly resembles. There are information switchers, control centers and substations. They are clustered and distributed. These are the wheel-works; the cloud is their avatar.[20]

TIME–SPACE SHRINKING TECHNOLOGIES

As Figure 3.3 shows, *processes of circulation* are fundamental to the operation of production circuits and networks; indeed, to the operation of society as a whole. Circulation technologies – transportation and communications technologies – overcome the frictions of space and time.[21] Although these certainly cannot be regarded as the cause of globalization, without them today's complex global economic system simply could not exist. Transportation and communications technologies perform two distinct, though closely related and complementary, roles:

- *Transportation systems* are the means by which materials, products and other tangible entities (including people) are transferred from place to place.
- *Communications systems* are the means by which information is transmitted from place to place in the form of ideas, instructions, images, and so on.

For most of human history, transportation and communications were effectively one and the same. Before the invention of electric technology in the nineteenth century, information had to be physically carried. It could move only at the same speed, and over the same distance, as the prevailing transportation system allowed. Electric technology broke that link, making it increasingly necessary to treat transportation and communications as distinct, though intimately related, technologies. Such developments have transformed societies in all kinds of ways. From a specifically economic and business perspective, they strongly influence how – and where – business organizations are able to operate. As a consequence, these technologies have helped progressively to transform the economic–geographical landscape, at increasing geographical scales and over shorter periods of time. Figure 4.6 summarizes this process. We will focus on how such transformations in firms' activities and their geographies are actually being worked out later in this chapter and in Chapter 5. Before that, we need to identify some of the major innovations in transportation and communications, which have been so important in helping to transform the economic landscape.

Accelerating geographical mobility

A shrinking world

In terms of the time it takes to get from one part of the world to another there is no doubt that the world has 'shrunk' dramatically (Figure 4.7). Throughout most of human history, the speed and efficiency of transportation were staggeringly low and the costs of overcoming the friction of distance prohibitively high. Movement over land was especially slow and difficult before the development of the railways. Indeed, even as late as the early nineteenth century, the means of transportation were not really very different from those prevailing almost 2000 years earlier.

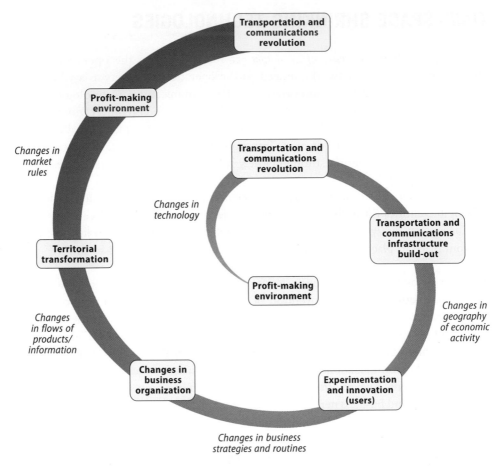

Figure 4.6   **Transportation/communications revolutions and economic transformation**

Source: based on Fields, 2004: Figure 2.1

The major breakthrough came with two closely associated innovations in K2 (Figure 4.3): steam power as a means of propulsion and the use of iron and steel for trains, railway tracks and ocean-going vessels. These, coupled with the linking together of overland and oceanic transportation (e.g. with the cutting of the canals at Suez and Panama), greatly telescoped geographical distance at a global scale. The railway and the steamship introduced a new, and much enlarged, scale of human activity. The decline in global transportation cost was truly amazing.[22] Flows of materials and products were enormously enhanced and the possibilities for geographical specialization greatly stimulated. Such innovations were a major factor in the massive expansion in the global economic system during the nineteenth century.

The past few decades have seen an acceleration of this process of global shrinkage. For example, transportation costs fell 'from an average of 8 per cent of total

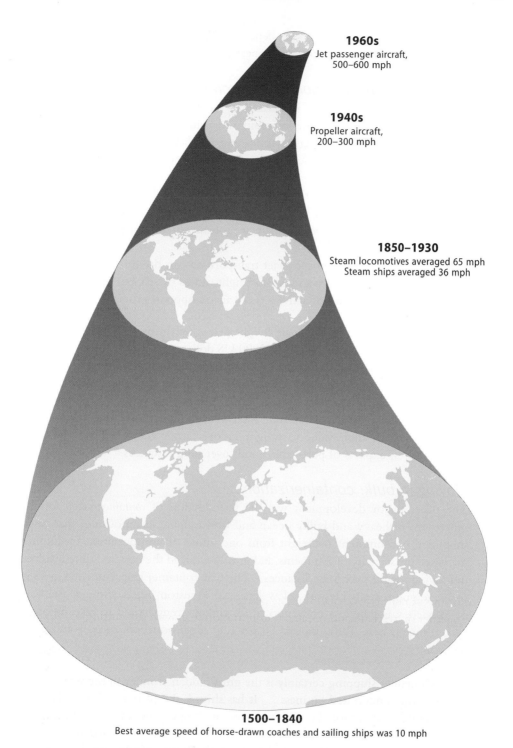

1960s
Jet passenger aircraft,
500–600 mph

1940s
Propeller aircraft,
200–300 mph

1850–1930
Steam locomotives averaged 65 mph
Steam ships averaged 36 mph

1500–1840
Best average speed of horse-drawn coaches and sailing ships was 10 mph

Figure 4.7 **Global shrinkage: the effects of transportation innovations on 'real' distance**

Source: based on McHale, 1969: Figure 1

import costs in 1970 to about 3 per cent in 2002'.[23] Two developments have been particularly important, both of them appearing for the first time during the 1950s.

Take-off: the introduction of jet aircraft

One was the introduction of *commercial jet aircraft*. This had two major effects. First, it enabled unprecedentedly rapid individual travel over vast distances, allowing face-to-face meetings at times and in places hitherto unrealistic. For TNCs, in particular, jet transport made possible the coordination and control of geographically dispersed operations. Direct control at a distance became a reality. It is no coincidence that the take-off of TNC growth and the (more literal) take-off of commercial jets both occurred during the 1950s. One estimate is that '320 million people meet annually at professional and corporate events after travelling by air'.[24]

The second significant effect of jet transport was on the movement of certain kinds of freight. Most heavy and bulky freight moves by sea, but for certain kinds of good and certain kinds of activity faster air transport is crucial:

> Between 1950 and 2004, air freight prices fell from $3.87 per ton-kilometer to less than $0.30, in 2000 US dollars ... Of the world's $12 trillion of merchandise trade, 35 per cent by value was shipped by air in 2006 ... [for example] ... air transport fills an important niche in just-in-time production systems. While shipments by sea are routine, firms use air cargo to fine-tune intermediate input flows and to ship goods with high value-to-weight ratios ... [air transport] ... also enabl[es] exports of perishable goods over long distances.[25]

Moving in bulk: containerization

The other major development was the introduction of *containerization* for the movement of heavy and bulky ocean and land freight, an innovation that vastly simplified transhipment of freight from one mode of transportation to another, increased the security of shipments, and greatly reduced the cost and time involved in moving freight over long distances.[26] The first container ship, launched in 1956 to move goods from Newark, New Jersey, to Houston, Texas, through the Gulf of Mexico, was merely a conventional oil tanker strengthened to take 58 boxes each 9 metres long. Today, around 90 per cent of all non-bulk cargo is moved in containers:

> Container shipping certainly is the great hidden wonder of the world, a vastly underrated business ... It has shrunk the planet and brought about a revolution because the cost of shipping boxes is so cheap. People talk about the contribution made by the likes of Microsoft. But container shipping has got to be among the 10 most influential industries over the past 30 years.[27]

However, the very success of containerization, in a world in which trade has grown very rapidly, especially on certain routes such as those from China to North America and to Europe, has created immense problems, notably port congestion. In 2004, a new generation of container ships, more than 300 metres long, more than 40 metres wide and capable of carrying 8000 containers each 6 metres long, entered service. In 2013, the new Triple-E container ships appeared, each able to accommodate 18,000 containers each 6 metres long. Relatively few ports have the capacity to take such huge vessels and this will, inevitably, enhance their dominance over smaller ports. In any case, there are already massive problems of delays at most major world ports because of the sheer volume of freight traffic and the physical and human problems of handling it quickly. Although the shrinkage of world trade created by the 2008 financial crisis created huge over-capacity in the container shipping industry, there is clearly a drive to introduce bigger and more efficient container ships. There is already talk of ships capable of carrying 25,000 containers.[28]

The unevenness of time–space convergence

Although the world has indeed shrunk in relative terms, such shrinkage has been, and continues to be, highly uneven. This is contrary to the impression given by Figure 4.7. In fact, technological developments in transportation have a very strong tendency to be geographically highly concentrated. The big investments needed to build transportation infrastructures tend to go where demand is greatest and financial returns are highest. Consequently, *time–space convergence* affects some places more than others. While the world's leading national economies and the world's major cities are being pulled closer together in relative time or cost terms, others – less developed countries or smaller towns and rural areas – are, in effect, being left behind. The time–space surface, then, is highly plastic; some parts shrink while other parts become, in effect, extended. By no means everywhere benefits from technological innovations in transportation.

'Everywhere is at the same place': innovations in communications technologies

> We know that telecommunication tends to push the meaning of space towards zero, nevertheless, the earth still has simultaneous night and day, and depending on one's location an inconsiderate phone call can still get people out of bed.[29]

Developments in transportation technologies would have been impossible without parallel developments in communications technologies: *the* key technologies transforming relationships at the global scale. As Figure 4.4 shows, global communications systems have been transformed radically during the past 20 or 30 years through a whole cluster of significant innovations in information technologies.

In terms of communications infrastructure – the transmission channels through which information flows – two innovations have been especially significant: satellite communications and optical fibre technologies.

Transmission channels: satellites and optical fibre cables

Satellite technology began to revolutionize global communications from the mid-1960s when the Early Bird or Intelsat I satellite was launched.[30] This was capable of carrying 240 telephone conversations or two television channels simultaneously. Since then, the carrying capacity of communications satellites has grown exponentially. Satellite technology made possible remarkable levels of global communication of both conventional messages and the transmission of data. A message could be transmitted in one location and received in another on the other side of the world almost simultaneously. Today, there are more than 100 geostationary satellites in orbit.

However, for most parts of the world, satellite communications have been increasingly challenged by *optical fibre* technology carried within submarine cables:

> Satellites were ideal for broadcasting … as well as providing a larger number of telephone circuits than the combined capacity of all submarine cables. The life of satellites, however, is much shorter than that of cables and the number of 'parking spots' available in geosynchronous orbit is limited … Satellites also forced a shift from analogue to digital transmission and digital signals are optimally carried by fibre-optic cables, which appeared in the 1980s, making both old telephone cables and even most satellites themselves obsolete.[31]

The first commercially viable optical fibre system was developed in the USA in the early 1970s. Since then, the speed, carrying capacity and cost of optical fibre transmission cables have changed dramatically. Optical fibre systems have a huge carrying capacity, and transmit information at very high speed and, most importantly, with a high signal strength. By the end of the 1990s, for example,

> a single pair of optical fibres, each the thickness of a human hair … [could] … carry North America's entire long-distance communications traffic. Gemini, a transatlantic undersea cable … completed … [in 1998] … ha[d] more capacity than all existing transatlantic cables combined.[32]

Since then, optical fibre technology has continued to accelerate, vastly increasing the speed and capacity of communications networks. At the same time, the geographical spread of optical fibre systems has increased dramatically (Figures 4.8 and 4.9). Today, more than 90 per cent of all international telecommunications are transmitted using optical fibre cables. The system continues to expand as a response to rapidly increasing demands, especially from the growth of Internet

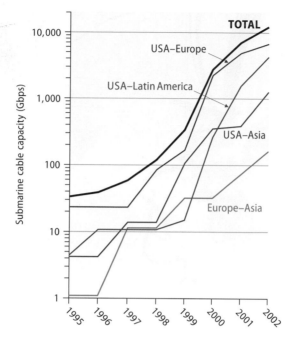

Figure 4.8 **Growth in the information carrying capacity of submarine cable systems**

Source: based on material in the *Financial Times*, 15 November 2000

traffic. In particular, video and data transmissions require much higher bandwidth than speech. There is also a need to build in extra capacity to cope with cable failure (as happened in mid-2008 when three submarine cables serving the Middle East and South Asia were damaged).

The Internet: the 'skeleton of cyberspace'

> The Internet is the decisive technology of the Information Age, as the electrical engine was the vector of technological transformation of the Industrial Age.[33]

The phenomenally rapid spread of the Internet has been one of the most remarkable developments of recent decades.[34] Its origins go back to the early 1970s and are to be found within the US Department of Defense. It spread initially through the linking of more specialized academic computer networks and, for some time, it seemed that it would remain a niche technology. Not so. As Figures 4.10 and 4.11 show, the growth of the Internet has been dramatic. Most important of all have been the development of the World Wide

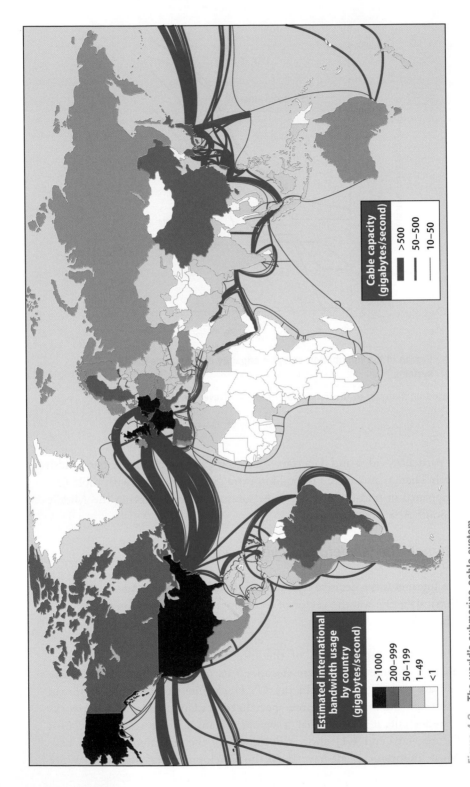

Figure 4.9 The world's submarine cable system

Source: based on material in the *Guardian* (1 February 2008; 18 August 2008)

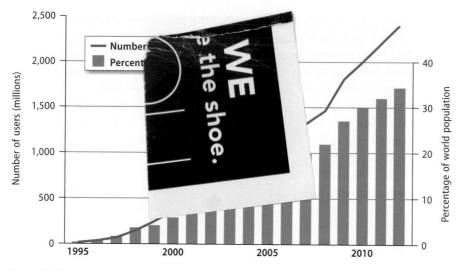

Figure 4.10 Exponential growth of the Internet

Source: based on material in www.internetworldstats.com

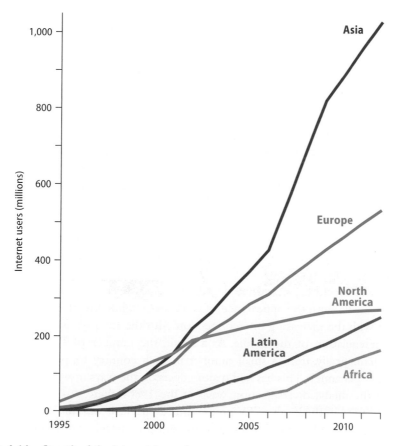

Figure 4.11 Growth of the Internet by region

Source: based on material in www.internetworldstats.com

Web (invented by Tim Berners-Lee in the mid-1990s) and the rapid increase in access to broadband and wireless transmission.

Internet communication has replaced (in whole or in part) a huge swathe of conventional communications methods. A large proportion of business communication is now conducted through the Internet. Similarly for millions of individuals, email and, more recently, the 'new' social media such as Facebook and Twitter have become the preferred means of communication. At the same time, the Internet gives access to a phenomenal amount of information on virtually everything under the sun through the World Wide Web. Without doubt, the Internet is changing the world and how we perceive and understand it – at least for those with access to it (see below).

The electronic mass media

The development of electronic mass media (radio, TV) during the twentieth century revolutionized the ways in which people living in one part of the world learn about what is happening in other parts of the world. Such media are especially powerful and influential not only because of their apparent immediacy, but also because they do not require the high level of literacy of books or newspapers. This is, of course, very important both commercially and politically. For example, large business firms require large markets to sustain them; global firms aspire to global markets. The existence of such markets obviously depends on income levels, but it depends, too, on potential customers becoming *aware* of a firm's offerings and being persuaded to purchase them. Even where consumer incomes are low, the ground may be prepared for possible future ability to purchase by creating an aspirational image.

Today, TV is the mass medium that has the most dramatic impact on people's awareness and perception of worlds beyond their own direct experience. Although the electronic media transmit messages of all kinds, a very large proportion of these messages (either explicitly or implicitly) are *commercial* messages aimed at the consumer. Because commercial advertising is a feature of most mass media networks throughout the world, the communications media open the doors of national markets to the heavily advertised, branded products of the transnational producers.

However, during the past three decades there has been a major 'phase shift' in the mass media with the appearance of cable and satellite broadcasting and, most recently, with the increasing interconnection with the Internet as well as a widespread deregulation of the media. As a result, the number of TV channels has grown dramatically, from a small number in each country to, potentially, many hundreds of channels. This has had major effects on the ways in which TV is used. Prior to the media diversification wave of the 1980s, there was a high level of standardization in the kinds of TV programme available. It was this kind of 'mutual experience' that led Marshall McLuhan to coin the metaphor of the *global village* in which certain images are shared and in which events take on the immediacy of participation.

But the increasing segmentation of TV messages means that the global village idea is no longer an accurate picture of reality:

> the fact that not everybody watches the same thing at the same time, and that each culture and social group has a specific relationship to the media system, does make a fundamental difference vis-à-vis the old system of standardized mass media … While the media have become indeed globally interconnected, and programs and messages circulate in the global network, *we are not living in a global village, but in customized cottages globally produced and locally distributed.*[35]

These trends are intensified through increasingly diverse ways of viewing TV programmes (e.g. on a variety of devices) and also at different times (through the use of on-demand TV services). Many of these trends, of course, are related to the development of wireless technologies and the rapid growth of smartphones and tablets.

Communications on the move: towards a wireless world

Telecommunications depend traditionally on a massive physical infrastructure. But within that infrastructure, one of the most significant developments of recent years has been the phenomenal growth of *mobile* communications, especially the mobile telephone or cellular phone. One of the first patents for a 'radio-telephone' system linked to base stations was taken out by Motorola in 1973. But development was slow. In the early 1980s, what was then still a relatively rare, and very prestigious, instrument – the mobile phone – was the size of a brick, weighed around 800 grams and cost almost $4000. Today, the weight is down to 90 grams and the typical cost of a basic handset is well below $100. At the same time, the geographical range and sophistication of mobile phones and their operating systems have increased dramatically. Hence, there has been an explosion in mobile phone ownership throughout the world. In the early 1990s, there were only a few hundred thousand subscribers to mobile systems; now there are more than 6 billion.[36] Mobile phone subscriptions now vastly exceed fixed telephone lines and at an increasing rate. In 2008, mobile subscriptions were a little over three times those of fixed subscriptions; by the end of 2011 they were five times greater. The fastest growth in mobile phone subscriptions is in developing countries: these made up more than four-fifths of new world mobile subscriptions in 2011.[37]

Much of this increase is being driven by the development of faster 3G and super-fast 4G systems, which enable a huge increase in the speed and quality of mobile Internet services. The spectacular recent development of the 'smartphone', a multi-purpose, integrated communications device, has been revolutionary. Indeed, smartphones (and tablets) have become the means by which increasing numbers of people access the Internet. The ITU estimate is that there were more than 1 billion mobile broadband subscriptions by the end of 2011 and that this has become the fastest-growing ICT service, increasing by 40 per cent in that year.

Such developments are revolutionary in many ways, especially in terms of their impact on conventional telecommunications and on social behaviour:

> The growth of mobile broadband services is erasing the boundaries between telephony and the Internet altogether ... As telephony has become increasingly digitized, the boundaries between traditional data and communications markets have become blurred ... texting has come to rival or surpass voice messages on many world telecommunications networks ... Instant messaging services such as Twitter and interactive Web pages such as Facebook, which permit online chat ... greatly enhanced the popularity of texting, which often bypasses the format of conventional email ...

> A clear sign of the mutually transformative impacts of the Internet and the world's telephony system is Voice Over Internet Protocol (VOIP), that is, telephone traffic conducted entirely through cyberspace, allowing users to bypass the toll charges ubiquitous among public switched networks ... The world's most popular VOIP application by far is Skype ... now the world's largest international provider of telephone services ... One half of Skype calls are between countries, and account for one-fourth of all calls that cross national borders.[38]

What we are experiencing, therefore, is a very rapid transition from a fixed to an increasingly wireless world of telecommunications in which the technological *convergence* between computing and communications, shown in Figure 4.4, has entered a new phase. Such developments have the potential to generate enormous social and economic changes as they free users (whether they be businesses or individuals) from the physical tie to fixed communications infrastructure.

Digital divides: an uneven world of communications

Although technological developments in communications have transformed space–time relationships between virtually all parts of the world, the outcomes – as in the case of physical movement – are immensely uneven. Not all places are equally connected in 'communications space'. The time–space surface is highly plastic; some parts shrink while other parts become, in effect, extended in relative, though not, of course, in absolute terms. By no means everywhere benefits equally from technological innovations in communications. As in the case of transportation facilities, the places that benefit most tend to be the already 'important' places. New investments in technology are market related; they go to where the returns are likely to be highest. The cumulative effect is both to

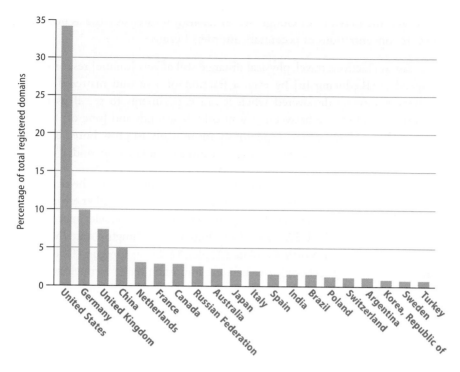

Figure 4.12   The uneven geography of Internet domain names

Source: based on data provided by Matthew Zook

reinforce certain communications routes at the global scale and to enhance the significance of the nodes (cities/countries) on those routes.

Even the Internet is far from being the placeless/spaceless phenomenon so often envisaged. For example, Figure 4.12 shows the highly uneven geography of registered Internet domain names at the end of 2012. Although there has been some spreading out, the pattern remains highly concentrated. North America and Europe have over 77 per cent of world domain names. The USA alone has one-third of the world total.

The seemingly spaceless 'cloud computing' also has a geography, and it, too, is very uneven. Its basic infrastructure (including the server farms referred to earlier on p. 82) is overwhelmingly an urban – especially a big city – phenomenon:

> This is partly an historical accident ... the Internet's fibre-optic cables often piggyback on old infrastructure where a right-of-way has already been established: they are laid alongside railways and roads or inside sewers ... Building the Internet on top of existing infrastructure in this way merely reinforces real-world geography. Just as cities are often railway and shipping hubs, they are also the logical places to put network hubs and servers, the powerful computers that store and distribute data.[39]

For example, the network of Google server farms is located as close as possible to the largest concentrations of potential customers because

> as fast as electrons travel, physical distance still affects [online] response speed ... Reducing [it] by even a fraction of a second mattered to users as Google discovered when it ran experiments to see if users noticed a difference between [a wait of] 0.9 seconds and [one of] 0.4 seconds ... Users were conspicuously more likely to grow bored and leave the Google site after waiting that interminable 0.9 seconds.[40]

To a considerable extent, therefore, the map of the Internet mirrors the network of global cities. At the same time, however, the particular energy and other environmental requirements of server farms are leading to their location in smaller, more remote, places. For example, in the USA, towns like Quincy in Washington state (Microsoft, Yahoo, Dell), Maiden in North Carolina (Apple), Dalles in Oregon (Google) and Prineville in Oregon (Facebook) have become important server farm clusters.

But it is at the *global* scale that the uneven geography of communications access is most serious. There is a real, and serious, *digital divide* between those places and people with access to communications technologies and those without.[41] Because such access is the key to so much information and knowledge, this poses severe developmental problems. Figure 4.13 summarizes some of these global inequalities in access to the communications media.

One of the biggest obstacles to communications growth and access in poor countries is the lack of fixed line infrastructures and the immense cost of providing them in poor and, especially, in rural areas. Wireless communications have the potential to overcome this:

> Mobile phones do not rely on a permanent electricity supply and can be used by people who cannot read or write. Phones are widely shared and rented out by the call, for example by the 'telephone ladies' found in Bangladeshi villages. Farmers and fishermen use mobile phones to call several markets and work out where they can get the best price for their produce. Mobile phones are used to make cashless payments in Zambia and several other African countries ...
>
> The digital divide that really matters, then, is between those with access to a mobile network and those without.[42]

Figure 4.13 shows that there has, indeed, been a huge change in the percentage of the population in developing countries having direct access to mobile telephones and the Internet. In the case of mobile phones, only 22.9 per cent had mobile subscriptions in 2005; by 2011 this had grown to 77.8 per cent. In the case of the Internet, only 7.7 per cent of the population in developing countries had access in 2005; by 2011 this had grown to 24.4 per cent. However, these figures are greatly distorted by developments in China, in particular, and in a small number of other

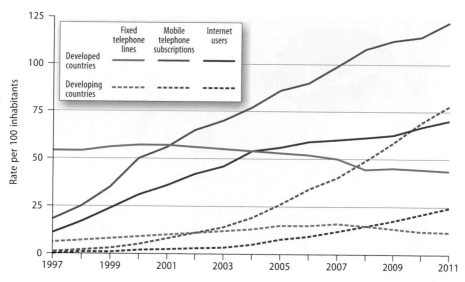

Figure 4.13 **Digital divides: uneven access to communications facilities**

Source: based on material in www.itu.int/ITU-D/ict/statistics

developing countries. For the majority, the digital divide remains alarmingly wide. Figure 4.14 demonstrates this very clearly.[43]

The digital divide between the 'global north' and the 'global south' is reflected in many ways, not least in the immense unevenness in geographical coverage in Wikipedia, as an analysis of geotagged articles has shown:

> There is clearly a highly uneven geography of information in Wikipedia. The US has the most articles about places or events (almost 100,000), while some smaller countries such as Tonga have fewer than 10 ... But it's not just size that is correlated with extremely low levels of wiki representation. Almost the entire continent of Africa is geographically poorly represented in Wikipedia. Remarkably, there are more Wikipedia articles written about Antarctica than all but one of the 53 countries in Africa.[44]

As Mark Graham argues,

> these highly uneven geographies of information matter. They shape what is known and what can be known, which in turn influences the myriad ways in which knowledge is produced, reproduced, enacted, and re-enacted ... The stickiness of information cores and peripheries, even in an age of supposed friction-free communications, is concerning because ... spatial configurations of information both have power and reproduce power ... Knowledge clusters that are reinforced by repeated rounds of spatial fixes thus result in, and reinforce, a landscape of uneven geographic development.[45]

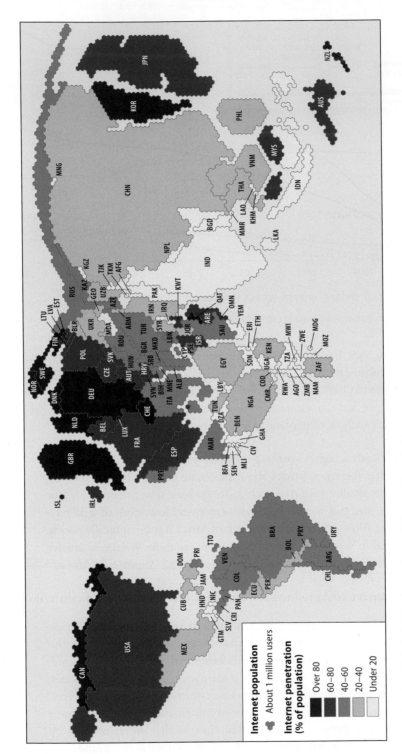

Figure 4.14 Digital divide: Internet population and penetration

Source: Mark Graham and Stefano de Sabbata, geography.oii.ox.ac.uk

The world is certainly not 'flat' – even in the supposedly spaceless 'information world' of the popular imagination.

TECHNOLOGICAL INNOVATIONS IN PRODUCTS, PRODUCTION SYSTEMS AND ORGANIZATIONAL FORMS

Product life cycles

Although a firm's profitability can be enhanced through increased penetration of existing markets or expansion into new geographical markets, there are limits. In an intensely competitive environment the introduction of a continuous stream of new products becomes essential to a firm's profitability and, indeed, to its very survival. However, all products have a limited life span: what is generally referred to as the *product life cycle* (PLC). Figure 4.15 shows the major characteristics of an idealized PLC: the growth of sales follows a systematic path from initial innovation through a series of stages. There are clear similarities with the innovation trajectory shown in Figure 4.1.

This kind of development path has very important implications for the growth of firms and for their profit levels. Of course, the rate at which the cycle proceeds will vary from one product to another. In some highly ephemeral products the cycle may run its course within a single year or even less. In others the cycle may be very long. However, in general, product cycles have become shorter, increasing the pressure on firms to develop new products or to acquire them from other firms. There are three major ways in which a product's sales may be maintained or increased:

- to introduce a new product as the existing one becomes obsolete so that 'overlapping' cycles occur;
- to extend the cycle for the existing product, either by making minor modifications in the product itself to 'update' it or by finding new uses;
- to make changes to the production technology itself to make the product more competitive.

However, product innovation alone is inadequate as a basis for a firm's survival and profitability. Firms must strive to produce their products as efficiently as possible. Recent developments in *process* technology – and, especially, in ICT – are having profound effects upon production processes in all economic sectors (see the next section). There is a close relationship between a product's trajectory through its life cycle and the way it is made, as Figure 4.15 shows. Each stage tends to have

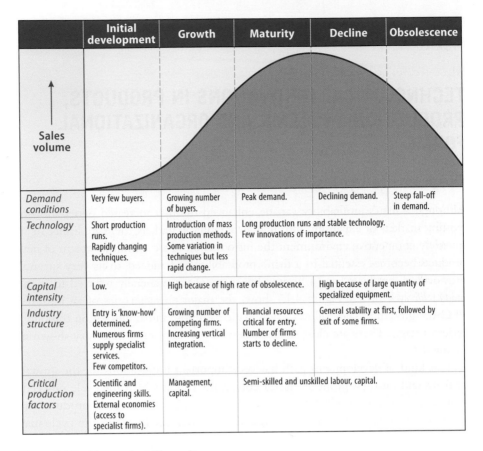

	Initial development	Growth	Maturity	Decline	Obsolescence
Demand conditions	Very few buyers.	Growing number of buyers.	Peak demand.	Declining demand.	Steep fall-off in demand.
Technology	Short production runs. Rapidly changing techniques.	Introduction of mass production methods. Some variation in techniques but less rapid change.	Long production runs and stable technology. Few innovations of importance.		
Capital intensity	Low.	High because of high rate of obsolescence.		High because of large quantity of specialized equipment.	
Industry structure	Entry is 'know-how' determined. Numerous firms supply specialist services. Few competitors.	Growing number of competing firms. Increasing vertical integration.	Financial resources critical for entry. Number of firms starts to decline.	General stability at first, followed by exit of some firms.	
Critical production factors	Scientific and engineering skills. External economies (access to specialist firms).	Management, capital.	Semi-skilled and unskilled labour, capital.		

Figure 4.15   **The product life cycle**

particular production characteristics. In general, as the cycle proceeds, the emphasis shifts from product-related technologies to process technologies and, in particular, to ways of minimizing production costs. In this respect, the relative importance of labour costs – especially of semi-skilled and unskilled labour – increases. More generally, different types of geographical location are relevant to different stages of the product cycle.

This view of systematic changes in the production process as a product matures is appealing and has some validity. There undoubtedly are important differences in the nature of the production process between a product in its very early stages of development and the same product in its maturity. But this linear, sequential notion of change is overly simplistic and deterministic. At any stage, the production process may be 'rejuvenated' by technological innovation. There may not necessarily be a simple sequence leading from small-scale production to standardized mass production.

Changes in production systems: towards greater flexibility and leanness

Most technological developments in production processes are, as we observed earlier, gradual and incremental: the result of 'learning by doing' and 'learning by using'. But periods of radical transformation of the production process have occurred throughout history. Over the long timescale of industrialization, the production process has developed through a series of stages, each of which represents increasing efforts to mechanize and to control more closely the nature and speed of work.

Five stages are generally identified:

- *Manufacture*: the collecting together of labour into workshops and the division of the labour process into specific tasks.
- *Machinofacture*: the application of mechanical processes and power through machinery in factories together with further division of labour.
- *Scientific management* ('Taylorism'): the subjection of the work process to scientific study in the late nineteenth century. This enhanced the fineness of the division of labour into specific tasks together with increased control and supervision.
- *Mass production* ('Fordism'): the development of assembly-line processes that controlled the pace of production and permitted the mass production of large volumes of standardized products.
- *Flexible and lean production*: the development of new production systems based upon the deep application of ICT.

These stages map closely onto the long-wave sequence shown earlier in Figure 4.3. The first K-wave was associated with the transition from manufacture to machinofacture. The application of scientific management principles to the production process emerged in the late phase of K2 and developed more fully in K3. The bases of mass production were established during K3, but reached their fullest development during K4. The key to production flexibility in K5 lies in the deep and extensive use of ICT, which provides more sophisticated control over production. Two particularly important processes are those of *flexible specialization* and *flexible mass production*. The potential of such flexible technologies is immense, and their implications are enormous. They involve three major tendencies:[46]

- A trend towards information intensity, rather than energy or materials intensity, in production.
- A much enhanced flexibility of production that challenges the old best-practice concept of mass production in three central respects:
  - A high volume of output is no longer necessary for high productivity; this can be achieved through a diversified set of low-volume products.

o Because rapid technological change becomes less costly and less risky, the 'minimum change' strategy in product development is less necessary for cost effectiveness.

o The new technologies allow a profitable focus on segmented rather than mass markets; products can be tailored to specific local conditions and needs.

- A major change in labour requirements in terms of both volume and type of labour. This involves a shift towards multitasking, rather than narrow labour specialization; a greater emphasis on teamworking; and individualized payments systems.

Largely because of the accelerating pace of development of ICT in production, the frontier of production process technology is changing very rapidly. One of the latest examples is 3D printing (sometimes known as 'additive manufacturing'):

> Machines based on advances in electronics, laser technology and chemistry can now 'print' complex three-dimensional objects, building them up layer-by-layer from granules of plastic or metal.

> The flexibility of 3D printing means that things can be made in much smaller numbers and much greater variety than was previously economically viable.[47]

However, 3D printing is still in its infancy: 'production equipment is expensive; technical experience with 3D printing is poorly established; making load-bearing or structural parts from 3D printing using metal is fairly difficult – most 3D printing so far has been used for plastic parts or non-structural metal objects'.[48] But its use is growing rapidly, especially for the production of prototypes. For example, Nike and Adidas are using 3D printing to increase the speed with which they can make multiple prototypes of their shoes,[49] and auto manufacturers to produce design samples and prototypes. More radically, Siemens is using 3D printing to manufacture spare parts and components for gas turbines: 'Siemens believes 3D printing could "revolutionise" the supply of spare parts … Soon they will be able to be printed exactly where they are needed – close to the customer.'[50]

The current position, therefore, is that of a *diversity* of production systems (Figure 4.16), but where the relative importance of specific processes is changing. In fact, no single production system is ever completely dominant. Even during the heyday of Fordist mass production there were firms and sectors in which smaller-scale, more craft-based, production persisted. Today, when all the emphasis is on flexible production, there is still a good deal of mass production and, indeed, of craft production. Figure 4.17 summarizes some of the contrasts between the three systems of production.

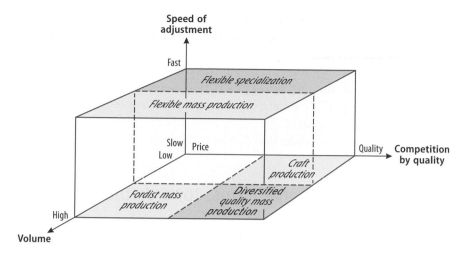

Figure 4.16 Ideal types of production system

Source: based on Hollingsworth and Boyer, 1997: Figure 1.3

Characteristic	Craft production	Mass production	Flexible/lean production
Technology	Simple but flexible tools and equipment using non-standardized components.	Complex but rigid single-purpose machinery using standardized components. Heavy time and cost penalties in switching to new products.	Highly flexible production methods using modular component systems. Relatively easy to switch to new products.
Labour force	Highly skilled in most aspects of professional production.	Very narrowly skilled workers design products but production itself performed by unskilled/semi-skilled 'interchangeable' workers. Each performs a relatively simple task repetitively and in predefined time sequence.	Multi-skilled, polyvalent workers operate in teams. Responsible for several manufacturing operations plus simple maintenance and repair.
Supplier relationships	Very close contact between customer and supplier. Most suppliers located within single city.	Distant relationships with suppliers, both functionally and geographically. Large inventories held at assembly plant 'just in case' of supply disruption.	Very close relationships with functionally-tiered system of suppliers. Use of 'just-in-time' delivery systems encourages geographical proximity between customers and suppliers.
Production volume	Relatively low.	Extremely high.	Extremely high.
Product variety	Extremely wide: each product customized to specific requirements.	Narrow range of standardized designs with only minor product modifications.	Increasingly wide range of differentiated products.

Figure 4.17 The major characteristics of craft production, mass production and flexible/lean production

Source: based, in part, on material in Womack et al., 1990

Thus, we can see a trend towards:

- *increasingly fine degrees of specialization* in many production processes, enabling their fragmentation into a number of individual operations;

- *increasing standardization and routinization* of these individual operations, enabling the use of semi-skilled and unskilled labour (this is especially apparent during the mature stage of a PLC);
- *increasing flexibility* in the production process that is altering the relationship between the scale and the cost of production, permitting smaller production runs, increasing product variety, and changing the way production and the labour process are organized;
- *increasing modularity* of production (see next section).

Changing organizational forms: towards the network organization

Just as changes in production processes and systems can be broadly mapped onto the long-wave sequence shown in Figure 4.3, so, too, can changes in organizational form. In broad-brush terms, organizational change has followed a path from an early focus on individual entrepreneurs in K1, through small firms, but of larger average size, in K2, to the monopolistic, oligopolistic and cartel structures of K3, the centralized, hierarchical TNCs of K4 and the 'network' and alliance organizational forms of K5. I will have much more to say about such business networks in Chapter 5. Here I focus briefly on two aspects most closely related to recent ICT-led changes in production.

The first one is the *modular production network*, what Suzanne Berger calls the 'Lego' model of production involving networks of firms:

> For many industries, the changes of the past twenty years mean that *organizing production has become more like playing with a set of Legos* than building a model airplane or a car. In other words, it's now possible to create many different models using the same pieces. New components can be added on to old foundations; elements from old structures can be reused in new configurations; parts can be shared by many players with different construction plans in mind … *the myriad possibilities of organizing a company have grown out of new digital technologies that create countless opportunities for using resources, organizations, and customers all over the world to build businesses that did not even exist ten years ago.*[51]

The development of modular production networks[52] depends largely on the fact that some modern production circuits have 'natural' breakpoints, where there is a transition from dependence on tacit knowledge to one where information can be codified through standard, agreed protocols. Figure 4.18 shows how such modular production networks differ from that of a traditionally vertically integrated firm.

A second type of new network organization, again heavily dependent on ICT, is the *virtual firm* or the *cellular network* organization[53] (Figure 4.19). Organizationally,

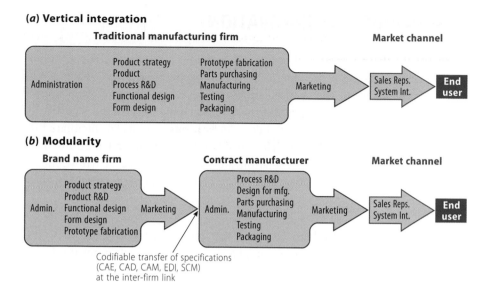

Figure 4.18 **From vertical integration to a modular production network**

Source: based on Sturgeon, 2002: Figure 1

the entire network structure is relatively 'flat' and non-hierarchical. Its essence is that the participants are all separate firms with no common ownership. Network forms of this broad type are rapidly emerging in such 'knowledge businesses' as advanced electronics, computer software design, biotechnology, design and engineering services, health care, and the like.

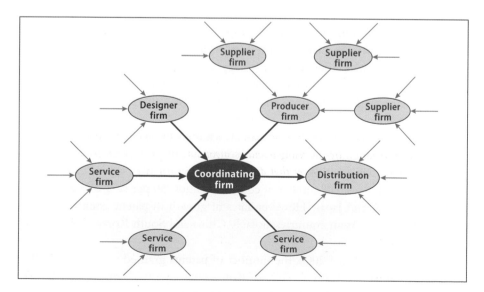

Figure 4.19 **A cellular network organization**

Source: based, in part, on Miles and Snow, 1986: Figure 1

GEOGRAPHIES OF INNOVATION

Innovation – the heart of technological change – is fundamentally a *learning* process. Such learning – by doing, by using, by observing and sharing with others – depends upon the accumulation and development of relevant knowledge. These processes have a very distinctive geography. Despite the fact that the development of highly sophisticated communications systems has facilitated the diffusion of knowledge at unparalleled speed and over unprecedented distances, 'conditions of knowledge accumulation are highly localized'.[54] Knowledge is *produced in specific places* and often used, and enhanced most intensively, in those same places. Hence,

> to understand technological change, it is crucial to identify the economic, social, political and geographical context in which innovation is generated and disseminated. This space may be local, national or global. Or, more likely, it will involve a complex and evolving integration, at different levels, of local, national and global factors.[55]

National innovation systems

The idea underlying the notion of national innovation systems is that the specific combination of social, cultural, political, legal, educational and economic institutions and practices varies systematically between national contexts.[56] Such nationally differentiated characteristics help to influence the kind of technology system that develops there. These underlying forces help to explain the gradual shifts in national technological leadership evident in successive K-waves (see Figure 4.3). Despite the claims of the hyper-globalists that national distinctiveness is declining, the evidence strongly suggests that national variations in technology systems – and therefore in technological competence – persist. Certainly there is a lot of evidence to show that the volume and characteristics of technological innovation vary greatly by country.

One indicator is the number of patents granted by country. Patents are the mechanism by which an individual or a company can protect an invention for a period of years. As Figure 4.20 shows, the patent map is highly uneven. Patent grants are concentrated in a small number of countries: almost 50 per cent of patent grants went to the USA and Japan. However, rates of growth in patent grants have been fastest in some East Asian countries, notably China and South Korea. For example:

> Between 2000 and 2006, the number of patents granted to applicants from China and the Republic of Korea grew by 26.5% and 23.2% a year, respectively (average annual growth rate).[57]

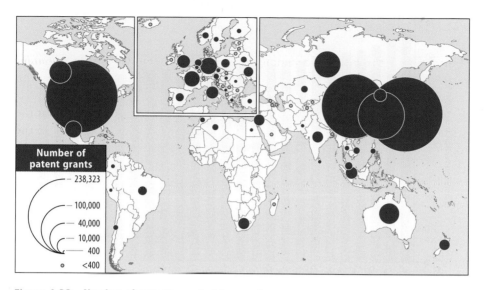

Figure 4.20 **Number of patents granted by country**

Source: based on data in WIPO-INSEAD, 2012: Table P2

The rapid growth of Chinese patents is matched by the 'awe-inspiring expansion of Chinese science' and its emergence as 'the second largest producer of scientific knowledge' as revealed by an analysis of 10,500 scientific journals worldwide for the period 1981–2008.[58]

Patents are one way of measuring innovative activity but there are many other ways. One is the *Global Innovation Index* (GII), a composite measure based upon 84 indicators encompassing both innovation inputs (institutions, human capital and research, infrastructure, market sophistication, business sophistication) and innovation outputs (knowledge and technology outputs and creative outputs). On this measure, as Figure 4.21 shows, smaller countries head the rankings. But, of course, in both the patent grant data and the GII, it is wealthier countries that figure most strongly. The map of the geography of innovation closely corresponds to the map of overall development.

Localized knowledge clusters

National systems of innovation are not homogeneous entities. They consist of aggregations of *localized* knowledge clusters.[59] One reason for the significance of 'localness' in the creation and diffusion of knowledge lies in a basic distinction in the nature of knowledge itself, which is broadly of two kinds:[60]

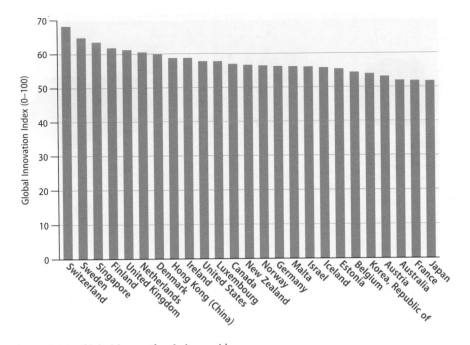

Figure 4.21   Global Innovation Index rankings

Source: based on data in WIPO-INSEAD, 2012: p. xviii

- *codified (or explicit) knowledge:* the kinds of knowledge that can be expressed formally in documents, blueprints, software, hardware, etc.;
- *tacit knowledge:* the deeply personalized knowledge possessed by individuals that is virtually impossible to make explicit and to communicate to others through formal mechanisms.

Although knowledge creation is more complex than this tacit/codified distinction implies it does help us to understand the role of space and place in technological diffusion. Codified knowledge can be transmitted relatively easily across distance. It is through such means that, throughout history, political, religious and economic organizations, for example, have been able to 'act at a distance'; to exert control over geographically dispersed activities.[61] Developments in transportation and communications technologies have enabled such 'acting' or 'controlling' to take place over greater and greater distances. Tacit knowledge, on the other hand, has a very steep 'distance-decay' curve. It generally requires direct experience and interaction; it depends to a considerable extent − though not completely by any means − on geographical proximity. It is much more 'sticky'. However, it is a mistake to take the 'tacit = local', 'codified = global' contrast too far because 'both tacit and codified knowledge can be exchanged locally and globally'.[62]

The specific socio-technological context within which innovative activity is embedded − what is sometimes called the *innovative milieu* − is a key factor in knowledge creation. This context consists of a mixture of both tangible and intangible elements:

- economic, social and political institutions;
- knowledge and know-how which evolve over time in a specific context (the 'something in the air' notion identified many decades ago by Alfred Marshall);
- 'conventions, which are taken-for-granted rules and routines between the partners in different kinds of relations defined by uncertainty'. [63]

The basis of localized knowledge clusters, therefore, lies in several characteristics of the innovation process that are highly sensitive to geographical distance and proximity:[64]

- *Localized patterns of communication*: geographical distance greatly influences the likelihood of individuals within and between organizations sharing knowledge and information links.
- *Localized innovation search and scanning patterns*: geographical proximity influences the nature of a firm's search process for technological inputs or possible collaborators. Small firms, in particular, often have a geographically narrower 'scanning field' than larger firms.
- *Localized invention and learning patterns*: innovation often occurs in response to specific local problems. Processes of 'learning by doing' and 'learning by using' tend to be closely related to physical proximity in the production process.
- *Localized knowledge sharing*: because the acquisition and communication of tacit knowledge is strongly localized geographically, there is a tendency for localized 'knowledge pools' to develop around specific activities.
- *Localized patterns of innovation capabilities and performance*: geographical proximity, in enriching the depth of particular knowledge and its use, can reduce the risk and uncertainty of innovation.

Local innovative milieux, therefore, consist primarily of a *nexus of untraded interdependencies* set within a temporal context of *path-dependent* processes of technological change. We outlined the major elements of such processes in general terms in Chapter 3. The point of emphasizing the 'untraded' nature of the interdependencies within such milieux is to distinguish the social 'cement' (especially face-to-face contact) which binds this kind of localized agglomeration from that which may be associated with the minimization of transaction costs (e.g. of materials and components transfers) through geographical proximity. The 'buzz' derived from 'being there' is at the heart of these social processes.[65]

But that is not the entire story. Localized knowledge clusters cannot be sustained and developed entirely through such incestuous relationships. A key additional process involves the connections between some of the actors in a given locality with outsiders (e.g. firms with suppliers, customers or sources of specific information and knowledge). In other words, as well as 'local buzz' there also have to be 'pipelines': channels of communication to other actors in other places. The processes of knowledge creation and innovation, therefore, consist of a complex set of networks and processes operating *within and across* various spatial scales, from the global, through the national, the regional and the local.

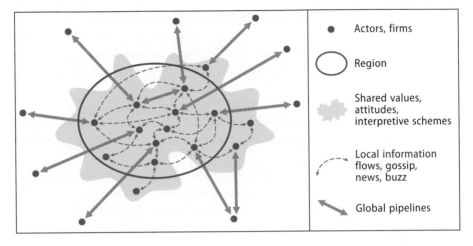

Figure 4.22   **Localized knowledge clusters in a wider context: local buzz and global pipelines**

Source: based on Bathelt et al., 2004: Figure 1

Figure 4.22 provides an idealized picture of this very complex process. It is based on the argument that

> the existence of local buzz of high quality and relevance leads to a more dynamic cluster … These actors and their buzz are, however, of little relevance if firms are not 'tuned in' … It is likely that a milieu, where many actors with related yet complementary and heterogeneous knowledge, skill and information reside, provides a great potential for dynamic interaction …

A well-developed system of pipelines connecting the local cluster to the rest of the world is beneficial for the cluster in two ways. First, each individual firm can benefit from establishing knowledge-enhancing relations to actors outside the local cluster. Even world-class clusters cannot be permanently self-sufficient in terms of state-of-the-art knowledge creation. New and valuable knowledge will always be created in other parts of the world and firms who can build pipelines to such sites of global excellence gain competitive advantage. Second, it seems reasonable to assume that the information that one cluster firm can acquire through its pipelines will spill over to other firms in the cluster through local buzz ... That is why a firm will learn more if its neighbouring firms in the cluster are globally well connected rather than being more inward-looking and insular in their orientation.[66]

The importance of localized knowledge/technology clusters to potential economic development has put them at the heart of economic policy in most countries. Who would not want to have a Silicon Valley as the driver of economic transformation? Everybody wants one, it seems, judging by the number of projects with the label 'silicon' in their title (a few examples: Silicon Alley, Silicon Fen, Silicon Glen, Silicon Gulf, Silicon Beach, even Silicon Roundabout in East London – the list is almost endless). Scores of places throughout the world have been labelled as the 'new' Silicon Valley.[67] Too often, however, such policies are driven by a desire to make a quick fix without much understanding of the complexity of the processes involved in the creation of such clusters. It is not difficult to recognize a successful cluster when one sees one; it is far more difficult (although not necessarily impossible) to be able to create or to replicate one as a matter of policy. Most are the outcome of the historical process of cumulative, path-dependent growth processes (see Chapter 3).

NOTES

1   The term 'creative gales of destruction' is borrowed from Schumpeter (1943).
2   Schumpeter (1943: 83).
3   Borrus, quoted in Cohen and Zysman (1987: 183; emphasis added).
4   Edgerton (2007).
5   This approach is essentially 'neo-Schumpeterian'. See Dosi et al. (1988), Freeman (1982, 1987, 1988), Freeman and Louçã (2001), Metcalfe and Dilisio (1996), Perez (1983, 1985, 2010).
6   Freeman and Perez (1988), Perez (2010).
7   Lipsey et al. (2005) use the term 'General Purpose Technologies (GPTs)'.
8   Freeman (1987: 130; emphasis added).
9   Perez (1983).
10 Perez (2010: 186).
11 See Freeman et al. (1982), Freeman and Louçã (2001), Freeman and Perez (1988), Hall and Preston (1988), Perez (2010), Rennstich (2002).
12 Hall and Preston (1988: 6).
13 Perez (2010: 189).
14 Gleick (2012: 8). Gleick provides a highly readable account of the development of what he calls *The Information*. See also Castells (1996), Hall and Preston (1988).
15 Rennstich (2002: 174).
16 Henderson and Castells (1987: 6).
17 Perez (2010: 189).

18   Carr (2008b).

19   Carr (2008a: 2; emphasis added).

20   Gleick (2012: 396).

21   For broad-ranging discussions of these technologies see Brunn and Leinbach (1991), Castells (1996), Graham and Marvin (1996), Hall and Preston (1988), World Bank (2009b: chapter 6).

22   See O'Rourke and Williamson (1999: chapter 3) for a detailed discussion of these developments.

23   Dean and Sebastia-Barriel (2004: 314).

24   World Bank (2009b: 177).

25   World Bank (2009b: 177).

26   Levinson (2006) provides a comprehensive and highly readable account of the development of containerization. See also Cudahy (2010: 73–86).

27   *Independent* (30 August 2000).

28   *Guardian* (7 March 2013).

29   Luhmann (1998: 85). Thanks to Roger Lee for this.

30   Malecki and Hu (2006) and Warf (2006, 2007) provide useful analyses of satellite and cable systems.

31   Malecki and Hu (2006: 7).

32   *Financial Times* (28 July 1998).

33   Castells (2013: 132).

34   Zook (2005) provides an excellent analysis of the development of the Internet. See also Castells (1996, 2008, 2013), Dodge and Kitchin (2001), Graham (2010), Malecki (2002).

35   Castells (1996: 341).

36   International Telecommunication Union statistics. For a detailed accounts of the global spread of mobile phones see Comer and Wikle (2008). Castells et al. (2007) explore the social implications of mobile communications.

37   International Telecommunication Union (ITU) statistics.

38   Warf (2013: 224, 225, 226).

39   *The Economist* (11 August 2001: 18).

40   Stross (2008) quoted in the *Guardian* (1 November 2008).

41   Major contributions include Dodge and Kitchin (2001), Graham (2012, 2014), Graham et al. (2012), Zook (2001, 2005, 2007).

42   *The Economist* (12 March 2005: 9).

43   See Graham (2014).

44   Graham (2009: 3). See also Graham et al. (2011).

45   Graham (2012: 156, 157).

46   Perez (1985).

47   *Financial Times* (4 June 2012).

48   Marsh (2012).

49   *Financial Times* (10 June 2013).

50   *Financial Times* (27 December 2013).

51   Berger (2005: 61; emphasis added).

52   See Berger (2005), Sturgeon (2002, 2003).

53   Miles et al. (1999).

54   Metcalfe and Dilisio (1996: 58).
55   Archibugi and Michie (1997: 2).
56   See Archibugi and Michie (1997), Archibugi et al. (1999), Freeman (1997), Lundvall (2007), Lundvall and Maskell (2000), Patel and Pavitt (1998).
57   WIPO (2008: 7).
58   *Financial Times* (26 January 2010).
59   There is a vast literature on this topic. See, for example, Asheim (2007), Asheim and Gertler (2005), Bathelt et al. (2004), Bunnell and Coe (2001), Gertler (1995, 2003), Gertler et al. (2000), Mattsson (2007), Morgan (2004), Sonn and Storper (2008), Storper (1997), Storper and Venables (2004).
60   Gertler (2003). See also Asheim (2007), Howells (2012a, b).
61   Fields (2004), Law (1986).
62   Bathelt et al. (2004: 32).
63   Storper (1995: 208).
64   Howells (2000: 58–9).
65   Bathelt et al. (2004), Gertler (1995), Storper and Venables (2004), Sturgeon (2003).
66   Bathelt et al. (2004: 45–6).
67   See, for example, Manning (2013: 380–1).

Want to know more about this chapter? Visit the companion website at **www.guilford.com/dickenGS7** for free access to author videos, suggested reading and practice questions to further enhance your study.

Five

TRANSNATIONAL CORPORATIONS: THE PRIMARY 'MOVERS AND SHAPERS' OF THE GLOBAL ECONOMY

THE MYTH OF THE 'GLOBAL' CORPORATION

A transnational corporation is a firm with the power to coordinate and control operations in more than one country, even if it does not own them.

The popular view is that TNCs are gargantuan, global firms whose giant footprints extend across the world and whose size makes them comparable with, or even in some cases, greater than entire nation-states. Of course, the precise numbers and identities of TNCs and states used in such comparisons vary over time (the figures below refer to the years 1999–2000) but the theme is constant. The typical argument runs as follows:[1]

- 'Of the 100 largest economies in the world, 51 are corporations; only 49 are countries (based on a comparison of corporate sales and country GDPs) ... To put this in perspective, General Motors is now bigger than Denmark; DaimlerChrysler is bigger than Poland; Royal Dutch/Shell is bigger than Pakistan.'
- 'The 1999 sales of each of the top five corporations (General Motors, Wal-Mart, Exxon Mobil, Ford Motor and DaimlerChrysler) are bigger than the GDPs of 182 countries.'

These are, indeed, very striking comparisons, the inference being that leading TNCs are not only bigger but also more powerful than states. But are they really meaningful? The answer is that, beyond their value as polemic, they are not. They are superficial and misleading, although they certainly make eye-catching head-lines. In fact, the statistics do not measure the same thing quantitatively, and they certainly do not capture the qualitative differences between TNCs and states.

One of the central claims of the hyper-globalists is that transnational firms are abandoning their ties to their country of origin and converging towards a universal *global* organizational form. Technological and regulatory developments in the world economy, it is argued, have created a 'global surface' on which a dominant organizational form is developing and wiping out less efficient competitors no longer protected by national or local barriers. Such an organization, it is asserted, is 'placeless' and 'boundary-less'. Throughout this book we challenge such a view.

How 'global' are the world's largest TNCs?

If the 'global corporation' hypothesis were valid then we would expect that at least the majority of the world's largest TNCs would have most of their operations dispersed widely outside their home country. One crude measure of such geographical spread is the *Transnationality Index* (TNI) of each of the largest 100 TNCs.[2] The TNI is a weighted average of three indicators: foreign sales as a percentage of total sales; foreign assets as a percentage of total assets; and foreign employment as a percentage of total employment. The higher the value, the greater the extent of a firm's transnationality; the lower the value, the more a firm is domestically oriented.

Figure 5.1 compares TNIs for firms from individual countries over a 20-year period. As might be expected, it shows that the degree of transnationality among the 100 largest TNCs has indeed increased progressively. In 1993 the average TNI was 51.6; in 2012 it was 67.8. Nevertheless, this still means that on average around one-third of their activities are based in their home countries. Of course, the composition of the top 100 did not remain constant over the 20-year period. However, the degree of transnationality continues to vary substantially between firms of different geographical origins. Part of this is explained by country size: the smaller the country, in general, the more transnational its companies tend to be. But that is not the entire story. Although the US average increased substantially from 36.7 to 58.3, the overall extent of transnationality of the largest US TNCs remains significantly lower than that of other major countries, except Japan. Many leading US TNCs still have a large proportion of their activities in the USA itself. Thus, despite many decades of international operations, the largest TNCs – at least in quantitative terms – remain strongly connected with their home base.

But the TNI goes only a very small way towards answering the question of how global the world's largest TNCs are. It tells us very little about the relative *geographical extent* of TNC activities outside the home country, only distinguishing between home and foreign. A firm might have a TNI of, say, 80 (meaning that 80 per cent of its activities were outside its home country) but all of those activities

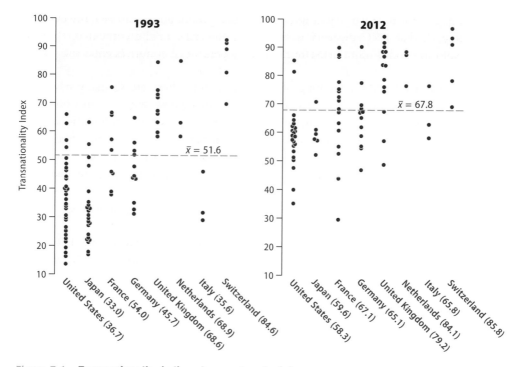

Figure 5.1 **Transnationality indices by country of origin**

Source: calculated from UNCTAD, *World Investment Report*, various issues

might be located in just one foreign country. An example would be the large number of US firms that operate only in Canada. Neither does it help us to establish whether or not TNCs of different national origins are becoming similar in their modes of operation. It is at least possible that TNCs may retain more of their assets and employment in their home country but still be converging organizationally and behaviourally towards a universal, global form. On the basis of these data, the jury is still out.

A different perspective: the highly diverse population of TNCs

Clearly, the very largest TNCs are immensely important in the global economy. The 100 largest TNCs, for example, employed around 15 million workers directly in 2011, of which 9 million were located outside the firm's home country.[3] This represented around 13 per cent of the foreign employment in the total number of TNCs identified by UNCTAD. However, the overall population of TNCs is far more diverse than the stereotype suggests: in terms of size, geographical origins, organizational structure and ways of becoming transnational. In fact, the evidence suggests that TNC diversity is increasing, especially in the context of the ICT explosion and as more firms from formerly peripheral countries enter the picture:

> Indeed at the beginning of the 21st century there are so many new kinds of internationally active firms – so many new 'species' – that one might legitimately talk of the new 'zoology' of the international economy … It is inhabited by a few giants, true, but mostly by a large number of SMEs [Small and Medium-size Enterprises] which are internationally active. Their modes of internationalizing, their reasons for doing so, their organizational and strategic innovations – are scarcely captured by existing theories and conceptual frameworks.[4]

Thus, TNC diversity, not uniformity, is the norm in today's world in which global production networks are the predominant form of organization. TNCs, whatever their size and shape, are deeply embedded in such networks, whether as lead firms or as suppliers, collaborators or customers. This chapter, then, is concerned with explaining why and how such TNCs develop, and how they configure and reconfigure their internal and external networks, both organizationally and geographically.

WHY FIRMS TRANSNATIONALIZE

Although state-owned TNCs have certainly become more important, they represent, according to UNCTAD, less than 1 per cent of the world total. Most TNCs are private *capitalist* enterprises. As such, they must behave according to the basic 'rules' of capitalism. The most fundamental is the drive for *profit* in a highly competitive environment, which is both increasingly global in its extent and also extremely volatile: 'This creates an environment of hyper-competition – an environment in which advantages are rapidly created and eroded.'[5] Firms are no longer competing largely with national rivals but with firms from across the world. Given these circumstances, therefore, one way of explaining TNCs is simply as a reflection of the 'normal' expansionary tendencies of the *circuits of capital*.[6] In these terms, the question of 'Why transnationalize?' might almost be better put as 'Why *not* transnationalize?'

Although a firm's motivation for engaging in transnational operations may be highly individual we can classify them into two broad categories (although the boundary between these is less sharp than this dichotomy suggests):

- market seeking;
- asset seeking.

Market seeking

Most FDI, whether engaged in producing goods or services or in marketing and sales, is designed to serve a specific geographical market by locating inside that market. The good or service produced abroad may be virtually identical to that being produced in the firm's home country, although there may well be modifications to suit the specific local tastes or requirements. In effect, such specifically market-oriented investment is a form of horizontal expansion across national boundaries. Three attributes of markets are especially important:

- *Size*: the most obvious attraction measured, for example, in terms of per capita income. Figure 5.2 shows the enormous global variation in per capita income levels. The largest geographical markets in terms of incomes, although not in terms of population, are obviously the USA and Western Europe. Such variations in per capita income provide a crude indication of how the *level* of demand will vary from place to place across the world.
- *Structure*: countries with different income levels tend to have a different structure of demand, thus as incomes rise, so does the aggregate demand for goods and services. But this does not affect all products equally. Populations in countries with low income levels tend to spend a larger proportion of their income on basic necessities while, conversely, people in countries with high income levels spend a higher proportion of their income on 'higher-order' manufactured goods and services. *Growth* in income, and not just its level, therefore, is highly significant in attracting foreign investment. Hence the attraction of the fast-growing emerging market economies of East Asia in particular.
- *Accessibility*: in the past, a major barrier was the cost of transportation. Today, this is far less significant, although not totally unimportant, especially for some products. However, political constraints in the form of various kinds of trade barrier do remain highly significant (see Chapter 6).

Asset seeking

Most of the assets needed by a firm to produce and sell its specific products and services are unevenly distributed geographically. This is most obviously the case in the natural resource industries, where firms must, of necessity, locate their extractive activities at the sources of supply. Often, such investments form the first element in an organizational sequence of vertically integrated operations whose later stages (processing) may be located quite separately from the source of supply itself, in some cases close to the final market. Natural resource-oriented foreign investments have a very long history and remain highly significant in the global economy (see Chapter 12).

Technological changes in production processes and in transportation have evened out the significance of location for some of the traditionally important

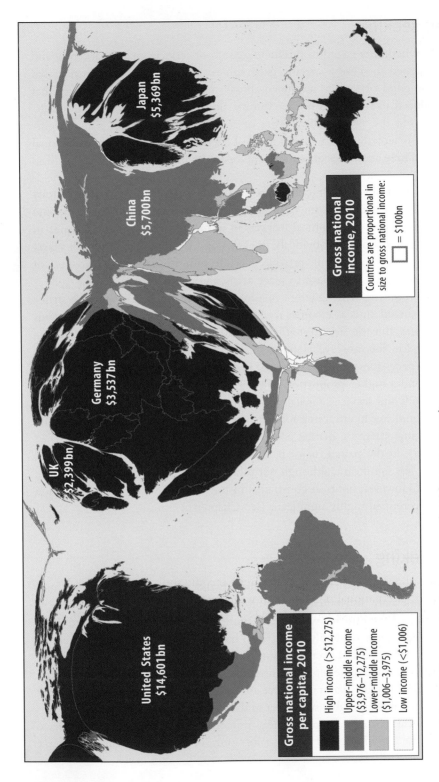

Figure 5.2 **Variations in market size: gross national income per capita**

Source: World Bank 2012 data. Cartograms produced by Danny Dorling and Benjamin Hennig, School of Geography and the Environment, University of Oxford

factors of production. At the global scale, arguably the two most important location-specific factors today are socially created, rather than occurring in nature:

- access to *knowledge*;
- access to *labour*.

The strong tendency for *knowledge* creation, dissemination and technological innovation to appear in *geographical clusters* (see Chapter 4) creates a major locational incentive. Particularly in those activities in which technological change is especially rapid and unpredictable, the incentive to locate 'where the knowledge and the action are' becomes very powerful. Such knowledge may be based in specific kinds of institution (such as universities, research institutes, industry associations). Fundamentally, however, it derives from the skills and knowledge embodied in *people*.

From a TNC's perspective, the locational significance of *labour* as a 'production factor' is reflected in a number of ways, although, of course, working people are very much more than 'crude abstractions in which ... [they are] ... reduced to the categories of wages, skill levels, location, gender, union membership and the like, the relative importance of which is weighed by firms in their location decision-making'.[7] Such characteristics vary, of course, in their significance according to the specific kind of labour being sought, as the cases in Part Four demonstrate. For some activities, it is cheap, unskilled, non-unionized labour that is sought; for others, it is highly skilled and educated 'knowledge workers'. In general terms, however, four especially important attributes of labour show large geographical variations:

- *Knowledge and skills.* Knowledge and skills depend on such conditions as the breadth and depth of education and on the particular history of an area's development. As a result, there are wide geographical variations in the availability of different types of labour. One very approximate indicator at the global scale is the variation in educational levels (e.g. extent of literacy, enrolment in various stages of education, public expenditure on education, etc.). Figure 5.3 maps one such indicator: the proportion of the relevant population in tertiary education. As might be expected, there is a very high correlation between these measures and the distribution of per capita income shown in Figure 5.2.
- *Wage costs.* International differences in wage levels can be staggeringly wide, as Figure 5.4 shows. These figures should be treated with some caution; they are averages across the whole of manufacturing industry and are therefore affected by the specific industry mix. Some industries have much higher wage levels than others. Even so, the contrasts are striking.
- *Labour productivity.* Spatial variations in wage costs are only a partial indication of the geographical importance of labour as a production factor. What matters from a firm's perspective is the scale of output per worker for a given wage or salary. The productivity of labour varies enormously from place to place, a reflection of a number of influences including: education, training, skill, motivation, as well as the kind

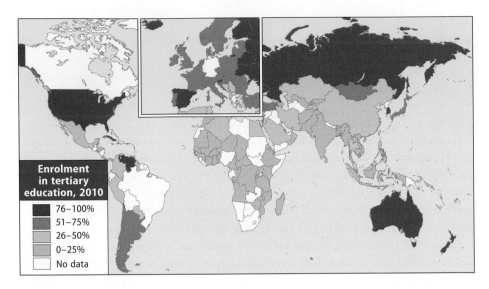

Figure 5.3   **Enrolment in tertiary education**

Source: based on data in USAID, *Global Education Database*

of capital equipment (machinery etc.) in use. Simply chasing low wage costs, without taking into account differences in productivity, is not a good corporate strategy.

• *Labour 'controllability'.* Largely because of historical circumstances, there are considerable geographical differences in the degree of labour 'militancy' and in the extent to which labour is organized through labour unions. The proportion of the workers who are members of labour unions has declined markedly in some countries, as we noted in Chapter 3. The fact that many firms are very wary of 'highly organized' labour regions is demonstrated by their tendency to relocate from such regions or to make new investments in places where labour is regarded as being more malleable.

Global variations in production costs are a highly significant element in the transnational investment–location decision. This is obviously the case for asset-oriented investments but it is also a critical consideration for market-oriented investments. In that case there is always a trade-off to be made between the benefits of market proximity on the one hand and geographical variations in production costs on the other. But the problem is not merely one of variations in production costs at a single moment in time or even the obvious point that such costs change over time. A particularly important consideration is the *uncertainty* of the level of future production costs in different locations. One way of dealing with such uncertainty is for the TNC to locate similar plants in a variety of different locations or to outsource to independent firms and then to adopt a flexible system of production allocation between plants. However, this strategy is made more complex by the

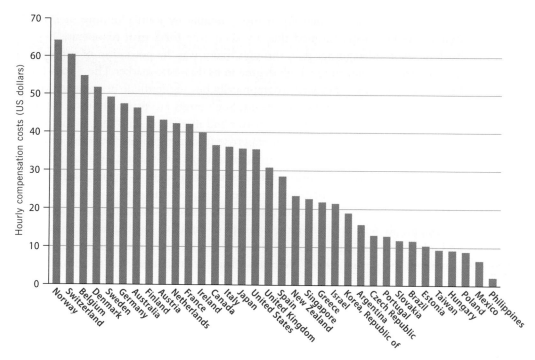

Figure 5.4 **Geographical variations in hourly compensation costs in manufacturing**

Source: based on US Bureau of Labour statistics, 2012

volatility of currency exchange rates between different countries. What appears to be a least-cost source with one set of exchange rates may look very different if there is a major change in these rates.

HOW FIRMS TRANSNATIONALIZE

Is there an identifiable *evolutionary sequence* of TNC development? Does the transition from a firm producing goods or services entirely for its domestic market to one engaged in foreign production of those goods and services follow a systematic development path?

The conventional view: a process of sequential development

The conventional view in the international business literature is of a linear, sequential trajectory to a firm's development from being domestically oriented to becoming a TNC. A vast literature, beginning with Stephen Hymer's pioneering work in the 1960s,[8] and developed most notably by John Dunning in his self-styled 'eclectic' theory,[9] argued that a prerequisite for a firm to operate beyond its domestic borders (other than through trade) was the possession of some firm-specific assets, developed to a high degree in its domestic market. These could then be transferred – across borders geographically but inside the firm organizationally (i.e. internalized) – to foreign locations. Such assets are primarily those of: firm size and economies of scale; market power and marketing skills (e.g. brand names, advertising strength); technological expertise (product, process, or both); or access to cheaper sources of finance. The implicit assumption is that only a firm that has reached a substantial size will have the resources to begin to operate transnationally. The TNC, therefore, became associated unequivocally with bigness.

This notion of beginning with a strong domestic position and then expanding geographically was captured in the concept of the PLC (see Figure 4.15), adopted and adapted as an explanation of the evolution of international production by Raymond Vernon in 1966.[10] Vernon's major contribution was to introduce an explicitly *locational* dimension into the product cycle. Figure 5.5 shows Vernon's PLC model, based upon the experience of US TNCs, especially during the 1960s.

Vernon assumed that domestic firms are more likely to be aware of the possibility of introducing new products in their home market than non-domestic firms The kinds of new products introduced would reflect the specific characteristics of the domestic market. In the US case, high average-income levels and high labour costs encouraged the development of new products aimed at high-income consumers and which were also labour saving. In this first phase of the locational PLC, all production would be located in the USA and overseas demand served by exports (Figure 5.5). But this situation could not last indefinitely. US firms would eventually set up production facilities in the overseas market either because they

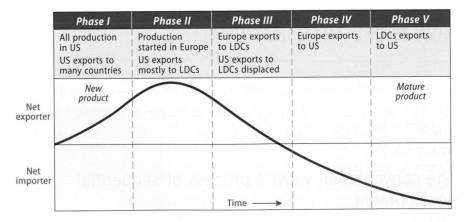

Figure 5.5   **The PLC as an evolutionary sequence of US TNCs' development**

Source: based on Wells, 1972: Figure 15

saw an opportunity to reduce production and distribution costs or because of a threat to their market position.

It follows from the nature of the PLC model that the first overseas production would occur in other high-income markets. The newly established foreign plants would serve these former export markets and thus displace US exports. These would be redirected to other areas where production had not yet begun (phase II in Figure 5.5). Eventually, the production cost advantages of the newer overseas plants would lead the firm to export from them to other, third-country, markets (phase III) and even back to the USA itself (phase IV). Finally, as the product became completely standardized, production would be shifted to low-cost locations in less developed countries (LDCs) (phase V). It is intriguing to note that Vernon regarded this as a 'bold projection'. At that time (the mid-1960s) there was still little evidence of developing country export platforms in East Asia serving European and US markets. How times have changed!

There is no doubt that a good deal of the *initial* overseas investment by US firms, and by some firms from other countries, fitted the PLC sequence quite well. But it cannot explain the increased diversity of TNC investment. It is no longer realistic to assume a simple evolutionary sequence from the home country outwards. Even within strongly innovative TNCs, the initial source of the innovation and of its production may be from any point in the firm's global network. In addition, as we saw in Chapter 2, much of the world's FDI is reciprocal or cross-investment between countries, which cannot easily be explained in product cycle terms.

Diverse trajectories: latecomers, newcomers and 'born globals'

> Latecomer and newcomer [TNCs] do not depend for their international expansion on prior possession of resources, as was the case for most traditional [TNCs] … expanding abroad in past decades. Instead, these new firms utilize international expansion in order to tap into transient advantages; they are not concerned to establish solid international structures, but rather quickly develop flexible and 'lattice-like' structures spanning diverse countries and markets.[11]

Figure 5.6 shows some of this diversity. The traditional developmental sequence is shown in the centre: overseas expansion occurs initially through exports, using the services of independent overseas sales agents. However, the potential benefits of exerting greater control may stimulate the firm to establish its own overseas sales outlets: for example, by setting up an entirely new facility or by acquiring, or merging with, a local firm (possibly the previously used sales agency itself). Actual production of goods and services overseas may eventually follow.

There is a good deal of anecdotal material to support such a sequence of development among firms that actually became TNCs. Apart from Vernon's US evidence,

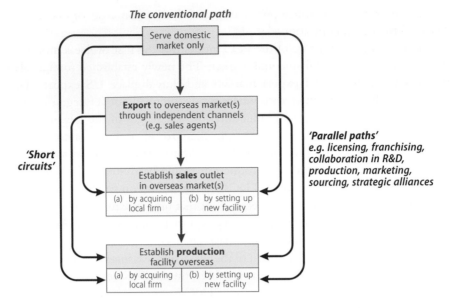

The conventional path

Figure 5.6   Diverse pathways of TNC evolution

Japanese firms investing in Europe showed a similar path. Actual manufacturing operations came rather late following a long period of development of Japanese service investments, mainly in the form of the general trading companies (*sogo sho-sha*), banks and other financial institutions, and the sales and distribution functions of the manufacturing firms themselves.[12]

However, there is nothing inevitable about a progression through all or any of the stages. Figure 5.6 shows that 'short circuits' and 'parallel paths' both may occur. For example, overseas production facilities may be established without using inter-mediaries. This has been especially common among firms from small countries, such as the Netherlands, Switzerland or Sweden. For example,

> Switzerland is a small country. Within five months of its creation, Nestlé was already manufacturing abroad. The mentality here was never to export from the home market but to produce locally.[13]

Increasingly, firms now engage in a bewildering variety of collaborative arrange-ments with other firms and these provide further diverse paths of TNC develop-ment. For example, a firm may tap into existing TNC networks (e.g. as suppliers of specific products, functions and services). Alternatively, a firm may take on various kinds of transnational networking roles and yet remain relatively small.

Virtually all TNCs have grown, at least partially, through acquisition and merger, which offers the attraction of an already functioning business compared with the more difficult, and possibly risky, method of starting from scratch in an unfamiliar environment. Certainly it is the way in which a new generation of TNCs from developing countries, like China and India, are becoming major global players. For example, the Chinese computer firm Lenovo acquired IBM's PC business in 2004, while the Indian Tata Group acquired the luxury car company Jaguar Land Rover, from Ford, in 2008.[14]

Although these examples illustrate increasing diversity in TNC development, they still imply a more or less lengthy temporal sequence. However, there is growing evidence of new entrepreneurial ventures starting out internationally from the very beginning: the so-called 'born globals'.[15] These are firms which

> started and operated from day one in global markets as global players, servicing their customers wherever they are to be found … they are all characterized by their accelerated internationalization … and they are thereby changing the dynamics of international competition … *The new species of [TNC] are different from traditional multinationals in that they are created by internationally experienced individuals and global in their outlook already from inception, seizing the opportunities offered by an increasingly integrated and interconnected global economy* … firms identified as born globals or international new ventures have been found to target and penetrate international markets from very early on, and in some cases from the outset organize operations around internationally dispersed knowledge and resources.[16]

Two examples can be used to illustrate this new form of TNC. First, Proteome Systems Ltd (PSL) was established by academics at Macquarie University in Australia as a biotech company. The firm

> sought to develop its customer base internationally from inception. Its pattern of market expansion was rapid and opportunistic, and focused on gaining access to resources wherever they might be available. In the US it expanded by acquisition of the pieces left after a biotech firm in Boston went out of business. In Japan it entered into a strategic alliance with an established trading house, Itochu … In Malaysia it entered the market through the services of an agent. In other words, there was a heterogeneous entrepreneurial process of market entry and resource deployments as and when circumstances and opportunities presented themselves, but always with a view to sustaining a global market presence from the outset.[17]

Second, Momenta Corporation of Mountain View, Colorado, was a

> 'start-up' in the emerging pen-based computer market. Its founders were from Cuba, Iran, Tanzania, and the US. From its beginning in

1989, the founders wanted the venture to be global in its acquisition of inputs and in its target market … Thus, software design was conducted in the US, hardware design in Germany, manufacturing in the Pacific Rim, and funding was received from Taiwan, Singapore, Europe, and the US.[18]

'Born global' TNCs are very different from traditional TNCs. Not only do they inject much greater diversity into the TNC population, but also they emphasize the *importance of social networks and networked knowledge.* Many of these new-style firms are in sectors where technology is changing very rapidly, where it is vital to get new products or processes to market very quickly. The ability to tap into geographically dispersed networks of firms and individuals, as well as into knowledge networks using the Internet, is vital. Of course, such quick ventures are highly vulnerable: Momenta Corporation, for example, folded within three years. But there are many more being created all the time. Clearly, therefore, it is no longer valid to equate transnationality with firm size. Although many TNCs are, indeed, very large, many others are not. Size does not always matter. TNCs come in all shapes and sizes.

The dilemma of 'going global' or 'being local'

Whatever their precise developmental trajectory, TNCs face a fundamental problem. The intensification of global competition in a world that retains a high degree of local differentiation creates an internal tension between globalizing forces on the one hand and localizing forces on the other. As Figure 5.7 shows, there are

Advantages	Costs and risks
✓ The firm's oligopoly power is increased through the exploitation of scale and experience effects beyond the size of individual national markets.	✗ The TNC may be vulnerable to disruption of its entire operations (or part of them) because of labour unrest or government policy changes affecting a particular unit.
✓ The TNC is placed in a better position to exploit the growing discrepancy between a relatively efficient market for goods (created by freer trade) and very inefficient markets for production factors.	✗ Fluctuations in currency exchange rates may disrupt integration strategies, drastically altering the economies of intrafirm transactions of intermediate of final goods.
✓ The possibility of exploiting differences in tax rates and structures between countries is increased and so, therefore, is the possibility of engaging in transfer pricing.	✗ Governments may impose performance requirements or other restrictions which impede the optimal operation of the firm's integrated production chain.
✓ The specialized and integrated function of individual country operations makes hostile government action less rewarding and less likely.	✗ The task of managing a globally integrated operation is more complex and demanding than that of managing separate national subsidiaries.

Figure 5.7 **Advantages and disadvantages of a globally integrated strategy**

Source: based on material in Doz, 1986b

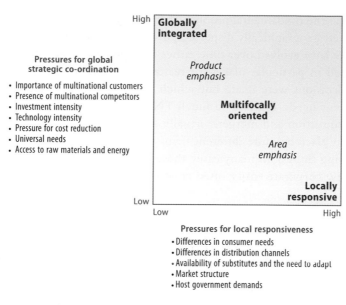

High

Globally integrated

Pressures for global strategic co-ordination

- Importance of multinational customers
- Presence of multinational competitors
- Investment intensity
- Technology intensity
- Pressure for cost reduction
- Universal needs
- Access to raw materials and energy

Product emphasis

Multifocally oriented

Area emphasis

Locally responsive

Low

Low   High

Pressures for local responsiveness

- Differences in consumer needs
- Differences in distribution channels
- Availability of substitutes and the need to adapt
- Market structure
- Host government demands

Figure 5.8   **A global integration–local responsiveness framework**

Source: based on material in Prahalad and Doz, 1987: Figure 2.2; pp. 18–21

considerable incentives for a firm to pursue a globally integrated strategy. But there are also substantial disincentives. Figure 5.8 captures this basic 'global–local tension'.

In reality, TNCs face far more complex decisions about the geographical con-figuration and organizational coordination of their operations than the simple global–local dichotomy suggests. Production circuits and production networks are immensely intricate structures, made up of many different functions and activities. Operating in many different economic, political, social and cultural environments means that very difficult decisions have to be made about every one of them:

- Which functions are to be performed internally (in-house) and which are to be outsourced to other firms?
- Where should each of the firm's own internalized functions be located?
- Which functions need to be located close to each other? Which ones can be separated out and located accordingly to enhance efficiency? What should the balance be between domestic production and producing offshore?
- Where should suppliers be located? Should they be close to the firm's home base or should they be in other countries (i.e. offshore)? Do suppliers need to be located nearby or can they be geographically dispersed to take advantage of lower costs or other locationally specific attributes?
- How is control over geographically dispersed activities – both internal and external – to be exercised?

There is also the fundamental problem that TNCs are not dealing with a 'clean surface': their geographically dispersed portfolio of functions, offices, factories, and the like have evolved over time rather than being planned. Some will have been located in particular places for reasons that may have been valid at the time the decisions were made but which may no longer be optimal for the firm's current needs. Because so much TNC growth and expansion has been through acquisition and merger, virtually all TNCs consist of elements originally put in place by quite different firms (often of different nationalities and ways of doing things). In many cases, these have been only partially integrated into the new corporate entity, often creating a veritable 'dog's breakfast' of bits and pieces.

TNCs AS 'NETWORKS WITHIN NETWORKS'

Although TNCs come in 'all shapes and sizes', they share two basic characteristics:

- TNCs are *networks within networks*, structured through a myriad of complex relationships, transactions, exchanges and interactions within their own internal corporate network and between that network and those of the other key actors with whom TNCs must interact (see Figures 3.1 and 3.4).
- The fact that a TNC's networks are spread across, and embedded within, *different national jurisdictions and contexts* means that coordinating and controlling its internal and external networked activities is vastly more complex than is the case for a purely domestic firm.

Adopting such a *relational network* view raises the question of where a TNC's organizational boundaries begin and end.[19] In a *legal* sense, of course, the boundary of a firm is clear: companies have to be registered in the jurisdictions in which they operate. But for firms that operate across national boundaries, there is no international legal framework. Nevertheless, at a TNC's core is the set of formally organized rules and conventions, regulated and institutionalized through the firm's own internal mechanisms. But in a *functional* sense – especially when we see firms as networks within networks – a TNC's boundaries are much less clear. The distinction between what goes on inside and what goes on outside is not only very fuzzy but also continuously changing. In the following sections, we explore these complex internal and external relationships of TNCs in order to show how – and where – their operations are coordinated, controlled and configured.

Figure 5.9 sets out the basic framework for this analysis. It shows that different parts of a TNC have network relationships both inside and outside the firm's boundaries. The important point to note is that a subsidiary is not solely embedded within a rigid hierarchical corporate structure, but is likely to have networked business relationships outside that structure:

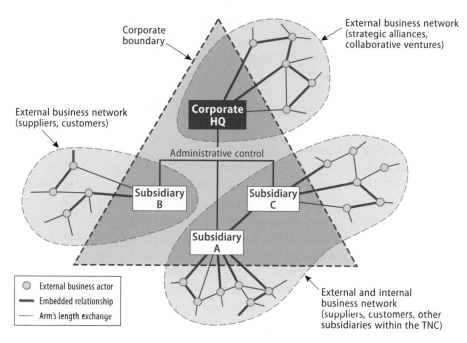

Figure 5.9   **TNCs as networks within networks**

Source: based, in part, on Forsgren et al., 2005: Figure 7.3

The configuration of a business network is specific to each individual subsidiary. First, some subsidiaries may be embedded in relationships that are both external and internal *vis-à-vis* the [TNC], as in the case of subsidiary A, while other subsidiaries like subsidiary B have external business relationships only. Thus we can distinguish between external and corporate embeddedness. Second, individual business relationships can range from arm's-length exchange to a high degree of mutual adaptation of resources and activities, that is to a high degree of embeddedness. A subsidiary may be dominated by highly embedded relationships – external, internal or both. Other subsidiaries, in contrast, may have only relationships consisting of arm's-length exchanges – external, internal or both. Since every relationship has its own specific characteristics and history, we would expect to find a high degree of variation as regards embeddedness both within the individual subsidiary and between the different subsidiaries in [a TNC].[20]

The precise manner, therefore, in which TNCs organize and configure their networks arises from a number of interrelated influences,[21] notably:

- the nature and complexity of the *industry environment(s)* in which the firm operates, including the nature of competition, technology, regulatory structures, etc.;
- the firm's specific history and geography, including

- o its *culture and administrative heritage* in the form of accepted practices built up over a period of time, producing a particular 'strategic predisposition';[22]
- o characteristics derived from its *home-country embeddedness*.

The geographical embeddedness of TNCs

Home-country influences

It is too often assumed that TNCs are all much the same, regardless of their geographical origin. This is emphatically not the case.[23] TNCs are 'produced' through an intricate process of embedding, in which the cognitive, cultural, social, political and economic characteristics of the national home base continue to play a dominant part. This does not mean that TNCs from a particular national origin are identical. This is self-evidently not the case. Within any national situation there will be distinctive corporate cultures, arising from the firm's own specific corporate history, which predispose it to behave strategically in particular ways. But, in general, the similarities between TNCs from one country will be greater than the differences between them. For example, a detailed study of US, German and Japanese firms found

> little blurring or convergence at the cores of firms based in Germany, Japan, or the US ... Durable national institutions and distinctive ideological traditions still seem to shape and channel crucial corporate decisions ... the domestic structures within which a firm initially develops leave a permanent imprint on its strategic behavior ... our findings underline, for example, the durability of German financial control systems, the historical drive behind Japanese technology development through tight corporate networks, and the very different time horizons that lie behind American, German, and Japanese corporate planning.[24]

One reason for such continuing national distinctiveness is the fact that most TNCs continue to recruit many of their senior executives from their home country. This is especially apparent among US firms whose senior executives tend to have far less direct international experience than, say, those in UK companies.[25] Within Europe, too, distinct differences continue to exist between TNCs from different European countries, despite the high level of economic integration within the EU. For example, an analysis of the national diversity of executive positions in large European companies showed that the overwhelming majority were from the TNC's home country:

> The recruitment dynamics on the executive board level in the EU are still strongly determined by characteristics of national government regimes and, as a result, their managerial labour markets seem highly segmented along national borders.[26]

Similarly, although there are similarities between firms from East Asia, there are also distinct differences between them.[27] The major similarities are:

- formation of intra- and inter-firm business relationships;
- reliance on personal relationships;
- strong relationships between business and the state.

However, it is wrong to think in terms of *one* East Asian business model.

Japanese companies, for example, have tended to be characterized by highly structured and formal relationships between firms within groups known as *keiretsu* (Figure 5.10).[28] Five distinctive characteristics of these groups can be identified:[29]

- Transactions are conducted through alliances of *affiliated* companies. This creates a form of organization intermediate between vertically integrated firms and arm's-length markets.
- Inter-firm relationships tend to be *long term* and stable, based upon mutual obligations.
- These inter-firm relationships are *multiplex* in form, expressed through cross-shareholdings and personal relationships as well as through financial and commercial transactions.
- Bilateral relationships between firms are embedded within a broader 'family' of *related companies*.
- Inter-corporate relationships are imbued with *symbolic significance* which helps to sustain links even where there are no formal contracts.

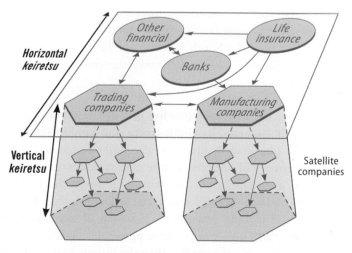

Figure 5.10   **Basic elements of the Japanese *keiretsu***

Source: based, in part, on Gerlach, 1992: Figure 1.1

Firms from other East Asian countries, for example South Korea and Taiwan, also have strong and distinctive relational structures. Despite sharing a common heritage of Confucian-based familism, they have developed different corporate systems. In South Korea, the dominant type of business group is the *chaebol*, modelled on the pre-Second World War Japanese *zaibatsu*, the giant family-owned firms which had been so important in the development of the Japanese economy. The *chaebol*

> are highly centralized, most being owned and controlled by the founding patriarch and his heirs through a central holding company. A single person in a single position at the top exercises authority through all the firms in the group. Different groups tend to specialize in a vertically integrated set of economic activities.[30]

As a result, the South Korean economy became highly concentrated and oligopolistic, with a relatively underdeveloped small- and medium-sized firm sector. Not only this, but many of these are tightly tied into the production networks of the *chaebol*, which have developed into some of the most highly vertically integrated business networks in the world:

> the firms in the *chaebol* are the principal upstream suppliers for the big downstream *chaebol* assembly firms ... in Samsung electronics, most of the main component parts for the consumer electronics division are manufactured and assembled in the same compound by Samsung firms.[31]

Taiwanese business networks, in contrast, have tended to have low levels of vertical integration. The more horizontal Taiwanese networks consist of two main types: 'family enterprise' networks and 'satellite assembly' networks (independently owned firms that come together to manufacture specific products primarily for export).

These contrasts between the South Korean and Taiwanese business groups – despite the strong similarities between the two countries – have been explained as arising from

> differences in social structures growing out of the transmission and control of family property. In South Korea, the kinship system supports a clearly demarcated, hierarchically ranked class structure in which core segments of lineages acquire elite rankings and privileges. These are the 'great families' ... In Taiwan, however, the Confucian family was situated in a very different social order ... Unlike Korea the Chinese practiced partible inheritance, in which all sons equally split the father's estate ... This set of practices preserved the household and made it the key unit of action, rather than the lineage itself ... In summary, although based on similar kinship principles, the Korean and the Chinese kinship systems operate in very different ways.[32]

Such differences in socio-cultural practices largely explain the contrasts between the ways that business firms are organized in the two neighbouring countries.

Convergence or differentiation?

My basic argument is that TNCs retain distinctive characteristics derived from their country of origin. But this does not imply that they are unchanging. On the contrary, the intense interconnectedness of the contemporary global economy means that influences are rapidly transmitted across boundaries. Corporations are *learning* organizations: they strive to tap into appropriate practices wherever they occur. This will, inevitably, affect the way business organizations are configured and behave. There 'is essentially a process of co-evolution through which different business systems may converge in certain dimensions and diverge in other attributes'.[33]

The very fact that TNCs are *trans*national – that they operate in a diversity of economic, social, cultural and political environments – means that they will, inevitably, take on some of the characteristics of their host environments. Non-local firms invariably have to adapt some of their domestic practices to local conditions: it is virtually impossible to transfer the whole package of a firm's practices to a different environment. For example, Japanese overseas manufacturing plants tend to be 'hybrid' forms rather than the pure organizations found in Japan itself. The same applies to US firms operating abroad. Even in the UK, where the apparent 'cultural distance' between the USA and the UK is less than in many other cases, there is a very long history of US firms having to adapt some of their business practices to local conditions.

We can find plenty of evidence of change within TNCs in response to these various forces. For example, although the *keiretsu* have been at the centre of Japanese economic development since the end of the Second World War, the financial crisis in Japan that has persisted since the bursting of the 'bubble economy' at the end of the 1980s has put them under considerable pressure to change at least some of their practices. In particular, the recent influx of foreign capital to acquire significant, sometimes controlling, shares in some of these companies has had a catalytic effect. The most notable example was the acquisition by the French automobile company Renault of 44 per cent of the equity of Nissan (see Chapter 15). There are strong pressures, particularly from Western (notably US) finance capital, for Japanese business groups to open up to outsiders, to reduce or eliminate the intricate cross-shareholding arrangements, and to become more like Western (i.e. US) firms with their emphasis on 'shareholder value' rather than the broader socially-based 'stakeholder' interests intrinsic to Japanese companies. However, the 2008 financial crisis has greatly reduced the 'attractiveness' of the US model.

While changes are certainly occurring, we should not assume that Japanese firms will suddenly be transformed into US clones. The Japanese have a very long history of adapting to external influences by building structures and practices that still remain distinctively Japanese. Similarly, Korean and other East Asian firms have come under enormous pressure to change some of their business practices in the aftermath of the region's financial crisis of the late 1990s. In Korea, the *chaebol* are being drastically restructured and the relationships with the state diluted. Among overseas Chinese businesses, the strong basis in family ownership and control is being challenged both by internal and external forces. Greater involvement in the global economy is forcing these firms to modify some of their practices.[34] Similar observations apply to firms from other home countries. In the case of Germany, for example, while some of the established characteristics of German business are under threat, the evidence suggests that many of the core elements remain in place.[35]

It would be extremely surprising, therefore, if the distinctive nature of nationally based TNCs were to be replaced by a universal form. Continued differentiation is the most likely scenario, although undoubtedly containing elements of change and some degree of convergence.

CONFIGURING THE TNCs' INTERNAL NETWORKS

Coping with complexity: a diversity of organizational architectures

One of the basic 'laws' of growth of any organism or organization is that as growth occurs its internal structure has to change. In particular, the *functional role* of its component parts tends to become more *specialized* and the links between the parts become more *complex*. In other words, its 'organizational architecture' has to change. Hence, as the size, organizational complexity and geographical spread of TNCs have increased, the internal interrelationships between their geographically separated parts have become a highly significant element in the global economy.

The traditional approach to changing a TNC's organizational architecture – based primarily on the hierarchical Western (i.e. US) model – depicts it as a sequential process, whereby firms transform their organizational structures from a *functional* form, in which the firm is subdivided into major functional units (production, marketing, finance, etc.), into a *divisional* form (usually product based). In such a divisional structure, each product division is responsible for its own functions, particularly of production and marketing, although some functions (especially finance) tend to be performed centrally for the entire corporation. Each product division also usually acts as a separate profit centre.

The main advantage of the divisional structure is its greater ability to cope with product diversity. However, operating across national boundaries poses additional problems of coordination and control. Largely through trial and error, TNCs have groped their way towards more appropriate organizational structures. Figure 5.11 shows four commonly used structures. Which one is actually adopted depends upon a number of factors, including the age and experience of the enterprise, the nature of its operations and its degree of product and geographical diversity.

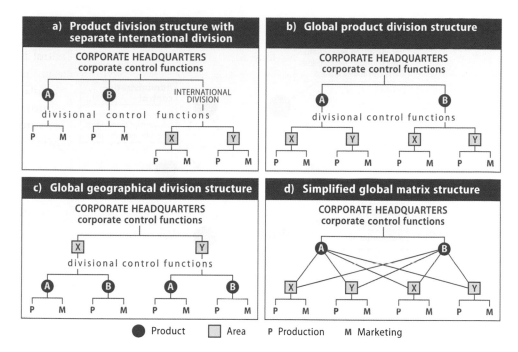

a) **Product division structure with separate international division**

b) **Global product division structure**

c) **Global geographical division structure**

d) **Simplified global matrix structure**

● Product ■ Area P Production M Marketing

Figure 5.11 Types of TNC organizational architecture

The form most commonly adopted in the early stages of TNC development is simply to add on an *international division* to the existing divisional structure (Figure 5.11a). This tends to be a short-lived solution to the organizational problem if the firm continues to expand its international operations because problems of coordination and tension inevitably arise between the parts of the firm organized on product lines (the firm's domestic activities) and those organized on an area basis (the international operations).

There are two obvious possible solutions. One is to organize the firm on a *global product* basis: that is, to apply the product division form throughout the world and to remove the international division (Figure 5.11b). The other possibility is to organize the firm's activities on a *worldwide geographical* basis (Figure 5.11c). But neither of these structures resolves the basic tension between product- and area-based systems. In response, some of the largest TNCs adopted complex *global grid* or *global matrix* structures (Figure 5.11d), containing elements of both product and area structures and involving dual reporting links.

Although there is plenty of evidence to support such a sequence, there is also plenty of evidence to demonstrate far greater organizational diversity. In this regard, Bartlett and Ghoshal's organizational typology, though far from perfect, is very useful (Figures 5.12 to 5.15).

The *'multinational organization'* model (Figure 5.12) emerged particularly during the 1930s. A combination of economic, political and social factors forced firms to

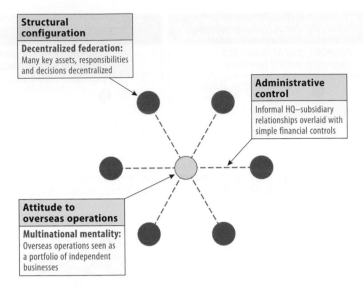

Figure 5.12   'Multinational organization' model

Source: based on Bartlett and Ghoshal, 1998: Figure 3.1

organize their operations in response to national market differences. The result was a decentralized federation of overseas units and simple financial control systems, overlain on informal personal coordination. The firm's worldwide operations are organized as a portfolio of national businesses. This was the kind of transnational

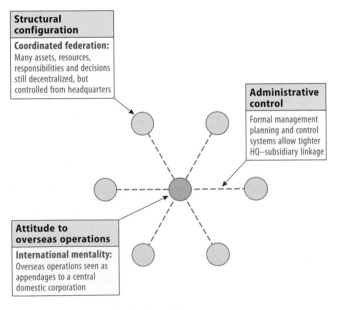

Figure 5.13   'International organization' model

Source: based on Bartlett and Ghoshal, 1998: Figure 3.2

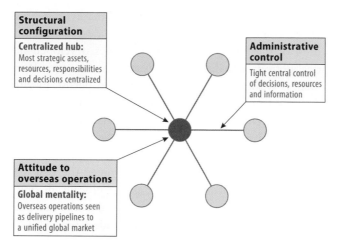

Figure 5.14 **'Global organization' model**

Source: based on Bartlett and Ghoshal, 1998: Figure 3.3

organizational form used extensively by expanding European companies. Each of the firms' national units has a very considerable degree of autonomy and a predominantly 'local' orientation. It is able, therefore, to respond to local needs, but its fragmented structure lessens scale efficiencies and reduces the internal flow of knowledge.

The *'international organization' model* (Figure 5.13) came to prominence in the 1950s and 1960s as large US corporations expanded overseas to capitalize on their firm-specific assets of technological leadership or marketing power. This ideal type involves far more formal coordination and control by the corporate headquarters over the overseas subsidiaries. Whereas 'multinational' organizations are, in effect, portfolios of quasi-independent businesses, 'international' organizations see their overseas operations as appendages to the controlling domestic corporation. Thus, the international subsidiaries are more dependent on the corporate centre for the transfer of knowledge and the parent company makes greater use of formal systems of control. The 'international' TNC is better equipped to utilize the knowledge and capabilities of its parent company but its particular configuration and operating systems tend to make it less responsive than the 'multinational' model. It is also rather less efficient than the next ideal type.

The *'global organization' model* (Figure 5.14) was one of the earliest forms of international business (used, for example, by Ford and by Rockefeller in the early 1900s, as well as by Japanese firms in their much later internationalization drive of the 1970s and 1980s). It is based upon a tight centralization of assets and responsibilities in which the role of the local units is to assemble and sell products and to implement plans and policies developed at the centre. Overseas subsidiaries have far less freedom to create new products or strategies or to modify existing ones. Thus, the 'global' TNC capitalizes on scale economies and on centralized knowledge and expertise. But this implies that local market conditions tend to be ignored and the possibility of local learning is precluded.

Although each of these three organizational types developed initially during specific historical periods, one did not simply replace the other. Because each has strengths (as well as weaknesses), each has tended to persist, in either a pure or hybrid form, helping to produce today's diverse TNC population.[36] There is also some correlation between organizational type and nationality of parent company but it is by no means perfect; it is better to regard firms of different national origins as having a predisposition to one or other form of organization.

The dilemma facing TNCs is that, ideally, they need the best features of each organizational form: to be globally efficient, geographically flexible, and capable of capturing the benefits of worldwide learning – all at the same time. Hence, it is argued, we are seeing the emergence of a fourth ideal-type TNC: the *'integrated network organization' model* (Figure 5.15), characterized by a distributed network configuration and a capacity to develop flexible coordinating processes. Such capabilities apply both inside the firm – displacing hierarchical governance relationships with a *heterarchical* structure[37] – and outside the firm through a complex network of inter-firm relationships.

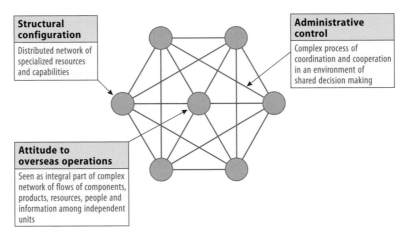

Figure 5.15   **'Integrated network organization' model**

Source: based on Bartlett and Ghoshal, 1998: Figure 5.1

The point to emphasize is the continuing diversity of organizational architectures: TNCs come in all shapes, sizes and forms of governance. Their internal architecture reflects not only the external constraints and opportunities they have to face – including the structures made possible by ICT – but also a strong element of path dependency. Firms organized on hierarchical principles not only still exist, but may still be in a majority. The newer, 'flatter', organizational forms tend to be confined to a limited number of firms in certain sectors. However, John Mathews argues that latecomer and newcomer TNCs, in particular, have

> adopted a variety of global organizational forms, from highly unconventional global cellular clusters (Acer, Li and Fung) to weblike integrated global operations like Ispat. In all cases they dispensed with conventional 'international division' style organization, which demonstrated that they began their internationalization already equipped with a global outlook. In the case of Acer, the organizational innovation has been the creation of a remarkable cluster of semi-autonomous businesses, interacting with each other through multiple connections, as well as with suppliers and customers.[38]

Headquarters–subsidiary relationships

The various TNC architectures discussed in the preceding section, and especially those shown in Figures 5.12 to 5.14, assume a clear distinction between a TNC's organizational centre – its headquarters – and its subsidiary operations. In a pure hierarchical model, the relationship is assumed to be top-down. In reality, headquarters–subsidiary relationships tend to be highly contested, even in a hierarchical organization. In a *heterarchical* organization (Figure 5.15) the position is far more complex.[39] The roles played by a subsidiary, therefore, vary between different organizational structures and in terms of a TNC's specific strategy. Within all of this, the roles – and the powers – of subsidiary managers are in a continuous state of flux.

Three broad types of subsidiary role can be identified:[40]

- *The local implementer*: limited geographical scope and functions. Its primary purpose is to adapt the TNC's products for the local market.
- *The specialized contributor*: specific expertise tightly integrated into the activities of other subsidiaries in the TNC. Narrow range of functions and a high level of interdependence with other parts of the firm.
- *The world mandate*: worldwide (or possibly regional) responsibility for a particular product or type of business.

These different subsidiary roles have important implications for the impact of TNC activities on national and local economies (see Chapter 8). How these roles develop and possibly change – for example, from local implementer to world mandate – depends upon the nature of the bargaining relationships within the TNC. Relationships within firms reflect internal power structures and bargaining relationships. In a similar way, a firm's individual affiliates (its subsidiaries, branches, etc.) continuously compete to improve their relative position within the organization by, for example, winning additional investment or autonomy from the corporate centre. At the same time, the performance of each affiliate is continuously monitored against the relevant others (internal benchmarking) and this is used as an integral part of the internal bargaining processes within the firm.

In fact, the *geography* of a TNC influences these internal bargaining processes as well:

> Different 'places' within the firm, organizationally and geographically, develop their own identities, ways of doing things and ways of thinking over time … The firm's dominant culture, created by and expressed through the activities and understandings of top management at headquarters, necessarily contains multiple subcultures. Some of these may revolve around functions and cut across places (engineers versus sales people, for example), but some will have real geographical locations – they will have grown up in specific plants in particular places.[41]

'Grounding' the TNC: mapping the firm's internal geographies

> Every business is a package of functions and within limits these functions can be separated out and located at different places.[42]

Given their chosen organizational architecture, how and where do TNCs choose to locate their productive assets and capabilities? This is a fundamental issue for all TNCs, regardless of the kind of business they are in; whether they produce manufactured goods or business services; whether their product is 'hard', like cars or semiconductors or food, or 'soft', like information or money (another kind of information) or retailing.

Different business functions have different locational needs and, because these needs can be satisfied in various types of geographical location, each function tends to develop rather distinctive spatial patterns. Some tend to be geographically dispersed; others geographically concentrated and co-located with other parts of the firm. In the following sections, we look at the geographical orientations of four of the major business functions:

- control and coordination;
- research and development;
- marketing and sales;
- production.

Centres of strategic control and coordination

The *corporate headquarters* is the locus of overall control of the entire TNC.[43] It is the *strategic centre* responsible for all the major investment and disinvestment decisions that shape and direct the enterprise: which products and markets to enter or leave, whether to expand or contract particular parts of the enterprise, whether to acquire other firms or sell off existing parts:

> The headquarters has to prevent subsidiaries from pursuing strategic initiatives that diverge from the [TNC's] strategy. In addition, the headquarters assesses the value of strategic resources distributed across the [TNC] network and coherently affects their mobility so as to assure that resources are made available where they are actually necessary.[44]

The corporate headquarters is also the *legal* core of the TNC, responsible for complying with all the legal, financial and regulatory functions required of the firm by the various national jurisdictions in which it operates. One of its key roles is *financial*: the corporate headquarters ultimately holds the purse strings and decides the allocation of the corporate budget between its component units. Headquarters offices are, above all, handlers, processors and transmitters of *information* to and from other parts of the enterprise and also between similarly high-level organizations outside. The most important of these are the major business services on which the corporation depends (financial, legal, advertising) and also, very often, major departments of government, both foreign and domestic. There is evidence that the size and complexity of corporate headquarters varies substantially between firms from different home countries.[45]

Regional headquarters offices constitute an intermediate level in the corporate organizational structure, having a geographical sphere of influence encompassing several countries. Regional headquarters offices perform several distinctive roles.[46] Most commonly, their primary responsibility is to *integrate* the parent company's activities within a region, that is to coordinate and control the activities of the firm's affiliates: to act as the intermediary between the corporate headquarters and its affiliates within its particular region and to 'respond to local imperatives that cannot be effectively handled by distant head offices'.[47]

Regional headquarters offices, therefore, are both *coordinating and controlling* elements within the TNC and also an important part of its 'intelligence-gathering' system. A regional headquarters may also have an *entrepreneurial* role: to act as a base to initiate new regional ventures or to demonstrate to governments that the company has a commitment to their region. In either case, regional headquarters offices act as 'strategic windows' on regional developments and opportunities.[48] In some cases, regional headquarters offices are located close to the firm's major production facilities in a particular country or region. But that is not always the case.

These characteristic functions of corporate and regional headquarters define their particular *locational* requirements:

- A *strategic location* on the global transportation and communications network in order to keep in close contact with other, geographically dispersed, parts of the organization.

- Access to *high-quality external services* and a particular range of *labour market skills*, especially people skilled in information processing.
- Since much corporate headquarters activity involves interaction with the head offices of other organizations, there are strong *agglomerative forces* involved. Face-to-face contacts with the top executives of other high-level organizations (including government) are facilitated by close geographical proximity. Such high-powered executives invariably prefer a location that is rich in social and cultural amenities.

These locational criteria are met in only a small number of major cities in the world. In particular, the so-called 'global cities' exert a huge pull on the locational decisions of TNCs,[49] not least because they contain all the major high-level advanced business and financial services (see Figure 16.8). For example, not only are the headquarters of the world's largest TNCs located in a relatively small number of cities, but four cities — New York, Tokyo, London and Paris — stand head and shoulders above all the others.[50] For such reasons, these four *global cities* are sometimes described as the geographical 'control points' of the global economy.[51] Below them is a tier of other key headquarters cities in each of the three major economic regions of the world: Europe (e.g. Amsterdam, Brussels, Düsseldorf, Frankfurt); North America (e.g. Atlanta, Chicago, Houston, Los Angeles, Montreal, San Francisco, Toronto); Asia (e.g. Beijing, Hong Kong, Osaka, Seoul, Shanghai, Singapore, Taipei).

One of the most striking features of the geography of corporate headquarters (as opposed to regional headquarters) is their *geographical inertia*. Very few, if any, major TNCs have moved their ultimate decision-making operations outside their home country. An analysis of headquarters' international relocations of the Fortune Global 500, covering the period 1994–2002,[52] found only one! And this was the result of the (ultimately failed) merger between Daimler of Germany and Chrysler of the USA. Such geographical fixedness is a further strong indicator of the continuing significance of the home base for corporate behaviour. TNCs often make *threats* to relocate — usually as bargaining weapons against state regulation, including taxation (see Chapter 7) — but relatively few actually materialize. On the other hand, TNCs are more willing to shift regional headquarters to meet changing circumstances. In East Asia, for example, there is an identifiable shift northwards as some firms move their regional headquarters from Singapore to Shanghai (although Singapore remains a major regional focus).[53]

Within individual countries, on the other hand, the locational pattern of both corporate — and especially regional — headquarters is far from static, with substantial geographical decentralization of corporate headquarters out of the city centres of New York and London. In the case of London, most of these shifts are a short distance to the less congested outer reaches of the metropolitan area. In the USA, on the other hand, there is a much higher degree of locational change in headquarters functions. Nevertheless, corporate headquarters tend not to be spread very widely within any particular country. In the UK, for example, there are very few corporate headquarters of major firms or regional headquarters of foreign TNCs outside London and the South East; in France few locate outside Paris. In Italy the most important centre is Milan, in the highly industrialized north, which is more important than Rome as a location for foreign TNCs.

Apart from corporate and regional headquarters, there are other key coordination functions that may be separated out geographically. For example, although a TNC's supply chain management is normally located at or near the corporate headquarters, or at one or more of the regional headquarters sites, there are cases where this function has been located beyond this part of the network. The Anglo-Dutch consumer products company Unilever has concentrated all its European supply chain coordination and management at a completely new site at Schaffhausen in Switzerland. IBM has moved its global procurement headquarters from New York to Shenzhen, China.

Research and development

Given the constant need for firms to innovate, the process of research and development (R&D) is absolutely fundamental.[54] It is a complex sequence of operations (Figure 5.16) consisting of three major phases, each of which tends to have rather different locational requirements, although, in each case, the TNC has to reconcile

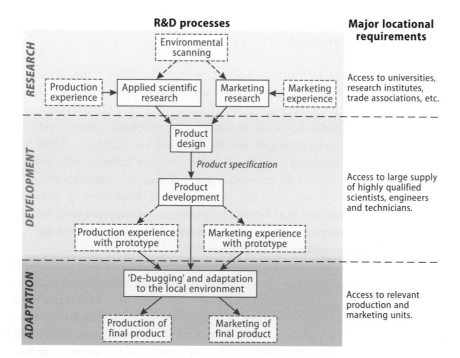

Figure 5.16 **Corporate R&D processes**

Source: based, in part, on Buckley and Casson, 1976: Figure 2.7

a number of factors. One is the advantage of gaining scale economies from concentrating R&D in one or a few large establishments. Another is the possible benefit of locating R&D close to corporate headquarters or, alternatively, close to production units to enhance communications and the sharing of ideas. Yet another possible locational pull is to markets, in order to benefit from closeness to customer needs, tastes and preferences. For cutting edge research, there are strong pulls to locations with science-intensive institutions and people.

The type of R&D undertaken by TNCs within their own transnational network can be classified into three major categories:

- The *support laboratory*, whose primary purpose is to adapt parent company technology to the local market and to provide technical back-up. It is by far the most common form of overseas R&D facility.
- The *locally integrated R&D laboratory* is a much more substantial unit, in which product innovation and development are carried out for the market in which it is located.
- The *international interdependent R&D laboratory* is of a quite different order. Its orientation is to the integrated global enterprise as a whole rather than to any individual national or regional market.

Of course, these categories are not fixed and unchanging. In particular, the development of so-called 'open innovation' is transforming the nature of, and the relationships between, corporate R&D units:

> Corporate R&D in this new context is changing from a model of closed and internal laboratories, becoming 'open' to knowledge found in many places. R&D becomes connect and develop (C&D), with links to networks of all kinds, which are needed to sense (that is identify and access) innovative technologies, and local market knowledge … What were merely 'listening posts' two decades ago have become sites for 'prospecting' and constant environmental scanning to obtain knowledge outside the firm … In the new model of distributed or *open innovation*, the internal R&D effort by a company is supplemented by an inflow of external research projects, venture investing, technology in-licensing, and technology acquisition.[55]

There is disagreement over the extent to which TNCs are dispersing their R&D geographically. On the one hand, they continue to show a very strong preference for keeping high-level R&D at home, as a recent study of 156 major research-intensive firms from Europe, the USA and Japan reveals.[56] Why should such home-country bias persist? The answer lies in the importance of the kinds of *untraded interdependencies* and of knowledge clusters discussed earlier (see Chapters 3 and 4). On the other hand, there is evidence of increasing geographical dispersal of R&D activities *within* TNC networks. For example, by the late 1990s, there was 'an increasing share of company-financed R&D performed abroad by US firms *as compared to domestically financed* industrial R&D ... US firms' investment in overseas R&D increased three times faster than did company-financed R&D performed domestically.'[57] In this regard, Asia is playing an increasingly important role as a location for certain kinds of R&D, especially in product development:[58]

> Asia's greatest overall advantage is its huge supply of scientists and engineers, particularly in China and India, at a time when students in the west are turning away from science and engineering. Companies in the US and Europe ... can exploit Asia's trained workforce by building research and development centres there or collaborating with Asian companies and universities ... The relative costs of doing research in Asia vary enormously according to circumstances ... [However] ... the pay of newly graduated researchers in India and China is around one-quarter of US levels. For more senior staff, it is usually at least half the US level and in exceptional circumstances may even exceed it.[59]

The phenomenal growth of some East Asian consumer markets – especially in China and, to a lesser extent, India – has led large consumer product TNCs to invest heavily in local product development facilities. The major incentive is the need both to develop products specifically for those markets and to get those products to the market as quickly as possible. For example,

> Pepsi's $40m–$45m new facility includes kitchens where Pepsi chefs develop new flavours from traditional Chinese cuisine, laboratories where they taste-test them on consumers, and plants where prototypes are produced. Doing all that in China means products can hit the shelves in as little as two weeks.[60]

Support laboratories are the most widely spread geographically, insofar as they generally locate close to production units. But the larger-scale, and more complex, R&D activities tend to be confined to particular kinds of location. The need for a large supply of highly trained scientists, engineers and technicians, together with proximity to universities and other research institutions, confines such facilities to large urban complexes. These are often those that are also the location of the firm's corporate headquarters. A secondary locational influence is that of 'quality of living' for the highly educated and highly paid research staff: an amenity-rich setting, including a good climate and potential for leisure activities as well as a stimulating intellectual environment.

Corporate R&D, therefore, is still predominantly a big-city activity despite recent growth in smaller urban areas. The pull of the amenity-rich environment is illustrated by the considerable concentration of R&D activities in locations such as Los Angeles, San Francisco and San Diego in California, Denver–Boulder in Colorado, Boston in Massachusetts and the 'Research Triangle' in North Carolina. In the UK, corporate R&D, like corporate headquarters and regional offices, is disproportionately concentrated in South East England. Almost two-thirds (61 per cent) of the research undertaken by foreign affiliates in the UK is located in London and the south east region of the country (compared with only 40 per cent of domestic firms' research).[61] A recent example is the decision by the Anglo-Swedish pharmaceuticals company AstraZeneca to close its long-established R&D laboratories in Cheshire and relocate them to Cambridge to be close to the bioscience cluster there. This is 'part of a plan to create strategic global research and development centres in the UK, US and Sweden'.[62] In East Asia, a big-city effect is also apparent: Beijing and, to a lesser extent, Shanghai in China; Tokyo–Yokohama and Osaka–Kobe in Japan.

Marketing and sales

Of all the various TNC functions it is the marketing, and especially the sales, units that are the most geographically dispersed. The reason is obvious. These functions need to be as close as possible to the firm's markets. They must be sensitive to local conditions in order to be able to feed back relevant information. They must be in a position to help to tailor the firms' products to local tastes. Not least, they must be in a position to prevent the firm from making costly, and often embarrassing, mistakes in misreading the various consumer cultures in which the firms are operating. The marketing literature is full of examples of insensitive, sometimes culturally insulting branding or packaging decisions made by foreign TNCs, which have not fully understood local conditions. It is for such reasons that firms such as the Swiss company Nestlé have developed a strategy in which

> every decision has to be made as close to the consumer as possible. It makes no sense for us in Vevey to decide on the taste of a soup to be sold in Chile.[63]

Apart from the obvious tendency to locate marketing and/or sales units in the firm's most important geographical markets, there is a good deal of flexibility in the precise geographical articulation of such activities. Marketing functions, in particular, are often concentrated either at corporate headquarters or, increasingly, within regional headquarters where they are responsible for all the marketing decisions in the specific region. In some cases, they are located close to the firm's R&D operations, especially development activities to facilitate positive synergy between product development and market needs. Of course, with sophisticated internal communications systems, virtual geographical proximity may replace physical proximity. Sales units, on the other hand, tend to be smaller and very widely dispersed.

Production

There are clearly some geographical similarities in the patterns of TNC headquarters, R&D, and marketing and sales activities, regardless of the particular activities – 'hard' or 'soft' – in which they are involved. This is because their

a) Globally concentrated production

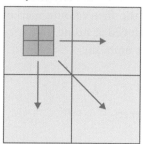

All production occurs at a single location. Products are exported to world markets.

b) Host-market production

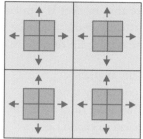

Each production unit produces a range of products and serves the national market in which it is located. No sales across national boundaries. Individual plant size limited by the size of the national market.

c) Product specialization for a global or regional market

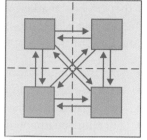

Each production unit produces only one product for sale throughout a regional market of several countries. Individual plant size very large because of scale economies offered by the large regional market.

d) Transnational vertical integration

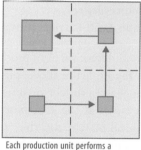

Each production unit performs a separate part of a production sequence. Units are linked across national boundaries in a 'chain-like' sequence – the output of one plant is the input of the next plant.

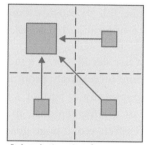

Each production unit performs a separate operation in a production process and ships its output to a final assembly plant in another country.

Figure 5.17　**Alternative ways of organizing the geography of transnational production**

locational needs are broadly similar for all firms. This is not so for production units, whose locational requirements vary not only according to the *specific* organizational and technological role they perform within the enterprise, but also with the geographical distribution of the relevant location-specific resources they need. It is certainly true that, compared with corporate headquarters and R&D, production units of TNCs have become increasingly dispersed geographically. But there is no single and simple pattern of dispersal, either at the global scale or within individual countries; the pattern varies greatly from one industry to another. Figure 5.17 illustrates in an idealized way four types of geographical orientation that a TNC might adopt for its production units.

Figure 5.17a presents the simplest case. All production is concentrated at a single geographical location (or, at least, within a single country) and exported to world markets through the TNC's marketing and sales networks. This is a procedure consistent with the classic global strategy shown in Figure 5.14. In contrast, in Figure 5.17b, production is located in, and oriented directly towards, a specific host market. Where that market is similar to the firm's home market the product is likely to be virtually identical to that produced at home. The specific locational criteria for the setting up of host-market units are:

- size and sophistication of the market;
- structure of demand and consumer tastes;
- cost-related advantages of locating directly in the market;
- government-imposed barriers to market entry.

Although the need to establish a production unit in a specific geographical market has become less necessary in purely cost terms, there are two main reasons for the continued development of host-market production:

- the need to be sensitive to variations in customer demands, tastes and preferences, or to be able to provide a rapid after-sales service;
- the existence of tariff and, particularly, non-tariff barriers to trade.

During the past five decades or so a radically different form of production organization has become increasingly prominent. Figure 5.17c shows production being organized geographically as part of a rationalized product or process strategy to serve a global, or a large regional, market (such as the EU, North America or East Asia). The existence of a huge geographical market, together with differences in locationally specific characteristics between countries within a region, facilitate the establishment of very large, specialized units of TNCs to serve an entire regional market, rather than single national markets. The key locational consideration, therefore, involves the trade-off between

- economies of large-scale production at one or a small number of large plants and;
- additional transportation costs involved in assembling the necessary inputs and in shipping the final product to a geographically extensive regional market.

This trade-off is once again becoming increasingly problematic as rising energy prices feed through to increased transportation costs. Firms that have been moving towards a network of fewer but very large production units are having to rethink this strategy.

A rather different kind of transnational production strategy involves geographical specialization by process or by semi-finished product, in which different parts of the firm's production system are located in different parts of the world. Figure 5.17d shows two ways in which such transnational process specialization might be organized as part of a vertically integrated set of operations across national boundaries within a *global production network*. Materials, semi-finished products, components and finished products are transported between geographically dispersed production units in a highly complex web of flows. In such circumstances, the traditional geographical connection between production and market is broken.

The output of a plant in one country may become the input for a plant belonging to the same firm located in another country. Alternatively, the finished product may be exported to a third-country market or to the home market of the parent firm. In such cases, the host country acts as an 'export platform'.

Such *offshore sourcing* and the development of vertically integrated global production networks were virtually unknown before the early 1960s. The pioneers were US electronics firms that set up offshore assembly operations in East Asia as well as in Mexico. Since then, the growth of such global production networks has been extremely rapid in most sectors. Indeed, there has been a veritable avalanche of firms in the older industrialized countries of the West shifting some of their manufacturing or lower-level service operations (like call centres or basic information processing) to cheaper developing country locations.

The choice of location for a production unit at the global scale is by no means as simple as it is often made out to be. It is not just a matter of looking at differences in labour costs between one country and another or at the subsidies, grants or tax incentives offered by governments to attract investment. Despite the enormous shrinkage of geographical distance, the relative geographical location of parent company and overseas production unit may still be significant. The sheer organizational convenience of geographical proximity may encourage TNCs to locate offshore production in locations close to their home country even when labour costs there are higher than elsewhere.

Of course, just as geographical proximity may override differentials in labour costs, so, too, other locational influences may dominate in any particular case. For the largest TNCs the world is indeed their oyster. Their production units are spread globally, often as part of a strategy of *dual or multiple sourcing* of components or products. This is one way of avoiding the risk of overreliance on a single source whose operations may be disrupted for a whole variety of reasons. In a vertically integrated production sequence, in which individual production units are tightly interconnected, an interruption in supply can seriously affect the other units, perhaps those located on the other side of the world. In an extreme case, a whole segment of the TNC's operations may be halted.

Nevertheless, major TNCs have developed highly complex and geographically extensive networks of control, R&D, sales and marketing, and production facilities. Figure 5.18 provides just one example: the electronics firm Solectron:

> Solectron was concentrated in a single campus in Silicon Valley until 1991, when its key customers, Sun Microsystems, Hewlett Packard and IBM, began to demand global manufacturing and process engineering support. Within ten years, the company's footprint had expanded to nearly 50 facilities worldwide ... [consisting of] a set of global and regional headquarters, high and low mix manufacturing facilities, purchasing and materials management centers, new product introduction centers, after-sales repair service centers for products manufactured by Solectron and others, and technology centers to develop advanced process and component packaging technologies.[64]

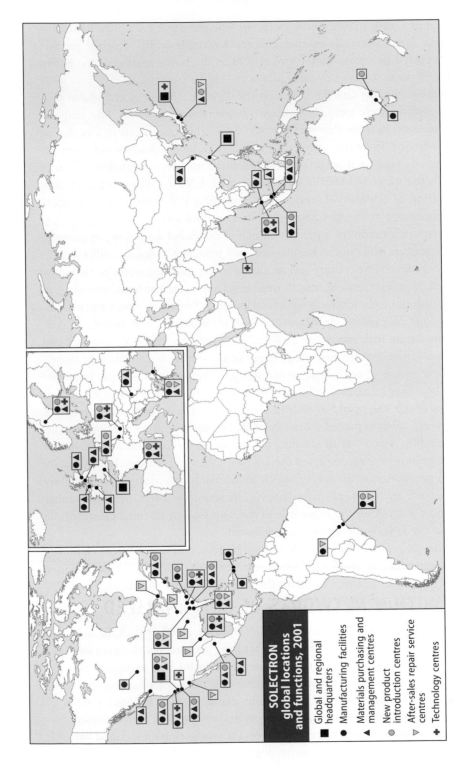

Figure 5.18 Solectron's global network

Source: based on Sturgeon, 2002: Table 2

Solectron was taken over by Flextronics in 2008 and a process of rationalization has inevitably changed the shape of the network shown in Figure 5.18. But it serves as a good example of the kind of TNC geographical structures that have become increasingly common.

However, there are dangers in simply shifting production offshore and this is reflected in what appears to be a recent countertrend towards what is variously termed *near-shoring or reshoring*: returning some aspects of production to a firm's home country. For example:

> Some 65 per cent of the senior [US] executives questioned by Accenture [in 2012] said they had moved their manufacturing operations in the past 24 months, with two-fifths saying the facilities had been relocated to the US ... the respondents cited freight and the speed of fulfilling orders as their main reasons for moving factories ... manufacturers were increasingly moving production closer to end markets.[65]

A number of high-profile cases seem to validate this trend. For example, in 2012, Apple announced that it planned to invest $100 million to shift parts of its Mac computer production back to the USA from China.[66] GE announced that it would relocate some of its domestic appliances business to the USA from China and Mexico.[67]

Of course, this and similar evidence from Europe should not be interpreted as heralding a complete reversal of long-distance networks. On the contrary:

> Moving production abroad remains, by far, the dominant trend. But ... for a wide variety of reasons, ranging from poor decision-making and preparation and rising transport and labour costs, some European companies [are] moving production back closer to home.[68]

In fact, what are sometimes presented as inexorable trends in one particular direction are often far less determinate and can change quite rapidly. The scale of 'reshoring' remains quite modest.

TNCs WITHIN NETWORKS OF EXTERNALIZED RELATIONSHIPS

In the previous section, the focus was on how TNCs organize and geographically configure their internalized networks. However, TNCs are also locked into *external* networks of relationships with a myriad of other firms: transnational and domestic, large and small, public and private (see Figure 5.9). As we saw earlier, the *boundary* between what is inside and what is outside the firm has become far more blurred.

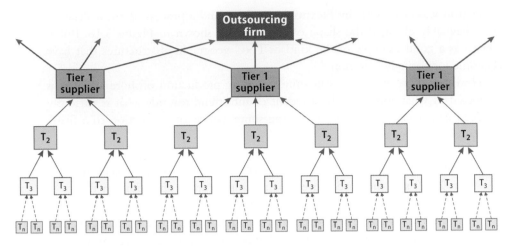

Figure 5.19   **Outsourcing as a multi-tiered process**

Outsourcing

No firm is completely self-sufficient. Overall, between 50 and 70 per cent of manufacturing costs are to purchase inputs. Indeed, a very strong general trend among both manufacturing and service firms in recent years has been for a greater proportion of activities to be *outsourced* to supplier firms:[69]

> The increasing implementation of outsourcing strategies is one of the most remarkable changes that has characterized firm behavior in the last decades. This strategy allows firms to concentrate their capabilities and resources in their respective core businesses, giving up those activities where firms do not have any competitive advantage.[70]

As a consequence, specialist outsourcing logistics firms have emerged (see Chapter 17).

Outsourcing, especially through longer-term relationships, is a kind of halfway house between, on the one hand, complete internalization of procurement and, on the other, arm's-length transactions through the open market. It is a *multi-tiered* process, as Figure 5.19 suggests, in which firms in each tier may themselves, in turn, outsource some of their activities. There are, broadly, two major types of outsourcing, both based on a supplier firm producing a good or service to a principal firm's specifications:

- *Commercial outsourcing*: the manufacture of a finished product. The supplier plays no part in marketing the product, which is generally sold under the principal's brand name and through its distribution channels. The principal firm may be either a producer firm, that is one that is also involved in manufacturing, or a retailing or wholesaling firm whose sole business is distribution.

Benefits and costs to principal firm	Types of relationship between principal firm and supplier	Benefits and costs to supplier
• Avoids need to invest in new production capacity • Flexible: easier to change suppliers • Externalizes some risks, while retaining some control • Possible problems of controlling how suppliers work (including labour issues)	• Time period may be long term, short term, single batch • Principal may provide some or all materials or components • Principal may provide detailed design or specification • Principal may provide finance, e.g. loan capital • Principal may provide machinery and equipment • Principal may provide general and/ or technical assistance and advice • Principal is invariably responsible for all marketing arrangements	• Access to markets • Continuity of orders • Access to technical knowledge, possible injection of finance • Risk of being 'expendable' if principal firm changes its priorities • Possible over-dependence on one or a small number of customers

Figure 5.20   **Outsourcing relationships**

- *Industrial outsourcing:*

  o *Speciality* outsourcing involves the carrying out, often on a long-term basis, of specialized functions which the principal chooses not to perform for itself but for which the supplier has special skills and equipment.

  o *Cost-saving* outsourcing is based upon differentials in production costs between principal and supplier for specific processes or products.

  o *Complementary or intermittent* outsourcing is a means adopted by principal firms to cope with occasional surges in demand without expanding their own production capacity. In effect, the supplier is used as extra capacity, often for a limited period or for a single operation.

Figure 5.20 summarizes some of the major features of the outsourcing relationship.

Outsourcing obviously has profound geographical implications. Initially, it depended on close proximity between firms and suppliers and was a major factor underlying the development and persistence of traditional 'industrial districts' – clusters of linked firms. However, innovations in transportation and communications have greatly increased the geographical extensiveness of outsourcing networks. Much of the increase in long-distance sourcing has been driven by the desire to take advantage of the wide global differentials in labour costs. As the distance between customers and suppliers increased, however, problems inevitably arose in terms of the reliability of supplies. Many firms had to establish sophisticated – and very costly – systems of stock/inventory holding to insure against interruptions in the supply of finished goods or components. This is the kind of 'just-in-case' system shown on the left-hand side of Figure 5.21.

However, as we saw in Chapter 4, production processes have changed dramatically. The emphasis is increasingly on rapid product turnover, speed to market and responsiveness to customer needs: what has come to be called 'lean' production. In such a production system, holding large stocks of inventory in warehouses is to

'Just-in-case' system	'Just-in-time' system
Characteristics	*Characteristics*
• Components delivered in large, but infrequent, batches	• Components delivered in small, very frequent, batches
• Very large 'buffer' stocks held to protect against disruption in supply or discovery of faulty batches	• Minimal stocks held – only sufficient to meet the immediate need
• Quality control based on sample check after supplies received	• Quality control 'built in' at all stages
• Large warehousing spaces and staff required to hold and administer the stocks	• Minimal warehousing space and staff required
• Use of large number of suppliers primarily on the basis of price	• Use of small number of preferred selected suppliers within a tiered supply system
• Remote relationships between customer and suppliers	• Very close relationships between customer and suppliers
• No incentive for suppliers to locate close to customers	• Strong incentive for suppliers to locate close to customers
Disadvantages	*Disadvantages*
• Lack of flexibility – difficult to balance flows and usage of different components	• Must be applied throughout the entire supply chain
• Very high cost of holding large stocks	• Reliance on small number of preferred suppliers increases risk of interruption in supply
• Remote relationships with suppliers prevents sharing of developmental tasks	
• Requires a deep vertical hierarchy of control to coordinate different tasks	

Figure 5.21   'Just-in-case' and 'just-in-time' systems of supplier relationships

Source: based on material in Sayer, 1986

be avoided. Supplies must be delivered precisely when (and where) they are needed, that is *just-in-time* (JIT). The major features of a JIT system are shown on the right-hand side of Figure 5.21.

Benefits, costs and risks of outsourcing

The highly complex, multi-tiered, globally extensive sourcing networks that have developed have greatly transformed the economic landscape. For the *outsourcing firm* the process is a way of enabling it to focus on its 'core competences' and to shed activities that do not fit. The logic is that costs will be reduced and profits enhanced through such concentration on core activities. For *supplier firms*, one of the major benefits of the increasing trend for firms to outsource some of their major functions is that it provides opportunities to fill the gap and to gain access to valuable markets (see Figure 5.20).[71]

One very high-profile (and controversial) example of this is the Taiwanese electronics manufacturer Foxconn Technology, founded by a Taiwanese entrepreneur in 1974 with capital of just $7500. Today it is the largest contract electronics manufacture in the world, supplying a vast range of leading manufacturers in many branches of electronics including, most notably, Apple. But you do not find Foxconn's name (or that of its parent company, Hon Hai) on any products. It manufactures entirely for others. For example, Foxconn in China is the largest manufacturer of iPhones and iPads.

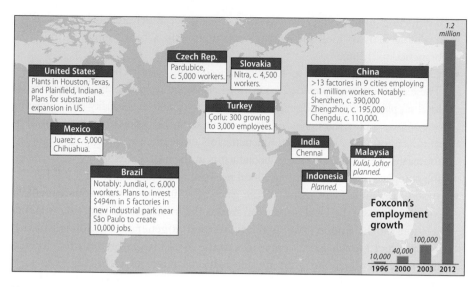

Figure 5.22   Some of Foxconn's global production facilities

Source: press and company reports

Foxconn's growth has been phenomenal: in 1996, the company employed around 10,000 workers; today it employs somewhere between 1 million and 1.2 million (estimates vary). As Figure 5.22 shows, the vast majority of Foxconn's workers are located in China, mostly in huge complexes such as those in Shenzhen, Zhengzhou and Chengdu which together employ over 700,000 workers. But Foxconn has also expanded significantly outside China, often to follow its major customers. Frequently, such expansion has been through the acquisition of customers' plants: for example, Sony's LCD operations in Slovakia, Cisco's video and telecoms plants in Mexico, HP's desktop PC operations in Turkey. Most recently, Foxconn announced it planned to expand operations in the USA (where it already has some activities) and this has been linked to Apple's announcement that it plans to manufacture some of its products in the USA.

In the outsourcing context it is tempting to regard suppliers as always being in a subservient position; merely small cogs in a much larger structure over which they have no influence, invariably being squeezed on price, quality and delivery times by their major customers. Often that is the case (see Part Four), although much depends on the position supplier firms occupy within a production network and also the kind of network involved (see the next section). Clearly, however, it does not apply to the Foxconns of this world. More generally, Andersen and Christenson argue that some subcontractors act as important 'connective nodes in supply networks'.[72] They identify five such 'bridging roles':

- *Local integrator:* firms able to provide access to additional production capacity through their relationships with other firms in the same locality. 'Local integrators may take on a host of different roles in the supply network, depending on fluctuations in the demand situation … [they] … may even take over commercial contracting, functioning as end producers – e.g. act as private label producers for a trading firm or look for market opportunities in a broad range of industrial branches' (p. 1266).

- *Export base*: such firms act as 'the gate of access to a local technological district … These subcontractors provide … superior knowledge regarding the competences of local suppliers … This bridging role is most likely found in speciality subcontracting or systems supplies, through which the subcontractor adds knowledge to the products of the customer … Export base subcontractors utilize their relations with customers to marshal relations with other subcontractors in their local area. Often, they take on the complex task of coordinating a local network of suppliers' (pp. 1266, 1267).

- *Import base*: these firms represent 'the gateway to international resources or skills for customers in the local or national area, as the international customer–supplier relations of the import base suppliers are used as generators of foreign market and product knowledge … compared to the local integrator, this firm depends heavily on representing a specific international range of technologies to local customers … the important task of the subcontractor is to foresee demand fluctuations and buffer them accordingly, either via extended information exchange with subcontractors or by keeping an extended inventory' (p. 1268).

- *International spanner*: often, such firms have evolved from being an export or import base subcontractor as their supply sources and buyers have internationalized. 'The position of the international spanner is a precarious one. There are pressures at both ends of the supply chain, which seek to attract the subcontractor further into the supply source or further to the logistical basis of the buyer … international spanners sometimes base their business potential on information asymmetries between subcontractors and buyers … The ability to orchestrate these activities globally is the required coordinative capability of these firms' (p. 1269).

- *Global integrator*: 'A hybrid form of subcontractor … responsible for all bridging activities of the international supply chain … connecting internationally dispersed buyers and subcontractors and supplying the necessary logistical infrastructure for carrying out exchange. The primary strategic asset … is its developed infrastructure and its ability to often manage quite different streams of manufactured goods … Compared to the roles taken by the other subcontractors in the typology, the global integrator has a strong bargaining position towards buyers as well as subcontractors' (p. 1270).

Nevertheless, global outsourcing carries substantial costs and risks, especially where there are several tiers of suppliers involved (see Figure 5.19). For example, there are inevitably huge logistical problems in organizing highly complex supply chains as well as ensuring product quality in suppliers over which control at a distance is difficult. A survey of 131 UK firms in 2013 found that 'almost one in five businesses … do not know who their suppliers' suppliers are'.[73] An example of the problems of controlling geographically and organizationally extended production networks occurred in 2007 when toys produced under outsourcing arrangements by Wal-Mart were found to contain lead:

> Wal-Mart squeezes Mattel [the toy maker], Mattel squeezes its supplier, that supplier squeezes its supplier, and at the end of the chain you have a remote business far out in the countryside that takes a different approach. They don't put lead in paint because they are wicked, it's just what works for them. China is so large, and industrialization has been so rapid, that maintaining any control over multiple sites is extremely difficult.[74]

Recently, there has been growing awareness of the dangers posed by supply chain disruption caused by major environmental events, such as earthquakes and floods (the case of the earthquake/tsunami that hit Japan in 2011 had a major impact on firms across the world, especially in automobiles and electronics). But perhaps the major problem is related to labour conditions in some supplier factories. Allegations of labour exploitation, including the use of child labour, excessive working hours, poor factory conditions, lack of workers' basic rights, are widespread. These have led to major investigations by international labour and human rights organizations and much adverse publicity for the firms themselves and pressure on them to ensure adherence to labour standards. These are issues we will discuss in some detail in later chapters, especially in the context of corporate social responsibility.

Different ways of coordinating GPNs

In Chapter 3 we noted that production networks can be coordinated in a variety of different ways, involving a mix of intra-firm and inter-firm structures. It is now time to examine this more closely.[75] Figure 5.23 shows one way of categorizing types of network coordination. In this discussion we will concentrate on three of the five coordination types shown in Figure 5.23: captive, relational and modular production networks. In all three networks, what we are interested in are the changing relationships between 'lead' firms and suppliers. We will encounter examples of these different types of network in the case studies of Part Four.

Captive production networks

These are networks in which a lead firm is dominant and effectively controls – although it does not own – all the major components in the network:

> Lead firms seek to lock-in suppliers in order to exclude others from reaping the benefits of their efforts. Therefore, the suppliers face significant switching costs and are 'captive'. Captive suppliers are frequently confined to a narrow range of tasks – for example, mainly engaged in simple assembly – and are dependent on the lead firm for complementary activities, such as design, logistics, component purchasing, and process technology upgrading.[76]

In such networks, the instructions to suppliers are highly codifiable while power is highly asymmetrical and lies unequivocally with the lead firm.

Coordination mechanism	Complexity of transactions	Ability to codify transactions	Capabilities of potential suppliers	Degree of explicit coordination and power asymmetry
Hierarchy Vertical integration within a firm with governance of subsidiaries and affiliates based on head-quarters' managerial control.	HIGH	LOW	LOW	HIGH
Captive Small suppliers transactionally dependent on larger buyers. Suppliers face significant switching costs.	HIGH	HIGH	LOW	
Relational Complex interactions between buyers and sellers often creating mutual dependence and high levels of asset specificity.	HIGH	LOW	HIGH	
Modular Production to customer's specification.	HIGH	HIGH	HIGH	
Market May involve repeat transactions but switching costs low for both parties.	LOW	HIGH	HIGH	LOW

Figure 5.23   **Different ways of coordinating transnational production networks**

Source: based on material in Gereffi et al., 2005

The hierarchically organized networks of major Japanese and Korean companies are captive networks. An especially graphic (although not necessarily a typical) example is the US sports footwear company Nike.[77] Nike does not wholly own any production facilities but consists entirely of a complex tiered and tightly coordinated network of subcontractors that perform specialist roles controlled from the corporate headquarters in Beaverton, Oregon, where most of the firm's R&D is also carried out (Figure 5.24).

Nike employs indirectly more than 800,000 workers in its 'contract supply chain' in around 600 factories (Figure 5.25). In terms of its geographical extensiveness it is certainly global. However, there is a strong bias towards East Asia, which contains almost 64 per cent of total suppliers. Of these, the vast majority are located in China (167 factories), followed by Vietnam and Thailand. Indonesia and Malaysia are also significant elements in the network. Only around 8 per cent of the total suppliers are in South Asia (mostly in Sri Lanka and India); 12 per cent in Central/Latin America (mostly in Mexico and Brazil); 5 per cent in Europe (Turkey has the most).

Relational production networks

Relational production networks are governed less by the authority of lead firms, and more by social relationships between network actors, especially those based on trust and reputation.[78]

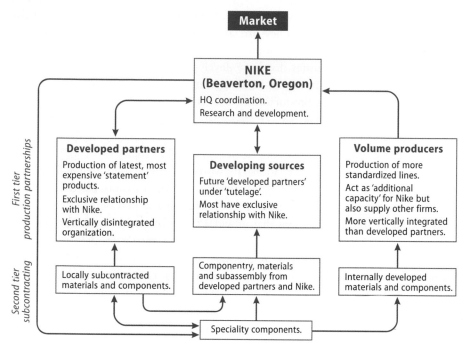

Figure 5.24 **Organization of the Nike production network**

Source: based on Donaghu and Barff, 1990: Figure 4; pp. 542–4.

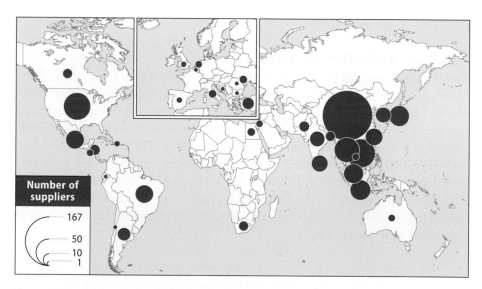

Figure 5.25 **Nike's global supplier network**

Source: based on data in Nike Inc., 2012, *Nike Contract Disclosure List*

Relational production networks have more symmetrical power relationships than captive production networks. They are the kinds of network that exist among overseas Chinese businesses and some other ethnic/social groups. The 'technical' transnational communities that have developed in the US electronics industries around Taiwanese, Chinese and Indian immigrants have facilitated rapid and extensive growth of global production networks based on relational processes.[79] In many cases, these individuals have created relational production networks in their home countries that are integrated into global networks. Many of these are the kinds of 'born global' enterprises discussed on pages 127–8.

Within Europe, examples of relational networks have been identified in Germany (the complex contracting relationships between small and medium-sized firms) and in Italy. In such cases, it is argued that it is the close *spatial proximity* between both firms and other social institutions that provides the 'relational cement' for the networks to exist. During the 1980s, in particular, it became extremely popular to eulogize such 'industrial districts' as the way forward from the old rigidities of Fordist mass production systems. However, important as close spatial proximity may be in facilitating the development of relational production networks, it is not, on its own, sufficient, as we saw in discussing localized knowledge clusters in Chapter 4.

One view of relational networks is that they may point the way towards the emergence of the *virtual firm* or the *cellular network* organization,[80] as we saw in Chapter 4 (see Figure 4.19). Organizationally, the entire network structure – consisting of separate firms – is relatively 'flat' and non-hierarchical. There is no common ownership; they are cooperative, *relational*, structures between independent and quasi-independent firms based upon a high degree of trust, something that takes time to develop. However, this does not mean that there are not *power* differentials within the network. There certainly are.

Modular production networks

We discussed modular production networks in Chapter 4 (See Figure 4.18). Their development, as we saw, depends largely on the fact that some modern production circuits have 'natural' breakpoints, where there is a transition from dependence on tacit knowledge to one where information can be codified through standard, agreed protocols. This has led, in an increasing number of industries, to a situation in which lead firms concentrate primarily on product development, marketing and distribution, while what are termed *turnkey suppliers* concentrate on producing those functions outsourced by lead firms and sell them, in effect, as services to a wide range of customers. To achieve this, turnkey suppliers develop three types of cross-cutting specialization:[81]

- '*base process*, one which is used to manufacture products sold in a wide range of end-markets (e.g. pharmaceutical manufacture, semiconductor wafer fabrication, plastic injection molding, electronics assembly, apparel assembly, brewing, telecommunications backbone switching)';

- '*base component*, one that can be used in a wide variety of end-products (e.g. semiconductor memory, automotive braking systems, engine controls)';
- '*base service*, one that is needed by a wide variety of end-users (e.g. accounting, data processing, logistics), rather than processes or services that are idiosyncratic or highly customer-specific'.

The development of contract manufacturing in the electronics industry provides a clear example of the development of modular production networks.[82] The increasing scale and complexity of outsourcing by US electronics firms in the 1980s and 1990s created a demand for suppliers to develop large capabilities at a global scale in order to serve the increasingly transnationalized lead electronics firms. The result was the emergence of a small number of very large electronics contract manufacturers from North America – Solectron, Sanmina/SCI, Celestica, Jabil Circuit – operating a global network of establishments serving the leading brand-name electronics manufacturers. The largest of all, as we have seen, is the Taiwanese company Foxconn (Figure 5.22) but there are others from East Asia, including TSMC (Taiwan) and Flextronics (Singapore).[83]

These different types of production network – hierarchical, captive, relational and modular – coexist in varying combinations in different industries and in different parts of the world. There is some evidence to suggest that firms from particular national origins tend to adopt particular types of production network. For example, the modular network form has developed most clearly in the USA and reflects a relative openness of procedures and a desire to reduce the degree of mutual dependence. Key to this system is the extensive and intensive use of 'IT suppliers that provide widely applicable "base processes" and widely accepted standards that enable the codifiable transfer of specification across the inter-firm link. These preconditions lead to generic (not product-specific) capacity at suppliers that has the potential to be shared by the industry as a whole.'[84] The extent to which such a system will be adopted more widely and lead to convergence of practice is an open question and relates to the comments made about the persistence of nationally grounded variations in TNC structures and practices discussed earlier in this chapter.

Transnational strategic alliances

Collaborative ventures between firms across national boundaries are nothing new. What is new is their current scale, their proliferation and the fact that they have become *central to the global strategies* of many firms rather than peripheral to them.[85] Most strikingly, many, if not most, strategic alliances are *between competitors*; as such they reflect a 'new rivalry … in the way collaboration and competition interact'.[86] Many companies are forming not just single alliances but *networks of alliances*, in which relationships are increasingly multilateral rather than bilateral, polygamous rather than monogamous. In effect, they create new *constellations* of economic power.

Strategic alliances are formal agreements between firms to pursue a *specific* strategic objective; to enable firms to achieve a specific goal that they cannot achieve alone. It involves the sharing of risks as well as rewards through joint decision-making responsibility for a specific venture. Note, however, that strategic alliances are not the same as mergers, in which the identities of the merging companies are completely subsumed. In a strategic alliance only *some* of the participants' business activities are involved; in every other respect the firms remain not only separate but also usually competitors.

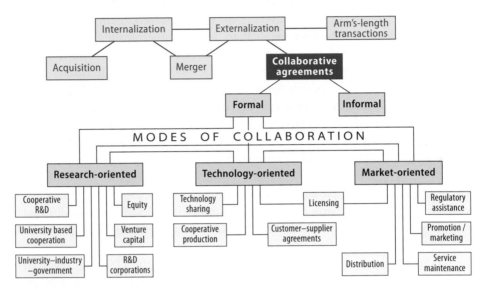

Figure 5.26   Types of inter-firm collaboration

Source: based on Anderson, 1995: Figure 1

Three major modes of collaboration are involved in strategic alliances (Figure 5.26): research-oriented, technology-oriented and market-oriented. Alliances offer the following (potential) kinds of advantage to the participants:

- overcoming problems of access to markets;
- facilitating entry into new/unfamiliar markets;
- sharing the increasing costs, uncertainties and risks of R&D and of new product development;
- gaining access to technologies;
- achieving economies of synergy, for example by pooling resources and capabilities, and rationalizing production.

Very often, the motivations for strategic alliances are highly specific. In the case of R&D ventures, for example, cooperation is limited to research into new products and technologies while manufacturing and marketing usually remain the responsibility of the individual partners. Cross-distribution agreements offer firms ways of widening their product range by marketing another firm's products in a specific market area. Cross-licensing agreements are similar but they also offer the possibility of establishing a global standard for a particular technology. Joint manufacturing agreements are used both to attain economies of scale and to cope with excess or deficient production capacity. Joint bidding consortia are especially important in very large-scale projects in industries such as aerospace or telecommunications, where the sheer scale of the venture or, perhaps, the specific regulatory requirements of national governments put the projects out of reach of individual companies.

The majority of strategic alliances, therefore, are in sectors with high entry costs, scale economies, rapidly changing technologies and/or substantial operating risks:

> Pharmaceuticals, chemicals, electronic equipment, computers, telecommunications, and financial and business services are examples of industries characterized by a large number of strategic alliances ... Although a large number of alliances are still formed in manufacturing industries, more and more strategic alliances are taking place in the services ... As the world economy becomes more service-based, strategic alliances are playing a more important role in cross-border restructuring in service sectors.[87]

Advocates of strategic alliances claim that companies can combine their capabilities in ways that will benefit each partner. But not everybody shares this rosy view. Many fear that entering into such alliances will result in the loss of key technologies or expertise by one or other of the partners. More broadly, strategic alliances are clearly more difficult to manage and coordinate than single ventures; the potential for misunderstanding and disagreement, particularly between partners from different cultures, is greater. Certainly many such alliances have relatively short lives.[88] Nevertheless, the obvious attractions of transnational strategic alliances in today's volatile and intensely competitive global economy guarantee their continued growth as a major organizational form.

PERPETUAL CHANGE: RESHAPING TNCs' INTERNAL AND EXTERNAL NETWORKS

Transnational corporate networks – both internal and external – are always in a state of flux. At any one time, some parts may be growing rapidly, others may be stagnating, yet others may be in steep decline. The functions performed by the component parts and the relationships between them may alter. Change itself may be the result of a planned strategy of adjustment to changing internal and external circumstances or the 'knee-jerk' response to a sudden crisis.

Forces underlying reorganization and restructuring

One of the diagnostic characteristics of TNCs is that they continuously monitor the performance of each of their individual operations and benchmark them against some best-practice metric. Hence, transnational corporate networks are almost always in a state of rationalization and restructuring, either in whole or in part. Precisely because TNC operations are located in different countries, such adjustments – perhaps involving the closure, downsizing or functional status of individual establishments – have very sensitive political implications.

In general, corporate reorganization and restructuring is driven by two, often overlapping, forces:

- *External conditions.* These may be negative pressures, such as declining demand, increased competition in domestic or foreign markets, changes in the cost or availability of production inputs, militancy and resistance of labour forces in particular places, the pressure of national governments to modify their activities or even to cede control. Conversely, changes in external conditions may be positive, for example the growth of new geographical markets or the availability of new production opportunities. A good illustration is the formation of regional economic groupings, where the creation of a large regional market provides an unprecedented opportunity for TNCs to restructure their production activities to serve the regional market. Investments that had made sense in the context of an individual national context are no longer necessarily rational in the wider context (see Figure 5.17).
- *Internal pressures.* These may relate to the enterprise as a whole or to one or other individual parts: for example, sales may be too low in relation to the firm's target, production costs may be too high. In a TNC the performance of individual plants in widely separate locations can be continuously monitored and compared to assess their efficiency. A key influence is often the 'new-broom factor': a new chief executive who undertakes a sweeping evaluation of the enterprise's activities and makes changes that stamp his/her authority on the firm.

In reality, external and internal pressures may be so closely interrelated that it is often difficult to disentangle one from the other. More than this, precisely how firms both identify and respond to changes in their circumstances is very much conditioned by the firm's culture.[89]

Complex corporate restructuring occurs at all geographical scales, from the global to the local, as strategic decisions are made about the organizational coordination and geographical configuration of the TNC's production network. Decisions to outsource or internalize particular functions, to centralize or to decentralize decision-making powers, or to concentrate or disperse some or all of the firm's functions in particular ways, are, however, *contested* decisions. They are the outcome of power struggles within firms, both within their headquarters and between headquarters and affiliates. How they are resolved depends very much on the nature and the location of the dominant coalition within the company.

The geography of reorganization and restructuring

Whether corporate reorganization is the result of a consciously planned strategy for 'rational' change or simply a reaction to a crisis (internal or external), its geographical outcome may take several different forms (Figure 5.27). The very large global corporations are *global scanners*. They use their immense resources to evaluate potential production locations in all parts of the world. The performance of existing corporate units and external suppliers is continuously monitored and evaluated against competitors, against the rest of the corporate network and also against potential alternative locations. Those existing plants or suppliers that fall short of expectations created by such *benchmarking* procedures[90] may be disposed of. As plants become obsolete in one location they are closed down. Whether or not new investment occurs in the same locality depends upon its suitability for the TNC's prevailing strategy. The chances are, in many cases, that the new investment will be made at a different location – quite possibly in a different country altogether.

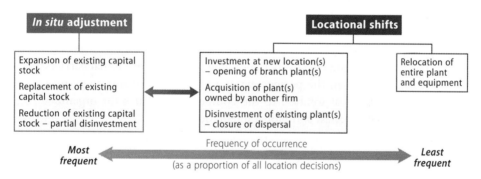

Figure 5.27 Reorganization, restructuring and geographical change

However, we should beware of exaggerating the speed and ease with which TNCs can, and do, radically restructure their operations; there are always 'barriers to exit'. Production units represent huge capital investments – sunk costs – which 'once undertaken, cannot be fully recovered through their transfer or sale'.[91] Political pressures may also inhibit firms from closing plants, especially in areas of economic and social stress. On the other hand, TNCs do have a highly tuned capacity to *switch* and *re-switch* operations within their existing corporate network. They also have the resources to alter the shape of their geographical network through locational shifts.

Hence, the processes of reorganization and restructuring are complex, dynamic and far from predictable. Overall, however, four continuing general tendencies are especially apparent:

- redefining core activities by stripping away activities that no longer 'fit' the firm's strategy;
- placing greater emphasis on downstream service functions;
- geographically reconfiguring production networks transnationally to redefine the roles and functions of individual corporate units;
- redefining the boundary between internalized and externalized transactions.

Regionalizing transnational production networks

We suggested earlier in this chapter that the notion of the 'global' corporation is something of a myth. In fact, a growing body of research suggests that rather than being globally organized, most of the largest TNCs have a stronger propensity to organize their production networks *regionally* (i.e. at the multinational scale of groups of contiguous states).[92] For example, 'for Western core companies, regionalism has become the institutional framework of choice within which the struggle for preservation of their core positions is played out … *the acceleration in the rate of internationalization after 1995 was an intra-regional phenomenon*'.[93] In 2004, four-fifths of the 500 largest TNCs in the world had almost 80 per cent of both their sales and their assets concentrated in their home region.[94] 'Global' this certainly is not.

The basis for such a regional orientation is evident in Figure 5.17c. In effect,

> a regional strategy offers many of the efficiency advantages of globalization while more effectively responding to the organizational barriers it entails … From the perspective of a TNC, a regional strategy may represent an ideal solution to the competing pressures for organizational responsiveness and global integration.[95]

In particular:[96]

- Regional-scale manufacturing facilities may represent the limits of potential economies of scale.
- Regionalization allows for faster delivery, greater customization and smaller inventories than would be possible under globalization.
- Regionalization accommodates organizational concerns and exploits subsidiary strengths.

The tendency we noted earlier for firms to draw back somewhat from all-out 'global' sourcing (whether intra- or inter-firm) is strongly reflected at the regional scale:

> Manufacturers are abandoning global supply chains for regional ones in a big shift brought about by the financial crisis and climate change concerns … Companies are increasingly looking closer to home for their components, meaning that for their US or European operations they are

more likely to use Mexico and Eastern Europe than China, as previously. 'A future where energy is more expensive and less plentifully available will lead to more regional supply chains', Gerard Kleisterlee, chief executive of Philips, one of Europe's biggest companies.[97]

In some instances, TNC regionalization is reinforced by regional political structures (as in the cases of the EU or the NAFTA). But not necessarily: simple geographical proximity is, itself, a very powerful stimulus for integrating operations.

Transnational production networks organized at the regional scale are evident in Europe, North America and East Asia, as we will see in several of the case study chapters in Part Four. In North America, the establishment of the NAFTA has led to a reconfiguration of corporate activities to meet the opportunities and constraints of the new regional system.[98] Mexico, in particular, has become increasingly important, especially as labour costs in China have risen relatively more quickly. In that context, Mexico's proximity to the USA becomes even more critical:

> It takes between 20 days and two months to ship goods from China to the US. In the case of Mexico, it takes a maximum of seven days – and often as little as two.

> The quicker times have gained relevance as US companies that depend on inputs from third parties embrace just-in-time manufacturing, which has become more popular since the 2008 recession because it allows companies to reduce costs by holding smaller inventories.[99]

The increasing integration and enlargement of the EU has led to substantial reorganization of existing corporate networks and the establishment of pan-EU systems by existing and new TNCs. Indeed, 'the EU can be seen as a gigantic international production complex made up of the networks of TNCs which straddle across national boundaries and form trade networks in their own right'.[100]

There is abundant evidence of US and Japanese TNCs – as well as many European firms themselves – creating regional networks within the EU. Some Japanese companies, for example, have adopted

> a three-tier European operation, partly centralised and partly decentralised. A number of them have set up small, new, pan-European head offices, with a purely strategic role: financial control, overall direction, high-level brand management … The real work is done, however, by the next two tiers of the business: the operational centres (production, distribution, logistics) organised on a pan-European basis and sited where convenient. For distribution, this means in the heartland of western Europe, with easy access to France and Germany; for production it will increasingly mean in eastern and central Europe, where costs are lower. Sales and tactical marketing are handled at a national

level. Perhaps where two or three countries have very similar characteristics, such as the Nordic region, they can be aggregated together.
But, in general, national markets are sufficiently distinctive to require
their own local sales operations.[101]

The process is complicated. On the one hand, supply-side forces are stimulating a
pan-EU structure of operations to take advantage of scale efficiencies. On the other
hand, demand-side forces are still articulated primarily at the country-specific level,
where linguistic and cultural differences play a major role in the demands for goods
and services. In effect, the strategic tensions between global integration and local
responsiveness, discussed earlier in this chapter, are played out at the EU regional level.

Although East Asia does not have the same kind of regional political framework
as the EU or NAFTA, there is very strong evidence of the existence of regional
production networks organized primarily by Japanese firms, although non-Asian
as well as some other Asian firms (from Korea, Hong Kong, Singapore and Taiwan,
for example) also tend to organize their production networks regionally.[102] Within
East Asia, a clear intra-regional division of labour has developed consisting of four
tiers of countries: (1) Japan; (2) Hong Kong, Korea, Singapore and Taiwan; (3)
China; (4) Malaysia, Thailand, Indonesia, the Philippines, Vietnam. Of course, the
rapid emergence of China as both a huge potential market and as a production
location is transforming intra-regional networks in East Asia.

NOTES

1   Anderson and Cavanagh (2000: 3).
2   The data are derived from the annual UNCTAD *World Investment Report*.
3   UNCTAD (2012: Table I.9).
4   Mathews (2006: 7, 8).
5   D'Aveni (1994: 2).
6   See Harvey (2011).
7   Herod (1997: 2).
8   Hymer (1976).
9   Dunning (1992, 2000). For a critique see Mathews (2006).
10   Vernon (1966, 1979), Wells (1972).
11   Mathews (2006: 22).
12   Dicken and Miyamachi (1998), Mason (1994).
13   Peter Brabeck, CEO of Nestlé, quoted in the *Financial Times* (22 February 2005).
14   Mathews (2006) provides a wide variety of examples.
15   See Eurofound (2012), Gabrielsson and Kirpalani (2004), Mathews and Zander (2007),
     Melén and Nordman (2009), Oviatt and McDougall (2005), Sasi and Arenius (2008).
16   Mathews and Zander (2007: 390; emphasis added).
17   Mathews and Zander (2007: 388).
18   Oviatt and McDougall (2005: 38).
19   See Badaracco (1991), Blois (2006), Cerrato (2006), Dicken and Malmberg (2001),
     Forsgren et al. (2005), Markusen (1999).

20 Forsgren et al. (2005: 97–8).
21 Bartlett and Ghoshal (1998), Faulconbridge (2008), Forsgren et al. (2005), Hedlund (1986), Heenan and Perlmutter (1979), Morgan et al. (2004), Schoenberger (1997), Whitley (2004).
22 Heenan and Perlmutter (1979).
23 Dicken (2000, 2003b).
24 Pauly and Reich (1997: 1, 4, 5, 24).
25 *Financial Times* (4 December 2007).
26 Van Veen and Marsman (2008: 196).
27 Yeung (2000: 408).
28 Fruin (1992), Gerlach (1992).
29 Gerlach (1992: 4).
30 Wade (2004: 324).
31 Hamilton and Feenstra (1998: 128–9).
32 Hamilton and Feenstra (1998: 134, 135).
33 Yeung (2000: 425); see also Yeung (2004).
34 Yeung (2004).
35 See, for example, Bathelt and Gertler (2005), Buck and Shahrim (2005).
36 Harzing (2000), Malnight (1996).
37 Hedlund (1986: 218–30).
38 Mathews (2006: 14).
39 Birkinshaw (2001), Birkinshaw and Morrison (1995), Cerrato (2006), Phelps and Fuller (2000).
40 Birkinshaw and Morrison (1995: 732–5).
41 Schoenberger (1999: 210–11).
42 Haig (1926: 426).
43 See Baaij et al. (2004), Cerrato (2006), Collis et al. (2007), Young et al. (2000).
44 Cerrato (2006: 261).
45 Collis et al. (2007), Young et al. (2000).
46 Lasserre (1996), Edgington and Hayter (2013).
47 Edgington and Hayter (2013: 651).
48 Yeung et al. (2001: 165).
49 Goerzen et al. (2013).
50 Alderson and Beckfield (2004). See also Carroll (2007).
51 Friedmann (1986), Sassen (2001), Taylor (2004).
52 Baaij et al. (2004: 143).
53 *Financial Times* (19 March 2007).
54 Malecki (2010) provides a comprehensive review. See also Blanc and Sierra (1999), Cantwell (1997), Hotz-Hart (2000), Howells (2012a, b), Patel (1995), Zanfei (2000).
55 Malecki (2010: 1037).
56 Belderbos et al. (2013).
57 Blanc and Sierra (1999: 188).
58 *Financial Times* (23 June 2005).
59 *Financial Times* (9 June 2005).
60 *Financial Times* (14 November 2012).
61 Cantwell and Iammarino (2000: 322).
62 *Financial Times* (19 March 2013).
63 CEO of Nestlé, cited in the *Financial Times* (22 February 2005).

64 Sturgeon (2002: 461–2).
65 *Financial Times* (21 May 2012).
66 *Financial Times* (7 December 2012).
67 *Financial Times* (3 April 2012).
68 *Financial Times* (5 June 2008).
69 Mol et al. (2005), Berggren and Bengtsson (2004).
70 Merino and Rodriguez (2007: 1147).
71 See UNCTAD (2011: chapter IV) for a detailed treatment of contract manufacturers.
72 Andersen and Christensen (2004: 1261).
73 *Financial Times* (7 May 2013).
74 Teagarden, quoted in the *Financial Times* (4 September 2007).
75 This section draws, in part, on Gereffi et al. (2005), Sturgeon (2002, 2003). See also UNCTAD (2011: chapter IV).
76 Gereffi et al. (2005: 87).
77 Donaghu and Barff (1990), Rothenberg-Aalami (2004).
78 Sturgeon (2003: 482).
79 Saxenian (2002: 186).
80 Miles et al. (1999).
81 Sturgeon (2002: 466–7).
82 Sturgeon (2002, 2003), Lüthje (2002).
83 UNCTAD (2011: Table IV.6).
84 Sturgeon (2002: 486).
85 See Anderson (1995), Gomes-Casseres (1996), Kang and Sakai (2000), Mockler (2000), Ulset (2008).
86 Gomes-Casseres (1996: 2).
87 Kang and Sakai (2000: 20).
88 Ulset (2008).
89 Schoenberger (1997: 204).
90 See Sklair (2001: chapter 5).
91 Barham and Coomes (2005: 162). See also Schoenberger (1997: 88).
92 Elango (2004), Kozul-Wright and Rowthorn (1998), Morrison and Roth (1992), Muller (2004), Rugman and Brain (2003), Rugman and Verbeke (2004, 2008).
93 Muller (2004: ix, 219; original emphasis).
94 Rugman and Verbeke (2008: Tables 1 and 2).
95 Morrison and Roth (1992: 45, 46).
96 Morrison and Roth (1992: 46–7).
97 *Financial Times* (10 August 2009).
98 Eden and Monteils (2002), Holmes (2000).
99 *Financial Times* (17 April 2012).
100 Amin (2000: 675).
101 *Financial Times* (8 November 2001).
102 Abo (2000), Borrus et al. (2000), Coe (2003a), Dicken and Yeung (1999), Yeung (2001), Yeung et al. (2001).

Six

THE STATE *REALLY DOES* MATTER

'THE STATE IS DEAD' – OH NO IT ISN'T!

That was then; this is now

'State denial'[1] has formed a central claim of the 'hyper-globalizers' (and many social scientists) over the past 40 years: that we live in a borderless world where states no longer matter. A combination of the revolutionary technologies of transportation and communications (see Chapter 4) and the increasing power of TNCs (see Chapter 5) has, it was argued, shifted economic power out of the control of nation-states to 'the market'. 'Market fundamentalism' – a neo-liberal agenda urging the reduction of state involvement in the economy, the privatization of state economic and social assets, lower direct taxation, unfettered trade and financial movements, a reduction in the state's social welfare role – became the mantra, especially in the USA and the UK. 'Government', argued the US President, Ronald Reagan, in the early 1980s, 'was not a solution to our problem, government is the problem.' A similar sentiment was echoed by the UK government of Margaret Thatcher (and revived by the Conservative-dominated UK coalition government of 2010–15). Such a free market ideology formed the basis of what came to be called the 'Washington Consensus', the set of views that exerted immense influence on both developed and, especially, developing countries.

That was then.

This is now – and how the world has changed! The cataclysmic events that stunned the global economy in 2008 saw a dramatic reversal in the apparently unchallenged dominance of the free market and a revival of the view that 'states really do matter'. The change was most apparent in the financial sector (see Chapter 16), where the 'Masters of the Universe'[2] had to go on bended knee to the state to be rescued, but also in such industries as automobiles (see Chapter 15). Governments poured billions of dollars, pounds and euros into propping up the financial sector. In some cases, notably in the USA and the UK, this amounted to little short of nationalization, a *bête noire* of the market fundamentalists. Quite how this will play out over the next few years is not yet clear. However, there is a generally held view that things will never be quite the same. The state is back.

In fact, the state never really went away. The notion that the power of the state had been totally emasculated by globalizing forces was always highly misleading. While some of the state's capabilities were reduced, and there may well have been a process of 'hollowing out',[3] the process was not a simple one of uniform decline on all fronts:[4]

> Much of the *'end of the state'* … *literature focuses on western notions of statehood and experiences* … Implicit is a common experience of the emergence of the state in the nineteenth century and its zenith in the postwar Fordist regime of accumulation … *In many parts of the world, however, experiences of statehood have followed a quite different trajectory and*

are, in a postcolonial context, still being actively constructed, strengthened and extended rather than weakened.[5]

The state unquestionably remains a most significant force in shaping the world economy, despite the hyper-globalist rhetoric. It has *always* played a fundamental role in the economic development of *all* countries[6] and, indeed, in the process of globalization itself. After all, an increased facility to transcend geographical distance made possible by transportation and communication technologies is of little use if there are political barriers to such movement. An important enabling factor underlying globalization, therefore, has been the progressive reduction in political barriers to flows of commodities, goods, finance and other services.

In fact, the more powerful states have *used* globalization as a means of increasing their power:

> States actively construct globalization and use it as soft geo-politics and to acquire *greater* power over, and autonomy from, their national economies and societies respectively … [for example] … The US and the G-7's other dominant members design and establish the international trade agreements, organizations, and legislation that support and govern the trans-border investments, production networks, and market-penetration constitutive of contemporary economic globalization. Advanced capitalist states, particularly, use these political instruments to shape international economic decision-making and policy in their interests.[7]

Governments have also used the rhetoric of the supposedly unstoppable forces of globalization to justify particular kinds of domestic policy (including not taking certain kinds of action) on the argument that 'there is no alternative'.

States, nations, nation-states

We need to be clear about what we mean by the terms 'state', 'nation' and 'nation-state':[8]

- A *state* is a portion of geographical space within which the resident population is organized (i.e. governed) by an authority structure. States have externally recognized sovereignty over their territory.
- A *nation* is a 'reasonably large group of people with a common culture, sharing one or more cultural traits, such as religion, language, political institutions, values, and historical experience. They tend to identify with one another, feel closer to one another than to outsiders, and to believe that they belong together. They are clearly distinguishable from others who do not share their culture.' A nation is an *imagined community*. Note that whereas a state has a recognized and defined territory, a nation may not.

- A *nation-state* is the situation where 'state' and 'nation' are coterminous. 'A nation-state is a nation with a state wrapped around it. That is, it is a nation with its own state, a state in which there is no significant group that is not part of the nation.'

Although it is often regarded as a natural institution (for all of us it has always been there), the nation-state is actually a relatively recent phenomenon. It emerged from the particular configuration of power relationships in Europe following the Treaty of Westphalia that ended the Thirty Years War in 1648. Since then, the map of nation-states has been redrawn continuously, sometimes peacefully and incrementally, often violently through revolution. During the second half of the twentieth century, two particular events had a profound effect on the map of nation-states. First, the waves of decolonization that swept through Africa and Asia in the 1960s created a whole new set of nation-states. Second, the collapse of the former Soviet Union, after 1989, resulted in the creation not only of a new Russian Federation, but also of a number of newly independent states throughout Eastern Europe. As a result, the number of nation-states, as measured by UN membership, has grown dramatically (Figures 6.1 and 6.2).

But that is not all. An important feature of today's world is the tension between the triad of nation, state and nationalism. Increasingly, it seems, there are more and more 'nations without states', manifested in separatist movements engaged in conflict with the state in which they are (wrongly in their view) embedded (obvious

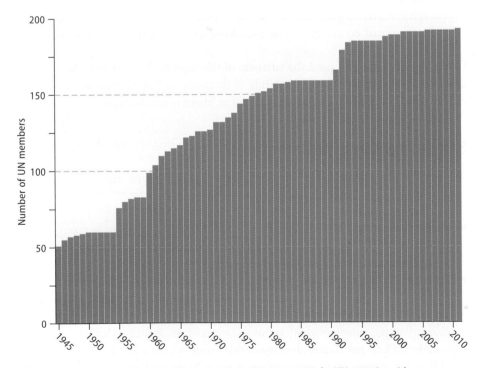

Figure 6.1   **The increasing number of nation-states: growth in UN membership**

Source: United Nations

Figure 6.2 **A world of nation-states**

#	Country	#	Country
1	Denmark	17	Macedonia
2	Netherlands	18	Romania
3	Belgium	19	Moldova
4	Germany	20	Bulgaria
5	Luxembourg	21	Albania
6	Czech Republic	22	Greece
7	Slovakia	23	Georgia
8	Switzerland	24	Armenia
9	Liechtenstein	25	Azerbaijan
10	Austria	26	Turkmenistan
11	Hungary	27	Lebanon
12	Slovenia	28	Israel
13	Croatia	29	Jordan
14	Bosnia-Herzegovina	30	Bahrain
15	Serbia	31	Qatar
16	Montenegro	32	Burkina Faso

#	Country	#	Country
33	Guinea Bissau	41	Antigua & Barbuda
34	Ghana	42	St. Kitts & Nevis
35	Togo	43	Dominica
36	Benin	44	St. Lucia
37	Cameroon	45	St. Vincent & Grenadines
38	Central African Republic	46	Barbados
39	South Sudan	47	Grenada
40	Equatorial Guinea	48	Trinidad & Tobago

examples include the Basques in Spain and France, the indigenous groups in Chiapas, Mexico, the East Timoreans in Indonesia, the Palestinians in Israel).

STATES AS CONTAINERS

The 'black box' of the state acts as a kind of 'container' of distinctive practices and institutions. Of course, the term 'container' should not be taken literally. It is used here as a loose metaphor to capture the idea that nation-states are *one* of the major ways in which distinctive cultures, practices and institutions are 'bundled together'.[9] Of course, such containers are not (except very rarely) hermetically sealed off from the outside world. A major impact of modern communications systems, especially the Internet, is to make national containers even more permeable. But that does not mean that the container no longer exists. Indeed, there is a good deal of compelling evidence to show the persistence of national distinctiveness – although not necessarily uniqueness – in structures and practices which help to shape local, national and global patterns of economic activity.

States as cultural containers

All economic activity is enmeshed in broader cultural structures and practices,[10] although 'culture' is an extremely slippery concept to define. Here it is taken to be

> a learned, shared, compelling, interrelated set of symbols whose meanings provide a set of orientations for members of a society. These orientations, taken together, provide solutions to problems that all societies must solve if they are to remain viable.[11]

From an economic perspective, there are relatively few comprehensive and robust analyses of how cultures vary between countries. The most widely known is Geert Hofstede's classic study of more than 100,000 workers employed by the US company IBM in 50 different countries.[12] Hofstede claimed that, by focusing on a controlled population within a common organizational environment, he was able to isolate *nationality* as a variable. On this basis he identified four distinct cultural dimensions:

- *Individualism versus collectivism*: societies vary between those in which people, in general, are motivated to look after their own individual interests – where ties between individuals are very loose – and those in which ties are very close and the collectivity (family, community, etc.) is the important consideration.
- *Large or small power distance*: societies vary in how they deal with inequalities (e.g. in power and wealth) between people. This is reflected in the extent to which authority is centralized and in the degree of autocratic leadership within society.

- *Strong or weak uncertainty avoidance*: in some societies, the inherent uncertainty of the future is accepted; each day is taken as it comes, that is the level of uncertainty avoidance is weak. In other societies, there is a strong drive to try to 'beat the future'. Efforts (and institutions) are made to try to create security and to avoid risk. These are strong uncertainty avoidance societies.
- *Masculinity versus femininity*: societies can be classified according to how sharply the social division between male and females is drawn. Societies with a strong emphasis on traditional masculinity allocate the more assertive and dominant roles to men. They differ substantially from societies where the social gender role division is small and where such values are less evident.

Hofstede went on to show how different countries could be characterized in terms of their positions on varying combinations of these four dimensions (Figure 6.3).

Group	1. Anglo	2. Germanic	3. Nordic	4. More developed Asian

Characteristics	Low power distance
	Low to medium
	  uncertainty avoidance
	High individualism
	High masculinity
		Low power distance
		High uncertainty avoidance
		Medium individualism
		High masculinity
			Low power distance
			Low to medium
			  uncertainty avoidance
			Medium individualism
			Low masculinity
				Medium power distance
				High uncertainty avoidance
				Medium individualism
				High masculinity

Countries	Australia Ireland Britain New Zealand Canada U.S.A.	Austria Italy Germany South Africa Israel Switzerland	Denmark Norway Finland Sweden Netherlands	Japan
Group	**5. Less developed Asian**	**6. Near Eastern**	**7. More developed Latin**	**8. Less developed Latin**
Characteristics	High power distance Low uncertainty avoidance Low individualism Medium masculinity	High power distance High uncertainty avoidance Low individualism Medium masculinity	High power distance High uncertainty avoidance High individualism Medium masculinity	High power distance High uncertainty avoidance Low individualism Whole range on masculinity
Countries	India Singapore Pakistan Taiwan Philippines Thailand	Greece Iran Turkey	Argentina France Belgium Spain Brazil	Chile Peru Colombia Portugal Mexico Venezuela

Figure 6.3   **National variations in cultural characteristics**

Source: based on Hofstede, 1980: p. 336

Although Hofstede's work has stood the test of time remarkably well,[13] it has its critics. For example, Shalom Schwartz[14] argued that not enough countries were included fully to capture national cultural variation and that the respondents were too narrowly drawn to be truly representative of the entire population. Using rather different methods, he identified the following seven distinctive cultural dimensions:

- *Conservatism*: places an emphasis on preserving the status quo and in restricting behaviour likely to disrupt the traditional order.
- *Intellectual autonomy*: the extent to which people are free to pursue their own intellectual ideas.
- *Affective autonomy*: the extent to which people are free to pursue their own personal and emotional desires.

- *Hierarchy*: the extent to which an uneven allocation of power and resources is legitimized.
- *Egalitarian commitment*: the extent to which individuals are prepared to subjugate self-interest for the greater communal good.
- *Mastery*: the extent to which individual self-assertiveness is legitimized as a means to achieve specific goals.
- *Harmony*: the importance placed on fitting harmoniously into the environment.

Although there is obviously some overlap between these two schemes, what matters here is not so much the detail as the fact that there *are* identifiable cultural attributes that appear to vary across countries and that this, in turn, affects both how the major actors we identified in Chapter 3 are likely to behave and the kinds of institutions within which such behaviour is organized and regulated. Although it is always rather dangerous to classify phenomena into statistical boxes, the categories shown in Figure 6.3 seem intuitively reasonable. Most of us would be able to recognize our own national contexts, while also realizing the danger of using simple stereotypes without due care.

For example, East Asia's emergence as the most dynamic growth region in recent decades has often been attributed to its having a very distinctive set of value systems: specifically an emphasis on collective responsibility rather than individualism and on the roles and responsibilities of the state, which is seen as essentially paternalistic. Figure 6.4 sets out the major components of this concept of 'Asian values' which, in effect,

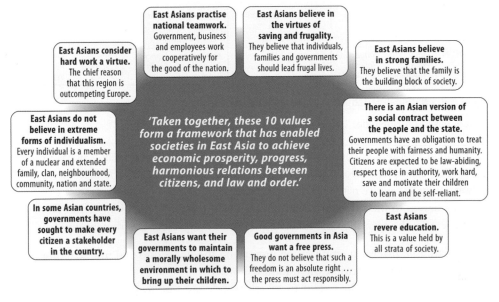

Figure 6.4 'Asian values'?

Source: based on material in Koh, 1993

'recast "Asia" as a moral opposite of the West. Thus … the Asian penchant for hard work, frugality and love of the family are unproblematically figured as things the West lacks or has lost.'[15] It is extremely doubtful that this reflects the situation across the whole of East Asia (let alone of Asia as a whole). This is, after all, a region of immense social, cultural and religious diversity. But insofar as these attributes reflect at least *some* of the social and political characteristics of *some* successful East Asian economies, they form a considerable contrast with the situation in other parts of the world.[16]

Variegated capitalisms

The specific cultural and institutional forms that have evolved over time in different national contexts have resulted in distinctive modes of economic organization, even within the apparently universal ideology of capitalism. Capitalism, in other words, is *variegated*, not uniform.[17] The traditional 'varieties of capital' literature focuses on just two broad categories of 'national' capitalism:

- the *liberal market economy* (LME), generally associated with the USA and, to a large extent, the UK;
- the *coordinated market economy* (CME), most commonly associated with such countries as Germany, Sweden and Japan.

This is not a very satisfactory classification.[18] In particular, the CME category encompasses enormous diversity and needs to be further unpacked. Here we identify four variants of capitalist organization, based on differing conceptions of the 'proper' role of government in regulating the economy:

- *Neo-liberal market capitalism.* Market mechanisms are used to regulate all, or most, aspects of the economy. Individualism is a dominant characteristic; short-term business goals tend to predominate. The state does not overtly attempt to plan the economy strategically. Capital markets are decentralized, open and fluid. The dominant philosophy is 'shareholder value' – facilitating maximum returns to the owners of capital. Exemplified by the USA and, to a large extent, the UK.
- *Social market capitalism.* In contrast to neo-liberal market capitalism, a higher premium is placed upon collaboration between different actors in the economy with a broader identification of 'stakeholders' beyond that of solely the owners of capital. The concept of 'social partnership' is more prominent. Capital markets tend to be bank centred. Exemplified by Germany, Scandinavia and many other European countries.
- *Developmental capitalism.* The state plays a much more central role (although not necessarily through public ownership of productive assets). The state sets substantive social and economic goals within an explicit industrial strategy. Capital

markets tend to be bank centred. There is a strong emphasis on tight business networks. Exemplified by Japan, South Korea, Taiwan, Singapore and most other East Asian countries (excluding China). Variants on this model include 'the "democratic development capitalism" of India and Brazil, with their strong social agendas to go with their growth aspirations'.[19]

- *Authoritarian capitalism*. Here, a highly centralized political system is combined with an increasingly open capitalist–market system. The prime example is China, where the process of liberalizing the economy (in a highly controlled way) began in 1979. Nevertheless, the Chinese Communist Party retains tight political control. In the case of Russia, the system is rather messier. Both political and economic structures were liberalized after 1991 but the Russian state still exerts strong control (though less effectively than in China).

Of course, this four-fold typology is also highly simplistic and, like all such schemes, should be seen in dynamic rather than static terms. However, there is little doubt that a *variegated*, rather than a single, system of capitalism (of whatever kind) is likely to persist in the future:

> There are inherent obstacles to convergence among social systems of production of different societies, for where a system is at any one point in time is influenced by its initial state ... Existing institutional arrangements block certain institutional innovations and facilitate others ... There are critical turning points in the history of highly industrialized societies, but the choices are limited by the existing institutional terrain. Being path dependent, a social system of production continues along a particular logic until or unless a fundamental societal crisis intervenes.[20]

An alternative view is that the pressures exerted by globalizing forces will inevitably produce a convergence of economic governance systems towards a 'best-practice' form. Until recently, many argued that the neo-liberal model, based on the success of its leading advocate, the USA, would come to replace national systems. In other words,

> even though the unique kinds of state capacities found in Japan and Germany have deep-rooted political preconditions, these face the prospect of 'permanent dismantling' by way of gradual 'liberal erosion'.[21]

But, as we have seen, the 'pure gold' of the neo-liberal model is now looking distinctly tarnished and it is difficult to imagine that it will retain its attractiveness. If this is so, then variegated capitalisms will continue to be the norm although in a dynamic, not static, form in which the state is likely to have a larger (though varied) role:

The wide divergences among high-income countries over the size of the state, the generosity of welfare systems, the structure of corporate governance and the pervasiveness of financial markets all demonstrate the possible divergences.[22]

We can safely predict ... that the Anglo-American view will become less influential ... [while] ... virtually all Asian models of capitalism involve a more active role for government. And the rise of these models is taking place as the US approach is discredited by abuse, shrivelling opportunities and a shrinking middle class. Among the alternatives, the US model is now the outlier.[23]

STATES AS REGULATORS

Recognizing that countries continue to differ as 'containers' of distinctive structures and practices is important in emphasizing that we do not live in a homogenizing world. In this section, we focus specifically on some of the ways states *regulate* how their economies operate as they attempt to control what happens within, and across, their boundaries.

The competition state

The transformation of the nation-state into a 'competition state' lies at the heart of political globalization.[24]

Books, government reports, newspaper articles, TV programmes in virtually all countries resonate with the language and imagery of the competitive race between states for a bigger slice of the global economic pie. Indeed, the Swiss business school IMD publishes an annual *World Competitiveness Yearbook* with a 'competitiveness scoreboard' (or 'league table') of 49 countries based on no fewer than 286 individual criteria!

States compete to enhance their international trading position in order to capture as large a share as possible of the gains from trade. They compete to attract productive investment to build up their national production base that, in turn, enhances their international competitive position. One of the most graphic expressions of competition between states is their intense involvement in what have been called 'locational tournaments': the attempts to entice investment projects into their own national territories. There has been an enormous escalation in the extent of *competitive bidding* between states (and between local communities within the same state) to attract the relatively limited amount of geographically mobile investment (see Chapter 7).

Most states continually search for a magic key to enhance their economic competitiveness. One of the most widely adopted has been Michael Porter's 'competitive diamond' framework, in which he argues that national competitive advantages are created through highly localized processes internal to the country. Figure 6.5 shows these as an interconnected, mutually reinforcing, system of four major determinants.

Porter's 'competitive recipe' has been adopted by many governments in their attempts to improve their competitive position, although he sees government itself as merely an 'influence'; a contingent, rather than a central, factor. In fact, *all* states perform a key role in the operation of their economies, although they differ substantially in the specific measures they employ and in the precise ways in which such measures are combined.

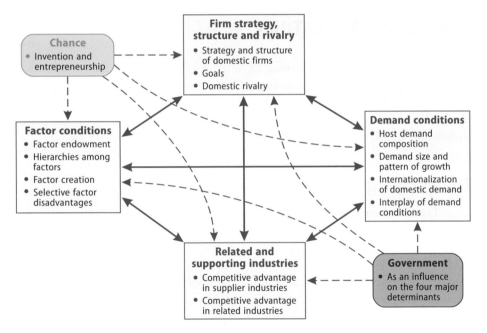

Figure 6.5   **National competitive advantage: the Porter 'diamond'**

Source: based on material in Porter, 1990: chapter 3

Managing national economies

> The institutions of the state … are not simply involved in regulating economy and society, for *state activity is necessarily involved in constituting economy and society* and the ways in which they are structured and territorially organized.[25]

In other words, states do not merely 'intervene' in markets; they underpin and help to constitute their very existence.

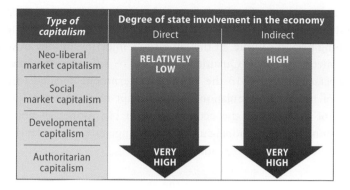

Type of capitalism	Degree of state involvement in the economy	
	Direct	Indirect
Neo-liberal market capitalism	RELATIVELY LOW	HIGH
Social market capitalism		
Developmental capitalism		
Authoritarian capitalism	VERY HIGH	VERY HIGH

Figure 6.6   State economic involvement in different types of capitalism

Although a high level of contingency may well be involved in how states strive to manage their economy, certain common themes are evident. These reflect the kinds of cultural, social and political structures, institutions and practices in which the state is embedded. Specifically, the degree of direct and indirect state participation in economic management varies with the type of capitalism involved (Figure 6.6). The precise policy mix adopted by a state will also be influenced by:

- the *size* of its national economy;
- its *resource endowment*, both physical and human;
- its *relative position* in the world economy, including its level of economic development and degree of industrialization.

Two basic types of macroeconomic policy are used by the state to manage its national economy:

- *Fiscal policies* to raise or lower taxes on companies and/or individual citizens and to determine appropriate levels and recipients of government expenditure. Raising taxes (either direct or indirect) dampens down domestic demand, lowering taxes stimulates demand. However, such automatic responses to changes in fiscal policy do not always occur. For example, consumers may choose to save rather than spend any tax gain they receive. Similarly, raising or lowering public expenditure or targeting specific types of expenditure can influence the level of economic activity in the economy.
- *Monetary policies* aimed at influencing the size of the money supply within the country and at either speeding up, or slowing down, its rate of circulation. The main mechanism employed is manipulation of the interest rate on borrowing. Lowering interest rates should stimulate economic activity through increased investment or private expenditure while, conversely, raising interest rates should dampen down activity. Again, however, rapid and automatic adjustment

does not always occur. The 2008 financial crisis has led most countries to keep their interest rates at exceptionally low levels (close to zero in some cases) for a very long period of time. At the same time, injecting money into the economy (sometimes called 'Quantitative Easing' – QE) has become common. Most spectacularly, in 2013 the Japanese government decided to double the volume of money in circulation in an attempt to reverse the long-standing problem of deflation in the economy. Inevitably, monetary policies impact upon a country's international currency exchange rate, whose level and volatility affect the costs of exports and imports.

Such policies are also underpinned by the state's regulation of financial services (see Chapter 16).

At a more tangible and material level, governments generally provide – or at least secure the provision of – those 'conditions of production that are not and cannot be obtained through the laws of the market'.[26] One example is the *physical infrastructure* of national economies – roads, railways, airports, seaports, telecommunications systems – without which private sector enterprises, whether domestic or transnational, could not operate. They are the providers, too, of the *human infrastructure*, in particular of an educated labour force as well as of sets of laws and regulations within which enterprises must operate.

For several decades after the end of the Second World War in 1945, the role of the state in the developed economies progressively expanded, notably through the provision of welfare benefits for particular segments of the population and the development of a considerable (though varied) degree of public ownership of productive assets. The majority of economies, outside the command economies of the state-socialist world, became *mixed economies*. In many countries certain economic sectors, such as telecommunications, railways, energy, steel and the like, became state owned or controlled. As a result, government spending as a percentage of GDP rose very substantially. In the OECD countries, such spending increased from less than 20 per cent of GDP in the early 1960s to 35 per cent in the early 1990s. In the developing countries, the average growth was from around 15 per cent to 27 per cent. Of course, the pattern varied a lot between countries.

Starting in the mid-1980s, many states reduced their direct involvement in their economies, most notably through a systematic process of *marketization*: extending the principles of market transactions into more and more aspects of public life. This was apparent not only in the older industrialized countries, but also in many developing countries and, most dramatically of course, in the former state-socialist countries of Eastern Europe, the former Soviet Union and in China. Such *market liberalization* consisted of two related processes:

- *Deregulation.* Virtually all industrialized countries jumped aboard the deregulation bandwagon to varying degrees. However, the issues are far less simple than the 'deregulationists' claim. Because no activity can exist without some form of regulation (otherwise anarchy ensues), 'deregulation cannot take place without the creation of new regulations to replace the old'.[27] In effect, what is often termed *de*regulation is really *re*regulation. Processes of deregulation spread to most economic sectors, most notably in financial services (see Chapter 16), telecommunications and utilities (such as energy and water). The labour market also became a particularly significant focus of deregulation (see below).

- *Privatization.* The state pulled out of a variety of activities in which it was formerly centrally involved and transferred them to the private sector. The selling of state-owned assets, and the greater participation of the private sector in the provision of both 'private' goods (the 'de-nationalization' of state-owned economic activities) and 'public' goods (such as health care or education), has been a pervasive, continuing, though uneven, movement. However, this has not reduced government expenditure as much as might have been expected; the rhetoric has often been stronger than the reality, as Figure 6.7 shows. The average GDP share of government spending in the 26 countries shown was 46.6 per cent in 2011 compared with 43.1 per cent in 2000.

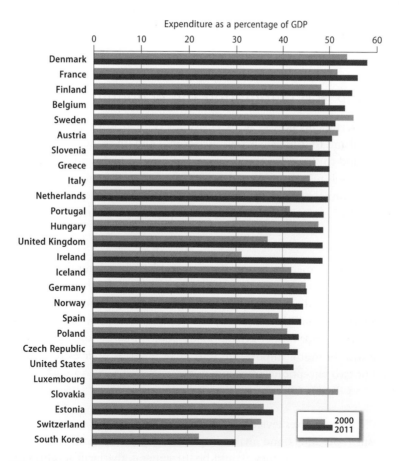

Figure 6.7   Central government spending as a share of GDP

Source: OECD data

In response to the post–2008 crisis, all governments intervened massively to re-stimulate their economies. The figures involved are astronomical.[28] The combined stimulus expenditure of the G20 countries for 2009 was $692 billion, the equivalent of 1.4 per cent of their GDP. The USA accounted for almost 40 per cent of this. The other countries with very large stimulus packages were China ($204 billion), Germany ($130 billion) and Japan ($104 billion). Since then, the debate has focused around either continuing or increasing stimulus expenditure to kick-start economic growth or cutting expenditure in key areas as part of austerity programmes. This debate has been especially acute within the EU but is by no means confined to Europe and continues within the G20 countries.

Such large-scale intervention during a period of economic recession reflects the influence of John Maynard Keynes, whose analysis of the 'Great Depression' of the 1930s demonstrated that markets do not necessarily correct themselves.[29] Under certain circumstances, they have to be stimulated by government actions – possibly in a very large-scale way – through, for example, reducing interest rates, providing financial assistance to specific firms and sectors, and investing heavily in infrastructure.

Regulating and stimulating the economy

National governments possess an extensive kit of regulatory tools with which to try to control and to stimulate economic activity and investment within their own boundaries and to shape the composition and flow of trade and investment across them. These tools may be employed as part of a deliberate, cohesive, all-embracing national economic strategy or, alternatively, individual policy measures may be implemented ad hoc with little attempt at strategic coordination.

Trade

Of all the measures used by nation-states to regulate their international economic position, policies towards trade have the longest history. The shape of the emerging world economy of the seventeenth and eighteenth centuries was hugely influenced by the mercantilist policies of the leading European nations. Figure 6.8 summarizes the major types of trade policy pursued by national governments. In general, policies towards imports are restrictive whereas policies towards exports, with one or two exceptions, are stimulatory.

Policies on *imports* fall into two distinct categories:

- *Tariffs*. These are taxes levied on the value of imports that increase the price to domestic consumers and make imported goods less competitive (in price terms) than otherwise they would be. In general, the tariff level tends to rise with the stage of processing, being lowest on basic raw materials and highest

Policies towards imports	Policies towards exports
1. Tariffs	Financial and fiscal incentives to export producers
2. Non-tariff barriers	
Import quotas (e.g. 'voluntary export restraint', 'orderly marketing agreements')	Export credits and guarantees
Import licences	Setting of export targets
Import deposit schemes	
Import surcharges	Operation of overseas export promotion agencies
Rules of origin	
Anti-dumping measures	
Special labelling and packaging regulations	Establishment of Export Processing Zones and/or Free Trade Zones
Health and safety regulations	
Customs procedures and documentation requirements	'Voluntary export restraint'
Subsidies to domestic producers of import-competing goods	
Countervailing duties on subsidised imports	Embargo on strategic exports
Local content requirements	
Government contracts awarded only to domestic producers	Exchange rate manipulation
Exchange rate manipulation	

Figure 6.8   **Major types of trade policy**

on finished goods. The purpose of such 'tariff escalation' is to protect domestic manufacturing industry while allowing for the import of industrial raw materials. Thus, although tariffs may be regarded simply as one means of raising revenue, their major use has been to *protect* domestic industries: either 'infant' industries in their early delicate stages of development or 'geriatric' industries struggling to survive in the face of external competition.

- *Non-tariff barriers (NTBs)*. While tariffs are based on the value of imported products, NTBs are more varied: some are quantitative, some are technical. Although, in general, tariffs have continued to decline, the period since the mid-1970s witnessed a marked increase in the use of NTBs. Indeed, today NTBs are more important than tariffs in influencing the level and composition of trade between nation-states. It has been estimated that NTBs affect more than a quarter of all industrialized country imports and are even more extensively used by developing countries. Certainly much of what has been termed the 'new protectionism' consists of the increased use of NTBs.

National trade policy is unique in that since the late 1940s it has been set within an *international* institutional framework: the GATT/WTO. We will have much more to say about this in Chapter 11. Here we merely need to note the basic features of this regulatory system. The purpose of the GATT was to create a set of *multilateral rules* to facilitate free trade through the reduction of tariff barriers and other types of trade discrimination. The GATT was eventually replaced by the WTO in 1995, an institutional change which greatly broadened the remit of the trade regulator. Today, around 97 per cent of world trade is covered by the WTO framework.

FDI

In a world of transnational corporations and of complex flows of investment at the international scale, national governments have a clear vested interest in the effects of FDI, whether positive or negative. Few national governments operate a totally closed policy towards FDI, although the degree of openness varies considerably.

Figure 6.9 summarizes the major types of national FDI policy. Most are concerned with inward investment, although governments may well place restrictions on the export of capital for investment (e.g. through the operation of exchange control regulations) or insist that proposed overseas investments be approved before they can take place. Historically, there have been large differences in national policy positions towards inward FDI. In general, developed countries have tended to adopt a more liberal attitude towards inward investment than developing countries,[30] although there were exceptions. For example, among developed countries France had a much more restrictive stance than most other European countries. Among developing countries, Singapore had a particularly open policy, far more so than most other Asian countries. In the past two decades, however, national FDI policies have tended to converge in the direction of liberalization. Attempts to regulate at the international scale have not been successful (see Chapter 11).

Policies relating to inward investment by foreign firms

Entry
Government screening of investment proposals.
Exclusion of foreign firms from certain sectors or restriction on the extent of foreign involvement permitted.
Restriction on the degree of foreign ownership of domestic enterprises.
Compliance with national codes of business conduct (including information disclosure).

Operations
Insistence on involvement of local personnel in managerial positions.
Insistence on a certain level of local content in the firm's activities.
Insistence on a minimum level of exports.
Requirements relating to the transfer of technology.
Locational restrictions on foreign investment.

Finance
Restrictions on the remittance of profits and/or capital abroad.
Level and methods of taxing profits of foreign firms.

Incentives
Direct encouragement of foreign investment: competitive bidding via overseas promotional agencies and investment incentives.

Policies relating to outward investment by domestic firms

Restrictions on the export of capital (e.g. exchange control regulations).
Necessity for government approval of overseas investment projects.

Figure 6.9   **Major types of FDI policy**

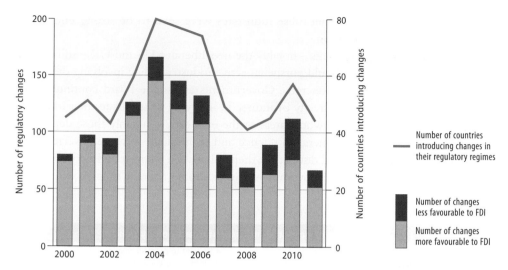

Figure 6.10 **Changes in national regulation of FDI**

Source: based on UNCTAD, 2009: Table I.14; 2012: Table III.1

Although national differences still exist, therefore, they are now rather less stark than in the past. Figure 6.10 summarizes the major regulatory changes towards FDI between 2000 and 2011. The proportion of regulatory changes that are more favourable to FDI continues to far outweigh those that are unfavourable, although 'in the last three years, 30 or 40 per cent of the laws have gone in the direction of being less welcome to investment'.[31]

Industry and technology

There is much debate about whether or not governments can, or should, attempt to pursue a focused industry strategy, especially in the more neo-liberal, free market economies. In fact, ever since Britain emerged as the world's first fully industrialized nation in the late eighteenth and early nineteenth centuries,

> every successful industrial power at some point in its history has carried out an activist industrial policy.[32]

Most influential historically were the ideas of the nineteenth-century German economist Friedrich List.[33] List heavily criticized Britain for advocating free trade policies only after it had attained a position of global industrial leadership. In fact, all the 'newly industrializing economies' of the nineteenth century – in particular the USA, Germany, France, other European nations, as well as Japan – adopted a set of policies that were strongly protectionist and developmental in order to nurture their infant industries, before relaxing some of the trade barriers when these industries were seen to be strong enough to face external competition.

Today, some governments – notably the neo-liberalist US and UK – still tend to be in denial that they should pursue an active industry policy involving the public sector. But this is a smokescreen. Governments across the board continue to be heavily engaged, either directly or indirectly, in trying to stimulate their industrial sectors. Indeed, there are whole areas of the economy – notably those dependent on big, long-term investments in science and technology – where government is absolutely central. The real distinction, then, is between an overt and a covert stance, for example over whether government can or should attempt to 'pick winners'.[34]

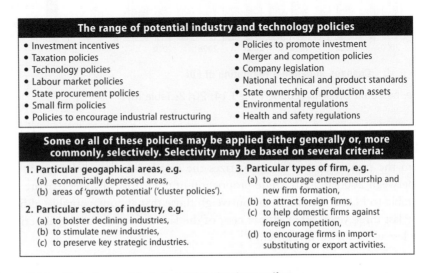

The range of potential industry and technology policies	
• Investment incentives	• Policies to promote investment
• Taxation policies	• Merger and competition policies
• Technology policies	• Company legislation
• Labour market policies	• National technical and product standards
• State procurement policies	• State ownership of production assets
• Small firm policies	• Environmental regulations
• Policies to encourage industrial restructuring	• Health and safety regulations

Some or all of these policies may be applied either generally or, more commonly, selectively. Selectivity may be based on several criteria:	

1. **Particular geographical areas, e.g.**
  (a) economically depressed areas,
  (b) areas of 'growth potential' ('cluster policies').
 	
2. **Particular sectors of industry, e.g.**
  (a) to bolster declining industries,
  (b) to stimulate new industries,
  (c) to preserve key strategic industries.
	3. **Particular types of firm, e.g.**
	  (a) to encourage entrepreneurship and new firm formation,
	  (b) to attract foreign firms,
	  (c) to help domestic firms against foreign competition,
	  (d) to encourage firms in import-substituting or export activities.

Figure 6.11   Major types of industry and technology policy

Figure 6.11 outlines the major types of industry and technology policies that may be used by national governments. Such policies may be applied *generally* across the whole of a nation's industries or they may be applied *selectively*. Such selectivity may take a number of forms: particular sectors of industry, particular types of firms (including, for example, the efforts to attract foreign firms), particular geographical locations. Especially, there has been a deluge of interest, in most countries, in trying to encourage the development of *growth clusters*: an attempt to capture the virtual circle of growth that has come to be associated with the kinds of technology clusters described in Chapter 4.

Related to this is the almost universal adoption of various kinds of *technology (R&D) policy* by national governments in an attempt to develop and exploit technological innovations. At one level, such policies tend to focus on stimulating investment and entrepreneurship through, for example, various kinds of tax incentive. But at the macro level, the major role of governments is in providing the basic, high-risk, exceedingly costly scientific and technological infrastructures and innovations upon which companies depend. Mariana Mazzacuto develops a very powerful case to show that in most of the 'high-tech' sectors, such as ICT, pharmaceuticals and nano-technology, most of the spectacularly successful private companies have depended on being able to 'piggyback' on the huge, long-term investments by government:

> Most of the radical, revolutionary innovations that have fuelled the dynamics of capitalism – from railroads to the Internet, to modern-day nanotech-nology and pharmaceuticals – trace the most courageous, early and capital-intensive 'entrepreneurial' investments back to the State ... [for example] all of the technologies that make [Apple's] iPhone so 'smart' were government funded (Internet, GPS, touch-screen display and the recent SIRI voice activated personal assistant). Such radical investments – which embedded extreme uncertainty – did not come about due to the presence of venture capitalists, nor of 'garage tinkerers'. It was the visible hand of the State which made these innovations happen. Innovation that would not have come about had we waited for the 'market' and business to do it alone – or government simply to stand aside and provide the basics.[35]

Labour markets

States, especially in the older industrialized economies, have become increasingly involved in labour market policies, particularly in attempting to make labour markets more *flexible*. A new conventional wisdom has emerged: the need to remove *rigidities* in the labour market to make it more in tune with what are seen to be the dominant characteristics of a globalizing world economy. The 'flexibilization' of labour markets through deregulation involves greatly increased pressures and restrictions on labour organizations, the drastic cutting back of welfare provisions, and the move away from welfare towards *workfare*.[36]

The process has gone furthest in the USA. Its apparent success in continuing to create large numbers of jobs (albeit with the widening of income gaps) has 'been the most persuasive argument for neo-liberal policies'.[37] It certainly stimulated the UK government to move along the same path. As yet, the countries of continental Europe have not moved as far, or as fast, down the labour market flexibility path. Most European governments are concerned that the social costs of reducing unemployment using the US model may be politically unacceptable in a system in which the social dimension of the labour market is very strongly entrenched. But there are clear signs of change as governments become increasingly concerned about the financial costs of sustaining existing practices and the continuing loss of competitive edge. As a result, a variety of labour market measures, employed in various combinations in different European countries, has emerged (Figure 6.12).

The range of potential labour market policies

- The use of more temporary and fixed term contracts
- The introduction of different forms of flexible working time
- Moves to encourage greater wage flexibility by getting the long-term unemployed and the young to take low-paid jobs
- Increased vocational training to provide more transferable skills
- Reforms in state employment services
- Incentives to employers to take on workers
- Measures to encourage workers to leave the labour market
- Reductions in the non-wage labour cost burdens on employers
- Specific schemes to target the long-term unemployed

Figure 6.12   Elements of labour market policies

Economic strategies in the older industrialized economies

As we saw earlier, the continental European countries, on the one hand, and the USA and the UK on the other, represent distinctively different types of capitalism. Historically, a major difference has been the centrality of industrial policy, together with a greater degree of social accountability of business in Europe, and the absence of such policy and accountability in the USA.[38] The UK occupies an intermediate position between the virtually pure market capitalism of the USA and the kinds of social market capitalism practised in continental Europe, but with a tendency in some areas (notably labour market policy) to be closer to the USA.

The policy stance of the *USA* reflects both the sheer scale and wealth of its domestic economy and also a basic philosophy of non-intervention by the federal government in the private economic sector. But, as we have seen, US governments have been immensely important in funding fundamental science and technology research, which has underpinned the growth of high-tech private sector firms. As far as industry in general is concerned, the role of the federal government has generally been *regulatory*: to ensure the continuation of competition. Action at the federal level has been based primarily on fiscal and monetary macroeconomic policies. The aim has been to create an investment climate in which private sector institutions could flourish. This has not, however, prevented the federal government from rescuing specific firms – especially very large ones – from disaster. At the other end of the size spectrum, the Small Business Administration has provided aid to stimulate new and small firms. Federal procurement policies are generally non-discriminatory but the sheer size of federal government purchases, particularly in the defence and aerospace industries, has exerted an enormous influence on US industry. Entire economic sectors, regions and communities are heavily dependent on the work created by federal defence and other procurement

contracts and on subsidies in such sectors as agriculture (Chapter 13) and automobiles (Chapter 15).

US policy towards international trade during most of the post-war period has
been one of urging liberalization through *multilateral* negotiations through the
GATT/WTO. However, there has been an increasing willingness to develop bilateral trading arrangements with other countries. US trade policy is complicated by
the structure and composition of the US Congress and the ways that new trade
policies have to be negotiated with domestic interest groups.[39] As the strongest
economy, the USA, like Britain in the nineteenth century, has been the leading
advocate of free trade. Even so, the federal government has intervened with the
use of tariff and non-tariff barriers to protect particular interests. A 'Buy American'
initiative was part of the Obama administration's stimulus measures introduced in
2009.

In the eyes of many parts of the world, the USA is seen as having a strong *unilateralist* tendency, very much at odds with its traditional multilateral trading stance.
The USA has become increasingly embroiled in a whole series of trade disputes,
particularly with East Asian countries (primarily this means China) and with the
EU. There is also concern that the USA has a tendency to introduce *extra-territorial*
trade legislation to achieve its broader political objectives.

Within *Europe*, despite the existence of the EU, an ideological divide continues
to exist between the so-called 'market' and 'social' models of how the economy
should be organized, that is between the UK's more 'neo-liberal' position and that
of France and Germany, where the principle of the 'social market' remains strongly
entrenched. However, the lines are not always quite as clear as is often claimed.
Although the *UK's* policy position does contrast in a number of ways with that
of continental European countries, and is closer to that of the USA, the UK has
been more interventionist than the USA, at least until recently.[40] Nevertheless, the
UK has strongly adopted economic policies of privatization and deregulation. Its
labour market policies, in particular, are far closer to the US model than to the
EU model.

There are considerable differences in policy emphasis between continental
European member states. Of the leading EU states, *France* maintains the most
'nationalistic' economic position, having long had the most explicit state industrial policy, a reflection of a tradition of strong state involvement dating back to
the seventeenth century. A major component of French industrial policy has
been the promotion of 'national champions' in key industrial sectors, often
through state ownership of large-scale enterprises. France's current policy position retains many of these traditional qualities (and an especially strong antago-
nism to the Anglo-American neo-liberal economic model). Despite considerable
privatization the French state retains a very considerable direct involvement in
the economy.

Germany is the major exception among the continental European nations to a
more centralized approach to industrial policy. In part, at least, this reflects its

federalist political structure, with power divided between the federal government and the provinces (*Länder*). But although often described as 'light', the federal government's role has been far from insubstantial. It has pursued policies of active intervention in industrial matters, including a substantial programme of financial subsidy. Such involvement has to be seen within the German model of a social market economy.[41] The German economy is characterized both by a considerable degree of competition between domestic firms and by a high level of consensus between various interest groups, including labour unions, the major banks and industry. The major challenge facing Germany after 1990, of course, was to cope with the fundamental transformation of the economy brought about by reunification. Putting together the strongest economy in Europe (the former West Germany) with one that, for half a century, had existed in a completely different ideological system, was an immense undertaking. It placed enormous strains on the federal budget because of the huge problems of rebuilding infrastructure and dealing with problems of unemployment brought about by restructuring.[42]

Among the older industrialized economies, *Japan* stands apart in its policy stance. Japan can be regarded as the archetypal *developmental capitalist state*.[43] There has long been a high level of consensus between the major interest groups in Japan on the need to create a dynamic national economy. This consensus is often regarded as a cultural characteristic of Japanese society, with its deep roots in familism. But it also reflected the poor physical endowment of Japan and the limited number of options facing the country when, in the 1860s, it suddenly emerged from its feudal isolation. In other words, consensus was also a pragmatic stance built up over more than a hundred years. Given virtually no natural resources and a poor agricultural base, Japan's only hope of economic growth lay in building a strong manufacturing base, both domestically and internationally, through trade. In this process, the state played a central role not through direct state ownership, but rather by *guiding* the operation of a highly competitive domestic market economy.

For more than 50 years after the end of the Second World War, the key government institution concerned with both industry policy and trade policy was *MITI* – the *Ministry of International Trade and Industry* (renamed *METI*, the *Ministry for Economy, Trade and Industry*, in 2001). After its establishment in 1949, MITI became the real 'guiding hand' in Japan's economic resurgence. Until the 1960s Japan operated a strongly protected economy and it was not until 1980 that full internationalization of the Japanese economy was reached. During the 1950s and early 1960s MITI, together with the Ministry of Finance, exerted very stringent controls on all foreign exchange, on foreign investment and over the import of technology.

Initially, MITI focused on the basic industries of steel, electric power, shipbuilding and chemical fertilizers, but then progressively encouraged the development of petrochemicals, synthetic textiles, plastics, automobiles and electronics. Japan was transformed from a low-value, low-skill economy to a high-value, capital-intensive economy. The foundation of this transformation was the clearly targeted, selective nature of Japanese industry policy together with a strongly protected domestic economy.

A key element in Japanese economic policy was the specific treatment of inward FDI which, for much of the post-war period, was extremely tightly regulated. The technological rebuilding of the Japanese economy was based on the purchase and licensing of foreign technology and not on the entry of foreign branches or subsidiaries. Since the early 1990s, Japanese policy has been especially exercised by the problem of a high-value currency, with contentious trading relationships with the USA and Europe, and especially with the deep domestic recession which accompanied the collapse of the so-called 'bubble economy' at the end of the 1980s.

These diverse characteristics of industry policy in the older industrialized economies persist. However, the post-2008 financial crisis dramatically changed their context and called into question at least some of their elements. Faced with the enormous problems of huge financial deficits and sluggish economic growth, all of the older industrialized economies are struggling to redefine their strategies. Here, the ideological position of individual governments is extremely important. For example, a 'new' UK industrial strategy was in process of construction in 2013 but the coalition government's persistence with a deep austerity programme – and the overhang of the banking crisis – inevitably limited the scope for industrial policy initiatives. In late 2013, France set out a new 10-year industrial policy based around 34 sectors.[44] In Germany and France, where explicit industry policy is the norm, the problem is less ideological than practical, given the problems of the eurozone (see later in this chapter). In the USA, the position is rather different, given the long-standing reluctance to accept even the notion of an industry policy. In fact, of course, the USA always had an industry policy – it was the label that was avoided. In Japan, a developmental strategy never went away; the problems there have been the two-decade stagnation since the 1990s.

Jump-starting economic development

As we saw earlier, activist trade and industry policies were fundamental to the early economic development of all of today's older industrialized economies. A similar strategy has been followed by the new wave of NIEs of East Asia and Latin America – the 'latecomers' – in the second half of the twentieth century:

> Countries arriving late on the industrial scene suffer from enormous disadvantages … The latecomers have to meet the powerful incumbents with only their temporary advantages of lower costs. They have to devise strategies that capitalize on these lower costs … In this, they do have two potential advantages, in (1) not being burdened with past

technological and organizational commitments ... and (2) being able
to devise institutions that make up for the deficits found in underdeveloped countries. These potential advantages are not handed on a
plate to latecomers, or achieved automatically through operation of
some 'economic law' ... They are only achieved through strategizing,
which is through the formulation of firm- and national-level policies
and programmes designed to mesh with the current situation and
capture the potential advantages that can be identified.[45]

From import substitution to export orientation

The essence of most policies aimed at 'jump-starting' the process has been one of
an initial emphasis on import-substituting industrialization (ISI): the manufacture
of products that would otherwise be imported, based upon protection against
such imports. The aim is to protect a nation's infant industries so that the overall
industrial structure can be developed and diversified and dependence on foreign
technology and capital reduced. To this end, many of the policies listed in Figures
6.8, 6.9 and 6.11 have been employed.

The ISI strategy, in theory, is a long-term *sequential* process involving the progressive domestic development of industrial sectors through a combination of
protection and incentives. The realization that an import-substituting strategy
cannot, on its own, lead to the desired level of industrialization began to dawn in
a growing number of countries, some during the 1950s, rather more during the
1960s. Generally it was the smaller industrializing countries that first began to shift
towards a greater emphasis on *export orientation* because of the constraints imposed
upon such a policy by their small domestic market. Increasingly, an export-oriented industrialization (EOI) strategy became the conventional wisdom among
such international agencies as the Asian Development Bank and the World Bank.

Such a shift was facilitated by a number of factors:

- the rapid liberalization and growth of world trade during the 1960s;
- the 'shrinkage' of geographical distance through the enabling technologies of
  transportation and communications;
- the global spread of TNCs and their increasing interest in seeking out low-cost
  production locations for their export platform activities.

Export orientation was invariably based upon a high level of government involvement. The usual starting point was a major devaluation of the country's currency to
make its exports more competitive in world markets, together with the whole battery of export trade policy measures shown in Figure 6.8. In effect, these amounted
to a subsidy on exports that greatly increased their price competitiveness. Of course,
the major domestic resource on which this EOI rests was the labour supply – not
only its abundance and relative cheapness, but also its adaptability and, very often,

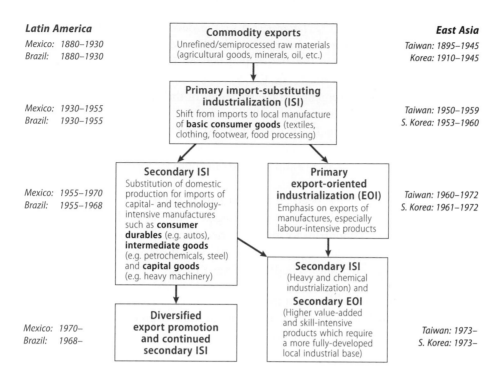

Latin America

Mexico: 1880–1930
Brazil: 1880–1930

Mexico: 1930–1955
Brazil: 1930–1955

Mexico: 1955–1970
Brazil: 1955–1968

Mexico: 1970–
Brazil: 1968–

Commodity exports
Unrefined/semiprocessed raw materials
(agricultural goods, minerals, oil, etc.)

**Primary import-substituting
industrialization (ISI)**
Shift from imports to local manufacture
of **basic consumer goods** (textiles,
clothing, footwear, food processing)

Secondary ISI
Substitution of domestic
production for imports of
capital- and technology-
intensive manufactures
such as **consumer
durables** (e.g. autos),
intermediate goods
(e.g. petrochemicals, steel)
and **capital goods**
(e.g. heavy machinery)

**Primary
export-oriented
industrialization (EOI)**
Emphasis on exports of
manufactures, especially
labour-intensive products

Secondary ISI
(Heavy and chemical
industrialization) and
Secondary EOI
(Higher value-added
and skill-intensive
products which require
a more fully-developed
local industrial base)

**Diversified
export promotion
and continued
secondary ISI**

East Asia

Taiwan: 1895–1945
Korea: 1910–1945

Taiwan: 1950–1959
S. Korea: 1953–1960

Taiwan: 1960–1972
S. Korea: 1961–1972

Taiwan: 1973–
S. Korea: 1973–

Figure 6.13   **Paths of industrialization in Latin America and East Asia:
common and divergent features**

Source: based on material in Gereffi, 1990: Figure 1.1; p. 17

its relative docility. Indeed, in many cases, the activities of labour unions have been
very closely regulated and often suppressed.

In fact, the 'paths of industrialization' followed by individual NIEs have been
rather more complex than is often suggested.[46] Figure 6.13 sets out a five-phase
sequence of industrialization based upon the experiences of the Latin American
and East Asian NIEs into the 1990s. A number of important points can be made:[47]

- The distinction commonly drawn between inward-oriented Latin American
  industrialization strategies and outward-oriented East Asian industrialization
  strategies is misleading.
- The initial stages of industrialization were common to NIEs in both regions;
  'the subsequent divergence in the regional sequences stems from the ways in
  which each country responded to the basic problems associated with the continuation of primary ISI'.[48]
- 'The duration and timing of these development patterns varied by region.
  Primary ISI began earlier, lasted longer, and was more populist in Latin
  America than in East Asia … The East Asian NICs began their accelerated
  export of manufactured products during a period of extraordinary dynamism

in the world economy … [after 1973] … the developing countries began to encounter stiffer protectionist measures in the industrialized markets. These new trends were among the factors that led the East Asian NIEs to modify their EOI approach in the 1970s.'[49]

• Some degree of convergence in the strategies of the Latin American and East Asian NIEs began to occur in the 1970s and 1980s. Each 'coupled their previous strategies from the 1960s (secondary ISI and primary EOI respectively) with elements of the alternate strategy in order to enhance the synergistic benefits of simultaneously pursuing inward- and outward-oriented approaches'.[50]

The attraction of FDI has been an integral part of both ISI and EOI in many developing countries, although to varying degrees. Among all the measures used by many developing countries to stimulate their export industries and to attract foreign investment one device in particular – the *export processing zone* (EPZ) – has received particular attention.[51] The ILO defines EPZs as:

> Industrial zones with special incentives set up to attract foreign investors, in which imported materials undergo some degree of processing before being (re-)exported again.[52]

Figure 6.14 shows the rapid growth in EPZs, especially during the past 30 years. Some 90 per cent of all EPZs in the developing countries are located in Latin America, the Caribbean, Mexico and Asia. However, in terms of employment, Asia is by far the most important region for EPZs, with 85 per cent of the total. Of these, the biggest concentration is in China, which has 40 million of the world total of 66 million EPZ workers.[53]

EPZs come in a number of different forms: 'free trade zones, special economic zones, bonded warehouses, free ports, and *maquiladoras*'.[54] Within developing countries, EPZs have been located in a variety of environments. Some have been incorporated into airports, seaports or commercial free zones or located next to large cities. Others have been set up in relatively undeveloped areas as part of a regional development strategy. EPZs themselves vary enormously in size, ranging from geographically extensive developments to a few small factories; from employment of more than 30,000 to little more than 100 workers.

EPZs in developing countries share many common features. The overall pattern of incentives to investors is broadly similar, as is the type of industry most commonly found within the zones. Historically, the production of textiles and clothing and the assembly of electronics – both employing predominantly young female labour – dominated. However, the position is not static:

> Zones have evolved from initial assembly and simple processing activities to include high tech and science zones, logistics centres and even tourist resorts. Their physical form now includes not only enclave-type zones but also single-industry zones (such as the jewellery zone in

Thailand or the leather zone in Turkey); single-commodity zones (like coffee in Zimbabwe); and single-factory (such as the export-oriented units in India) or single-company zones (such as in the Dominican Republic).[55]

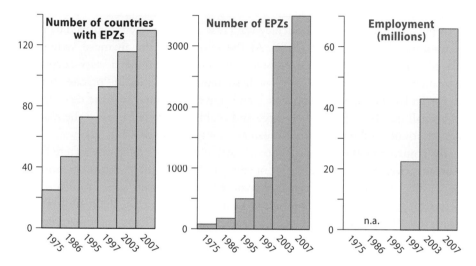

Figure 6.14   Growth in EPZs

Source: ILO, 2003: Table 1; 2007a: pp. 1–2

Variations on a theme

The recurring theme running through the development of all NIEs is the central involvement of the state. But its precise nature varies, a reflection of each country's particular historical, cultural, social, political and economic complexion.[56] In some cases, state ownership of production has been very substantial; in others it has been insignificant. In some cases, the major policy emphasis has been upon attracting FDI; in others FDI has been tightly regulated and the emphasis placed on nurturing domestic firms.

As we noted earlier (Figure 6.13), NIEs in East Asia and Latin America initially followed similar, though distinctive, 'paths to industrialization'. Of the two geographical areas, the East Asian NIEs have been significantly more successful in creating dynamic economies.[57] Three examples from East Asia can be used to illustrate how the state has been involved in each case.

South Korea (the Republic of Korea) came into being in 1948, following partition. From 1910 to 1945, Korea was a Japanese colony, very tightly integrated into the imperial system. Between 1948 and 1988, when political liberalization occurred, South Korea was governed by a succession of authoritarian, military-backed and strongly nationalistic governments that operated a strong state-directed economic policy articulated through a series of five-year plans.[58] Indeed, 'South Korea [represented] perhaps the strongest form of the developmental state among the three [East Asian NIEs].'[59] Two important developments during the 1950s helped to provide the basis for industrialization: the land reform of 1948–50, which removed the old landlord class and created a more equitable class structure; and the redistribution of Japanese-owned and state properties to well-connected individuals which helped to create a new Korean capitalist class.[60]

A powerful economic bureaucracy was created, with a key role played by a new Economic Planning Board (EPB). At the same time, the financial system was placed firmly in the hands of the state. This highly centralized 'state-corporatist' bureaucracy, in effect, 'aggressively orchestrated the activities of "private" firms'.[61] In particular, the state made possible – and actively encouraged – the development of a small number of extremely large and highly diversified firms – the *chaebol* – that continue to dominate the Korean economy (see page 134).

By controlling the financial system, particularly the availability of credit, the Korean government was able to operate a strongly interventionist economic policy. The *chaebol* were consistently favoured through their access to finance and very strong, long-term relationships were developed between them and the state. From the 1960s Korean policy had a strong sectoral emphasis as the state decided which particular industries should be supported through a battery of measures, including financial subsidy and protection against external competition.

Like Japan at a similar stage in its development, Korea generally eschewed the use of inward FDI to acquire technology. Indeed, Korea adopted the most restrictive policy towards inward foreign investment of all the four leading Asian NIEs. Korean government policy has been to build a very strong domestic sector. As a consequence, the share of FDI in the Korean economy remains very low (Table 2.2).

In the early 1980s the policy emphasis shifted towards a greater degree of (restricted) liberalization. Indeed, much of Korea's traditional industry policy was gradually diluted.[62] Major changes were made in policies of financial regulation, exchange rate management and investment coordination. The formerly tightly controlled financial sector was significantly liberalized and the policy of exchange rate management virtually abandoned. The central pillar of South Korean industrial policy for 40 years – the coordination of investment – began to be dismantled.

When the East Asian financial crisis of 1997 hit Korea, the country's problems – as for the other affected East Asian economies – were attributed by the IMF, and by the Western financial community in general, to an over-regulated, state-dominated economy with excessively close (even corrupt) relationships between government and business. Yet, in the case of Korea, that was no longer entirely the case. It could be argued, in fact, that the Korean government had already gone too far in abandoning the principles on which its spectacular economic growth had been based. Clearly, certain reforms were needed as both the Korean economy itself and the broader global environment were changing. Not least was the need to reform the *chaebol*, which distort the economy by, in effect, 'choking the development of small and medium-sized companies'[63] and which were, themselves, in great financial difficulty. That battle is still being fought. The *chaebol* argue that the proposed reforms will leave them vulnerable to foreign takeover; the government argues that reform of cross-shareholdings will make them more competitive. The issue of 'foreign takeover' remains, however, a very sensitive issue in Korea as a whole.

Singapore demonstrates a very different model of industrialization, albeit one in which the state has also played a dominant role.[64] Singapore is by far the smallest of all the East Asian NIEs: a city-state with a population of only around 5 million. Like both Korea and Taiwan, it had a very long history as a colony (in Singapore's case as a British colony). But it was less tightly integrated into its imperial system, although its strategic geographical position gave it a highly significant role as a commercial *entrepôt*. Singapore became fully independent in 1965 when it separated from Malaysia. Since then, although Singapore is a parliamentary democracy, it has been governed by one political party (the People's Action Party).

From the outset, the Singapore government pursued an aggressive policy of export-oriented, labour-intensive manufacturing development. Concentration on manufacturing – especially labour-intensive manufacturing – was adopted because of the need to reduce a very high unemployment rate in a society that, at the time, had one of the fastest population growth rates in the world. The twin pillars of the policy were those of complementary economic and social planning, the latter being much more overt than in other East Asian NIEs.

In contrast to both Korea and Taiwan, the central pillar of Singapore's export-oriented strategy was attracting FDI.[65] As a result, the economy has become over-whelmingly dominated by foreign firms (Table 2.2). The most explicit industrialization measures, therefore, were those of incentives to inward investors, using a sectorally selective process. The government agency responsible was the Economic Development Board (EDB), which still plays an extremely influential role in the Singapore economy. With a few exceptions, Singapore operated a free port policy with little use of trade protectionist measures. The second set of direct measures used to promote industrial development was the establishment of a high-quality physical infrastructure.

At the same time, a series of *social policy* measures was introduced aimed at creating an amenable environment for foreign investment. Most notably, the labour unions were effectively incorporated into the governance system: 'Strikes and other industrial action were declared illegal unless approved through secret ballot by a majority of a union's members. In essential services, strikes were banned altogether ... These labour market regulations resulted in the creation of a highly disciplined and depoliticised labour force in Singapore.'[66] Thus, through a whole battery of interlocking policies, the Singapore government created a very high-growth, increasingly affluent, industrialized society in which foreign firms played the dominant economic role in production but within a highly regulated political and social system.

Today, Singapore promotes itself as a global business centre on the basis of the very high quality of its physical and human infrastructure, its strategic geographical location and its business-friendly policies. Government policy incorporates an explicit strategy to 'regionalize' the Singaporean economy by encouraging domestic firms to set up operations in Asia, while Singapore develops as the 'control centre' of a regional division of labour. The government introduced a series of initiatives using government-linked corporations to develop major infrastructural projects in Asia and, more broadly, to develop international networks.[67] At the same time, the emphasis on high-technology research and development and technological upgrading[68] has intensified with, for example, specific emphasis on biotechnology to enhance its already significant role as a pharmaceuticals centre and on IT. Two recent policy initiatives have been the greater liberalization of the financial system and a push for greater 'Asian regionalism'. The key question, however, is the extent to which this highly paternalistic state is able to loosen its grip on the country's political and social life without damaging its economic influence.

The dominant role of the state is, of course, most obvious in the case of *China*.[69] The People's Republic of China (PRC) came into existence in 1949 with the replacement of the nationalist government by a communist government led by Mao Zedong. For the next 30 years, China followed a policy of economic self-reliance. This policy was pursued through a series of major, often extreme, measures. Initially, the new government followed the example of the Soviet Union in establishing a Five-Year Plan (1953–57). This relatively successful policy was jettisoned in 1958 when Mao announced the 'Great Leap Forward': a total transformation of economic planning, with the emphasis on small-scale and rural development. Although this initiated rural industrialization, the Great Leap Forward had disastrous consequences, including mass famine. In 1966, policy changed again with the introduction of the 'Cultural Revolution', a phase that lasted for some 10 years with, once more, disastrous human and social implications.

The period after Mao's death in 1976 was one of political hiatus that was eventually resolved by the emergence of Deng Xiaoping as leader. It was under Deng's leadership that China began to jettison the self-reliance policy of the previous 30 years and to make links with the world market economies. This has been done, however, without substantial political change. In the words of the new Party Constitution of 1997, it is 'Socialism with Chinese characteristics'; in our terminology, it is an *authoritarian capitalist state*.

The pivotal year was 1979, when China began its 'open policy' based upon a carefully controlled trade and inward investment strategy. This was set within the so-called 'Four Modernizations' (concerned with agriculture, industry, education, and science and defence). A central element was the opening up of the Chinese economy to foreign direct investors. As we saw in Chapter 2, FDI has grown very rapidly indeed in China since the early 1980s and now accounts for 10 per cent of GDP (Table 2.2). The organizational form of these investments varies from wholly owned foreign subsidiaries to equity joint ventures with Chinese partners and other partnership arrangements.

A distinctive feature of the open policy has been the explicit use of *geography*. Partly in order to control the spread of capitalist market ideas and methods within Chinese society, and partly to make the policy more effective through external visibility and agglomeration economies, FDI was originally steered to specific locations. Initially, these were the four Special Economic Zones (SEZs) established in 1979 at Shenzhen, Zhuhai, Shantou and Xiamen (Figure 6.15). Significantly, each of these was located to maximize their attraction to investors from overseas Chinese, notably in Hong Kong, Macau and Taiwan. The Chinese SEZs offered a package of incentives, including tax concessions, duty-free import arrangements and serviced infrastructure. The original SEZs were located in areas well away from the major urban and industrial areas in order to control the extent of their influence. However, since the mid-1980s, there has been considerable development and geographical spread of Economic and Technological Developments Zones (ETDZs), as Figure 6.15 shows.

Despite massive inflows of foreign capital and technologies, China remains a centrally controlled economy in which state-owned enterprises (SOEs) predominate,

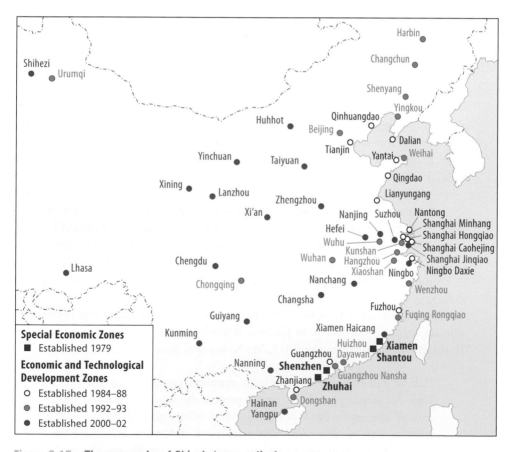

Figure 6.15 The geography of China's 'open policy'

despite more than halving in numbers. Reform of the SOEs is an immense task and one surrounded by massive controversy. A major problem for a country trying to 'modernize' its economy is the sheer inefficiency (by Western standards) and high levels of corruption in many of the SOEs. SOEs are embedded within the Communist Party system and this fact pervades their operations.[70]

The problems posed by the SOEs were intensified with China's accession to the WTO in 2001. Although this greatly enhanced China's economic potential it also imposed severe stresses on the domestic economy and institutions. Not only have tariff levels fallen from their previously high levels, thus exposing Chinese enterprises to intense competition, but also NTBs, matters relating to intellectual property rights, safety regulations, financial and telecommunications regulations were all affected. It is notable that the Chinese government now actively encourages Chinese businesses to invest overseas and there have been a number of significant Chinese acquisitions of foreign businesses, notably the IBM PC business by Lenovo in 2004. Financially, China continues to be under pressure to revalue the *renminbi*, not least because it has the largest trade surplus in the world.

Overall, the institutional structure of the Chinese economy is in a state of flux, with a greater variety of forms. As in the past, however, the key lies in the internal political power struggles between the 'modernizers', who wish to sustain and develop the open policies of the recent past, and those who wish to retain a degree of isolation. So far, China's reform policies have proved remarkably successful. But the key test of the survival of such policy is its continued success in delivering economic growth and raising incomes for the majority of Chinese, and not just those in the more developed parts of the country. For a country so large geographically, so populous and still heavily rural, this is a very tall order indeed:

> China has an unsustainable growth pattern and it will have to pay a cost in the form of slower growth ... To make its growth sustainable China must shift to a new growth pattern that relies more on domestic rather than external demand and consumption instead of investment, especially real estate investment.[71]

In this context, the arrival of a new president, Xi Jinping, in 2013 is highly significant for the next decade of Chinese economic development. In a speech to a Business Forum in Hainan in 2013, Mr Xi asserted that

> 'China will sustain relatively high economic growth, but not superhigh economic growth ... would protect the lawful rights and interests of foreign-invested companies and ensure their rights to equal participation in government procurement and independent innovation ... China will never close its doors to the outside world.' Mr Xi said a slowing of the pace of growth would help China rebalance its

economy towards a domestic-consumption-led model rather than an export-driven model, something it has been trying to achieve for years. 'It does not mean that we cannot maintain economic growth at a very fast pace, but because we don't want it any more.'[72]

STATES AS COLLABORATORS

As we saw in an earlier section of this chapter, states – like firms – are competitors in the global economy. But they are also – again like firms – often *collaborators*: involved in trade agreements with other states. Indeed, what the WTO terms *regional trade agreements* (RTAs) have become a pervasive feature of the global economy. At least one-third of total world trade occurs within RTAs.

The basis of RTAs is the preferential trading arrangement (PTA). Technically, PTAs are not necessarily 'regional', that is involving states that are geographically proximate. They simply involve states agreeing to provide preferential access to their markets to other specified states wherever they are located – primarily through tariff reductions, at least initially. However, the WTO uses the term *regional trade agreement* for all such arrangements. RTAs have a two-sided quality: they liberalize trade between members while, at the same time, discriminating against third parties.[73]

The proliferation of regional trade agreements

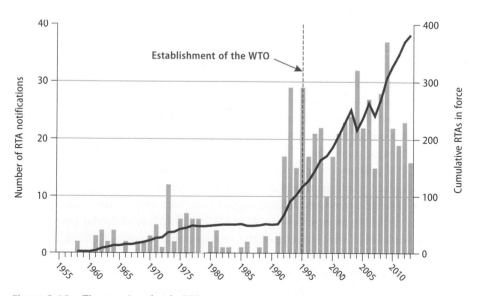

Figure 6.16   **The acceleration in RTAs**

Source: WTO data

There has been an especially marked acceleration in RTA formation since the early 1990s (Figure 6.16) and the development of a complex tangled web of interstate connections (Figure 6.17). Most have a strongly defensive character; they represent an attempt to gain advantages of size in trade by creating large markets for their producers and protecting them, at least in part, from outside competition. There is also an undoubted 'bandwagon' effect: a 'fear of being left out while the rest of the world swept into regionalism, either because this would be actually harmful to excluded countries or just because "if everyone else is doing it, shouldn't we?"'.[74]

Despite a widespread view that RTAs are a relatively new phenomenon they have been an important feature of the global economic landscape since the middle of the nineteenth century. But their basis and their nature have changed over time. Historically, four 'waves of regionalism' can be identified:[75]

- During the second half of the nineteenth century there were a number of trade agreements in place, especially in Europe: for example, the German *Zollverein*, the customs unions between the Austrian states, and between several of the Nordic countries. 'As of the first decade of the twentieth century, Great Britain had concluded bilateral arrangements with forty-six states, Germany had done so with thirty countries, and France had done so with more than twenty states' (p. 596).

- After the disruption of the First World War (1914–18) a new wave of regional arrangements occurred but, this time, in a more discriminatory form. 'Some were created to consolidate the empires of major powers, including the customs union France formed with members of its empire in 1928 and the Commonwealth system of preferences established by Great Britain in 1932. Most, however, were formed among sovereign states ... The Rome Agreement of 1934 led to the establishment of a PTA involving Italy, Austria and Hungary. Belgium, Denmark, Finland, Luxembourg, the Netherlands, Norway, and Sweden concluded a series of economic agreements throughout the 1930s ... Outside of Europe, the US forged almost two dozen bilateral commercial agreements during the mid-1930s, many of which involved Latin American countries' (p. 597).

- Since the end of the Second World War (1939–45) there have been two distinct waves of regionalism. 'The first took place from the late 1950s through the 1970s and was marked by the establishment of the EEC, EFTA, the CMEA, and a plethora of regional trade blocs formed by developing countries. These arrangements were initiated against the backdrop of the Cold War, the rash of decolonisation following World War II, and a multilateral commercial framework, all of which coloured their economic and political effects' (p. 600).

- A further wave of economic regionalism – from the late 1980s onwards – occurred in the drastically changed geopolitical circumstances of the collapse of the Soviet-led system and the increased uncertainties of a more fragmented political and economic situation. 'Furthermore, the leading actor in the

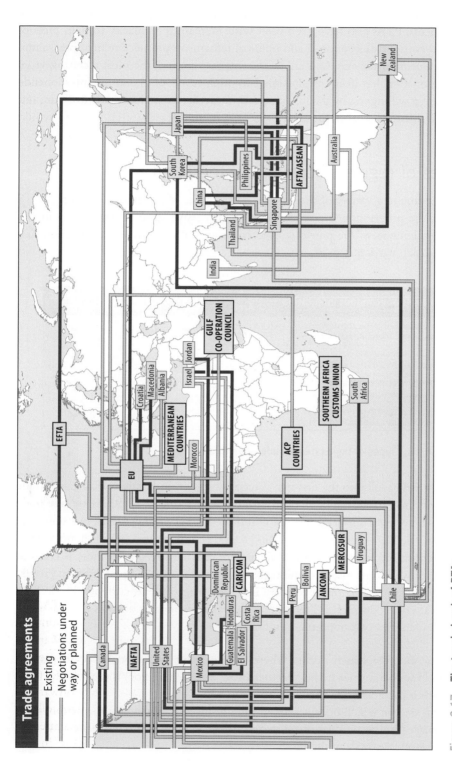

Trade agreements

— Existing

— Negotiations under way or planned

Figure 6.17 **The tangled web of RTAs**

Source: based on WTO data; *Financial Times*, 19 November 2003; press reports

international system (the US) is actively promoting and participating in the process. PTAs also have been used with increasing regularity to help prompt and consolidate economic and political reforms in prospective members, a rarity during prior eras. And unlike the interwar period, the most recent wave of regionalism has been accompanied by high levels of economic interdependence, a willingness by the major economic actors to mediate trade disputes, and a multilateral (that is, the GATT/WTO) framework' (p. 601).

Types of regional economic integration

RTAs come in a variety of shapes, sizes and degrees of integration. As Figure 6.18 shows, the progression is cumulative: each successive stage of integration incorporates elements of the previous stage, together with the additional element that defines each particular stage.

Levels of economic integration	Free Trade Area	Customs Union	Common Market	Economic Union
Removal of trade restrictions between member states	✓	✓	✓	✓
Common external trade policy towards non-members		✓	✓	✓
Free movement of factors of production between member states			✓	✓
Harmonization of economic policies under supra-national control				✓

Figure 6.18   Types of regional economic integration

Most RTAs fall into the first two categories shown in Figure 6.18: the free trade area and the customs union. Indeed, around 90 per cent of all RTAs are free trade areas. There are a small number of common market arrangements, but only one group – the EU – comes close to being a true economic union. In fact, not only is there enormous variation in the scale, nature and effectiveness of these RTAs, but also there is, in some cases, a considerable overlap of membership of different groups. Figure 6.19 shows the major regional integration agreements currently in force.

What effects do such RTAs have? The classic economic analysis of their trade effects identifies two opposing outcomes:

- *trade diversion* which occurs where, as the result of regional bloc formation, trade with a former trading partner (now outside the bloc) is replaced by trade with a partner inside the bloc;
- *trade creation* which occurs where, as the result of regional bloc formation, trade replaces home production or where there is increased trade associated with economic growth in the bloc.

In addition, regional trading blocs have a major influence on *flows of investment* by TNCs. The effects of regional integration on direct investment, like that on trade, can also be conceptualized in terms of 'creation' and 'diversion'. In the latter case, the removal of internal trade (and other) barriers may lead firms to realign their organizational structures and value-adding activities to reflect a regional rather than a strictly national market (see Figure 5.17). This, by definition, 'diverts' investment from some locations in favour of others.

Regional group	Membership	Date(s)	Type
EU (European Union)	Austria, Belgium, Bulgaria, Croatia, Cyprus, Czech Republic, Denmark, Estonia, Finland, France, Germany, Greece, Hungary, Ireland, Italy, Latvia, Lithuania, Luxembourg, Malta, Netherlands, Poland, Portugal, Romania, Slovakia, Slovenia, Spain, Sweden, UK	1957 (European Common Market) 1992 (European Union)	Economic union
NAFTA (North American Free Trade Agreement)	Canada, Mexico, US	1994	Free trade area
EFTA (European Free Trade Association)	Iceland, Lichtenstein, Norway, Switzerland	1960	Free trade area
Mercosur (Southern Cone Common Market)	Argentina, Brazil, Paraguay, Uruguay, Venezuela (2006)	1991	Common market
ANCOM (Andean Common Market)	Bolivia, Colombia, Ecuador, Peru, Venezuela	1969 (revived 1990)	Customs union
CARICOM (Caribbean Community)	Antigua and Barbuda, Bahamas, Barbados, Belize, Dominica, Grenada, Guyana, Haiti, Jamaica, Montserrat, St Kitts and Nevis, St Lucia, St Vincent and the Grenadines, Suriname, Trinidad and Tobago	1973	Common market
AFTA (ASEAN Free Trade Agreement)	Brunei Darussalam, Cambodia, Indonesia, Laos, Malaysia, Myanmar, Philippines, Singapore, Thailand, Vietnam	1967 (ASEAN) 1992 (AFTA)	Free trade area
China–ASEAN Free Trade Agreement	Brunei Darussalam, Cambodia, China, Indonesia, Laos, Malaysia, Myanmar, Philippines, Singapore, Thailand, Vietnam	2010	Free trade area

Figure 6.19   Major RTAs

Regional integration within Europe, the Americas, East Asia and the Pacific

In Chapters 2 and 5 we identified a strong tendency for a disproportionate share of global production, trade and FDI to be 'regionalized'. Such geographical concentrations reflect, first and foremost, the basic economic–geographical processes of preference for proximity to markets and suppliers and a general tendency to 'followership' in location decision making. But there are also rather different kinds of regional integration agreement in each of the three major regions.

The EU

> The European Union is the duck-billed platypus of the political
> world: a curious-looking animal that defies simple categorization.
> Some people think it resembles a bird, others a reptile or a mammal.
> Similarly, everyone interprets the EU according to their own precon-
> ceptions rather than seeing it for the singular institution it is.[76]

The EU is by far the most highly developed and structurally complex of all the
world's regional economic blocs. Although initially established as a six-member
European *Economic* Community (EEC) in 1957, it was always – and remains today –
more than simply an economic institution. The EU is a *political*, as well as an economic, project. Indeed, the initial stimulus was the desire to bring together France
and Germany in such a way that their traditional enmities could no longer find
their outlet in another round of European wars and also to strengthen Western
Europe in the face of the perceived Soviet threat. Figure 6.20 shows how the EU

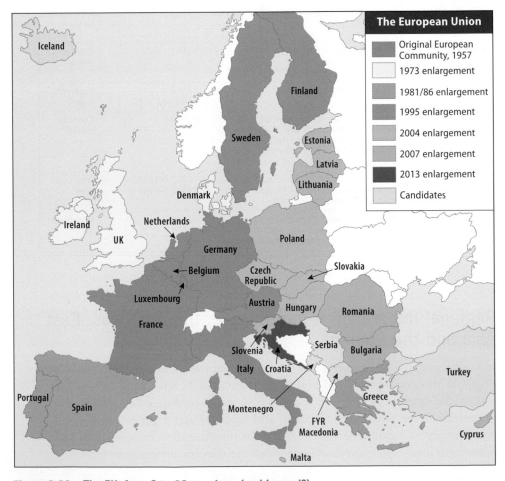

Figure 6.20   **The EU: from 6 to 28 members (and beyond?)**

has grown from its original 6 member states in 1957, to 12 in the 1970s and 1980s, 15 in the 1990s, 25 in 2004, to its current 28 member states.

Since the early 1990s, four developments have been especially important for the EU.

The *first* significant development was the completion of the *Single European Market* in 1992. Almost 40 years after the Treaty of Rome, individual countries were still resorting to tactics which prevented, or delayed, the import of certain products from other member nations through the use of various kinds of NTB. The Single European Act aimed at the removal of the remaining physical, technical and fiscal barriers; the liberalization of financial services; the opening of public procurement; and other measures. Such internal liberalization and deregulation, it was argued, would create a virtuous circle of growth for the European Community as a whole, its member states and for those business firms successfully taking advantage of the changes.

The *second* major development in the EU since the early 1990s was the *Treaty on European Union* (TEU), signed at Maastricht in 1991. This introduced a far more ambitious political agenda, aimed at creating a fully fledged *economic union*. In particular it:

- strengthened social provisions by (a) the incorporation of the Social Charter, (b) the enlargement of the EC Structural Funds, (c) the creation of a new Cohesion Fund to assist poorer areas of the Union;
- set out the mechanisms for the creation of a single European currency and monetary union (EMU).

European Monetary Union (the *eurozone*) came into effect in 1999, when 11 (later 12) of the 15 member states joined the system. Today, 18 of the 28 member states are in the eurozone. The issue of monetary union, and the adoption of a single European currency (the *euro*), crystallized some of the most difficult political problems within the EU, notably the sensitive issue of national sovereignty. Within the eurozone national control over monetary policy – notably the setting of interest rates – has been passed upwards to the European Central Bank (ECB) based in Frankfurt. The ECB, therefore, has an immense influence over the economies of individual member states. Each member state in the eurozone has to comply with the Stability and Growth Pact, which sets limits on permissible budget deficits and debts. We will return to the problems within the eurozone towards the end of this section.

The *third* major development was the dramatic *enlargement of membership* from the mid-2000s to 28 states, with the potential of further enlargement. In this regard, the most contentious outstanding applicant is Turkey. The majority of the new members were previously embedded within the Soviet-dominated system, with very different recent histories and socio-political structures from the existing EU members. Others are smaller countries like Cyprus and Malta. Significantly, the income gap between existing and new members was much wider than in previous rounds of enlargement. The average GDP per head of the 10 new members in 2004 was only 46.5 per cent of the existing EU average. This compares with the average of 95.5 per cent for Denmark, Ireland and the UK, when they joined in 1973, and the 103.6 per cent for Austria, Finland and Sweden on their accession in 1995. Such huge income differences pose massive problems for the already stressed EU budget.

The greatly increased size and diversity of EU enlargement make the process of consensus in decision making even more difficult, hence the *fourth* major development was the implementation of the Lisbon Treaty on 1 December 2009. This was an immensely tortuous and contested process over several years, with a number of states refusing to ratify the original 'EU Constitution'. The result was a considerably less ambitious structure but one that, nevertheless, involved some important changes. In particular, the position of the European Parliament was strengthened with greater powers regarding EU legislation, the EU budget and international agreements. National parliaments were to have greater involvement, especially in ensuring that the EU only acts where it will result in better results than would occur at the national level (the principle of 'subsidiarity'). The aim was to create 'a more efficient Europe, with simplified working methods and voting rules, streamlined and modern institutions for a EU of 27 [now 28] members and an improved ability to act in areas of major priority for today's Union'.[77] Significantly, it made it possible for a member state to leave the EU.

Political–economic integration in the EU is unique in its extent and depth. Many – though not all – of the economic policies of individual member states have been 'relocated' to the supra-national EU level. For example, there is just one EU trade commissioner representing the EU in the WTO and in all other inter-national trade negotiations. There are EU-wide policies on competition, on sub-sidies (both industrial and agricultural) and on investment incentives. On the other hand, there are significant areas where policy is set at the national level: for example, in labour markets and taxation.

However, even in areas of 'common' EU policy, the differing ideological posi-tions of individual member states clearly affect the process of reaching consensus. Trade negotiations, for example (including issues relating to the Common Agricultural Policy – CAP), have become increasingly contested within the EU, with a sharp divide opening up between states with a more protectionist stance (notably France, but also Poland) and those espousing more open trade policies (notably the UK and some of the Northern European states). In the sphere of competition policy, as well, there is much heated argument over the acquisition of domestic firms even by firms from other EU member states.

In the post-2008 world, not surprisingly, major cleavages have developed within the EU, both between members of the eurozone and between the eurozone and the other EU member states. The pros and cons of a single European currency were always finely balanced. The major benefits are the reduced costs and uncer-tainties associated with having to deal with many separate currencies within a single market and the overall stability this is intended to produce. Set against this is the fact that an individual state's ability to use monetary mechanisms to deal with periodic economic crises is hugely reduced. Such constraints on national freedom of manoeuvre become especially apparent during major financial crises, as has happened since 2008. Massive crises developed, initially in Ireland and Greece, necessitating large-scale bailouts of both economies. Bigger EU economies, notably Spain and Italy, as well as Portugal, have been drawn into the financial morass and others may well follow. The ECB undertook to take 'whatever measures were necessary' to sustain the eurozone but the cost has been draconian austerity measures imposed on struggling economies as the price of financial help. The tension between the EU's strongest economy, Germany, and these states has become acute.

The result is the intensification of social tensions within and between EU states:

> The big challenge is unemployment and growth. About 26m people are out of work across the EU and the unemployment rate for the 17-nation eurozone has hit a record 11.8 per cent ... Worse, the eurozone-wide rate conceals stark country-by-country differences. Joblessness is still near two-decade lows in Germany but in Spain and Greece one-in-four people are out of work with the rate nearing 60 per cent among those under 25 ... These social strains have started to be expressed in a rekindling of smouldering separatist and regionalist tensions ... Many countries are experiencing the most severe economic crises in living memory ... The social contract around which a country coalesces may become increasingly strained.[78]

Inevitably, therefore, there is intense speculation about the future of the euro itself and, more broadly, over the future shape of the EU as a whole. In the case of the euro, some argue that it will inevitably fail; others that it will survive, primarily because 'they underestimate Europe's deep political commitment to the euro's survival, in some form or other ... The euro will neither fail nor succeed. Defective but defended, it will simply endure.'[79] One distinct possibility is that the 'geometry' of the EU will change, perhaps into a three-tier structure:

> The first tier will probably – as France and Germany are proposing – have its own budget separate from the EU budget, to help countries that suffer economic shocks or are introducing painful structural reforms ... A second tier, consisting of countries that aspire to join the euro, is already known as 'eurozone plus'. This group, which includes Poland, will accept much of the same supervision of budgetary and economic policy as the first tier ... The third tier will consist of the UK and a few others that do not wish to give up any more economic

sovereignty. They will, however, wish to remain involved in the single market, trade policy, farm policy, foreign policy cooperation and other things that the EU does.[80]

Of course, this is all speculation. Only time will tell how the EU will turn out.

The Americas

Whereas the history of political–economic integration in Europe has been one of progressive deepening and widening – albeit with many interruptions and uncertainties – the history of attempts to create regional integration agreements in the Americas has been far more fragmented and shallow. To a great extent, this reflects the overwhelming dominance of the USA in the region and the fact that, until very recently, the USA had chosen not to enter into bilateral or regional trading arrangements. It reflects, too, the limited success of Latin American countries in creating robust and lasting regional agreements. The picture in the Americas, therefore, is of a mosaic of regional trade agreements of different type and scope (Figure 6.21).

The *North American Free Trade Agreement* (NAFTA) is by far the most important RTA in the Americas. By integrating two highly developed countries (the USA and Canada) and one large developing country (Mexico) into a single free trade area it radically changed the economic map of North America. The NAFTA came into force in 1994, but its origins can be traced back into the 1980s. One important building block, although this was not its intent, was the Canada–US Free Trade Agreement (CUSFTA) signed in 1988 and implemented in 1989. As the CUSFTA was being signed, two other developments were also occurring. President George Bush (Senior) had made freer trade with Mexico a campaign issue in 1988. At the same time, President Carlos Salinas of Mexico made clear his determination to negotiate a free trade area with the USA. Within a short time of bilateral talks starting, Canada had joined in an obvious defensive response.

The arguments in favour of creating the NAFTA varied among the three parties. For the USA, it formed part of its long-term objective of ensuring stable economic and political development in the western hemisphere and also gave access to Mexican raw materials (especially oil), markets and low-cost labour. The Canadian government was anxious to consolidate the recent CUSFTA. The motives of the Mexican government were primarily to help to lock in the economic reforms of the previous few years, to create a magnet for inward investment, not only from the USA but also from Europe and Asia, and to secure access to the US and Canadian markets.

The aims of the NAFTA were gradually to eliminate most trade and investment restrictions between the three countries over a 10- to 15-year period. The possibility of other countries joining the NAFTA was left open to negotiation. The NAFTA is not a customs union; it does not incorporate a common external trade policy. Each member is free to make trade agreements with other states outside the NAFTA. In contrast to the EU, political–economic integration is minimal so that, unlike the EU, there are no social provisions within the NAFTA.

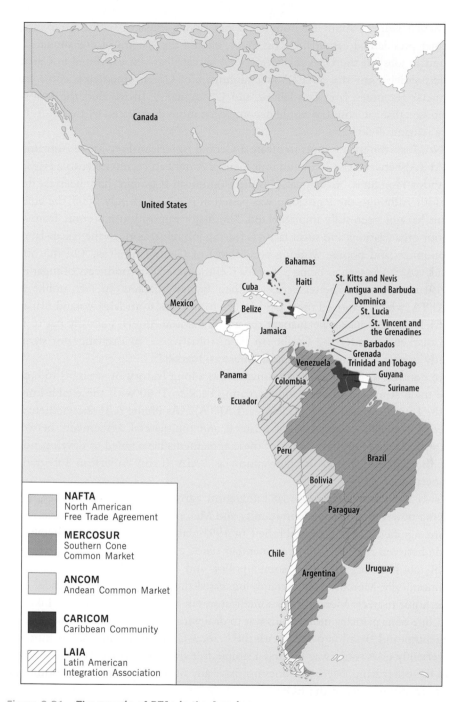

Figure 6.21 **The mosaic of RTAs in the Americas**

The NAFTA remains a highly controversial issue in all three countries. Against the claimed benefits of an enlarged economic space (from both a production and marketing point of view) is set a number of concerns. In the USA, there were particular worries about environmental and labour impacts. In the latter case, a former presidential candidate, Ross Perot, offered the spectre of a 'giant sucking sound' as jobs left the USA for Mexico.[81] A similar fear was expressed in Canada. One politician saw the NAFTA as a 'nightmare of US continentalists come true: Canada's resources, Mexico's labour, and US capital'.[82] In Mexico, the fear was expressed that the country would become even more dominated by the USA. The jury remains divided.

Not surprisingly, attempts to create a Central American Free Trade Agreement (CAFTA) between the USA and four Central American countries (Costa Rica, El Salvador, Honduras, Nicaragua), plus the Dominican Republic, have been far from smooth. Although the legislation was passed in the USA in July 2005, the agreement has not been fully implemented. The major opposition has come from US labour organizations and sugar farmers fearing job relocations to the cheap-labour economies (and poorer working conditions) of Central America. On the other hand, CAFTA is seen as being a way for Central American producers of sugar and of garments to gain better access to their biggest markets. In fact, unlike the NAFTA, which removed most US barriers to imports from Mexico and Canada, 'CAFTA largely makes permanent the access Central America already has to the US market … under the Caribbean Basin Initiative … in exchange for significantly greater access to the Central American market.'[83]

In contrast to the USA, Latin America has a long history of attempts to create free trade areas and customs unions, dating back to 1960 with the establishment of the Latin American Free Trade Area (LAFTA).[84] As Figure 6.21 shows, there has been a complex overlapping of bilateral and multilateral agreements between Latin American countries. Some of these agreements have failed to develop, notably the LAFTA, despite its reinvention as LAIA (Latin American Integration Association) in 1980.

Two Latin American regional integration agreements have had rather more staying power: the Andean Community and Mercosur. Of the two, *Mercosur* is the more significant.[85] It was established in 1991 with the intention of liberalizing trade between the four founding member states, establishing a common external tariff, coordinating macroeconomic policy and adopting sectoral agreements. Economically, Mercosur has certainly increased the degree of internal trade.

In some respects Mercosur has some features in common with the EU. Like the EU, one of its primary motivations was to deal with security relationships between Argentina and Brazil (a parallel with the Franco-German relationship in Europe). It certainly goes some way beyond a simple free trade area (such as the NAFTA). On the other hand, Mercosur does not have any of the supra-national institutions that are at the heart of the EU:

> Conflict continues to plague the organization because of a lack of coordinated economic policies and supranational institutions. Deepening of the integration process has slowed because member

states have not established common mechanisms for coordinated macro-economic policy nor have they truly committed themselves, despite the rhetoric, to establishing a regional institutional framework ... rather, loose regulations and shallow institutionalism have been maintained at a relatively low political cost ... Put simply, the member states of Mercosur want the maximum economic and political benefits from integration while foregoing as little sovereignty as possible.[86]

Looming over all attempts to create a more vigorous regional economy in Latin America is the USA, which aspires to create a pan-hemispheric Free Trade Area of the Americas (FTAA), encompassing North, Central and South America. So far, progress in the negotiations involving 34 countries have stalled. Partly to subvert an FTAA, there are counter-moves to create a South America Community of Nations, whose core would be a merger, over 15 years, between Mercosur and the Andean Community.

East Asia and the Pacific

Regional trading arrangements in the Asia-Pacific are much looser, less formalized and more open than the EU and NAFTA.[87] Until 2010 there were two main regional economic collaborations (AFTA and APEC) and a host of bilateral agreements. The *ASEAN Free Trade Agreement* (AFTA) was initiated in 1992 between the ASEAN countries. ASEAN itself had been established in 1967 as a group of four, then six, South East Asian countries (Singapore, Malaysia, Thailand, Indonesia, the Philippines, Brunei). ASEAN's membership grew to 10 countries in the 1990s, with the addition of Cambodia, Laos, Myanmar and Vietnam (see Figure 6.22):

> ASEAN as an intergovernmental institution established to promote regional cooperation, offers a striking contrast to the Western institutions such as EU and NAFTA ... it is ... based on a different concept of institutionalisation ...
>
> Paying full respect for the sovereignty and independence of each member state is one of the fundamental principles of the Association ... most of the decisions have been made by consensus through the 'consultation based on the ASEAN tradition', which means to negotiate and consult thoroughly till achieving an agreement ...
>
> [The] mechanism for dispute settlement also reflects ASEAN's preference for an informal approach. This is a striking contrast with the Western approach to dispute settlement in which preference is clearly on the side of judicial settlement based on clear rules and binding decisions.[88]

Such a system has both strengths and weaknesses.[89] A strength is that it has helped what is a very diverse group of countries to maintain positive relationships. A weakness is that a firm and rapid response to problems is often difficult, especially in light of the principle of non-interference in domestic matters of member states. ASEAN has had only limited success in stimulating economic activity. As a consequence, in 1992, the original six member states agreed to initiate an ASEAN Free Trade Agreement (AFTA).

Increasing competitive pressures on the ASEAN region from other East Asian countries (notably China) has forced the organization to look towards making agreements with other countries in East Asia. Some ASEAN members, notably Singapore, have negotiated bilateral trade agreements with China, South Korea,

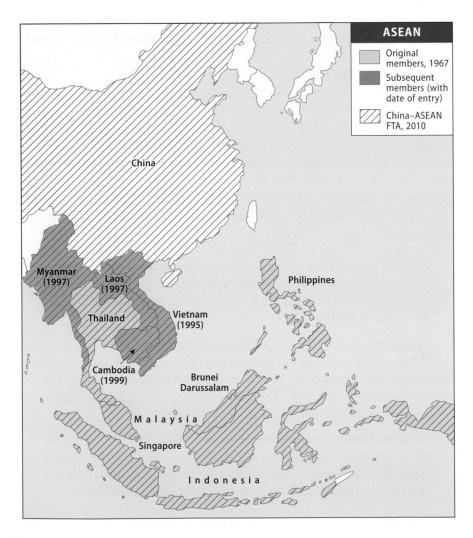

Figure 6.22   The China–ASEAN Free Trade Agreement

Japan, and with the EU, the USA, Canada, Mexico and Chile. However, the China–ASEAN agreement (Figure 6.22), which came into being in January 2010, is at a different scale:

> The deal creates the third largest regional trading agreement by value after the European Union and the North American Free Trade Agreement, covering countries with mutual trade flows of $231bn (€161bn) in 2008 and combined gross domestic product of about $6,000bn … However, the deal remains short of genuine free trade. The trade in goods agreement provides for each country to register hundreds of sensitive goods on which tariffs will continue to apply, in many cases until at least 2020.[90]

At the same time, a free trade agreement has been reach between ASEAN, Australia and New Zealand. An agreement has also been negotiated with India to establish an Indo-ASEAN free trade area by 2012.

The other major regional economic organization in East Asia is the Asia-Pacific Economic Cooperation Forum (APEC), established in 1989 on the initiative of the Australian government. Figure 6.23 shows the extremely diverse composition of

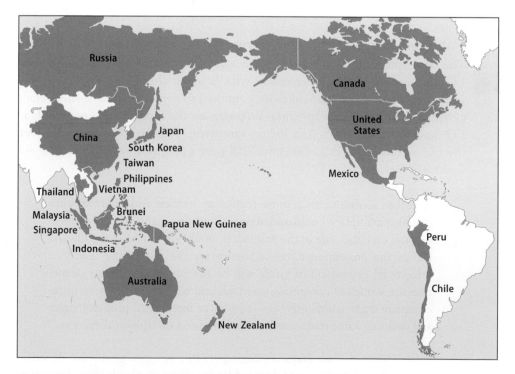

Figure 6.23   **The Asia-Pacific Economic Cooperation Forum (APEC)**

APEC. It includes not only the obvious East and South East Asian states themselves (including China and Taiwan), but also Australia and New Zealand on the one hand and the USA, Canada, Mexico, Peru and Chile on the other. However, APEC is, so far, little more than a broadly based 'forum' and little real progress has been made in fulfilling its stated goal of 'open regionalism'. Particularly following the Asian financial crisis of 1997, APEC became increasingly criticised by Asian participants:

> APEC's failure to provide any meaningful response to the biggest economic crisis in the Asia-Pacific region since 1945 made it, if not irrelevant, then less important for many Asian members ... Increasingly, Asian observers evaluated APEC as a tool of American foreign economic policy. And the resistance of Asian policy makers to a strengthened APEC was caused by their fear of US dominance ... APEC has not been successful in creating a joint identity as the basis for further pan-Pacific cooperation and the lack of tangible benefits has been progressively criticized ... APEC has failed to provide much needed political legitimacy for the wider regional liberal economic project.[91]

At its summit meeting in 2012, APEC's 21 members promised to find ways of stimulating economic growth but in rather vague ways.

This failure of APEC has led to various initiatives within East Asia to create a more robust regional economic (and financial) framework. None, so far, has come to fruition.

Potential Transatlantic and Trans-Pacific Initiatives

The development of new regional trade agreements continues. For example, the EU is discussing one such agreement with Japan (it already has a recent agreement with Korea). The USA, likewise, continues to explore various bilateral trade agreements. But the most ambitious proposals are those involving a possible US–EU agreement and a US–Asia-Pacific agreement. Formal negotiations between the EU and the USA began in early 2013 over a potential *Transatlantic Trade and Investment Partnership* (TTIP):

> A deal to abolish tariffs, remove regulatory barriers and create an integrated marketplace could add about 0.5 per cent annually to national income on either side of the Atlantic. It would also establish the US and EU as the pre-eminent standard-setter for the rest of the world ... [However] getting rid of tariffs will be the easy bit ... Delve deeper into the worlds of competing standards and cultural preferences, intra-company trade, competitive tax regimes or intellectual property rights and defining a free trade area becomes almost a metaphysical exercise.[92]

Negotiations over a *Trans-Pacific Partnership* (TPP) agreement involve Australia, Brunei, Canada, Chile, Japan, Malaysia, Mexico, New Zealand, Peru, Singapore,

USA and Vietnam. Although less ambitious than the TTIP, it is likely to take some considerable time to negotiate and implement. Of course, neither project may actually happen, given the complexity of the politics (both domestic and international) involved. The current atmosphere of distrust between the USA and others over the revelations of the wholesale monitoring of communications by US intelligence agencies (helped, to a degree, by the UK) certainly does not augur well. This should remind us that, even though such projects are ostensibly economic in focus, they are, like all such projects, fundamentally *political*.

NOTES

1   Weiss (1998: chapter 1).
2   This was the term coined by the novelist Tom Wolfe in *The Bonfire of the Vanities* (1988).
3   Jessop (1994).
4   See Gilpin (2001), Gritsch (2005), Hirst et al. (2009), Hudson (2001), Jessop (2002), Wade (1996), Weiss (1998, 2003).
5   Kelly (1999: 389–90; emphasis added).
6   Rodrik (2011).
7   Gritsch (2005: 2–3). Nye (2002) also addresses the question of 'soft power' in the context of the geopolitical position of the USA.
8   Glassner (1993: 35–40).
9   Agnew and Corbridge (1995) and Taylor (1994) discuss the general notion of states as 'containers' and the nature and significance of territoriality and space in geopolitics.
10 See Granovetter and Swedberg (1992), Lee (2009), Smelser and Swedberg (2005).
11 Terpstra and David (1991: 6).
12 Hofstede (1980).
13 A study of 700 managers across a large number of countries confirmed the persistence of significant cultural differences (*Financial Times*, 15 October 2004). See also Drogendijk and Slangen (2006).
14 Schwartz (1994), Drogendijk and Slangen (2006).
15 Yao (1997: 238).
16 Jacques (2012: chapter 5) provides an extensive discussion of these issues.
17 See Berger and Dore (1996), Brenner et al. (2010), Hall and Soskice (2001), Hollingsworth and Boyer (1997), Peck and Theodore (2007), Whitley (1999, 2004).
18 Peck and Theodore (2007: 750–8).
19 Rothkopf (2012).
20 Hollingsworth and Boyer (1997: 266, 267–8).
21 Peck and Theodore (2007: 756).
22 Wolf (2008: 1).
23 Rothkopf (2012).
24 Cerny (1997: 251).
25 Hudson (2001: 48–9; emphasis added).
26 Hudson (2001: 76).

27   Cerny (1991: 174).
28   Brookings Institution (2009), www.brookings.edu/articles/2009/03_g20_stimulus_prasad.aspx.
29   Keynes (2007). See Skidelsky (2010).
30   Mortimore and Vergara (2004) and Mytelka and Barclay (2004) discuss FDI policies with particular reference to developing countries.
31   *Financial Times* (25 April 2008).
32   Gilpin (2001: 201).
33   List (1928).
34   Mazzucato (2013) provides an excellent analysis. See also Chang (2011: chapter 12).
35   Mazzucato (2013: 3).
36   Peck (2001: 10).
37   Faux and Mishel (2000: 101).
38   See Gilpin (2001: chapter 7).
39   See Chorev (2007).
40   See, for example, Beath (2002).
41   Contributors to Vitols (2004) explore the extent to which the 'German model' is sustainable.
42   Gretschmann (1994: 471).
43   Accounts of Japanese economic policy are provided by Dore (1986), Johnson (1985), Porter et al. (2000).
44   *Financial Times* (13 September 2013).
45   Mathews (2009: 9–10). See also Yeung (2014).
46   See, for example, Rodrik (2011).
47   Gereffi (1990: 18).
48   Gereffi (1990: 21).
49   Gereffi (1990: 21).
50   Gereffi (1990: 22).
51   ILO (2003, 2007a), Farole and Akinci (2011).
52   ILO (2003: 1).
53   ILO (2007a).
54   ILO (2003: 1).
55   ILO (2003: 2).
56   Douglass (1994: 543).
57   Yeung (2014) explores the relationship between East Asian developmental state policies and global production networks. Henderson (2011) and Studland (2013) discuss variations in economic policy within East Asia.
58   Especially useful accounts of Korean industrialization policy are by Amsden (1989), Chang (2007), Koo and Kim (1992), Pirie (2012), Wade (1990, 2004).
59   Yeung (2014: 85).
60   Koo and Kim (1992).
61   Wade (2004: 320). See also Amsden (1989).
62   See the detailed analyses provided by Chang (1998a), Pirie (2012).
63   *Financial Times* (17 July 2013).
64   Singapore's developmental policies are discussed by Lall (1994), Ramesh (1995), Rodan (1991), Yeung (1998, 2006a,b,c, 2014).
65   Yeung (2014: 86).

66 Yeung (1998: 392).
67 See Yeung (1998, 1999, 2006b,c).
68 Coe (2003b), Yeung (2006a).
69 Spence (2013) provides a comprehensive account of the development of modern China. See also Benewick and Wingrove (1995), Crane (1990), Jacques (2012), Nolan (2001), Zheng (2004).
70 Nolan (2001).
71 Yu Yongding, quoted in the *Financial Times* (23 January 2013).
72 BBC News Business (8 April 2013).
73 Mansfield and Milner (1999: 592).
74 Schiff and Winters (2003: 9).
75 Mansfield and Milner (1999: 595–602). Numbers in parentheses refer to pages in this work.
76 Thornhill (2008).
77 www.europa.eu/lisbon_treaty/glance/index_en.html.
78 *Financial Times* (23 January 2013).
79 Cohen (2012: 689).
80 Grant (2012).
81 Lawrence (1996: 72–3).
82 Quoted in McConnell and MacPherson (1994: 179).
83 *Financial Times* (23 February 2005).
84 See Grugel (1996), Gwynne (1994), Kaltenthaler and Mora (2002).
85 This discussion of Mercosur is based upon Kaltenthaler and Mora (2002).
86 Kaltenthaler and Mora (2002: 92, 93).
87 Bowles (2002), Dieter and Higgott (2003), Haggard (1995), Hamilton-Hart (2003), Higgott (1999).
88 Liao (1997: 150–1).
89 Narine (2008).
90 *Financial Times* (2 January 2010).
91 Dieter and Higgott (2003: 433).
92 Stephens (2013).

Want to know more about this chapter? Visit the companion website at **www.guilford.com/dickenGS7** for free access to author videos, suggested reading and practice questions to further enhance your study.

PART THREE

WINNING AND LOSING IN THE GLOBAL ECONOMY

Seven

THE UNEASY RELATIONSHIP BETWEEN TRANSNATIONAL CORPORATIONS AND STATES: DYNAMICS OF CONFLICT AND COLLABORATION

Our focus in Parts One and Two has been on the *patterns* and *processes* of global shift: on the *forms* being produced by the globalizing of economic activities and on the *forces* producing these forms. These transformations of the geographies of the global economy are the outcome of extraordinarily complex processes, involving major changes in the nature of production, distribution and consumption. The central argument in this book is that the reshaping of the global economic map is being driven more and more by the emergence of increasingly intricate organizational and geographical *networks* of production, distribution and consumption:

what we have called global production networks (GPNs). The precise form of such networks – how they are controlled and coordinated, as well as the shape and extent of their specific geographies – varies enormously, as the case studies of Part Four show.

As we have seen, TNCs operate through a complex mix of intra-organizational and inter-organizational networks: the internalized networks of TNCs themselves, varying from centrally controlled hierarchies to flatter 'heterarchies'; the external-ized captive, relational and modular networks created through strategic alliances and various kinds of subcontracting and supplier relationships within GPNs. Fundamental to these networks are the dynamic *relationships between TNCs and states*. In the preceding two chapters we focused on the major characteristics of TNCs and of states as separate actors. In this chapter we focus explicitly on the relationships between them because these relationships are, in many ways, at the very centre of the processes of global shift and of global economic transformation. They are integral to the issues of 'winning and losing in the global economy', which are the concern of Part Three.

THE TIES THAT BIND

The popular view tends to see the state as always in a subservient position to the invariably dominant TNC. In fact, relationships between TNCs and states are far more complex and ambiguous:

> [they are] both cooperative and competing, both supportive and con-flictual. They operate in a fully dialectical relationship, locked into unified but contradictory roles and positions, neither the one nor the other partner clearly or completely able to dominate.[1]

This quotation captures the essence of the intricate relationships between TNCs and states: they contain elements of both rivalry and collusion.[2] On the one hand, there is no doubt that the fundamental goals of states and TNCs differ. In ideal-type terms, whereas the basic goal of business organizations is to maximize profits and 'shareholder value', the basic economic goal of the state is (or should be) to maximize the material welfare of its society. Figure 7.1 indicates some of the dimensions of these conflicting objectives of TNCs and states.

On the other hand, although their relationships may often be conflictual, *states and firms need each other*. Clearly, *states need firms* to generate material wealth and provide jobs for their citizens. They might prefer such firms to be domestically bounded in their allegiance but that is not an option in a capitalist market econ-omy. Indeed, some states regard TNCs as important extensions of their state for-eign policy. For example, in addition to ensuring control of key natural resources,

	TNC objectives	State objectives
Performance	Maximize profits and shareholder value. Minimize cost base consistent with customer need.	Maximize growth of GDP. Maximize quantity and quality of employment opportunities.
Technology	Undertake R&D at locations optimal to the needs of the firm as a whole. Gain access to all necessary technology.	Stimulate the development of locally-rooted technology.
High-order functions	Locate headquarters and other high-order functions to fit optimal pattern of the firm's overall operations.	Maintain indigenous headquarters. Attract and retain key operations of TNCs.
Responsiveness	Retain flexibility to move profits in optimal manner. Retain flexibility to modify the geographical configuration of the firm's production network to meet changing conditions. Retain flexibility to use the labour force as required.	Retain power to gain a fair return on local operations of TNCs through taxation policies. Maximize the extent and benefits of local supplier linkages. Prevent the closure/scaling down of local TNC operations. Develop a flexible, high-skill, high-earning labour force.

Figure 7.1   **Some conflicting objectives of TNCs and states**

Source: based, in part, on Hood and Young, 2000: Table 1.1

American political leaders have believed that the national interest has also been served by the foreign expansion of US corporations in manufacturing and services. Foreign direct investment has been considered a major instrument through which the US could maintain its relative position in world markets, and the overseas expansion of multinational corporations has been regarded as a means to maintain America's dominant world economic position.[3]

Conversely, *TNCs need states* to provide the infrastructural basis for their continued existence: not only physical infrastructure, in the form of the built environment, but also social infrastructures, in the form of legal protection of private property, institutional mechanisms to provide a continuing supply of educated workers, and the like. TNCs, invariably, look to their home-country government to provide them with diplomatic protection in hostile foreign environments:

> In the last resort … [a TNC's] … directors will always heed the wishes and commands of the government which has issued their passports and those of their families.[4]

As we saw in Chapter 6, states are both *containers* of distinctive business practices and cultures – within which firms are embedded – and *regulators* of business activity. National boundaries, therefore, create significant differentials on the global political–economic surface; they constitute one of the most important ways in which location-specific factors are 'packaged'. They create discontinuities in the flow of economic activities that are extremely important to the ways in which TNCs can operate. In particular, states have the potential to determine two factors of fundamental importance to TNCs:[5]

- the terms on which TNCs may have *access* to markets and/or resources;
- the *rules of operation* with which TNCs must comply when operating within a specific national territory.

At the same time, the fact that TNCs not only span national boundaries but also, in effect, *incorporate parts* of national economies within their own firm boundaries (Figure 7.2) creates major potential problems for states. There is, in other words, a *territorial asymmetry* between the continuous territories of states and the dis-continuous territories of TNCs. The nature and the magnitude of the problem created by such asymmetry vary considerably according to the kinds of strategies pursued by TNCs. Most important is the extent to which TNCs pursue globally integrated strategies within which the roles and functions of individual units are related to that overall global strategy.[6] As we saw in Chapter 5, geographical seg-mentation and fragmentation of transnational production networks has become increasingly common. States tend to be fearful about the autonomy and stability of those TNC units located within their national territory as well as concerned about the leakage of tax revenues. At the extreme, of course, TNCs have the potential capability to move their operations out of specific countries.

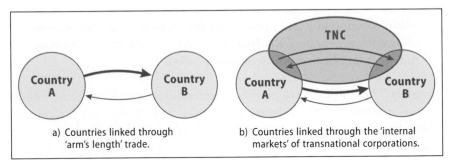

a) Countries linked through 'arm's length' trade.   b) Countries linked through the 'internal markets' of transnational corporations.

Figure 7.2   **Territorial interpenetration: the 'incorporation' of parts of a state's territory into a TNC**

At first sight it seems obvious that TNCs would seek the removal of all regula-tory barriers that act as constraints and impede their ability to locate wherever, and to behave however they wish, including:

- freedom to enter a national market, through either imports or a direct presence;
- freedom to export capital and profits from local operations;
- freedom to import materials, components and corporate services;
- freedom to operate unhindered in local labour markets.

Certainly, given the existence of differential regulatory structures in the global economy, TNCs will seek to overcome, circumvent or subvert them. Regulatory mechanisms are, indeed, constraints on a TNC's strategic and operational behaviour.

Yet it is not quite as simple as this. TNCs may see such regulatory structures as *opportunities*, enabling them to take advantage of regulatory differences between states by shifting activities between locations according to differentials in the regulatory surface – that is, to engage in *regulatory arbitrage*. One aspect of this is the ability of TNCs to stimulate competitive bidding for their mobile investments by playing off one state against another as states themselves strive to outbid their rivals to capture or retain a particular TNC activity. Perhaps more contentious is the use of regulatory differences to minimize tax payments through the use of transfer pricing (see below).

More generally, TNCs seem to have a rather ambivalent attitude to state regulatory policies:

> TNCs have favoured minimal international coordination while strongly supporting the national state, since they can take advantage of regulatory differences and loopholes ... While TNCs have pressed for an adequate coordination of national regulation, they have generally resisted any strengthening of international state structures ... Having secured the minimalist principles of national treatment for foreign-owned capital, TNCs have been the staunchest defenders of the *national state*. It is their ability to exploit national differences, both politically and economically, that gives them their competitive advantage.[7]

More specifically, TNCs may well support a home-country strategic trade policy, in expectation that this will open up market access in foreign countries and enable them to benefit from large economies of scale and learning curve effects.[8]

BARGAINING PROCESSES BETWEEN TNCs AND STATES

It is clear that the relationships between TNCs and states are exceedingly complex. In the final analysis, such relationships revolve around their relative bargaining power: the extent to which each can implement its own preferred strategies. The situation is especially complex when TNCs pursue a strategy of transnational integration – but geographical fragmentation – of their activities, in which individual units in a specific host country form only a part of the firm's overall operations. In such circumstances, governments have a number of legitimate concerns:[9]

- that integrated TNCs might relocate their operations to other countries because of relative differences in factor costs;

- that integrated TNCs use their operations to engage in transfer pricing to reduce the taxes they pay;
- that integrated TNCs retain their key competences outside host countries (typically in the firm's home country) and locate only lower-skill, lower-technology operations in host countries;
- that national decision centres no longer operate within an integrated TNC making negotiations difficult between host-country governments and the local affiliate.

Although the degrees of freedom of TNCs to move into and out of territories at will are often exaggerated, the *potential* for such locational mobility obviously exists. In fact, the TNC–state bargaining process is immensely complex and highly variable from one case to another. Despite such contingency, we need to try to understand some of the *general* features of the bargaining process. Here, for the sake of simplicity, we assume that a host country can be regarded as a single entity in the bargaining relationship. In fact, of course, many competing interest groups are involved, including domestic business interests, labour organizations and other CSOs, each of which will have different attitudes towards TNCs. In other words, it is, in reality, a *multi-party* bargaining situation.[10]

Figure 7.3 is a highly simplified, hypothetical example. The vertical axis of the graph shows the rate of return a TNC may seek for a given level of investment (XA) on the horizontal axis. The bargaining range for this level of TNC investment is shown to vary between:

- a lower limit (XY), which is the minimum rate of return that the TNC is prepared to accept for the amount of investment XA; and
- an upper limit (XZ), which is determined by the cost to the host economy of developing its own operation, or finding an alternative investor, or managing without the particular advantages provided by the TNC.

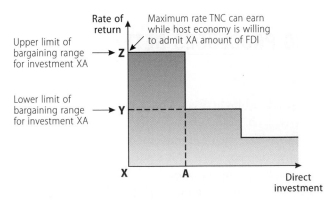

Figure 7.3   A simplified model of the bargaining relationship between a TNC and a host country

Source: based on Nixson, 1988: Figure 1

XZ is the maximum return the TNC can make for the amount of direct investment (XA) permitted by the host economy. It is in the interests of the TNC to try
to raise the upper limit (XZ). Conversely, it is in the interests of the host economy
to try to lower that upper limit: 'The higher is the cost to the host economy of
losing the proposed [investment], the greater are the possibilities for the TNC of
setting the bargain near the maximum point.'[11]

On the other hand, the more possibilities the host economy has of finding
alternatives, the greater are its chances of lowering that upper limit. The greater
the competition between TNCs for the particular investment opportunity, the
greater the opportunities for the host country to reduce both the upper and lower
limits: 'In addition, the host economy has an interest in lowering the lower limit,
through the creation of an advantageous 'investment climate' (political stability,
constitutional guarantees against appropriation, etc.) which might persuade the
TNC to accept a lower rate of return.'[12]

Seducing investors: 'locational tournaments' and competitive bidding

The greater the competition is between potential host countries for a specific
investment, the weaker will be any one country's bargaining position, because
countries will tend to bid against one another to capture the investment. Indeed,
one of the most striking features of the last few decades has been the development of so-called *locational tournaments*. There has been an enormous intensification in *competitive bidding* between states (and between communities within the
same state) for the relatively limited amount of internationally mobile investment. It has also become increasingly common for TNCs to try to lever various
kinds of state subsidies in order to persuade them to keep a plant in a particular
location. Otherwise, it is threatened, the plant will be closed or much reduced
in scale.

Such cut-throat bidding undoubtedly allows TNCs to play off one state against
another to gain the highest return for their investment. An example from the USA
illustrates this:

> The latest [2008] cheap manufacturing site for European companies is
> not in Asia or eastern Europe but the US … The reason is less the
> value of the dollar … but rather the large number of incentives that
> some US states are offering companies to set up factories in their
> region. Tennessee has disclosed that it agreed to give German car-
> maker Volkswagen $577m in incentives for its $1bn plant in
> Chattanooga. A senior executive of Fiat … said: 'with the amount of
> money US states are willing to throw at you, you would be stupid to
> turn them down at the moment' …

ThyssenKrupp, the German steelmaker and industrial group, is receiving more than $811m to build a steel mill in Alabama. It turned down an offer from Louisiana, which is reported to have offered as much as $2bn, as well as an additional $900m in cheap debt from Alabama ...

A VW official suggested that the US had a competitive advantage because European Union state aid rules made support for factories complicated. 'It is more difficult in Europe.' The chairman of a large Swiss group said: 'States are willing to pay for new roads, re-train workers and offer huge tax breaks – that is a competitive package that not many parts of the world can match when you look at how productive US workers are and where the dollar is.'[13]

The EU has strong state aid rules to control such competitive subsidization but it is always a highly sensitive and contested process. For example, the tortuous saga of the on–off sale of General Motors' European operations in 2009 raised the issue of countries where the plants are located outbidding each other in subsidies to retain employment. The situation has become especially complex within the expanded EU. After 1989, but prior to the accession of Eastern European states into the EU, firms from the West had moved rapidly into the newly emerging market economies attracted by very generous state incentives:

Generous deals were made across eastern Europe to spur investment in fields as diverse as banking, sugar production and agribusiness. Subsidies, tax breaks, import quotas and other commercial advantages were granted to those willing to invest and help create jobs. But the subsequent need to adhere to EU rules has meant an end to the highly lucrative arrangements for the companies involved, and that, in turn, has provoked calls for compensation.[14]

However, it is far from certain that the use of EU subsidies to attract TNCs to relocate from one EU state to another has ceased. An investigation in 2010 suggested that it had not:

EU rules specifically forbid grants from its structural funds from going to subsidise the relocation of businesses ... but a joint investigation ... found companies ranging from British teamaker Twinings to automotive company Valeo were at the very least receiving EU subsidies to help with the establishment of new factories, the extension of existing ones and the training of workers in their new homes. While a direct link between the relocation of companies and the use of structural funds in destination countries is not always clear-cut, it does raise questions about whether the EU's oversight of the use of grants is strong enough.[15]

Corporate tax and the contentious issue of transfer pricing

International variations in corporate tax levels

At the international scale, the use of relatively lower tax levels as an incentive to attract and retain TNCs is virtually universal. Corporate tax rates vary widely and it has become a frequent practice for TNCs to threaten to leave a particular country because of perceived high tax rates. Although often the threat is more apparent than real, states do not necessarily know that; it can be very much like a game of poker. Such games are especially marked in regions like Europe where, as Figure 7.4 shows, there are very substantial differences in national rates of corporate tax offering many possible locational options within what is a huge regional market and production space. Evidence suggests that tax competition has increased sharply in Europe, driven not only by the influx of new member states, but also by the aggressive competition for FDI by countries like Ireland and Switzerland:

> Studies show that location of FDI is becoming more sensitive to taxation, and that corporate income tax rates can influence a TNC's decision to undertake FDI, especially if competing jurisdictions have similar 'enabling conditions'. For instance, EU investors were found to increase their FDI positions in other EU member states by approximately 4% if the latter reduced their corporate income tax rates by one percentage point relative to the European mean.[16]

The threat of increased taxation on companies following the 2008 financial crisis provoked a wave of predictions that TNCs would relocate operations to lower-tax

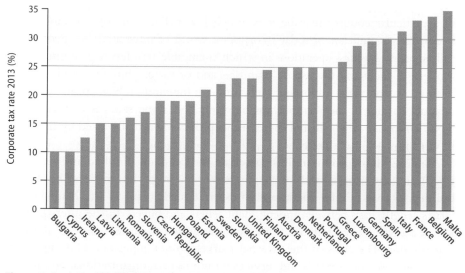

Figure 7.4   **Intra-EU differences in corporate taxation**

Source: based on KPMG data

countries. In the UK, for example, a number of TNCs relocated (or threatened to relocate) their headquarters to countries like Ireland or Switzerland to avoid higher taxes. Examples include WPP, the world's second largest advertising company, Shire Pharmaceuticals, UBM (United Business Media) and Henderson Global Investors. Conversely, reports of firms thinking of moving to the UK because of its tax attractiveness continue to appear. Indeed, WPP and UBM moved their headquarters back to the UK in response to changes in UK tax on how overseas profits are taxed. US firms taking over UK companies may move their HQs from the US to the UK to avoid US taxes (so-called 'inversion'). That was a major motivation for Pfizer's unsuccessful takeover of AstraZeneca in 2014. It is a game that is constantly being played out across the world as firms make noises about potential relocations, many of which never materialize. Nevertheless,

> the independent influence of taxes on the location of production is statistically significant and growing over time ... the impact of tax competition is particularly intense between locations where much of the output is destined for export. Case study evidence reveals that TNCs typically identify three or four roughly comparable investment sites, and then unleash their negotiators to bring back the biggest tax breaks as a 'tiebreaker'.[17]

The transfer pricing problem

The corporate tax rates shown in Figure 7.4 are, in fact, not an accurate reflection of the rate that companies actually pay because different countries have different rules governing the 'allowable' costs that can be set against tax. In reality, the 'headline' rate of corporate tax can be misleading; the actual rate of tax paid by a TNC in a particular country may be very much lower. This issue of 'allowable costs' is especially significant in today's corporate world of integrated, but geographically separate, business operations in which 'intangible' transfers (e.g. of intellectual property – including the use of 'brands' – and of various business services) have become exceptionally important. Hence, one of the most problematical – yet most opaque – issues in the relationships between TNCs and states is that of how a TNC's *internal transactions*, and therefore its profits, are actually taxed by the states in which a TNC has a presence.

All TNCs move both tangible materials and products (finished and semi-finished), and also various kinds of corporate services, across international borders to the various parts of their operations. In external markets, prices are charged on an 'arm's-length' basis between independent sellers and buyers. In the internal 'market' of a TNC, however, transactions are between *related* parties – units of the *same* organization. The rules of the external market do not apply. The TNC itself sets the *transfer prices* of its goods and services within its own organizational boundaries and, therefore, has very considerable flexibility in setting those transfer prices to help achieve its overall goals.

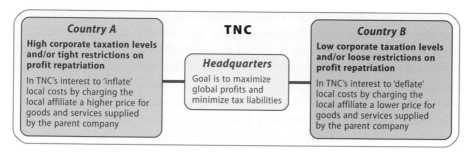

Figure 7.5   The incentives for TNCs to engage in transfer pricing

The ability to set its own internal prices – within the limits imposed by the vigilance of the tax authorities – enables the TNC to adjust transfer prices either upwards or downwards and, therefore, to influence the amount of tax payable to national governments. For example, as Figure 7.5 suggests, it would be in a TNC's interest to charge more for the goods and services supplied to its subsidiaries located in countries with high tax levels and less for those supplied to countries with low rate taxes. A similar incentive exists where governments restrict the amount of a subsidiary's profits that can be remitted out of the country.

In general, the greater the geographical differences in levels of corporate taxes, tariffs, duties and exchange rates, the greater the incentive for the TNC to manipulate its internal transfer prices. The very large, highly centralized, global TNC has the greatest potential for doing so:

> Picture a General Motors plant in Windsor, Ontario, producing hundreds of items for assembly in [autos] … that will be sold in the Canadian market as well as for assembly by its sister plants in Michigan. No independent public market exists for many of the items, since no other firm produces these products. Nor is it obvious what the production cost may be of the items that cross the US-Canadian border – that kind of estimate will depend heavily on how the fixed costs of the Windsor plant are allocated among the many items produced, an allocation that cannot fail to be arbitrary. Without an obvious selling price or an indisputable cost price, all the ingredients exist for a pitched battle over the transfer price.
>
> When the item crossing the border is intangible, such as a right bestowed by the parent on a foreign subsidiary to use the trademark of the parent or to draw on its pool of technological know-how, the indeterminateness of a reasonable price becomes even more apparent. How much is the use of the IBM trade name worth to its subsidiary in France? How valuable is the access granted to a team of engineers in an Australian subsidiary to the databank of a parent in Los Angeles?[18]

A US House of Representatives study claimed that more than half of almost 40 foreign companies surveyed had paid virtually no taxes over a 10-year period. The US Internal Revenue Service estimated that some $53 billion was lost through the transfer pricing mechanism in 2001 alone.[19] According to a UK House of Commons Report, one in four of the largest companies in the UK paid zero corporation tax in 2006–7.[20] In 2009, both the US and the UK governments began investigations into the tax disclosure practices of TNCs.[21] However, the controversy over the tax-avoiding practices of TNCs operating in the UK reached a new level of acrimony in 2012 when the tax strategies of Starbucks and Amazon, among others, were revealed to a public feeling battered by recession:

- *Starbucks* UK employed around 8500 workers and had a turnover of £398 million in 2011. But it showed a *loss* of £33 million. In total, Starbucks paid only £8.6 million in UK tax over 14 years of operations. It achieved this through a transfer pricing strategy which involved:[22] (1) paying royalties for the use of the brand and its associated 'intellectual capital' to Starbucks in the Netherlands; (2) acquiring its coffee from Starbucks in Switzerland where the company's global coffee buying operations are located; (3) paying high levels of interest on an intra-group loan to its US parent company.
- *Amazon* UK employed around 15,000 workers, and made £3.35 billion of sales in 2011 – but showed a *profit* of only £74 million and paid a mere £1.8 million in UK tax. The key to this is the way in which Amazon has structured its European operations. In 2006, Amazon UK's status was defined as a 'fulfilment' centre. 'The practical effect of this was to reduce the UK business to little more than a delivery service. From 2006, sales made in Britain were billed from Luxembourg and any profits from those sales were taxed not in Britain but in Luxembourg … [which] … employed only 134 people in 2010 … At first glance, corporation tax rates in Luxembourg and the UK are similar, but the Luxembourg authorities have a different view of costs that can be offset against income, which reduces taxable profit. So Amazon EU Sarl's €7.5bn of income in 2010 was almost entirely offset by €7.4bn of charges, enabling it to disclose a tax charge of just €5.5m.'[23]

In 2013, a US Senate Committee focused its attention on Apple, and the way it structures its global operations in order to minimize tax. This revealed some fascinating features, shown in some detail in Figure 7.6.[24] By any reasonable measure, Apple is a US-based company. Two-thirds of its 80,000 worldwide employees in 2012 were located in the USA. Its R&D – the basis of Apple's entire business – is overwhelmingly *located* in the USA:

> The vast majority of Apple's engineers, product design specialists, and technical experts are physically located in California. ASI and AOE employees conduct less than 1% of Apple's R&D and build only a small number of speciality computers. In 2011, 95 per cent of its R&D was conducted in the United States.[25]

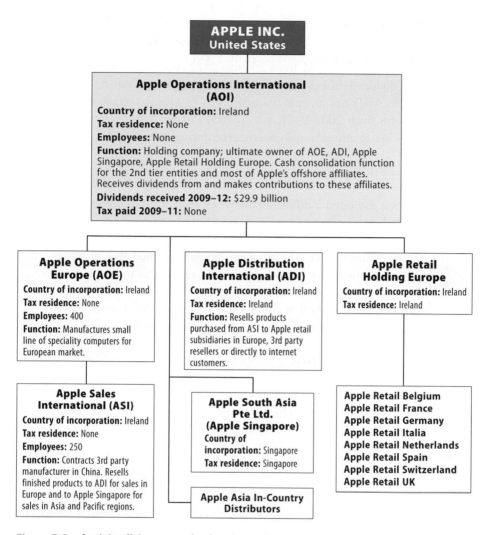

Figure 7.6   Apple's offshore organizational structure

Source: based on material in US Senate Committee on Homeland Security and Governmental Affairs, 2013

Yet, according to the Senate Committee, Apple avoided paying huge amounts of tax by using its Ireland-based affiliates. So, for example,

> ASI contracted with Apple's third-party manufacturer in China to assemble Apple products and acted as the initial buyer of those finished goods. ASI then re-sold the finished products to ADI for sales in Europe, the Middle East, Africa, and India; and to Apple Singapore for sales in Asia and the Pacific region. When it re-sold the finished products, ASI charged the Apple affiliates a higher price than it paid for the goods and, as a result, became the recipient of substantial income, a

portion of which ASI then distributed up the chain in the form of dividends to its parent. AOE, in turn, sent dividends to AOI.[26]

Over a four-year period, from 2009 to 2012, AOI received $29.9 billion in dividends from lower-tiered offshore Apple affiliates. According to Apple, AOI's net income made up 30% of Apple's total worldwide net profits from 2009–2011, yet … AOI did not pay any corporate income tax to any national government during that period.[27]

All of this was made possible because

> Apple has exploited a difference between Irish and US tax residency rules. Ireland uses a management and control test to determine tax residency, while the United States determines tax residency based upon the entity's place of formation. Apple explained that, although AOI is incorporated in Ireland, it is not tax resident in Ireland because AOI is neither managed nor controlled in Ireland. Apple also maintained that because AOI was not incorporated in the United States, AOI is not a US tax resident under US tax law either.[28]

As Senator Carl Levin observed,

> Apple wasn't satisfied with shifting its profits to a low-tax offshore tax haven. Apple sought the Holy Grail of tax avoidance. It has created offshore entities holding tens of billions of dollars, while claiming to be tax resident nowhere.[29]

There is, in fact, nothing inherently illegal in these and other transfer pricing and tax avoidance practices by TNCs. Indeed, to some extent they reflect the practices by states to attempt to attract and retain investment by various kinds of tax incentive. So, for example, at the same time as the UK Chancellor of the Exchequer, George Osborne, was calling for a severe clampdown on corporate tax practices in 2012, he was in the process of reducing the UK's corporate tax rate to 20 per cent by 2015 and also introducing a special 'cut-price tax rate for certain types of intellectual property and an offshore finance company regime to enhance the UK's ability to attract headquarters'.[30] Clearly, major *international* reform is needed to address these issues. We will look at this problem again in Chapter 11.

Relative bargaining powers of TNCs and states

In general, TNCs wish to maximize their locational flexibility to take advantage of geographical differences in the availability, quality and cost of production inputs in serving their existing and new markets. Their ideal would be to pursue such goals without any hindrance from the regulatory practices of states. States, on the other hand, strive to capture as much as possible of the value created from production within their territories. In this latter sense, a primary aim of a host state is to try to *embed* a TNC's activities as strongly as possible in the local/national economy.

One way of thinking about this specific process is to conceive of two ideal types of embeddedness:[31]

- *Active* embeddedness: where a TNC seeks out localized assets and incorporates them, *as a matter of choice*, within its operations. Where such localized assets are widely available in different geographical locations then the power of such choice rests primarily with the TNC. However, the less widely available the assets (or where access to them is controlled by the state), the more likely the state is to have a greater degree of bargaining power over the terms on which the TNC can utilize them. In such circumstances, obligated embeddedness is likely to occur.
- *Obligated* embeddedness: where a TNC is forced to comply with state criteria in order to gain access to, and use of, the desired asset. Obligated embeddedness, therefore, is most likely to occur where two conditions exist:
  - there must be a localized asset that is highly important to a TNC (this may include a natural resource, a human resource and/or a significant market) and to which it needs access in order to achieve its business goals;
  - access to that resource must be controlled by the state within whose territory the asset is located and the state must have the power to exert that control.

The extent to which a state feels the need to offer large incentives (subsidies, tax concessions, etc.) to attract a foreign investment or to retain an existing investment, or is able to impose access or performance requirements, will depend on its relative bargaining strength in any specific case. Conversely, the extent to which a TNC is able to obtain such incentives, or to operate as it wishes, will depend on its relative bargaining strength. The outcome will depend on a number of factors.

On the one hand, the price a *host country* will ultimately pay depends upon:

- the number of foreign firms independently competing for the investment opportunity;
- the recognized measure of uniqueness of the foreign contribution (as against its possible provision by local entrepreneurship, public or private);
- the perceived degree of domestic need for the contribution.

On the other hand, the terms the *TNC* will accept depend upon:

- the firm's general need for an investment outlet;
- the attractiveness of the specific investment opportunity offered by the host country, compared with similar or other opportunities in other countries;
- the extent of prior commitment to the country concerned (e.g. an established market position).

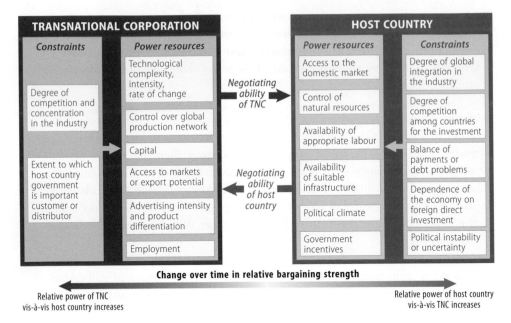

Figure 7.7 Components of the bargaining relationship between TNCs and host countries

Source: based on material in Kobrin, 1987

Figure 7.7 sets out the major components of the bargaining relationship between TNCs and host countries. Both possess a range of 'power resources' that are their major bargaining strengths. Both operate within certain constraints that will restrict the extent to which these power resources can be exercised. The relative bargaining power of TNCs and host countries, therefore, is a function of three related elements:

- the *relative demand* by each of the two participants for resources which the other controls;
- the *constraints* on each which affect the translation of potential bargaining power into control over outcomes;
- the *negotiating status* of the participants.

Figure 7.7 suggests that, in general, host countries are subject to a greater variety of constraints than are TNCs, a reflection of the latter's greater potential flexibility to switch their operations between alternative locations. In particular,

> it is the TNC which orchestrates the value chain. Thus, the most important source of TNC bargaining power ... is its role as the coordinator of the GVC itself ... The TNC's governance of its integrated international production network and of the web of loosely

dependent entities that make it up allows it to regulate access to the network and to set the conditions ... the segmentation or 'fine-slicing' of value chains into ever more numerous and discrete activities that can be carried out by partner firms in any location plays into the hands of TNCs.[32]

Nevertheless, the extent to which a TNC can implement a globally integrated strategy may be constrained by nation-state behaviour. Where a company particularly needs access to a given location and where the host country does have leverage, then the bargain that is eventually struck may involve the TNC in making concessions. In general, the scarcer the resource being sought (whether by a TNC or a host country), the greater the relative bargaining power of the controller of access to that resource and vice versa.

For example, states that control access to large, affluent domestic markets have greater relative bargaining power over TNCs pursuing a market-oriented strategy than states whose domestic markets are small (China is the obvious case). It is in this kind of situation that the host country's ability to impose performance requirements – such as local content levels – on foreign firms is greatest. It may also give the host country sufficient leverage to persuade the inward investor to establish higher-level functions such as R&D facilities. On the other hand, the nature of the domestic market may not be a consideration for a TNC pursuing an integrated production strategy. Where, for example, the TNC's need is for access to low-cost labour that is very widely available, then an individual country's bargaining power will be limited. On the whole, cheap labour is not a scarce resource at a global scale.

On the other hand, 'host countries wield the power to limit the extent of, or even to dismantle, the [T]NC integrated manufacturing and trade networks with more regulations and restrictions on foreign investments and market access'.[33] At the extreme, of course, both institutions – TNCs and governments – possess sanctions which one may exercise over the other. A TNC's ultimate sanction is not to invest in a particular location or to pull out of an existing investment:

> The meta-power that global business interests have in relation to nation-states is based on the *exit option* ... It is the experience ... of actual or threatened *exclusion of states* from the world market that demonstrates and maximizes the power of global business in contrast to isolated individual states.[34]

A nation-state's ultimate sanction against a TNC is to exclude a particular foreign investment or to appropriate an existing investment.

The problem, of course, is that the whole process is *dynamic*. The bargaining relationship changes over time, as the bottom section of Figure 7.7 suggests. In most studies of TNC–state bargaining the conventional wisdom is that of the so-called 'obsolescing bargain' in which once invested, fixed capital becomes 'sunk', a hostage and a source of bargaining strength. The high risk associated with exploration and development diminishes when production begins. Technology, once arcane and proprietary, matures over time and becomes available on the open market. Through development and transfers from FDI the host country gains technical and managerial skills that reduce the value of those possessed by the foreigner.[35]

In this view, after the initial investment has been made, the balance of bargaining power shifts from the TNC to the host country; in other words, it moves to the right in Figure 7.7. But although this may well be the case in natural-resource-based industries (see Chapter 12), it is far less certain that this applies in those sectors in which technological change is frequent and/or where global integration of operations is common. In such circumstances, 'the bargain will obsolesce slowly, if at all, and the relative power of [T]NCs may even increase over time'.[36]

Not surprisingly, there are few detailed studies of TNC–state bargaining processes outside the resource extractive sectors (see the example of the Kazakhstan oil industry in Chapter 12). The participants regard them as being far too sensitive (and possibly embarrassing). A rare example is Edouard Seidler's study of Ford's strategy to enter the Spanish market in the early 1970s.[37] This case demonstrates just how powerful a large TNC can be in persuading a host-country government to change its existing regulations. The Spanish automobile market in the early 1970s was heavily protected. Not only were tariffs on imports very high (81 per cent on cars, 30 per cent on components), but also cars built in Spain had to have 95 per cent local content. In addition, no foreign company could own more than 50 per cent of a company operating in Spain. Such restrictions were very much in conflict with Ford's own preferences for a Spanish operation. Ford's aim was not only to penetrate the local market, but also to create an export platform from which to serve the entire European market. As such, it wanted the lowest possible import tariffs on components and a minimal level of local content so that it could source components from other parts of its transnational network. Ford's preferred policy was also to have complete ownership of its foreign affiliates. On the other hand, the Spanish government was very anxious to build up its automobile industry and especially to increase exports.

Two years of negotiations at the highest political level ensued, a reflection of the 'new' diplomacy in the global economy in which heads of TNCs talk directly to heads of government. And Ford certainly did that across Europe. The eventual agreement showed just how powerful Ford's position was. The fact that virtually all other European governments were trying to entice Ford to locate in their countries gave the company substantial negotiating leverage. On the other hand, Ford regarded a Spanish location as vital to its future European operations, although the Spanish government could not be sure of this. Under the agreement finally signed, virtually all of Ford's demands were met. In particular, for Ford the tariff on imported components was reduced from 30 per cent to 5 per cent; the local content requirement was reduced from 95 per cent to 50 per cent, provided that two-thirds of production was exported (precisely what Ford wanted to do anyway); and Ford was allowed 100 per cent ownership of its Spanish subsidiary. But, of course, the benefits were not all one way. In return, Spain gained a massive boost to its automobile industry, which was subsequently enhanced by the entry of other TNCs, including General Motors. As a result, Spain became one of the world's leading automobile producers (see Chapter 15).

However, states are not always as weak as is often assumed. Or at least in certain circumstances this is the case. A prime example is China and its policy towards automobile firms.[38] The prospect of access to the world's largest and fastest-growing market led many automobile firms to try to enter China. But the Chinese government has complete control over such entry and has adopted a policy of limited access for foreign firms. Here, then, we have the obverse of the usual situation. Whereas in most cases, TNCs play off one country against another to achieve the best deal, in the Chinese case it is the state whose unique bargaining position enables it to play off one TNC against another. Of course, China is something of a special case. But although 'some developing countries have few attractive productive assets or locational advantages for which TNCs will compete with each other, and as a result may not be able to play off one TNC against another ... equally there are many others who can play this game, as they have at least some "bargaining chips"'.[39]

It is important, therefore, not to fall into the usual trap of assuming that the bargaining advantage *always* lies with the TNC and that the state is *always* in a weak position. Neither should we assume that a state's bargaining power remains unchanged. The transitional economies of Eastern Europe illustrate this very clearly.[40] As highly centralized, state-controlled economies (though to differing degrees) before 1989, they were in a position to determine the terms on which TNCs could enter, and operate within, their economies. With political liberalization after 1989 came a headlong rush into neo-liberal, market-driven economic policies. This considerably reduced their relative bargaining power as individual states in relation to TNCs:

> Western multinationals enjoyed more favourable terms of entry in Eastern Europe than in other capital-importing regions during earlier phases of FDI. The small size, economic weakness, and geopolitical vulnerability of the East European states prompted local officials to offer foreign investors unusually generous tax holidays and profits repatriation allowances. The international economic conditions prevailing at the time of Eastern Europe's opening further bolstered MNCs' bargaining position. The global ascent of economic liberalism simultaneously lowered national barriers to FDI and intensified bidding for foreign investment among capital-importing countries,

allowing Western companies to obtain local-content waivers and other concessions from post-communist governments.[41]

However, the increasing political integration of the Eastern European states into the EU, with its particular regulations on the concessions and incentives that can be granted to TNCs, has enabled those states to retrieve some of their bargaining power. Ford's experience in Hungary is a case in point: 'The dramatic developments of 1989 thwarted the company's plan to use Ford Hungária as a trade-balancing instrument, while Hungary's subsequent convergence toward Western trade norms hindered Ford's attempts to extract concessions from post-communist governments.'[42] But this was only possible because, in effect, the EU acted as a 'strong state'. Left alone, the post-communist Eastern European countries would have been relatively powerless. Nevertheless, their degrees of bargaining freedom should not be over-exaggerated. As experience throughout Europe shows, the intensity of competition between states for mobile investment is extremely high. There are far more substitutable locations within Europe for potential investors to retain considerable bargaining strength.

TNCs and states, therefore, are continuously engaged in intricately choreographed negotiating and bargaining processes. On the one hand, TNCs attempt to take advantage of national differences in regulatory regimes (such as taxation or performance requirements, like local content). On the other hand, states strive to minimize such 'regulatory arbitrage' and to entice mobile investment through competitive bidding against other states. The situation is especially complex because, while states are essentially territorially fixed and clearly bounded geographically, a TNC's 'territory' is more fluid and flexible.[43] Transnational production networks slice through national boundaries (although not necessarily as smoothly as some would claim). In the process parts of different national spaces become incorporated into transnational production networks (and vice versa).

Such territorial asymmetry translates into complex bargaining processes in which, contrary to much conventional wisdom, there is no unambiguous and totally predictable outcome. TNCs do not always possess the power to get their own way, as some writers continue to assert. In the complex relationships between TNCs and states – as well as with other institutions – the outcome of a specific bargaining process is highly contingent. States still have significant power vis-à-vis TNCs, for example to control access to their territories and to define rules of operation. In collaboration with other states, that power is increased (the EU is an example of this). So, the claim that states are universally powerless in the face of the supposedly unstoppable juggernaut of the 'global corporation' is nonsense; the question is an empirical one.

NOTES

1   Gordon (1988: 61).
2   Pitelis (1991).
3   Gilpin (1987: 242). See also Lynn (2005).
4   Stopford and Strange (1991: 233).
5   See Reich (1989).
6   Doz (1986a) provides an extensive discussion of these issues.
7   Picciotto (1991: 43, 46).
8   Yoffie and Milner (1989).
9   Doz (1986a: 231–4).
10 See Levy and Prakash (2003).
11 Nixson (1988: 379).
12 Nixson (1988: 380).
13 *Financial Times* (8 September 2008).
14 *Financial Times* (23 June 2009).
15 *Financial Times* (2 December 2010).
16 UNCTAD (2005: 22–3).
17 Moran (2011: 89).
18 Vernon (1998: 40).
19 *Financial Times* (3 February 2005).
20 Cited in the *Financial Times* (21 October 2008).
21 *Financial Times* (6 May 2009), *Guardian* (16 June 2009).
22 *Financial Times* (15 December 2012).
23 Griffiths (2012).
24 US Senate Committee on Homeland Security and Governmental Affairs, Permanent
    Subcommittee on Investigations (21 May 2013). See also Mazzucato (2013: chapter 8).
25 US Senate Committee on Homeland Security and Governmental Affairs, Permanent
    Subcommittee on Investigations (21 May 2013: 28).
26 US Senate Committee on Homeland Security and Governmental Affairs, Permanent
    Subcommittee on Investigations (21 May 2013: 25–6).
27 US Senate Committee on Homeland Security and Governmental Affairs, Permanent
    Subcommittee on Investigations (21 May 2013: 22–3).
28 US Senate Committee on Homeland Security and Governmental Affairs, Permanent
    Subcommittee on Investigations (21 May 2013: 23).
29 US Senate Committee on Homeland Security and Governmental Affairs, Permanent
    Subcommittee on Investigations Press release (20 May 2013).
30 *Financial Times* (14 January 2013).
31 Liu and Dicken (2006).
32 UNCTAD (2011: 129).
33 Doz (1986b: 39).
34 Beck (2005: 53).
35 Kobrin (1987: 611–12).
36 Kobrin (1987: 636).
37 Seidler (1976).

38   Chang (1998b), Liu and Dicken (2006).
39   Chang (1998b: 234).
40   Bartlett and Seleny (1998).
41   Bartlett and Seleny (1998: 320).
42   Bartlett and Seleny (1998: 328).
43   Dicken and Malmberg (2001).

Want to know more about this chapter? Visit the companion website at **www.guilford.com/dickenGS7** for free access to author videos, suggested reading and practice questions to further enhance your study.

Eight

'CAPTURING VALUE' WITHIN GLOBAL PRODUCTION NETWORKS

PLACING PLACES IN GPNs

GPNs are grounded in specific places; organizational networks connect into geographical networks:

- GPNs integrate *firms* (and parts of firms) into structures which blur traditional organizational boundaries. They do this through both direct ownership and a diversity of non-equity relationships, particularly with supplier firms (see Chapter 5, Figure 5.23).[1]

- In so doing, GPNs also integrate *places* (national and local economies) in ways that have enormous implications for their economic development. It is this *place dimension* that provides the specific focus of this chapter. The questions posed are those relating to the ways in which a place's insertion (or non-insertion) into GPNs affects its developmental prospects.

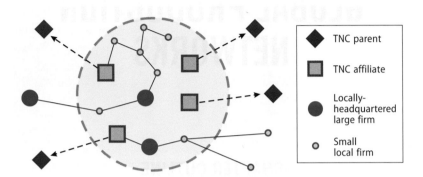

Figure 8.1   **A place's 'organizational ecology'**

We can think of places, at whatever geographical scale, as having an *organizational ecology* (Figure 8.1): a mix of firms and parts of firms, large and small, old and new, foreign and domestically owned, connected together through geographically extensive production circuits and networks. The branches and affiliates of TNCs are obviously part of a specific corporate structure and are constrained in their autonomy by parent company policy. The extent to which they are functionally connected into the local economy is enormously variable. But even the apparently 'independent' firms in a local economy may, in fact, be less independent than they appear at first sight. Many are deeply integrated into the multi-tiered supply networks of larger firms, whose decision-making functions are very distant. Other local firms may be linked together through strategic alliances and non-equity modes or they may be a part of the flexible business networks coordinated by key 'broker' firms.

In this context, four highly interconnected sets of relationships are especially important:

- *intra-firm relationships*: between different parts of a corporate network, as each part strives to maintain or to enhance its position vis-à-vis other parts of the organization;
- *inter-firm relationships*: between firms belonging to separate, but overlapping, networks as part of customer–supplier transactions and other inter-firm interactions;

- *firm–place relationships*: as firms attempt to extract the maximum benefits from the communities in which they are embedded and as communities attempt to derive the maximum benefits from the firms' local operations;
- *place–place relationships*: between places, as each community attempts to capture and retain the investments (and especially the jobs) of the component parts of GPNs.

Each of these sets of relationships is embedded within and across *national/state* political and regulatory systems that help to determine the parameters within which firms and places interact.

The key issue addressed in this chapter, therefore, is the extent to which a place's involvement in GPNs creates net benefits (or net costs) for its inhabitants. There is a good deal of disagreement about this, as there is about the more specific issue of the impact of TNCs on local and national economies. In that respect, virtually every aspect of TNC operations – economic, political and cultural – has been judged in diametrically opposed ways, depending upon the ideological viewpoint adopted. Thus, TNCs are seen:

- either to expand national or local economies or to exploit them;
- either to act as a dynamic force in economic development or to act as a distorting influence;
- either to create jobs or to destroy them;
- either to spread new technology or to pre-empt its wider use.

Similar polarization of opinion applies to the impact of GPNs. From the viewpoint of particular places, then, are GPNs a 'good' thing or a 'bad' thing?

> [Global production networks] can be seen as opportunity structures for organizational learning on the part of developing countries. Not only can local firms access international markets via such [networks], but the implication is that firms can actively seek to *change* the way that they are linked to global [networks] in order to increase the benefits they derive from participating in them – a process of repositioning that is called upgrading ... [On the other hand] particular strategies to increase the competitiveness of suppliers in global [networks] may look like upgrading from the vantage point of the firm but in fact constitute a form of downgrading for the workers involved.[2]

CREATING, ENHANCING AND CAPTURING VALUE IN GPNs

Each stage in a production circuit (Figure 3.3), each node in a global production network, *creates value* through the combined application of labour skills, process and product technologies, and the organizational expertise involved in coordinating complex production and logistical processes and in marketing and distribution. In this sense, value is a *surplus* over and above the costs involved in performing the transformations and transactions at that particular stage or node. In the economists' terminology, it would be called *economic rent*.[3] By definition, the process is dynamic: the aim is continuously to *enhance value* – to increase profits and/or to reduce competition – through a whole variety of means: product and process innovation, improved labour productivity, more efficient logistical systems, and so on.

When we turn to *value capture* – who (or where) gets what – the situation is far more complicated. Analyses of the value chains for the production of the Apple iPod[4] and the iPhone[5] show just how complicated the capture of value can be and also the extent to which the highest value capture tends to be at the high end of the value chain (design, brand ownership and control) while assembly is far less significant in the total value added. Geographically, in the case of the iPod, this means that the USA captures most of the value even though all iPods are actually manufactured in China (in Taiwanese-controlled factories) and the hard disk drive (the most expensive component) is manufactured by the Japanese firm Toshiba but mostly in factories located in China and the Philippines.

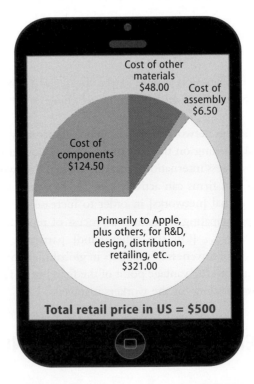

Figure 8.2   The distribution of value capture in the production of the iPhone

Source: based on UNCTAD, 2011: Box IV

Figure 8.2 shows this geographically uneven value capture for the iPhone:

> It is estimated that only $6.50 of the $179 production cost (retail price, $500 in the US market) is captured by Foxconn (Taiwan Province of China), the company's ... partner in China ... The share captured by domestic Chinese companies is even less, limited to packaging and local services. This is, in part, because iPhones are assembled from components made mostly in other countries, such as the United States, Japan, Germany and the Republic of Korea. The remaining $321 of the $500 retail price is accounted for by Apple and other companies' returns to R&D, design, distribution and retailing etc.[6]

However, there is evidence that some Chinese companies are beginning to buck that trend:

> Chinese companies are increasingly designing sophisticated components for Apple's iPhone and iPads instead of just supplying low-cost labour for assembling the high-tech devices ... [for example] The number of Chinese companies supplying Apple with components such as batteries has doubled from eight in 2011 to 16 this year [2013].[7]

So, the key questions addressed in this chapter are:

- Who captures the value created within production networks?
- Who benefits from value creation and enhancement?

These questions raise issues way beyond the narrow confines of firm competitiveness and profitability to encompass all the different *stakeholders* involved in GPNs in different geographical locations. As we saw in the discussion of transfer pricing and taxation in Chapter 7, *where* taxes are paid may bear little relationship to the *actual geography* of production, distribution and sales. The key issue is the *configuration of power* within GPNs which, as we have seen, tends to be highly asymmetrical and subject to complex bargaining processes. One dimension of this is the relationship between capital and labour. In general over the past few decades, there has been a pronounced shift in which capital has gained massively at the expense of labour, not least because of the increased *financialization* of all parts of the economy (see Chapter 3). This is shown, for example, in the increased unevenness in the distribution of incomes in many developed economies (see Chapter 10). Another dimension is the relationship between lead firms and their multilayered tiers of suppliers; the extent to which lead firms are able to squeeze their first-tier suppliers who, in turn, squeeze their suppliers, and so on through the entire production network. This is apparent in several of the cases discussed in Part Four.

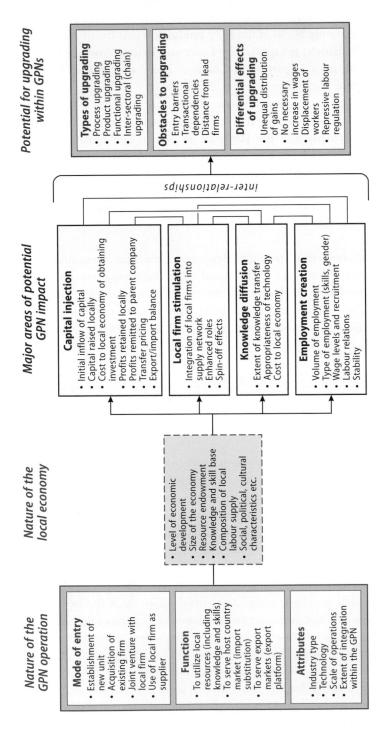

Figure 8.3 Major dimensions of potential GPN impact on local economies

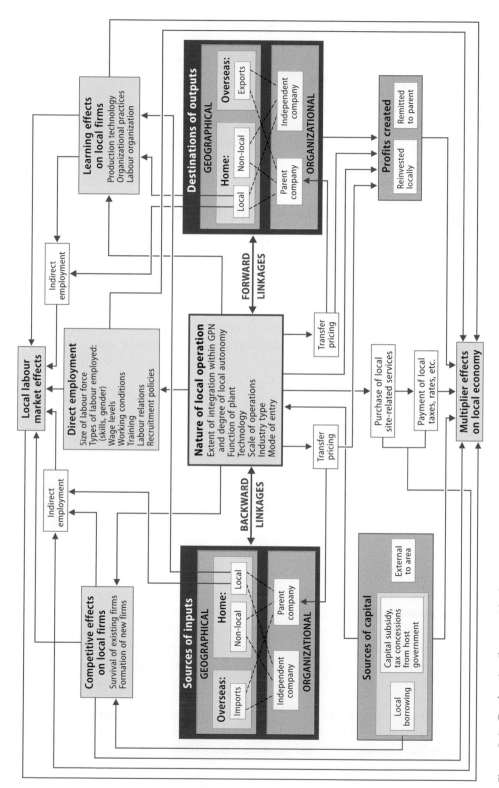

Figure 8.4 Tracing the direct and indirect connections of a GPN in a local economy

In this chapter, however, we are concerned with how value within GPNs is created, enhanced and captured in the *places* – the national and local economies – in which the component elements are located. In other words, the focus is developmental at the 'community' level:

- To what extent is the value created within GPNs captured for the benefit of the places in which the activities occur?
- To what extent does participation in GPNs offer the potential to *upgrade* a place's economic well-being?

UPGRADING (OR DOWNGRADING) OF LOCAL ECONOMIES WITHIN GPNs

The potential effects of GPNs on local economies involve a whole range of complex direct and indirect interactions, as Figures 8.3 and 8.4 show. These effects are contingent upon the relationships between the nature of the GPN operations themselves and the nature and characteristics of the local economy. In the following sections we focus on four especially important dimensions of a place's involvement in a GPN: capital injection, local firm stimulus, knowledge diffusion and local employment creation.

Injecting capital?

The inflow of capital is the most obvious impact of foreign investment, especially for those countries suffering from capital shortage. TNCs have certainly been responsible for injecting capital into host economies, both developed and developing. But not all new overseas ventures undertaken by TNCs involve the actual transfer of capital into the host economy. One estimate for the 1990s was that around 50 per cent of US foreign direct 'investment' was actually raised on host-country capital markets and not imported.[8] Thus, local firms may be bought with local money. Local firms may even be squeezed out of local capital markets by the perceived greater attractiveness of TNCs as an outlet for local savings.

Even where capital inflow does occur, there will, eventually, be a reverse flow as the local operation remits earnings and profits back to its parent company (see the section on transfer pricing in Chapter 7). This outflow may, in time, exceed the inflow. An analysis of the impact of FDI on the Mexican economy concluded that

> when profit remittances are deducted from gross FDI flows, the economic impact of the resulting 'net' FDI capital per worker variable is reduced in magnitude and statistical significance.[9]

Any net financial gain to the host country also depends on the trading practices of the TNC. A host economy's balance of payments will be improved to the extent that the local plant exports its output and reduced by its propensity to import production or service inputs. A vital issue, therefore, is the extent to which financial 'leakage' occurs from host economies through the channel of the TNC. This raises the question of the ability of host-country governments to obtain a 'fair' tax yield from foreign-controlled operations whose parent companies are capable of manipulating the terms of their intra-corporate transactions through transfer pricing and tax avoidance (see Chapter 7).

Stimulating local firms?

The extent to which local firms may be stimulated by involvement in a GPN depends upon the roles such firms perform and upon whether or not TNCs create positive linkages within the local economy, either directly or indirectly:

- Which level in the supply network do local firms occupy?
- Are they first-, second- or lower-tier suppliers?
- What kinds of operations do they perform?
- What is the skill and technology level involved?
- If the local operation is a subsidiary of a TNC, what kinds of subsidiary responsibilities does it have?

Inter-firm linkages are the most important channels through which technologies are transmitted. By placing orders with local suppliers for materials or components that must meet stringent specifications, technical expertise is raised. The experience gained in new technologies by local firms enables them to compete more effectively in broader markets, provided, of course, that they are not tied exclusively to a specific customer. The sourcing of materials locally may lead to the emergence of new domestic firms to meet the demand created, thus increasing the pool of local entrepreneurs. The expanded activities of supplying firms, and of ancillary firms involved in such activities as transportation and distribution, will result in the creation of additional employment. But such beneficial spin-off effects will occur *only if* the foreign affiliates of TNCs *do* become linked to local firms. Where TNCs do not create such linkages they remain essentially foreign enclaves within a host economy, contributing little other than some direct, often low-level, jobs.

As far as local linkages are concerned, the most significant are *backward* or *supply* linkages (Figure 8.4). Here, the crucial issue is the extent to which TNCs either import materials and components or procure them from local suppliers. The actual incidence of local linkage formation by foreign-controlled plants depends upon three major influences:

- *The particular strategy followed by the TNC and the role played by the local operation in that strategy.* TNCs that are strongly vertically integrated globally are less likely to develop local supply linkages than firms with a lower degree of corporate integration. But even where vertical integration is low the existence of strong links with independent suppliers in the TNC's home country or elsewhere in the firm's GPN may inhibit the development of local linkages in the host economy. Familiarity with existing supply relationships may well discourage the development of new ones, particularly where the latter are perceived to be potentially less reliable or of lower quality. Foreign plants that serve the host market are more likely to develop local supply linkages than export platform plants.

- *The characteristics of the local economy.* In general, we would expect to find denser and more extensive networks of linkages between TNCs and domestic enterprises in developed, compared with developing, economies. Within developing countries such linkages are likely to be greatest in the larger and more industrialized countries than in others. In many developing countries, the existing supplier base is simply not sufficiently developed to meet TNC criteria; that is, the *absorptive capacity* is too low. However, host-country governments can play an important role in stimulating local linkages, either by implementing policies to upgrade local suppliers or through local content policies. But much depends on the relative strength of the host country's bargaining power vis-à-vis the TNC. Again, it tends to be in the larger and the more industrialized developing countries that local content policies have the greatest impact, and also in those TNC activities serving the local market. Indeed, it could be that the export-oriented industrialization strategies of developing countries actually inhibit the development of local supply linkages.

- *Time.* Local supply capabilities do not develop over night. Particularly in view of the closer relationships between firms and their suppliers (see Chapter 5) it should not be expected that a foreign plant, newly established in a particular host economy, would immediately develop local supplier linkages. Not only do appropriate suppliers have to be identified, but also it takes time for supplier firms to 'tune-in' to a new customer's needs and to develop sufficient expertise to meet the standards required.

More important than the number of local linkages is their *quality* and the degree to which they involve a beneficial transfer of technology (either production or organizational) to supplier firms. A common criticism is that many TNCs tend to procure only 'low-level' inputs from local sources. This may be because of deliberate company policy to keep to established suppliers of higher-level inputs or because such inputs are simply not available locally (or are perceived not to be so). Where development of higher-level supply linkages occurs, there does seem to be a positive effect on supplier firms. Figure 8.5 summarizes the differences between 'dependent' and 'developmental' linkages. Clearly, from a local economy's

Attribute	Dependent structure	Developmental structure
Form of local linkages	Unequal trading relationships. Conventional subcontracting. Emphasis on cost-saving.	Collaborative, mutual learning. Basis in technology and trust. Emphasis on added value.
Duration and nature of local linkages	Short-term contracts.	Long-term partnerships.
Degree of local embeddedness of inward investors	Weakly embedded. Branch plants restricted to final assembly operations.	Deeply embedded. High level of investment in decentralized, multi-functional operations.
Benefits to local firms	Markets for local firms to make standard, low-technology components. Subcontracting restricts independent growth.	Markets for local firms to develop and produce their own products. Transfer of technology and expertise from inward investor strengthens local firms.
Prospects for the local economy	Vulnerable to external forces and 'distant' corporate decision-making.	Self-sustaining growth through cumulative expansion of linked firms.
Quality of jobs created	Predominantly low-skilled, low-paid. May be high level of temporary and casual employment.	Diverse, including high-skilled, high-income employment.

Figure 8.5 **Dependent and developmental linkage structures**

Source: based on Turok, 1993: Table 1

perspective, the aim must be to achieve a linkage structure that is developmental. In this respect, much will depend upon the local economy's bargaining power (see Chapter 7).

Empirical evidence of local linkage formation by TNCs presents a very uneven picture.[10] Studies within smaller developing countries, particularly those with a short history of industrial development, tell a fairly uniform story of shallow and poorly developed supply linkages between local firms and foreign-controlled plants. A common observation is that foreign plants located in export processing zones (EPZs) are particularly unlikely to develop supplier linkages with the wider economy. In the case of the Mexican *maquiladora* plants, for example, less than 5 per cent of the inputs used are sourced from within Mexico. Additionally, most of those inputs are low-value and low-technology products whose production does little to upgrade the local technological and skill base. However, this may be changing:

> There is a difference in impact between traditional first generation maquiladora firms on the one hand and second and third generation maquiladora firms on the other … younger generation maquiladora firms may start to generate a larger positive impact on the Mexican economy, compared to the notoriously small impact of first generation maquiladora firms.[11]

In some cases, there may be a considerable amount of local sourcing but with relatively little involvement of genuinely local firms. For example, although the new foreign manufacturing plants established in the Johor region of southern Malaysia 'are sourcing a large part of their inputs in Johor ... the regional effect is confined to foreign, mainly Japanese and Singaporean, suppliers. As a result, the linkages of the new manufacturing plants are only in part beneficial to the local economy.'[12] Overall, Japanese firms in the Malaysian electronics industry tend 'to rely more heavily on relocated suppliers from their home country, supporting the general belief about the effect of Japanese business ties'.[13] This latter point is confirmed by a study of 227 Japanese electronics firms operating in 24 countries,[14] which found that although local procurement was widespread, such increase in local content did not necessarily involve local suppliers.

The Japanese case suggests that nationality of ownership may be an important variable in helping to determine the degree and kinds of local linkage. A recent study of Taiwanese TNCs in different countries, for example, showed much higher levels of local procurement than the average:

> The local sourcing ratio, defined as the share of intermediate inputs procured locally, is about 32% for the Taiwanese affiliates as a whole, of which more than half (54%) goes to local firms ... compared with the average reported local sourcing ratio that ranges between 10% and 20% in most studies.[15]

The same research showed that not only the particular nature of Taiwanese production networks but also country-specific factors influence the creation of local linkages:

> The local linkage effects in China have something to do with culture and ethnic ties, and institutional risks. Similar culture and ethnic links provide the level of trust needed ... which lowers the cost of searching, learning, adjustment, and adaptation, and therefore makes local sourcing more appealing. Risks inherent in local institutions in China help facilitate the formation of the network supply chain among Taiwanese affiliates. These effects are reinforced by the fact that Taiwanese firms face lower costs in switching their supplies from home firms to those in China, as their relationship with home suppliers often is noncommittal. This stands in stark contrast to Japanese firms, which tend to have relatively small local linkages because they face higher costs of switching from long-standing suppliers (e.g. within keiretsu) to those in host countries.[16]

Nevertheless, involvement in a GPN may well create opportunities for the enhancement of local businesses. Existing firms may receive a boost to their fortunes or new firms may be created in response to the stimulus of demand for materials or components The formation of new enterprises may be stimulated through the 'spin-off' of managerial staff setting up their own businesses on the basis of the experience and skills gained in participation in a GPN. For example, 'one third [of MNCs in Mexico] had cases of employees leaving the company to create their own business … the overall spinoff from TNCs amounts to 3,667 new companies, of which 38.5% became suppliers of their former MNC employer'.[17]

Diffusing knowledge?

> GPNs in their operations … disseminate important knowledge to local suppliers in low-cost locations, which could catalyze local capability formation.[18]

> 'Technology transfer' in a horizontal direction from TNCs is somewhat of an oxymoron. Manufacturing TNCs try assiduously to prevent the leakage of technology, production techniques, and trained personnel to other firms that might become rivals. Luckily – from a developmental point of view – they are not always successful, as workers and managers carry on-the-job experience around the industry.[19]

Simply by locating operations outside its home country a TNC engages in the geographical transfer of knowledge. Insofar as a foreign affiliate employs local labour, there will be a degree of knowledge transfer to elements of the local population through training in specific skills and techniques. But the mere existence of a particular technology within a foreign-controlled operation does not guarantee that its benefits will be widely diffused through a host economy. The critical factor here is the extent to which the technology is made available to potential users outside the firm either directly, through linkages with indigenous firms, or indirectly via 'demonstration effects'.

In fact, the very nature of the TNC inhibits the spread of its proprietary technologies beyond its own organizational boundaries. Such technologies are not lightly handed over to other firms. Control over their use is jealously guarded: the terms under which technologies are transferred are dictated primarily by the TNC itself in the light of its own overall interests. TNCs tend to transfer the results of innovation but not the innovative capabilities – the 'know-how' rather than the 'know-why'. A major tendency, as we saw in Chapter 5, is for TNCs to locate most of their technology-creating activities either in their home country or in the more advanced industrialized, and some of the more advanced newly industrializing, countries. So far, relatively little R&D, other than lower-level support laboratories, has been relocated to developing countries. In some cases this is a direct result of host-government pressure on TNCs to establish R&D facilities in return for entry. Such leverage is greatest where the TNC wishes to establish a branch plant to serve the host-country market itself.

The evidence for TNCs transferring technologies beyond a fairly basic level to developing countries is very mixed. A study of the electronics industry in Malaysia, the Philippines and Thailand was fairly positive:

> Their [TNCs'] participation has at least produced latent technological capabilities for absorption by local firms ... foreign firms' participation and the high levels of ... [human resource and process technology] ... capabilities generated have at least transformed the local environment to facilitate export manufacturing in these countries involving a high-tech industry.[20]

The Ford auto complex in Hermosillo provides another example of the potentially positive knowledge and technology spin-offs:

> As some employees depart from the leading company, their new technical skills, their first hand knowledge on how the supplier relations work, and the organizational capabilities developed to provide the levels of efficiency, quality, and lead times required to do business with Ford, become invaluable assets. The tendency towards regionalization of supplier networks, and the need for increased geographical proximity of critical operations also explains the openness of Ford and its global suppliers to find and help establishing local suppliers, especially if these firms can meet the rigorous standards imposed by MNCs.[21]

On the other hand, the conclusions of a study of two Caribbean countries (Trinidad and Tobago and Costa Rica) were more pessimistic:

> Despite the attractiveness of both countries to foreign investors, foreign investment has made only a minimal contribution to strengthening local innovation systems in these countries.[22]

A critical issue, however, is the ability of local firms to actually *absorb* new knowledge and technologies.

> Knowledge transfer ... is not automatic. It requires a significant level of absorptive capacity on the part of local suppliers and a complex process to internalize disseminated knowledge ... Of course, knowledge transfer is not a sufficient condition for effective knowledge diffusion. Diffusion is completed only when transferred knowledge is internalized and translated into the capability of the local suppliers. Much depends on the types of knowledge involved and the mechanisms that [lead firms] use to disseminate different types of knowledge.[23]

In Chapter 4 we distinguished between two types of knowledge: *codified (or explicit) knowledge*, the kinds of knowledge that can be expressed formally in documents, blueprints, software, hardware, etc.; and *tacit knowledge*, the deeply personalized knowledge possessed by individuals that is virtually impossible to make explicit and to communicate to others. Codified knowledge can be transmitted relatively easily across distance. Tacit knowledge, on the other hand, has a very steep 'distance-decay' curve. It is much more 'sticky'. Both types of knowledge are essential ingredients in the knowledge diffusion process within GPNs, whether that occurs within the organizational boundaries of a TNC's internal network or across organizational boundaries to other firms within the GPN. However,

> local suppliers can only effectively absorb knowledge disseminated by global network flagships if they have developed their own capabilities. Knowledge internalization and capability building require individual and organizational learning.[24]

Creating good jobs?

For most ordinary people, as well as for many governments, the most important issue is the effect of GPNs on local jobs:

- Do they create new jobs?
- What kinds of jobs are they?
- Do local firms embedded within GPNs pay higher or lower wages than other, non-GPN firms?
- Do GPN firms operate an acceptable system of labour relations and working conditions?

In other words, do GPNs create a 'high-road' job scenario, in which the emphasis is on quality, skill, good labour conditions, or a 'low-road' scenario, characterized by low wages, low skills, job insecurity and poor labour conditions?[25]

Number of jobs

The number of jobs created (or displaced) by a GPN operation in a local economy consists of both those created in the operation itself and those created or displaced elsewhere in the local economy (Figure 8.4).

The number of *direct jobs* created in a particular operation depends upon two factors:

- the *scale* of its activities;
- the *technological* nature of the operation, particularly on whether it is capital intensive or labour intensive.

The number of *indirect* jobs created also depends upon two major factors:

- the extent of *local linkages* forged with local firms;
- the *amount of income generated* by the TNC and *retained* within the local economy. In particular, the wages and salaries of employees and of those in linked firms will, if spent on locally produced goods and services, increase employment elsewhere in the domestic economy (Figure 8.4).

Against the number of local jobs *created* in GPNs we need to set the number of jobs *displaced* by any possible adverse effects on other local enterprises. Hence, the overall employment effect depends upon the balance between job-creating and job-displacing forces. The *net* employment contribution of a GPN to a local economy, or the net jobs (NJ), can therefore be expressed as:

$$NJ = DJ + IJ - JD$$

where DJ is the number of direct jobs created locally in the GPN, IJ is the number of indirect local jobs in firms linked to the GPN, and JD is the number of jobs displaced in other local firms.

Quality of jobs

The number of jobs created by GPNs in local economies is only part of the story. What kind of jobs are they? Do they provide employment opportunities that are appropriate for the skills and needs of the local labour force? The answer to these questions depends very much on the attributes of the GPN operation (see Figure 8.4). In particular, where the operation 'fits' into the GPN's overall structure and how much decision-making autonomy it has are key factors. In general, the fact that TNCs tend to concentrate their higher-order decision-making functions and their R&D facilities in the developed economies produces a major geographical bias in the pattern of types of employment at the global scale.

In developing countries, the overwhelming majority of jobs in GPN plants are *production* jobs. In EPZs, low-level production jobs, especially for young females, are the norm, although this partly reflects the types of industry that dominate in EPZs. Overall, the proportion of higher-skilled workers employed within GPNs in developing countries has tended to increase over time, as has the proportion of local professional and managerial staff. Such changes have progressed furthest in the more advanced industrializing countries of Asia. For example, the shift of IT activities to India involves more than low-level call centre jobs:

> Anyone who assumes J. P. Morgan will simply be doing low-level 'back office' tasks in the country — a bit of data entry and paper-shuffling — would be flat wrong. One task for the new recruits is to settle complex structured-finance and derivative deals, what one insider calls 'some of the most sophisticated transactions in the world'.[26]

Even so, the GPN labour force in developing countries remains concentrated in low-skill production and assembly occupations. The experience of individual developing countries varies in the extent of TNC-induced labour upgrading, as a study of the TV industry in East Asia shows.[27] In each case, the extent of human capital formation in the industry was very limited prior to the mid-1990s:

- In Malaysia, specialized staff were still foreign but there was significant training by leading firms and for their partners in their regional production networks. There was evidence of rising skill levels and increasing numbers of specialized technical and managerial staff.
- In Mexico, the first signs of upgrading were apparent as a result of significant training efforts and linking with local education institutions, rising labour skill levels, and increasing numbers of specialized technical and managerial staff.
- In Thailand, the skill levels of the labour force were low but rising with increased emphasis on labour training. But there was not much evidence of an increasing involvement of more highly educated specialist staff.

Wages and salaries

Insofar as TNCs take advantage of geographical differences in wage rates between countries, they do, in effect, 'exploit' certain groups of workers. The exploitation of cheap labour in developing countries at the expense of workers in developed countries is one of the major charges levelled at the TNC by labour unions in Western countries. The general response of TNCs to such allegations is that they do not have complete control over what goes on in independent factories, an issue we will return to later in this chapter.

However, as far as their *directly owned affiliates* are concerned, the general consensus is that TNCs generally pay either at or above the 'going rate' in the host economy. Figure 8.6 shows two aspects of the wage comparison. First, the relative height of the columns shows that TNCs pay very much more to workers in high-income countries than to those in middle- and low-income countries. This differential reflects a number of factors, including the composition of economic activity, educational and skill levels, cost of living, and so on. Second, although TNCs certainly pay higher wages overall than domestic firms in the same country group (a ratio of 1.5), the pattern varies between country groups: 1.4 in high-income countries, 1.8 in middle-income countries and 2.0 in low-income countries.

TNCs that do pay above the local rate may, as a consequence, 'cream off' workers from local firms and possibly threaten their survival, rather than recruiting from the ranks of the unemployed. Another aspect of recruitment, at least in some industries, is the extent to which TNCs recruit particular types of workers to keep labour costs low. In the textiles, garments and electronics industries, for example, there is a very strong tendency to prefer females to males in assembly processes and, in some cases, to employ members of minority groups as a means of holding down wage costs and for ease of dismissal. But such practices appear to be specific to particular industries and should not necessarily be regarded as universally applicable to all TNCs in all industries.

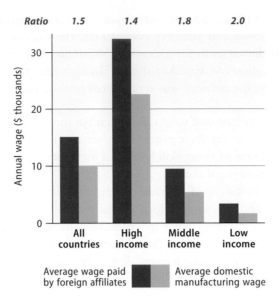

Figure 8.6 **Differences in average wages paid by foreign affiliates of TNCs and domestic firms**

Source: based on Crook, 2001: p. 15

Labour relations and working conditions

In many developing countries labour is either weakly organized or labour unions are strictly controlled (or even banned) by the state. Even in developed economies some major TNCs simply do not recognize labour unions in their operations, while state deregulation of labour markets has become widespread (see Chapter 6). But most TNCs, however reluctantly, do accept labour unions where national or local circumstances make this difficult to avoid. Whether labour unions are involved or not, the question of the nature of labour relations within TNCs focuses on whether they are 'good' or 'bad', that is harmonious or discordant. Some studies suggest that TNCs tend to have better labour relations in their own plants than domestic firms; others point to a higher incidence of strikes and internal disputes in TNCs. But it is often difficult to separate out the 'transnational' element. In the case of strikes, for example, it may be plant or firm size that is the most important influence rather than nationality of ownership.

One of the most acute concerns of organized labour is that decision making within TNCs is too remote: that decisions affecting work practices and work conditions, pay and other labour issues are made in some far-distant corporate headquarters which has little understanding or even awareness of local circumstances. Some labour relations decisions are far more centralized than others, either being made at corporate headquarters or requiring its approval. However, there is considerable variation between TNCs in their degree of headquarters' involvement in labour relations.

The dispersed nature of TNC operations and the tendency towards remoteness in decision making have made it very difficult for labour unions to organize effectively to counter such issues as plant closure or retrenchment. Two developments, although relatively limited so far, are significant.[28] One is the initiation by global union federations (such as the International Confederation of Free Trade Unions – ICFTU) of networks of workers within specific TNCs in an attempt to move industrial relations issues to the global level. The second development has occurred within the EU:

> As part of the social protocol of the 1993 Maastricht Treaty, at least 15 million employees in some 1500 [TNCs] operating in Europe now have rights to information and consultation on all matters that affect more than one member state ... Each company that employs more than 1000 people, of whom at least 150 are located in two (or more) member states, has to meet the representation, transportation, accommodation, and translation costs of bringing employee representatives from across the European Union on an annual basis ... they provide a new opportunity for workplace representatives to meet their counterparts from every division of their companies' operations in Europe.[29]

Despite such developments, labour unions remain primarily contained within national state boundaries while TNCs are not. This structural difference creates inevitable tensions.

A key issue is the kind of employment contract involved. It is increasingly common for firms to differentiate between *core workers* (employed on secure contracts and with good conditions of employment) and *non-core workers* (with less secure contracts and fewer fringe benefits and who can be more easily dismissed if the firm wishes to scale down its labour force). Labour force flexibility is a key element in GPNs. Non-core workers are frequently hired through employment and temporary staffing agencies.[30]

Working conditions in the directly owned affiliates of TNCs are generally high standard – and often better than those in locally owned plants. But the situation in supplier firms within GPNs, especially lower-tier suppliers, is far more problematical. The longer the supply chain, the less control a lead firm has over what happens in the more remote supplier firms ('remote' in both an organizational and a geographical sense). That there are serious problems surrounding working conditions in supplier firms with GPNs is beyond dispute in such industries as consumer electronics, garments (Chapter 14), agro-foods (Chapter 13) and others where the pressure on labour costs is especially intense.

For example, the world's largest electronics contract manufacturer, Foxconn, has been embroiled in a whole series of workers' rights disputes at its Chinese factories. An especially egregious case is the garment industry of Dhaka in Bangladesh where, in late 2012, 117 workers were killed at a fire in a garment factory. Less than six months later, more than a thousand workers were killed when a building housing five garment firms collapsed. In both of these tragedies, the Bangladeshi firms were producing garments for leading Western brands and retailers. As we will see in Chapter 11, many TNCs, in the context of corporate social responsibility (CSR) programmes, now operate various codes of conduct in an attempt to respond to criticisms that they condone, and take advantage of, poor working conditions in developing countries.

The two key aspects of working conditions in GPNs are:[31]

- *measurable standards* including: 'wages, physical wellbeing (e.g. health and safety, working environment, and working hours) and employment security (e.g. type of contract, social protection)';
- *enabling rights* including: 'freedom of association and collective bargaining, the right to freely choose employment, non-discrimination, and voice … Enabling rights are the … manifestation of more balanced power relations between workers and management in the context of sound industrial relations. Their enforcement is therefore also tightly dependent on institutions and actors beyond the factory floor.'

The importance of being there

> One main challenge is to use globalization as a lever for local development, by helping local firms and workers take advantage of the opportunities opened up by the global economy … the development of transnational networks of economic activities generates unprecedented possibilities for accessing new markets and resources, acquiring new skills and capabilities and developing international competitive advantage.[32]

Indeed, the fact that GPNs have become the predominant mode within which production is organized means that it is extremely difficult for local firms/economies to prosper outside them. *Being there* – as an insider – is virtually a prerequisite for development. However, whether or not a local firm is able to gain entry into a particular GPN depends on the extent to which a GPN is actually accessible:

> The degree of network openness varies according to industry-specific characteristics and the features of the business systems within which network firms are embedded. Buyer-driven networks in garments and footwear tend to be more open than producer-driven networks in, say, automobiles, mainly as a result of lower entry barriers in the low-skilled, labour-intensive production activities … [In addition] lead firms in the same industry might exhibit different networking behaviours depending on the idiosyncrasies of their national environments … The most successful production networks, however, are neither closed nor open but

'permeable' ... They are characterized by an evolving tiered structure in which a first-tier of selected, stable partners is surrounded by a more mobile row of second-tier suppliers.[33]

But just being there is not enough

Gaining access to a GPN may be a necessary step in the short run, but in the long run it is not sufficient. For sustainable developmental benefits to occur it is necessary for a local firm to *upgrade* its performance – to achieve a 'better' position within its GPN. *Economic upgrading* can take a number of forms (Figure 8.3):[34]

- *Process upgrading*: the more efficient transformation of inputs into outputs through improved technology and/or better organization of the production process.
- *Product upgrading*: diversification into more sophisticated, higher-value product lines.
- *Functional upgrading*: taking on new functions; that is, moving up the skill ladder.
- *Inter-sectoral (chain) upgrading*: 'shifting to a more technologically advanced production chain – involves moving into new industries or product markets'.[35]

An example of economic upgrading involves East Asian clothing firms (see Chapter 14). This involves moving progressively from the simple assembly of imported inputs, through increased local production and sourcing, to the design of products sold under a buyer firm's label and, finally, to own-brand production.[36]

However, such a progression is by no means inevitable. There are a number of *obstacles* to local industrial upgrading within GPNs (Figure 8.3):[37]

- 'Local firms are likely to face substantial entry barriers into the most profitable parts of value chains, nowadays increasingly associated with strategic services such as marketing and R&D. As global networks evolve towards greater functional integration, entry barriers also rise in network positions that previously provided a port of entry into more profitable activities, such as first-tier supplying.'
- 'Local supply firms face the difficulty of overcoming transactional dependency *vis-à-vis* lead firms ... the learning process by which suppliers can evolve towards more complex and remunerative activities involves a phase of high concentration in which lead firms might account for as much as 80 per cent of suppliers' revenues. Serving one major customer facilitates the development of trust and the acquisition of specific competences ... but also increases suppliers' vulnerability. The next step for suppliers is thus to diversify their clientele, a phase that requires some degree of standardization of products and production.'
- 'The advantages provided by geographical proximity in strengthening network relations might impede industrial upgrading in distant locations ... Global

transactions might thus remain limited to standard arm's-length exchanges involving few interdependencies between lead firms and their remote suppliers … [however] … remoteness from lead firms' core locations is not an insurmountable obstacle to local industrial upgrading.'

Even if, despite the existence of such obstacles, economic upgrading does occur, a key question remains: does economic upgrading lead to *social upgrading* in GPNs?

> Social upgrading … is the process of improvement in the rights and entitlements of workers as social actors, which enhances the quality of their employment … This includes access to better work … But it also involves enhancing working conditions, protection and rights.[38]

Social upgrading, therefore, encompasses the two areas identified earlier: measurable standards and enabling rights. And even if upgrading does occur, there are likely to be *differential effects*:[39]

- 'The gains derived from industrial upgrading may be unequally spread among different groups of workers. Vulnerable groups include "guest workers" imported in response to local labour shortages, as well as workers employed by smaller suppliers and subcontractors that perform lower value-added activities within global networks … Accordingly, upgrading *per se* does not correct the inequalities in employment conditions that are inherent to outsourcing practices. On the contrary, such practices might contribute towards explaining the rising wage inequalities observed in developed and developing countries over the last decades.'
- 'The value created through industrial upgrading does not seem to be shared with workers under the form of higher wages … higher wage levels appear to depend more on tight local labour market conditions and/or demanding collective agreements and labour laws, than on individual firms' upgrading strategies. These results underline the role of local institutions in improving employment conditions, in the face of global downward pressures on workers' wages.'
- 'Industrial upgrading typically involves some forms of workers' displacement, either directly, through declining numbers of production workers, or indirectly, through the emergence of new job profiles that make workers' skills obsolete or less valuable in the local labour market.'
- 'In a number of countries such as the Republic of Korea, Singapore and Malaysia, the "high road" has been combined with elements of a "low road" including union repression and/or restrictive labour laws.'

In other words, what 'may look like upgrading from the vantage point of the firm … [may] … in fact constitute a form of downgrading for the workers involved'.[40]

The ability both of local firms to participate in GPNs and of a local economy to capture value created in those parts of a GPN located there depends, therefore,

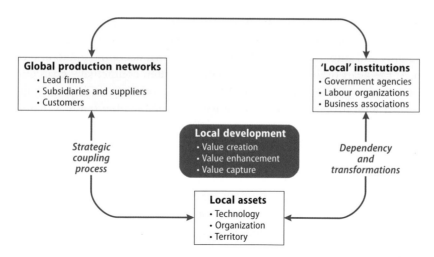

Figure 8.7 Relationships between local economic development and GPNs

Source: based on Coe et al., 2004: Figure 1

on far more than just what happens inside, or between, GPN firms. The *local context* itself matters enormously. Figure 8.7 summarizes the kinds of relationships involved in what has been called a 'strategic coupling' process.[41] In effect, this means that to participate successfully in a GPN a local economy needs to develop institutions and practices (including training and education, support for local entrepreneurial activities, development of high-quality physical infrastructure, etc.) which meet the needs of GPNs.

Of course, this will not guarantee success in capturing GPN value. As we have seen, TNCs have enormous potential flexibility in deciding where to locate their operations or source their inputs. The relative bargaining power of firms and states is critical (see Chapter 7). This poses a huge dilemma for local economic development in a GPN-dominated world. Not to try to create the 'right' conditions to attract GPN activities will, undoubtedly, close off a major avenue for economic development. On the other hand, to try to couple local assets too closely to specific GPNs also has its dangers, not least that of being left stranded if the local operation is relocated elsewhere, or of becoming too tightly locked in.

The dangers of external dominance

Whereas the involvement of some foreign activities in a local/national economy will generally have beneficial effects – not only in creating employment but also in introducing new technologies and business practices – *overall dominance* by foreign firms is undesirable. There are real dangers in acquiring the status of a 'branch plant economy' or of being totally at the mercy of shifting configurations within GPNs.

But precisely what constitutes an undesirable level of foreign penetration? A high level of dependence on foreign enterprises *potentially* reduces a host economy's sovereignty and autonomy – its ability to make its own decisions and to implement them. At the heart of this issue are the different – often conflictual – goals pursued by nation-states on the one hand and TNCs on the other (see Chapter 7). Each is concerned with maximizing its own 'welfare' (in the broadest sense). Where most of a host country's economic activity is effectively controlled by foreign firms, non-domestic goals may well become dominant. It may be extremely difficult for the host government to pursue a particular economic policy if it has insufficient leverage over the dominant firms.

The tighter the degree of control exercised by TNCs within their production networks, and the lower the degree of autonomy of individual plants, the greater this loss of host-country sovereignty is likely to be. In the *individual* case this may not matter greatly, but where such firms *collectively* dominate a host economy or a key economic sector it most certainly does matter. The most significant aspect of dependence upon a high level of FDI is *technological*: the inability to generate the knowledge, inventions and innovations necessary to generate self-sustaining growth. As we have seen, TNCs have a strong propensity to keep their higher-level R&D, design and decision-making functions close to home. When a domestic firm is taken over by a foreign firm there is, almost inevitably, a loss or downgrading of such functions in the acquired firm. However, this is not to argue that foreign investment should be avoided completely. On the contrary. What should be avoided by host economies is an *excessive* degree of foreign domination. In other words, *ownership still matters*. This is an especially vital message for those economies – like the UK's – which take a totally laid-back view of the indiscriminate acquisition of domestic firms by foreign firms. Seller beware!

The other side of the employment coin: exporting jobs from 'headquarters countries'

As TNCs establish GPNs, they inevitably engage in significant reconfiguration of the balance between their home-country and foreign activities, both through FDI and outsourcing. What are the implications of this? Does it adversely affect the home country's economic welfare by, for example, drawing away investment capital, displacing exports or destroying jobs? Does it represent a 'hollowing out' of a local or national economy? Is it an inevitable feature of today's highly competitive global economy that forces firms to expand abroad in order to remain competitive?

- *Proponents* of overseas investment argue that the overall effects on the domestic economy will be positive, raising the level of exports and of domestic activity to a level above that which would prevail if overseas investment did not occur.

Profits from overseas operations will flow back to the home economy, enhancing the firm's competitive position and making funds available for investment in appropriate activities in the home economy, as well as overseas.

- *Opponents* of overseas investment argue that the major effect will be to divert capital that could have been invested at home and to displace domestic exports. Profits earned overseas will be reinvested in other overseas ventures, rather than in creating new job opportunities at home.

A critical issue is the extent to which domestic investment could realistically be *substituted* for overseas investment. This raises a whole series of questions:

- What would have happened if the investment had not been made abroad?
- Would that investment have been made at home?
- Would the resources that went into the foreign investment have been used in higher levels of consumption and/or public services?
- What would have been the effect of foreign investment on domestic exports?
- Would the foreign sales of the product of the investment have been filled by exports from the home economy in the absence of the investment?
- Or would they have been taken over by foreign competitors?

It is impossible to say, with any certainty, that overseas investment could equally as well have been made in the firm's home country. We can make various *assumptions* about what might have happened, but that is all. Ultimately, the key lies with the *motivations* that underlie specific investment decisions. As we have seen, firms invest abroad for a whole variety of reasons, for example:

- to gain access to new markets;
- to defend positions in existing markets;
- to circumvent trade barriers;
- to diversify the firm's production base;
- to reduce production costs;
- to gain access to specific assets and resources.

It might be argued that foreign investment undertaken for *defensive* reasons – to protect a firm's existing markets, for example – is less open to criticism than *offensive* overseas investment. The argument in the case of defensive investment would be that, in its absence, the firm would lose its markets and that domestic jobs would be lost anyway. Such investment might be made necessary by the erection of trade barriers by national governments, by their insistence on local production, or by the appearance of competitors in the firm's international markets. But, presumably, defensive investment can also include the relocation of production to low-wage countries in order to remain competitive. Here, the alternative might be the introduction of automated technology that would lead to a loss of jobs anyway even without any outward investment. Although there may well be some clear-cut cases – particularly where access to markets is obviously threatened or where proximity to a localized material is mandatory – there will inevitably be many instances where there is substantial disagreement over the need to locate or source abroad rather than at home.

The possible direct employment effects of such outward investment fall into four categories:[42]

- *Export-stimulus effect* (XE): employment gains from the production of goods for export created by the foreign investment which would not have occurred in the absence of such investment.
- *Home office effect* (HE): employment gains in non-production categories at the company's headquarters made necessary by the expansion of overseas activities.
- *Supporting firm effect* (SE): employment gains in other domestic firms supplying goods and services to the investing firm in connection with its overseas activities.
- *Production-displacement effect* (DE): employment losses arising from the diversion of production to overseas locations and the serving of foreign markets by these overseas plants rather than by home–country plants, that is the displacement of exports.

Thus, the *net employment effect* (NE) of overseas investment on the home economy is:

$$NE = XE + HE + SE - DE$$

Unfortunately, the data needed to disaggregate employment change into these components are rarely available so that, once again, large assumptions have to be made. That is why the estimates of the numbers of jobs either created or destroyed vary so widely – often by hundreds of thousands.

Figure 8.8 summarizes the potential positive and negative aspects of both direct and indirect employment effects of outward investment in terms of three attributes: quantity of jobs, quality of jobs and the location of jobs. We need to bear in mind that the precise effects of outward investment on home-country employment are highly contingent on the specific circumstances involved. But even though we cannot put precise numbers on jobs gained or lost through FDI, one thing is clear: *the winners and the losers are rarely the same.* At one time, it could be said with some accuracy that the dominant losers were usually blue-collar production workers while the major gainers were white-collar, managerial workers. But this simple distinction no longer holds, as the recent rapid increase in the outsourcing/offshoring of white-collar jobs has shown. Also, given the complex geography of TNC networks (Chapter 5), it is almost inevitable that jobs created in the home country through outward investment effects (XE, HE, SE in the above formula) will be in *different places* from those where jobs are lost.

Area of impact	DIRECT		INDIRECT	
	Positive	Negative	Positive	Negative
Quantity	Creates or preserves jobs in home location, e.g. those serving the needs of affiliates abroad.	Relocation or 'job export' if foreign affiliates substitute for production at home.	Creates or preserves jobs in supplier/service industries at home that cater to foreign affiliates.	Loss of jobs in firms/ industries linked to production/activities that are relocated.
Quality	Skills are upgraded with higher-value production as industry restructures.	'Give backs' or lower wages to keep jobs at home.	Boosts sophisticated industries.	Downward pressure on wages and standards flows on to suppliers.
Location	Some jobs may depart from the community, but may be replaced by higher-skilled positions, upgrading local labour market conditions.	The 'export' of jobs can aggravate regional/local labour market conditions.	The loss of 'blue-collar' jobs can be offset by greater demand in local labour markets for high-value-added jobs relating to exports or international production.	Demand spiral in local labour market triggered by layoffs can lead to employment reduction in home-country plant locations.

Figure 8.8 **The potential effects of outward investment on home-country employment**

Source: based on UNCTAD, *World Investment Report*, 1994: Table IV

NOTES

1 See UNCTAD (2011: chapter IV), UNCTAD (2013a: chapter IV).
2 Bair (2009: 29, 30).
3 Kaplinsky (2004) discusses economic rent in the context of global value chains. See also Coe et al. (2004), Henderson et al. (2002), Palpacuer (2008).
4 Dedrick et al. (2010).
5 UNCTAD (2011: 154, 156).
6 UNCTAD (2011: 156).
7 *Financial Times* (30 September 2013).
8 UNCTAD (1995: 142–3).
9 Ramirez (2006: 812).
10 See, for example, Contreras et al. (2012), Giroud and Mirza (2006), Jordaan (2011), Liu (2011), Moran (2011), Tavares and Young (2006), UNCTAD (2000, 2001, 2011).
11 Jordaan (2011: 629).
12 Van Grunsven et al. (1995: 3).
13 Linden (2000: 210).
14 Belderbos and Capannelli (2001).
15 Liu (2011: 633).
16 Liu (2011: 644).
17 Contreras et al. (2012: 1020).
18 Ernst and Kim (2002: 2).
19 Moran (2011: 86–7).
20 Rasiah (2004: 619).
21 Contreras et al. (2012: 1021).
22 Mytelka and Barclay (2004: 553).
23 Ernst and Kim (2002: 2, 6).

24   Ernst and Kim (2002: 8).
25   See Coe and Hess (2013), Jürgens and Krzywdzinski (2009: 29), Palpacuer and Parisotto (2003: 109–11).
26   *The Economist* (17 December 2005).
27   UNCTAD (2001).
28   Wills (1998).
29   Wills (1998: 122).
30   See, for example, Coe et al. (2008b).
31   Rossi (2013: 224).
32   Palpacuer and Parisotto (2003: 97).
33   Palpacuer and Parisotto (2003: 105–6).
34   Barrientos et al. (2011), Gereffi (2014), Humphrey and Schmitz (2002), Rossi (2013).
35   Barrientos et al. (2011: 324).
36   Gereffi (1999: 38).
37   Palpacuer and Parisotto (2003: 107–8).
38   Barrientos et al. (2011: 324).
39   Palpacuer and Parisotto (2003: 110–11).
40   Bair (2009: 30).
41   Coe et al. (2004).
42   Hawkins (1972).

Want to know more about this chapter? Visit the companion website at **www.guilford.com/dickenGS7** for free access to author videos, suggested reading and practice questions to further enhance your study.

Nine

DESTROYING VALUE? ENVIRONMENTAL IMPACTS OF GLOBAL PRODUCTION NETWORKS

PRODUCTION–DISTRIBUTION–CONSUMPTION AS A SYSTEM OF MATERIALS FLOWS AND BALANCES

Throughout our discussion of GPNs, we have focused on the *creation* of value at various points in a network. Such value, as we saw in Chapter 8, takes on different forms for different actors within a network. Firms make profits, shareholders receive dividends, workers are paid wages or salaries. In a developmental context, what matters is how much – and what kinds of – value are 'captured' for the benefit of the local community. However, there is another – darker – side to the picture. We can see this more clearly using Figures 9.1 and 9.2. In Figure 9.1, the basic production circuit, shown originally in Chapter 3 as Figure 3.3, has been set within a much broader framework which presents the production–distribution–consumption circuit as a *system of materials flows and balances*. Figure 9.2 provides a more detailed picture of the ways in which material flows involved in the processing, residual recycling and residual discharging are configured within a production system.

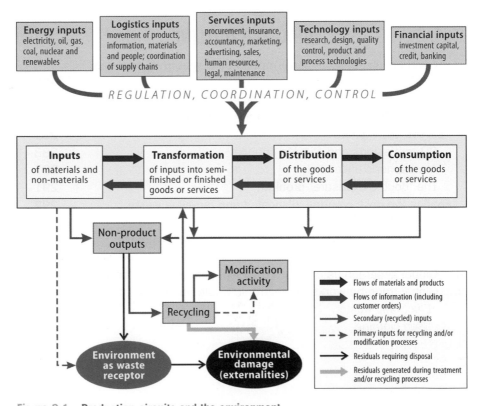

Figure 9.1   Production circuits and the environment

Source: based, in part, on Turner et al., 1994: Box 1.2

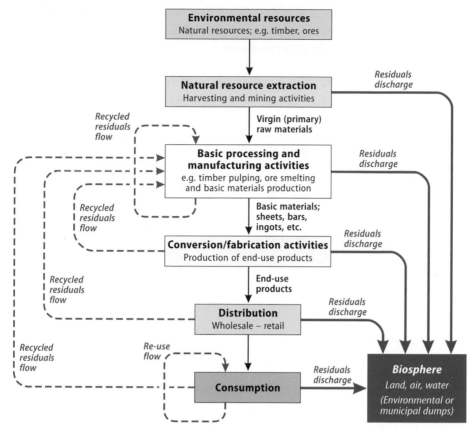

Figure 9.2 **Material flows in the process of production**

Source: based on Turner et al., 1994: Box 1.3

Negative spillovers: unintentional effects of production

Figures 9.1 and 9.2 demonstrate that there are unintentional external effects (*negative externalities* or *spillovers*) involved in all economic activities. In other words, just as production creates value it also has the capacity – albeit perhaps unintentionally – to *destroy* value. Three aspects of such environmental damage are especially important:[1]

- overuse of non-renewable and renewable resources (including exploitation of fossil fuels, water resources, clearance of forests);
- overburdening of natural environmental 'sinks' (e.g. the increasing concentration of greenhouse gases in the earth's atmosphere and of heavy materials in the soil, the dumping of waste);
- destruction of increasing numbers of ecosystems to create space for urban and industrial development.

The key point of all production processes is that what goes in has to come out again, albeit transformed, but without being reduced. In Figures 9.1 and 9.2 the materials used in the production process are

> dispersed and chemically transformed. In particular, they enter in a state of low entropy (as 'useful' materials) and leave in a state of high entropy (as 'useless' materials, such as low temperature heat emissions, mixed municipal wastes, etc.) ... No material recycling processes can therefore ever be 100 per cent efficient.[2]

Thus, even after all efforts are made to recycle the unused energy and materials involved in production, there will still be 'things' left over in the form of residual waste and environmental damage. This is simply because the fundamental laws of thermodynamics cannot be overruled:

> the total mass of inputs to a transformation process is equal to the total mass of outputs. If inputs do not emerge as desired products, they must therefore appear as unwanted by-products or wastes.[3]

Such negative externalities are of various kinds and of varying geographical extent. For example, the negative externalities from a factory or from an airport are, at one level, geographically localized. The impact is greatest at the location of the facility itself and its immediate neighbourhood but then declines with increasing distance away from that location. On the other hand, the smoke pollution from the factory or the effect of aircraft fuel combustion may have much more extensive geographical effects, particularly on the atmosphere. The problem is that many adverse environmental effects cannot be contained within geographical boundaries. Some are, indeed, global.

The environmental problems that are inherent in all aspects of production, distribution and consumption raise serious questions about the future sustainability of economy and society as we know them. They raise big issues relating to the future of the world's economic and trading system and, indeed, to most aspects of contemporary economic life. In this chapter, we will focus on two aspects of negative environmental impacts of production: atmospheric damage (including climate change, atmospheric pollution) and waste disposal. The question of environmental regulation will be addressed in Chapter 11.

DISTURBING THE DELICATE BALANCE OF LIFE ON EARTH: DAMAGING THE EARTH'S ATMOSPHERE

Human life is only made possible by a complex, and extremely delicate, balance of processes: atmospheric, hydrological and biological. As the history of the earth clearly shows, such a critical balance may be – indeed often has been – disturbed by natural forces. Periods of widespread freezing and glaciation, drought and high temperatures, rises and falls in sea level, are all evident in the earth's geological record. Until relatively recently, it was generally assumed that human activity would have little effect on natural processes; it was simply too small in relative terms to influence such enormous natural forces. No longer. Despite the views of some sceptics, the evidence of not only large-scale, but potentially irreversible, damage to the natural environment by human activity is accumulating day by day. By far the most contentious aspect of negative environmental externalities relates to potential *atmospheric damage*, that is damage to the gaseous membrane that sustains all life on earth.

The processes of material transformation involve the use of massive quantities of energy, especially of fossil fuels whose combustion products are the major source of damage to the earth's atmosphere. The problems arise because some of the key gaseous components of the earth's atmosphere – notably carbon dioxide, methane and ozone – are becoming excessively concentrated in the atmosphere. The issue is one of balance. Without these, and other, gases the earth would have a surface temperature like that of the planet Mars; it would be uninhabitable. The earth's surface remains habitable precisely because of the presence of such gases in the atmosphere. In combination, they act like a 'greenhouse', preventing both excessive solar heating and excessive cooling. But it is a very delicate balance. It is now abundantly clear that this balance is dangerously disturbed by human action.

CO_2 emissions and climate change

> Warming of the climate system is unequivocal, as is now evident from observations of increases in global average air and ocean temperatures, widespread melting of snow and ice, and rising global mean sea level ... The linear warming trend over the last 50 years ... is nearly twice that for the last 100 years.[4]

The overwhelming scientific consensus is that human-induced climate change has become the dominant factor:[5]

> The causes of contemporary and future changes in climate, their rate and their potential significance for the human species ... are all notably different from anything that has occurred previously in history or prehistory. The *causes* are now dominated by human perturbation of the atmosphere, the *rate* of warming already exceeds anything experienced in the last 10000 years and is set to be more rapid, probably, than anything experienced in human history, and the *significance* for humanity is qualitatively different from the previously given ecological imprint made by our current and growing population of 6 billion and more.[6]

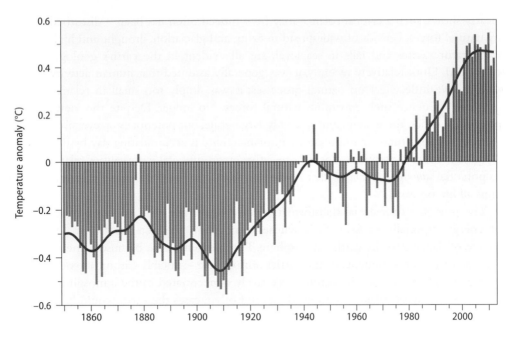

Figure 9.3   **Changes in global land and sea temperatures**

Source: based on www.cru.uea.ac.uk/cru/info/warming (2013)

Figure 9.3 plots these rising trends in global temperature between 1850 and 2012 compared with the mean temperature for the period 1961–90. As the graph shows, although the overall trend is clearly upwards, there are always annual variations in temperature change. The acceleration in rising average temperatures is due to the fact that

> global atmospheric concentrations of carbon dioxide, methane and nitrous oxide have increased markedly as a result of human activities since 1750 and now far exceed pre-industrial values determined from ice cores spanning many thousands of years. The global increases in carbon dioxide concentration are due primarily to fossil fuel use and land use change, while those of methane and nitrous oxide are primarily due to agriculture.[7]

The latest IPCC Report, published in 2013, confirms such trends. Because carbon dioxide is the main 'greenhouse gas', its increasing concentration in the atmosphere is *the* major cause of global climate change. The association between rising CO_2 levels and the growth of economic activity is abundantly clear. There was a significant acceleration after around 1800.[8] Before that time, CO_2 levels in the atmosphere remained fairly stable at between 270 and 290 parts per million (ppm). Since then, the following escalation in levels has occurred:

- 1900: 295 ppm
- 1950: between 310 and 315 ppm
- 1995: 360 ppm
- 2008: 387 ppm
- 2013: 400 ppm.

The 2013 levels were measured at the Mauna Loa monitoring site in Hawaii, the primary global benchmark site with the longest continuous CO_2 time series. They are especially significant because it is the first time in human history that a CO_2 level of 400 ppm has been experienced. It is now increasing at a rate of 2 ppm every year, 'a rate of increase … more than 100 times faster than the increase that occurred when the last ice age ended':[9]

> When the concentrations were last this high 'the world was warmer on average by three or four degrees Celsius than it is today. There was no permanent ice sheet on Greenland, sea levels were much higher, and the world was a very different place, although not all of these differences may be directly related to CO_2 levels.'[10]

As we might expect, there is a clear geography to CO_2 emissions as Figure 9.4 shows. These emissions map primarily onto the usage of fossil fuels (mainly coal and oil for industrial production, transportation and domestic use), which accounts for almost two-thirds of total CO_2 emissions. Within that figure, emissions from power plants account for 27 per cent, industry for 14 per cent, road transport for 12 per cent, refineries for 6 per cent and international transport for 2 per cent.[11] A further one-third is created by emissions from global biomass (mainly forest fires). In absolute terms, the world's biggest emitters of CO_2 in 2011 were China (26.8 per cent) and the USA (17.9 per cent). Together, these two countries produced no less than 44 per cent of the world's total emissions. Europe contributed around 13 per cent. But the picture is rather different when we look at the volume of emissions per head of population. From such a per capita perspective, China ranks as low as 74th.

But there is a further complication in interpreting the geography – and, therefore, the politics – of CO_2 emissions. The emissions data shown in Figure 9.4 are *production* data. What happens if we take a different perspective: that of *consumption*? The CO_2 emission figures, especially for countries like China, India and other developing countries, particularly in East Asia, are greatly influenced by the fact that much of those countries' industrial production is for export to the developed markets of the USA and Europe. For example, Chinese CO_2 emissions grew by 45 per cent between 2002 and 2005. One estimate is that half of that increase was associated with production for export and 60 per cent of that export production was for Western economies.[12] In effect:

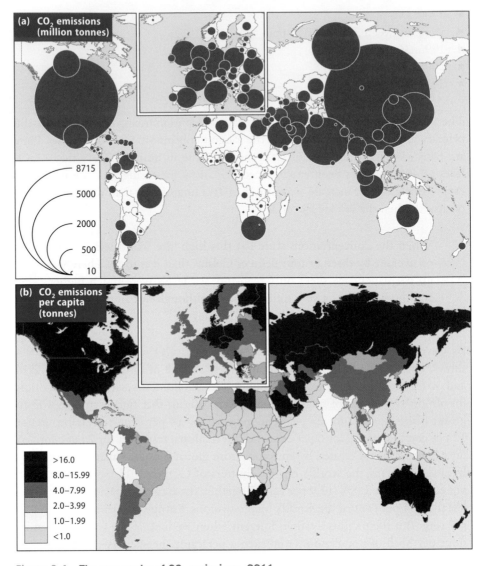

Figure 9.4   The geography of CO_2 emissions, 2011

Source: based on US Energy Information Administration data (www.eia.gov/environment)

Quite a lot of carbon production was simply outsourced abroad. We then imported the carbon intensive goods back to Britain and then consumed that carbon ... It is not the Chinese who are consuming the outputs from its coastal economic boom. The extra two large coal stations per week in China are being built for export manufacturers. And since it is likely that the efficiency of coal-fired generation is lower in China than in developed countries, outsourcing carbon intensive industries may be more polluting – before adding in the pollution from shipping and other transport back to developed countries.[13]

Predicting the precise effects of climate change is, like all predictions of the out-come of highly complex processes, far from easy. However, it is abundantly clear that the current upward trend in temperatures is potentially catastrophic for many parts of the world, as the IPCC reports show. But the effects will be far from geo-graphically evenly spread. Shifting climatic zones will create intensified drought in some areas but higher rainfall and increased frequency of flooding in others. The geography of food production will be very different from that of today. Rising sea levels produced by the melting of polar ice will drastically change the shape of coastlines, with especially serious effects on those cities located on low-lying land. The global economic map will be drastically reshaped. The extreme climatic events of recent years – for example, the catastrophic floods in New York, in east-ern Australia and throughout much of East and South Asia in 2012 and 2013 – may well be harbingers of what is to come.

Atmospheric pollution

Industrial processes (including transportation) create other forms of atmospheric damage in addition to the effect of CO_2 emissions on climate change. Some of these types of atmospheric pollution are invisible to the naked eye; others are very visible indeed, most notably the dense clouds of yellow polluted air found in major cities and industrial agglomerations. One of the most important types of 'invisible' atmospheric damage occurs in the earth's *ozone layer*. Ozone is formed in the stratosphere through the chemical reaction of oxygen and sunlight. At this level, ozone is vital to the sustainability of human life on earth because it absorbs almost all the ultraviolet radiation from the sun, which would otherwise make human life impossible. Equally, an excess of ozone in the atmosphere is inimical to temperature change and to human health. Any damage to this vital protective shield poses a serious problem.

Just such thinning of – or even holes in – the ozone layer (beyond natural occurrences) began to be identified in certain part of the world in the early 1970s. One of the major effects of ozone depletion is an increase in the incidence of skin cancer. A primary cause was believed to be the chemical chlorofluorocarbon (CFC), which had become extensively used in refrigeration and aerosols. Although CFCs are now heavily restricted, the fact that the chemical is immensely stable means that the amount already in the stratosphere will still be affecting the ozone layer until about 2087.[14] Evidence for the Antarctic ozone layer in 2013 showed that the hole there was shrinking, although there is no guarantee that holes in the ozone layer will not continue to appear and even to grow.

The most significant types of atmospheric pollution induced by the processes of production, distribution and consumption result from the emission of a whole range of tiny particles of sulphur dioxide, nitrogen oxides, lead, copper, zinc and other products of combustion. Such particles may remain in the atmosphere as solid particulate matter (SPM) or in a dissolved state in rainfall or in rivers and lakes. In each case, the result is a serious environmental and health problem. Although such pollution may have localized sources, it frequently spreads very widely, depending on the nature of the pollutant and the prevailing atmospheric conditions, notably air mass and wind directions and intensities. What is usually called *acid rain*, for example, is generated at specific locations (coal-fired power stations, metallic ore smelters) but can travel across considerable distances to affect places far from the point of generation. It causes acidification of rivers and lakes, damages vegetation, degrades soils and corrodes buildings. Such acidic pollutants are classic cases of global – or at least, trans-boundary – environmental damage.

Figures 9.5 and 9.6 provide two examples of pollution through the concentration of particulate matter that are closely linked to the operation of GPNs. Figure 9.5 maps the particulate matter emitted by ocean-going ships, a key element in the movement of materials, commodities, products and wastes within GPNs. This is a much bigger source of environmental pollution than air transport. It is estimated that merchant shipping emits 1.2 billion tonnes of CO_2 per year. For example:

> When the world's largest merchant ship ferries its monthly cargo of 13,000 containers between China and Europe it burns nearly 350 tonnes of fuel a day … its giant diesel engine can emit more than 300,000 tonnes of CO_2 a year – equivalent to a medium-sized coal power station.[15]

Most significant is the fact that ships use the most polluting type of oil – what is known as 'bunker fuel' – which is the residue from crude oil refining after all the cleaner elements have been removed. It is an extremely potent source of pollution-induced health problems:

> Our results indicate that shipping-related emissions from maritime shipping contribute approximately 60,000 deaths annually at a global scale, with impacts concentrated in coastal regions on major trade routes. Most mortality effects are seen in Asia and Europe where high populations and high shipping-related PM concentrations coincide.[16]

Apart from such concentrated sources of atmospheric pollution as power stations, metal smelters and oceanic shipping routes, one of the most significant locations of health-threatening pollution are the world's major cities. Figure 9.6 shows the variation in concentrations of particulate matter across major world cities. Virtually all cities have levels of concentration above the World Health Organization (WHO) guidelines of 20 micrograms per cubic metre. However, the biggest problems are clearly in big cities in developing countries, where there has been rapid industrialization, inefficient power generation and an accelerated increase in car ownership (often of old polluting vehicles). One extremely serious by-product of such high levels of atmospheric pollution is the high number of premature deaths (Figure 9.7).

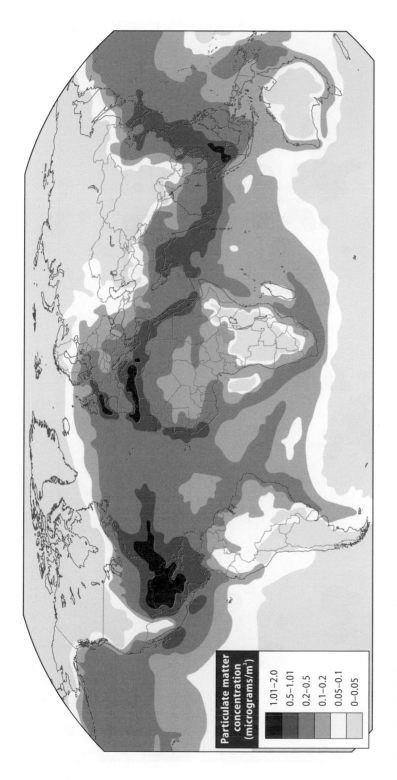

Figure 9.5 **Pollution from maritime transport**

Source: based on Corbett et al., 2007: Figure 1; *Guardian* (13 February 2008)

Particulate matter
concentration
(micrograms/m³)

1.01–2.0
0.5–1.01
0.2–0.5
0.1–0.2
0.05–0.1
0–0.05

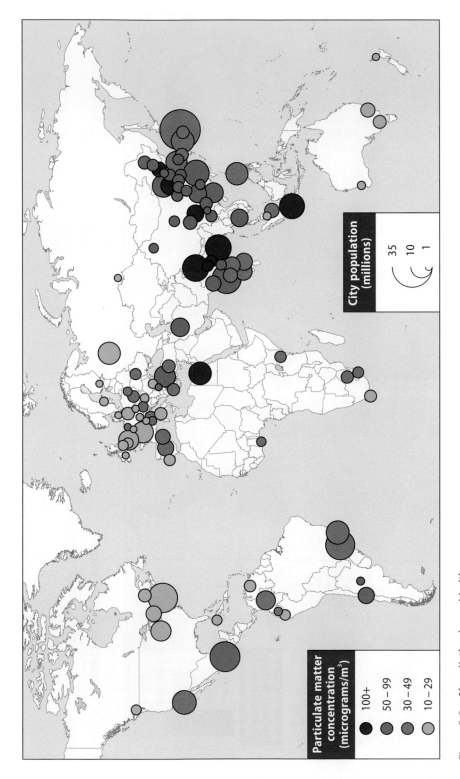

Figure 9.6　Air pollution in world cities

Source: based on data from World Bank, 2008a: Table 3.14

Legend (within figure):

Particulate matter concentration (micrograms/m³)
100+
50 – 99
30 – 49
10 – 29

City population (millions)
35
10
1

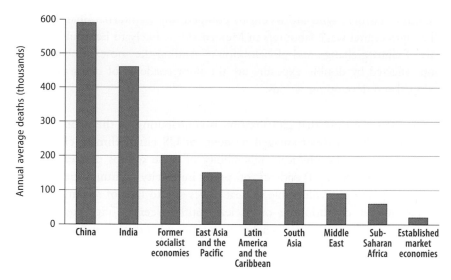

Figure 9.7   **Premature deaths due to urban air pollution**

Source: data from World Bank; WorldWatch Institute, cited in the *Financial Times*, 27 January 2006

The 'double exposure' problem

> Climate change is ... highly inequitable, as the greatest risks are to the poorest populations, who have contributed least to greenhouse gas (GHG) emissions. The rapid economic development and the concurrent urbanization of poorer countries mean that developing-country cities will be both vulnerable to health hazards from climate change and, simultaneously, an increasing contributor to the problem.[17]

> Climate change is claiming 300,000 lives a year and costing the global economy $125bn annually, with the damage set to escalate rapidly ... A further 300m people around the world are seriously affected by climate change through, for instance, malnutrition or disease and by being displaced from their homes.[18]

The highly uneven incidence and impact of climate change and atmospheric pollution, in conjunction with the immense variations in global economic well-being generated by globalization (see Chapter 10), create what has been called a 'double exposure' problem, 'where a particular region, sector, ecosystem or social group is confronted by the impacts of both climate change and economic globalization ... *different outcomes emerge when the two processes are considered together*'.[19]

It is the world's poorest countries that are most seriously threatened.

But although Africa is a 'double loser' overall, the situation is more varied than this generalization suggests. There are sectoral effects, as in the case of Mexican agriculture: 'farmers who are trying to compete in ... international markets as well as agricultural wage labourers in Mexico are ... likely to be double losers in terms of climate change and globalization'.[20] Among the most vulnerable social groups affected by double exposure are the poor residents of cities in both the developed and developing worlds:

> At the same time that globalization is contributing to the economic vulnerability of disadvantaged residents of US cities, climate change may increase the physical vulnerability of these groups to weather-related events ... Residents of poor, inner-city communities are among the most vulnerable to heat waves due to lack of resources to pay for air conditioning or to leave stifling central city areas ... Globalization and climate change thus represent a dual threat to these groups.

> For poor residents of cities in the developing world, the double impacts of globalization and climate change may be even more severe ... In conjunction with increased financial vulnerability as the result of globalization, poor residents of developing world cities are also among the groups that are most vulnerable to climatic change. Many of the urban poor live in shantytowns and squatter settlements located in precarious areas such as on hillsides ... Such areas are especially vulnerable to mudslides or flooding as the result of severe storms, events that may increase in both frequency and magnitude as the result of climate change. In addition to direct physical hazards, the urban poor are also vulnerable to climate change related health-hazards, particularly outbreaks of diseases such as cholera and malaria, both of which increase with warm spells and heavy rains.[21]

The argument, therefore, is that different sets of winners and losers from globalization may emerge when the effects of the two sets of global processes – economic globalization and environmental change – are superimposed on both those who are vulnerable and those who may benefit.

FOULING THE NEST: CREATING, DISPOSING AND RECYCLING WASTE

Environmental degradation is a major social problem throughout the world. It is especially problematic in many of the newly industrialized, and emerging market, economies where the 'single-minded pursuit of rapid economic growth has caused particularly severe environmental degradation'.[22]

An inexorable avalanche of waste

It is almost impossible to calculate the exact amount of waste generated at a global scale by producers and consumers. According to the United Nations Environment Programme (UNEP), many countries do not report waste levels at all or, where such reporting does exist, there are large inconsistencies in reporting practices.[23] The Basel Convention supposedly monitors the situation but only for those states that are signatories, and these exclude the USA.[24] However, some specific examples can give us an indication of the size of the waste avalanche:

- 4 billion tonnes of waste generated by the OECD countries in 2001;
- 254 million tonnes of municipal solid waste (MSW) generated by the USA in 2007;
- 155 million tonnes of MSW generated by China in 2005, growing at an annual rate of 8 to 10 per cent;
- 1.3 billion tonnes of industrial waste generated by China;
- 108 million tonnes of hazardous waste produced by the countries covered by the Basel Convention in 2001.

These levels are now almost certainly higher.

Hazardous wastes, which may come in liquid, gaseous or solid form, are especially problematical. They have four distinctive characteristics:[25]

- *ignitability*: wastes that may be spontaneously combustible or create fires under certain conditions;
- *corrosivity*: acids or bases that corrode metals;
- *reactivity*: wastes that are unstable under normal conditions and can cause explosions when mixed with water;
- *toxicity*: wastes that are harmful, even fatal, if ingested or absorbed. May pollute groundwater through the leaching of toxins from the waste.

Radioactive waste – from nuclear power plants and military installations, as well as from research and medical facilities – poses especially difficult problems.

Not surprisingly, some activities produce more – and nastier – waste than others. Mineral extraction (Chapter 12) is an especially potent creator of waste as earth is stripped away to gain access to the desired material. It has been estimated that

> at a typical copper mine around 125 tonnes of ore are excavated to produce just one tonne of copper. The amount of earth moved is mind-boggling and mining now strips more of the Earth's surface each year than does natural erosion.[26]

In addition, the waste rock and the 'tailings' (waste products created during mineral recovery) include toxic chemicals.

Food and beverages	Furniture and wood
Animal waste Cleaning wastes Refrigerants	Ignitable wastes Spent solvents Paint wastes
Metals	**Chemicals**
Paint wastes containing heavy metals Strong acids and bases Cyanide wastes Sludges containing heavy metals	Strong acids and bases Reactive wastes Ignitable wastes Discarded commercial chemical products
Construction	**Paper and printing**
Ignitable wastes Paint wastes Spent solvents Strong acids and bases	Ink wastes including solvents and metals Photography waste with heavy metals Ignitable and corrosive wastes Heavy metal solutions
Vehicle maintenance shops	**Cleaning and cosmetics**
Paint wastes Ignitable wastes Spent solvents Acids and bases	Heavy metal dust and sludges Ignitable wastes Solvents Strong acids and bases

Figure 9.8   **Typical hazardous wastes generated by selected manufacturing industries**

Source: based on UNEP, 2004: p. 20

Different industries obviously generate different kinds of hazardous wastes. The industries shown in Figure 9.8 are 'traditional' industries. Newer industries create different problems. What has come to be called 'e-waste' is now the biggest and fastest-growing source: 'Anywhere between 20 and 50 million tonnes of e-waste are generated globally, an amount growing at a rate nearly three times faster than the overall municipal solid waste stream.'[27] Such e-waste is highly problematic:

> On average a computer is 23% plastic, 32% ferrous metals, 18% non-ferrous metals (lead, cadmium, antimony, beryllium, chromium and mercury), 12% electronic boards (gold, palladium, silver and platinum) and 15% glass. Only about 50% of the computer is recycled, the rest is dumped. The toxicity of the waste is mostly due to the lead, mercury and cadmium – non-recyclable components of a single computer may contain almost 2 kilograms of lead. Much of the plastic used contains flame retardants, which make it difficult to recycle.[28]

The above examples of waste are producer generated. But, as consumers, we also generate huge volumes of what is usually classified as MSW:

> Our trash, or municipal solid waste (MSW), is made up of the things we commonly use and then throw away. These materials include items such as packaging, food scraps, grass clippings, sofas, computers, tires, and refrigerators. MSW does not include industrial, hazardous or construction waste.[29]

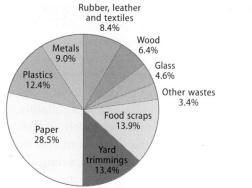

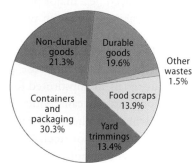

(a) **MSW generation (by material) 2010**
    250 million tons (before recycling)

(b) **MSW generation (by category) 2010**
    250 million tons (before recycling)

Figure 9.9   **The composition of municipal solid waste in the USA**

Source: based on USEPA, 2011: Figures 5, 6

As the figures above show, the volume of MSW is astronomical and poses huge disposal problems. Figure 9.9 shows the broad breakdown of MSW for the USA. Although the largest share of the total materials is organic in nature – paper, yard (garden) trimmings and food scraps – the biggest single category is containers and packaging, followed by non-durable goods. The throwaway consumer society is the major source of MSW, at least in developed countries. Indeed, the trend is clear: 'as countries get richer, the organic share decreases whereas the paper and plastic ones increase'.[30]

Distinguishing between 'valueless waste' and 'valuable materials': recreating value

> Wastes are materials that are not prime products (that is, products produced for the market) for which the generator has no further use in terms of his/her own purposes of production, transformation or consumption, and which he/she wants to dispose.[31]

However, actually distinguishing between 'waste' (valueless or useless materials) and valuable or useful materials is far from straightforward.[32] As Figure 9.2 shows, at each stage in the production–distribution–consumption circuit, some waste is recycled and emerges in a different form. The process is *circular*, not linear. As transformation processes change over time – and over space – new uses are found for what was previously regarded as useless waste. Indeed, waste almost always has the *potential* once again to become a valued and valuable material.

The problems inherent in dumping waste in landfill sites, or the burning of waste in incinerators (other than to generate energy), are so great that the recovery and recycling of waste at all stages of the production–distribution–consumption circuit has become a major priority. All countries now operate some kind of waste recycling strategy, although its scale and effectiveness vary widely:

> The most valuable benefit of recycling is the saving in energy and the reduction in greenhouse gases and pollution that result when scrap materials are substituted for virgin feedstock ... Recycling aluminium, for example, can reduce energy consumption by as much as 95%. Savings for other materials are lower but still substantial: about 70% for plastics, 60% for steel, 40% for paper and 30% for glass. Recycling also reduces emissions of pollutants that can cause smog, acid rain and the contamination of waterways.[33]

Recycling activity is now on such a large scale that it forms the basis of entirely new businesses and industries. In that respect, it could be said that *value is being recreated*. However, the economics of recycling are quite volatile. At times of very high commodity prices in, say, steel or paper, the market for scrap steel or recycled paper will be very buoyant. When such commodity prices weaken, the obverse applies. Recycling may be seen as too expensive, although national regulations will invariably insist that it is carried out.

Global geographies of waste disposal and recycling

In many cases, wastes are dealt with locally: at, or close to, the point of their generation. However, 'the tightening of waste legislation in industrialized countries during the 1980s significantly increased the costs of domestic disposal and created a financial incentive to export waste for processing and disposal'.[34] Hence, one of the most notable developments of recent years is the *re*location of waste on an international or global scale. In other words, there is a *global shift in waste*. In large part, this arises from the existence of wide geographical differentials in the nature and stringency of environmental regulations. Just as firms may seek out tax havens or union-free labour havens, so, too, some may seek out *pollution havens*:

> This differential capacity to pollute and produce dangerously in part reflects the increasing involvement of national states with environmental regulation, which creates opportunities and constraints for companies in their locational strategies. As a result of this, and changes in production and transportation technologies, 'dirty' industries and the production of pollutants can *to a degree* be shifted to spaces where their localized impacts are more tolerated ... [With the tightening of] environmental regulation ... companies began to relocate 'dirty', hazardous and polluting production activities, initially to peripheral regions within their home national territories but increasingly to parts

of the global periphery ... Companies were often encouraged to do this by financial inducements and low (or no) levels of environmental regulation as national governments eagerly encouraged the perceived benefits of modernization via industrial growth, regardless of environmental or social cost.[35]

However, the view that TNCs habitually relocate their more noxious activities to pollution havens needs to be treated with caution.[36] A study of US companies in the late 1980s, at a time when environmental regulatory differentials were steeper than today, did not show such firms engaging in industrial flight to pollution havens on a large scale. The period following the introduction of stringent environmental regulations in the USA was not characterized by the widespread relocation of pollution-intensive industries to countries with lower regulatory standards.[37]

The general tendency for TNCs to relocate their environmentally noxious production has almost certainly been exaggerated, especially as regulatory pressures have intensified. However, there is another dimension to the global shift in waste that is most certainly on the increase: *international trade*.[38]

Between 1993 and 2001 the amount of waste crisscrossing the globe increased from 2 million tonnes to more than 8.5 million tonnes ... Unfortunately data on waste movements are incomplete – not all countries report waste movements to the Basel Convention. However, we do know that the movement of waste is big business.[39]

It is also *highly contentious* business, not least because of the argument that developed countries are, in effect, dumping their waste – especially their hazardous waste – onto poor countries. Although there is certainly some truth in this, it is not the whole story.[40]

Only 2 per cent of the waste generated worldwide in 2000 was actually traded. However, the vast majority of the waste that was traded (around 90 per cent) was hazardous waste, consisting of radioactive materials, toxic heavy metals and printed circuit boards. The biggest single waste component by volume was lead and lead compounds. The most contentious material, however, is that of radioactive waste:

Over 50 countries currently have spent fuel stored in temporary locations, awaiting reprocessing or disposal. Major commercial reprocessing plants operate in France, the UK and the Russian Federation with a capacity of some 5000 tonnes per year. Countries like Japan have sent 140 shipments of spent fuel for reprocessing to Europe since 1979.[41]

The image of container ships moving such hazardous materials round the world is not a very comforting one. But it is going on all the time and is likely to increase.

Where does traded waste end up? Although most of the publicity focuses on China, in fact the majority of the world's waste (around 75 per cent in 2000) is actually traded between developed countries. For example, during the late 1990s, Germany was the biggest exporter and France the biggest importer of waste. Nevertheless, there is no doubt that China plays a huge role in international trade in waste. In large part this is because of China's recent insatiable appetite for industrial materials (see Chapter 12). For example, in 2004 the USA exported $3.1 billion in scrap to China, making scrap the USA's biggest dollar-value export to China, outstripping aircraft parts and electronics.[42] Some 70 per cent of the UK's exports of plastic waste go to Hong Kong and, thence, to the mainland; 50 per cent of the UK's exports of paper waste go to China.[43] A similar situation applies to most other developed countries: China is a magnet for waste, though not the only one.

One repercussion is that it has become more difficult for domestic recycling firms to compete with Chinese recyclers, who may offer prices for plastic waste some two-and-a-half times higher than UK companies:

> [The result is that] … China drives the waste trade … But the trade is being driven equally by tough EU legislation forcing local authorities and businesses to recycle more. Landfill charges are rising steeply, making it relatively cheaper to send the waste abroad. Meanwhile, major companies have moved in, offering to collect and dispose of large quantities. The trade is made possible by the vast numbers of shipping containers arriving in Britain with Chinese exports … the return waste trade to China is accelerating rapidly.[44]

This, in effect, takes us back full circle. Not only are waste materials reused in further manufacturing processes, but also the huge imbalance in trade between China and the West creates yet another form of reverse trade. Not least, some of the packaging materials used in the consumer goods exported from China go back to their origin.

Global trade networks in electronic waste and used clothing

A growing number of studies, particularly by geographers, provide enormously valuable insights into the nature and complexity of international trade in waste and, especially, the development of complex global recycling networks. Two examples are illustrated here: global trade in electronic waste[45] and in used clothing[46]. Both of these studies show how 'waste' may become new forms of 'value' as it is moved across the world.

Electronic waste

> We flew to Dhaka, spent 4 months tracking what we thought was e-waste, but we couldn't find any. We found used printers. Old monitors (tons and tons of them). Hard drives … Old silicon chips,

mother-boards and piles of circuitry. *Amidst all this stuff we could hardly find any waste. Almost everything had value.* Every component. Every material. They were all being bought and sold, assembled, disassembled and reassembled … They also dwindled into their constituent materials – plastics, glass, metals. Plastic printer chasses were smashed by hand and hammer but not because they were garbage. The plastic shards were collected, sorted, baled and hefted down the street. Then they were sold … All those bags of plastic shards were washed, then sorted by hand into categories of colour and hardness. They were washed again in a machine like an industrial dough mixer. Then they were ground into chunks, melted, extruded like gooey spaghetti … Then the grinding happened. Out came the pellets. Not done yet. Some of this was bagged and sold to the plastic wholesalers down the street. The rest went right next door to a hot plastic press, manned by a single male worker, churning out CD and DVD cases … Some of these cases sold domestically; others were exported to China. To India … Was this the *end* of a global production network? Or the *beginning* of one?[47]

This graphic vignette from Bangladesh reflects just one of the moments in what has developed into the highly complex and dynamic global trade networks in e-waste shown in Figure 9.10. These maps of e-waste flows in 2001 and 2006 illustrate how the geography of such trade has evolved. In particular, the significance of Asia as a destination for e-waste trade from all the other major regions increased markedly between 2001 and 2006:

> In 2001, Asia accounted for over 50 per cent of exports from the Americas and Europe, nearly 80 per cent of exports from Oceania and all exports from the Middle East. However, by 2006, Asia received over 96 per cent of exports from the Americas, over 99 per cent of exports from Europe, over 98 per cent of exports from the Middle East and over 99 per cent of exports from Oceania.[48]

This detailed analysis of global trade flows in e-waste also makes clear that the situation is far more complex than simply that of 'rich' countries dumping waste in 'poor' ones. On the one hand, there is considerable trade in e-waste between developed countries and, on the other, between developing countries themselves. So, although Lepawsky and McNabb find 'some support for the pollution haven hypothesis as an explanation of the geographies of the e-waste trade … [it] is not as robust as might be expected'.[49]

Used clothing

Lepawsky and Mather's conclusion from their study of e-waste – that 'rather than finding "waste", we kept finding "value"'[50] – could also apply to the used clothing sector. In both cases, we see the development of complex GPNs in which 'one

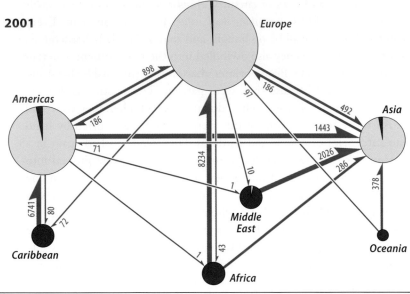

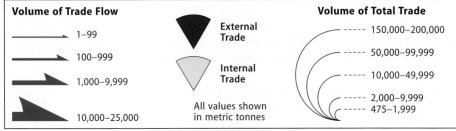

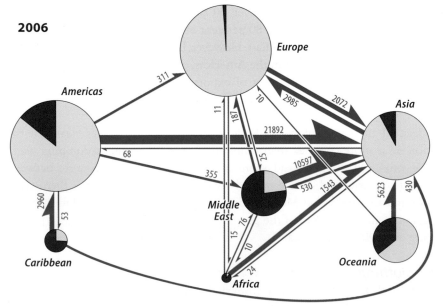

Figure 9.10   **Global trade networks in e-waste**

Source: based on Lepawsky and McNabb, 2010: Figures 1 and 2

country's waste or discarded goods become resources recovered for further rounds of commodity production in another'.[51]

International trade in used clothing has grown very rapidly; it roughly doubled between 2001 and 2009, from $1.26 billion to $2.5 billion. The USA is the largest source, exporting around 500,000 tonnes of used clothing per year to some 100 countries:[52]

> Five countries (the USA, UK, Germany, South Korea and Canada) account for more than half of all exports of second-hand apparel, while 15 countries account for half of all imports (Ghana, Poland, India, Malaysia, Pakistan, Russia, Cameroon, Kenya, Benin, Tunisia, Angola, Ukraine, Canada, Germany and Cambodia) – though among these are significant re-exporters … [in fact] used clothing exhibits complex flows within and between multiple countries.[53]

One of the most significant features of the used clothing network is that the primary source of the inputs – the used clothing – derives mainly from *gifts* made to charitable organizations in developed countries. In other words, 'value appears from something that is not only at the end of one life, but given away for nothing. The process is a recommodification of something that was once purchased, then had personal values and then became a gift.'[54] The bags of used clothing collected by, or for, the charities are highly heterogeneous, in terms of both their reusability as garments and as sources for materials of various kinds. Hence, to extract value from them involves an immensely complex, and often geographically dispersed, set of sorting operations. It has been compared with the process of 'panning for gold':

> [T]here are multiple layers of agents, brokers, importers, wholesalers, retailers and remanufacturers, located in different countries, involved in the sorting and re-sorting of the garments to fit consumers at different destinations. Given the fixed nature of the supply, dealers have to work hard to develop increasingly differentiated markets for the flow of goods available … This is not just a matter of fashions, and matching the climatic needs between global North and global South. Differentiated valuing also responds to body sizes and patterns of wear.[55]

The used clothing sector, therefore, involves 'a multi-layered process of sequentially stripping out value' in which:[56]

- consumers discard what they do not want;
- charity organizations discard what they do not think they can resell themselves;
- domestic recyclers sift the discarded garments for 'vintage' or 'retro' clothes and sell the remainders to international traders;
- international traders re-sort for different destination countries;
- in those countries, wholesalers and dealers sort the shipment again, breaking it into smaller bundles to fit their own market niches;
- intermediaries sell to final, small-scale, often family-run, enterprises, from small reselling stalls in Africa to fabric processors in India.

Both of these examples – e-waste and used clothing – raise important issues about the nature of GPNs. One is that such 'waste' networks, and others like them, constitute GPNs in their own right. They are not merely the final stage in a conventional manufacturing process. What may conventionally appear to be the *end* of one network (waste) in fact may form the *beginning* of a new network.[57]

In other words, it re-emphasizes the non-linearity of GPNs. A second issue relates to the form of governance that characterizes such GPNs. Although, in some cases, very large firms may be involved, for the most part the key actors tend to be medium and small-sized firms. These networks are 'complexly brokered' and strongly relational in terms of our discussion in Chapter 5 (see Figure 5.23). Above all, they demonstrate the continuous recreation of *value* – rather than its destruction.

NOTES

1   Simonis and Brühl (2002: 98).
2   Turner et al. (1994: 17).
3   Hudson (2001: 288).
4   IPCC (2007: 4).
5   IPCC (2013).
6   Hulme (2004: 48).
7   IPCC (2007: 2).
8   McNeill (2000: 109).
9   Scripps Institution of Oceanography press release (10 May 2013).
10   Director of the Grantham Institute for Climate Change, quoted in Wolf (2013: 13).
11   *Financial Times* (9 July 2008).
12   Guan et al. (2009).
13   Helm (2009: 7–8).
14   McNeill (2000: 114).
15   *Guardian* (13 February 2008).
16   Corbett et al. (2007: 8517).
17   Campbell-Lendrum and Corvalán (2007: 109).
18   Global Humanitarian Forum, cited in the *Guardian* (30 May 2009).
19   O'Brien and Leichenko (2000: 227; emphasis added). See also Leichenko and O'Brien (2008), Leichenko et al. (2010).
20   O'Brien and Leichenko (2000: 229).
21   O'Brien and Leichenko (2000: 229).
22   Brohman (1996: 126, 127). See also Bello and Rosenfeld (1990).
23   The following section draws extensively on UNEP (2004).
24   Lepawsky and McNabb (2010: 178–80) discuss some of the shortcomings of the Basel Convention.
25   UNEP (2004: 34).
26   UNEP (2004: 16).
27   Lepawsky and McNabb (2010: 178).

28   UNEP (2004: 36).

29   USEPA (2011: 2).

30   UNEP (2004: 22).

31   UNEP (2004: 1). See also Taylor and Morrissey (2004), USEPA (2011).

32   See Crang et al. (2012), Lepawsky and Mather (2011), Lepawsky and McNabb (2010).

33   *The Economist Technology Quarterly* (9 June 2007: 22).

34   Lepawsky and McNabb (2010: 178).

35   Hudson (2005: 194).

36   Hudson (2005: 195). See also Smarzynska and Wei (2001).

37   Leonard (1988).

38   See, for example, Beukering (2001), Beukering and Bouman (2001), Crang et al. (2012), Lepawsky and Mather (2011), Lepawsky and McNabb (2010), UNEP (2004).

39   UNEP (2004: 30).

40   UNEP (2004: 30).

41   UNEP (2004: 31).

42   Goldstein (2007).

43   UK Department for Environment, Food and Rural Affairs (Defra) figures.

44   *Guardian* (20 September 2004).

45   Iles (2004), Lepawsky and Mather (2011), Lepawsky and McNabb (2010).

46   Crang et al. (2012), Brooks (2013), Rivoli (2005: Part IV).

47   Lepawsky and Mather (2011: 242–3; emphasis added).

48   Lepawsky and McNabb (2010: 185).

49   Lepawsky and McNabb (2010: 188).

50   Lepawsky and Mather (2011: 247).

51   Crang et al. (2012: 12–13). See also Brooks (2013), Siegle (2011: chapter 11). This section is based primarily on those studies.

52   Brooks (2013: 11).

53   Crang et al. (2012: 17).

54   Crang et al. (2012: 18).

55   Crang et al. (2012: 18).

56   Crang et al. (2012: 18).

57   Lepawsky and Mather (2011: 243).

Want to know more about this chapter? Visit the companion website at **www.guilford.com/dickenGS7** for free access to author videos, suggested reading and practice questions to further enhance your study.

Ten

WINNING AND LOSING: WHERE YOU LIVE REALLY MATTERS

LOCATION MATTERS

The real *effects* of globalizing processes are felt not at the global or the national level but at the *local* scale: the communities within which people struggle to meet the needs of their daily lives. It is at this scale that physical investments in economic activities are actually put in place, restructured or closed down. It is at this scale that most people make their living and create their own family, household and social communities. Despite the undoubtedly large volumes of migration that have occurred throughout human history, most people live out their lives within the country – often even the locality – of their birth. A person's place of birth or residence, therefore, is a key determinant of the range of 'life chances' that are available. These are highly unevenly distributed across the earth's surface at all geographical scales: between countries, within countries, even within individual cities.

The contours of the well-being map show a landscape of staggeringly high peaks of affluence and deep troughs of deprivation interspersed with plains of greater or lesser degrees of prosperity. Writing before the onset of the 2008 global economic crisis, the UN *Human Development Report* observed:

> The era of globalization has been marked by dramatic increases in technology, trade and investment – and an impressive increase in prosperity. Gains in human development have been less impressive. Large parts of the developing world are being left behind. Human development gaps between rich and poor countries, already large, are widening … *The scale of the human development gains registered over the past decade should not be underestimated – nor should it be exaggerated.* Part of the problem of global snapshots is that they obscure large variations across and within regions … Progress towards human development has been uneven across and within regions and across different dimensions.[1]

Today, this statement is even more valid.

Looking at the world through the lens of GPNs leads us to think of the map of economic activities as a set of variably interconnected 'islands', rather than as a continuous surface. Figure 10.1 is one such representation by Allen Scott, in which

the developed areas of the world are represented as a system of polarized regional economies each consisting of a central metropolitan area
and a surrounding hinterland (of indefinite extent) occupied by ancillary communities, prosperous agricultural zones, smaller tributary
centers, and the like … Each metropolitan nucleus is the site of intricate networks of specialized but complementary forms of economic
activity, together with large, multi-faceted labour markets, and each is
a locus of powerful agglomeration economies and increasing returns
effects … These entities can be thought of as *the regional motors of the
new global economy* … Equally, there are large expanses of the modern
world that lie at the extensive economic margins of capitalism …
Even so, underdeveloped areas are occasionally punctuated by islands
of relative prosperity.[2]

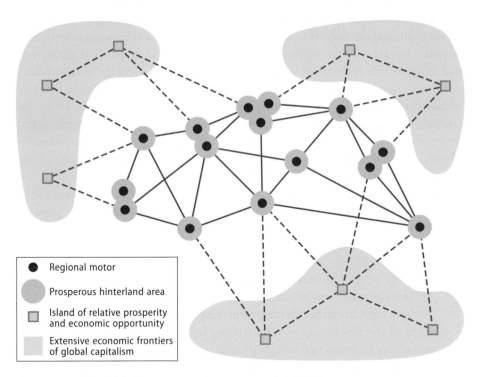

● Regional motor

⬤ Prosperous hinterland area

☐ Island of relative prosperity
and economic opportunity

▨ Extensive economic frontiers
of global capitalism

Figure 10.1   **The global economy as interconnected 'islands'**

Source: based on Scott, 1998: Figure 4.2

This notion of 'islands of relative prosperity' resonates with the more general metaphor of the global economy as an *archipelago* (literally, a sea studded with many
islands).[3]

The processes of winning and losing in the global economy are highly interconnected. Development and underdevelopment are, in a very real sense, two sides

of the same coin, although the relationships are more complex than is often suggested. Hence,

> establishing a link between globalization and inequality is fraught with difficulty, not only because of how globalization is defined and how inequality is measured, but also because the entanglements between globalization forces and 'domestic' trends are not that easy to separate out ... However, there is sufficient evidence to conclude that contemporary processes of globalization have been accompanied by a rise in global inequality and vulnerability.[4]

At the global scale, the development gap is stunningly wide. The developed countries are clearly 'winners'. They continue to contain a disproportionate share of the world's wealth, trade, investment and access to modern technologies (especially of information technologies). The 20 per cent of the world's population living in the highest-income countries have well over 80 per cent of world income, trade, investment and communications technology. The 20 per cent of the world's population living in the poorest countries have around 1 per cent.

In developed countries, at least until the 2008 financial crisis, the trajectory was of generally increasing affluence, although by no means everybody was a winner. The picture in developing countries is very different. Although there are some undoubted winners, there are also many losers. In large part, though not entirely, the economic progress and material well-being of developing countries are linked to what happens in the developed economies. Buoyant economic conditions in those economies, stimulating a general expansion of demand for both primary and manufactured products, would undoubtedly help developing countries. But the old notion that 'a rising tide will lift all boats' ignores the enormous variations that exist between countries. The shape of the 'economic coastline' is highly irregular; some economies are beached and stranded way above the present water level. Indeed, the global financial and economic crisis that erupted in 2008 is redrawing the economic coastline in rather dramatic ways, just as the effects of climate change threaten to redraw the physical coastline.

For the poorest countries, however, there is no automatic guarantee that a rising tide of economic activity would, on its own, do very much to refloat them. The internal conditions of individual countries – their histories, cultures, political institutions, forms of civil society, resource base (both natural and human) – obviously influence their developmental prospects. However, despite the claims of the 'neo-environmental determinists', low levels of development cannot be explained simplistically in terms of the natural environment (e.g. climatic conditions). As always, it is the *specific combination* of external and internal conditions which determines the developmental trajectories of individual countries. For the developing world as a whole, the basic problems are those of extreme poverty, continuing rapid population growth, and a lack of adequate employment opportunities. Apart from the yawning gap between developed and developing countries, there are also enormous disparities within the developing world itself.

In this chapter, we focus on two tightly interconnected dimensions of the problems posed by globalizing processes for both developed and developing countries, namely incomes and jobs:

- *Income* is the key to an individual's or a family's material well-being. But income – or the lack of it in the form of *poverty* – is not an end in its own right, rather a means towards what Amartya Sen calls 'development as freedom'. In that sense, poverty is an 'unfreedom': 'a deprivation of basic capabilities, rather than merely a low income'.[5]
- *Employment* or *self-employment* is the major source of income (for all but the exceptionally wealthy). Hence, the question of *where will the jobs come from?* is a crucial one throughout the world. The major employment changes that have been occurring in both developed and developing countries are the result of an intricate interaction of processes. Job losses in the developed market economies, for example, cannot be attributed simply to the relocation of production to low-cost developing countries. There is far more to it than this. What is clear, however, is that the industrialized economies face major problems of adjusting to the decline in manufacturing jobs in particular but also, increasingly, of some service jobs, especially in the current global crisis. However, the problems facing developing countries are infinitely more acute, despite the spectacular success of a small number of newly industrialized economies.

INCOMES AND POVERTY

The contours of world poverty

Before the beginning of the nineteenth century the differences in levels of income between different parts of the world were relatively small:

> At the dawn of the first industrial revolution, the gap in per capita income between Western Europe and India, Africa, or China was probably no more than 30 per cent. All this changed abruptly with the industrial revolution.[6]

Figure 10.2 shows in graphic terms how much this changed; how dramatically the gap between the richest and the poorest countries progressively widened as industrialization (and globalization) proceeded. In 1820, the ratio between the richest and the poorest countries was 3:1; by 2007 it had grown to a staggering 92:1. Figure 10.3 shows the massive unevenness in the map of incomes between countries today, while Figure 10.4 provides 'a general simultaneous impression of

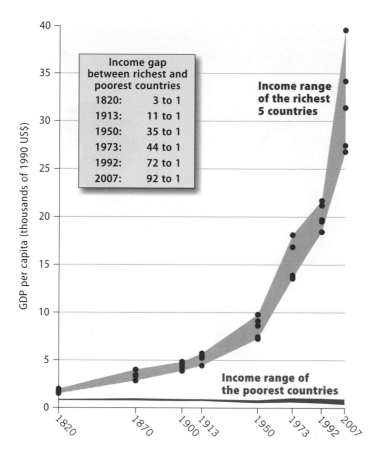

Figure 10.2   The widening income gap between countries

Source: based on UNDP, *Human Development Report*, 1999: Figure 1.6; World Bank, 2009b: Table 1

two distributions – between countries (the longer axis ascending from left to right) and between income groups (the shorter axis from left to right'.[7]

But what are the *current trends* in global income distribution over time? Is the poverty gap getting bigger? Are the numbers living in poverty increasing or falling? There is no simple and straightforward answer to these questions. The extent to which the income gap is widening, narrowing or staying about the same is controversial and depends on how it is measured. Not only this, but also the statistical data are incomplete and often out of date.

Wherever they are located, the poor are poor; the poorest are very poor indeed. In 2010, approximately 1.2 billion people lived below the international poverty line (less than $1.25 per day). This was some 700 million fewer than in 1990: a real improvement, but one that was highly uneven geographically, as Figure 10.5 shows.

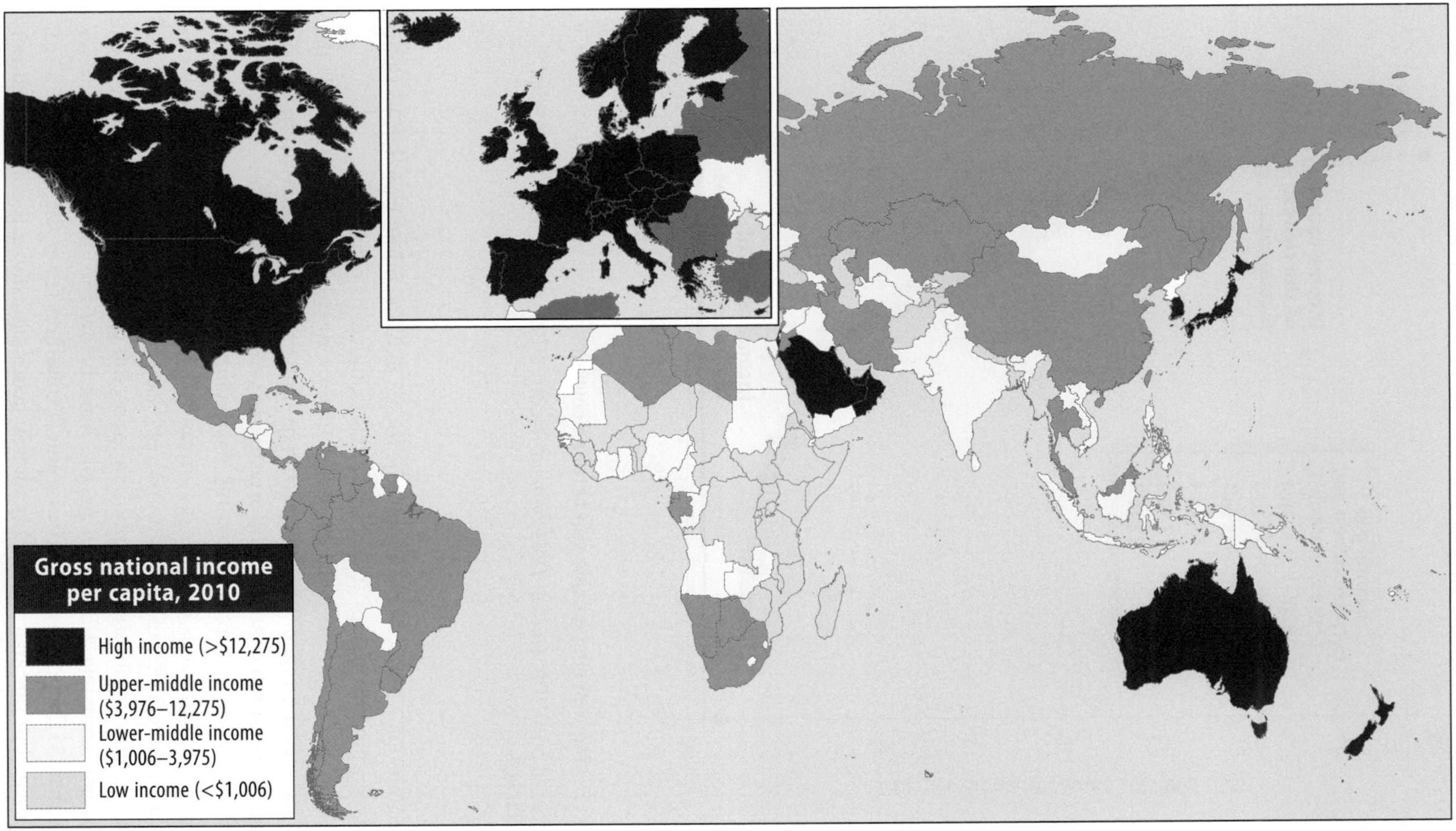

Gross national income
per capita, 2010

High income (>$12,275)

Upper-middle income
($3,976–12,275)

Lower-middle income
($1,006–3,975)

Low income (<$1,006)

Figure 10.3   The huge global unevenness in per capita income

Source: based on World Bank, 2012: Table 1

Annual income (international $), 2008

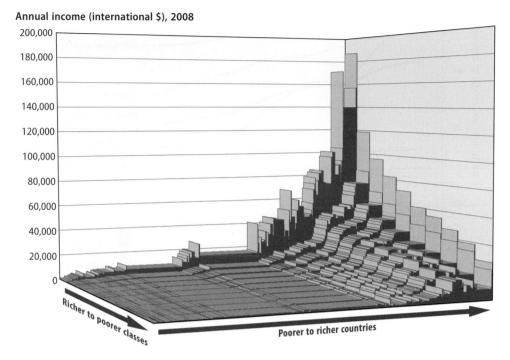

Figure 10.4   **Global distribution of per capita income**

Source: graph compiled by Bob Sutcliffe (December 2009)

The biggest improvement was in East Asia and the Pacific, whose share of the world's poorest people fell from almost 49 per cent in 1990 to 21 per cent in 2010. Much of this was accounted for by China, where there has been very substantial progress in reducing poverty. Of course, as we saw in Chapter 2, the spectacular economic growth of a relatively small number of East Asian developing countries has been one of the most significant developments in the global economy in the past 50 years. In particular, the four East Asian 'tigers' industrialized at a rate 'unmatched in the nineteenth and twentieth centuries by Western countries and, for that matter, by Latin American economies'.[8] The spread of the growth processes to encompass some other East Asian countries during the 1980s and 1990s – Malaysia, Thailand, the Philippines, Indonesia and, most of all, China – means that

> in little more than a generation, hundreds of millions of people have been lifted out of abject poverty, and many of these are now well on their way to enjoying the sort of prosperity that has been known in North America and Western Europe for some time.[9]

In contrast, the share of the world's poorest population increased from 32 per cent to 42 per cent in South Asia and in Sub-Saharan Africa from 15 per cent to 34 per

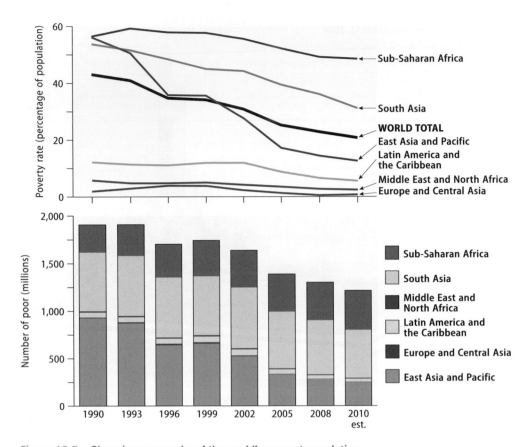

Figure 10.5   Changing geography of the world's poorest population

Source: based on data in World Bank, *World Development Indicators*, 2013: Table 2.8

cent. In other words, three-quarters of the world's most impoverished people live in those two regions. In no fewer than 16 African countries, for example, over half the population has to survive on less than $1.25 a day, while in 5 of those countries, more than four-fifths of the population live below that poverty level. Nevertheless, the percentage of the population in poverty fell from 54 to 31 per cent in South Asia, and from 57 to 49 per cent in Sub-Saharan Africa between 1990 and 2010.

Poverty, of course, is *multidimensional*; it is associated with a whole host of other problems. The Multidimensional Poverty Index (MPI)[10] (based upon 10 indicators along three dimensions: health, education, living standards) provides a broader and more nuanced picture. The findings for the MPI in 2013, covering 104 countries, showed that:[11]

- 1.6 billion people lived in multidimensional poverty – over 30 per cent of the population in the countries covered;
- 51 per cent of these people lived in South Asia, 29 per cent in Sub-Saharan Africa; 72 per cent of the MPI population lived in middle-income countries.

Almost 10 per cent of the world's poorest billion people live in high-income or upper-middle-income countries.

- Changes in MPI in a sample of 22 countries for which time-series data exist showed some significant improvements:
  - In 18 of the 22 countries, multidimensional poverty fell significantly.
  - 'The biggest absolute reductions in multidimensional poverty were seen in countries with relatively high poverty levels. Nepal, Rwanda and Bangladesh were the top performers ... followed by Ghana, Tanzania, Cambodia and Bolivia' (p. 2).

- '[I]f the study's "star" performers continue to reduce poverty at the current rate, they will halve MPI in less than 10 years and eradicate it within 20. Other countries are closing in more slowly. At the current rate of reduction, it will take Ethiopia 45 years to halve multidimensional poverty, while India will need 41 years and Malawi 74 years to eradicate acute poverty as measured by the MPI' (p. 3).

Inequalities within countries

Focusing the analytical lens at the country level provides a useful first cut at mapping the contours of poverty and income. But, of course, such a focus obscures the detail of the economic landscape both at smaller geographical scales and in terms of non-geographical criteria (e.g. gender, social class, and so on). For example, even though most people in developed countries are significantly better off than in the past,

> it is remarkable that the extent of deprivation for particular groups in very rich countries can be comparable to that in the so-called third world. For example, in the US, African Americans as a group have no higher – indeed have a lower – chance of reaching advanced ages than do people born in the immensely poorer economies of China or the Indian state of Kerala (or in Sri Lanka, Jamaica or Costa Rica).[12]

The fact that a significant proportion of people with high multidimensional poverty are found in higher-income countries is a graphic illustration of the extreme unevenness of incomes *within*, as well as between, countries.

Income inequalities within developed countries

One measure of income inequality is the Gini coefficient, a summary statistic whose potential value ranges from zero (complete income equality) to one (complete income inequality). The extent to which individual countries tend towards one or the other extreme is a useful, if crude, indicator of inequality.[13] A striking feature of Figure 10.6 is the relative income equality within the Nordic countries (Sweden, Norway, Denmark, Finland), as well as in Austria, Belgium and Germany, and, in contrast, the fact that the USA and UK have a much more unequal income distribution than any other leading developed economies. Figure 10.6 also shows

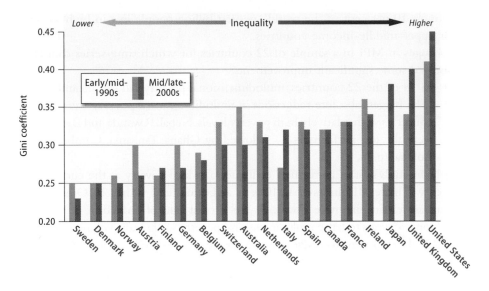

Figure 10.6   Variations in income inequality within developed countries

Source: calculated from data in *CIA World Fact Book, 2013*

the trend in individual countries' income distribution. The UK, USA and Japan all became less equal in income terms: the UK from 0.34 to 0.40; the USA from 0.41 to 0.45; and Japan from 0.25 to 0.38.

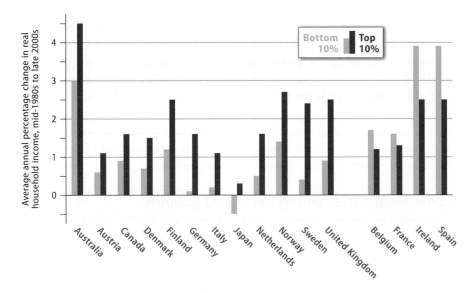

Figure 10.7   The top end wins: changes in the incomes of the top and bottom segments of the population

Source: based on OECD, 2011: Table 1

Such changes in income distribution are complex. However, what is very clear is that, in most developed countries, it is the 'top end' of the income distribution that has grown significantly faster in recent years than the 'bottom end'.[14] Figure 10.7 shows the average annual change in real household income for the lowest 10 per cent and the highest 10 per cent between the mid-1980s and late 2000s in a number of major developed countries. In 12 of the 16 countries shown the income of the top 10 per cent grew significantly faster than the bottom 10 per cent. The income gap has widened:

> In OECD countries today, the average income of the richest 10% of the population is about nine times that of the poorest 10% – a ratio of 9 to 1. However, the ratio varies widely … It is much lower than the OECD average in the Nordic and many continental European countries, but reaches 10 to 1 in Italy, Japan, Korea and the United Kingdom; around 14 to 1 … in the United States … *The latest trends in the 2000s showed a widening gap between rich and poor not only in some of the already high-inequality countries … but also – for the first time – in traditionally low-inequality countries, such as Germany, Denmark and Sweden (and other Nordic countries) where inequality grew more than anywhere else in the 2000s.*[15]

In fact, the capture of bigger and bigger shares of income by the small minority at the top is even greater than these figures suggest. Figure 10.8 shows the extent to which the share of national income held by the *top 1 per cent* has increased dramatically, especially in the UK and North America. In the USA, the share of the top 1 per cent increased from around 8 per cent in 1970 to almost 19 per cent in 2007;

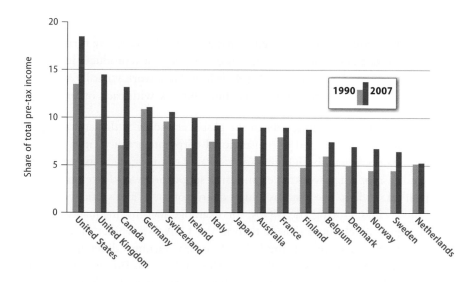

Figure 10.8   **The very top end wins even more: the increasing share of the top 1 per cent of incomes**

Source: based on OECD, 2011: Figure 12

in the UK, the increase was from 7 per cent in 1970 to 15 per cent in 2005. And the trend continues. As Joseph Stiglitz shows for the USA:[16]

- In the five years to 2007, the top 1 per cent captured more than two-thirds of the increase in US national income. By 2010, the top 1 per cent had captured more than 90 per cent of the gain.
- In the past 30 years, the bottom 90 per cent have increased their wages by 15 per cent; the top 1 per cent had a staggering 150 per cent increase.

In the case of the UK, Danny Dorling shows that, between 1997 and 2007:[17]

- the average income of the top 1 per cent increased by 60 per cent while that of the bottom 90 per cent grew by only 18 per cent;
- the income of the top 0.1 per cent of the population in 1997 was 61 times greater than the 90 per cent at the bottom; by 2007 this had risen to 95 times.

One of the major causes of the extreme inequalities that have developed particularly in the UK and USA in recent years has been the growing dominance of the financial services sector. In the UK case in particular:

> If you look at who is racing away, then half the top 1% of high earners work in financial services … almost all the increase in inequality has come from financial services in the past 12 years.[18]

The effect is most apparent within the 'global cities' of London and New York, where wealth tends to be highly concentrated but where there is also huge income inequality:

> The great cities are becoming elite citadels … Global cities are turning into vast gated communities where the one per cent reproduces itself. Elite members don't live there for their jobs. They work virtually anyway. Rather, global cities are where they network with each other.[19]

Because of their particular functions in the global economy as the 'control points' of global financial markets and of transnational corporate activity, cities like New York and London contain both highly sophisticated economic activities, with their highly paid cosmopolitan workforces, and large supporting workforces in low- and medium-level services. The result is a high degree of social and spatial *polarization* within these cities. During the 1990s, for example, income inequality in New York City grew much more sharply than in the USA as a whole: 'New York has the worst income inequality in the U.S.'[20] Similarly, earnings differentials within London have increased substantially since the mid-1980s. But in addition, the extremely high, and increasing, concentration of wealth in London has hugely adverse effects on the rest of the country.

The UK, in particular, is a highly unbalanced economy, both geographically and socially, not least because of the sheer scale of the City's financial sector and associated wealthy population. Indeed, Eurostat figures for 2010 indicate that the UK has the most geographically uneven income distribution anywhere in the EU:

> Measured by per capita incomes, the gap between the best-performing and the worst-performing regions of the UK is the widest of any of the European Union's 27 member states ... in inner London GDP per head was 328% of the EU average, while in West Wales it was 70% of the average. No other country came close to the gap of 258 percentage points between extremes that exists in the UK ... Britain, in other words, has islands of prosperity in a sea of relative poverty. Of the 37 regions studied by Eurostat, 27 have GDP per capita below the EU average. Only one region in the north of England had per capita incomes above €24,500, the average for the EU as a whole; none did in the West Midlands, Northern Ireland or Wales.[21]

Differences in income inequality between, and within, individual countries reflect many forces, both external (such as globalization and technological change) and internal (such as economic and social policies), as we will discuss later. Specifically, the contrasts between the neo-liberal market capitalist systems of the USA and UK and the social market systems of continental Europe are extremely important.

Such extreme inequality within the UK and the USA, especially, raises questions about its longer-term effects, especially on *social mobility*. As Thomas Piketty

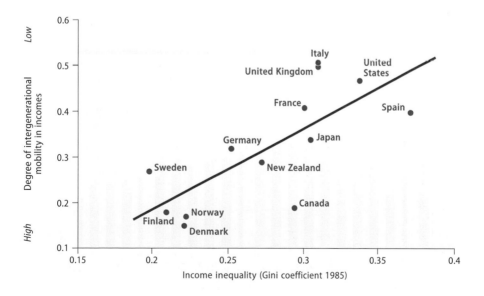

Figure 10.9   **Inequality and intergenerational mobility**

Source: based on Council of Economic Advisers, 2012: Figure 6.7

argues, 'it is hard to imagine an economy and society that can continue functioning indefinitely with such extreme divergence between social groups.'[22] Highly
uneven income distributions are potentially dysfunctional in social terms. This is
because

> family (or individual) incomes in one generation are … highly cor-
> related with family (or individual) incomes in the next generation. In
> other words, the children of parents who are poor are more likely than
> the children of well-off parents to be poor when they grow up …
> [Evidence suggests that] in the past 30 years … intergenerational
> mobility has fallen … Moreover, the widening of income inequality
> has meant that it is harder for someone born into the bottom to move
> to the middle or the top of the income distribution[23]

So, as Figure 10.9, the so-called 'Great Gatsby Curve',[24] shows, countries with low
levels of income inequality at one point in time (e.g. the Nordic countries) tend
to have a higher level of intergenerational income mobility than those with high
levels of income inequality (like the USA and UK).

Income inequalities within developing countries

A widely voiced criticism of industrialization in developing countries is that its
material benefits have not been widely diffused to the majority of the population. There is indeed evidence of highly uneven income distribution within many
developing countries, as Figure 10.10 shows. Comparison with Figure 10.6 shows

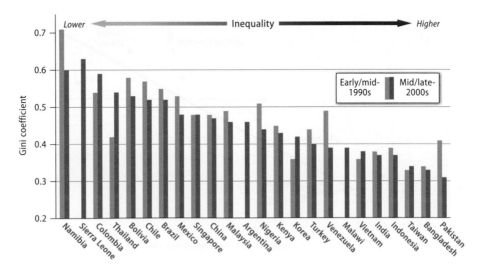

Figure 10.10   **Variations in income inequality within developing countries**

Source: calculated from data in *CIA World Factbook, 2013*

Table 10.1   Distribution of income within selected developing countries

Country (year)	Lowest 10%	Lowest 20%	Highest 20%	Highest 10%
Brazil (2009)	1	3	59	43
Chile (2009)	2	4	58	43
Mexico (2000)	2	5	53	38
Malaysia (2009)	2	5	51	35
Philippines (2009)	3	3	50	34
Singapore (1998)	2	5	49	33
China (2009)	2	5	47	30
India (2010)	4	9	43	29
Korea (1998)	3	8	37	22

Source: based on World Bank, *World Development Indicators,* 2013: Table 2.9

that the majority have a more unequal income distribution than the least equal developed countries (the USA and UK). On the other hand, the trend in many of the countries shown was for some improvement. Table 10.1 shows this in a different way. It is clear that the East Asian countries have a more equitable income distribution than the Latin American countries, where there is a 'hugely unequal distribution of income and wealth. A disproportionately large number of Latin Americans are poor – some 222m or 43% of the total population.'[25] However, in some cases, notably Korea and Singapore, the figures in Table 10.1 are quite old. Recent evidence suggests that, in both cases, inequality may have been increasing.

Such differences reflect specific historical experiences and social policies, in particular the different patterns of land ownership and reform. In Korea and in Taiwan, for example, post-war reform of land ownership had a massive effect, increasing individual incomes through greater agricultural productivity, expanding domestic demand and contributing to political stability.[26] This has not happened in most Latin American countries:

> In 1953, while Taiwan was still recovering from World War II, the island had a level of income inequality that was about the level found in *present-day* Latin America. Ten years later it had dropped to the level *now found* in France. At the same time, growth rates in this period were of the order of 9 per cent per annum … this outcome was due primarily to improved income distribution in Taiwan's agriculture sector. This improvement, in turn, rested on a specific set of governmental policies, that focused in the first instance on agricultural reforms – especially land reform, infrastructure investment, and price reform – coupled with a rapid proliferation of educational opportunities for Taiwanese students at all levels. In terms of distributive measures, land reform was of greatest significance.[27]

However, especially in geographically extensive countries, like Brazil, China or India, aggregative income distribution data are misleading. As always, there are vast

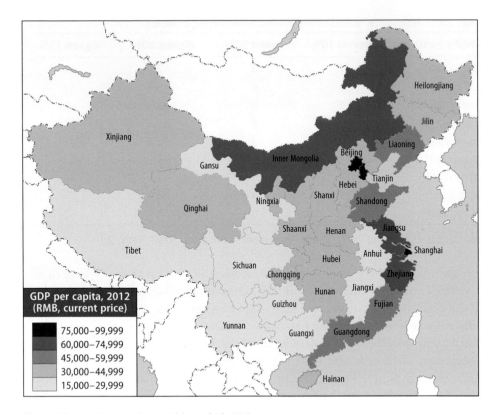

Figure 10.11   **Income inequalities within China**

Source: based on data in *Statistical Yearbook of China, 2013*

differences in income levels (and in other measures of well-being) between different parts of the same country. China, for example, faces massive internal problems. Its spectacular economic growth since its opening up in the early 1980s has created vast inequalities between different parts of the country (Figure 10.11), especially between inland and rural areas on the one hand and coastal and urban areas on the other:

> Currently, rural incomes are less equally distributed than urban incomes. However, urban inequality is increasing faster than rural inequality. At its current rate, urban inequality will eventually overtake rural inequality. Moreover, this trend would further accelerate the increase in inequality as people move to urban areas. On the other hand, the Chinese government restricts free migration from rural to urban areas. Even if such migration were permitted, it probably is not possible for the urban economy to accommodate the majority of the gigantic rural population. Thus ... gaps between rural and urban incomes may persist and cause overall inequality to rise for an extended period.[28]

We discussed the '1 per cent' – the top end of the income distribution in developed countries – earlier in this chapter. A similar phenomenon is emerging in

Asia in particular, where the growth of the extremely wealthy has accelerated markedly:

> There are more millionaires and 'super rich' people than ever before as the rapid growth in Asia's emerging markets propels private wealth to record levels ... Asia, excluding Japan, was the fastest growing region with private wealth increasing to $28tn, a 17 per cent jump on 2011. The figure is projected to nearly double to $48.1tn over the next five years.[29]

Winners and losers

How we identify the winners and losers in terms of incomes depends very much on the scale of analysis we adopt. As we have seen, there are huge income differentials both between and within countries. However, there are two broad groups of winners and losers that merit our brief attention at this stage. These two groups cut right across the broad development divide.

The clear winners are the elite *transnational capitalist class* (TCC)[30] whose members are predominantly, although no longer exclusively, drawn from developed countries. Indeed, the emergence of a substantial class of extremely wealthy and influential individuals within most developing countries, who see themselves as global players, has become a major feature of the global economy. The dominant group within the TCC consists of the owners and controllers of the major corporations and leading financiers – the globe-trotting, jet-setting TNC executives, whose bases are primarily the affluent, often gated, communities of the global cities. To these we can add globalizing bureaucrats and politicians, globalizing professionals (with particular technical expertise – even including some academics), merchants and media people. Without question, these are winners in the global economy and are highly influential in global policy discourses.[31]

This TCC displays a number of significant characteristics:[32]

- Economic interests increasingly globally linked rather than exclusively local and national in origin.
- Behaviour based on specific forms of global competitive and consumerist rhetoric and practice.
- Outward-oriented global, rather than inward-oriented local, perspectives on most economic, political and culture ideology issues.
- Similar lifestyles, especially patterns of higher education (e.g. in business schools) and consumption of luxury goods and services: 'Integral to this process are exclusive clubs and restaurants, ultra-expensive resorts in all continents, private as opposed to mass forms of travel and entertainment and, ominously, increasing residential segregation of the very rich secured by armed guards and electronic surveillance.'
- Self-projection as citizens of the world as well as place of birth.

While transnational elites are clear winners, *women* – at least in many parts of the world – tend to be losers in the global economy. Most strikingly, some two-thirds of the world's population living on less than $1 per day are women, living 'on the margins of existence without adequate food, clean water, sanitation or health care, and without education'.[33] The 2012 World Bank Report on gender inequality and development listed several major problems facing women, especially – though not exclusively – in developing countries:[34]

- different work and less pay;
- housework and care still predominantly a woman's domain;
- less control over resources;
- more vulnerable to domestic violence;
- less voice and less power;
- less likely to hold political office.

In Sen's terms of 'development as freedom', then, women are significantly more disadvantaged than men. At the same time, because of their key role in nurturing children, women hold the key to development, especially in the poorest countries of the world. The problem is that in many developing countries (as opposed to developed countries) women have a much higher mortality rate and lower survival rate than men. As a result, the female/male ratio is lower than in developed countries, implying a phenomenon of 'missing women'. Where this occurs – as in China and India, for example – the main explanation would seem to be 'the comparative neglect of female health and nutrition, especially, but not exclusively, during childhood'.[35]

WHERE WILL THE JOBS COME FROM?

People strive to make a living in a whole variety of ways: for example, exchanging self-grown crops or basic handcrafted products; providing personal services in the big cities; working on the land, in factories or in offices as paid employees; running their own businesses as self-employed entrepreneurs; and so on. For the overwhelming majority of people, *employment* (full- or part-time or as self-employment) is the most important source of income and, therefore, one of the keys to 'development as freedom'. However, there are simply not enough jobs to meet the growing demand. In 2013, almost 202 million people were unemployed globally, compared with around 197 million in 2012 and some 175 million in 2000.[36]

Between 1980 and 2005, the effective global labour supply quadrupled. Half of that increase was in East Asia, primarily the result of China entering the world market economy. As Figure 10.12 shows, the vast majority (85 per cent) of the world's labour force is in low- and middle-income countries. Only 1 per cent of the projected growth of the global labour force between 1995 and 2025 will be in the high-income countries while more than two-thirds of the projected growth will occur in developing countries:

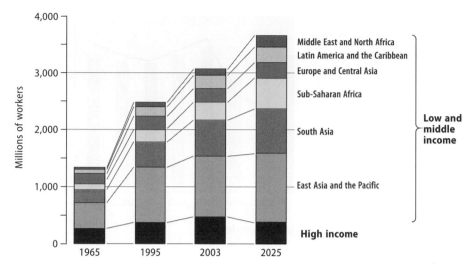

Figure 10.12 **Distribution of the global labour force**

Source: calculated from World Bank, *World Development Reports*, 1995: Table 1; 2005: Table 2

Some 46 million new workers will be joining the world's labour force every year in the future, the bulk of them in developing countries. While the world's labour force is concentrated in developing countries, its capital and skills are concentrated in advanced industrial countries. The global employment situation reflects this huge asymmetry in the distribution of the world's productive resources.[37]

In many developing countries, extremely high rates of population growth mean that the number of young people seeking jobs will continue to accelerate for the foreseeable future.

Writing in 2006 – well before the onset of the current global financial crisis – the Director-General of the ILO warned:

> We are facing a global jobs crisis of mammoth proportions, and a deficit in decent work that isn't going to go away by itself.[38]

How true it is turning out to be – especially for young people. Globally, around 74.5 million 15–24 year olds are now unemployed.[39] Figure 10.13 shows how global youth unemployment has grown during the 2000s. By 2013, it had reached 13.1 per cent: 'almost three times as high as the adult unemployment rate'.[40] In fact, the youth unemployment rate in many countries is far higher than these aggregate figures suggest, reaching levels of around 24 per cent in some cases and up to 50 per cent in countries such as Greece and Spain.

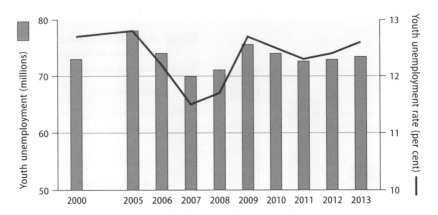

Figure 10.13   **Growth in global youth unemployment**

Source: based on ILO, 2013b: Table A1

Employment and unemployment in developed countries

Figure 10.14 shows that the annual rate of employment growth among developed economies since 2001 has been far weaker than that for the world as a whole. Indeed, in 2009 and 2010, the annual growth rate was negative. Of course, there

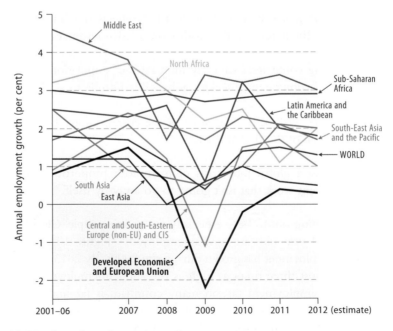

Figure 10.14   **Annual employment growth**

Source: based on ILO, 2013a: Table A6

were variations between individual countries but the general pattern is clear. The developed economies are creating very few new jobs.

Changing employment structures

During the past 50 years, two major trends have occurred in the employment structures of developed economies:

- the displacement of jobs in manufacturing industries by jobs in services;
- the increasing participation of women in the labour market.

Figure 10.15 shows that between three-quarters and four-fifths of the labour forces of the major developed countries are now employed in service occupations – even higher in the UK and North America. In recent years, virtually all the net employment growth in the developed economies has been in services, although manufacturing employment remains relatively stronger in such countries as Germany, Italy and Japan.

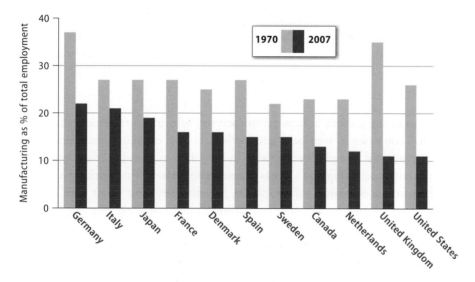

Figure 10.15   The declining share of manufacturing in total employment

Source: calculated from ILO data

Within the older industrialized countries, three broad geographical trends in these processes of manufacturing employment decline are apparent:

- *Broad interregional shifts* in employment opportunities, as exemplified by the relative shift of investment from 'Snowbelt' to 'Sunbelt' in the USA, from north to south within the UK.
- *Relative decline of the large urban–metropolitan areas* as centres of manufacturing activity and the growth of new manufacturing investment in non-metropolitan and rural areas.

- *Hollowing out of the inner cities of the older industrialized countries*: in virtually every case, the inner urban cores have experienced massive employment loss as the focus of economic activity shifted first from central city to suburb and subsequently to less urbanized areas.

Thus, deindustrialization has been experienced most dramatically in the older industrial cities as well as in those broad regions in which the decline of specific industries (including agriculture) has been especially heavy. In many cases, the vacuum left by the decline of traditional manufacturing remains unfilled. The physical expression of these processes is the mile upon mile of industrial wasteland; the human expression is the despair of whole communities, families and individuals whose means of livelihood have disappeared. One outcome of these cataclysmic changes has been the growth of an *informal* or *hidden economy*, a world of interpersonal cash transactions or payments in kind for services rendered, a world much of which borders on the illegal and some of which is transparently criminal.

A common general criticism levelled at the new service jobs is that they are essentially poorly paid, low skilled, part-time and insecure – at least compared with the kinds of jobs in manufacturing that were characteristic of the developed countries up until the 1960s. There is certainly some truth in this. Many of the new service jobs are, indeed, 'McJobs', and these may well have become even more pervasive in the current recession. But it is not the entire story. An OECD report suggested that

> most of the growth in new private services jobs in western industrialized countries is well-paid and skilled ... the expansion in service employment brought faster growth in the 1990s in high-paid than low-paid work ... While the US has a higher proportion of its working-age population employed in low-paying jobs than in most other OECD countries, it also has a higher proportion in higher-paying jobs.[41]

The shift in the balance of employment towards services has been closely associated with the second major trend: *the increasing participation of women in the labour force*.[42] In all developed economies, the changing roles of women, away from an automatically assumed domestic role, has gone hand in hand with the growth of service jobs. Although women are certainly employed in manufacturing industries, their relative importance is far higher in service industries. This is especially so where there are greater opportunities for part-time work, which allows women with families a degree of flexibility to combine a paid job with their traditional gender roles.

Female participation in the labour market has increased in virtually all countries. In the USA, for example, it was around 38 per cent in 1960; today it is 60 per cent. In the UK, a similar trend is evident: from 40 per cent in 1971 to 55 per cent today. But, as Figure 10.16 shows, there is considerable variation between

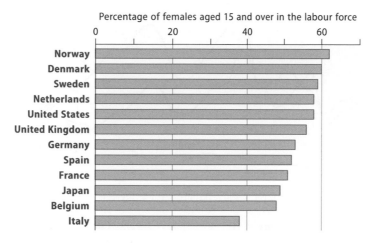

Percentage of females aged 15 and over in the labour force

Figure 10.16   Variations in female participation in the labour markets of developed countries

Source: based on World Bank, *World Development Indicators*, 2013: Table 2.2

countries. The highest female participation rates are found in the Scandinavian countries and the Netherlands; significantly lower rates are found in Germany, France, Spain, Belgium and Italy.

Resurging unemployment

The obverse of employment growth is, of course, *unemployment* growth. Figure 10.17 demonstrates just how volatile unemployment rates have become since the so-called 'golden age of growth' of the 1960s and early 1970s. Since then, unemployment rates in the industrialized countries have increased dramatically, though very unevenly. The overall pattern of change in unemployment rates is clearly related to the 'roller-coaster' of production and trade shown in Figure 2.3. Over the entire period, the trend has been one of significantly higher levels of unemployment in the major European economies, excluding the UK, compared with both the USA and, especially, Japan. However, the unemployment situation in Japan has undergone a particularly significant change. Historically, unemployment rates in Japan were extremely low (well below 2 per cent throughout the 1960s and most of the 1970s). A combination of a rapidly growing economy and a very strong orientation towards job security in the large-company sector of the economy sustained lower rates of unemployment than in any other industrialized country for almost 30 years. But the burst of the bubble economy at the end of the 1980s and persistent domestic recession throughout the 1990s changed all that. The lifetime job system has crumbled.

The current financial crisis has drastically altered the situation once again; unemployment rates have risen sharply in several countries. Reports from

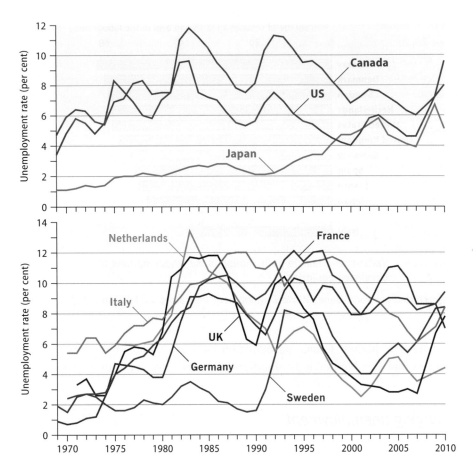

Figure 10.17   **Unemployment rates**

Source: ILO data

virtually all the developed economies suggest huge job losses, either actual or in the pipeline. Increases in unemployment rates have been especially high in parts of the EU – notably Greece, Ireland, Spain and Portugal – as the region struggles to cope with financial crises in those eurozone countries. In early 2012, according to one estimate, unemployment in Greece had reached 22 per cent, in Spain 24 per cent, in Portugal 15 per cent and in Ireland 15 per cent.[43]

Whatever its precise level at any point in time, unemployment is always a *selective* process. The drastic collapse of financial services employment in 2008 clearly affected particular groups of workers and particular places where such activities are concentrated. Some manufacturing industries (automobiles being a prime example) were also hit very hard. More generally, however, males aged between 25 and 54 years, with a good education and training, are less likely to be unemployed, on average, than women, younger people, older workers and minorities. Most of these latter categories tend to be unskilled or semi-skilled workers.

The vulnerability of women and young people to unemployment reflects two major features of the labour markets of the older industrialized countries. First, as we have seen, the increased participation of women in the labour force – particularly married women – has increased dramatically. A large proportion of these are employed as part-time workers in both manufacturing and services, especially the latter. Second, youth unemployment during the 1980s partly arose from the entry onto the labour market of vast numbers of 1960s' 'baby boom' teenagers. In most industrialized countries, therefore, unemployment rates among the young (under 25 years) have been roughly twice as high as that for the over-25s. In some cases youth unemployment is three times higher than adult unemployment. As we saw earlier (Figure 10.13), there has been a huge surge in youth unemployment. Not surprisingly, this has been especially steep in those EU countries whose overall unemployment rates have increased dramatically during the eurozone crisis. Cutting across these patterns is the fact that unemployment tends to be especially high among *minority groups* within a population.

Why is it happening?

Put this question to most politicians, journalists, quite a lot of academics and many ordinary people and you are likely to get a simple answer: 'it's globalization, stupid'; or, in light of the post-2007 crisis, it is the fault of evil bankers and financiers. In fact, it is not as simple as this. These highly uneven trends in employment, unemployment and incomes in the industrialized economies cannot be explained simplistically in terms of a single set of causes. It is a matter of searching for explanatory needles in very messy haystacks.

For example, the most general explanation of an overall high level of unemployment in the older industrialized countries between the early 1970s and mid-1980s, in the 1990s and, again, in the 2010s is the effect of global recession. Recession, whatever its causes, drastically reduces levels of demand for goods and services. By this explanation, the bulk of unemployment in the older industrialized countries is cyclical: it is *demand-deficient* unemployment. But the general force of recession does not explain the *geographical variation* in unemployment between and within countries. In fact, a whole set of interconnected processes operates simultaneously to produce the changing map of employment, its reverse image, unemployment, and the increasingly uneven map of income.

Technological change?

Technological developments in products and processes are widely regarded as being a major factor in changing both the number and the type of jobs available. In general, *product innovations* tend to increase employment opportunities overall as they create new demands. On the other hand, *process innovations* are generally introduced to reduce production costs and increase productive efficiency. They tend to be labour saving rather than job creating. Such process innovations are characteristic of the mature phase of product cycles (see Figure 4.15) and became a dominant phenomenon from the late 1960s onwards.

The general effect of process innovations, therefore, is to increase labour productivity: an increased volume of output from the same, or even a smaller, number of workers. But, again, the impact of such technological change on jobs tends to be uneven. In most cases, it has been the semi- and unskilled workers who have been displaced in the largest numbers. Initially, it was manual workers rather than professional, technical and supervisory workers whose numbers were reduced most of all, although this is no longer the case.

There is no doubt that changes in process technology have adversely affected the employment opportunities of less-skilled members of the population. However, there is much disagreement about the overall contribution of technological change to unemployment. Some argue that the 'end of work' is nigh, and that much of this is due to the job-displacing effects of technological change. The explosive spread of new information and communications technologies would seem to confirm such apocalyptic views. But do they? Not in the opinion of the ILO,[44] which argues that:

- ICT does not destroy jobs.
- In the 'core' ICT sector, the jobs being lost in manufacturing are more than compensated for by rapid growth in the services segment of these industries (software, computer and data processing services).
- There is huge potential for high-cost economies to move up the value chain and to create higher-skill jobs.
- For most workers, employment stability remains the norm.
- However, these changes in employment tend to reinforce gender inequalities.

The ILO study was published in 2001; by definition, the world of technology does not stand still. Although technological change may continue to create, in net terms, more jobs than it destroys, the problem is the actual *distribution* of such new jobs in relation to those destroyed. Certainly, the ever-increasing pervasiveness of computerization in all areas of the economy is dramatically transforming existing divisions of labour and contributing towards a 'hollowing out' of labour market structures.[45] New technologies redefine the nature of the jobs performed, the skills required and the training and qualifications needed. They alter the balance of the labour force between different types of worker, involving processes of deskilling and reskilling. The geography of the employment effects of technological change is also extremely uneven. The 'anatomy of job creation' is rather different from the 'anatomy of job loss'. To change the metaphor, the terms 'sunrise' and 'sunset' industries imply (probably unconsciously) a geographical distinction (the sun does not rise and set in the same place).

Globalization of production?

In Chapter 8 we explored the impact of GPNs on local economies. The development of complex GPNs in virtually all sectors of the economy has a major impact on the geographical distribution of employment and incomes. In an increasingly volatile competitive environment, TNCs continuously reconfigure their operations across, and within, national boundaries. As a result, *which* jobs are created/destroyed *where* is contingent upon the specific strategic behaviour of TNCs headquartered in different countries. The strong tendency to locate certain functions in particular kinds of place creates a corporate geographical division of labour which, inevitably, is highly uneven by type of employment (and by income). As we have seen, TNCs are increasingly connected into external networks of suppliers and collaborators and this creates indirect effects on employment patterns and more complex implications for local communities.

One way in which these externalized relationships impact on employment and incomes is through the currently highly controversial processes of outsourcing/offshoring of white-collar activities, especially in financial and business services (Chapter 16) but also in other sectors. Estimates of the scale and likely future trajectory of such offshoring vary enormously; scare stories abound. In fact, the numbers involved are minuscule compared with the number of job changes that occur within individual countries all the time. For example, "'an average of 4.6m Americans started work with a new employer every month" in the year to March 2005'.[46] However, as always, the effects are experienced differentially, by different groups of people in different places. It is not so much the aggregate numbers affected by the reconfiguration of global production networks that counts but, rather, their distribution.

Trade competition from developing countries?

One of the most widely accepted explanations for the employment and income problems facing workers in the older industrialized countries is the competition from imports of cheaper manufactured goods from developing countries. The rapid development of manufacturing production in a small number of NIEs, and their accelerating involvement in world trade, has been a major theme of this book. It is one of the most striking manifestations of global shifts in the world economy.

The basic question is: how far has the industrialization of these fast-growing economies – as expressed through *trade* – contributed towards the *de*industrialization of the older industrialized countries, to the increased levels of unemployment and to the pauperization of workers at the bottom end of the labour market? This has become an even more contentious issue with the recent emergence of China (and, to a lesser extent, India) as a major global economic force:

> China is no longer a marginal supplier ... China's low production costs arise from and are coupled with growing industrial competence ... developments in these labour forces, when these economies are integrated into the global labour force, have the capacity to significantly affect global wage levels.

It is not just the wages of unskilled labour in the global economy which are being and will increasingly be undermined by the size of the labour reservoir in China (and India). One of the most striking features of the Chinese labour market is its growing level of education and skilling.[47]

There is a wide range of views on the relationship between developing country trade and employment and income changes in industrialized countries. On the one hand, analysts like Adrian Wood argue that trade with developing countries has had a very considerable impact, especially in widening the gap between skilled and unskilled workers:

> Countries in the South have increased their production of labour-intensive goods (both for export and domestic use) and their imports of skill-intensive goods, raising the demand for unskilled but literate labour, relative to more skilled workers. In the North, the skill composition of labour demand has been twisted the other way. Production of skill-intensive goods for export has increased, while production of labour-intensive goods has been replaced by imports, reducing the demand for unskilled relative to skilled workers … up to 1990 the changes in trade with the South had reduced the demand for unskilled relative to skilled labour in the North as a whole by something like 20 per cent … Thus expansion of trade with the South was an important cause of the de-industrialization of employment in the North over the past few decades. However, it does not appear to have been the sole cause.[48]

On the other hand, the ILO regards the evidence as 'inconclusive':

> Although international trade has contributed to income inequality trends to some extent, it has not played a major role in pushing down the relative wage of less-skilled workers … [in the case of the USA] … employment patterns in industries least affected by trade moved in the same direction as those in trade-affected manufacturing industry, increasing the share of high-wage employment. This pattern of change in the employment structure is not well explained by the argument relying on the trade effect.[49]

However, given the *particular* ways in which the internal geographies of national economies have evolved, there will inevitably be a correspondingly uneven impact of trade on different parts of the same country. But such effects are very complex, as a study of US regions shows:

> Many regions benefited from cheaper imports. The Southeast and South Central regions, however, both of which are dominated by low-wage,

import-sensitive manufacturing industries, were made worse off by both cheaper imports and by greater orientation toward the production of import-competing goods. By contrast, the Great Lakes, a region with industries that are highly reliant on imported intermediate inputs, was helped by cheaper imports and a greater orientation toward the production of goods in import-competing sectors. On the export side, cheaper exports hurt most regions, but helped states on the West Coast, a highly export-oriented region.[50]

At a finer geographical scale, research into the Los Angeles labour market suggests that:

> An increase in foreign competition significantly reduces the wages of less-skilled workers in the Los Angeles CMSA. The wages of more highly educated workers are unaffected by imports and appear to rise with exports. Between 1990 and 2000, the negative impact of import competition moves up the skills ladder, suggesting that higher education may not insulate all workers from the pressures of the global economy over the long-run … the impact of trade on wage inequality eclipses the influence of technological change through the 1990s, at least in our study region.[51]

Searching for explanatory needles in messy haystacks

Which of these forces are responsible for changing employment and income levels and distribution in developed economies? Is one more important than the others? In fact, efforts to separate out individual influences, and to calculate their precise effects, have not been very successful. The basic problem in all of the individual factor explanations is that each of the factors is treated *independently* of one another. It is as though changes in one of the variables are unrelated to the others. But this is clearly not the case.

For example, although the *direct* effects of trade may be relatively small, the *indirect* effects may be larger because of the ways in which firms respond to the threat of increased global competition. They may, for instance, invest in labour-saving technologies to raise labour productivity and to reduce costs. This would appear as a 'technology effect' whereas the underlying reason for such technological change may be quite different: a response to low-cost external competition. How do we separate out 'trade' effects from 'TNC' effects when so much of global trade is either intra-firm trade or controlled and coordinated by TNCs within GPNs? In some cases, a major driving force in import penetration has actually been the direct – or indirect – involvement of domestically owned TNCs. Is this a trade effect or a TNC effect?

In fact, the long-term decline in overall manufacturing (and increasingly some service) employment in the older industrialized countries is primarily the result of increased productivity. But this has affected the labour force differentially with the greatest relative losses of jobs and of income falling on the least-skilled, least-educated workers. The geographies of such effects are highly uneven, depending on the particular circumstances of individual regional and local economies.

At the level of individual countries, of course, the kinds of domestic policies pursued by national governments are extremely important. How governments respond to pressures on their economies depends very much on their ideological position. Nowhere is this more clearly illustrated than by the UK, where the Conservative-led coalition between 2010 and 2015 has followed such a draconian austerity policy that even the IMF has urged some relaxation of the debt reduction policies and a greater emphasis on measures to stimulate demand, including infrastructure projects.

In summary, Figure 10.18 sets out a rough balance sheet of the positive and negative effects of the globalizing processes on employment in developed economies.

Positive effects	Negative effects
Cheaper imports of relatively labour-intensive manufactures promote greater economic efficiency through the demand side while releasing labour for higher productivity sectors.	Particularly in relatively labour-intensive industries, the rising imports from developing countries, together with competition-driven changes in technology and other factors, lead to inevitable losses in employment and/or quality of jobs, including real wages. This increases inequality between skilled and unskilled workers, and causes extreme redeployment difficulties.
Growth in developing countries through industry relocation and export-generated income leads to (a) increased demand for industrialized country exports and (b) shifts in production in industrialized countries from lower- to higher-valued consumer goods, to more capital- and/or skill-intensive manufacturing and services.	Employment gains from rising industrialized country exports are unlikely to compensate fully for the job losses, especially if (a) industrialized country wages remain well above those of the NIEs and other emerging developing countries and (b) the rates of world economic growth are relatively low, and/or excessively concentrated in East and South East Asia.
Employment growth and job quality improvement for skilled workers are likely to be significant in the short and medium term, even though in the long run the effects are unclear.	The employment growth and job quality improvement for skilled workers will dwindle in the long run, as a result of relatively cheaper and more productive skilled labour in the NIEs.
Relocation of production and/or imports causes negative short-term effects on workers but promotes labour market flexibility and efficiency through greater mobility of workers within countries (and, to a lesser extent, within regional economic spaces) to economic activities and areas with relative scarcity of labour.	Increased trade will further reduce demand for unskilled labour. This exacerbates unemployment because, in a world of mobile capital, the industrialized countries no longer retain a capital-based comparative advantage.

Figure 10.18   **A balance sheet of effects of globalizing processes on employment in developed economies**

Source: based on ILO, 1996: Table Int. 1

Employment and unemployment in developing countries

Changing employment structures

As in the case of developed countries, the employment structures of developing countries have undergone considerable transformation over the past few decades. Some, as we saw in Chapter 2, have become highly significant manufacturing centres;

others have begun to develop important higher-level service sectors. Nevertheless, many developing countries remain predominantly agricultural economies. More than 50 per cent of the labour force in the lowest-income countries is employed in agriculture. Even in the upper-middle-income group (in which most industrial development has occurred) agriculture employs almost 20 per cent of the labour force. In each category the relative importance of agriculture has declined even though the numbers employed in agriculture continued to grow. The balance of employment has shifted towards the other sectors in the economy: industry and services. However, as Figure 10.19 shows, there is a clear geography to these developing country employment structures.

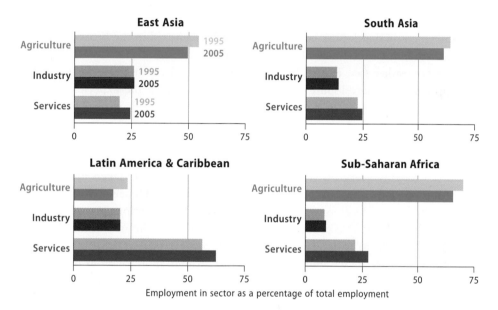

Figure 10.19   **Geographical variations in employment structures in developing countries**

Source: ILO, 2006: Table 5

Some of the biggest changes are taking place within Asia:

> The rapid transition from predominantly rural and agricultural employment to urban-based manufacturing and service-oriented activities in developing Asian countries will continue, and the trend is expected to even accelerate in some countries. Between 2006 and 2015, total employment in agriculture is expected to contract by nearly 160 million, with employment in industry and services expanding by 172 million and 198 million respectively ... Not only will the services sector be the main source of job creation but, by 2015, will also become the largest sector, representing about 40.7 per cent of the region's total employment ... Yet, given its size and importance for

poverty alleviation, agriculture will remain an important sector, even
though the main engines of the region's growth will be elsewhere ...
The stage and speed of the structural change will vary across the
region.[52]

As in the case of developed countries, there has also been a trend towards increased
participation by women in the labour force (quite apart from their huge role in
the informal sector – see below). But its extent varies enormously between different developing countries, ranging from East Asia and Sub-Saharan Africa, where
around two-thirds of women of working age are in the labour force, to one-
quarter in North Africa and the Middle East. Within Asia, female participation
rates are lowest in South Asia (around one-third). These broad structural changes in
employment in developing countries have to be seen within the broader context
of growth in the overall size of the labour force.

We saw earlier (see Figure 10.12) that virtually all the increase in the global
labour force is in developing countries. The contrast with the experience of the
industrialized countries in the nineteenth century is especially sharp. During that
earlier period, the European labour force increased by less than 1 per cent per year
on average; in today's developing countries the labour force is growing at more
than 2 per cent every year. Thus, the labour force in the developing world has
doubled roughly every 30 years compared with the 90 years taken in the nineteenth century for the European labour force to double. Hence, it is very much
more difficult for developing countries to absorb the exceptionally rapid growth
of the labour force. The problem is not likely to ease in the near future because
labour force growth is determined mainly by past population growth with a lag
of about 15 years. As we will see later in this chapter, more than 90 per cent of
the world's population growth since around 1950 has occurred in the developing
countries.

There is, therefore, an enormous difference in labour force growth between the
older industrialized countries on the one hand and the developing countries on
the other. But the scale of the problem also differs markedly between different
parts of the developing world itself. The situation is especially acute in low-
income Asian countries like Bangladesh, India and some in South East Asia. It is
also a major problem even for fast-growing East Asian economies, which are not
creating sufficient numbers of jobs for their burgeoning labour forces. In the case
of China, for example, it is estimated that 15 million jobs need to be created every
year.[53] The basic dilemma facing most developing countries, therefore, is that the
growth of the labour force vastly exceeds the growth in the number of employment opportunities available.

Formal and informal labour markets

It is extremely difficult to quantify the actual size of the unemployment problem in many developing countries. Published figures often show a very low level

of unemployment, in some cases lower than those recorded in the industrialized countries. But the two sets of figures are not comparable. One reason is the paucity of accurate statistics. But the major reason is that unemployment in many developing countries is not the same as unemployment in industrial economies. To understand this we need to appreciate the strongly segmented nature of the labour market in developing countries, in particular its division into two distinctive, though closely linked, sectors, namely *formal* and *informal*:

- In the *formal sector*, employment is in the form of wage labour, where jobs are (relatively) secure and hours and conditions of work clearly established. It is the kind of employment characteristic of the majority of the workforce in the developed market economies. But in most developing countries the formal sector is not the dominant employer, even though it is the sector in which the modern forms of economic activity are found.
- *The informal sector* encompasses both legal and illegal activities, but it is not totally separate from the formal sector: the two are interrelated in a variety of complex ways. The informal sector is especially important in urban areas; some estimates suggest that between 40 and 70 per cent of the urban labour force may work in this sector. It is especially important for women, who depend on the informal sector to a much greater extent than men. But measuring its size accurately is virtually impossible. By its very nature, the informal sector is a floating, kaleidoscopic phenomenon, continually changing in response to shifting circumstances and opportunities.

In a situation where only a minority of the population of working age are 'employed' in the sense of working for wages or salaries, defining unemployment is, thus, a very different issue from that in the developed economies, although even there an increasing informalization of the economy is apparent. The major problem in developing countries is *underemployment*, whereby people may be able to find work of varying kinds on a transitory basis, for example in seasonal agriculture, as casual labour in workshops or in services, but not permanent employment.

Positive and negative effects of globalizing processes on developing country employment

There is no question that the magnitude of the employment and unemployment problem in developing countries is infinitely greater than that facing the older industrialized countries. The high rate of labour force growth in many developing countries continues to exert enormous pressures on the labour markets of both rural and urban areas. Such pressures are unlikely to be alleviated very much by the development of manufacturing industry alone. Despite its considerable development in at least some developing countries, manufacturing industry has made barely a dent in the unemployment and underemployment problems of most developing countries.

Only in small, essentially urban, NIEs (like Hong Kong and Singapore) has manufacturing growth absorbed large numbers of people. Indeed, Singapore has a labour shortage and has had to resort to controlled in-migration while Hong Kong firms have relocated most of their manufacturing production to southern China. In most other cases, the problem is not so much that large numbers of people have not been absorbed into employment – they have – but that the *rate of absorption* cannot keep pace with the growth of the labour force. Globalizing processes, while offering some considerable employment benefits to some developing countries, are, again, a double-edged sword as Figure 10.20 shows.

Positive effects	Negative effects
Higher export-generated income promotes investment in productive capacity with a potentially positive local development impact, depending on intersectoral and inter-firm linkages, the ability to maintain competitiveness, etc.	The increases in employment and/or earnings are (in contradiction to the supposed positive effects) unlikely to be sufficiently large and widespread to reduce inequality. On the contrary, in most countries, inequality is likely to grow because unequal controls over profits and earnings will cause profits to grow faster.
Employment growth in relatively labour-intensive manufacturing of tradeable goods causes (a) an increase in overall employment and/or (b) a reduction of employment in lower-wage sectors. Either of these outcomes tends to drive up wages, to a point which depends on the relative international mobility of each particular industry, labour supply-demand pressure and national wage-setting/bargaining practices.	Relocations of relatively mobile, labour-intensive manufacturing from industrialized to developing countries, in some conditions, can have disruptive social effects if – in the absence of effective planning and negotiations between international companies and the government and/or companies of the host country – the relocated activity promotes urban-bound migration and its length of stay is short. Especially in cases of export assembly operations with very limited participation and development of local industry and limited improvement of skills, the short-term benefits of employment creation may not offset those negative social effects.
These increases in employment and/or wages – if substantial and widespread – have the potential effect of reducing social inequality if the social structure, political institutions and social policies play a favourable role.	
Exposure to new technology and, in some industries, a considerable absorption of technological capacity leads to improvements in skills and labour productivity, which facilitate the upgrading of industry into more value-added output, while either enabling further wage growth or relaxing the downward pressure.	Pressures to create local employment, and international competition in bidding for it, often put international firms in a powerful position to impose or negotiate labour standards and management practices that are inferior to those of industrialized countries and, as in the case of some EPZs, even inferior to the prevailing ones in the host country.

Figure 10.20   **A balance sheet of effects of globalizing processes on developing country employment**

Source: based on ILO, 1996: Table Int. 1

Over-dependence on a narrow economic base

There is no single explanation for the deep poverty of low-income countries (and of some of the lower-middle-income countries too). There is no doubt, for example, that problems of inadequate internal governance (including corruption) play a major role in some cases. But in the context of the global economy, one factor is especially significant in many cases: an over-dependence on a very narrow economic base, together with the nature of the conditions of trade. We saw earlier that the overwhelming majority of the labour force in low-income countries is employed in agriculture. This, together with the extraction of other primary products, forms the basis of these countries' involvement in the world economy. Two-thirds of developing countries have more than a 50 per cent dependence on commodity exports (including agricultural food and non-food products, ferrous metals, industrial raw materials and energy). In most Sub-Saharan African countries, the level of dependence is around 80 per cent.

In the classical theories of international trade, based upon the comparative advantage of different factor endowments, it is totally logical for countries to specialize in the production of those goods for which they are well endowed by nature. Thus, it is argued, countries with an abundance of particular primary resources should concentrate on producing and exporting these and import those goods in which they have a comparative disadvantage. This was the rationale underlying the 'old' international division of labour in which the core countries produced and exported manufactured goods and the countries of the global periphery supplied the basic materials (Figure 2.1). According to traditional trade theory, *all* countries benefit from such an arrangement. But such a neat sharing of the benefits of trade presupposes:

- some degree of equality between trading partners;
- some stability in the relative prices of traded goods;
- an efficient mechanism – the market – which ensures that, over time, the benefits are indeed shared equitably.

In the real world – and especially in the trading relationships between the industrialized countries and the low-income, primary-producing countries – these conditions do not necessarily hold. In the first place, there is a long-run tendency for the composition of demand to change as incomes rise. Thus, growth in demand for manufactured goods and services tends to be greater than the growth in demand for primary products. This immediately builds a bias into trade relationships, favouring the industrialized countries at the expense of the primary producers.

Over time, these inequalities tend to be reinforced through the operation of the *cumulative* processes of economic growth. The prices of manufactured goods tend to increase more rapidly than those of primary products and, therefore, the *terms of trade* for manufactured and primary products tend to diverge. (The terms of trade are simply the ratio of export prices to import prices for any particular country or group of countries.) As the price of manufactured goods increases relative to the price of primary products, the terms of trade move against the primary producers and in favour of the industrial producers. For the primary producers it becomes necessary to export a larger quantity of goods in order to buy the same, or even a smaller, quantity of manufactured goods. In other words, they have to run faster just to stand still or to avoid going backwards. Although the terms of trade do indeed fluctuate over time (as the recent commodities boom demonstrated – see Chapter 12), there is no doubt that they have generally, and systematically, deteriorated for the non-oil primary-producing countries over many years.[54]

In other words, one of the major problems facing these economies, especially those rich in extractive resources, is that of the so-called *resource curse*.[55] This is the apparent paradox that an abundant endowment of resources does not necessarily create rapid economic growth and development:

> In a ... study covering a sample of 95 developing countries, a negative relationship was found between natural-resource-based exports (including agricultural products, metallic minerals and energy minerals) and economic growth during the period 1970–1990 ... relatively poor per capita growth performance has generally characterized resource-rich developing countries, especially mineral-exporting countries ... Oil exporters have not been immune either to the 'resource curse' in terms of low growth ... Many studies also emphasize that countries rich in oil and solid minerals have performed worse in terms of alleviating poverty compared with countries with little or no such mineral wealth.[56]

The reason seems to be that the apparent ease of exploitation of natural resources makes it a 'soft option' and that such low-growth commodities tend to 'crowd out' potentially more profitable activities.[57] However, the evidence is more mixed than this suggests:

> In aggregate terms, the finding that natural resource abundance is associated with lower than expected national growth is *highly sensitive to the time period selected*, with numerous counter-trend examples. The negative outcomes in Angola, Equatorial Guinea, Democratic Republic of Congo and Nigeria are countered by positive developmental impacts in Argentina, Botswana, Brazil, Chile, Colombia, Indonesia and Malaysia. The specific problems with the 'Dutch disease' have proved readily manageable with appropriate macroeconomic policies.[58]

POPULATIONS ON THE MOVE

The contours of world population

Geographical variations in population growth rates, in age composition and in migration, exert an extremely important influence on how globalizing processes are worked out in different places. They also relate, very clearly, to issues of poverty, to the ability of people in different places to make a living through employment, and to issues of environmental impact.

Population growth

In 2013, the world's population reached a total of 7.1 billion. A hundred years earlier, it was less than 2 billion. Not unreasonably, then, was the twentieth century called 'the century of population' and the 'explosion of population … [as] … one of its defining characteristics':[59]

> This is an absolute increase that far exceeds that which has occurred in any other period of human experience. It took until 1825 to reach one billion humans *in toto*; it took only the next 100 years to double; and the next 50 years to double again, to 4 billion in 1975. A quarter of a century later, as we were celebrating the millennium, the total jumped to six billion. True, the pace of increase has been slowing in the last decade or so but, like a large oil tanker decelerating at sea, that slowdown is a protracted process.[60]

The UN's latest medium projection is that world population in 2100 will be around 10.1 billion, although it could be significantly higher or lower, depending on what happens to fertility rates.[61]

The most striking feature of world population growth is that it now occurs overwhelmingly in developing countries. In 2011, more than four-fifths of the world's population was in developing countries. Figure 10.21 shows this massive – and accelerating – divergence in population growth between developed and developing countries from 1950, which was an especially significant turning point. That year marked the beginnings of the 'population explosion' brought about by the rapid fall in death rates in Africa, Asia and Latin America coupled with continuing high fertility rates in those areas. Since then, the contrast between the very low population growth rates of the developed countries and the very high rates in many developing countries has become even more marked.

Just to replace an existing population requires a fertility rate of 2.1 children per woman. In most developed countries, fertility rates are now well below the replacement level – at 1.7 and declining in some cases – although with an expected rise in the mid-twenty-first century to just below replacement levels. In contrast, fertility rates in the least-developed countries remain exceptionally high, currently at 4.4, and the UN estimates that they will not fall to replacement levels until 2100; hence their projected continued population growth. Figure 10.21 shows that Asia will continue to be the world's most populous region throughout the century (in 2011 it contained 60 per cent of the world's population). But Asia's population is predicted to reach its maximum around 2050 and then slowly decline. In contrast, Africa's population will continue to grow, from its current 1 billion to 3.6 billion.

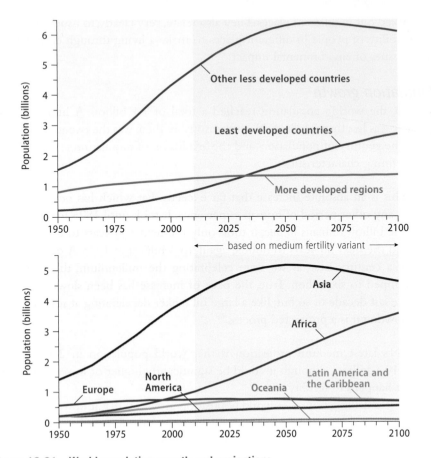

Figure 10.21 **World population growth and projections**

Source: based on data in UN Population Division, *World Population Prospects*, 2012

'Old' and 'young' populations

Persistent unevenness in fertility rates between developed and developing countries creates significant differentials in the *age composition* of the population. Put in a nutshell, developed countries are ageing while most developing countries continue to be youthful. Table 10.2 shows the marked geographical variations in the relative importance of different age groups. Europe, North America and Japan all have relatively old populations; 'young' countries (in population terms) are overwhelmingly in the developing world, particularly in Africa, which is the youngest region in the world. Over the next few decades, both the Japanese and European populations will age very significantly. Such wide variations in age structure are enormously important for economic and social development, especially in terms of the dependency of an ageing population on support from the working population. Of course, migration may help to change this situation because migrants tend to be younger and also more likely to produce children.

Table 10.2 Geographical variations in the age composition of the population (% in region)

Region	Under 15 years		15–64 years		Over 65 years	
	2005	2050	2005	2050	2005	2050
World	28.2	20.2	64.5	63.7	7.4	16.1
Africa	41.5	28.7	55.1	64.7	3.4	6.7
Asia	27.8	18.3	65.8	64.3	6.4	17.5
Japan	13.8	11.2	66.3	50.9	19.9	37.8
Europe	15.9	15.0	68.3	57.4	15.9	27.6
Latin America & Caribbean	30.0	18.1	63.9	63.6	6.1	18.4
North America	20.5	17.1	67.1	61.8	12.4	21.1
Oceania	24.8	18.0	65.1	62.7	10.0	19.3

Source: based on data in UN Population Division, *World Population Prospects*, 2009

This is, of course, an increasingly contentious political issue in some countries, notably in Europe.

An urban explosion

> The urban population of the world is estimated to increase from 2.86 billion in 2000 to 4.98 billion by 2030 ... By comparison, the size of the rural population is expected to grow only very marginally, going from 3.19 billion in 2000 to 3.29 billion in 2030.[62]

In 2007, a major threshold was passed: more than half of the world's total population lived in cities. By 2050 it is estimated that almost three-quarters will live in cities. The extent to which populations are urbanized, however, varies significantly from one part of the world to another. Not only is most of the world's population, and population growth, located in developing countries, but also that population is increasingly concentrated in cities. In complete contrast to the older industrialized countries, therefore, where a *counter-urbanization* trend has been evident for some years, urban growth in most developing countries has continued to accelerate. The highest rates of urban growth are now in developing countries, where the number of very large cities has increased enormously (Figure 10.22). Three-quarters of the world's 'megacities' (populations of more than 10 million) are in developing countries and this is projected to increase to four-fifths by 2025.

In some cases, notably the cities within the rapidly growing economies of East Asia, urban growth is driven, and sustained, by the forces of economic dynamism. But, in most cases, the link between economic growth and urban growth is less clear, and owes more to high rates of population fertility coupled with rural poverty, which drive millions of people towards what are seen to be the economic

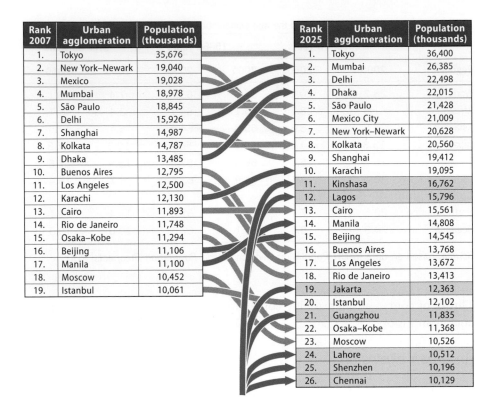

Rank 2007	Urban agglomeration	Population (thousands)
1.	Tokyo	35,676
2.	New York–Newark	19,040
3.	Mexico	19,028
4.	Mumbai	18,978
5.	São Paulo	18,845
6.	Delhi	15,926
7.	Shanghai	14,987
8.	Kolkata	14,787
9.	Dhaka	13,485
10.	Buenos Aires	12,795
11.	Los Angeles	12,500
12.	Karachi	12,130
13.	Cairo	11,893
14.	Rio de Janeiro	11,748
15.	Osaka–Kobe	11,294
16.	Beijing	11,106
17.	Manila	11,100
18.	Moscow	10,452
19.	Istanbul	10,061

Rank 2025	Urban agglomeration	Population (thousands)
1.	Tokyo	36,400
2.	Mumbai	26,385
3.	Delhi	22,498
4.	Dhaka	22,015
5.	São Paulo	21,428
6.	Mexico City	21,009
7.	New York–Newark	20,628
8.	Kolkata	20,560
9.	Shanghai	19,412
10.	Karachi	19,095
11.	Kinshasa	16,762
12.	Lagos	15,796
13.	Cairo	15,561
14.	Manila	14,808
15.	Beijing	14,545
16.	Buenos Aires	13,768
17.	Los Angeles	13,672
18.	Rio de Janeiro	13,413
19.	Jakarta	12,363
20.	Istanbul	12,102
21.	Guangzhou	11,835
22.	Osaka–Kobe	11,368
23.	Moscow	10,526
24.	Lahore	10,512
25.	Shenzhen	10,196
26.	Chennai	10,129

Figure 10.22   **The world's megacities**

Source: based on data in UN-HABITAT, 2008

honeypots of the city. In these latter cases, therefore, what we have is a process of *over-urbanization*: circumstances where the basic physical, social and economic infrastructures are not commensurate with the sheer size and rate of growth. The sprawling shanty towns endemic throughout the developing world are the physical expression of this explosive growth.

In the developing countries, virtually all industry growth is in the big cities. Stark polarization between rich and poor is one of the most striking features of developing country cities. UN data show that 80 per cent of the urban population of the 30 least-developed countries live in slums.[63] Increasingly, very high levels of poverty tend to be concentrated in urban areas. Whereas rural dwellers may be able to feed themselves and their families from the land, such an option is not available in the cities. In addition, there is a whole syndrome of urban pathologies to contend with:

> About 220 million urban dwellers, 13 per cent of the world's urban population, do not have access to safe drinking water, and about twice

this number lack even the simplest of latrines. Women suffer the most from these deficiencies ... poverty also includes exposure to contaminated environments and being at risk of criminal victimization ... Poverty is closely linked to the wide spread of preventable diseases and health risks in urban areas.[64]

People on the move: migration

Global migration trends

The subtitle of this chapter – 'where you live really matters' – reflects the fact that most people tend to stay close to where they are born. According to the International Organization for Migration,[65] the number of international migrants in the world represents only around 3 per cent of the total global population. This is significantly lower than in the nineteenth century, when international migrants accounted for 10 per cent of the world population.[66] On the other hand, in absolute terms, international migration is higher today than it has ever been. There are around 214 million international migrants, to which must be added a further 20–30 million unauthorized migrants. Some international migrants – asylum seekers – are fleeing various kinds of persecution, and these tend to reflect very specific political, social and religious conditions in their home countries. But the majority of international migrants are *migrant workers*.

The geographical distances over which international migration occurs are enormously varied. A large proportion of migrant flows are to countries close to the place of origin – for fairly obvious reasons, including cost, greater knowledge of closer opportunities, possibly greater cultural or linguistic compatibility. But over and above such short-distance migrations are the long-distance, often intercontinental, flows. Certain migration paths are especially important, as Figure 10.23 indicates for the world's major regions. In the case of large countries, like China, there is also a vast amount of internal migration whose geographical scale is greater than much cross-border migration. The Chinese government estimates that there are 130 million internal migrant workers in China, of whom around 80 million have moved from poorer interior regions to the coastal cities.[67]

One of the most important outcomes of international migration is the creation of geographically dispersed *transnational migrant communities*, particularly in cities in developed countries.[68] These complex networks created by migrants – especially labour migrants – between their places of origin and their places of settlement constitute particular kinds of transnational social spaces held together by financial remittances and social networks derived from ethnic ties. Such transnational communities play an extremely significant role not only in channelling subsequent migrant flows, but also in investment patterns and in the creation of distinctive forms of entrepreneurship.

Region	International migrants (millions)	Percentage of region's population	Migration characteristics
Europe	72.1	8.7	Substantial migration from outside, but most is internal migration within the EU. Large flows from the east following enlargement of EU.
North America	50.0	6.1	Dominated by very strong south–north migrant flows from Latin America/Caribbean to US and Canada. Increasing flows to Europe from Latin America.
Latin America & Caribbean	7.5	1.2	
Asia	32.5	0.8	Huge intra-regional flows of migrant workers, both between Asian countries and within large countries. China has 130 million internal migrant workers. Asia is world's largest source of temporary contractual migrant workers.
Middle East	26.5	19.0	Major destinations: Saudi Arabia, United Arab Emirates, Jordan.
Africa	19.3	1.9	Most migration is to other African countries. Most important migration foci are Southern Africa, Côte d'Ivoire and Ghana.
Oceania	6.0	16.8	Australia and New Zealand are the large destination countries, with increasing migration from Asian countries.

Figure 10.23   International migration trends by region

Source: based on data from www.iom.int/jahia/Jahia/about-migration/facts-and-figures

Home-country effects of out-migration

At one level, the decision to migrate abroad in search of work is an individual decision, made in the context of social and family circumstances. When successful – that is, when the migrant succeeds in obtaining work and building a life in a new environment – the benefits to the individual and his/her family are clear, although there may be problems of dislocation and emotional stress. There is invariably discrimination against migrant workers in host countries. In many cases, migrants are employed in very low-grade occupations, they may have few, if any, rights, and their employment security is often non-existent. They may also be subject to abuse and maltreatment.

But what are the effects of out-migration on the exporting country? From a *positive* perspective, out-migration helps to reduce pressures in local labour markets. Most significantly, the remittances sent back home by migrant workers make a huge contribution, not only to the individual recipients and their local communities, but also to the home country's balance of payments position and to its foreign exchange position. Indeed, migrants' remittances have reached epic proportions: almost $480 billion in 2011. And this is certainly an underestimate because a large volume of remittances is transmitted through unrecorded and informal channels. Annual remittances to Latin America and the Caribbean in 2005 were greater than the combined flows of FDI and development aid.[69] Frequently, the value of foreign remittances is equivalent to a large share of the country's export earnings; in a few cases, they are worth between one and three times *more* than total exports. However, migrant remittances are highly sensitive to downturns in host economies. For example, the annual growth of remittances from the USA to Latin America fell from 25 per cent in early 2006 to zero in early 2008.[70]

Figure 10.24 maps migrant workers' remittances in 2011. Ten countries accounted for 51 per cent of the destination remittances: notably India ($64 million), China ($40.5 million), Mexico ($23.6 million) and the Philippines ($23 million). Remittance origins were more concentrated: 10 countries accounted for 67 per cent of the total. By far the biggest source of worker remittances was the USA ($51.4 million), followed by Switzerland ($30.8 million) and Saudi Arabia ($28.5 million).

Paradoxically, remittances do not always help the poorest people back home, as some Mexican research indicates:

> 'For some people, remittances allow them to buy a basic basket of essential goods,' says Rodolfo Tuiran, of Sedesol, Mexico's social development ministry. 'But overall, in terms of poverty, remittances do not have a significant impact. They do, however, have an important impact on inequality – they increase it. Of every $100 received, $75 goes to homes that aren't poor.' Anecdotal evidence supports this. In areas of high migration, the houses in good repair, with a satellite dish, are the ones that receive remittances.[71]

On the other hand, again in Mexico, there are schemes which capitalize on the fact that migrants from the same home town often tend to cluster together in their host country. As a result, there is now a network of Mexican 'home-town associations' across the USA. Collective remittances to a home town in several Mexican states are organized in a 'three-for-one' programme, where each dollar from the home-town association for a development project is matched by a dollar each from the municipal, state, and federal governments'.[72] Unsurprisingly, the 2008 financial crisis has had a disastrous effect on remittances, as many labour migrants lost their jobs and incomes.

However, there are important *negative* consequences of out-migration. The migrants are often the young and most active members of the population. Further,

> returning migrants are rarely bearers of initiative and generators of employment. Only a small number acquire appropriate vocational training – most are trapped in dead-end jobs – and their prime interest

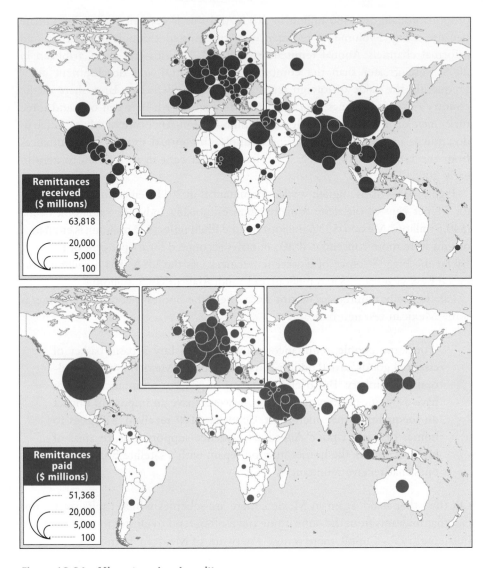

Figure 10.24   **Migrant workers' remittances**

Source: based on World Bank, *World Development Indicators*, 2013: Table 6.13

on return is to enhance their social status. This they attempt to achieve by disdaining manual employment, by early retirement, by the construction of a new house, by the purchase of land, a car and other consumer durables, or by taking over a small service establishment like a bar or taxi business; there is also a tendency for formerly rural dwellers to settle in urban centres. There is thus a reinforcement of the very conditions that promoted emigration in the first place. It is ironic that those migrants who are potentially most valuable for stimulating development in their home area – the minority who have acquired valuable skills abroad – are the very ones who, because of successful adaptation abroad, are least likely to return. There are also problems of demographic imbalance stemming from the selective nature of emigration.[73]

Of course, there are important exceptions to this pattern. One is the large number of ethnic Chinese, part of the Chinese *diaspora* after 1949, who have returned to their homeland as the Chinese economy has opened up. Another is what Annalee Saxenian calls 'the new Argonauts' of Silicon Valley:

> A small but meaningful proportion of individuals who left their home countries for greater opportunities abroad have now reversed course, transforming a brain drain into a 'brain circulation.' They are returning home to establish business relationships or to start new companies, while maintaining their professional and social ties to the US … In the early 1980s, emigrants returning from Silicon Valley began to transfer the model of early-stage high-risk investing to Taiwan and Israel. These native born investors brought cultural and linguistic know-how as well as the capital needed to operate profitably in these markets. They also brought technical and operating experience, knowledge of new business models, and networks of contacts in the US. Today, Israel and Taiwan boast the largest venture capital industries outside of North America, and both support high rates of new firm formation.[74]

Host-country effects of in-migration

> Without migration, the population of more developed regions as a whole would start declining in 2003 rather than in 2025, and by 2050 it would be 126 million less than the 1.18 billion projected under the assumption of continued migration.[75]

It may seem paradoxical to think of migration as helping to solve the adjustment problems of the older industrialized countries. After all – especially in Europe – we have been talking about not enough jobs to meet the demands of the existing populations. To add further to what appears to be an over-supplied labour market seems perverse to say the least. It is such considerations, together with fears of social unrest between indigenous and immigrant populations, that have made current immigration policies in most developed countries so rigid. But, as ever, things are not as simple as aggregate figures suggest. In addition to humanitarian concerns for refugees, asylum seekers or people simply trying to improve their lives, there are two reasons why developed countries need to create a sensible policy towards in-migration. One reason is immediate, the other is longer term.

The immediate reason for asserting the need for more enlightened immigration policies is the fact that, in most developed countries, there is a *severe shortage of labour*. This applies as much in high-skill sectors such as ICT and health care as in some low-skill service sectors. The longer-term reason is that the populations of such countries are *getting older* (see Table 10.2). Their active populations are shrinking. There will not be enough people of working age to support future dependent populations. For both short- and longer-term reasons, then, there is a pressing need to rethink immigration policies. But, of course, there are major political obstacles to doing so.

Fears (sometimes justified, often not) of being squeezed out of jobs by incomers, or of local cultures and practices being diluted by 'foreign ways', generate powerful forces of opposition.[76] Such fears are easily exploited by political groups of the extreme right, as can be seen today in many European countries, as well as in the USA. Labour force displacement does, indeed, happen. But not invariably so – and not on the scale so often imagined. One of the biggest obstacles to popular support for more liberal migration polices is that the size of the host country's immigrant population tends to be greatly overestimated.[77] For example, foreign workers make up a very small percentage of the working population in EU states.

However, immigrants tend to be highly unevenly distributed geographically within individual countries and this is an important factor in people's perceptions. Specific transnational communities tend to develop specific local geographies, some of which are more apparent than others, and that is where the greatest tension tends to develop. One of the most serious repercussions of the financial collapse of some eurozone countries, notably Greece, is that it has reignited racial tensions and increased the prominence of far-right fascist organizations. 'Get rid of the foreigners and all will be well' is the message. These, and other similar organizations in other EU countries (like the EDL in the UK), may be small but they pose a serious challenge to social cohesion, especially as the growth of the social media facilitates their activities.

Controls on immigration are now much tighter than in the past. Despite the fact that labour migration is an integral part of the EU, the enlargement of 2005 to incorporate a further 10 countries, mostly from the former Soviet bloc, led to 12 of the existing 15 EU member states imposing 'transitional' restrictions on migration from Eastern Europe (the exceptions are the UK, Sweden and Ireland). This is despite pleas from the European Commission for an open-door policy for new members and the fact that 'in most EU15 countries, workers from the new members make up less than 1% of the workforce'.[78] Similar problems exist in the case of Mexican migration into the USA. Indeed, proposals to build a more robust physical barrier along the border to reduce the roughly 400,000 Mexicans who cross the border into the USA illegally every year appear to be supported by a majority of the US population.

Yet, many parts of the European and US economies – as well as many public services – simply could not operate without the employment of migrant workers.

The need for an influx of new workers will not go away. On the contrary, given the demographic trends in all the developed countries, the need will increase. It can also be argued that not only do in-migrants fill important needs – often performing tasks that, otherwise, will go unperformed – but also this need not have the negative effects claimed by opponents. A study of Europe claimed that increased immigration leads to economic expansion rather than to job losses.[79] Indeed, the sharp decline in the value of the UK pound against the euro in 2008 led to large numbers of Eastern European nationals returning home.[80] Migration is, indeed, a highly volatile – and increasingly a highly contentious and sensitive – process.

NOTES

1   UNDP (2005: 19, 21; emphasis added).
2   Scott (1998: 68, 70).
3   Veltz (1996). For an elaboration of this concept within a GPN framework, see Hess (2009).
4   Amin (2004: 218).
5   Sen (1999: 20).
6   Bairoch quoted in Cohen (1998: 17).
7   Sutcliffe (2009: 764).
8   Ito (2001: 77).
9   Henderson (1998: 356–7).
10 OPHI (Oxford Poverty and Human Development Initiative): Alkire et al. (2013).
11 Alkire et al. (2013).
12 Sen (1999: 21).
13 Piketty (2014: 266) points out the limitations of such 'synthetic indices as the Gini coefficient'.
14 There is now a big literature on income inequality, especially in the UK and the US. Most important is the magisterial book by Thomas Piketty (2014) *Capital in the Twenty First Century*. See, for example, Dorling (2012), ILO (2012), OECD (2011), Stiglitz (2012), Wilkinson and Pickett (2009).
15 OECD (2011: 22; emphasis added).
16 Stiglitz (2012).
17 Dorling (2012: 1).
18 Paul Johnson, cited in the *Guardian* (6 December 2011).
19 Simon Kuper interview with Saskia Sassen, *Financial Times* (15 June 2013).
20 Sassen (2001: 270).
21 Eurostat data quoted in the *Observer* (26 May 2013).
22 Piketty (2014: 297).
23 Council of Economic Advisers (2012: 175).
24 So called because the last time that US incomes were so unequal was in the 1920s. The allusion is to the novel by F. Scott Fitzerald, *The Great Gatsby*, published in 1926.
25 *The Economist* (17 September 2005).
26 Kapstein (1999: 118).

27 Kapstein (1999: 119).

28 Wu and Perloff (2005: 23).

29 Boston Consulting Group report, quoted in the *Financial Times* (31 May 2013).

30 Sklair (2001), Struna (2013).

31 Carroll (2007), Carroll and Carson (2003).

32 Sklair (2001: 18–23).

33 Department of International Development (2000: 12).

34 World Bank (2012: chapter 2).

35 Sen (1999: 106), World Bank (2012: 77).

36 ILO (2013a, 2014).

37 Ghose et al. (2009: 1).

38 ILO Press Release (24 January 2006).

39 ILO (2014: 11).

40 ILO (2014: 11).

41 *Financial Times* (22 June 2001).

42 See ILO (2004b).

43 *Financial Times* (3 May 2012).

44 ILO (2001: 140–1).

45 Levy and Murname (2004).

46 *The Economist* (2 July 2005).

47 Kaplinsky (2001: 56–7).

48 Wood (1994: 8, 11, 13).

49 ILO (1997: 71, 73).

50 Silva and Leichenko (2004: 283).

51 Rigby and Breau (2006: 18).

52 ILO (2007b: 10).

53 *The Economist* (14 January 2006), *Financial Times* (7 October 2005).

54 Kaplinsky (2004: 78–9).

55 See Bridge (2008b), Farooki and Kaplinsky (2012: chapter 3), Sachs and Warner (2001), UNCTAD (2007: 93–4).

56 UNCTAD (2007: Box III.3, p. 94).

57 Sachs and Warner (2001: 833).

58 Moran (2011: 73; emphasis added).

59 Population Reference Bureau (1999: 1).

60 Kennedy (2002: 3).

61 UN Population Division (2009).

62 Cohen (2004: 27).

63 UN Centre for Human Settlements (2003).

64 UN Centre for Human Settlements (2001: 14).

65 International Organization for Migration (2012) Facts and Figures. www.iom.int/jahia/Jahia/about-migration/facts-and-figures.

66 Castles and Miller (2009) provide a comprehensive review of migration.

67 *Financial Times* (8 January 2009).

68 Coe et al. (2003).

69 *Financial Times* (30 March 2006).

70 *Financial Times* (4 June 2008).

71 *Financial Times* (13 December 2005).
72 *Financial Times* (13 December 2005).
73 Jones (1990: 250).
74 Saxenian (2006: 7–8).
75 UN Population Division (2001: vii).
76 See, for example, Goodhart (2013).
77 Dustmann and Glitz (2005).
78 *The Economist* (11 February 2006).
79 Dustmann and Glitz (2005).
80 Pollard et al. (2008).

Want to know more about this chapter? Visit the companion website at **www.guilford.com/dickenGS7** for free access to author videos, suggested reading and practice questions to further enhance your study.

Eleven

MAKING THE WORLD A BETTER PLACE

CHAPTER OUTLINE

'THE BEST OF ALL POSSIBLE WORLDS'?

As we have seen, the world has changed dramatically over the past several decades. It is, in very many ways, a different place. But is such a 'globalized' world a 'better' world? Voltaire, the eighteenth-century French writer, wrote a wonderful satirical novel, *Candide*, in which the eponymous hero lives in a world of immense suffering and hardship, yet whose tutor, Dr Pangloss, insists that Candide's world is 'the best of all possible worlds, where everything is connected and arranged for the best'.[1] Today, such a Panglossian view is held by those to whom an unfettered capitalist market system – based on the unhindered flow of commodities, goods, services and investment capital – constitutes the 'best of all possible worlds'. Although they might agree that globalization is a savage process, they also argue that it is a beneficial one, in which, they claim, the winners far outnumber the losers.[2] But it is arguable that 'now is the best time in history to be alive'.[3]

Certainly, there is considerable divergence in the views of ordinary people in different parts of the world. For example, a poll of 34,500 people in 34 countries, commissioned by the BBC World Service in 2008, concluded that

> in 22 out of 34 countries around the world, the weight of opinion is that 'economic globalization, including trade and investment' is growing too quickly … Related to this unease is an even stronger view that the benefits and burdens of 'the economic developments of the last few years' have not been shared fairly … In developed countries, those who have this view of unfairness are more likely to say that globalization is growing too quickly … In contrast, in some developing countries, those who perceive such unfairness are more likely to say globalization is proceeding too slowly.[4]

There is, in fact, a highly differentiated geography of attitudes towards globalization.[5]

Without doubt, large numbers of people in the developed economies, and also in the rapidly growing economies of East Asia, have benefited from much increased material affluence: 'The average person is about eight times richer than a century ago, nearly one billion people have been lifted out of poverty over the past two decades.'[6] There has been immense growth in the production and consumption of goods and services and, through international trade, a huge increase in the variety of goods available. But the evidence discussed in Chapters 7 to 10 suggests a very different reality for a substantial proportion of the world's population, not only in the poorest countries and regions, but also among certain sectors of the population in affluent countries, who have not benefited – or have benefited very little – from the overall rise in material well-being. The fact remains that there is vast inequality between the haves and the have-nots (or, as some have put it more ironically, between the 'have-yachts' and the 'have-nots'). And that gap has been widening, despite the operation of precisely those globalizing processes that are supposed to create benefits for everybody. For many, *insecurity* has become the norm, much exacerbated by the impact of the 2008 financial crisis:

> Globalization increases objective and subjective insecurities among a great many workers and producers … different faces of economic globalization can be expected to have different implications for risk. For instance, some faces of globalization more than others are visible, direct, and palpable with respect to job risks – for instance, via threats of outsourcing by companies rather than via trade competition.[7]

What can or should be done? How can the world be made a better place for all, including those at the bottom of the heap? There is no simple answer. Choices are never unconstrained:

> Our choices … are shaped by systems and structures over which we, as individuals, have no control. Economic, political, technological and social dynamics make some choices available and remove others from the table.[8]

We are all deeply embedded in specific contexts, structures and places and constrained by our knowledge and resources. As we have seen, the map of such constraints is immensely uneven; for many people, in many parts of the world, the exercise of choice is extremely limited. More broadly, of course, it depends on one's political and ideological point of view. It is about values.[9] It is about where we want to be. In terms of 'making the world a better place', one person's 'utopia' is another person's 'dystopia'.

For example, GCSOs vary widely both in their agendas and in how these agendas are pursued: from vociferous, often violent, confrontation through to more reformist movements. Anti-capitalist groups advocate the replacement of the capitalist system,[10] although precisely what the alternative should be varies between groups. For some, it would be a democratically elected world government; for others, a structure in which the means of production and distribution were controlled by a nationally elected government. For some, it would be a system of locally self-sufficient communities in which long-distance trade would be minimized. This is the position, for example, of the 'deep green' environmental groups. For some, the focus is on 'fair', rather than 'free', trade – although who decides what is 'fair' is a crucial issue. For the more nationalist–populist groups, and for some labour unions, the agenda is one of protecting domestic industries and jobs from external competition (especially from developing countries) and restricting immigration. For some, the objective is removing the burden of debt from the world's poorest countries or improving labour standards in the developing world (especially of child labour). The problem is that, very often, these agendas are contradictory.

Not surprisingly, GCSOs have themselves attracted considerable criticism from some quarters, questioning their legitimacy and, in some cases, their abilities to further economic and social development goals for the poor. Although the proliferation of GCSOs has 'unquestionably projected the globalization debate into the popular political consciousness in important ways … the movements themselves have a severe democratic deficit: representing humanity ultimately requires legitimation through some sort of people's mandate'.[11] Nevertheless, GCSOs undoubtedly force people – including politicians and business leaders – to recognize, and to engage with, the uncomfortable reality that both the benefits and the costs of globalization are very unevenly distributed and that there are severe and pressing problems that need resolution:

> The advocatory movements of global civil society are the originators, advocates and judges of global values and norms. The way they create and hone this everyday, local and global awareness of values is by sparking public outrage and generating global public indignation over spectacular norm violations. This they do by focusing on individual cases.[12]

In fact, the major responsibility for making the world a better place lies with two dominant sets of actors/institutions: *TNCs* and *states*. The central argument of this book has been that, among the multiplicity of actors involved in the global economy, these two – whether in conflict or collaboration – are responsible for much of the shaping and reshaping of the global economic map. As such, they bear the primary responsibility for improving the lives and livelihoods of people throughout the world. For that reason they form the focus of the next two sections of this chapter. First, we will look at the role of TNCs in terms of their corporate social responsibility (CSR). Second, we will focus on states in the context of global governance issues.

TNCs AND CORPORATE SOCIAL RESPONSIBILITY

'The business of business is business'

This statement, generally attributed to Milton Friedman, the free market economist, implies that the primary purpose of firms is to maximize *shareholder* value. In other words, the only actors who matter are the shareholders (stockholders): the ultimate owners of the company. Everybody and everything else – employees, customers, suppliers, members of the communities in which the company's facilities are located, the environment – are not the company's direct concern. This is the ideology of business that dominates the USA and the UK economies in particular: the neo-liberal model of free market capitalism. It is demonstrated most clearly in the context of company takeovers, where the views of employees are usually ignored, even though they are much more directly engaged in the company than many of the shareholders (which are predominantly huge financial institutions for whom a firm is simply part of a broader portfolio), and have more at stake (their incomes and livelihoods). In fact, such a narrow view of business responsibilities is far from universal. In many European countries, for example, a broader concept of *stakeholder* capitalism exists in which other actors ('stakeholders', such as labour, consumers, suppliers) are explicitly recognized as having legitimate interests in business decisions.

Issues of corporate responsibility impinge on virtually all aspects of modern life and span the entire spectrum of relationships between firms, states and civil society.[13] We cannot explore all of these. Instead we will concentrate on those aspects of CSR that have an explicitly *international* dimension.[14]

Approaches to CSR

Rob van Tulder and his colleagues identify four approaches to CSR (Figure 11.1), each of which reflects different degrees of relationship to the social environment and to external stakeholders:[15]

- *Inactive* CSR is essentially that embodied in the 'business of business is business' philosophy: 'the only responsibility companies (can) have is to generate profits … no fundamental ethical questions are raised about what they are doing' (p. 143).
- *Reactive* CSR is slightly different: it 'shares the focus on efficiency but with particular attention to not making any mistakes … entrepreneurs monitor their environment and manage their primary stakeholders so as to keep mounting issues in check … Entrepreneurs … respond specifically to actions of external actors that could damage their reputation' (p. 143).
- *Active* CSR 'represents the most ethical entrepreneurial orientation. Entrepreneurs … are explicitly inspired by ethical values … on the basis of which company objectives are formulated. These objectives are subsequently realised in a socially responsible manner regardless of actual or potential social pressures by stakeholders' (p. 145).
- *Proactive* CSR occurs where an entrepreneur involves 'external stakeholders right at the beginning of an issue's life cycle' (p. 145). It implies active and ongoing discussion with stakeholders: a 'discourse ethics' approach.

International CSR and GPNs

As we have seen throughout this book, the production, distribution and consumption of goods and services are primarily organized within GPNs, usually controlled and coordinated by TNCs. Such networks raise hugely important questions, particularly regarding relationships between lead firms and suppliers and the treatment of labour throughout the network. In Chapter 8, we discussed the developmental implications of involvement (or non-involvement) in GPNs for people and businesses in local economies using the criterion of various types of *upgrading*. Of these, *social upgrading* relates specifically to work and labour standards. This includes a

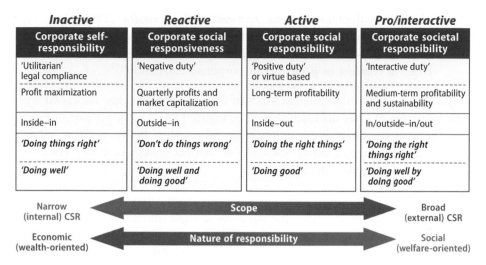

Inactive	Reactive	Active	Pro/interactive
Corporate self-responsibility	**Corporate social responsiveness**	**Corporate social responsibility**	**Corporate societal responsibility**
'Utilitarian' legal compliance	'Negative duty'	'Positive duty' or virtue based	'Interactive duty'
Profit maximization	Quarterly profits and market capitalization	Long-term profitability	Medium-term profitability and sustainability
Inside–in	Outside–in	Inside–out	In/outside–in/out
'Doing things right'	'Don't do things wrong'	'Doing the right things'	'Doing the right things right'
'Doing well'	'Doing well and doing good'	'Doing good'	'Doing well by doing good'

Narrow (internal) CSR ←——— **Scope** ———→ Broad (external) CSR

Economic (wealth-oriented) ←——— **Nature of responsibility** ———→ Social (welfare-oriented)

Figure 11.1 **Differing approaches to CSR**

Source: based on van Tulder with van der Zwart, 2006: Table 8.1; van Tulder et al., 2009: Table I

whole spectrum of social, economic and ethical issues, including pay, work conditions, occupational health and safety, and human rights. Questions of CSR, therefore, are *intrinsically* involved in the operation of GPNs.[16] We examine some specific examples in the cases of agro-food (Chapter 13) and clothing (Chapter 14).

The primary mechanism for attempting to ensure social upgrading in GPNs is the *code of conduct*. Such codes have proliferated to the extent that they often overlap in highly confusing ways. In 2006, for example, it was estimated that there were around 10,000 different codes of labour practice.[17] Two-thirds of the 100 largest firms in the world operated a code of conduct by the early 2000s.[18] A major reason for such proliferation is the increased geographical extent and organizational complexity of GPNs:

> Codifications are triggered by *intrinsic* motivations … [including] … the greater strategic need to coordinate and control the firm's activities spread over a large number of countries and constituencies … This is often the area of 'internal codes of conduct' or 'codes of ethics'. The strategic need for the formulation and implementation of external codes of conduct as a coordination mechanism becomes bigger when firms engage in sourcing out activities to dependent affiliates (offshoring) or to independent suppliers (outsourcing) in developing countries, where the governance quality is often relatively low and the cultural and institutional distance … is relatively high. A large number of (procurement) codes thus addresses supply chain issues such as human rights, labour standards or the right to association … In this case firms have an incentive not only to formulate codes of conduct,

but also to implement them. *Extrinsic* motivations for [TNCs] are gaining in importance as well: the risk of reputation damage triggered by critical NGOs precipitates [TNCs] to formulate international codes of conduct or principles of 'corporate citizenship'.[19]

Figure 11.2 sets out the different kinds of CSR supplier strategy associated with the four types of CSR discussed above (see Figure 11.1). The upper part of Figure 11.2 sets out the variations in supply chain relationships between different CSR positions; the lower part shows how codes of conduct strategy may vary. The codes are classified along two dimensions:[20]

- *Specificity* includes 'how many issues it covers, how focused it is, the extent to which it refers to international standards and guidelines, and to what extent aspects of the code are measured' (p. 402).
- *Compliance* 'is generally enhanced by clear monitoring systems in place, combined with a more independent position of the monitoring agency and the possibility of these organizations to formulate and implement sanctions' (p. 402).

	Inactive	*Reactive*	*Active*	*Pro/interactive*
	Corporate self-responsibility	**Corporate social responsiveness**	**Corporate social responsibility**	**Corporate societal responsibility**
	Supply chain relationships			
	Price only. Strong competition for customers. Active use of power position in chain. Suppliers responsible for labour conditions.	Price and quality. Suppliers responsible for labour conditions.	Fair prices and high quality. Suppliers selected on basis of approach to e.g. labour conditions.	Joint responsibilities. Prices and quality set together. Definition of fair wages and labour conditions based on consultation and strategic dialogues.
	Cost, control, risk aversion.	Cost, control, quality.	Control and quality.	Co-development and quality.
	CSR only if not too costly and does not mean higher purchasing prices.	CSR only if needed and/or available and does not mean higher purchasing prices.	Upgrading according to own standards.	Upgrading according to joint and/or open standards.
	Below 5% CSR of purchases.	Below 25% CSR of purchases.	Target of 25–60% CSR of purchases.	Target of 60–100% CSR of purchases.
	Buy	Make or buy	Make	Cooperate
	Global	Global	Regional	Local
	Codes of conduct strategy			
Type of code	Internal	Specific supplier	General supplier	Joint/dialogues
Specificity	Low	Medium/high	Medium/low	High
Compliance	Low	Medium/low	Medium/high	High
Implementation	Low	Medium/low	Medium/high	High

Chain liability ⟵⟶ Chain responsibility

Figure 11.2   **Types of CSR strategy towards suppliers**

Source: based on van Tulder et al., 2009: Table II; van Tulder, 2009: Table 4

Firms positioned at the left-hand side of Figure 11.2 tend to opt (if they do so at all) for internal corporate codes or for codes drawn up in collaboration with other firms without prior dialogue with non-firm stakeholders. On the other hand, firms positioned towards the right-hand side of Figure 11.2 tend to participate in more open agreements with non-firm stakeholders. The pressure from GCSOs is to move as many firms as possible to that more open, cooperative position. Much will clearly depend upon the relative bargaining power of the participants as well as the 'social conscience' of firms. There has certainly been some movement. Even among the hard-line business-is-business community there is now a considerable (albeit often reluctant) recognition that companies do have broader social responsibilities.

Hence, there has been a rush to formulate *corporate responsibility* statements. Some of this may well be altruistic, in other cases mere self-interest. However, it is difficult to avoid the conclusion that a major catalyst for CSR has been the increasing pressure on TNCs to recognize their social responsibilities and to conform to acceptable ethical standards.[21] For example, there is no doubt that such pressures led to such leading companies as Apple and Nike to publish a list of their global suppliers in their CSR reports. This was an unprecedented step for companies which had always been highly secretive about their supply networks.

Types of code of conduct

There are four major types of code of conduct:

- Codes devised by individual TNCs, or groups of TNCs, with no involvement of other stakeholders. Example: the Global Social Compliance Programme established by Wal-Mart, Tesco, Carrefour and Metro.
- Codes drawn up by coalitions of interest groups in specific industries, such as clothing.[22] Example: the Global Alliance for Workers and Communities involving Nike, and Gap, together with the World Bank and the International Youth Foundation.
- Codes formulated by TNCs in association with some of their stakeholders. Examples: Global Framework Agreements (GFAs) between a TNC and a global labour union federation;[23] the UK Ethical Trading Initiative (ETI), an alliance of companies, NGOs and labour unions.[24]
- Codes established by international NGOs. Example: the UN Global Compact,[25] which is based upon the ILO Declaration of Fundamental Principles and Rights to Work. Figure 11.3 sets out its 10 principles.

All such codes are, of course, the outcome of complex bargaining processes:

> They need to be understood as part of a contradictory process, involving collaboration and conflict between commercial and civil society actors, in which inherent tensions play out.[26]

Human rights
Principle 1: Support and respect the protection of international human rights within their sphere of influence.
Principle 2: Make sure their own corporations are not complicit in human rights abuses.

Labour standards
Principle 3: The freedom of association and the effective recognition of the right to collective bargaining.
Principle 4: The elimination of all forms of forced and compulsory labour.
Principle 5: The effective abolition of child labour.
Principle 6: The elimination of discrimination in respect of employment and occupation.

Environment
Principle 7: Support a precautionary approach to environmental challenges.
Principle 8: Undertake initiatives to promote greater environmental responsibility.
Principle 9: Encourage the development and diffusion of environmentally friendly technologies.

Anti-corruption
Principle 10: Work against all forms of corruption, including extortion and bribery.

Figure 11.3 **Principles of the UN Global Compact**

TNCs clearly have an interest in being seen as having a positive relationship with GCSOs, not least because it provides a 'seal of approval'. GCSOs need to find ways of increasing their influence on TNC decision making. But there are problems for both of them in too cosy a relationship. In the final analysis, they have very different aims and objectives. But that need not mean that such collaboration is not worth pursuing.

How effective are codes of conduct?

Are such codes mainly a cosmetic exercise? How fully are they implemented? How are they monitored? These are the questions commonly posed by critics, to which there are no unambiguous answers. Inevitably, there is a good deal of scepticism about voluntary codes, whether at the individual firm or collective level. This is not only because they are 'voluntary', but also because they are rather marginal in their scope and effect. Without some degree of compulsion – and the monitoring of compliance – there is always the danger that such codes will amount to little more than a gesture or that companies will be able to influence how the process works.

In one sense, of course, anything that contributes to better conditions for people and communities should be welcomed:

> Whilst in themselves codes of labour practice are limited, they do have a role in wider strategies to promote economic and social rights of vulnerable workers. But they are not sufficient (nor have they aimed) to achieve more sustainable systems of global production that address inherent inequalities and poverty ... The issue, therefore, is whether and how codes contribute to a wider process that promotes the rights of the most vulnerable workers.[27]

Very often, the impacts are mixed. For example, a study of the effects of the Ethical Trading Initiative (ETI) reached the following conclusions:

> ETI company codes have had a positive impact in relation to certain code principles, particularly health and safety, documented minimum (not living) wages and employment benefits. Company codes were found to have had little or no impact on other code principles, particularly freedom to join an independent trade union, collective bargaining and discrimination ... In general, permanent and regular workers were found to have fared better from company codes of labour practice ... [However] ... whilst there had been positive impacts on regular workers, codes of labour practice were failing to reach more vulnerable casual, migrant and contract workers, many of whom were women.[28]

A detailed analysis of GFAs involving firms from the USA, Europe and Japan identified two important factors in how such codes of conduct tend to be implemented:[29]

- The extent to which the various stakeholders participate in a code's formulation. This tends to affect the likelihood of different levels of implementation and compliance, the nature of the codes themselves and the degree of compromise involved.
- A country of origin effect: 'All Japanese firms scored low on both specificity and compliance, indicating inactive codes, whereas the only examples of high specificity and compliance, i.e. active codes, could be found with European firms ... The US companies fall somewhere in between and generally represent the reactive CSR strategy. The difference in approach between US and European companies is particularly remarkable, but could be largely explained by the bigger involvement of stakeholders. The implementation likelihood of almost all European codes is higher than that of their American or Japanese counterparts.'[30]

Codes of conduct, therefore, are useful mechanisms in the progress to greater CSR. They are clearly better than nothing. But they are insufficient, not least because they are partial in terms of both their coverage and their essentially voluntary nature.

STATES AND ISSUES OF GLOBAL GOVERNANCE

Global–national tensions

> The world's economy is global; its politics are national. This, in a nutshell, is the dilemma of global governance.[31]

> While the world has become much more highly integrated economi-
> cally, the mechanisms for managing the system in a stable, sustainable
> way have lagged behind.[32]

Virtually the entire world economy is now a *global capitalist market economy* although, as we saw in Chapter 6, there are several variants. The collapse of the state social-ist systems at the end of the 1980s and the headlong rush to embrace the market, together with the more controlled opening up of the Chinese economy after 1979, created a very different global system from the one which emerged after the Second World War. The massive flows of goods, services and, especially, finance in its increasingly bewildering variety created a world whose rules of governance have not kept pace with such changes.

In Chapter 3 (see Figure 3.2), we noted the 'thickening web' of public and private institutions that make up the institutional macro-structures of the global economy. Now we focus on the *core* institutions, a mixture of bodies established in different circumstances, and at different times, in the seven decades since the end of the Second World War. They consist of widely differing memberships (Figure 11.4), with widely different methods of reaching agreement. Many of them – especially those set up in the immediate aftermath of the war, like the IMF and the World Bank – have power structures and sets of rules that were put in place in a very different world. Essentially, they reflect the prevailing dominance of the Western nations, most notably the USA and the bigger European nations. Since then, of course, while the world has changed dramatically the global institu-tions have seriously lagged behind this new reality. The various 'G groups', espe-cially the G7 and G8, are totally unrepresentative of today's world. Only very recently has the voice of some of the growing developing countries been accom-modated through the emergence of the G20. The significance of the G20 lies in its much wider membership, especially the involvement of developing countries.

These global governance institutions reflect intricate bargaining, based upon asymmetrical power configurations within and between member institutions, in

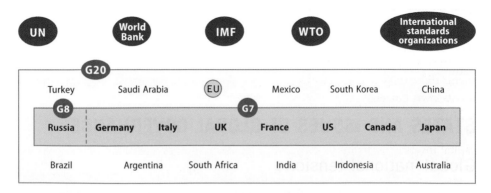

Figure 11.4   **The core of global governance institutions**

which the exercise of 'soft' power predominates.[33] Such bargaining involves very much more than just states. It is a

> multi-actor process among NGOs, states, firms, and international organizations. Indeed, even states may be represented by multiple authorities, such as departments of environment and state, with conflicting interests … Organizations representing labor, environmentalists, scientists and other elements of civil society have been particularly active in negotiations over environmental regimes … Even when not seated directly at the negotiating table, activist groups have exerted considerable influence through street demonstrations and through the disseminations of information … Thus firms and governments exert less control over the bargaining process, and bargain outcomes are more uncertain.[34]

In what follows, we focus specifically on the *global* scale of governance and regulation in four of the most important and most contentious areas:

- international finance
- international trade
- TNCs
- the environment.

Regulating the global financial system

The established 'architecture' of the global financial system

The regulatory 'architecture' of the modern global financial system came into being formally at an international conference at Bretton Woods, New Hampshire, in 1944. Two international financial institutions were created: the *International Monetary Fund* (IMF) and the *International Bank for Reconstruction and Development* (later renamed the *World Bank*). The IMF's primary purpose was to encourage international monetary cooperation between nations through a set of rules for world payments and currencies. Each member nation contributes to the fund (a quota) and voting rights are proportional to the size of a nation's quota. A major function of the IMF has been to aid member states in temporary balance of payments difficulties. A country can obtain foreign exchange from the IMF in return for its own currency, which is deposited with the IMF. A condition of such aid is IMF supervision or advice on the necessary corrective policies – the *conditionality* requirement. The World Bank's role is to facilitate development through capital investment. Its initial focus was Europe in the immediate post-war period. Subsequently, its attention shifted to the developing economies.

The primary objective of Bretton Woods was to stabilize and regulate international financial transactions *between nations* on the basis of fixed currency exchange rates, in which the US dollar played the central role. In this way it was hoped to provide the necessary financial 'lubricant' for a reconstructed world economy. However, through a whole series of developments, the relatively stable basis of the Bretton Woods system was progressively undermined, particularly after the early 1970s. In effect, a state-led system was transformed into a market-led system.[35]

What we do not have, therefore, is a comprehensive and integrated global system of governance of the financial system. Instead, there are various areas of regulation performed by different bodies, each of which is *nationally*, rather than globally, based. For example:

- The 'G' groups (e.g. G7, G8 and, recently, G20) take an overall view of the monetary, fiscal and exchange rate relationships between themselves. The 'G' groups have no real institutional base; they are informal arrangements structured around periodic summits of national leaders.
- The international payments system is operated through the national central banks rather than through an international central bank.
- The supervision of financial institutions is carried out through the Bank for International Settlements (BIS), established in 1975. The Basel II Accord (currently being replaced by Basel III) sets out standards of banking supervision but their implementation is down to national governments, and not all governments follow these standards.

Within such a lightly regulated financial system, developing countries are particularly vulnerable to the volatilities of global capital flows. Indeed, one of the major weaknesses of the various reforms to the global financial architecture following the breakdown of the Bretton Woods system was that they maintained a separation between the problems facing developed countries and those facing developing countries, instead of seeing them as inextricably linked. In fact, the IMF/World Bank's conditionality 'medicine' often made the patient worse rather than better. By imposing massive financial stringency on countries in difficulty – including raising domestic interest rates, insisting on increased openness of the domestic economy, reducing social spending, and the like – it became extremely difficult for countries to help themselves out of difficulty:

> Conditionality, at least in the manner and extent to which it has been used by the IMF, is a bad idea; there is little evidence that it leads to improved economic policy, but it does have adverse political effects because countries resent having conditions imposed on them … In some cases it even *reduced* the likelihood of repayment.[36]

In the absence of a more coordinated and institutionalized system, the global financial system could easily spiral out of control. Indeed, this is what appeared to be happening following the East Asian financial crisis of 1997, with its subsequent spillover effects on countries like Russia and Brazil. There was particular concern over the volatile nature of global capital flows in terms of their impact on both the financial system itself and the individual countries and their populations most seriously affected by unpredictable flows of 'hot money'. To many observers, especially in the West, the causes of the 1997 East Asian crisis lay in structures and practices inside the affected countries (including so-called 'crony capitalism'). The remedy was obvious: apply the usual 'Washington Consensus' formula in which all answers lie in the unfettered operation of markets and in the conditionality applied to financial assistance. In fact, the major (though not the only) cause of the East Asian crisis was to be found in flows of speculative capital into (and then out of) the region. It also transpired that corrupt financial practices were by no means unique to East Asia. The collapse of two massive US companies, LTCM and Enron, in 2000–1, demonstrated this in graphic terms.

Not surprisingly, there were calls for a new, or reformed, *financial architecture* to ensure that a similar crisis could not recur. In fact, very little happened. It was back to business as usual and the further headlong growth and diversification of finan-cial markets and esoteric financial products (see Figure 16.5). From a broad devel-opmental viewpoint, the problem still remained that

> the global financial market is heavily dominated by financial interests in the industrialized countries. The governments of these countries, especially the economically strongest, determine the rules governing the market through their influence on the IFIs [International Financial Institutions]. These latter institutions in turn exercise great leverage over the macroeconomic and financial policies of developing countries. At the same time, the banks and financial houses from these same countries enjoy tremendous market power within the global financial system. The system is also characterized by severe market failures and is unstable. The upshot of all this is that most of the risks and the negative consequences of financial instability have been borne by the middle-income countries, currently the weakest players in the system.[37]

Ten years after the East Asian crisis, the much bigger – and potentially catastrophic – financial crisis of 2008 erupted. This time it could not be argued that the causes lay in 'inefficient' or 'corrupt' markets in developing countries. The origins of the much bigger 2008 financial crisis lay in the very heart of the 'Washington Consensus'. The much lauded, solely market-driven, financial system did not work. This time, it has to be fixed or, rather, replaced. The discrediting of the existing, very lightly regulated, financial system means that, this time, new solutions have to be found.

Towards a new global financial architecture?
It is too early to say what kind of new financial architecture will emerge or how stable it will be. What we can say is that the immediate response of national gov-ernments to the 2008 crisis was quite impressive, in the sense that total financial

meltdown was avoided. All governments implemented short-term rescue packages for their own financial sectors. But what about the bigger – global – picture?

Potentially, the most important development has been the emergence of the G20 as the central focus of attempts to build a reformed global financial system. The G20 was created in 1999 in the aftermath of the East Asian crisis but it was not until 2007 that it came to real prominence when the G20 finance ministers agreed to pump liquidity into financial markets at the beginning of the global financial crisis. In subsequent meetings in 2008 and 2009, the G20 was at the centre of initiatives to deal with the crisis. At its London summit in April 2009, $500 billion was committed to refinance the IMF; at the Pittsburgh summit in September 2009, the national leaders agreed to expand the G20's role, placing it at the centre of international economic policy making. Figure 11.5 outlines the major aspects of the G20's proposed global financial reform programme.

Area	Purpose
Financial regulation	Implement higher global standards consistently to ensure a level playing field and avoid fragmentation of markets, protectionism and regulatory arbitrage.
Establish Financial Stability Board (FSB)	Includes all G20 countries, plus Spain and the EC with strengthened mandate to promote financial stability, enhance openness and transparency of the financial sector, implement international financial standards.
International cooperation	Collaborate with IMF to conduct early warning exercises of potential macroeconomic and financial risks. Home authorities of each major financial institution should ensure that the group of authorities with a common interest in that financial institution meets at least annually. Systemically important financial firms should develop internationally-consistent firm-specific contingency and resolution plans. Establish supervisory colleges for significant cross-border firms. Advanced economies, the IMF and other international organizations should provide capacity-building programmes for emerging market economies and developing countries on the formulation and implementation of new major regulations, consistent with international standards.
Prudential regulation	Raise the quality, consistency and transparency of the Tier 1 capital base. Require banks to build buffers of resources in good times that they can draw on when conditions deteriorate. Level of capital in the banking system to be raised relative to pre-crisis levels. All major G20 countries to adopt the Basel II capital framework. Financial institutions should provide enhanced risk disclosures in all their reporting.
Compensation	Align compensation with long-term value-creation, not excessive risk-taking by (i) avoiding multi-year guaranteed bonuses; (ii) requiring a significant portion of variable compensation to be deferred, tied to performance and subject to appropriate clawback; (iii) making firms' compensation policies transparent through disclosure requirements; (iv) ensure compensation committees can act independently.

Figure 11.5   **Examples of measures proposed by the G20 to reform the global financial system**

Source: based on *Progress Report on the Actions to Promote Financial Regulatory Reform*, www.g20.org

How far have these, and other, reforms progressed? The report by the G20 Financial Stability Board (FSB) in late 2013 showed that some progress has been made but that there is still a long way to go.[38] Among areas where reform is urgently needed are the following:

- A restriction on the overall size of banks, in particular ending the 'too big to fail' situation in which taxpayers have to pick up the bill for failure.
- Separating the 'utility' and 'casino' functions of banks to prevent cross-contamination from the risky speculative activities (like hedge and private equity funds) to those activities needed to finance the 'real' economy. This harks back, at least in spirit, to the US Glass–Steagall Act of 1933 (see Chapter 16).
- Limiting the size of bonuses paid to bankers. There has been universal condemnation of the obscene sums derived from those financial activities described as 'socially useless' by the chair of the UK's Financial Services Authority.
- Dealing with the risks posed by 'shadow banking': institutions which perform some of the roles traditionally performed by banks, but are outside regulatory control.

There are, of course, many other possibilities for reform. One is the imposition of a small tax on every financial transaction: the so-called 'Tobin tax', first proposed by James Tobin in the 1970s, with the aim of 'throwing some sand in the wheels of cross-border financial transactions'. The idea was to discourage excessive flows of 'hot' money: short-term capital flows which can so easily destabilize financial systems, especially of weaker countries. In its present form it is seen as a way of raising capital for broader developmental purposes:

> A small global tax on financial transactions (say on the order of one tenth of 1 per cent) would generate tens of billions of dollars to address global challenges such as climate change or health pandemics at little economic cost.[39]

Of course, substantial reform of the global financial system can only happen with the consent of states themselves. One of the lessons of the post-2008 crisis is that, once the immediate crisis seems to have passed (it has not), then the tendency to adopt parochial positions tends to return. Narrow, short-term national political agendas too often prevail over longer-term global needs.

Regulating international trade

The evolution of world trade regulations

Compared with the international financial system, the governance of international trade is much clearer (though just as controversial).[40] In 1947, the General Agreement on Tariffs and Trade (GATT) was established as the third international institution formed in the aftermath of the Second World War, along with the IMF and the World Bank – completing what some have called the 'unholy trinity.'[41] Establishment of the GATT reflected the view that the 'beggar-my-neighbour' protectionist policies of the 1930s should not be allowed to recur. The objective

was to be 'free' trade based upon the *principle of comparative advantage*, first introduced by David Ricardo in 1817. This states that a country (or any geographical
area) should specialize in producing and exporting those products in which it has a
comparative or relative cost advantage compared with other countries and should
import those goods in which it has a comparative disadvantage. Out of such specialization, it is argued, will accrue greater benefit for all.

Whether or not there is such a thing as 'free' trade is highly debatable. In order
to work, it needs some degree of equality between trading partners and this, as we
have seen, at the global scale simply does not exist. The purpose of the GATT was
to create a set of *multilateral rules* to facilitate free trade through the reduction of
tariff barriers and other types of trade discrimination. The GATT was eventually
replaced by the WTO in 1995, an institutional change which greatly broadened
the remit of the trade regulator. Today, there are 159 member states in the WTO
(Russia having joined in 2012) and around 97 per cent of world trade is covered
by the WTO framework. Figure 11.6 traces its evolution.

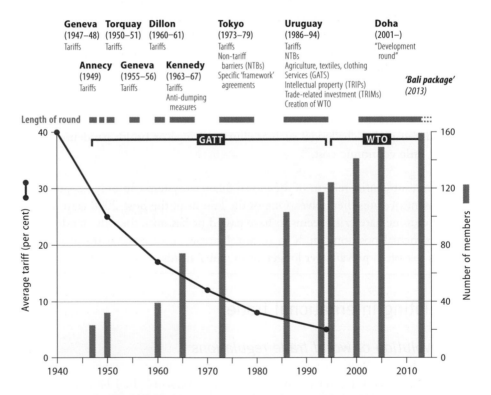

Figure 11.6   **Evolution of the international trade regulatory framework: from the
GATT to the WTO**

Since 1947 there have been nine 'rounds' of multilateral trade negotiations,
including the current Doha Round, initiated in 2001 and still not completed. Prior

to the mid-1960s, the GATT was mostly concerned with trade of manufactures between developed nations. As a result, widespread dissatisfaction emerged among developing countries. A particularly sensitive issue was the lack of access of developing country exports to developed country markets. Pressure led, in 1965, to the adoption within the GATT of a generalized system of preferences (GSP) under which exports of manufactured and semi-manufactured goods from developing countries were granted preferential access to developed country markets. In fact, there were a number of exclusions from the GSP, of which one of the most important was textiles and clothing (separately regulated under the MFA: see Chapter 14).

As Figure 11.6 shows, the first seven GATT rounds were both quite brief and also very limited in scope. It was the Uruguay Round, started in 1986 and eventually concluded in 1994, which constituted the most ambitious and wide ranging of all the GATT rounds to that point. For the first time, several additional trade issues were addressed. Notably, agriculture, textiles and clothing were brought into the GATT, and special agreements were concluded in services (GATS – the General Agreement on Trade in Services), intellectual property (TRIPS – Trade-Related Aspects of Intellectual Property Rights), and investment (TRIMS – Trade-Related Investment Measures). There was a further large reduction in overall tariff levels. The major organizational change was the creation of a new world trade organization.

The WTO, like the GATT, constitutes a *rule-oriented* approach to multilateral trade cooperation:

> Rule-oriented approaches focus not on outcomes, but on the rules of the game, and involve agreements on the level of trade barriers that are permitted as well as attempts to establish the general conditions of competition facing foreign producers in export markets.[42]

The fundamental basis is that of *non-discrimination*, based upon two provisions:

- The *most-favoured nation* (MFN) *principle* states that a trade concession negotiated between two countries must also apply to all other countries; all must be treated in the same way. The MFN principle is 'one of the pillars of the GATT' and 'applies unconditionally, the only major exception being if a subset of Members form a free-trade area or a customs union or grant preferential access to developing countries'.[43]
- The *national treatment rule* requires that imported foreign goods are treated in the same way as domestic goods.

Battles within the WTO

The WTO continues to be widely criticised from many directions and from interest groups in both developed and developing countries.[44] For example, unilateralist groups within the USA tend to regard the WTO as a basic infringement of the country's national sovereignty. Among developing countries there is resentment over what is regarded as the bullying and unfair behaviour of the powerful industrialized countries. To the anti-globalization protestors, the WTO is regarded as an undemocratic institution acting primarily in the interests of global corporations.

In one sense, in fact, the WTO is a far more democratic organization than the IMF. Whereas in the IMF the voting system is 'weighted', so that the more powerful states have a greater share of the vote, in the WTO each of the 159 member states has an equal vote. However, the position is not as straightforward as it seems. Decisions in the WTO are arrived at through negotiation in formal and informal meetings and through consensus, rather than by vote. Such processes depend heavily on the resources available to countries to lobby and exert influence:

> Most small delegations from developing countries do not have the appropriate resources either in Geneva or at home to service the increasingly frequent, complex, and resource-intensive negotiation process at the WTO …
>
> However, knowledge and resources are not enough for all countries to be effective in WTO negotiations. *An important reality is that the WTO rules do not entirely remove the inequality in the power of nations. It remains the case that countries with big markets have a greater ability than countries with small markets to secure market access and to deter actions against their exporters.*[45]

Two especially important sources of tension within the WTO relate to labour standards and the environment. How far do international differences in labour standards and regulations (such as the use of child labour, poor health and safety conditions, repression of labour unions and workers' rights) and in environmental standards and regulations (such as industrial pollution, the unsafe use of toxic materials in production processes) distort the trading system and create unfair advantages?

Several countries, led primarily by the USA but also including some European countries, have attempted to incorporate the issue of *labour standards* into the WTO. The attempt has failed, partly because not all industrialized countries support it, but also because developing countries are vehemently opposed. The argument of those opposed to its inclusion within the WTO's remit is that labour standards are the responsibility of the ILO. Indeed, all members of the ILO have agreed to a set of core principles. The counter-argument is that the ILO lacks any powers of enforcement. It is also notable that the USA, despite its current position on including labour standards in trade agreements, has not signed up to several of the ILO's core labour conventions, arguing that they do not comply with US law.

Similar questions apply to the relationship between trade regulations and the *environment*. To what extent should variations in environmental standards be incorporated into international trade regulations? At one level, the problem is exactly the same as that of labour standards. If a country allows lax environmental standards, it is argued, then it should not be able to use what is, in effect, a subsidy on firms located there to be able to sell its products more cheaply on the international market. The question then becomes one of whether the solution lies in using international trade regulations or in some other forms of regulation.

These labour and environmental questions posed by some developed countries arose in the aftermath of the Uruguay Round in the mid-1990s. But three-quarters of the WTO's membership consists of developing countries. They face, as we have seen in Chapter 10, immense economic and social problems. The Uruguay Round helped them in some respects but created major difficulties in others. In particular,

> of the three big agreements coming out of the Uruguay Round – on investment measures (TRIMS), trade in services (GATS), and intellectual property rights (TRIPS) – the first two limit the authority of developing country governments to constrain the choices of companies operating in their territory, while the third requires the governments to enforce rigorous property rights of foreign (generally Western) firms. Together, the agreements make comprehensively illegal many of the industrial policy instruments used in the successful East Asian developers to nurture their own industrial and technological capacities.[46]

In November 1999, a WTO meeting was held in Seattle to try to initiate a new round of trade negotiations. The meeting failed, not so much because of the anti-WTO/anti-globalization protests, but, as the UN Secretary-General, Kofi Annan, argued, because it failed to initiate a

> 'development round' that would at last deliver to the developing countries the benefits they have so often been promised from free trade, instead … [we] … saw governments – particularly those of the world's leading economic powers – unable to agree on their priorities. As a result, no round was launched at all.[47]

It was not until the end of 2001 that a new global trade round was announced at Doha in Qatar, with the official title of the 'Doha Development Agenda', to be concluded by 2004. It has effectively failed. The Doha Round has been possibly even more acrimonious than the Uruguay Round.[48] Deadlines have been missed with (un)impressive regularity. A 'make or break' Ministerial Meeting at Cancún in 2003 collapsed without producing any significant results. Subsequent meetings in Hong Kong (2005) and Geneva (2006, 2008) made very little progress.

The G20 has committed 'to reaching an ambitious and balanced conclusion to the Doha Development Round' noting that it is 'urgently needed'. But whether such rhetoric will make a difference is far from clear. The G20 also reaffirmed its commitment not to raise new barriers to trade. However, 17 of the 20 G20 members introduced some kind of trade protectionist measure in 2008–9.[49] A further complication is the resurgence of regional and bilateral trade negotiations outside the WTO, such as the proposed Transatlantic Trade and Investment Partnership and the Trans-Pacific Partnership (see Chapter 6). These call into question the willingness of some leading states to participate in the multilateral framework that is the WTO.

In late 2013, at a WTO meeting in Bali, an agreement was reached claiming to be 'worth' $1 trillion in global benefits. This is to be achieved primarily through 'trade facilitation': simplifying cross-border procedures to reduce costs and delays. There is also agreement to 'give improved terms of trade to the poorest countries, and offer developing countries leeway to bypass the normal rules on farm subsidies to feed the poor'.[50] In fact, the so-called 'Bali package' in no way completes the Doha Round; it is more symbolic than substantive ('Doha lite' it has been called). The need for a comprehensive trade and development agreement remains as urgent as ever.

Regulating TNCs

International guidelines and multilateral agreements

In the case of FDI and TNCs there is no international body comparable to the WTO, although the Uruguay Round included a set of *trade-related investment measures* (TRIMS). Within this framework, some of the industrialized countries, led by the USA, wish to prohibit or restrict a number of the measures listed in Figure 6.9, notably local content rules, export performance requirements, and the like. TRIMS' advocates argue that such measures restrict or distort trade. Its opponents see such measures as essential elements of their economic development strategies. They, in turn, wish to see a tightening of the regulations against the restrictive business practices of TNCs. Similarly, organized labour groups are generally opposed to measures that they feel will increase the ability of TNCs to affect workers' interests or to switch their operations from country to country.

In fact, there is a lengthy history of attempts to introduce an international framework relating to FDI and TNCs (apart from those agreed bilaterally or within the context of regional trade blocs):[51]

- OECD Guidelines for Multinational Enterprises (first introduced in 1976).
- ILO Tripartite Declaration of Principles Concerning Multinational Enterprises and Social Policy (1977).
- UN Code of Conduct for Transnational Corporations (initiated in 1982, abandoned in 1992).
- OECD Multilateral Agreement on Investment (MAI). The most recent attempt launched in the mid-1990s. Its main provisions were:

- o Countries were to open up all sectors of the economy to foreign investment or ownership (the ability to exempt key sectors in the national interest was to be removed).
- o Foreign firms were to be treated in exactly the same manner as domestic firms.
- o Performance requirements (e.g. local content requirements) were to be removed.
- o Capital movements (including profits) were to be unrestricted.
- o A dispute resolution process would enable foreign firms to be able to sue governments for damages if they felt that local rules violated MAI rules.
- o All states were to comply with the MAI.

Not surprisingly, the MAI generated a huge amount of opposition and was eventually blocked. Opposition was drawn from a very broad spectrum indeed, across both developed and developing countries:

> The choice of the OECD as the venue for the negotiations was a serious mistake because the OECD is a rich-country club and many LDCs were excluded from the discussions; why would LDCs accept an agreement that they had no part in formulating and that protected the interests of [T]NCs? Even many OECD countries objected to rules that would harm their own interests ... Labor and environmentalists objected that MAI would give [T]NCs license to disregard workers' interests and pollute the environment. Many critics charged that no protection was provided against the evils committed by [T]NCs. Even official American enthusiasm cooled when people realized that the MAI dispute mechanism could be used against the US and its [T]NCs.[52]

The major dilemma in any attempt to establish a global regulatory framework for FDI and TNCs is the sharp conflict of interest inherent in the process involving TNCs, states, labour groups and CSOs. Should the focus be on regulating the *conduct* of TNCs (the viewpoint of most developing countries, some developed countries, labour and environmental groups) or should it be concerned with the *protection* of TNCs' interests? Both TRIMS and the aborted MAI were stacked in favour of TNCs.

Dealing with problems of tax avoidance

Today, as we saw in Chapter 7, there is particular concern over tax avoidance by TNCs, especially through the practices of transfer pricing and establishing shell operations in lower-tax countries. Through such means, TNCs are able to manipulate their international tax liabilities and, hence, to deprive states (and their taxpayers) of legitimate revenue (see Figures 7.5 and 7.6). As a result, a variety of possible tax reforms have been put forward. One proposal is for a system of *unitary taxation*:

> Unitary taxation … does not allow the TNC to be taxed as if it were a collection of separate entities in different jurisdictions, but instead treats a TNC engaged in a unified business as a single entity, requiring it to submit a single set of worldwide consolidated accounts in each country where it has a business presence, then apportioning the overall global profit to the various countries according to a weighted formula reflecting its genuine economic presence in each country. Each country involved sees the combined report and can then tax its portion of the global profits at its own rate.[53]

However, the kind of international regulatory framework needed for such reforms certainly does not exist at present. But pressure is certainly building. Within the EU, for example, the European Commission is investigating the tax arrangements of countries such as Ireland, Luxembourg and the Netherlands. More broadly, the Commission is aiming to deal with so-called 'hybrid tax schemes' which exploit 'mismatches between different countries' tax systems that allow companies to minimise tax using hybrid instruments such as convertible preference shares or profit participating loans, which are treated as equity in some countries and debt in others'.[54]

But there is still a long way to go before a coherent international regulatory system is in place. In response to a request from the G20, the OECD in 2013 proposed a series of measures to address some of the most egregious international tax avoidance practices: for example, those relating to transfer pricing, the digital economy, rules on foreign-controlled companies, including the issue of 'permanent establishment status' (whereby companies claim non-residentiary status for their operations). The OECD's 15-point 'action plan'[55] aims to 'give governments the domestic and international instruments to prevent corporations from paying little or no taxes'. As such, it at least represents a potential step towards dealing with the very serious problems arising from the tax avoidance practices of TNCs.

There is clearly an urgent need to deal with the problem of *offshore financial centres* (OFCs), which operate as *tax havens* (not only for TNCs but also for very wealthy individuals). They attract investors through their low tax levels and 'light' regulatory regimes.[56] For example, although hundreds of banks are apparently located in countries such as the Cayman Islands, only a few actually have a physical presence there. Most are little more than 'a brass or plastic name plate in the lobby of another bank, as a folder in a filing cabinet or an entry in a computer system'.[57] Similarly, although there were roughly 300,000 companies registered in the Virgin Islands in the early 2000s, 'only 9,000 of them show any signs of activity locally':[58] 'The Netherlands has about 23,000 "letterbox companies", managed by 176 licensed trust firms … [which] attract huge flows of money through the Netherlands, making €8tn worth of transactions in 2011–13 times its gross domestic product.'[59]

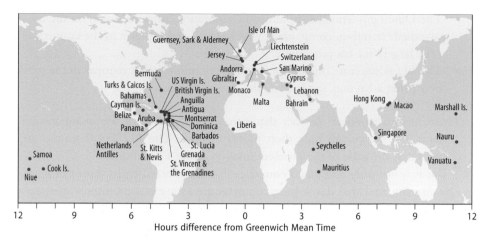

Figure 11.7 **The geography of offshore financial centres**

Source: based on OECD data

Figure 11.7 shows the geographical distribution of offshore financial centres. Each tends to fill a specific niche which it exploits in competition with other centres in the same geographical cluster and with similar niche centres elsewhere in the world. Much of their growth occurred in the 1970s, in places that were already operating as tax havens, to act as banks' 'booking centres' for their eurocurrency transactions:

> By operating offshore booking centres international banks could act free of reserve requirements and other regulations. Offshore branches could also be used as profit centres (from which profits may be repatriated at the most suitable moment for tax minimization) and as bases from which to serve the needs of multinational corporate clients.[60]

The location of these offshore centres, and especially their geographical clustering, is partly determined by time zones and the need for 24-hour financial trading.

There is now an intensifying international drive to crack down on offshore tax havens. Such action was initiated by the OECD but has been followed by specific actions by the USA, UK and other European governments.[61] For example:

- In 2013, the UK made an agreement with 10 British protectorate territories, including Bermuda, the British Virgin Islands, the Cayman Islands, Jersey, Guernsey and the Isle of Man to establish a register of the owners of foundations, trusts and shell firms in their jurisdictions.
- In 2010, the USA introduced a new law – the Foreign Accounts Tax Compliance Act – to force foreign bank accounts to declare assets held by US citizens.

- The Dutch government announced its intention 'to crack down on the use of so-called "letterbox companies", which do no real business in the country and exist largely for tax purposes'.[62]
- The EU is 'to create one of the toughest tax transparency regimes in the world by passing a Savings Tax Law by the end of the year'.

These initiatives reflect the fact that astronomical tax losses are being incurred as firms and individuals hide their profits offshore. The EU Tax Commissioner claimed that the scale of the problem involves about €1 trillion.

But it is not only developed countries that are affected by offshore tax havens. Oxfam estimated that developing countries are losing out on annual income of up to $124 billion because more than $6 trillion of developing country wealth is held in offshore accounts.[63] The Tax Justice Network claims that 'in tax revenue alone, at least $100billion was lost from developing countries through insufficient international tax policies'.[64]

Burning issues: global environmental regulation

As we saw in Chapter 9, the processes of production, distribution and consumption, articulated within and through GPNs, have the potential to create enormous and long-lasting environmental damage. And yet, compared with finance and trade regulation, there were few systematic attempts to build an appropriate global regulatory structure for the environment until the late 1980s.[65] Today, of course, environmental issues, and especially climate change, have become one of the (literally) hottest and most contentious policy issues of all – a veritable minefield, politically, economically and scientifically.

The evolution of climate change initiatives

From the outset, the UN has been at the centre of global climate change initiatives, beginning with its decision in 1968 to convene the 1972 Stockholm Conference on the Human Environment. This stimulated the setting up of national environmental agencies in most developed, and some developing, countries.[66]

In 1988, the UN established what was to become the scientific core of its environmental programme: the Intergovernmental Panel on Climate Change (IPCC). The first IPCC Assessment Report was published in 1990 and this formed the basis of the first comprehensive policy on climate change: the 1992 *Framework Convention on Climate Change* (FCCC). A key objective of the FCCC was to achieve

> the stabilization of greenhouse gas concentrations in the atmosphere at a level that would prevent dangerous anthropogenic interference with the climate system.[67]

The FCCC was based upon *voluntary* reduction of carbon dioxide levels: it merely 'encouraged industrialized countries to stabilize GHG emissions'.

Its (not surprising) lack of success led, in 1997, to the drafting of the *Kyoto Protocol*. In contrast to the FCCC, Kyoto incorporated *binding* emission targets over the period 2008–12 for 37 developed countries, based on 1990 levels. The Protocol came into force in 2005; 184 countries (excluding, most significantly, the USA) were signatories. After the Kyoto Protocol was finally ratified, there was much argument among the signatories and, with the USA, over the details of climate change regulation. In December 2005, the UN Conference in Montreal agreed the following measures:

- To strengthen the 'clean development mechanism', which allows developed countries to invest in sustainable development projects in developing countries while earning emission allowances.
- To launch the 'Joint Implementation' mechanism, which allows developed countries to invest in other developed countries, especially the transition economies of Eastern Europe. In doing so they can earn carbon allowances, which can be used to meet their emission reduction commitments.
- To implement the 'compliance regime' which ensures that countries have clear accountability for meeting their emission reduction targets.

Where are we now?

The Kyoto commitments were time limited (2012). A new agreement was to be negotiated and signed at the UN Conference on Climate Change at Copenhagen in December 2009.

Climate scientists believe that if global temperatures were to rise by more than 2°C above pre-industrial levels then climate change would become irreversible. To meet such a criterion, a number of specific, but highly variable, targets have been proposed, including the following:

- Developed countries to halve global CO_2 emissions, compared with 1990 levels, by 2050. This has the support of developed countries in general, while the G8 promised to cut their own emissions by 80 per cent.
- The EU promised to cut its emissions by 20 per cent by 2020 compared with 1990 levels and to increase this to 30 per cent if other countries also commit.
- The USA promised to reduce its emissions by 17 per cent by 2020, compared with 2005 levels.
- Japan promised to reduce its emissions by 25 per cent by 2020.
- China promised to reduce the growth in its CO_2 output by 40–45 per cent by 2020.

The most intractable problem is the extent to which developing countries should be expected to adopt measures that could prevent their future economic development. Since most of the 'stock' of CO_2 in the atmosphere was produced historically by developed countries then, it is argued, developing countries should be given preferential treatment. On the other hand, the developed country argument is that most of the growth in emissions in the future will be in developing countries, especially China, India and Brazil.

Given the 2°C 'bottom line', the major goals of the *Copenhagen* meeting were to reach agreement on the following issues and to embed them into a binding UN treaty with precise numbers and a timescale: developed countries to cut their CO_2 emissions; developing countries to curb their emissions; provision by developed countries of financial and technological assistance to developing countries to enable them to achieve their emission targets. On every issue, of course, views differed widely between different interest groups: developed and developing countries, environmental groups and other GCSOs, and business firms.

Despite all the pre-meeting hype – and all the dire warnings – no binding agreement was reached. At the last minute, and after highly acrimonious negotiations, an 'Accord' was reached, based primarily on a deal put together by a small group of countries: the USA, Brazil, China, India and South Africa. The most striking aspect of the Copenhagen Accord was its vagueness. The only numbers related to the commitment of financial assistance to developing countries.

Since Copenhagen, discussions have continued at annual UN Climate Change Conferences in Cancún (2010), Durban (2011), Doha (2012) and Warsaw (2013). The Warsaw meeting agreed that countries must set out their 'national contributions' to greenhouse gas emissions in time for the 2015 Climate Change Summit in Paris. The major scientific input for these meetings is the IPCC's Fifth Assessment Report (2013), which reaffirms the human influence on global warming and that 'limiting climate change will require substantial and sustained reductions of greenhouse gas emissions'.[68] However, the big issue, as always, is not the science but the *politics*.

A BETTER WORLD?

The future shape of the global economy is far from clear. Although the chances are that globalizing processes will continue to operate and that the world will continue to become increasingly interconnected, there is a huge amount of uncertainty. We should certainly not simply extrapolate from past trends. However, the key question is not so much what the world *might* be like in the future, but what it *should* be like. Most of all, then, we need to think about the *kind* of world we, and our children, would want to live in. There are choices to be made. What might these be? After all, globalization is not a force of nature; it is a social process.[69] What are the choices? In theory they are infinite; in practice they are not.

Alternative economies?

In thinking about alternative futures in the context of globalization debates, there is a depressing tendency towards polarization of positions of the kind we identified in Chapter 1. The gung-ho, neo-liberal hyper-globalizers see the solution in yet more openness of markets, unfettered flows of goods, services and capital. In other words, much, much more of the same. The anti-globalizers argue for exactly the opposite. Whereas the first strategy would almost certainly create a world of even greater inequality (as well as environmental damage) the second embodies the dangers of reverting to a set of medieval subsistence economies.

The diametrical opposition of these two positions can be illustrated by their polarized attitudes towards trade. To the hyper-globalizers, it is a central tenet that trade should be allowed to flourish without hindrance. The anti-globalizers' position is that the pursuit of ever-increasing international trade – which is clearly encouraged by a free trade regime like the WTO – should be totally abandoned, not merely regulated. The argument is basically that sustainable development is incompatible with the pursuit of further economic growth. An economic system based upon very high levels of geographical specialization inevitably depends upon, and generates, ever-increasing trade in materials and products.

A central criticism is that the energy costs of transporting materials and goods across the world are not taken into account in setting the prices of traded goods and that, in effect, trade is being massively subsidized at a huge short-term and long-term environmental cost. But by no means all environmentalists agree with this kind of viewpoint. As David Pearce argues, 'unquestionably, there are environmental problems inherent in the existing trading system … [but] there is also extensive confusion in the environmentalist critique of free trade'.[70] There are, in fact, very different 'shades of green', ranging from the position that human ingenuity and new technologies will find the solutions without necessitating a change in lifestyles (the Panglossian view) through to the 'deep green' arguments that only a return to a totally different, small-scale, highly-localized mode of existence will suffice. But such a path, rather than improving the position for the poor in the world economy, 'would condemn the vast majority of people to a miserable future, at best on the margins of the bare minimum of physical existence'.[71] It is not a socially acceptable policy:

> The alternative to an economic system that involves trade is not bucolic simplicity and hardy self-sufficiency, but extreme poverty. South Korea has plenty of problems, but not nearly so many as its neighbour to the north.[72]

But this emphatically does *not* mean that 'local' economies are irrelevant. On the contrary. There exists a wide diversity of economies[73] offering different kinds of possibilities and which occupy different positions in relation to the larger global economy. Many of these are, essentially, 'community economies'. Figure 11.8 summarizes the main ways in which such economies differ from the 'mainstream' economy: 'In some cases, these communities are geographically confined to the "local", whilst in others

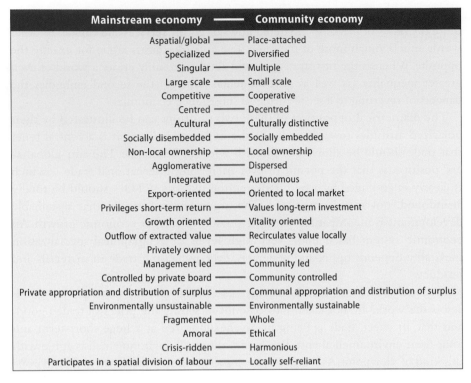

Mainstream economy	———	Community economy
Aspatial/global	———	Place-attached
Specialized	———	Diversified
Singular	———	Multiple
Large scale	———	Small scale
Competitive	———	Cooperative
Centred	———	Decentred
Acultural	———	Culturally distinctive
Socially disembedded	———	Socially embedded
Non-local ownership	———	Local ownership
Agglomerative	———	Dispersed
Integrated	———	Autonomous
Export-oriented	———	Oriented to local market
Privileges short-term return	———	Values long-term investment
Growth oriented	———	Vitality oriented
Outflow of extracted value	———	Recirculates value locally
Privately owned	———	Community owned
Management led	———	Community led
Controlled by private board	———	Community controlled
Private appropriation and distribution of surplus	———	Communal appropriation and distribution of surplus
Environmentally unsustainable	———	Environmentally sustainable
Fragmented	———	Whole
Amoral	———	Ethical
Crisis-ridden	———	Harmonious
Participates in a spatial division of labour	———	Locally self-reliant

Figure 11.8   Contrasting characteristics of mainstream and community economies

Source: based on Gibson-Graham, 2006: Figure 23

they span the "global".[74] The fair-trade networks discussed in Chapter 13 are examples of the latter. The Mondragón Cooperative Corporation is an example of a complex of cooperatives spread across 14 countries but grounded in the Basque region of Spain and organized on worker-owned principles. The LETS (Local Exchange Trading System) uses local 'currencies' to facilitate the exchange of services and self-produced or self-earned goods within a network of members in a local community.[75] A micro-finance scheme, which began as a local initiative in Bangladesh in the 1970s, subsequently spread across many other countries and has been a huge contributor to poverty reduction.[76] None of these initiatives are without their problems. For example, in late 2013, the Mondragón Cooperative cast adrift its Fagor domestic appliances member, which employed almost 6000 workers.[77]

The diversity of alternative economies is growing and offers significant possibilities for creating fulfilling and fair communities and, more generally, for reconsidering globalization as a transformable social process and not a force of nature. But they are, by definition, mostly small in scale and often highly local in scope. They raise important issues of how such economies connect into the bigger picture (unless they decide to opt out). And it is the 'bigger picture' that still demands our primary attention.

To be 'globalized' or not to be 'globalized': that is the question

> The main losers in today's very unequal world are not those who are too much exposed to globalization. They are those who have been left out.[78]

> Is the problem actually globalization or not-globalization? Is the difficulty being part of the system or not being part of it? How can globalization be the source of problems for those excluded from it?[79]

It is abundantly clear that the position of many of the world's poorest countries is highly marginal in terms of the global economy. The usual prescription of the IMF/World Bank 'doctors' is that they should open their economies more, for example by positively encouraging exports and by liberalizing their regulatory structures:

> For policymakers around the world, the appeal of opening up to global markets is based on a simple but powerful promise: international economic integration will improve economic performance ... *The trouble is ... that there is no convincing evidence that openness, in the sense of low barriers to trade and capital flows, systematically produces these consequences. In practice, the links between openness and economic growth tend to be weak and contingent on the presence of complementary policies and institutions.*[80]

'Openness' will only work if the playing field is relatively level – which, clearly, it is not. And it also has to work both ways – which, clearly, it does not. Tariffs imposed by developed countries on imports of many developing country products remain very high. It is common for tariffs to increase with the degree of processing (so-called tariff escalation), so that higher-value products from developing countries are discriminated against. At the same time, agricultural subsidies make imports from developing countries uncompetitive. In other words, the odds are stacked against them:[81]

> The human costs of unfair trade are immense. If Africa, South Asia, and Latin America were each to increase their share of world exports by one per cent, the resulting gains in income could lift 128 million people out of poverty ... When developing countries export to rich-country markets, they face tariff barriers that are four times higher than those encountered by rich countries. Those barriers cost them $100bn a year – twice as much as they receive in aid.[82]

However, simply opening up a developing economy will almost certainly lead to further disaster. There is the danger of local businesses being wiped out by more efficient foreign competition before they can get a toehold in the wider world. Hence a prerequisite for positive and beneficial engagement with the global economy is the development of robust internal structures: 'the development of a national economy is more about internal integration than about external integration'.[83]

Eradicating extreme poverty: the UN Millennium Development Project

Poverty is *the* major problem in many parts of the world. For many years, aid programmes have been devised to help alleviate its major manifestations but such aid has generally fallen far below needs. In 2002, a meeting of heads of state in New York adopted the *UN Millennium Declaration*. Its aim was nothing less than the eradication of extreme poverty by 2015, as part of a broad and comprehensive development programme. The precise goals and targets of the UN project are set out in Figure 11.9. They are, indeed, extremely ambitious – especially in light of the 2008 global financial crisis. The right-hand column of Figure 11.9 shows some of the progress reported by the UN in 2013. Its conclusion was that while 'progress can be reported in most areas, despite the impact of the global economic and financial crisis ... progress in many areas is far from sufficient'.[84]

Goals, aspirations and collective will

> Society is faced with a profound dilemma. To resist growth is to risk economic and social collapse. To pursue it relentlessly is to endanger the ecosystems on which we depend for long-term survival.[85]

The major global challenge is to meet the material needs of the world community as a whole in ways that reduce, rather than increase, inequality and which do so without destroying the environment. That, of course, is far easier said than done. It requires the involvement of all the major actors – business firms, states, international institutions, CSOs – in establishing mechanisms to capture the benefits of globalization for the majority and not just for the powerful minority. To some, this can only be achieved by an overarching global system of governance: in effect, a world democratic government. But, as Dani Rodrik argues, there is an irresolvable political trilemma, between democracy, national determination and economic globalization:

> Even though it is possible to advance both democracy and globalization, the trilemma suggests this requires the creation of a global political community that is vastly more ambitious than anything we have seen to date or are likely to experience soon. It would call for global rulemaking by democracy supported by accountability mechanisms that go far beyond what we have at present. Democratic global governance of this sort is a

Goal	Target	Progress by 2013
1: Eradicate extreme poverty and hunger	1: Halve, between 1990 and 2015, the proportion of people whose income is less than $1 a day. 2: Achieve full and productive employment and decent work for all, including women and young people. 3: Halve, between 1990 and 2015, the proportion of people who suffer from hunger.	1: Proportion of people in extreme poverty halved at global level by 2010. 3: Hunger reduction target within reach, but 1 in 8 people remain chronically undernourished.
2: Achieve universal primary education	1: Ensure that, by 2015, children everywhere, boys and girls alike, will be able to complete a full course of primary schooling.	1: Target of universal primary education by 2015 unlikely to be met.
3: Promote gender equality and empower women	1: Eliminate gender disparity in primary and secondary education, preferably by 2005, and in all levels of education no later than 2015.	
4: Reduce child mortality	1: Reduce by two-thirds, between 1990 and 2015, the under-five mortality rate.	1: Despite large reduction in under-five mortality rate, more rapid progress needed to meet the 2015 target. Increasingly, child deaths are concentrated in poorest regions and in first month of life.
5: Improve maternal health	1: Reduce by three-quarters the maternal mortality ratio. 2: Achieve universal access to reproductive health.	1: Despite considerable reduction in maternal mortality, meeting the three-quarters target needs accelerated intervention and stronger political backing for women and children.
6: Combat HIV/AIDS, malaria and other diseases	1: Have halted by 2015 and begun to reverse the spread of HIV/AIDS. 2: Achieve, by 2010, universal access to treatment for HIV/AIDS for all those who need it. 3: Have halted by 2015 and begun to reverse the incidence of malaria and other major diseases.	2: Target of universal access to antiretroviral therapy by 2010 missed, but reachable by 2015. 3: Remarkable gains made in fight against malaria and tuberculosis.
7: Ensure environmental sustainability	1: Integrate the principles of sustainable development into country policies and programmes and reverse the loss of environmental resources. 2: Reduce biodiversity loss, achieving, by 2010, a significant reduction in the rate of loss. 3: Halve, by 2015, the proportion of the population without sustainable access to safe drinking water and basic sanitation. 4: By 2020, to have achieved a significant improvement in the lives of at least 100 million slum dwellers.	3: The drinking water target reached by 2010, insufficient improvements in sanitation. 4: Proportion of slum dwellers in cities of developing world is declining. The 100 million MDG target of improved water resources, sanitation facilities, durable housing/sufficient living space exceeded by 2010.
8: Develop a global partnership for development	1: Address the special needs of least developed countries, landlocked countries and small island developing states. 2: Develop further an open, rule-based, predictable, non-discriminatory trading and financial system. 3: Deal comprehensively with developing countries' debt. 4: In cooperation with pharmaceutical companies, provide access to affordable essential drugs in developing countries. 5: In cooperation with the private sector, make available benefits of new technologies, especially information and communications.	

Figure 11.9 **The UN Millennium Development Goals**

Source: based on material in www.un.org/millenniumgoals; UN, 2013: pp. 4–5

chimera. There are too many differences among nation states ... for their needs and preferences to be accommodated within common rules and institutions ... A thin layer of international rules that leaves substantial room for manoeuvre by national governments ... can address globalization's ills while preserving its substantial economic benefits. *We need smart globalization, not maximum globalization.*[86]

Nevertheless, even this would require a high level of international cooperation between nation-states. Leaving 'substantial room for manoeuvre' must not involve facilitating 'beggar-my-neighbour' policies. Certainly, any system must be built on world trading and financial systems that are *equitable* and reflect the new realities of the changing global economic map. This must involve reform of such institutions as the WTO, the World Bank and the IMF or, alternatively, their replacement by more effective, and more widely accountable, institutions. Pressure for reform has come from a number of directions. Not the least of these has been the newly institutionalized self-awareness of the so-called BRICs. In 2012, the heads of state of the BRIC countries (including South Africa) urged the need for faster reform of the IMF and 'threatened to withhold additional financing requested by the International Monetary Fund to fight the European sovereign debt crisis unless they gained greater voting power at the fund'.[87] In July 2014, the BRIC leaders established a $100bn New Development Bank (NDB) aimed at redressing some of the obstacles created for developing countries by the established international organizations, notably the World Bank and the IMF. The NDB will have two major foci: (1) funding infrastructural projects; (2) helping members facing sudden foreign capital flight through establishing a Contingency Reserve Arrangement (CRA). The NDB will be headquartered in Shanghai and is planned to be in operation in 2016.

More broadly, the emergence of the G20 is undoubtedly a step in the right direction, but it is little more than that so far. The G20 has not, to date, delivered on the early promise of the major initiatives taken in 2009 to address the global financial crisis (see Figure 11.5). Much, much more needs to be done. As we have seen, the exercise of developed country power through the various kinds of conditionality and trade-opening requirements imposed on poorer countries has seriously negative results. Without doubt, trade is one of the most effective ways of enhancing material well-being, but it has to be based upon a genuinely fairer basis than at present. The poorer countries must be allowed to open up their markets in a manner, and at a pace, appropriate to their needs and conditions. After all, that is precisely what the USA and European countries did during their early phases of industrialization and as did Japan and the East Asian NIEs at a later date. At the same time, developed countries must operate a fairer system of access to their own markets for poor countries.

Of course, this will cause problems for some people and communities in developed countries and these must not be underestimated. As we saw in Chapter 10, there are, indeed, many losers in the otherwise affluent economies. Will the populations of the rich countries be prepared to make some sacrifices for the greater global good? The signs are not very promising. Even at the best of times, it is difficult to persuade people to look beyond their own needs and wants. And these are emphatically not the best of times. The chaos wrought by the near collapse of the financial system in 2008, and the debt burdens piling up to deal with its aftermath, have increased general feelings of insecurity. For example, there has undoubtedly been an increase in the opposition of developed country populations to trade and to foreign immigration. At one stage, it seemed that 'less-educated, lower-income workers are much more likely to oppose policies aimed at freer trade and immigration'.[88] However, this is changing as more highly educated workers are increasingly affected.

People whose lives are devastated by 'globalization' – especially through loss of their livelihood – must be assisted effectively and sensitively, whether through financial assistance or education and retraining. Governments must design and implement appropriate adjustment policies for such groups if trade policies helpful to developing countries are to be acceptable politically. Equally, governments of developing countries must engage in their own internal reforms: to strengthen domestic institutions, enhance civil society, increase political participation, remove corruption, raise the quality of education, and reduce internal social polarization. Although difficult, such policies are not impossible if the social and political will is there.

However, even increased material affluence does not necessarily make people 'happier' in proportion to their increased wealth.[89] Research by the ILO[90] suggests that it is 'economic security', rather than wealth, that 'promotes happiness':

> The global distribution of economic security does not correspond to the global distribution of income ... South and South East Asia have greater shares of economic security than their share of the world's income ... By contrast, Latin American countries provide their citizens with much less economic security than could be expected from their relative income levels ... income security is a major determinant of other forms of labour-related security ... [and] ... income inequality worsens economic security in several ways ... *highly unequal societies are unlikely to achieve much by way of economic security or decent work.*[91]

As we saw in Chapter 10, the trend in many countries has been for inequality to be widening, rather than narrowing.

There is a more general argument: that 'prosperity' needs to be defined in broader terms than just 'gross domestic product'; that 'well-being' is about more than just material affluence. A number of proposals to measure well-being have emerged, beginning with the rather exotic case of the Kingdom of Bhutan, which introduced the concept of GNH (Gross National Happiness) in the 1970s. A French government commission proposed that the components that go into the measurement of GDP need to be broadened to incorporate a whole range of other measures, such as health, education, security, social connectedness, environmental sustainability.[92] A rather more subjective set of measures proposed for national accounts focuses on two dimensions: personal well-being and social well-being.[93] Whether or not such well-being measures will replace or supplement the conventional measures like GDP is hard to say. But the fact that we must define growth/prosperity/well-being in more meaningful terms is incontrovertible if we are to build a better world.

A moral imperative

The problems facing us are both practical and moral. In practical terms, the continued existence across the world of vast numbers of people who are impoverished – but who can see the manifestations of immense wealth either at first hand or through the electronic media – poses a serious threat to social and political stability. But the moral argument is, I believe, more powerful. It is utterly repellent that so many people live in such abject poverty and deprivation (wherever they may be) while, at the same time, others live in immense luxury. This is not an argument for levelling down but for raising up. The means for doing this are there. What matters is the *will* to do it – the real acceptance of, to use David Smith's words,

> the imperative of developing more caring relations with others, especially those most vulnerable, whoever and wherever they are, within a more egalitarian and environmentally sustainable way of life in which some of the traditional strengths of community can be realised and spatially extended.[94]

We all have a responsibility to ensure that the contours of the global economic map in the twenty-first century are not as steep as those of the twentieth century. We all have a responsibility to treat others as equals. In a global context, this means being sensitive to the immense diversity that exists, to the world as a mosaic of people equally deserving of 'the good life'.

This also means, in my view, the need to question what Michael Sandel terms 'the moral limits of markets':

> We need to rethink the role that markets should play in our society … without quite realizing it, without ever deciding to do so, we drifted from *having* a market economy to *being* a market society. The difference is this: A market economy is a tool – a valuable and effective tool – for organizing productive activity. A market society is a way of life in which market values seep into every aspect of human endeavour. It's a place where social relations are made over in the image of the market … sometimes, market values crowd out nonmarket norms worth caring about.[95]

As Erica Schoenberger argues:

> We need to come up with a different way of producing choices from relying entirely on the blind forces of the market. We need a way of making big decisions about how things work that is not absolutely beholden to the drive for profits and does not hold private property absolutely sacrosanct. Profits and property are not evil. But if they are the only basis for making decisions about how we live on earth, then we cannot change our trajectory.[96]

Paradoxically, the 2008 global financial crisis seemed to offer a real opportunity for change. For the first time in several decades, both the economic inefficiencies and the social limitations of free, unregulated markets were exposed for all to see. In particular, an economic system based so heavily on financial speculation is, in any social and moral sense, dysfunctional. It has failed. The opportunity *must* be taken to build a new system to redress the imbalance that has developed between states and markets, between people and institutions and between the immensely wealthy and the rest. Such a project is global in both scale and scope, hence the need for coordinated international policy initiatives rather than individual national measures that would lead to destructive competition rather than collaboration. At the height of the crisis in 2008–9, it seemed that such a rebuilding might, indeed, be on the agenda. But subsequently, as the worst has seemed to some to be over (or is it?), there is a real danger of going 'back to the future'. It would be a tragedy, in every sense, if that were to happen. We can – we *must* – do better.

NOTES

1   Voltaire (1947: 8).
2   Micklethwait and Wooldridge (2000: ix).
3   *Oxford Martin Commission for Future Generations* (2013: 9).
4   BBC World Service (2008).
5   ILO (2004b: 12–23).
6   *Oxford Martin Commission for Future Generations* (2013: 9).
7   Burgoon (2009: 148).
8   Schoenberger (2014: xx).
9   See Lee (2007), Lee and Smith (2004), Sandel (2012), Singer (2004), Smith (2000).
10 Harvey (2011: chapter 8).
11 Taylor et al. (2002: 15–16).
12 Beck (2005: 238).
13 Scherer et al. (2014) explore the increasingly complex social and political issues facing business firms.
14 Van Tulder with van der Zwart (2006: Parts II and III) provide a comprehensive analysis of international corporate social responsibility (ICSR).
15 Van Tulder with van der Zwart (2006: 143–5).
16 Barrientos (2008), Hughes et al. (2008), van Tulder (2009), van Tulder et al. (2009), Barrientos (2008), Hughes et al. (2008).
17 Barrientos (2008: 979).
18 Van Tulder et al. (2009: 399).
19 Van Tulder (2009: 10).
20 Van Tulder et al. (2009: 402).
21 Gereffi et al. (2001).
22 See Chapter 14.
23 Cumbers et al. (2008: 380–4), van Tulder et al. (2009).
24 Barrientos (2008), Hughes et al. (2008).
25 See Moran (2011), Rasche (2009).

26 Barrientos (2008: 978).

27 Barrientos (2008: 978).

28 Barrientos (2008: 980).

29 Van Tulder et al. (2009).

30 Van Tulder et al. (2009: 408). See also Maignan and Ralston (2002).

31 Wolf (2007).

32 Commission on Global Governance (1995: 135–6).

33 Gritsch (2005).

34 Levy and Prakash (2003: 143, 144).

35 Hirst et al. (2009).

36 Stiglitz (2002: 44).

37 ILO (2004b: 88, 89).

38 Letter from the Chairman of the FSB to G20 leaders (5 September 2013).

39 Rodrik (2011: 264).

40 See Deese (2008), Hoekman and Kostecki (1995), Peet et al. (2003: chapter 5), Sampson (2001).

41 Peet et al. (2003).

42 Hoekman and Kostecki (1995: 24).

43 Hoekman and Kostecki (1995: 26).

44 See, for example, Deese (2008), Peet et al. (2003: chapter 5), Singer (2004: chapter 3).

45 Sampson (2001: 7–8; emphasis added).

46 Wade (2003: 621).

47 Quoted in Sampson (2001: 19).

48 Stiglitz and Charlton (2005) present a detailed critique of the Doha Round and show how 'fair' trade and development can go together.

49 Gamberoni and Newfarmer (2009).

50 *Guardian* (7 December 2013).

51 See Braithwaite and Drahos (2000: chapter 10), Gilpin (2000: chapter 6), Kolk and van Tulder (2005).

52 Gilpin (2000: 184–5).

53 Picciotto (2012: 1).

54 *Financial Times* (26 November 2013).

55 OECD (2013).

56 Eatwell and Taylor (2000: 189). See also Palan (2003), Roberts (1994).

57 Roberts (1994: 92).

58 *Financial Times* (7 December 2001).

59 *Financial Times* (29 April 2013).

60 Roberts (1994: 99).

61 'EU tax havens under pressure as leaks go public', euobserver.com (17 June 2013).

62 *Financial Times* (12 September 2013).

63 *The Guardian* (14 March 2009).

64 Tax Justice Network (19 September 2013).

65 See Braithwaite and Drahos (2000: chapter 12), Pearce (1995).

66 Braithwaite and Drahos (2000: 257).

67 Quoted in Pearce (1995: 149).

68 IPCC Fifth Assessment Report, *Approved Summary for Policymakers* (2013: SPM-14).

69 Massey (2000: 24).

70 Pearce (1995: 74).

71 Hudson (2001: 315).

72 Elliott (2002). See also Elliott (2000).

73 Gibson-Graham (2006).

74 Gibson-Graham (2006: 80).

75 Lee (1996).

76 Hulme and Arun (2009).

77 *Financial Times* (10 December 2013).

78 Kofi Annan, UN Secretary-General, Speech to UNCTAD Meeting in Bangkok, 2000.

79 Mittelman (2000: 241).

80 Rodrik (1999: 136–7; emphasis added).

81 See UNCTAD (2002).

82 Oxfam (2002: 1).

83 Wade (2003: 635).

84 UN (2013: 4).

85 Jackson (2009: 187).

86 Rodrik (2011: xix; emphasis added).

87 *Financial Times* (30 March 2012).

88 Scheve and Slaughter (2001: 87).

89 Jackson (2009), James (2007), Layard (2005), Oswald (1997), Wilkinson and Pickett (2009).

90 ILO (2004a). See also Scheve and Slaughter (2004).

91 ILO press release, www.ilo.org.

92 Stiglitz and Fitoussi (2009).

93 New Economics Foundation (2009).

94 Smith (2000: 208).

95 Sandel (2012: 7, 10–11, 113).

96 Schoenberger (2014: xxx).

Want to know more about this chapter? Visit the companion website at **www.guilford.com/dickenGS7** for free access to author videos, suggested reading and practice questions to further enhance your study.

PART FOUR

THE PICTURE IN DIFFERENT SECTORS

Twelve

'MAKING HOLES IN THE GROUND': THE EXTRACTIVE INDUSTRIES

BEGINNING AT THE BEGINNING

In a very real sense, the extractive industries represent the 'beginning of the beginning': the initial stage in the basic production circuit and in the web of GPNs that make up the global economy:[1]

> Minerals … [excluding oil] … account for a small share of world production and trade. Nonetheless, their supply is essential for the sustainable development of a modern economy. They are basic, essential and strategic raw materials … No modern economy can function without adequate, affordable and secure access to raw materials.[2]

The basis of the extractive industries is the notion of the *natural resource*: materials created and stored in nature through complex biophysical processes over vast periods of time. However, natural resources are not, in fact, 'naturally' resources. An element or material occurring in nature is only a 'resource' if it is defined as such by potential users. In other words, it is both a *socio-cultural* and a *political* construction. It is given meaning by its socio-cultural context and given differential priorities through political choices.[3] Basically, there must be an effective demand, an appropriate technology, and some means of ensuring 'property rights' over its use: 'If any of these conditions ceases to hold, resources could "unbecome".'[4] The resources that form the basis of the extractive industries (energy materials like oil, as well as ferrous and non-ferrous minerals like iron ore and copper) are, effectively, *non-renewable*. They are fixed in overall quantity, at least under known technological conditions. The more we use today, the less will be available for tomorrow.

   Quite apart from their finiteness, extractive resources are *locationally specific*. They are where they are. They have to be exploited, at least initially, where they occur, although later stages of refining might well be located elsewhere. In either case, their use involves vast investment and expenditure, not only on exploration, extraction and processing, but also on transportation infrastructures:

> The most significant differences about the extractive production network relate, in one way or another, to the 'landed' nature of assets … on the one hand, the nature-based character of extractive enterprises and the influence that the *materiality* of [the resource] exerts on the organization of production; and on the other … the *territoriality* of [the resource] in the sense of its embeddedness in the territorial structures of the nation-state … Resources are closely bound to notions of sovereign territoriality and national identity.[5]

This triadic combination of finite quantities, fixed locations and territorial embeddedness creates the specific shape and developmental path of the extractive industries.[6] It helps to explain why the extractive industries are so sensitive economically, politically, environmentally and even culturally; why they are the focus of such intense conflict and bargaining between firms, between states and between firms and states. To a greater extent than most other industries, the extractive industries are made up of a strong mix of private firms (TNCs) and state-owned enterprises (SOEs). They are also dominated by giant firms: a significant number of the 50 largest companies in the *Financial Times Global 500* are oil or mining companies. They are overwhelmingly *producer-driven* industries.

These industries, then, are at the heart of many of the most pressing and most controversial debates in the global economy. As we saw in Chapter 2, the roller-coaster trajectory of production and trade in the past 50 years has often been closely related to sharp fluctuations in the supply – and, therefore, the price – of oil and other natural resources. 'The race for resources' has been a central component of the development of a global economy for centuries.[7] It still is, as the insatiable growth of China's demand shows so very clearly.[8] The extractive industries are also at the centre of the development dilemma – the so-called 'resource curse' (see Chapter 10) – facing many resource-rich, but deeply impoverished, countries, especially in Africa.

PRODUCTION CIRCUITS IN THE EXTRACTIVE INDUSTRIES

As Figure 12.1 shows, the extractive industries fall into three broad categories based upon the kind of minerals involved. In this chapter we will focus primarily on two of these industries: oil and copper (one of the most important of the metallic metals industries, accounting for a little under one-fifth, by value, of world metallic mineral production).[9] Both oil and copper are employed in an enormous variety of end uses. In the case of oil, this includes both final consumer demand for transportation and heating fuel as well as providing the feedstock for chemicals and related industries. Copper, on the other hand, like most of the base and ferrous metals, is overwhelmingly a producer commodity:

> Copper is one of the oldest metals ever used … Because of its properties, singularly or in combination, of high ductility, malleability, and thermal and electrical conductivity, and its resistance to corrosion, copper has become a major industrial metal … Electrical uses of copper, including power transmission and generation, building wiring, telecommunication, and electrical and electronic products, account for about three quarters of total copper use.[10]

Figure 12.2 outlines the basic production circuit for extractive industries. At the most general level, it is a relatively straightforward sequence of stages, from exploration

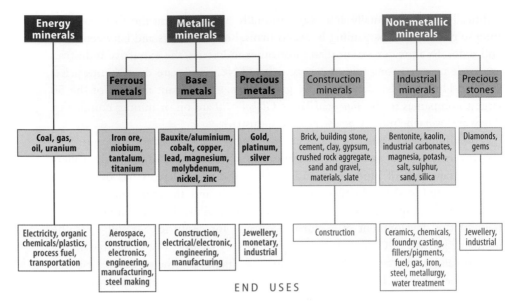

Figure 12.1   **Classification of extractive industries**

Source: based on UNCTAD, 2007: Box III.1.1

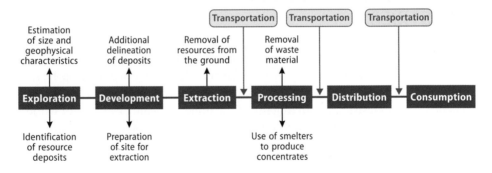

Figure 12.2   **The basic extractive industry production circuit**

Source: based, in part, on Turner et al., 1994: Box 16.4

through to final consumption, although, in fact, it is a highly complex and contested process. Something of that complexity is shown in Figure 12.3, which goes beyond the basic production circuit to depict the production of oil as a

> global production network of inter-firm and firm–state relations that link nationalized oil companies, resource-holding states and publicly traded, transnational firms. It reveals a number of lateral/horizontal relations not captured by the linear commodity chain.[11]

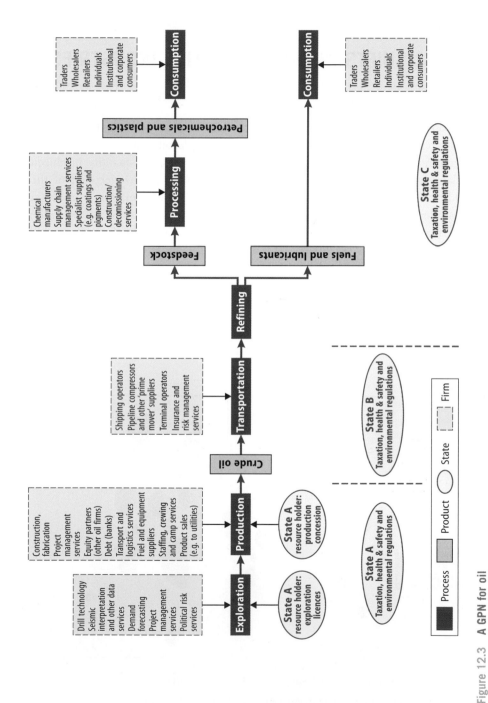

Figure 12.3 A GPN for oil

Source: based on Bridge, 2008b: Figure 3

Overall, the production circuits in the extractive industries are highly capital and technology intensive, involving primarily large firms (or consortia of firms), both private and state owned.

GLOBAL SHIFTS IN THE EXTRACTIVE INDUSTRIES

Oil

Between 1975 and 2012, world oil *production* grew by 54 per cent, from 56 billion barrels to 86 billion barrels. Production of crude oil is quite widely spread geographically, as Figure 12.4 shows. But, in many cases, the quantity produced is relatively small. In 2012, twelve countries accounted for 67 per cent of the world total, two of which – Saudi Arabia and the Russian Federation – produced more than one-quarter of the total. However, major changes have occurred in the global map of oil production since 1975 (immediately after the 'first oil shock'). Important new producers emerged. So, although the Middle East still accounted for 33 per cent of world oil production in 2012, the world production map is much more complex than it was 30 years ago. And it is changing even more as oil extracted from shale is becoming a major feature of the industry, particularly in the USA and the Russian Federation, but also elsewhere as the controversial 'fracking' industry expands its reach.

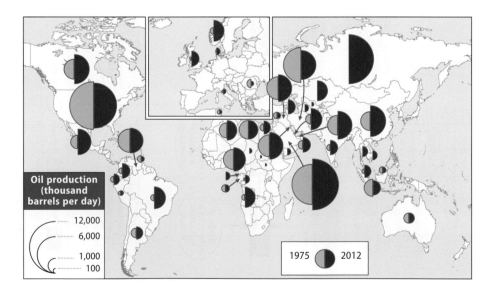

Figure 12.4   **The changing geography of global oil production**

Source: based on data in *BP Statistical Review of World Energy 2013*

The pattern of world *trade* in oil is shown in Figure 12.5. Almost half of total oil imports go to Europe and the USA, with a further one-quarter going to Japan and China. In particular, China's significance as an oil importer has increased at enormous speed as its economy has grown at the dramatic rates discussed in Chapter 2. In the early 1990s, China was the biggest exporter of oil in Asia; today it is the fastest-growing importer of oil in the world. Much of that shift has involved China's sourcing of oil from Africa, as we will see in later sections. For many of the world's major oil exporters, oil is by far the most important commodity, constituting, in some cases, virtually the entire basis of the country's export sector.

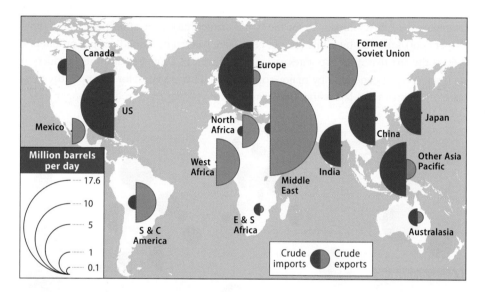

Figure 12.5   **Patterns of world trade in oil**

Source: based on data in *BP Statistical Review of World Energy 2013*

However, the global map of oil trade seems likely to change dramatically in the next few years if the predictions of the International Energy Agency are borne out. In particular:

> By around 2020, the United States is projected to become the largest oil producer (overtaking Saudi Arabia until the mid-2020s) ... the result is a continued fall in US oil imports, to the extent that North America becomes a net oil exporter by 2030. This accelerates the switch in direction of international oil trade towards Asia ... The United States, which currently imports around 20% of its total energy needs, becomes all but self-sufficient in net terms – a dramatic reversal of the trend seen in most other energy-importing countries.[12]

Copper

World copper production has increased even more rapidly than that of oil during the past two decades: by 84 per cent between 1988 and 2011 (from 8.8 million tonnes to 16.2 million tonnes). Such growth reflects the particular qualities of copper in a wide range of end uses and, again, the growth of China and its seemingly insatiable hunger for raw materials. Figure 12.6 maps the world distribution of both mine production and refined copper. Five countries produce 61 per cent of mined copper. Chile is by far the biggest producer, with 33 per cent of the world total; its share of world production doubled between 1988 and 2011. Copper production in Africa, notably in Zambia and the Democratic Republic of Congo, as well as in China, has also grown significantly. Indeed, China was the world's second-largest producer of mined copper in 2011 having overtaken the USA. China is by far the world's largest producer of refined copper (with 27 per cent), followed by Chile (16 per cent). The pattern of refined copper production reflects the fact that it incorporates about 20 per cent of copper scrap in its production, such scrap being generated by major copper users. This explains, for example, the presence of countries like Japan and Germany as major producers of refined copper only.

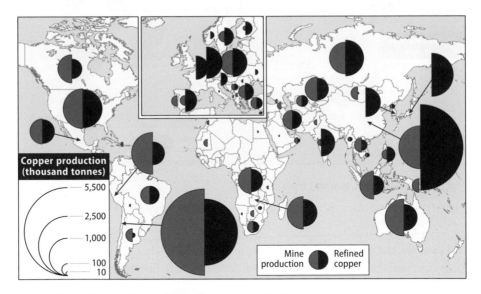

Figure 12.6   **The geography of world copper production**

Source: based on data in Brown et al., 2013: pp. 19, 21

VOLATILE DEMAND

Welcome to the new world of runaway energy demand
(*Financial Times*, 14 November 2007)
Global oil demand to collapse
(*Financial Times*, 10 December 2008)

These two headlines, separated by almost exactly one year, illustrate the extreme volatility of the market for the extractive industries. Periodic boom and bust are the norm. Periods of strong economic growth intensify the demand for commodities; periods of economic decline produce the opposite effect so that demand may collapse, at least until the next upturn. This means that the extractive industries are much more sensitive to the general state of the economy than most other sectors, although the speed of adjustment to ups and downs in the cycle may not be immediate and this can cause problems of over- and under-capacity.

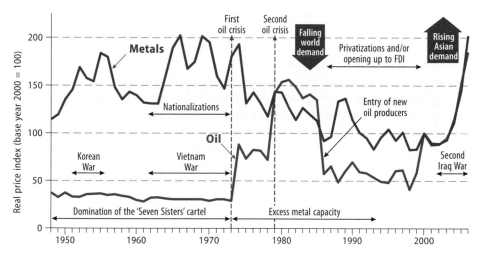

Figure 12.7 **Fluctuations in the prices of oil and metallic minerals (base year 2000 = 100)**

Source: based on UNCTAD, 2007: Figure III.1

Such massive swings in demand are, of course, reflected in equally massive fluctuations in prices. Figure 12.7 shows how the prices of oil and metallic minerals fluctuated in the six decades since the 1940s in response to changing market conditions:

> 1974 marked the end of the 30-year 'golden period' of strong world economic growth, and high demand for minerals that began after the Second World War ... From the first oil crisis in 1973–1974 until the early 1980s, oil prices began to climb steeply ... Metal prices, on the other hand, began a long-term declining trend ... Crude oil prices also began to decline in real terms in 1985 ... The depressed mineral prices of the 1980s and 1990s had important consequences: instead of being regarded as strategically important to economic development, oil and metals were increasingly treated as simple commodities ...

> It is only in recent years that the gradual decline in mineral prices has been reversed.[13]

In fact, this reversal, especially in the case of minerals, was unexpectedly sudden. The first half of the 2000s, especially after 2004, saw what were, in effect, 'gold rush' conditions. This acceleration in demand reflected, in general terms, the rapid overall growth of the global economy but it was especially driven by the vast increase in demand for resources from some developing countries, most notably China. Depiction of China as 'a ravenous dragon' became common:[14]

> There is no exaggerating China's hunger for commodities. The country accounts for about a fifth of the world's population, yet it ... has swallowed over four-fifths of the increase in the world's copper supply since 2000.[15]

In light of these new circumstances, the predictions in 2007 were that prices would remain high, and even accelerate:

> The economic ascendancy of China, India and other developing countries, along with the resource-intensive stages of their current development phase could well result in a long-running acceleration of commodity demand growth. *This can be seen as a new stage in international commodity markets, with prices remaining at unprecedentedly high levels ... there are no indications of an impending world recession.*[16]

Of course, this reflects China's increasingly significant role as an export producer of a whole range of metal-intensive (and energy-intensive) manufactured goods.

So much for prediction. One year later, the financial conflagration had resulted in a collapse of commodity prices. The price of oil fell from $150 per barrel in July 2008 to below $40 a few months later. The price of copper fell from more than $8000 per tonne in June 2008 to less than $3000 per tonne in June 2009. The bonanza was, apparently, over. Of course, if history is the guide, the process will occur again at some time in the future, although we cannot know when, and precisely how, this will happen. There has indeed been some recovery in prices: in mid-2013, oil was around $100 per barrel and copper around $7000 per tonne. It is likely, however, that virtually all the growth in the demand for oil and many other commodities over the next 20 years will come from developing countries. Of course, these shifts in demand reflected in price fluctuations are not only the result of changes in the market for oil or metals. Supply-side changes, especially those generated by changes in state policies and corporate strategies, play a highly significant role, as we will see in subsequent sections.

TECHNOLOGIES OF EXPLORING, EXTRACTING, REFINING, DISTRIBUTING

The core of the extractive industries, as Figure 12.2 shows, is the sequence of stages from exploration, through development, extraction, processing, distribution, to consumption. Each of these poses immense technological challenges. The reason lies in the basic characteristics of the resource-based industries alluded to earlier: their finiteness and their locational specificity. In general, highly expensive, sophisticated technologies have to be employed at all stages of the production circuit:

> Building a large base-metals mine can cost over a billion dollars. The magnitude of investments in the oil and gas industry is even greater. Constructing a pipeline, developing an oil deposit or revitalizing an ailing, underinvested mineral industry can run into many billions of dollars.[17]

As a consequence, capital intensity is extremely high while labour intensity is low. These industries employ comparatively few workers relative to their size. For example, the biggest non-state oil company in the world, ExxonMobil, employs around 80,000 workers. The biggest metal mining company, BHP Billiton, employs 42,000. In comparison, the retailer Wal-Mart employs 2,100,000 workers while the automobile company Toyota employs more than 300,000. The difference is especially dramatic if we compare sales per worker: ExxonMobil $4.83 million; BHP Billiton $1.43 million; Wal-Mart $180,000; Toyota $730,000.

Firms in the extractive industries face three closely related technological challenges: finding new sources of supply, extracting the highest yield from these sources, and getting them to the market. Of course, such challenges face firms in all industries. But the extractive industries are unique in that they are faced with 'managing a depleting asset'.[18] Unlike the agro-food industry, for example (see Chapter 13), a new crop cannot be grown next year. Once an oil well dries up or a copper mine becomes exhausted it cannot be regenerated, although in some cases technological innovation enables some further extraction to occur.

New sources of supply must continuously be sought as existing sources become exhausted and/or too expensive to exploit at prevailing market prices. This is not unlike searching for needles in haystacks. Immensely sophisticated techniques of geochemical, geophysical and satellite remote sensing techniques are involved:

> The exploration period may take up to 10 years, and in many cases such investments turn out to be unsuccessful ... Even if the exploration is successful and a new mine is developed and brought into production, the investor still faces various technical risks, market risks (related to demand and price forecasts), political risks (e.g. changes in mining laws, nationalizations), and social and environmental risks.[19]

In addition, the time (and investment) needed to develop a new resource – its gestation period – can be very long indeed. The situation is not unlike that in the pharmaceuticals industry, where vast investments are made over many years in the hope that a drug breakthrough will occur. In fact, of course, the majority fail, and that is also true of the extractive industries:

> [I]n the actual process of extraction, the raw materials tend to get more and more difficult to harvest as time goes on; for example, surface deposits of minerals are used up and people have to dig deeper, the most pure ores are depleted and users must shift to more amalgamated sources, etc. This requires the application of bigger, more powerful equipment, new techniques, etc.[20]

A major problem, therefore, is that most of the easily accessible sources have already been exploited. New resources almost invariably tend to be found in less accessible locations and also often in circumstances making their extraction extremely difficult and, therefore, costly. The deeper the resource below the surface, the greater the problems involved. The lower the degree of purity, the greater the cost involved in extraction and processing to the point where it becomes uneconomic. In the case of oil, for example,

> variations in the quality of crude include its density (lighter grades … are more highly valued than heavier grades because they contain a higher gasoline and kerosene fraction), the lack of sulphur compounds (a 'sweet' oil is more highly valued than a 'sour' oil because sulphur compounds require additional 'cleaning' for transportation and refining), the pouring point (related to the wax or bitumen content) and the presence of salt or metal (vanadium, nickel, iron).[21]

There is, inevitably, a close connection between explorative activity and market (i.e. price) conditions. Periods of high prices for oil and minerals stimulate a wave of exploration and the bringing into use of what are, in less favourable market conditions, marginal supplies. Conversely, when prices fall – especially when they fall very steeply and rapidly, as happened in 2008 – investors pull back from such risky ventures. A notable example is the Canadian oil sands project in Alberta:

> Until recently, Canada's oil sands were the venue for one of the most spectacular races for profit of modern times. The remote, boggy landscape contains between 1.7tn and 2.5tn barrels of oil, of which an estimated 173bn can be extracted using expensive, hi-tech filtering technology. Canada's reserves are second only to Saudi Arabia's, and a year ago 60 projects were being constructed … But since oil prices began a downward tumble, energy companies … have shelved more than US$90bn worth of oil sands investment.[22]

Boom and bust is the way the extractive world works – and will no doubt continue to do so in the future. Today, much of the attention in many parts of the world is on extracting oil and gas from shale deposits. Unlike the Canadian oil sands, shale oil and gas are very deeply buried and have to be extracted using a method known as 'fracking' or hydraulic fracturing. This technique combines deep vertical drilling with horizontal drilling. A combination of water, chemicals and sand is injected at immensely high pressure to crack the shale strata and then to extract the oil or gas. There are vast shale deposits in many parts of the world that have the potential to yield huge quantities of oil and, especially, gas. It is this technique that is revolutionizing the US energy industry and may well do the same globally if US Department of Energy estimates are accurate:

> 'technically recoverable' shale oil resources of 345bn barrels in 42 countries [were identified, equivalent to] ... 10 per cent of global crude supplies ... [the] assessment indicated that Russia had the largest shale oil resource with 75bn barrels. Russia and the US [with 58bn barrels] were followed by China at 32bn. The report estimated UK shale oil resources at 700m barrels. The US report looked at technically recoverable resources without regard to profitability ... 'the extent to which technically recoverable shale resources will prove to be economically recoverable is not yet clear'.[23]

This latter caveat is the crucial one.

Both the exploration and extraction/processing of oil and mineral resources involve very high sunk costs.[24] The same is also true of the distribution stage. Again, all industries face problems in getting their products to market. But the particular characteristics of the extractive industries – especially their bulk and remoteness from markets – generate the need for a massive scale of transportation infrastructure that is virtually unique. The trade-off between increasing the scale of production and being able to transport the outputs is a central problem in these industries. Massive investments in pipelines, supertankers, port facilities, and the like are a prerequisite. Not only are these costly but they, too, have a long gestation period. They represent a very high sunk cost indeed, not least because many of these facilities are highly specialized and not easily transferred to alternative uses.

The effects of such transience are graphically reflected in those places where the 'resource frontier' has moved on, leaving behind the relics of technology:

> Few sights are as impressive as the massive port works, open-pit mines, and 500-mile railways developed to tap the natural resources of frontier regions, or so bittersweet as the relic landscapes left behind in the wake of resource booms. Abandoned mines, idle processing facilities, vacant warehouses, empty ports, disused railroads, boarded-up buildings, and under-employed residents in once vibrant regions speak not only to the capricious nature of resource economies but also to the salience of 'rigidities' in investments in extractive industries.[25]

The environmental costs of resource exploitation are immense and long lasting.

THE CENTRALITY OF STATE INVOLVEMENT IN THE EXTRACTIVE INDUSTRIES

A central argument of this book is that the state plays a major role in *all* GPNs. However, nowhere is the degree of state involvement as deep or as pervasive as in the extractive industries. In these industries, the state is absolutely central. The reason, of course, lies in the unique *territorial embeddedness* of resources. Access to such resources is controlled, ultimately, by the national state in which they are located.

As Figure 12.3 shows, the state operates within an extractive GPN in two main ways:

- as a *regulator* (of access, taxation, health, safety and environmental issues);
- as an *operator* (an actual producer).

Where such dual roles exist, states have potentially enormous power over how such resources are exploited. How effective that power is, and how it is exercised, of course, depend very much on the nature of the state in question, notably its strength (both domestically and internationally) and its political orientation. This, of course, brings the state into sharp confrontation with private companies, especially TNCs, as well as with other states. The history of the resource extractive industries, therefore, is one of continuously shifting power struggles between firms and states, states and states, and firms and firms. Again, although this is true of virtually all industries, it is especially evident in the extractive industries. However, its precise form varies between different extractive industries, especially between oil on the one hand and metal mining industries on the other.

Nationalizing the assets

The central problem facing all resource-rich states is how to exploit their resources to achieve the maximum gain when, as we have seen, the costs of finding, developing, extracting, processing and distributing the product can be astronomically high. Given that such a large proportion of the world's extractive resources are located in poorer countries, this poses immense problems. To what extent can a state develop its own indigenous resources using domestic capital and know-how? How far must it depend on outside investment by foreign TNCs which will, inevitably, result in some loss of control? Over time, these problems have been approached in different ways.

In most cases, the initial development of a country's resource industry has depended on outside investment. Indeed,

> in the early twentieth century, FDI went mostly into these industries, reflecting the international expansion of firms that originated from the colonial powers. The objective of TNCs in the extractive industries was to

gain direct control over the mineral resources required as inputs for their growing manufacturing and infrastructure-related industries. During the Great Depression (1929–1933), the international expansion of oil companies continued unabated despite the crisis in other overseas investments.[26]

However, by the 1960s, this situation had changed radically:

> As former colonies gained independence after the Second World War and with the creation of the Organization of the Petroleum Exporting Countries (OPEC), many governments chose to nationalize their extractive industries, resulting in a declining involvement of the TNCs that hitherto had been dominant.[27]

In fact, nationalization in the extractive industries – the complete transfer of ownership from a private firm to the state – has a long history. This is especially true in the case in the oil industry:[28]

> Outright nationalization of oil and gas … first took place in the context of the Russian Revolution in 1917. This was followed by nationalizations in Bolivia (1937, 1969), Mexico (1938), Venezuela (1943), Iran (1951), and Argentina, Burma, Egypt, Indonesia and Peru in the 1960s … In the 1970s, nationalizations occurred in Algeria, Iraq, Kuwait, Libya and Nigeria and there was a gradual increase in Saudi ownership of Aramco … [Such nationalizations] have changed the global landscape of petroleum extraction and contributed to the emergence and subsequent strengthening of State-owned firms.[29]

A clear indication of such a change in the global landscape is provided by the prominent position of state-owned firms among the world's largest oil companies (see Table 12.1, p. 414). Indeed, national oil companies (NOCs) control the vast majority of the world's oil reserves.

Controlling prices

The nationalization of oil production makes possible (though far from inevitable) collaboration between oil producing countries to control production levels and, therefore, prices. The clearest example is OPEC, the Organization of the Petroleum Exporting Countries. OPEC was set up in 1960 as a reaction to the cut in the oil price made unilaterally by Standard Oil. Its aim was

> to defend the price of oil – more precisely, to restore it to its [1960] level. From here on, the member countries could insist that the companies consult them on the pricing matters that so centrally affected their national revenues.[30]

The original OPEC membership consisted of five oil producing countries: Iran, Iraq, Kuwait, Saudi Arabia and Venezuela. A further seven countries subsequently joined: Qatar (1961), Libya (1962), United Arab Emirates (1967), Algeria (1969), Nigeria (1971), Ecuador (1973; left and rejoined 2007), Angola (2007).

OPEC's influence was limited until the outbreak of the 1973 Arab–Israeli War when

> it was the oil weapon, wielded in the form of an embargo – production cutbacks and restrictions on exports – that ... altered irrevocably the world as it had grown up in the postwar period ... The embargo signalled a new era for world oil ... The international order had been turned upside down. OPEC's members were courted, flattered, railed against, and denounced. There was good reason. Oil was at the heart of world commerce, and those who seemed to control oil prices were regarded as the new masters of the global economy.[31]

Today, although OPEC's influence is lessening in the light of new oil discoveries elsewhere – notably shale oil – it remains highly significant and reminds us of the highly politicized nature of the oil industry. OPEC member countries produce around 40 per cent of the world's crude oil; their exports account for around 60 per cent of world oil exports.

A (partial) return to privatization

Nationalization has also been a strong trend in the metal mining industries. For example, the number of expropriations of foreign mining enterprises increased from 32 between 1960 and 1969 to 48 between 1970 and 1976.[32] As in the oil industry, this resulted in a squeeze on the private companies:

> For example, the share of the seven largest TNCs in copper mining outside the centrally planned economies fell from 60% in 1960 to 23% in 1981 as a result of nationalizations ... By the early 1980s, the participation of TNCs in many developing countries had become limited to minority holdings and non-equity agreements with State-owned enterprises. However, many of the nationalizations undertaken in Africa and Latin America in the metal mining industry turned out to be failures.[33]

As a result of such failures, the emphasis has shifted towards a greater liberalization of the ownership/exploitation laws in many mining countries. Between 1985 and the early 2000s, more than 90 states introduced new laws, or relaxed existing laws, in order to attract foreign investment.[34] Widespread privatization, often as part of a broader neo-liberalization project, became the norm: 'By the early 2000s, the privatization process in the [metal mining] industry worldwide, apart from China, had been more or less completed.'[35]

Power games: states and firms; states and states

As we saw in Chapter 7, the power relationships between states and firms are highly dynamic and contingent. In some cases, the balance of power lies one way, in other cases it lies the other way. That balance tends to shift over time. In Chapter 7, we met the term *obsolescing bargain* which refers to the situation in which once private capital is 'sunk' in a fixed form the advantage tends to move away from the investor to the state that controls access to the resource. Although this situation may not generally prevail in many sectors, it certainly applies in the extractive sector. A detailed study of the development of the oil industry in Kazakhstan[36] provides evidence of how a state can learn how to renegotiate contracts with a foreign investor; in other words, it shows how the balance of power can shift over time.

Kazakhstan achieved independence in 1991. It was rich in oil but lacked the technology to develop its resource. It needed foreign investors. Like many other former Soviet Republics and allies, Kazakhstan rushed into the wholesale privatization of its assets, primarily its resource extraction activities. By 2002, around half of the FDI entering Kazakhstan was concentrated in the petroleum industry. One-quarter of the country's oil production originates from the Tengiz oilfield in the west. It is a rich field, but difficult to exploit:

> it is the deepest high pressure deposit in the world, with oil that emerges from the ground scalding hot, at a very high pressure, and laden with poisonous hydrogen sulfide, which must be removed from the oil.[37]

Such a challenging field required a very sophisticated technology. The US company Chevron had started negotiations with the Soviet government in 1990. After independence, the negotiations shifted to Kazakhstan, a state with absolutely no experience in such complex political bargaining. In contrast, Chevron, one of the world's biggest and oldest oil companies, was a very old hand at this game. Ten years after the contract was signed, Kazakhstan attempted to renegotiate the terms, based on the kinds of circumstances implied in the obsolescing bargain concept:

> the agreement had been made, the investments were sunk, the oil was beginning to turn a profit for the corporation, and the state started to feel that the distribution of benefits were too much in favor of the MNC. The country called for renegotiations.[38]

Kazakhstan had already negotiated some improvements over a period of time but without a firm contractual basis. It was this that was now being sought:

In such an event, the renegotiations in question were not a simple affair and likely did not progress as Kazakhstan had predicted. The renegotiations involved the financing arrangements for major gas processing and recycling projects designed to reduce pollution as well as for projects to increase production at the TengizChevroil venture. Looking back ... it may seem surprising that Chevron would shut down its operations in protest of the renegotiations. Yet initially it did ... the result of Chevron's following through on its threat, and being taken by surprise that Kazakhstan indeed demanded renegotiations. After recalculating its costs, expected value, and strategic play, and given the strategy revealed by the State's move, Chevron reversed its decision after just two months. TengizChevroil's operations were resumed in January of 2003, with Chevron agreeing to some revisions in the contractual terms.[39]

On the basis of this learning experience, Kazakhstan subsequently managed to introduce a series of regulatory measures for its oil industry as a whole: renegotiations with other companies; more stringent rules for foreign investors; a reversal of over-generous VAT exemptions; power to cancel a contract that did not meet its economic expectations; introduction of a new oil export duty; better environmental provisions, including the banning of all gas flaring. Eventually, in 2002, the state set up its own NOC to ensure a more active role in its extractive sector.

This example is one of state–firm rivalry. But given the strategic importance of extractive resources for all states, these industries are also characterized by a high degree of *state–state rivalry*. This is especially true of the major users of resources: the established industrialized countries and the newer, fast-growing countries of Asia. For those countries possessing a substantial resource base of their own, like the USA, for example, a major aim is to sustain as much of that resource as possible for strategic reasons while importing resources to meet their needs. In this latter case, there is a strong incentive to attempt to control access to resources located overseas through either state-owned or private firm investment. In other words, it is in the resource extractive industries that direct state–state competition is most evident.

Currently, the most obvious example concerns the involvement of both the USA and China in the 'scramble' for oil and other minerals in Africa, through direct or indirect government participation:

> The US and China are competing to secure access for the oil riches of Africa ... Both the American and Chinese governments were important in paving the way for American and Chinese oil interests in expanding in Africa. The US government used diplomatic instruments ... economic incentives ... and military aid (the largest portion of US military aid to Africa was aimed at Nigeria and Angola). While the US government

assisted private US firms in obtaining oil concessions for oil exploration and production, the Chinese government focused instead on securing oil supplies through bilateral agreements. As the most notable example, Sinopec – a Chinese state-owned oil company – acquired oil concessions in [Angola] … on the back of a US$2 billion oil-backed credit from China's Eximbank in 2004 to rebuild the country's railways, government buildings, schools, hospitals, and roads … The Angola example demonstrates how China has adopted an aid-for-oil strategy.[40]

Interstate rivalry for resources is also apparent in international trade disputes. Again, it is not surprising that the most recent cases involve China. In mid-2009, the USA and EU initiated action in the WTO against China for its alleged restrictions on exports of key materials, such as silicon, coke and zinc:

China imposes restrictions, including minimum export prices and tariffs of up to 70% on a range of raw materials of which it is a major producer. The EU claims these not only break general WTO rules on world trade, but specific promises China made when it joined the organization in 2001, becoming a fully fledged player in global markets.[41]

CORPORATE STRATEGIES IN THE EXTRACTIVE INDUSTRIES

Consolidation and concentration

The oil industry

The top 10 companies shown in Table 12.1 account for around 60 per cent of world oil production. No fewer than 3 of the top 5, and 15 of the world's 25 largest oil producers, are fully or majority state owned, the result of the widespread nationalizations discussed in the previous section. This is in stark contrast to the situation that prevailed before the early 1970s:

Until the 1970s, a few major TNCs from the US and Europe dominated the international oil industry. In 1972, 8 of the top 10 oil producers were privately owned … including the so-called Seven Sisters … These were fully integrated oil companies, active in the extraction and transportation of oil as well as in the production and marketing of petroleum products.[42]

In order to compete on what the private oil companies see as a very uneven playing field, there has been a great deal of consolidation through merger and acquisition, as well as a proliferation of collaborative ventures between private firms and also

Table 12.1   The world's largest oil and gas companies, 2012

Rank 2012	Rank 1995	Company	Home country	State ownership (%)	Total production (million barrels/day)
1	1	Saudi Aramco	Saudi Arabia	100	12.5
2	3	Gazprom	Russia		9.7
3	3	NIOC	Iran	100	6.4
4	5	ExxonMobil	USA		5.3
5	7	PetroChina	China	100	4.4
6	13	BP	UK		4.1
7	6	Royal Dutch/Shell	UK/Netherlands		3.9
8	4	Pemex	Mexico	100	3.6
9	16	Chevron	USA		3.5
10	9	KPC	Kuwait	100	3.2
11	23	ADNOC	UAE	100	2.9
12		Sonatrach	Algeria	100	2.7
13	33	Total	France		2.7
14	20	Petrobras	Brazil	100	2.6
15		Rosneft	Russia		2.6
16		MoO	Iraq	100	2.3
17		QP	Qatar	100	2.3
18	11	Lukoil	UAE		2.2
19		ENI	Italy		2.2
20		Statoil	Norway	100	2.1

Source: based on material in Helman, 2012; UNCTAD, 2007: Table IV.8

between private firms and state-owned companies. The most recent – and biggest – was the acquisition by the Russian company Rosneft of TNK-BP for $55 billion in 2013. This made Rosneft the largest listed oil and gas company in the world in terms of total production and proven reserves, ahead of ExxonMobil.[43] Nevertheless, the private oil companies 'are increasingly being squeezed by the growing power of the national companies and by dwindling reserves and production in accessible and mature basins outside OPEC countries. The super-majors have been struggling to replace their proven reserves and expand production.'[44] At the same time, the capital intensity of production, refining and transportation reinforces the position of the major companies and raises the already high barriers to entry.[45]

The metal mining industries

Historically, the metal mining industries have been highly fragmented, but this is changing rapidly as a smaller number of very large companies control an increasing share of world production:

Worldwide … there are more than 4,000 metal mining firms, mostly engaged in exploration and extraction … Most of the 149 'majors' are TNCs, the majority of which have production facilities covering mining, smelting as well as refining. These companies account for some 60% of the total value at the mining stage of all non-energy minerals produced … The degree of concentration in the metal mining industries increased significantly between 1995 and 2005.[46]

The top 10 metal mining companies shown in Table 12.2 produced around one-third of total world output in 2007. Whereas the oil industry is now dominated by national companies, the degree of state ownership in metal mining is significantly lower. Only one of the top 10 mining companies, the Chilean company Codelco, is fully state owned and only one other, the Brazilian company Vale, has significant state involvement. This is a consequence, as we saw in the previous section, of the widespread adoption of privatization policies by many national resource holders in recent years.

At the same time, there has been a wave of mergers and acquisitions in the metal mining industries, largely stimulated by the surge in commodity prices that occurred in the mid-2000s (see Figure 12.7). In 2006 alone, the value of mergers and acquisitions in these industries was $55 billion. Two of the biggest acquisitions in that year were of Inco (Canada) by the Brazilian company Vale, and of Falconbridge (Canada) by Xstrata, the Swiss mining company. The pace accelerated in 2007 and included Rio Tinto's acquisition of the alumina producer Alcan, and the attempted hostile acquisition of Rio Tinto by BHP Billiton. This latter case turned out to be highly

Table 12.2   **The world's largest metal mining companies**

Rank 2007	Rank 1995	Company	Home country	State ownership (%)	Percentage share of world production
1	6	Vale	Brazil	12	5.2
2	4	BHP Billiton Group	Australia		4.6
3	1	Anglo American plc	UK	–	4.3
4	2	Rio Tinto plc	UK	–	4.0
5	5	Codelco	Chile	100	3.4
6	11	Freeport McMoran	USA	–	3.3
7	7	Norislk Nickel	Russian Federation	–	2.7
8	8	Xstrata plc	Switzerland	–	2.4
9	14	Barrick Gold Corp.	Canada	–	2.3
10	22	Grupo Mexico	Mexico	–	1.6

Source: based on Ericsson, 2008: Table 1; UNCTAD, 2007: Table IV.4

contentious and was abandoned in 2008, largely because of the collapse in commodity prices. This situation was made especially complex because the Chinese state-owned company Chinalco attempted to double its equity stake in Rio Tinto in order to stop the BHP Billiton takeover. What would have been China's biggest overseas investment was acrimoniously prevented by Australian pressure. The disagreements were exacerbated by the proposal of BHP and Rio Tinto to form an iron ore joint venture. Again, we see the immensely political nature of the extractive industries. Talks also began in 2009 on a possible merger between Xstrata and Anglo American to create a rival to BHP Billiton and Rio Tinto. This venture was abandoned.

A far more revolutionary merger was concluded in 2013 between Xstrata and Glencore. This $90 billion merger brought together one of world's largest metal mining companies (Xstrata) and the leading commodities trading company and metal mining company (Glencore). The unique feature of this huge merger[47] is its creation of a fully vertically integrated company 'from the shovel to the shelf' whereby 'Glencore/Xstrata combined will cover all areas from exploration to marketing' with the intention of 'capturing each and every dollar along the supply chain'.

Whether or not this vertically integrated model will spread to other major companies in these industries is far from clear; if it were to do so it would dramatically reconfigure the mining industries. Whatever the ultimate outcome of this and other mergers, one thing is clear:

> The fragmented structure of mining is slowly disappearing … [T]he industry is getting more and more polarised, to the one side there are the large, established mining TNCs controlling a major share of global metal production and on the other side are the junior exploration companies without any production, only 'blue sky' hopes of future production. There is a lack of medium and small sized producers, which can grow organically and become major producers with time. These companies are important in that they concentrate on smaller deposits which often have good grades but which are discarded by the majors.[48]

Organizational and geographical restructuring

The geography of the extractive industries is, as we have seen, basically constrained by the distribution of the territorially embedded resources on which they are based, together with the need to transport outputs at each stage of the production circuit, particularly to the final market. In the case of the oil industry, it is also strongly influenced by the ownership of the firms involved. In general, most of the state-owned firms have a very restricted geography, mostly limited to their home territory. In contrast, the production spaces of the private companies are globally extensive. However, some state companies have begun to develop more extensive geographies. CNPC, for example, has operations in 14 foreign locations, Kuwait Petroleum Corporation and Petrobras in 8. Figure 12.8 maps the geographical distribution of some of the leading oil companies.

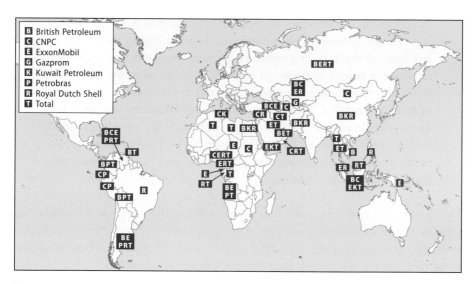

Figure 12.8 Geographies of oil production by some major companies

Source: based on data in UNCTAD, 2007: Table IV.10

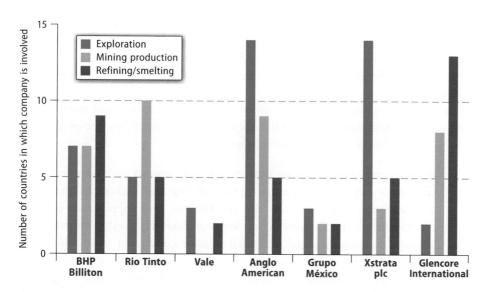

Figure 12.9 Distribution of exploration, production and refining/smelting projects by leading mining companies

Source: based on data in UNCTAD, 2007: Tables IV.5–IV.7

Figure 12.9 shows the distribution of some metal mining companies' operations. Their geographical extensiveness varies considerably both by size of firm and by type of operation (exploration, production, refining/smelting):

In *exploration*, the activities of certain TNCs, such as Anglo American and Xstrata (present in 14 countries each) were widely spread ... All but four of the top-25 producers ... were involved in exploration activities in at least one foreign country. In terms of *mining production*, Rio Tinto was the company with activities in the largest number (10) of host countries ... In *smelting and refining*, Glencore was the most internationalized top metal mining company, with a presence in 13 host countries, followed by BHP Billiton (9) ... Leading firms appear to be more internationalized in exploration and mining production than in smelting and refining.[49]

The major extractive companies vary enormously in their degree of *product diversification*. Some focus on one or two specific resources; others operate as highly diversified companies. They also differ in the extent of their *functional integration* along their production circuit. Four broad types can be identified:[50]

- *Vertically integrated companies*: active in all stages of exploration, development, extraction, refining and distribution. In the case of oil companies such vertical integration extends into retailing.
- *Independent producers*: specialize in upstream activities with very limited downstream activity.
- *Independent transporters, refiners and distributors*: specialize in the middle and/or the downstream segments of the production circuit.
- *Service companies*: provide 'drilling, interpretation and logistical services to producers'.

One of the most significant developments in the organization and operation of the extractive industries has been the huge increase in the influence of specialist services firms. In the case of oil, for example,

> drilling operations are often outsourced to a contract drilling company who may also provide the rig or drill-ship (e.g. Parker Drilling) and who undertakes to crew the rig. Drilling tool supply may be contracted to a specialist tool company (e.g. Baker Hughes), with data logging, data analysis and well maintenance contracted to another firm (e.g. Schlumberger). For many large projects, engineering, design and project management functions may also be outsourced (e.g. AMEC). These specialist upstream oil service companies operate on a global scale, with patterns of inter-firm relations developed in one geographical setting (e.g. Gulf of Mexico) often replicated in other regional contexts (e.g. offshore West Africa or the North Sea) ... This ... dramatic growth of the oil service market has led several commentators to suggest that the balance of power is shifting away from the majors as a number of oil service providers – Halliburton,

Schlumberger, Baker Hughes – assume an increasingly dominant role in the production chain.[51]

A similar trend towards the increasing importance of specialist service suppliers is also evident in the metal mining industries:

> The growing role of such suppliers is being driven by the reorganization of global mining production and technological rejuvenation of the industry, with continued improvements in exploration, mining and mineral processing. Suppliers are focused on specific niches in which they have a globally dominant position …

> Examples … include large international consulting firms that integrate engineering, project management, procurement and construction activities, such as Kvaerner (Norway), Hatch (Canada), and Bechtel Group (US); medium-sized specialized engineering consulting companies, such as Bateman (South Africa), SRK Consulting (South Africa), and AMC Consultants (Australia); and small- to medium-sized mining and geological software providers, such as Maptek (Australia).[52]

RESOURCES, RESERVES AND FUTURES

The dilemma facing all extractive industry producers, whether state owned or privately owned, is that 'as extractors of non-renewable resources … they *necessarily consume their resource base during production*'.[53] Hence, there is a continuous search for new sources of supply and for new techniques that enable the extraction of materials from less and less pure deposits. The big question, of course, is the extent to which the world is running out of viable resources. On this issue, views are highly polarized.

On the one hand, there is the 'Malthusian' view that resource exhaustion is inevitable; the only question is the timescale over which such exhaustion will occur. On the other hand, there is the view that new technologies of exploration leading to discoveries of new reserves (e.g. shale oil and gas), better means of exploitation leading to more efficient use of the resource (including recycling), and the development of appropriate substitutes will put off the dreadful day. Such polarization of views is reflected clearly in the arguments about 'peak oil': the assertion that oil production is about to peak and then move into inexorable decline.[54] The problem is that there are so many variables at work that it is extraordinarily difficult to assess the extent of future reserves of minerals. All the estimates of future are based on *assumptions*. A small change in one of the variables, whether on the demand or the supply side, can drastically change the predictions.

Figure 12.10 provides a framework (known as a McKelvey Box) for understanding the complex relationships between reserves and resources:

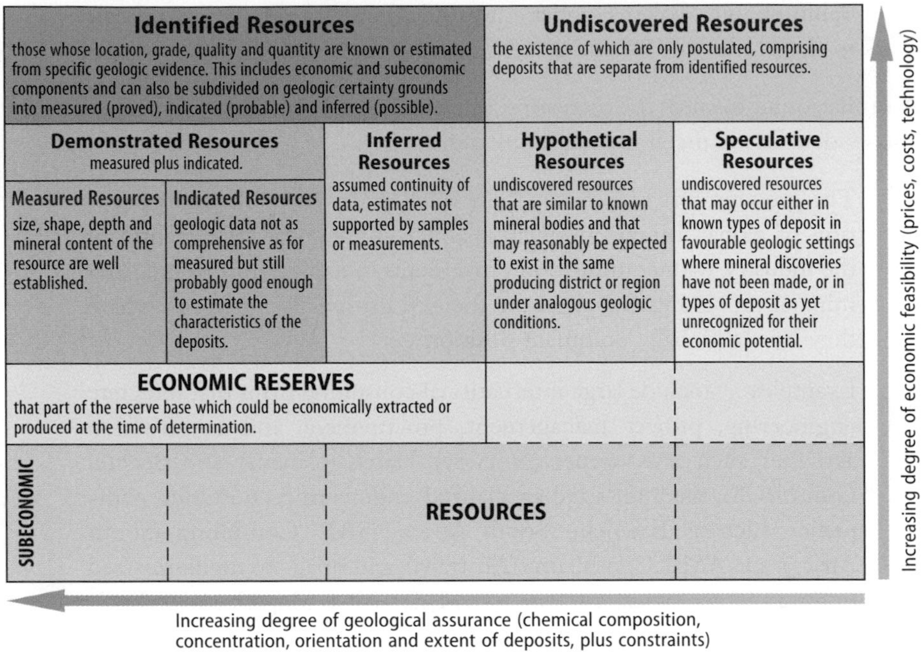

Identified Resources			Undiscovered Resources	
those whose location, grade, quality and quantity are known or estimated from specific geologic evidence. This includes economic and subeconomic components and can also be subdivided on geologic certainty grounds into measured (proved), indicated (probable) and inferred (possible).			the existence of which are only postulated, comprising deposits that are separate from identified resources.	
Demonstrated Resources measured plus indicated.		**Inferred Resources**	**Hypothetical Resources**	**Speculative Resources**
Measured Resources size, shape, depth and mineral content of the resource are well established.	**Indicated Resources** geologic data not as comprehensive as for measured but still probably good enough to estimate the characteristics of the deposits.	assumed continuity of data, estimates not supported by samples or measurements.	undiscovered resources that are similar to known mineral bodies and that may reasonably be expected to exist in the same producing district or region under analogous geologic conditions.	undiscovered resources that may occur either in known types of deposit in favourable geologic settings where mineral discoveries have not been made, or in types of deposit as yet unrecognized for their economic potential.
ECONOMIC RESERVES that part of the reserve base which could be economically extracted or produced at the time of determination.				
SUBECONOMIC			**RESOURCES**	

Increasing degree of economic feasibility (prices, costs, technology)

Increasing degree of geological assurance (chemical composition, concentration, orientation and extent of deposits, plus constraints)

Figure 12.10   McKelvey Box framework for resources and reserves

Source: adapted from Turner et al., 1994: Box 16.1

The reserves category includes all geologically identified deposits that can be economically recovered and is subdivided into proved, probable and possible reserves on the basis of geological certainty. All other deposits are labelled resources, either because they have not yet been discovered or because their exploitation is not currently feasible (technical and economic problems are inhibiting their extraction) ... Thus, resources are continuously reassessed in the light of new geologic knowledge, scientific and technical progress and changing economic and political conditions. Known resources are therefore classified on the basis of two types of information: geologic or physical/chemical characteristics (grade, quality, tonnage, thickness and depth of material in place); and financial profitability based on costs of extraction and marketing at a given point in time.[55]

This way of looking at resources and reserves is essentially techno-economic. But there are also environmental, ecological and geographical dimensions[56] that relate to the impact of continued resource exploitation on sustainable development and the effects of resource extraction on the places where it occurs and of transportation between places of extraction, production and consumption (see Chapter 9). In a sense overriding all of these considerations, however, is the fact that *the 'limits' to resources are, essentially, socially and, therefore, politically determined.* Choices have to be made, for example, as to how much money should be thrown at finding and extracting increasingly difficult resources or over what is the acceptable degree of environmental and ecological damage. The disastrous oil leakage in the BP operations in the Gulf of Mexico in 2010 demonstrated the potential scale of environmental damage posed by attempts to extract oil from very difficult locations. It surely will not be the last example. Indeed, the environmental implications of shale oil and gas exploitation are highly controversial, especially in Europe. Ultimately, then, the future shape of the extractive sectors 'will be determined not by natural limits but by social choice'.[57]

NOTES

1   Smith (2005) makes this argument in his plea for research on global commodity chains to take the extractive sector more seriously.
2   UNCTAD (2007: 83).
3   See Bridge (2009).
4   Hudson (2001: 301).
5   Bridge (2008b: 413).
6   See, for example, Bridge (2008b), Bunker and Ciccantell (2005), Yergin (1991).
7   Bunker and Ciccantell (2005).
8   Farooki and Kaplinsky (2012).
9   UNCTAD (2007: Table III.1).
10   USGS (2013: 1).
11   Bridge (2008b: 400).
12   International Energy Agency (2012: 1–2).
13   UNCTAD (2007: 88).
14   Farooki and Kaplinsky (2012), *The Economist* (15 March 2008).
15   *The Economist* (15 March 2008).
16   UNCTAD (2007: 90–1; emphasis added).
17   UNCTAD (2007: 92).
18   Bridge (2008b: 403).
19   UNCTAD (2007: 92).
20   Smith (2005: 152).
21   Bridge (2008b: 404).
22   *Guardian* (7 February 2009).
23   *Financial Times* (11 June 2013).
24   Barham and Coomes (2005).
25   Barham and Coomes (2005: 160).
26   UNCTAD (2007: 99).
27   UNCTAD (2007: 99).
28   Yergin (1991).
29   UNCTAD (2007: 115).
30   Yergin (1991: 523).

31   Yergin (1991: 588, 613, 633).
32   UNCTAD (2007: 108).
33   UNCTAD (2007: 107–8).
34   Bridge (2004: 407).
35   UNCTAD (2007: 108).
36   Hosman (2009). The following section draws from this analysis.
37   Hosman (2009: 19).
38   Hosman (2009: 19).
39   Hosman (2009: 20).
40   Frynas and Paulo (2006: 229, 238–9). See also Mohan (2013), Mohan and Lampert (2012), Power et al. (2012).
41   *Guardian* (24 June 2009).
42   UNCTAD (2007: 115).
43   *Financial Times* (3 April 2013).
44   International Energy Agency (2012: 10).
45   Bridge (2008b: 408).
46   UNCTAD (2007: 109).
47   *Financial Times* (8 February 2012).
48   Ericsson (2008: 114–15).
49   UNCTAD (2007: 111).
50   Bridge (2008b: 397–8). See also UNCTAD (2007: 113).
51   Bridge (2008b: 400, 408).
52   UNCTAD (2007: Box IV.3, p. 113).
53   Bridge (2004: 407).
54   See, for example, Clarke (2007), Monbiot (2012), Strahan (2007).
55   Turner et al. (1994: 222, 224).
56   Emel et al. (2002: 383–8).
57   Gavin Bridge, personal communication.

Want to know more about this chapter? Visit the companion website at **www.guilford.com/dickenGS7** for free access to author videos, suggested reading and practice questions to further enhance your study.

Thirteen

'WE ARE WHAT WE EAT': THE AGRO-FOOD INDUSTRIES

TRANSFORMATION OF THE FOOD ECONOMY: THE 'LOCAL' BECOMES 'GLOBAL'

The production of food addresses the most basic of all human needs. Like the activities discussed in the previous chapter, it is based upon the *extraction* of materials from the natural environment. In principle, food production is a *renewable* activity, although over-production, soil erosion and water shortages can, in effect, make agriculture impossible under certain conditions. Having changed relatively slowly over long periods of time,[1] the production, distribution and consumption of food have been transformed during the past four decades. They have become increasingly *industrialized*.[2] Basic subsistence is still the norm for millions of people, and starvation is always imminent, but for millions of others food has become as much a statement about lifestyle as about survival. According to the UN Food and Agricultural Organization, '842m people – one in eight – already go hungry. At the other end of the scale, many countries face ballooning health bills because of overweight populations.'[3] 'Abundance amidst scarcity' is a glaring paradox of today's world.[4]

In some respects, the modern agro-food industries may seem little different from other manufacturing industries. But, despite the industrialization of much food production, these are highly complex and geographically differentiated activities. The basic fact remains that food production is fundamentally different from other manufacturing industries in one particular way: it is literally *grounded* in biophysical processes:

> The role of biology in plant and animal growth is key … on a farm – unlike a factory – it is the biological time necessary for plant and animal growth that dictates the work schedule … In addition, the land-based character of farm production poses severe constraints to industrialization … because land is a fixed and limited resource, and because land markets are deeply colored by localized social conditions, farmers cannot easily or quickly adjust their investment in land.[5]

Food *production* remains an intensely *local* process, bound to specific climatic, soil – and often socio-cultural – conditions. At the same time, certain kinds of local production, notably high-value foods, have become increasingly *global* in terms of their *distribution* and *consumption*. For the affluent consumer, with access to the overflowing cornucopias of supermarket shelves, the seasons have been displaced by 'permanent global summertime' (PGST).[6] But such apparently idyllic circumstances for affluent consumers have a dark and contentious side.

Producing food for a global market requires huge capital investment and gives immense power to the transnational food producers and the big retailers. It creates serious problems – as well as opportunities – for food suppliers as they become increasingly locked into (or out of) transnational agro-food production networks. Global food production and distribution create huge environmental disturbances in terms of excessive exploitation of sensitive natural ecosystems, the application of chemical fertilizers and pest controlling agents, the increasing attempts to genetically modify seeds, plants and even animals and to 'patent life', and the transportation of high-value foods (HVFs) over vast geographical distances. These processes make agro-food an intensely sensitive industry, raising the fundamental question of 'who owns nature?'[7]

Food safety, including the ethics of genetic modification of seeds, plants and animals, has become a central issue. In the past few years, for example, there have been several serious food safety scares: BSE ('mad cow disease'), foot (hoof) and mouth disease, avian flu, swine flu and, most recently, the 'horse meat scandal' in Europe. These have a huge impact on agro-food trade and on the livelihoods of farmers, growers and distributors. They create massive fluctuations in consumer buying patterns, often out of ignorance. At the same time, there is widespread scepticism – and considerable fear – of genetic modification (GM). Both food safety and GM help to stimulate consumer resistance to the products of the global agro-food industries and to reinforce demands for a return to local sourcing of organically grown products. The agro-food industries have become a battleground with several 'fronts': between producers and producers, between producers and consumers, between producers and governments (not least because agro-food is one of the most heavily regulated industries), and between governments.

AGRO-FOOD PRODUCTION CIRCUITS

Production circuits in the agro-food industries are immensely varied. In the case of traditional commodities, like grains, the circuit is relatively simple (though more intricate than in the past). In the case of high-value foods, however, which are the primary focus of this chapter, the situation is far more complex. We provide several examples here.

Figure 13.1 shows the highly complex structure of the US chicken (broiler) production circuit, an industry which has become increasingly dominated by very large integrated producers. From a producer's perspective, a major advantage of integrated chicken production is that it facilitates the coordination of chicken raising processes which are subject to intrinsic biological lags. It is not possible to speed up the 'assembly line' as can be done in automobiles. It is, however, as much a 'just-in-time' system as that in automobile production. At the same time, integration gives closer control over product quality and food safety.

Figure 13.2 displays the fresh fruit and vegetable production circuit between Kenyan and Zimbabwean producers and European consumer markets. The key point to make about the fruit and vegetable production circuit is that it is driven by the large supermarket chains, rather than by the producers of the crops themselves.

Figures 13.1 and 13.2 both depict conventional agro-food production circuits. However, there are other, 'alternative', circuits which involve the production of organic food and/or the involvement of various kinds of non-economic actors, notably fair trade organizations. Such alternative food networks are driven by

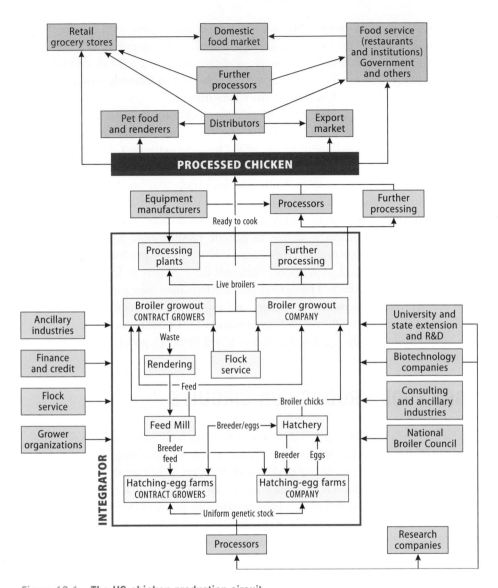

Figure 13.1   **The US chicken production circuit**

Source: based on Boyd and Watts, 1997: Figure 8.4

increasing concerns with food quality, food safety and fairer treatment of farmers/ growers in developing countries. These networks 'redistribute value through the network against the logic of bulk commodity production ... reconvene "trust" between food producers and consumers ... and ... rearticulate new forms of political association and market governance'.[8] Figure 13.3 provides one example of an alternative agro–food production circuit: fair trade coffee.[9]

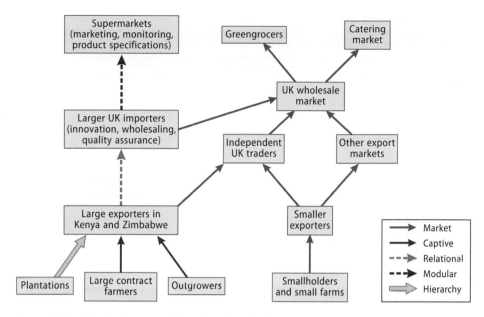

Figure 13.2 **The fresh vegetable production circuit**

Source: based on Dolan and Humphrey, 2002: Figure 3

The kind of food circuit shown in Figure 13.3 is just one of several alternatives to the tightly controlled, highly integrated, industrially based agro-food circuits that have become so dominant in recent years. Currently, there is also a growing (re-)emergence of explicitly *territorially based* food production networks.

Overall, the agro-food industries seem to be polarizing into:[10]

- *standardized–specialized* production processes responding to economic standards of efficiency and competitiveness;
- *localized–specialized* production processes trading on the basis of environmental, nutritional or health qualities.

GLOBAL SHIFTS IN THE HIGH-VALUE AGRO-FOOD INDUSTRIES

Globally, *chicken* production is dominated by three countries, the USA, China and Brazil, which, together, account for almost half the world total (Figure 13.4). Until very recently, the USA was also the world's leading exporter of chickens but it has been overtaken by Brazil.

Fresh fruit and vegetable production is also heavily concentrated at the global scale (Figure 13.5). China (38 per cent of the world total) is by far the world's biggest

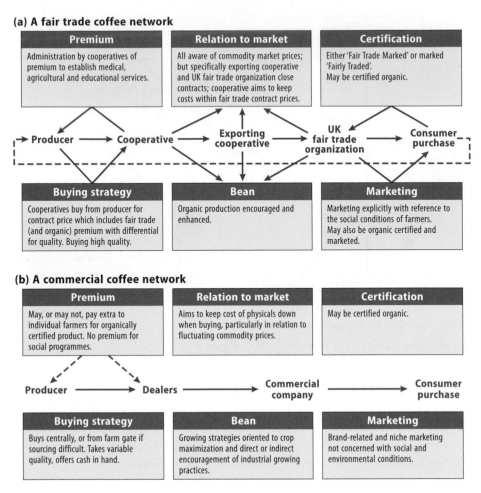

(a) A fair trade coffee network

Premium	Relation to market	Certification
Administration by cooperatives of premium to establish medical, agricultural and educational services.	All aware of commodity market prices; but specifically exporting cooperative and UK fair trade organization close contracts; cooperative aims to keep costs within fair trade contract prices.	Either 'Fair Trade Marked' or marked 'Fairly Traded'. May be certified organic.

Producer → Cooperative → Exporting cooperative → UK fair trade organization → Consumer purchase

Buying strategy	Bean	Marketing
Cooperatives buy from producer for contract price which includes fair trade (and organic) premium with differential for quality. Buying high quality.	Organic production encouraged and enhanced.	Marketing explicitly with reference to the social conditions of farmers. May also be organic certified and marketed.

(b) A commercial coffee network

Premium	Relation to market	Certification
May, or may not, pay extra to individual farmers for organically certified product. No premium for social programmes.	Aims to keep cost of physicals down when buying, particularly in relation to fluctuating commodity prices.	May be certified organic.

Producer → Dealers → Commercial company → Consumer purchase

Buying strategy	Bean	Marketing
Buys centrally, or from farm gate if sourcing difficult. Takes variable quality, offers cash in hand.	Growing strategies oriented to crop maximization and direct or indirect encouragement of industrial growing practices.	Brand-related and niche marketing not concerned with social and environmental conditions.

Figure 13.3 'Alternative' agro-food production circuits: fair trade and commercial coffee

Source: based on Whatmore and Thorne, 1997: Figure 11.2

producer. India is far behind at 9 per cent, followed by the USA (4.5 per cent), and Brazil (3.4 per cent). However, the composition and pattern of trade in fruits and vegetables has changed markedly during the past two decades.[11] Export growth rates of traditional products (e.g. oranges, canned pineapples, canned mushrooms, concentrated orange and apple juices) were very low. Non-traditional products grew most rapidly: 'Some commodities – mangoes, frozen potatoes, single-strength orange and apple juices, fresh mushrooms, garlic, sweet corn (prepared or preserved), and avocado – achieved, or were close to, double-digit growth rate in their exports.'[12]

The geography of global trade in fruits and vegetables (Figure 13.6) is strongly regionalized. Not only are Europe and North America the leading importers of such products (along with Japan), but they are also substantial exporters. Both

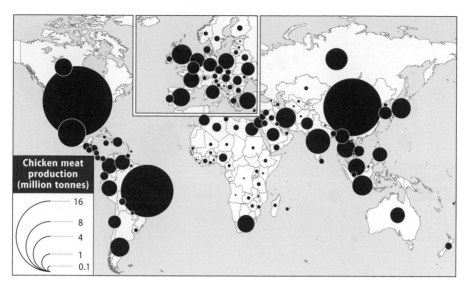

Figure 13.4   **Global production of chickens**

Source: FAO *Statistical Yearbook*, 2009: Table B11

regions contain a variety of climatic conditions conducive to certain kinds of fruit and vegetable production: the Mediterranean rim in the case of Europe; Mexico and the Caribbean in the case of North America. Increasingly, southern hemisphere countries have become especially significant, producing and exporting a wide variety of products for the affluent markets of the northern hemisphere. The key, of course, is the seasonal difference between the two hemispheres.

Finally, Figure 13.7 maps global exports of *coffee*. As coffee aficionados will know, there are two major types of coffee bean: arabica beans, grown at higher altitudes and more difficult to grow; and robusta beans, grown on the low lands in the humid tropics. In general, arabica beans are regarded as being of higher quality. Four countries generate 60 per cent of total coffee exports: Brazil (28 per cent, of which 95 per cent is arabica), Vietnam (17 per cent, all robusta), Colombia (8 per cent, all arabica) and Indonesia (6 per cent, 67 per cent robusta).

The geography of production and trade in high-value food combines elements of global, regional and local scales. Globally, the emergence of southern hemisphere producers, basing their advantage on their seasonal complementarity with the temperate markets of the northern hemisphere, generates massive flows of long-distance trade. Regionally, the existence of areas of more exotic production within the major regional markets of North America, Europe and East Asia has led to strong intra-regional trade flows of high-value foods. Locally, the increasing interest in alternative food networks, especially those which focus on local (often organic) production, has created much shorter movements of agro-food products.

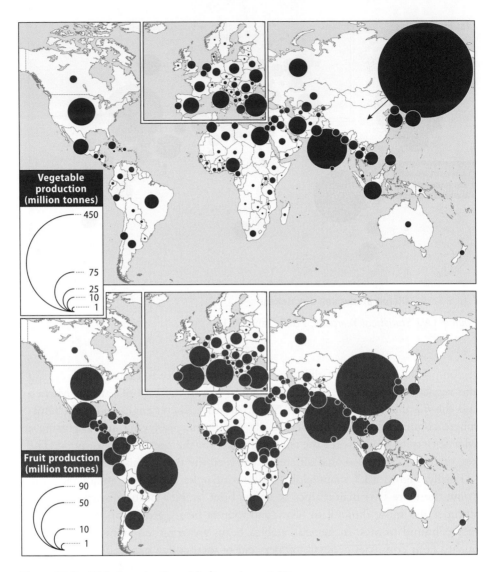

Figure 13.5   **Global production of fruits and vegetables**

Source: FAO *Statistical Yearbook*, 2009: Tables B6, B7

CONSUMER CHOICES – AND CONSUMER RESISTANCES

For most of human history people have had to struggle to obtain enough food to survive. Only a minuscule proportion of the population could afford to obtain the more exotic foods from distant places. That is still the case for millions of people

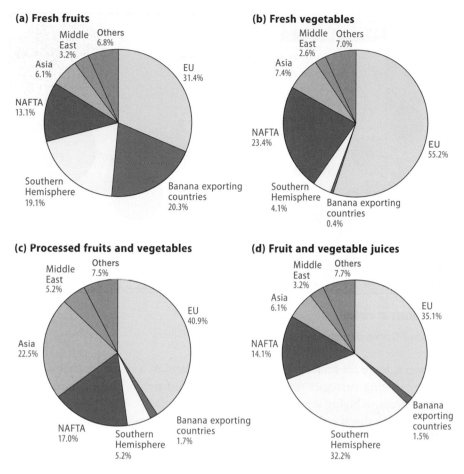

(a) Fresh fruits

- Others 6.8%
- Middle East 3.2%
- Asia 6.1%
- NAFTA 13.1%
- Southern Hemisphere 19.1%
- Banana exporting countries 20.3%
- EU 31.4%

(b) Fresh vegetables

- Others 7.0%
- Middle East 2.6%
- Asia 7.4%
- NAFTA 23.4%
- Southern Hemisphere 4.1%
- Banana exporting countries 0.4%
- EU 55.2%

(c) Processed fruits and vegetables

- Others 7.5%
- Middle East 5.2%
- Asia 22.5%
- NAFTA 17.0%
- Southern Hemisphere 5.2%
- Banana exporting countries 1.7%
- EU 40.9%

(d) Fruit and vegetable juices

- Others 7.7%
- Middle East 3.2%
- Asia 6.1%
- NAFTA 14.1%
- Southern Hemisphere 32.2%
- Banana exporting countries 1.5%
- EU 35.1%

Figure 13.6   Origins of imports of fruits and vegetables to the world's 30 leading importers

Source: based on Huang, 2004: Figure 2.2

in the poorest countries and for many people in affluent countries. But as incomes have risen for many through economic growth, and with the associated urbanization of the population, demand for food has changed dramatically.

The relationship between food production and consumption is complex. What we choose to eat has become a far more intricate process: a mix of taste, culture, religion, health concerns, ethical position and lifestyle as well as of disposable income. On the one hand, food producers strive to produce and market foods that will attract the largest number of consumers (and enhance profits); on the other hand, consumers themselves have widely varying 'food agendas'.

In the affluent consumer markets of North America, Europe and parts of East Asia, it is the *changing patterns* of demand and consumption, rather than the overall level of food consumption, that are especially important. Increasing affluence

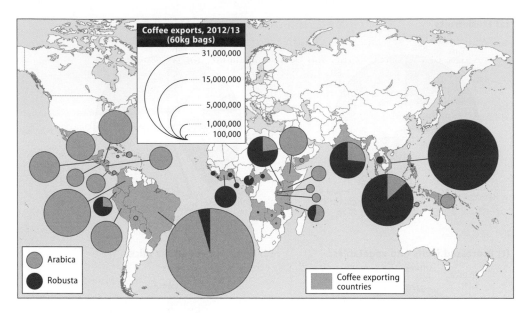

Figure 13.7   **Exporters of coffee**

Source: International Coffee Organization data, 2013

stimulates a desire for greater choice in food products. As a result – but also driven by the marketing strategies of the transnational food producers – the market for food has become highly segmented.

At one level, this is reflected in the huge diversity of products sold through the major supermarkets and, especially, their provision of all-year-round perishable foods from across the globe. It is reflected in the rapid growth of new food products such as the chilled convenience food market. It is reflected in the ever-changing dietary fashions of the affluent in search of the route to beauty and long life and in the development of specialist 'lifestyle' drinks markets, for example the 'coffee revolution' driven by Starbucks' colonization of much of the world.[13]

At the same time, however, there is increasing *consumer resistance* to many of the food products being sold through the big supermarkets, as well as to the more traditional providers of fast food. In the case of GM foods, there is considerable difference in consumer attitudes between the USA, where GM crops tend to be more acceptable, and Europe, where there is greater resistance.[14] There are also pressures to 're-localize' food production: both to rely more on local sources and to stimulate and protect areas of local production of key products. Such resistances derive from a combination of concern over environmental damage and fears about the safety of foods grown using what are increasingly regarded as suspect or ethically unacceptable methods. For example, 'fresh' supermarket food

> is predicated on a new nature-defying order where every conceivable
> fruit and vegetable grown anywhere is available all the time … PGST

> [Permanent Global Summertime] may look good, but in the name of consumer choice and public health the irregularity and diversity that is part of the natural order has been eliminated, not to benefit consumers but to fit the way our big food retailers like to do business. In essence, this means sourcing vast quantities of easy-to-retail, long shelf-life standard varieties, grown to rigid size and cosmetic specifications, that can be supplied 365 days a year ... 'Hi-tech, low-taste, odour-free produce is the norm.'[15]

Not surprisingly, there has been significant growth in the ethical consumer movement in the agro-food industries.[16] For example, some 7 million farmers and workers in around 60 developing countries are now covered by the 'Fairtrade' charitable scheme, which pays a guaranteed price covering basic costs and a surplus to reinvest in further development. Fairtrade is especially active in such foods as coffee (see Figure 13.3), tea, bananas and chocolate. According to the Fairtrade Foundation, 'Fairtrade accounts for 10% of all tea sold in the UK, just over 27% of all roast and ground retail coffee is Fairtrade certified.'[17]

Set against these kinds of consumer resistance, we have to recognize that such movements are, at least in part, facilitated by the choices of the affluent consumer. While there is no doubt that demand is growing from consumers for food whose quality and geographical provenance are regarded as being superior to food from the large-scale sources, for most people the overwhelming need is still for enough food to survive. For every 'enlightened' consumer pursuing their organic food, or for the lifestyler drinking designer coffee, there are many for whom such foods are out of reach. For people working long hours, for the poor and for the elderly, the availability of convenience foods is a major benefit. The fact that such foods may not be especially healthy is another issue. Clearly, demand for, and consumption of, food is an extremely complex set of processes. It has major implications for the changing technologies of food production, for state regulatory policies and for the strategies of the transnational food producers.

TRANSFORMING TECHNOLOGIES IN AGRO-FOOD PRODUCTION

Global cool chains

Traditionally, food production and consumption were predominantly local. No longer. Developments in transportation, together with innovations in refrigeration and food-freezing technologies – the development of 'global cool chains' – transformed the availability of a much wider range of agricultural products over vast geographical distances.[18] Long-distance trade in fresh foods depends critically on controlled atmosphere (CA) technologies to move fragile and perishable products without destroying their 'freshness'.[19] Technologies of fresh food preservation are also greatly enhanced by the use of air freight to transport low-weight/high-value exotic foods to distant, affluent markets.

Consequently – and controversially – many food products travel vast distances. For example, a basket of 20 fresh foods bought from major UK retailers was found to have clocked up a total of 100,943 miles.[20] On the other hand, long-distance movement of agricultural produce also makes possible the continued existence of many traditional producers through their access to a larger market (including that of Fairtrade production). The carbon footprint per pound of food of the biggest container ships is significantly lower than that of much 'local' sourcing.[21]

There is, in fact, no easy equivalence between long-distance movement and environmental impact, as an analysis of some New Zealand (NZ) products shipped to the UK reveals:[22]

- The UK uses twice as much energy per tonne of milk solids produced as NZ, even including the energy associated with transport from NZ to the UK.
- The energy used in producing lamb in the UK is four times higher than the energy used by NZ lamb producers, even after including the energy used in transporting NZ lamb to the UK.
- NZ energy costs for the production of apples are a third of those in the UK. Even when transport is added, NZ energy costs are approximately 60 per cent of those in the UK.

Industrialization of food production and the shift towards biotechnology

The technologies of agro-food production have been transformed by their *industrialization* and, most recently, through the introduction of *biotechnologies*. Such developments are intimately related to the increasing role of very large agro-food corporations in all aspects of food production.

The application of industrially produced chemicals to agricultural production (fertilizers to stimulate higher crop yields, pesticides to inhibit disease and insect damage) has been common for decades. The development of newer varieties of crops has also been a continuing process. The so-called 'Green Revolution' of the 1960s and 1970s was the most significant combination of such practices: an attempt to solve the food problems of poor countries through the development of new varieties of basic crops such as wheat, rice and maize, using fertilizers, pesticides and irrigation.

The Green Revolution was, in many ways, a precursor of what has become the most controversial aspect of agro-food production: genetic modification (GM). As before, the objective is to improve plants' resistance to disease and to herbicides, to increase yields and to improve nutritional value by changing basic genetic structures and producing new varieties of seeds.[23] Such GM techniques are immensely complex and costly. They involve massive levels of capital expenditure that can only be afforded by the big biotechnology and agro-food companies. Not least, they encourage the patenting of what had hitherto been regarded as 'public' goods: the seeds needed to produce the next generation of crops. This is the patenting of life itself. Traditionally, a farmer would set aside some seeds from one year for use in the following year. GM seeds, in contrast, 'belong' to the seed company, which produces 'terminator' seeds that cannot be reproduced by the user, who has to purchase the next year's seeds from the seed company. Planting of GM crops increased to 160 million hectares globally in 2011, an increase of 8 per cent over 2010. Growth was especially rapid in Brazil (+19 per cent) but the biggest area of GM crops is the USA. Around 90 per cent of the US production of maize, soya beans, cotton and oilseed rape is through GM.[24]

The application of biotechnologies is relatively recent, and mainly applied in the early stages of the agro-food production circuit. The use of chemical additives in food products themselves has been common for much longer. Increasing industrialization of food production can remove some of the desirable qualities of taste, texture, colour, and so on. To counteract these changes, and to enhance the attractiveness of food products, producers have developed a bewildering variety of food additives: preservatives, antioxidants, emulsifiers, flavourings, colourings. One calculation is that some 4,500 different flavouring compounds are available to food manufacturers and that 90 per cent of additives are purely cosmetic.[25]

What about the workers?

The impacts of technological transformations in how food is produced, and how far and how quickly it can be transported, are immense. In addition to their effect on what people eat – and the potential effects on health – they also impact greatly on those people who work in agriculture. The proportion of the labour force working on the land has fallen markedly, especially in developed countries. The industrialization of agro-food processes has, in effect, shifted the locus from the field to the factory or to the packaging plant. The seasonal rhythms of agricultural work have been displaced by the mechanical rhythms of food processing and packaging assembly lines. Indeed, many workers in the agro-food industries are more like workers in automobile or electronics production, engaged in 'lean and flexible production', than farmers.[26]

Because governments are heavily involved in regulating their food industries for health and safety reasons (see next section), the working conditions in processing and packaging plants are more tightly monitored than in some other industries (such as clothing). The work itself may be mind-numbingly boring and repetitive, but so, too, are many other jobs in today's society (and not just in manufacturing: think of telephone call centres). Of course, wide variations in working conditions exist despite, or perhaps because of, the ubiquitous involvement of the big super-market chains in sourcing from such plants.

Although some jobs in food processing and packaging are permanent or full-time, agro-food is the largest user of *casual labour* of all modern industries. These industries depend fundamentally on a huge floating labour force of workers, employed only when the producer needs them and often organized by subcon-tractors or 'gangmasters'. Since the supply of such labour invariably exceeds demand, wages are extremely low and working hours very long. The majority are migrants, with virtually no bargaining power and often very little protection from abuse. The seasonality of agricultural processes creates vast periodic movements of migrant workers within and across borders.[27] In the USA, the majority of these workers are Hispanic (especially Mexican); in Europe, they come predominantly from Eastern Europe or from North Africa.

An Oxfam Report on American agriculture provides graphic details of what the report terms 'sweatshops in the fields':

> Farmworkers are among the poorest – if not *the* poorest – laborers in the US … farm labor is also one of the most dangerous jobs in America. At work, farmworkers suffer higher rates of toxic chemical injuries than workers in any other sector of the US economy, with an estimated 300,000 suffering pesticide poisonings each year. They also suffer extremely high rates of workplace accidents …

> Farmworkers are much more likely to have temporary jobs … Just 14% of all workers in crop agriculture are employed full time in year-round positions, while fully 83% work on a seasonal basis … 56% of farmworkers in crop agriculture are migrant workers, travelling more than 75 miles to get a job …

> Thirty per cent of migrant workers (or 17% of all crop workers) are characterized as 'follow-the-crop' migrants, moving year-round like those portrayed in John Steinbeck's *The Grapes of Wrath* … Farmworkers in general and immigrant farmworkers in particular, have low levels of education … Their literacy and communication skills in English are especially limited …

> Finally, yet perhaps most significantly, these immigrant workers typi-cally lack work authorization … Given the vulnerabilities of their legal status, US farmworkers tend to face widespread workplace and human rights abuses, and are rarely able to take the risk of challenging abuses when they occur.[28]

While some of these characteristics of the agro-food workforce are far from new, they have intensified as agro-food production circuits have become more tightly controlled by larger and larger producers and buyers.

THE ROLE OF THE STATE

The agro-food industries are among the most highly regulated, heavily subsidized and vigorously protected of all economic activities. The involvement of the state is ubiquitous in these industries.

Regulating agro-food industries

A vast array of government agencies and departments operates to oversee various parts of the agro-food industries. Food safety is a primary focus, a problem greatly exacerbated by the growth of international trade in food. Before the 1970s, as much as 90 per cent of world food production was consumed in the producing country itself. That situation has changed dramatically. As a result, national food regulatory measures have become increasingly embedded in international codes, such as the Codex Alimentarius, set within the Food and Agricultural Organization and the WHO. This consists of 'over 200 standards, forty codes and guidelines for food production and processing, maximum levels for about 500 food additives, and 2700 maximum-residue limits for pesticide residues in foods and food crops'.[29]

A striking feature of regulatory policies in these industries is that they are deeply intertwined with the strategies of the major food producers:

> The biggest funder of the establishment of the Codex Alimentarius Commission was not the US state but the US food industry … Indeed, the Codex has become one of the more industry-dominated international organizations.[30]

In other words, there is a substantial amount of 'private' regulation in the agro-food industries sanctioned by national governments. A major problem facing food safety regulators is the continuing proliferation of new products that cross the boundaries between food and medicine: the development of so-called functional foods or 'nutriceuticals', which claim to improve various aspects of health.[31]

The vastly increased geographical complexity and lack of transparency in food supply chains has created huge problems for their regulation. This was demonstrated in graphic terms during the so-called 'horsemeat scandal' in Europe in early 2013. This involved, at least initially,

> horsemeat from a Romanian abattoir being sold to a French supplier by way of a Cypriot trader, and then passed on to a French food-processing company before landing on supermarket shelves in Britain and France.[32]

This case demonstrated just how difficult it is to trace the origins of contaminated materials in processed food when the supply chains involved are so complex and cross many national boundaries. In the EU, it is the *national* inspectors of the 27 member states who are responsible for tracking meat shipments and testing food samples; the EU acts as coordinator. Clearly, there is a need for much greater international regulation.

The case of GM food is one of the biggest sources of difference between states and one that spills over into trade disputes, especially between the USA and the EU. The US position is that GM foods are not only safe, but also vital to increasing food supply in poor countries. Driven by consumer resistance (see earlier), the EU has taken a more restrictive position. Although it lifted its six-year moratorium on GM food in 2004 and allowed limited approvals of GM products, several EU states continue to ban them.

There is also considerable variation in national regulations governing the operation of foreign food retailers. Retail markets tend to be a highly sensitive national and local issue. Many countries have protected their domestic retail sector either by keeping out or by constraining the entry and operations of foreign food retailers. Restrictions on ownership (e.g. by insisting on local partners or minority foreign ownership) have been very common and continue to exist, especially in emerging economies where there is a great fear of the domestic retailing sector (primarily a small-firm sector) being swamped by foreign incursion.

Subsidizing and protecting agro-food industries: *the major focus of trade conflict*

For reasons that lie deeply embedded in national emotions, as well as in the need to guarantee a secure food supply, most countries have adopted policies to nurture, sustain and, where felt necessary, protect their agro-food industries from external competition. Such policies include the trade measures shown in Figure 6.8, as well as direct financial support (subsidies) for domestic farmers. Agricultural subsidies are heavily concentrated in particular countries:

> More than 90 per cent of the dollar value of agricultural support in OECD countries is provided by the European Union (which alone provides about half); Japan; the US; and the Republic of Korea.[33]

For example, both Japan and Korea have adopted highly protectionist policies towards their rice industries, which have deep cultural, as well as dietary, significance. In Europe, the French, in particular, regard the rural economy as sacrosanct. In the USA, farming remains a national obsession, a reflection of the country's desire for food security as well as the emotional connotations of the development of the national space in the nineteenth century. Subsidies to US farmers began in the 1930s under the New Deal programme.

The EU's Common Agricultural Policy (CAP) has long absorbed the largest single share of the EU's total budget and has become a source of dissatisfaction for several member states. The CAP has become increasingly controversial, not only within the EU itself, but also in the context of the WTO trade negotiations. The CAP was reformed most recently in 2003, when the level of subsidy to farmers was separated from production, a practice which had led to notorious cases of over-production. Instead, subsidy was linked to 'compliance with environmental, food safety, and animal welfare standards' and part of the process of 'transforming the CAP from a sectoral policy of farm community support to an integrated policy for rural development'.[34] To some member states (Austria, Denmark, Finland, the Netherlands, Sweden and the UK) further radical reform of the CAP is regarded as essential.

The issue of agricultural subsidies has become possibly the biggest bone of contention in the current WTO negotiations, especially in the context of the Doha 'development round' (see Chapter 11). It has been pointed out, for example, that the average subsidy per cow in the EU is more than the $2 per day on which half the world's population has to live, while US farm subsidies allow 'farmers to export wheat at 28 per cent less than it costs to produce, corn at 10 per cent less and rice at more than a quarter less than cost price'.[35] Financial subsidization of some, or all, agricultural production continues to be common in many countries, although there has been some movement within OECD countries:

> The average support to agricultural producers fell from 37 per cent of the gross value of farm receipts in 1986–88 (the beginning of the Uruguay Round) to 30 per cent in 2003–05 … [however] … while the 7 percentage point decline in support is progress, the amount of support increased over the same period from $242 billion a year to $273 billion.[36]

Despite the general reduction in tariffs and subsidies, many agricultural products remain heavily protected to the detriment, especially, of poor countries.

A new phenomenon: state land grabs

Fears over future food shortages have led, in recent years, to 'land grabbing': state-supported actions to acquire agricultural land in foreign countries.[37] Although this is a highly complex situation which does not just involve powerful states and TNCs taking land from weaker states, it has become a major, and highly controversial, phenomenon:

> In just over one year, from March 2008 to April 2009, an estimated 40 million hectares of land changed hands; the latest figures from the World Bank suggest that this was twenty times higher than the average annual level of land transfers for the preceding forty years.[38]

While it is virtually impossible to establish the precise scale of land transfers, the identity of the major investors is clearer:

> The big investors tend to be capital-exporting countries with large worries about feeding their own people. Their confidence in world markets has been shaken by two food-price spikes in four years. So they have sought to guarantee food supplies by buying farmland abroad. China is by far the largest investor, buying or leasing twice as much as anyone else.[39]

These land deals invariably come with the promise of jobs for the local population, technology and skills transfer, and tax revenue for the local economy. But such promises rarely materialize:

> In Mozambique … one project had promised 2,650 jobs and created a mere 35–40 full-time positions … 99 smaller projects in Benin, Burkina Faso and Niger reported 'hardly any' rural job creation … Most land deals contribute little or nothing to the public purse. Because markets for land are so ill-developed in Africa and governments so weak, rents are piffling: $2 per hectare per year in Ethiopia; $5 in Liberia … It is not unusual for foreign investors to pay less tax than local smallholders. And upfront compensation to local farmers for use of their land is derisory: often just a few months of income for agreeing to a 100-year lease.[40]

CORPORATE STRATEGIES IN THE AGRO-FOOD INDUSTRIES

Concentration and consolidation

The massive transformation of the agro-food industries during the past few decades is inexorably bound up with the increasing dominance of very large transnational firms. This is apparent at all stages in the production circuit, from seeds, through growing, to processing and retailing. What was historically a highly fragmented set of industries – although some parts were always more concentrated than others – has become one in which a relatively small number of giant transnational firms shape what food is produced, how it is produced, who produces it, and how it is marketed and distributed to final consumers.

Figure 13.8 lists the 10 leading companies in the world in four agro-food industries: seeds, pesticides, food and beverage manufacture, food retailing. Although there have been some changes in detail since these data were compiled, the general pattern remains much the same today. Notably, there are many cross-links,

Top 10 seed companies		$m sales 2007
1. Monsanto	US	4,964
2. DuPont	US	3,300
3. Syngenta	Switzerland	2,018
4. Groupe Limagrain	France	1,226
5. Land O'Lakes	US	917
6. KWS AG	Germany	702
7. Bayer Crop Science	Germany	524
8. Sakata	Japan	396
9. DLF-Trifolium	Denmark	391
10. Taikii	Japan	347

Top 10 pesticide companies		$m sales 2007
1. Bayer	Germany	7,458
2. Syngenta	Switzerland	7,285
3. BASF	Germany	4,297
4. Dow AgroSciences	US	3,779
5. Monsanto	US	3,599
6. DuPont	US	2,369
7. Makhteshim Agan	Israel	1,895
8. Nufarm	Australia	1,470
9. Sumitomo Chemical	Japan	1,209
10. Arysta Lifescience	Japan	1,035

Top 10 food & beverage companies		$m sales 2007
1. Nestlé	Switzerland	83,600
2. Pepsi Co.	US	39,474
3. Kraft Foods	US	37,241
4. Coca-Cola	US	28,857
5. Unilever	UK/Netherlands	26,985
6. Tyson Foods	US	26,900
7. Cargill	US	26,500
8. Mars	US	25,000
9. ADM Co.	US	24,219
10. Danone	France	19,975

Top 10 food retailers		$m sales 2007
1. Wal-Mart	US	180,621
2. Carrefour	France	104,151
3. Tesco	UK	72,970
4. Schwarz Group	Germany	58,753
5. Aldi	Germany	55,966
6. Kroger	US	52,082
7. Ahold	UK	50,556
8. Rewe Group	Germany	49,651
9. Metro Group	Germany	49,483
10. Edeka	Germany	45,397

Figure 13.8 Dominant firms in the global agro-food industries

Source: based on data in ETC Group, 2008

especially between seed and pesticide companies as vertical integration has increased. For example, the Swiss company Syngenta has become 'the Apple of the agro-chemical world. By selling seeds, pesticides, fertilisers and advisory services it keeps farmers from their first purchase right through to – and beyond – harvesting.'[41]

Global seed production is dominated by European and US firms. US dominance increased following Monsanto's acquisition of Seminis in 2005 to create the world's largest seed company. US firms also dominate food and beverage production, although the world's biggest food manufacturer, Nestlé, comes from one of the smallest European countries, Switzerland, while the fifth largest is the Anglo/Dutch company Unilever. In global food retailing, on the other hand, eight of the top ten companies are European, and only two are American, including by far the largest, Wal-Mart.

Overall:

- Almost three-quarters of the world seed market is controlled by the leading 10 companies, compared with two-thirds in 1967.
- Almost 90 per cent of the world pesticide market is controlled by the leading 10 firms.
- Over a quarter (26 per cent) of the world packaged food market is controlled by the leading 10 firms.
- The leading 100 global food retailers account for 35 per cent of total world grocery sales. The top three produce half of the total revenues of the top ten.[42]

Virtually all of this increased concentration is the result of *merger and acquisition*. These have been among the most takeover-intensive industries in recent years, as firms have striven not only to acquire a wider portfolio of brands (as well as to drive out competition for their own existing brands), but also to extend their reach into new geographical markets. Much of this activity has been driven by the increased *financialization* of the leading firms: 'the prioritization of objectives to boost "shareholder value"'.[43]

Take the case of the US tobacco company Philip Morris. In 1985 Philip Morris acquired General Foods; in 1988 it acquired Kraft Foods; in 1989 these were combined to form Kraft General Foods, the largest food company in the USA; in 2000 it acquired Nabisco Holdings of the USA and integrated Nabisco brands into Kraft Foods worldwide; in 2007 the entire Kraft Foods business was sold and became the world's third-largest food company; in 2010, Kraft controversially acquired the major UK company Cadbury.

Among the diversified food companies, Unilever acquired Brooke Bond in 1984, to make it the world's leading tea company; in 2000, the company acquired the US food company Bestfoods, as well as Ben & Jerry's ice cream; in 2007 Unilever acquired the Buavita vitality drinks brand in Indonesia and Inmarko, the leading ice-cream business in Russia. The more narrowly specialized food companies have also grown through acquisition as well as through organic growth (no pun intended). Tyson Foods, for example, the world's biggest poultry company, began its 'expand or expire' strategy in 1963 by acquiring the Garrett Poultry Company of Arkansas and then made 19 further acquisitions between 1966 and 1989. In 1995, Tyson purchased Cargill's US broiler operations and has subsequently made acquisitions in other food companies outside poultry, notably IBP, the huge beef and pork company.

Merger and acquisition have also been important factors in the growth of the major transnational food retailers. One of the biggest deals was Wal-Mart's acquisition of the British supermarket chain Asda, for almost $11 billion. Because of national regulatory restrictions, the major food retailers have often had to enter foreign markets through joint ventures with local partners. Examples include Tesco's alliance with Samsung in Korea.[44]

Strategies of combining 'global' brands with 'local' products

The agro-food producers are dominated by the drive to introduce, develop and sustain *branded products*. Indeed, the degree of product differentiation through branding is probably greater in the agro-food industries than in most others. Each of the leading agro-food companies has a vast portfolio of brands serving different market segments. At the same time, all the leading food companies are actively rationalizing their brand portfolio through sell-offs.

The primary aim is to sell each brand to the largest number of consumers; the ideal would be brands that sell everywhere without any need for modification. But agro-food markets are not like that. A major problem for the big agro-food producers, therefore, is to create *global* brands in circumstances where much food consumption is still very strongly influenced by *local* tastes and preferences. A distinction must, of course, be made between the manufacture of a product for a global market (based on large-scale production plants serving geographically extensive markets) and the way that product is actually sold to the local consumer. A product may be sold overtly as a global brand but it may also be sold under a more local label and packaging, even if the product itself is the same everywhere.

While some food companies do market their products as global brands, others are less inclined to do so. Nestlé, for example, dismisses the idea of 'global brands':

> There is a trade-off between efficiency and effectiveness in global brands ... Operational efficiency comes from our strategic umbrella brands. But we believe there is no such thing as a global consumer, especially in a sector as psychologically and culturally loaded as food. As a result, Nestlé retains its brand strength by using ... very strong local brands.[45]

The increased consumer interest in food health and safety has important implications for food producers' strategies. Capitalizing on the enhanced interest in local and organic foods becomes increasingly important. All the big food companies have to deal with these market changes. They are doing so in various ways: for example, by acquiring local companies and by retaining their brand identities rather than rebranding them with the new corporate identity. Thus, Nestlé announced its intention to 'accelerate the evolution of Nestlé from a respected, trustworthy Food and Beverage Company to a respected, trustworthy *Food, Nutrition, Health and Wellness* Company'.[46] Note the very significant change of emphasis. This shift in emphasis towards 'healthy' products has become virtually universal among the large food companies. Unilever boasts about how it is 'bringing Vitality to life' and launched the 'Unilever Health Institute – a centre of excellence in nutrition, health and vitality'.[47] Likewise, Kraft Foods has a 'health and wellness strategy'.[48]

Changes in organizational and geographical architectures

Traditionally, the major food manufacturers expanded overseas by setting up (or acquiring) operations in each of their major geographical markets. The existence of highly protected domestic food markets, together with the idiosyncrasies of local consumer tastes, make each national market distinctive. As a result, the leading transnational food producers established organizational structures that were strongly *multi*national, with all the characteristics shown in Figure 5.12.[49] The agro-food industries, therefore, are the clearest example of the 'global–local tension' discussed in Chapter 5. Because the traditional organizational–geographical structures are less and less effective, all the major food producers are engaged in large-scale reorganization programmes. Two cases illustrate these processes.

Nestlé currently has operations in 80 countries and employs 250,000 people. Organizationally, Nestlé is changing from a decentralized multinational company to a global and, ultimately, a global multifocal company.[50]

In fact, Nestlé has been involved in substantial geographical reorganization for some time, as its actions within South East Asia reveal.[51] With the increasing liberalization of agro-food trade within ASEAN, Nestlé progressively rationalized its multidomestic operations there (in the early 1990s it had more than 40 factories in the region). Under the 'centres of excellence' programme, the company established such centres for production of breakfast cereals in the Philippines, chocolate and confectionery in Malaysia, non-dairy creamer in Thailand, soya sauce in Singapore and instant coffee in Indonesia. It has a major R&D centre in Singapore.

Unilever, like Nestlé, had long operated a decentralized multinational strategy but it, too, has made strenuous efforts to create a more efficient and responsive global structure. In the late 1990s, Unilever operated around 300 food factories, with a presence in virtually every country in the world. The acquisition of Bestfoods brought in a further 70 factories in 60 countries. In its various strategies since the late 1990s, Unilever has drastically rationalized and reorganized its entire food production and supply chain activities. The focus on a much smaller number of brands has involved closing a large number of plants in favour of concentrating production on a much smaller number of key sites.

Such organizational and geographical restructuring – often with a strong *macroregional* dimension – is typical of all the major multibrand food producers:

> Global firms had launched a restructuring process aimed at developing large macro-regional factories specialized by product lines and serving the entire region, with the objective of generating scale economies and productivity increases. These macro-regional factories had been progressively replacing traditional national factories through continuous restructuring and cost cutting programmes, involving plant closures and lay-offs at the national level ... [for example] ... in the early 2000s, Nestlé launched its own version of a macro-regional production system in ice cream, distinguishing between 'global factories' that would perform initial production stages for global or macro-regional markets, and 'finishing factories' in which products would be adapted to local markets ... The adoption of global strategies in marketing and production entailed a centralization of support functions such as sourcing, aimed at controlling and coordinating the activity of local buyers.[52]

'Big Food' and 'Big Retail': two sides of the same coin

These developments in the strategies of the major transnational food producers have to be seen within the context of the retailing systems through which their products are sold. There is a deep symbiotic relationship between the big food producers and the big supermarket chains:

> 'Big Food' and 'Big Retail' are really two sides of the same coin. Big global food manufacturers need big supermarket chains to get their products on to the shelves and our big supermarkets need big food processors ... Mass-produced food that can be churned out over and over again in vast, uniform quantities, made by a handful of big manufacturers who jump to the big retailers' tune, processed food lends itself to supermarket retailing: it gives them the ability to put a standard, regular product into every store nationwide, a product that does not require any specialist handling ... Industrial food lends itself to the supermarkets' heavily centralised, highly mechanical distribution systems.[53]

This is an arena of continuous power struggles in which power lies increasingly with the big transnational food retailers. And there is no doubt that the biggest food retailers have become increasingly *transnational* after being essentially domestically oriented for most of their histories.[54] But the extent of transnationalization differs between firms; the biggest food retailers are not invariably the most transnational, as the case of Wal-Mart shows. The world's biggest food retailer in overall sales is far less so in terms of international sales. Figure 13.9 maps the distribution of stores of three of the leading transnational food retailers. There are some significant differences between them in the specific geography of their overseas activities but all share a common characteristic: a very strong focus on their home region.

Wal-Mart has 68 per cent of its stores in North America (primarily the USA, plus Canada and Mexico). Its stores outside North America are concentrated in East Asia (China and Japan – it disposed of its Korean stores), Latin America (particularly Brazil, Chile, Argentina) and Central America, where it acquired a substantial equity stake in the region's largest retailer from Ahold. In contrast, Wal-Mart's only European base is in the UK through its acquisition of Asda. Its attempts to establish a presence in Germany failed, largely because of its inability to understand the fundamental differences between the German and the US retail food markets.

The French company *Carrefour* has 47 per cent of its stores in its home market and 90 per cent in Europe. Elsewhere, it has a significant presence in Latin America (primarily Argentina and Brazil) and in East Asia (particularly China). Brazil and China seem destined to be a major focus in the near future. Carrefour has a policy of getting out of countries in which it cannot become one of the top three retailers.[55] It withdrew from Japan and Mexico, and sold its stores in the Czech Republic and Slovakia to Tesco. At the same time, it bought Tesco's Taiwan

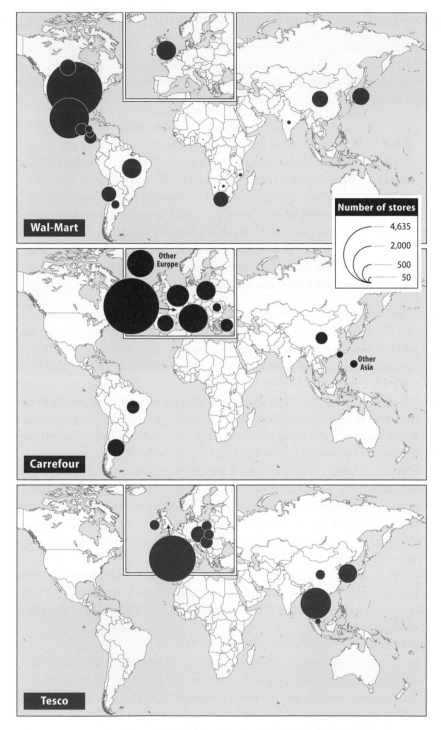

Figure 13.9   The global geographies of leading transnational food retailers

Source: company reports

operations. Significantly, Carrefour has no stores in North America, having failed to transfer its hypermarket model to the USA.

The biggest UK food retailer, Tesco, has pursued a very aggressive – but geographically focused – transnationalization strategy, based on expansion in East Asia and Eastern Europe. Tesco has no stores in Western Europe outside the UK and Ireland. Its recent buying and selling deals with Carrefour are part of this strategy, strengthening Tesco's position in Eastern Europe. In East Asia, Tesco's major store concentrations are in Thailand, Korea[56] and China. (Tesco sold its Japanese operations in 2012.) But Tesco's biggest setback occurred in 2013 when it announced it would dispose of its heavily loss-making US operations 'Fresh & Easy', established amid much fanfare only in 2008. Tesco's global ambitions have been severely dented.

Overall, therefore, there has been considerable growth in the transnational – or, more accurately, regional – operations of some of the leading retail chains. But such expansion has not been problem-free, as the sell-offs listed above demonstrate. The use of local partners within a joint venture often helps to avoid the problems of misunderstanding local market conditions. But even joint ventures are not without their difficulties, especially if the foreign partner fails to learn from the knowledge embedded in the local partner. While the strength of most of the leading retailers is based on their high levels of profitability in their home market, their returns on international operations are often far lower.

So, the transnationalization of food retailing is far from being a straightforward or unproblematic process. Competing head-to-head with local firms is particularly difficult in this sector. A major problem is identity. Because food retailing has traditionally been very much a domestic activity, there is little knowledge of foreign retail store brands (as opposed to product brands). For many customers outside the USA, for example, Wal-Mart is a totally unknown quantity. The same applies to non-French residents' knowledge of Carrefour, or non-UK residents' awareness of Tesco. Yet building up a respected and trusted brand identity takes a long time. Meanwhile, local competition remains, in most cases, a very serious problem for transnational food retailers.

Supplier relationships

A second dimension of food retailers' strategies is from whom, and from where, their products are sourced. The big retail chains have vastly increased the geographical extensiveness of their supply networks as well as exerting increasing power and influence over their suppliers. As in the case of clothing (Chapter 14), the major retailers dominate their supply networks, forcing suppliers to meet their increasingly stringent demands on price, delivery and quality. There is a great deal of criticism of the treatment of suppliers by the big supermarkets, although suppliers are often afraid to object out of fear of losing their contracts. An investigation of the accounts of transnational food retailers claimed that they gain huge financial benefits simply by delaying payments to their suppliers:

> stock is turned into cash at the check-out counters long before sup-
> pliers have to be paid … In effect, suppliers have acted as surrogate
> bankers … [however] … the burden is not shared equally … the most
> powerful manufacturers are able to shunt the burden of increased trade
> debt down the supply chain … life is very much tougher for smaller
> suppliers who do not have the luxury of their burden down the line.[57]

It is also increasingly common practice for the big supermarket chains to ask the
major food producers to pay for 'preferred status'.[58]

As the big food retailers have increased their direct presence in foreign countries
(especially in the emerging market economies) they have also drastically changed the
geography and organization of their sourcing networks, both for their local stores and
for their entire network.[59] Typically, the degree of centralization of procurement has
greatly increased. When a transnational retailer establishes operations in a specific
country, one of its first actions is to replace 'a per store procurement system with the
distribution centre (DC) model used in established markets. Each DC may have
responsibility for a particular range of products or a particular territory.'[60]

A further aspect of the changing procurement practices of transnational retailers
is the changing balance between global and local sourcing:

> On the one hand, transnational retailers have increased levels of global
> sourcing for their home markets … On the other hand … there are
> the supply chain impacts that result from the retailers establishing store
> operations *within* the various markets … The foreign subsidiaries of
> retailers such as Tesco, Ahold, and Carrefour commonly source over
> 90% of products from within the country … contra accounts of the
> continuing rise of global sourcing, local sourcing may actually *increase*
> over time as the supply base develops and retailers therefore import
> fewer products.[61]

However, the recent strategic shift of Wal-Mart towards a more global sourcing
system reflects what may become an increasingly common practice:

> Wal-Mart intends a drive … to cut billions of dollars from its supply
> chain by combining its store purchasing across national frontiers in a
> fresh stage of the globalization of its business … It is … shifting to
> direct purchasing of its fresh fruit and vegetables on a global basis,
> rather than working through supplier companies.[62]

The recent crises over food safety and contamination highlight the problems of
operating supply networks involving many suppliers in very different locations
across the world. As a result, food retailers like Tesco have had to issue high-profile
public apologies in the national media and to promise to reform their system:

The problems we've had with some of our meat lately is about more than burgers and bolognese. It's about some of the ways we get meat to your dinner table. It's about the whole food industry. And it has made us realise we really do need to make it better ... We know that our supply chain is too complicated. So we're making it simpler ... For farmers to do what they do best, they need to know they've got our support ... We know that, no matter what you spend, everyone deserves to eat well. We know that all this will only work if we are open about what we do.[63]

The need for such 'confessions' epitomizes one aspect of the sensitivity of the agro-food industries. But, of course, there are many others, as this chapter has demonstrated.

NOTES

1   Kiple (2007).
2   Bonanno et al. (1994), Roberts (2008), Ward and Almås (1997), Watts and Goodman (1997), Weiss (2007), Wilkinson (2002).
3   *Financial Times* (20 November 2013).
4   McMichael (2007: 218).
5   Page (2000: 245; emphasis added).
6   Blythman (2004: chapter 11).
7   ETC Group (2008).
8   Whatmore et al. (2003: 389).
9   Ponte (2002) examines the conventional coffee production circuit at a global scale.
10 Sonnino and Marsden (2006: 183).
11 This section draws heavily on Huang (2004).
12 Huang (2004: 3).
13 See Ponte (2002).
14 Munro and Schurman (2009).
15 Blythman (2004: 76, 77).
16 See Blowfield (1999), Hughes et al. (2008), Leclair (2002).
17 The Fairtrade Foundation, www.fairtrade.org.uk/press_office/press_releases (2013).
18 Friedland (1994: 223).
19 Huang (2004: 19).
20 *Guardian* (10 May 2003).
21 Murray (2007).
22 Saunders et al. (2006).
23 Whatmore (2002: 131).
24 *Financial Times* (8 February 2012).
25 Millstone and Lang (2003).

26 Raworth and Kidder (2009).

27 Phillips (2009).

28 Oxfam (2004: 2–3, 7, 8).

29 Braithwaite and Drahos (2000: 401).

30 Braithwaite and Drahos (2000: 401).

31 Wilkinson (2002: 338).

32 *Financial Times* (12 February 2013).

33 World Bank (2008b: 97).

34 Sonnino and Marsden (2006: 192).

35 US Institute for Agriculture and Trade Policy, quoted in the *Observer* (3 July 2005).

36 World Bank (2008b: 97).

37 *The Economist* (5 May 2011), UNCTAD (2009), Wolford et al. (2013).

38 Wolford et al. (2013: 189–90).

39 *The Economist* (5 May 2011).

40 *The Economist* (5 May 2011).

41 *Financial Times* (13 December 2012).

42 ETC Group, www.etcgroup.org (2008, 2012).

43 Palpacuer and Tozanli (2008: 81).

44 Coe and Lee (2006).

45 Nestlé CEO, quoted in the *Financial Times* (22 February 2005).

46 Nestlé company website: www.nestle.com; emphasis added.

47 Unilever company website: www.unilever.com/aboutus/ourhistory.

48 Kraft Foods company website: www.kraftfoodscompany.com/brands/healthand wellness.

49 For cases in the agro-food industries, see Pritchard (2000a,b,c).

50 Nestlé company website: www.nestle.com.

51 Pritchard (2000a: 252–4).

52 Palpacuer and Tozanli (2008: 82–3).

53 Blythman (2004: xvii, 73).

54 Coe and Wrigley (2009), Wrigley and Lowe (2007).

55 *The Economist* (16 April 2005).

56 Coe and Lee (2006).

57 *Financial Times* (7 December 2005).

58 *Financial Times* (30 March 2006).

59 Coe and Hess (2005), Durand (2007), Reardon et al. (2007).

60 Coe and Hess (2005: 464).

61 Coe and Hess (2005: 463).

62 *Financial Times* (4 January 2010).

63 Tesco advertisement in the *Guardian* (28 February 2013).

Want to know more about this chapter? Visit the companion website at **www.guilford.com/dickenGS7** for free access to author videos, suggested reading and practice questions to further enhance your study.

Fourteen

'FABRIC-ATING FASHION': THE CLOTHING INDUSTRIES

A HIGHLY CONTROVERSIAL INDUSTRY

Lucy Siegle's provocatively titled book, *To Die For*, captures in graphic terms some of the more egregious problems posed by the clothing industries. Although certainly not unique, these industries exemplify many of the intractable issues facing today's global economy, particularly those relating to labour conditions and corporate social responsibility as well as to trade tensions between developed and developed countries.

These industries were the first to take on a global dimension because of the low barriers to entry to clothing production; in the 1970s, they were the 'poster industries' of what came to be called the 'new international division of labour'.[1] The clothing industries are relatively rare instances of globally significant industries that are important in many developing countries, rather than in just a few. Yet despite the huge global shift to developing countries – where predominantly young female workers work in conditions that recall those of the sweatshops of nineteenth-century cities in Europe and North America – these industries continue to be important sources of jobs in the developed economies as well, employing many of the more 'sensitive' segments of the labour force, particularly females and ethnic minorities, often in tightly localized communities.

THE CLOTHING PRODUCTION CIRCUIT

The clothing industries form part of a larger production circuit involving textile production, in which each stage has its own specific technological and organizational characteristics and particular geographical configuration (Figure 14.1).

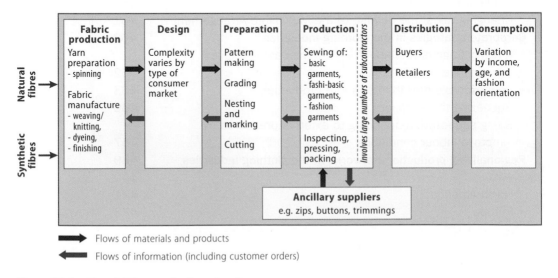

Figure 14.1   **The clothing production circuit**

The clothing industries are far more fragmented organizationally than textiles and far less sophisticated technologically. They are also industries in which outsourcing to subcontractors is especially prominent. The clothing industries produce an enormous variety of often rapidly changing products to a very diverse, and often unpredictable, consumer market. Increasingly, it is the corporate buyers of garments – particularly the retailers – who play the dominant role in shaping the organization and the geography of the clothing industries. These are overwhelmingly *buyer-driven* industries.[2]

GLOBAL SHIFTS IN THE CLOTHING INDUSTRIES

Figure 14.2 maps the world exports of clothing by country of origin. It shows a highly uneven pattern. China is by far the world's biggest clothing exporter, generating 37 per cent of the world total, significantly more than the entire EU of 27 states (28 per cent). Among individual countries other than China, the most significant are Bangladesh, India, Turkey and Vietnam. Clearly Asia dominates the map of clothing exports, generating almost 60 per cent of the world total.

Figure 14.3 shows the leading clothing exporters in terms of their world share in 2000 and 2011. China's share of world clothing exports doubled (in 1980, China generated a mere 4 per cent of world clothing exports). The EU maintained its position, but this aggregate figure includes intra-regional exports and

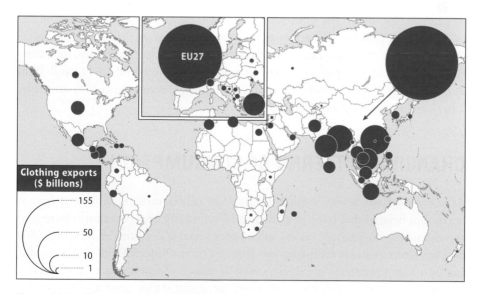

Figure 14.2 **The geography of clothing exports**

Source: based on WTO, *International Trade Statistics*, 2013: Table II.70

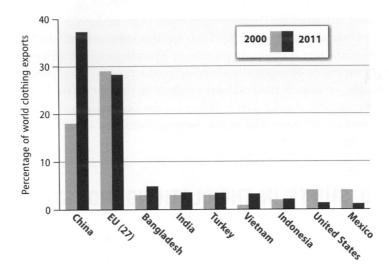

Figure 14.3   **Leading clothing exporters**

Source: based on WTO, *International Trade Statistics*, 2013: Table II.69

also masks significant geographical shifts within the EU, especially towards Eastern Europe. However, the US share of world clothing exports fell from 4.4 per cent to 1.3 per cent.

Not surprisingly, 65 per cent of world clothing imports are received by the USA and the EU. The net result is that both the USA ($84 billion) and the EU ($73 billion) have huge trade deficits in clothing. Between 2005 and 2011, imports of Chinese clothing to the USA accelerated by 9 per cent per year and to the EU by 11 per cent per year. Growth of clothing imports from smaller East Asian countries grew even more spectacularly. US clothing imports from Vietnam, for example, increased by 16 per cent per year between 2005 and 2011, and from Bangladesh by 11 per cent. In contrast, US clothing imports from Mexico fell by 7 per cent per year between 2005 and 2011.

CHANGING PATTERNS OF CONSUMPTION

At the most basic level, clothing satisfies one of the most fundamental human needs. But beyond that basic level, demand for clothing becomes more discretionary and subject to a whole variety of complex social and cultural forces, including people's desires to express themselves through their choice of clothing. Clothing can be a highly symbolic good, suggestive of certain self-perceptions and external self-projections. Such variables as income, age, social status, gender, ethnicity, and so on, play very important roles. It is a market full of uncertainty and volatility. Much of the business of producing and selling clothing, therefore, depends upon

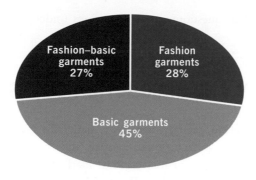

Figure 14.4 Composition of demand for different clothing categories in the USA

Source: based on Abernathy et al., 1999: Figure 1.1

firms' abilities to predict, or to influence, what consumers wish to buy. It is also, increasingly, about *fast fashion*: identifying fashion changes and producing garments very quickly, in small batches, at low cost to the producer.

Clothing can be divided broadly into three major types: basic garments; fashion–basic garments; and fashion garments (Figure 14.4). The fastest growth is occurring in the fashion–basic segment.[3] The primary determinant of both the *level* of demand and the *composition* of demand (in terms of these three basic categories) is the level and distribution of personal income. Since, as we have seen, personal incomes are so very unevenly distributed geographically at the global scale, it is the affluent parts of the world – including the newly affluent consumers in East Asia – that largely determine the level and the nature of the demand for garments. It is in these markets that demand for fashion–basic clothing is growing most rapidly.

The conventional economic wisdom is that, beyond the level of basic necessities, demand for clothing increases less rapidly than the growth of incomes. This poses a major problem for clothing manufacturers and retailers: they need to stimulate demand through *fashion change*, that is they need to shift consumer demand away from low-margin basic garments to higher-margin, more fashionable garments. Enormous expenditure goes into promoting fashion products and creating 'designer' labels. Designer labelling is basically a device to *differentiate* what are often relatively similar products and to cater to – and to encourage – the segmentation of market demand for garments. Such a practice covers a very broad spectrum of consumer income levels from the exceptionally expensive to the relatively cheap.

Consumer behaviour in the clothing industries is not just about fashion choice. It is also about concerns that some producers (and retailers) are utilizing dubious labour practices to reduce costs. Some segments of the clothing industry, and some high-profile retailers, have become the target of large-scale anti-sweatshop campaigns. Consumer resistance has come to be a major feature of these industries.[4] However, many consumers are more concerned about buying garments at very low prices rather than questioning the conditions under which they have been produced.

TECHNOLOGY AND PRODUCTION COSTS

In clothing manufacture capital intensity is generally low, labour intensity is generally high, the average factory size is small, and the technology is relatively unsophisticated. These characteristics contrast markedly with other parts of the textiles–clothing production circuit, as Figure 14.5 shows.

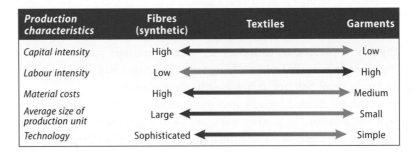

Production characteristics	Fibres (synthetic)	Textiles	Garments
Capital intensity	High	→	Low
Labour intensity	Low	→	High
Material costs	High	→	Medium
Average size of production unit	Large	→	Small
Technology	Sophisticated	→	Simple

Figure 14.5   **Variations in production characteristics between major segments of the textiles–clothing production circuit**

Technological change

Both the cost of production and the speed of response to changes in demand are greatly influenced by the technologies used. Technological innovation can reduce the time involved in the manufacturing process and make possible an increased level of output with the same size – or even smaller – labour force. As global competition has intensified in the clothing industries, the search for new, labour-saving technologies has increased, especially among developed country producers. Two kinds of technological change are especially important:

- those that increase the speed with which a particular process can be carried out;
- those that replace manual with mechanized and automated operation.

The nature of the clothing production process means that the potential for such innovation varies very considerably between the different stages shown in Figure 14.1.[5] In fact, there was relatively little change in clothing technology between the industry's initial emergence in the late nineteenth century and the early 1970s. Even today, clothing manufacture remains a complex sequence of related *manual* operations, especially in those items in which production runs are short:

The basic reason is the nature of the production process itself, where two-dimensional materials, i.e. cloth that is rather soft and limp in nature, are subjected to a series of individual labour-intensive handling/assembly steps, culminating in a product which then fits/drapes a three-dimensional human body.[6]

Hence, most of the recent technological developments in the industry have been in the non-sewing operations: grading, laying out and cutting material in the pre-assembly stage, and in warehouse management and distribution in the post-assembly stage. The application of computer-controlled technology to these operations can achieve enormous savings on materials wastage and greatly increase the speed of the process. For example, the grading process may be reduced from four days to one hour; computer-controlled cutting can reduce the time taken to cut out a suit from one hour to four minutes. But these developments do not reach the core of the problem. The sewing and assembly of garments account for 80 per cent of all labour costs in clothing manufacture. So far only very limited success has been achieved in mechanizing and automating the sewing process.

Current technological developments in the manufacture of clothing are focused on three areas:

- Increasing the *flexibility* of machines, to enable them to recognize oddly shaped pieces of material, pick the pieces up in a systematic manner and align them on the machine correctly, while also being able to sense the need to make adjustments during the sewing process.
- Addressing the problem of *sequential operations*, particularly the difficulty of transferring semi-finished garments from one workstation to the next while retaining the shape of the limp material.
- Developing the *unit production system* to deliver individual pieces of work to the operator on a conveyor belt system. This greatly reduces the amount of (wasted) production time spent by the operator on unbundling and rebundling work pieces. The handling process has been estimated to take up to 60 per cent of the operator's total time.

The drive to introduce such new technologies among developed country producers has been stimulated, of course, by very low-cost competition from developing countries. But cost reduction is not the only benefit derived from the new technologies. At least as important, if not more so, are the *time savings* that result from automated manufacture. This has two major benefits:

- Speeding up the production cycle reduces the cost of working capital by increasing the velocity of its use.
- It becomes possible for the manufacturer to respond more quickly to customer demand.

In addition, electronic point-of-sale (EPOS) technologies permit a direct, real-time link between sales, reordering and production. As the production circuit has become increasingly buyer driven, these IT-based innovations have become extremely important. They not only permit very rapid response to sales and demand at the point of sale, but also enable the buyer firm to pass on the costs of producing and holding inventory to the manufacturer. These technological developments, when combined with the pressures exerted by the big buyers to be faster and more flexible (see below), create enormous stresses on supplier firms and, consequently, on the labour force.[7]

Labour

Variations in labour costs

Labour costs are the most significant *variable* production factor in the clothing industries. Figure 14.6 shows just how wide the labour cost gap can be between different producer countries. The spread is enormous. The highly uneven geography of labour costs, and the increased ability of manufacturers to take advantage of such differences because of improvements in the speed and relative costs of transportation and communications, continue to drive most of the geographical shifts in the clothing industries. The major advantage of low-labour-cost producers lies in the production of basic items, which sell largely on price, rather than in fashion garments in which style

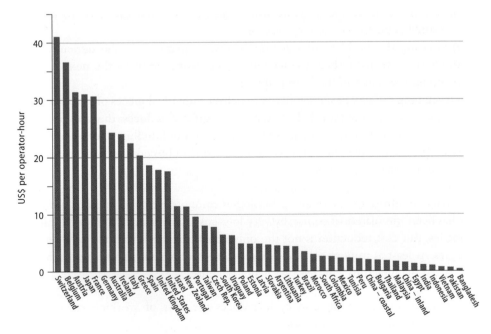

Figure 14.6   **Hourly labour costs in the clothing industries**

Source: Werner International

is more important. The difference between the two is one of *rate of product turnover.* Fashion and fashion–basic garments have a rapid rate of turnover reflecting the idiosyncrasies of particular markets. Geographical proximity to such markets is vital and this helps to explain the survival of many developed country clothing manufacturers. It also partly explains the relative advantage of low-cost countries located close to the major consumer markets of the USA (e.g. Mexico, the Caribbean), Europe (e.g. Central and Eastern Europe, the Mediterranean rim) and Japan (the Asian countries).

Characteristics of the labour force and working conditions

Some 80 per cent of the workers in the clothing industries are female.[8] A substantial proportion of the labour force is also relatively unskilled or semi-skilled. The specific socio-cultural roles of women, in particular their family and domestic responsibilities, also make them relatively immobile geographically. A further characteristic of the clothing workforce in the older industrialized countries is that a large number tend to be immigrants or members of ethnic minority groups. This is a continuation of a very long tradition. The early clothing industries of New York, London, Manchester and Leeds in the late nineteenth and early twentieth centuries were major foci for poor Jewish immigrants. Subsequent migrants from other origins have also seen the industry as a key point of entry into the labour market. The participation of Italians and Eastern Europeans in both the USA and the UK has been followed more recently by the large-scale employment of blacks, Hispanics and Asians in the USA and by non-white Commonwealth immigrants in the UK.

The history of these industries is not a pleasant one: appalling working conditions in sweatshop premises. At least in the clothing industries of the developed economies such conditions are now relatively rare; factory and employment laws have seen to this, although the sweatshop has certainly not disappeared entirely from the clothing industries of the big cities of North America and Europe.[9]

In contrast, sweatshop conditions are almost the industry standard in the rapidly growing clothing industries of the developing countries. Employment tends to be geographically concentrated in the large, burgeoning cities and in the EPZs. The labour force is overwhelmingly female and predominantly young (often extremely young). Many workers are first-generation factory workers employed on extremely low wages and for very long hours: a seven-day week and a 12- to 14-hour day are not uncommon. Employment in the clothing industry in particular tends to fluctuate very markedly in response to variations in demand.

Hence, a very large number of outworkers are used: women working as machinists or hand-sewers at home on low, piecework, rates of pay. Such workers are easily hired and fired and have no protection over their working conditions. Many are employed in contravention of government employment regulations. Yet there is no shortage of candidates for jobs in these fast-growing industries in some developing countries. Factory employment is often regarded as preferable to un- or underemployment in a poverty-stricken rural environment. A factory job does provide otherwise unattainable income and some degree of individual freedom. Often the wages earned are a crucial part of the family's income and there is much family pressure on young daughters to seek work in the city clothing factories or in the EPZs.

Too often, this argument is used as an excuse by buyers and retailers to avoid responsibility for clothing workers and their working conditions. As many highly publicized cases over many years have shown, this is an immensely problematic industry from a labour and human rights perspective. For example, while fire hazards in developed country clothing factories have been largely eradicated,

> [t]here are more fires in garment factories than ever before. The danger has merely been outsourced to countries where casualties are reported in numbers rather than by name, and often not at all.

> Fires continue to sweep through the rag trade ... Time and again retrospective inspections (surely the ultimate example of shutting the stable door far too late) reveal the same depressing reality. Young female garment workers without unions to represent them or the confidence to raise safety issues are locked into factories to fulfil Western orders.[10]

The deaths of more than 1100 workers in a Bangladeshi building collapse in 2013 are just one of the most recent cases. We will return to the responses of clothing manufacturers, buyers and retailers in a later section of this chapter.

THE ROLE OF THE STATE

In developing economies, textiles and clothing manufacture have occupied a key position in national industrialization strategies. Hence, the kinds of import-substituting and export-oriented measures outlined in Chapter 6 have been applied extensively. But it is in the older-established producing countries of Europe and North America and, more recently, Japan, faced with increasingly severe competition from low-cost producers, that government intervention has been especially marked. The political sensitivity of these industries has forced governments to intervene in three major ways:

- to encourage *restructuring and rationalization* through the use of subsidies and adjustment programmes;
- to *stimulate* offshore assembly (e.g. by granting tariff concessions on imports of products assembled abroad using domestic materials) and through preferential trading agreements;
- to *protect* from competition from low-cost producers in developing countries.

This third strategy is intimately bound up with the Multi-Fibre Arrangement.

Changing rules: the demise of the Multi-Fibre Arrangement

On 1 January 2005, the clothing industries entered a new era. The special international framework, which had regulated virtually all trade in the industries for four decades (the Multi-Fibre Arrangement – MFA), ceased to exist. Trade in clothing (as well as in textiles) was no longer to be subject to import quotas. This represented a massive change in the rules of the game. Cries of anguish emanated from developed country producers, fearing annihilation through competition from developing country producers, especially in Asia, most of all from China. On the other hand, developed country retailers were more sanguine, viewing with enthusiasm the prospect of being able to buy their garments more cheaply. But it was not only developed country producers that feared the repercussions of the MFA abolition. Many developing countries had been able to survive in these industries only because they had some degree of quota protection.

Initially formulated, in 1962, as the Long-Term Arrangement to cover cotton textiles, the framework was broadened in 1973 as the *Multi-Fibre Arrangement* (MFA).[11] From then until January 2005, the MFA regulated most of the world trade in textiles and clothing. Its provisions and their implementation – and their avoidance – were major factors in redrawing the global map of these industries.

The MFA was initially negotiated for a limited period of four years from January 1974. Its principal aim was to create 'orderly' development of trade in textiles and clothing that would benefit *both* developed and developing countries. Access to developed country markets was to increase at an annual average rate of 6 per cent, although this was far below the 15 per cent sought by the developing countries. At the same time, the developed countries were to have safeguards to protect the 'disruption' of their domestic markets. Within the MFA, individual quotas were negotiated setting precise limits on the quantity of textiles and clothing that could be exported from one country to another. For every single product, a quota was specified beyond which no further imports were allowed.

In practice it was the disruptive, rather than the liberalizing, aspect which was at the forefront of trading relationships in these industries. The MFA was renegotiated, or extended, four times (in 1977, 1982, 1986, 1991). Progressively, the MFA became more, rather than less, restrictive. Both the EU and the USA negotiated much tighter import quotas on a bilateral basis with most of the leading developing country exporters and, in several cases, also invoked anti-dumping procedures.

The effects of the MFA on world trade in textiles and clothing have been immense. Without doubt, it greatly restricted the rate of growth of exports from developing countries. A major initial beneficiary of this dampening of the relative growth of developing country exports was the USA, which increased its penetration of European textiles and clothing markets during the 1970s. During the early

1980s, however, it was the European producers who greatly increased their presence in the US market.

An inevitable consequence of the increased restrictiveness of developing country exports of textiles and garments was a parallel increase in evasive action. This took a variety of forms, for example:

- A producing country which had reached its quota ceiling in one product would switch to another item.
- False labelling was used to change the apparent country of origin (an illegal act).
- Firms relocated some of their production to countries which were not signatories to the MFA or whose quota was not fully used by domestic producers.

As a result, the entire clothing industry of some developing countries was, in effect, created by MFA quotas.

In 1995, the regulation of trade in textiles and clothing was incorporated into the WTO, with the MFA being phased out over a 10-year period (1995–2004), but in three stages. However, the process was 'heavily back-loaded, putting most of the difficult liberalization off to the future'.[12] Finally, on 1 January 2005, the MFA was abolished. But, of course, this was not the end of the story. Both the USA and the EU set up monitoring procedures and negotiated new import quotas with China, which lasted until the end of 2008.

The final phasing out of quotas in 2008 coincided with the global recession, which severely dampened down clothing exports and made it difficult to assess the long-term impact of the abolition of the MFA.[13]

Inevitably, most of the concern, voiced by both developed and developing country clothing producers focused on China, which appeared to be the most likely beneficiary of MFA abolition. The empirical evidence presented earlier tends to bear this out (see Figure 14.3). China's share of world clothing exports doubled to 37 per cent. But there were also other 'winners', notably Bangladesh and Vietnam, as well as countries in close proximity to large markets, such as Turkey. For example, the Moroccan garment industry has successfully increased its penetration of the fast fashion segment of the European market.[14]

CORPORATE STRATEGIES IN THE CLOTHING INDUSTRIES

A highly fragmented industry – but increasing retailer dominance

The *manufacture* of clothing is heavily fragmented, with a myriad of small and medium-sized firms, many of which operate as subcontractors within a multi-tiered system.[15] *Control* of the industry, however, lies increasingly in the hands of large buyers and retailers. Indeed, the most significant structural change in the clothing industry is, without doubt, the fact that the production circuit has become increasingly dominated by the purchasing policies of the major multiple and specialist retailing chains, as well as by the buying agents who integrate large numbers of different retail customers. The clothing production network is now overwhelming *buyer driven*.

An inexorable growth in offshore production

In many cases, domestic sourcing of clothing has virtually disappeared; in a few others it remains important, though to varying degrees. This shifting balance between domestic sourcing of garments and offshore sourcing by the large companies has occurred over several decades and taken a variety of forms.

For example, *Levi Strauss*, the US jeans company, once a major domestic producer, has gone entirely offshore. Its recent history is emblematic of the geographical transformation of the clothing industry in developed countries. In the 1980s, 70 per cent of Levi's global workforce of 40,000 was employed in the USA, 17 per cent in Europe and only 5 per cent in Asia. In the late 1980s, the company began to make massive cuts in its operations in the USA and Europe and to shift more of its operations to lower-cost locations. In 1998, the company closed 13 of its plants in the USA and 4 in Europe, shedding 7400 jobs. The following year (1999) Levi closed half of its remaining 22 US factories and eliminated 30 per cent of its US labour force (almost 6000 jobs). At the same time, the company reduced the proportion of its production manufactured in-house to 30 per cent (in 1980, Levi had manufactured 90 per cent of its own production). In 2002, a further six manufacturing plants were closed in the USA, with the loss of more than 3000 jobs. Finally, in 2003, the company announced the closure of its last four remaining North American manufacturing and finishing plants, with a loss of a further 2000 jobs.[16]

One US garment company bucking the offshoring trend is *American Apparel*, established in 1998 by a Canadian-born entrepreneur, which boasts of its all-American production from its 'campus' in downtown Los Angeles – 'the largest apparel manufacturing facility in North America'.[17] American Apparel operates a fully vertically integrated system, from design through manufacturing to distribution using US-based labour, paying higher wages in better working conditions than competitors using offshore contractors. The business model relies heavily not only on the advantages of being close to its market to respond quickly to demand changes, but also on its appeal to the consciences of consumers, branding itself as 'sweatshop free'. Whether or not this is a viable business operation in the long term is open to question. As of 2013, the company was losing money.[18]

Among European clothing firms, the adoption of offshore production strategies has been most pronounced among German and British companies. Already by the

1970s around 70 per cent of all the (then West) German clothing firms, including some quite small ones, were involved in some kind of offshore production. Roughly 45 per cent of the arrangements involved international subcontracting; a further 40 per cent involved varying degrees of equity involvement by German firms in local partners. The case of the high-end German fashion company *Hugo Boss* provides a good example. Faced with high domestic production costs in Germany, Hugo Boss has long used offshore subcontractors. In 1989, Hugo Boss acquired an American garments producer, Joseph & Feiss of Cleveland, Ohio. In 1991, Hugo Boss itself was acquired by Marzotto, the Italian textiles and clothing group, but is now two-thirds owned by a European private equity investor, Permira. In addition to sourcing an increasing proportion of its garments overseas, the company also moved strongly into retailing, initially through franchising its brand name in around 200 stores worldwide but increasingly controlling more of its own retail outlets.[19]

Until very recently, Italian firms were the major exception to this strong shift of production to low-cost foreign locations by European producers. Italy was the only major European country whose clothing industries continued to perform relatively well in the teeth of intensive global competition. In general, Italian producers have pursued a strategy of product specialization and fashion orientation with the aim of avoiding dependence upon those types of garments most strongly affected by low-cost competition. This involved mainly small firms in a decentralized production system, capitalizing on the traditional reputation of specific towns or regions, such as Como, Prato, and the like. More recently, however, some Italian firms have established international licensing or production agreements for high-fashion and designer-label products. Armani, for example, is now using some Chinese firms, although the company claims that most of its production remains in Italy. As a result, the localized Italian 'clothing districts' are undergoing major change.[20]

Benetton is the best-known Italian company to have developed an especially distinctive strategy. Benetton very much sold itself as an 'Italian' company, franchising thousands of stores around the world. Whereas most European firms shifted much of their production to Asia, most of Benetton's garments were, until recently, still manufactured in Europe, mostly in Italy, though not by Benetton itself. The company used around 500 subcontractors for its actual production, many of which were located in the Veneto region of north-east Italy. This system gave it considerable flexibility in responding to changing demand for its garments, Benetton itself performing only those functions – mainly design, cutting, dyeing and packing – considered crucial to maintain quality and cost efficiency.

For a long time, Benetton was the only major European clothing firm in the fashion–basic sector to have retained the bulk of its manufacturing operations in a higher-cost European location rather than relocating to low-cost Asian locations. It did so by producing a relatively limited range of garments, but differentiating them primarily on the basis of colour. But this changed. By 2007, Benetton was aiming to produce 80 per cent of its clothing outside Italy, mostly in Hungary, Croatia and Tunisia.[21] But Benetton is no longer the industry leader it was, not least because it has failed to keep up with new developments in the *fast fashion* sector.

The acknowledged pioneer of fast fashion is the Spanish firm *Inditex*, especially through its leading brand, *Zara*. Inditex is headquartered in La Coruña in north-west Spain, the traditional focus of the Iberian textile industry. Inditex has developed a highly distinctive business model. According to the Inditex chairman, it is 'all about reducing response time. In fashion, stock is like food. It goes bad quick.'[22]

> At Inditex's heart is a vertical integration of design, just-in-time production, delivery and sales. Some 300 designers work at the firm's head office … Fabric is cut in-house and then sent to a cluster of several hundred local co-operatives for sewing … Production is deliberately carried out in small batches to avoid oversupply. While there is some replenishment of stock, most lines are replaced quickly with yet more new designs rather than more of the same. This helps to create a scarcity value … The result is that Zara's production cycles are much faster than those of its nearest rival, Sweden's Hennes & Mauritz (H & M). An entirely new Zara garment takes about five weeks from design to delivery; a new version of an existing model can be in the shops within two weeks. In a typical year, Zara launches some 11,000 new items, compared with the 2,000 to 4,000 from companies like H & M or America's giant casual-fashion chain, GAP.[23]

In other words, not only does Zara use a manufacturing model long ago jettisoned by the major US and European garments companies (i.e. producing a large proportion of its garments in-house), but also it operates within a highly volatile part of the fashion–basic sector of the industry. Zara achieves dramatic results by combining highly efficient production and distribution logistics with a continuous monitoring of the fashion scene. In 2008, Zara's parent company, Inditex, became the world's largest clothing retailer.[24]

However, more recently, the geography of Zara's production network has become more diverse:

> According to Inditex, in 2006, 64% of the group's production was carried out in Europe and neighbouring countries while 34% was carried out in Asia. Products with a greater fashion component were manufactured in the group's own factories or by suppliers 'whose processes are significantly integrated with the group's dynamics' …

> China seems to account for 12% of Zara's production, less than that of its rivals … but still considerable for a firm with the reputation of being an anomaly to globalization … Today, Zara stores are full of garments made

in India, Pakistan, Bangladesh, Sri Lanka and Indonesia. And the supply chains of Zara also include Morocco, Bulgaria, Lithuania and Turkey.[25]

Even so, 50 per cent of Inditex's production still takes place in Spain, Portugal and Morocco.[26] In that respect, Inditex's strategy contrasts significantly with that of its nearest rival in the fast fashion sector, the Swedish company *H & M* (Hennes & Mauritz). H & M sources 80 per cent of its clothing from Asia and only 20 per cent from Europe and is looking at sourcing from Latin America and Africa for the first time. Nevertheless, H & M claims to be able to get its clothes into its stores as quickly as Inditex.[27]

Squeezing the suppliers

The highly concentrated purchasing power of the large retail chains and the major clothing brands gives them enormous leverage over clothing manufacturers. As Figure 14.7 shows, the modern 'lean' manufacturer–retailer system differs markedly from the traditional system, where the market was dominated largely by the mass market retailers and demand was for long production runs of standardized garments at low cost:

> Two to four fashion 'seasons' each year was once an industry standard for garment retailing; now the norm is six to eight, and the Spanish retailer Zara has led the move toward a model that puts out twelve seasons a year. Quick response means shorter production lead times – that is, the period from when the order is received to when the garments must be shipped off to the market ... these lead times are falling significantly, in step with the shorter seasonal cycles ...
>
> Fashion is fickle ... buyers typically demand rapid response flexibility from suppliers ... Lead firms are placing orders for smaller initial batches of garments and then following up with rapid reorders for styles that sell well.[28]
>
> A few years ago, a factory supplying a major retailer would have expected to manufacture 40,000 garments across four styles for 20 weeks. Today, it will be lucky to get commitment from the retailer to manufacture four styles at 500 garments per week for just five weeks. The remaining 30,000 will be ordered at the last minute, when the design team has worked out whether the mainstream consumer has been inspired [by the latest 'celebrity'].[29]

A further trend is for the big companies to use a smaller number of suppliers from fewer locations. In this respect, the demise of the MFA is having a considerable impact:

(a) Traditional retailing–apparel supplier relations

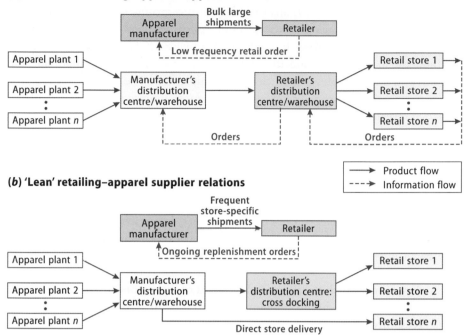

Figure 14.7 **Changing relationships between garment manufacturers and retailers**

Source: based on Abernathy et al., 1999: Figures 3.1, 4.1

Industry sources claim that large retailers and manufacturers such as Gap, JC Penney, Liz Claiborne and Wal-Mart that once sourced from 50 or more countries will source from only 10-15 countries when quotas no longer constrain their sourcing decisions.[30]

The 2008 recession accelerated this trend: the number of suppliers serving the US clothing market fell by 70 per cent in 2008[31] as buyers focused their purchasing more selectively.

Being squeezed: responding to external pressures to improve labour conditions

While big companies increasingly squeeze their suppliers, the companies themselves are becoming increasingly squeezed from external sources. There is no other global industry that is the focus of so much controversy over factory working conditions and labour exploitation. The persistence of the kinds of conditions in developing country garment factories, outlined earlier, explains why the number of labour and human rights pressure groups involved continues to grow. Organizations such as Oxfam, labour unions and anti-sweatshop organizations such as Sweatfree, the Clean Clothes Campaign (CCC), No Sweat, Labour Behind the Label (LBL), and the like, have become immensely important and effective in exerting pressure on clothing companies.[32] The squeeze on clothing firms to behave more responsibly has become more intense with each case of bad practice revealed by such groups.

As a result of such concerted pressure over a number of years, the major clothing companies have undertaken to monitor the operations of their suppliers and subcontractors to remove illegal practices, especially employment of child labour. The major UK retailers have promised to end contracts with firms that contravene their guidelines. Similarly in the USA, leading clothing firms (including Nike, Liz Claiborne, Nicole Miller, L.L. Bean and Reebok) subscribe to a voluntary code of conduct to eliminate domestic and overseas sweatshop conditions and to back the Fair Labor Association:

> Any brand worth its salt boasts big teams of inspectors: in 2009, Nike boasted 80 in-house employees working in Corporate Social Responsibility ... by 2001 Gap had 115 compliance officers keeping a beady eye on 4,000 factories ... Wal-Mart conducts 16,000 social audits across its supply chain every year, Tesco increased the number of 'high-risk' sites audited from 87 per cent to 94.7 per cent in 2010.[33]

Nevertheless, new cases of labour exploitation and factory safety in subcontracting factories continually appear in the media. The process of monitoring and detection is difficult. It is even more difficult to monitor the practice of home-working which is highly exploitative of the most disadvantaged groups who work at home for minimal rates of pay and no benefits. But in an industry as fragmented and organizationally complex as clothing this is an immense task: 'Codes of conduct are awfully slippery. Unlike laws, they are not enforceable.'[34] Despite such confusion, and continuing evasion of such codes by some companies, there is no doubt that some progress has been made in improving conditions in these industries, although problems certainly remain. A 2001 initiative, 'Better Factories Cambodia', for example – linked to the ILO and supported financially by such companies as Nike, Reebok, Levi Strauss, Wal-Mart and H & M – is being heralded as a model initiative in the industry.

And yet ... As the 2013 factory collapse in Dhaka, Bangladesh, demonstrated, immense problems remain. This was such an egregious case that it may well produce substantial change. In the immediate aftermath of the tragedy in which over 1100 workers died, various commitments were made by some of the Western firms involved in sourcing garments there:

Following the disaster, which involved manufacturers working for up to 40 companies … more than 50 brands have signed up to a legally binding building safety agreement backed by international trade union IndustriaALL and the Bangladeshi government … Under the terms of the agreement, brands including H & M and Marks & Spencer, as well as Primark, have each agreed to contribute up to $500,000 (£325,000) a year towards rigorous independent factory inspections and the installation of fire safety measures.[35]

But not all firms signed up to the agreement, including Wal-Mart and Gap, for example, as well as the large UK group Arcadia. There is still some way to go to improve conditions in this industry. The squeeze will continue.

REGIONALIZING PRODUCTION NETWORKS IN THE CLOTHING INDUSTRIES

Much of the explanation for the recent global shifts in the clothing industries can be explained in terms of the trade-off between labour costs on the one hand and the need for market proximity on the other. The result is increasing *regionalization* of clothing production networks.

Asia

Japanese clothing firms were among the earliest to make extensive use of offshore subcontracting. During the 1960s and 1970s Japanese companies established outsourcing arrangements in Hong Kong, Taiwan, South Korea and Singapore. Their production was mostly exported to the USA and not to Japan's own domestic market. The Japanese general trading companies (*sogo shosha*) were at the leading edge of these international outsourcing developments, often using minority investments in local firms. Probably 90 per cent of the remaining Japanese overseas garments operations are still located in East and South East Asia. Uniqlo is a major example of this.

More recently, firms from other East Asian countries have established large and complex clothing production networks.[36] For example, the Chinese trading and logistics company Li and Fung controls and coordinates all stages of the clothing supply chain, from design and production planning, through finding suppliers of materials and manufacturers of products, to the final stages of quality control, testing and the logistics of distribution (see Chapter 17). The company also 'produces' private-label brands for retailers which lack the resources to do this, especially smaller companies. By organizing and managing supply chains over the Internet for such smaller retail chains Li & Fung can combine many small orders and so achieve economies of scale in production and distribution.[37] China, Bangladesh and Vietnam are the major sources for Li & Fung. Other examples include the Taiwanese company Nien Hsing, the world's largest jeans manufacturer, and the Chinese company Luen Thai Holdings which

> has created a 'supply-chain city' in Dongguan (Guangdong Province in southern China) … including a two-million square foot factory, a 300 room hotel, a dormitory for the factory's 4,000 workers, and product development centers. The factory permits apparel manufacturer Liz Claiborne and other Luen Thai customers to work in a single location, so that designers can meet with technicians from the factory and fabric mills to plan production far more efficiently … Luen Thai is developing a second supply chain city in Qing Yuan (also in Guangdong Province) … [and] … maintains supply chain centers in the US and the Philippines.[38]

The key to the internal transformation of the industry in Asia lies in the changing strategies of the northern tier East Asian NIEs. As the clothing industry in Asia has matured – and especially in response to shifting market conditions – its organization has acquired a particular 'geometry', namely that of *triangle manufacturing*:

> The essence of triangle manufacturing … is that US (or other overseas) buyers place their orders with the NIE manufacturers they have sourced from in the past, who in turn shift some or all of the requested production to affiliated offshore factories in low-wage countries (e.g. China, Indonesia, or Guatemala). These offshore factories can be wholly owned subsidiaries of the NIE manufacturers, joint-venture partners, or simply independent overseas contractors. The triangle is completed when the finished goods are shipped directly to the overseas buyer … Triangle manufacturing thus changes the status of NIE manufacturers from established suppliers for US retailers and designers to 'middlemen' in buyer-driven commodity chains that can include as many as 50 to 60 exporting countries.

> Triangle manufacturing is socially embedded. Each of the East Asian NIEs has a different set of preferred countries where they set up their new factories … These production networks are explained in part by social and cultural factors (e.g. ethnic or familial ties, common language), as well as by unique features of a country's historical legacy.[39]

Asia remains the most globally connected region of clothing production. However, Asia has also become a major market in its own right: in 1980 less than 5 per cent of Asian garments trade was intra-regional; today it is around 22 per cent.

North America

Traditionally, the US clothing market was served primarily by domestic production. But, in the past few decades, the market has become increasingly dominated
by imports from low-cost producing countries, initially in Asia (notably China)
but also from Mexico and the Caribbean.[40] Most of these imports are organized through the buyer–retailer–supplier complex that has become increasingly
important.

Two sets of forces reinforce the development of regional clothing production
networks in North America:

- The trade-off between minimizing production costs and maximizing speed of
  access to consumer markets has become more critical. Proximity to markets
  has become a key factor in determining the geography of clothing production
  as the dominant buyers/retailers insist on fast product turnover.
- The development of regional economic initiatives by the USA, in particular the
  signing of the NAFTA and the preferential arrangements with the Caribbean
  countries (the Caribbean Basin Initiative), has reinforced the benefits of geographical proximity driven by changing buyer–supplier relationships.

Initially, apart from the rapid growth in Chinese imports, the major growth area for
clothing imports into the USA was the Caribbean Basin, whose share of the total
grew from less than 3 per cent in 1981 to 13 per cent in 1995. During the same
period, Mexico's share of US clothing imports grew from 3 per cent to 7 per cent.
However, by 2000, Mexico had overtaken China to become the leading source of
clothing imports into the USA, a dramatic turnaround indeed – or so it seemed.

Under the terms of the NAFTA, tariffs and quotas on clothing imported from
Mexico to the USA were eliminated. In addition, under the rules of origin for
garments in the NAFTA, clothing must be cut and sewn from fabric made from
fibre originating in North America in order to qualify for duty-free access. This
provided a stimulus for the development of a more integrated industry within
North America. Thus, 'through NAFTA, apparel and textile manufacturers are
acquiring the freedom and flexibility to create – duty and quota free – transborder
production networks that best suit their individual needs'.[41]

Because Mexico's comparative advantage lies in clothing production while the
US comparative advantage lies in textile manufacture, synthetic fibre production and
retailing, a clear division of labour emerged. The combination of the NAFTA and
the benefits of geographical proximity, together with low production costs, have
stimulated many clothing firms in the USA to source more of their garments from
Mexico.

The precise form of this geographical division of labour is still evolving.
Traditionally, Mexico's clothing industry was dominated by *maquiladora* production: simple sewing of garments made from imported fabrics and using extremely

cheap labour. In other words, it was dominated by the very basic operations in a vertically integrated system coordinated and regulated by US manufacturers and retailers. Although this is still the dominant mode of operation, there are signs of rather more sophisticated arrangements in which Mexican firms perform some of the higher-level functions in the production chain. There is some evidence of the development of *full-package production* in which selected local manufacturers are responsible for the entire process of clothing production. Figure 14.8 shows an example of this development in the Torreón district of Coahuila in northern Mexico. However, even this most developed full-package cluster in Mexico has 'experienced significant declines in both production and employment in recent years'.[42]

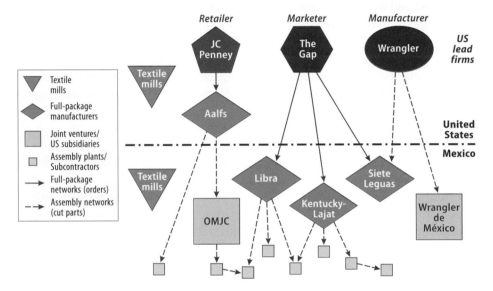

Figure 14.8   **Development of 'full-package' garments production in Torreón, Mexico**

Source: based on Bair and Gereffi, 2001: Figure 2

The rapid growth of Mexico as a local source of clothing imports into the USA has had a significant impact on the Caribbean Basin producers, to whom the level of preferential access to the North American market under NAFTA is denied. In particular, the Caribbean countries must still pay import duty on the value added in the clothing assembly process, a contentious issue for these producers.

But Mexico's greatly increased share of US clothing imports has proved to be ephemeral. In 2011, Mexico was the fifth-largest source of clothing imports into the USA, behind China, Vietnam, Indonesia and Bangladesh. Since the abolition of the MFA, the huge shadow of China and other Asian producers hangs over the North American clothing industries. China's share of US clothing imports had already once again overtaken those of Mexico by 2003, two years before the end of the MFA, and by 2011 Chinese clothing imports into the USA were more than eight times greater than Mexico's. Clearly, within the North American clothing market, the battle between low production costs and market proximity is still being waged.

Europe

As we have seen in earlier chapters, Europe is the most highly integrated regional market in the world and its clothing industries are no exception.[43] Historically, most European clothing production was located in the leading European economies themselves, notably France, Germany, Italy and the UK. But the clothing industries of these countries have experienced massive decline and restructuring. Some of this has been caused, of course, by the rise of the low-cost Asian producers. But much of the restructuring is the result of the geographical reconfiguration of clothing production within what might be called 'greater Europe': the EU28, together with non-member countries in Eastern and Central Europe (ECE), the CIS and the Mediterranean rim.

Through the 1980s and 1990s, European clothing production networks became geographically more extensive, but within an expanded regional context. This is a situation created by the intersection of the changing sourcing strategies of clothing firms and the changing political agreements with ECE and Mediterranean countries, some of which became – or will become in the future – members of the EU. It is a pattern with some clear geographical consistencies but also with considerable volatility, as some supplier countries lose their dominance and others emerge.

As in the case of Mexico and the Caribbean countries, the advantages of geographical proximity in the clothing industries of Europe (in terms of their effect on speed of delivery) can offset lower production costs at more distant locations: 'It takes 22 days by water to reach the UK from China, while products from Turkey can take as little as five days to arrive.'[44] Of course, both sets of forces operate. The continued attraction of low-cost sourcing of garments is shown most graphically by China's increased share of the EU clothing market, from 14 per cent in 1995 to 24 per cent in 2011. Thus, although a substantial proportion of the EU's sourcing of clothing still takes place in Asia, the countries on the immediate geographical periphery of the EU, like Turkey and Morocco,[45] have become tightly integrated into the production networks of European clothing manufacturers and the purchasing networks of European retailers.

This process of regionalization of European clothing production networks became increasingly common from the early 1980s, when Outward Processing Trade (OPT) provisions were introduced by the EU. These established import quotas between the EU and individual countries in Eastern and Southern Europe, which facilitated significant patterns of production relationship between EU clothing firms (both producers and retailers) and clothing manufacturers in lower-cost countries nearby.

The regional reconfiguration of the clothing industries in Europe, therefore, can be summarized as follows:[46]

- The phasing out of quotas in the final stages of the MFA (from 1994) favoured the ECE and Mediterranean countries far more than the Asian suppliers: 'Between 1991 and 1995 OPT quotas for the ECE grew at the rate of 36.2%, whereas those for Asia were growing at only 6.9%' (p. 2202).
- A series of preferential trade agreements was signed between the EU and applicant countries in the early 1990s, which facilitated greater integration of the region's clothing industries.
- 'Among the top ten suppliers … ECE and the Mediterranean countries increased their share of EU apparel imports from 26.8% in 1989 to 30.8% in 2000, with Romania, Tunisia, Morocco, and Poland being the largest suppliers from the region' (p. 2194). By 2005, their share had risen to 37 per cent.[47]
- 'ECE producers have become … much more important sources for the EU apparel market during the 1990s. Romania, Hungary, and Poland played the leading role in the early part of the 1990s; Bulgaria and, to a lesser extent, Slovakia, have also become increasingly important … albeit from smaller bases' (pp. 2194–5).
- Turkey has emerged as the second most important individual clothing supplier to the EU after China.

The processes of organizational and geographical restructuring of the clothing industries of 'greater Europe' will continue to produce changes in the sourcing map and could well see further inroads by Asian competitors. However,

> to the extent that production costs continue to shape the geographies of export production in conjunction with other demands on buyers and producers, such as proximity to market, time-to-delivery, and garment quality, the 'golden belts' of European clothing production may continue to supply EU markets as alternatives to the relentless pursuit of lower cost production elsewhere in the global economy.

> Yet the extent to which such cross-border geographies can withstand competitive pressures remains an open question … there is evidence of ECE shares of core EU markets seeing a decline in some product areas. In others, however, where sourcing strategies are different, time to delivery is more critical and quality considerations may be high. The result is that cross-border arrangements have been introduced as one way of tapping lower cost but regionalized production possibilities.[48]

NOTES

1   Fröbel et al. (1980).
2   See Gereffi (1994) and subsequent writings.
3   Abernathy et al. (1999: 9), Siegle (2011).
4   See, for example, Klein (2000), Rivoli (2005), Siegle (2011).
5   Detailed accounts of technology in the clothing industries are provided by Abernathy et al. (1999) and OECD (2004: chapter 4).
6   OECD (2004: 139).
7   Raworth and Kidder (2009).
8   See the contributions in Hale and Wills (2005).
9   Ross (2002).
10 Siegle (2011: 49).
11 See Hoekman and Kostecki (1995: chapter 8), ILO (2005), OECD (2004), Rivoli (2005).
12 Hoekman and Kostecki (1995: 209).
13 See Bair (2008).
14 Rossi (2013).
15 Hurley (2005: Figure 5.1).
16 *Financial Times* (26 September 2003).
17 Company website.
18 *Financial Times* (18 November 2013).
19 *Financial Times* (4 December 2012).
20 Dunford (2006).
21 *Financial Times* (23 July 2004).
22 Quoted in Siegle (2011: 22).
23 *The Economist* (18 June 2005).
24 *Guardian* (12 August 2008).
25 Tokatli (2008: 34).
26 *Financial Times* (14 September 2012).
27 *Financial Times* (20 May 2013).
28 Raworth and Kidder (2009: 174).
29 Siegle (2011: 20).
30 Appelbaum (2008: 71).
31 *Financial Times* (10 December 2008).
32 See Hale and Wills (2005), Siegle (2011).
33 Siegle (2011: 76).
34 Klein (2000: 430).
35 *Observer* (23 June 2013).
36 See Appelbaum (2008).
37 Schary and Skjøtt-Larsen (2001: 383–4).
38 Appelbaum (2008: 73).
39 Gereffi (1996: 97–8).
40 See Abernathy et al. (1999, 2004), Bair (2002, 2006), Bair and Gereffi (2003), Gereffi and Memedovic (2004), Gereffi et al. (2002), Kessler (1999).

41   Kessler (1999: 569).

42   Bair (2006: 2240).

43   Bair (2006), Begg et al. (2003), Palpacuer et al. (2005), Smith et al. (2005, 2008).

44   *Financial Times* (30 August 2005).

45   Rossi (2013).

46   Begg et al. (2003).

47   Smith et al. (2008: Table 1).

48   Smith et al. (2008: 304).

Want to know more about this chapter? Visit the companion website at **www.guilford.com/dickenGS7** for free access to author videos, suggested reading and practice questions to further enhance your study.

Fifteen

'WHEELS OF CHANGE': THE AUTOMOBILE INDUSTRY

ALL CHANGE?

The 2008 global financial crisis hit the automobile industry with cataclysmic force. Other than the financial services sector itself (see Chapter 16), no other major industry attracted such high-profile attention in the turmoil. Former corporate giants of the industry faced bankruptcy, massive corporate restructuring began to occur, especially in North America. Governments injected enormous financial assistance into the automobile industries within their territories to try to stem massive job losses and to ride out the crisis. All of this in what Peter Drucker once called 'the industry of industries'.[1] The internal combustion engine was, quite literally, the major engine of growth until the middle 1970s and is still seen as a key contributor to industrial development. The industry's significance lies in both its scale and in its linkages to many other manufacturing industries and services. Around 8 million people are employed directly in automobile production. If we add those involved in selling and servicing vehicles, we reach a total of up to 20 million workers.

The global automobile industry is made up of very large corporations, which have increasingly organized their activities on transnationally integrated lines. In so doing, they engage very closely – sometimes collaboratively, sometimes conflictually – with national governments, themselves anxious to establish, nurture or enhance automobile production within their territories. It is an industry in which, after decades of dominance by firms from developed economies, new global players – from India, from China, from South Korea – have arrived on the scene. The 'industry of industries' is beginning to look very different from the apparently stable picture of a few decades ago. Change is, indeed, in the air.

THE AUTOMOBILE PRODUCTION CIRCUIT

The automobile industry is an *assembly* industry, bringing together an immense number and variety of components. At the centre of the automobile production circuit (Figure 15.1) is the complex set of relationships between the assemblers of vehicles and the suppliers of components, which account for between 50 and 70 per cent of the cost price of the average car.[2] As Figure 15.1 shows, there are three major processes prior to final assembly: the manufacture of bodies, components, and engines and transmissions, which may be performed by the assemblers, as part of a vertically integrated sequence. However, there is a strong trend towards the de-verticalization of automobile production as assemblers pass more responsibility to the suppliers. Figure 15.1 shows just three tiers of suppliers, although there can be more.[3] First-tier suppliers supply major component systems direct to the assemblers and have significant R&D and design expertise. Second-tier suppliers generally produce to designs provided by the

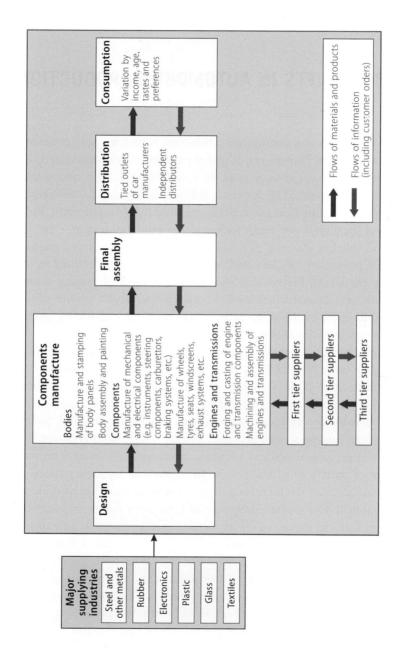

Figure 15.1   The automobile production circuit

assemblers or by the first-tier suppliers, while third-tier suppliers provide the more basic components. In essence, the automobile industry is a strongly *producer-driven* industry, as opposed to the predominantly buyer–driven nature of the clothing industries.

GLOBAL SHIFTS IN AUTOMOBILE PRODUCTION AND TRADE

Figure 15.2 shows that automobile production is very strongly concentrated geographically. Almost 70 per cent of global production is concentrated in just seven countries. Of these, China is now, by a very large margin, the world's leading automobile producer[4] (24.6 per cent), followed by Japan (13.7 per cent), Germany (8.5 per cent), South Korea (6.6 per cent), the USA (6.6 per cent), India (5.2 per cent) and Brazil (4.2 per cent). Today's global production map is the outcome of profound changes over the past five decades as new centres of production have emerged, particularly in Asia, and as older centres have declined in importance (notably the USA). Figure 15.3 shows these changes in graphic terms. Initially, by far the most dramatic development was the spectacular growth of the Japanese automobile industry. Most recently, it has been the remarkable growth of the Chinese automobile industry.

A high level of geographical concentration is also evident in the pattern of automobile trade (Figure 15.4). But, in this case, there are also huge differences in the balance of trade. On the one hand, the USA has an automobile trade *deficit* of $93 billion; on the other, Japan has an automobile trade *surplus* of $134 billion. In summary, an industry dominated in 1960 by the USA and, to a much lesser extent, Europe was transformed initially during the 1970s and 1980s by the spectacular growth of Japan as a leading automobile producer. This was reflected in terms of growth of production in Japan itself, of Japanese exports to the rest of the world, and of the increasing proportion of Japanese automobile production located abroad. The recent emergence of China as a major producer of automobiles may soon be enhanced by its increasing importance as an exporter of cars. In 2005, for the first time, China exported more cars than it imported, although it currently has a small trade deficit. At the same time, other potentially important new centres of automobile production and exports are emerging, notably in India and Russia. More broadly, the industry has become increasingly concentrated in the three major global regions of North America, Europe and East Asia. Much of this reconfiguration of global automobile production is related to developments at the 'macro-regional level', as we will see in the final section of this chapter.

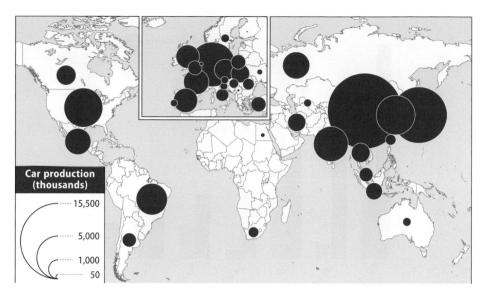

Figure 15.2   **Global production of passenger cars**

Source: calculated from OICA (International Organization of Motor Vehicle Manufacturers) statistics, 2013

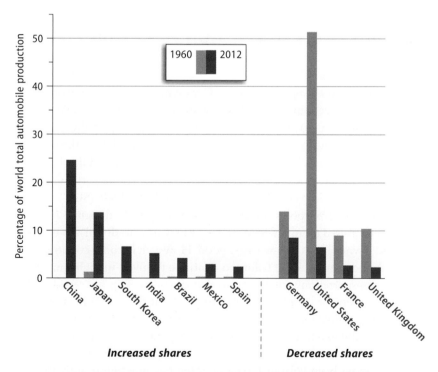

Figure 15.3   **Major changes in the relative importance of automobile producing countries**

Source: calculated from MVMA *World Motor Vehicle Data*; OICA statistics, 2013

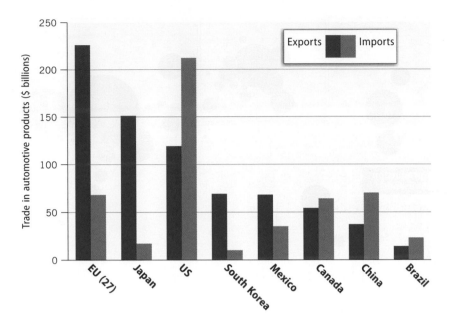

Figure 15.4   **The world's leading exporters and importers of automobiles**

Source: WTO, 2013: Table II.59

CHANGING PATTERNS OF CONSUMPTION

The intoxicating allure of private transportation has made the automobile one of the most significant of all *aspirational goods*. Car ownership offers (at least in theory) immense personal freedom to travel to places otherwise inaccessible (including travel to work, to shop, to engage in all kinds of recreation). It also – and just as importantly – embodies a complex range of symbolic attributes through which people can project their self-images, their social position, and indulge in the fantasies of driving. Certain kinds of vehicle become emblematic of particular lifestyles. The obvious example in recent years is the sports utility vehicle (SUV), which was rarely used for those purposes for which it was originally designed (how many SUV drivers ever used them off-road, or even knew how to do so?). In one respect, therefore, car ownership is a *discretionary* good. However, in some countries – notably the USA and the UK – the failure to continue to invest in high-quality, accessible public transportation systems means that car ownership has actually become an absolute *necessity* for people to be able to go about their daily lives.

Changes in personal income levels and in consumer tastes and preferences over time, as well as the extent to which car ownership has already spread through the population, are key variables in influencing the demand for automobiles. Such demand has always been volatile. However, it has become significantly more volatile – and more complex – in recent years. Three interrelated characteristics of the market for new automobiles are especially important:

- It is highly cyclical.
- There are long-term (secular) changes in demand.
- There is increasing market segmentation and fragmentation.

For several decades, demand has been growing very slowly in the mature markets of Europe and North America; the 2008 financial crisis produced a virtual overnight collapse. In the EU, car sales fell from 16 million in 2008 to around 12 million in 2013.[5] In particular, the demand for SUVs in the USA has plummeted. At one stage, SUVs (known as 'axles of evil' by critics of their environmental damage) accounted for three out of every four vehicles sold in the USA. In the mature markets in general there is huge excess capacity (at least 30 per cent: equivalent to several million automobiles). The major automobile manufacturers, therefore, are pinning their hopes on continuing high levels of growth in demand elsewhere, especially in Asia, Eastern Europe and Latin America.

Of these, it is in Asia that the major growth is expected to occur. According to World Bank data, the number of vehicles per 1000 population in the USA is almost 800; in India it is only 18 and in China it is around 58. The potential for growth is obvious. This can be seen already, especially in the cities of China where automobile sales have grown at such a phenomenal rate that it is now the largest automobile market in the world. In most developing countries the demand is primarily for small, cheap cars, but among the increasingly affluent segments of the population, demand for large luxury cars is growing at remarkable speed. While SUVs may have gone out of fashion in the USA this is not the case in China and India,[6] where their sales continue to grow apace. They, like such luxury marques as Mercedes or BMW, are significant aspirational goods among the newly rich.

The slow growth in demand for automobiles in the mature markets is more than merely cyclical. There are deeper *secular* or structural characteristics in these markets that limit future growth in car sales. Rapid growth in demand is associated with new demand. But as a market 'matures' and automobile ownership levels approach 'saturation', more and more car purchases become replacement purchases. In the mature automobile markets today some 85 per cent of total demand for automobiles is replacement demand. Such demand is generally slower growing, and also more variable, because it can be postponed. The increased reliability of cars – they do not corrode or break down as they did in the past – enhances this trend.

The third characteristic of today's automobile market is its increasing *segmentation and fragmentation*, as affluent consumers demand different types of vehicle for different purposes or want more sophisticated specifications, as the demographic profile of consumer markets changes, and as emerging customers demand basic (low-cost) cars:

> The need to respond to an increasingly diverse set of customers generated a large proliferation of segments and models ... the number of different vehicle models offered for sale in the US market alone doubled from 1980 to 1999, reaching 1,050 different models in 2000. In addition to the different models, there is also a myriad of features that can be added to each of the models.[7]

Taken together, the volatile and geographically uneven nature of demand for, and consumption of, automobiles create huge problems for the manufacturers. In particular, the continuing problems of excess capacity facing many of the companies result in changes in both *how* vehicles are manufactured and *where* they are manufactured.

TECHNOLOGICAL CHANGE IN THE AUTOMOBILE INDUSTRY

From mass production to lean production

The basic method of manufacturing automobiles changed very little between 1913, when Henry Ford introduced the moving assembly line, and the early 1970s. It was the mass production industry par excellence. This certainly brought the automobile within the reach of millions of customers. To do so, however, it had to produce a limited range of standardized products at huge production volumes – around 2 million vehicles per year – to obtain economies of scale, together with a very high level of worker specialization. It was the antithesis of craft production (Figure 4.17): automobile workers were, literally, cogs in the continuously running assembly-line machine.

This situation changed dramatically in the early 1970s. Highly efficient, and cost-competitive, Japanese automobile firms, led by Toyota, totally transformed the industry. What had appeared to be a stable, technologically mature industry, based on well-established technologies and organization of production, entered a phase of change (not unlike the first transformation in the early twentieth century when a mass production system displaced craft-based production). The basis of this second transformation was the displacement of mass production techniques by a system of *lean production* (see Figure 4.17). Within the broad framework of lean production systems, two of the most significant technological developments are related to the *architecture* of the vehicle.

The first is the increasing use of *shared platforms* between different vehicle models. Hitherto, each model produced by an individual manufacturer aimed at different market segments was distinctive not only on, but also below, the surface. By using a smaller number of common platforms, it is possible to share many components across what are, on the surface, very different vehicles (often in different price segments of the market). So, one of the paradoxes of the modern automobile industry is that, although the number of models has increased, such diversity is based on a much smaller number of platforms. Beauty, it seems, really may only be skin-deep as far as automobiles are concerned.

The second significant technological development linked to vehicle architecture is the *modularization* of certain components and the development of component *systems* (see Chapter 4). In the case of automobiles, a *module* is a group of components arranged close to each other within a vehicle, which constitute a coherent unit. A component *system* is a group of components 'located throughout a vehicle that operates together to provide a specific vehicle function. Braking systems, electrical systems and steering systems are examples.'[8] A modular and system-based architecture has become the norm. Hence,

> VW is lowering production costs and boosting commonality across a growing portfolio of diverse brands, while trying to avoid the pitfall that its cars end up looking the same ... [it uses] common, interchangeable modules – such as the crankshaft, bonnet or infotainment system – that can be assembled in a bewildering variety of combinations ... VW's modular system maintains only a few design parameters; for example the mounting position of the engine ... 'With the modular production toolbox we will in the future be able to build different models and different brands on the same production line.'[9]

The most significant developments in the technology of automobile manufacture, and of the automobiles themselves, are based upon the increasing use of *electronics*:

> The modern car has become completely dependent on electronics for engine management, satellite navigation, suspension controls and a raft of other enhancements from memory seats to rain-activated windscreen wipers. The next big step in the integration of electronics in the vehicle is the connection of all computers on a 'vehicle intranet' which will provide a simple and flexible installation with a minimum of wiring ... it is believed that electronics will continue to grow in all cars, accounting for more than 30% of a vehicle's value in the executive class to around 20% in 3-door hatchbacks.[10]

However, the very rapid introduction of complex electronic systems into vehicles poses problems for an industry whose expertise is in different areas. Not only does this make automobile manufacturers more dependent on electronics and software suppliers, but also 'the electronics in the car bring six or seven times more faults than normal mechanical parts'.[11] Problems of reliability, and their impact on brand image, have become important again, as in earlier stages of technological change.

The increased complexity of vehicle production produces huge pressures on materials costs, which have escalated in recent years:

> Steel, the price of which has nearly doubled over the last year, is the biggest single component in cars, which typically use 700kg to 800kg of the metal per unit. Car makers are also struggling with the surging cost of platinum, which they use in catalytic converters – up 135 per

cent since the beginning of 2005 – and plastics, which are rising in tandem with higher oil prices.[12]

As a result, automobile manufacturers are searching for ways of reducing the amounts of materials used. For example, Toyota is planning 'to reduce the thickness of resins it uses in its cars by more than 30 per cent, and to cut its use of sheet steel by 20 per cent'.[13]

Changing the product: the search for cleaner, more efficient cars

The drive for more efficient production processes is one part of the challenge facing automobile manufacturers. The other (not unrelated) challenge is to produce different kinds of vehicle to meet the pressures of environmental regulation on emissions and to reduce the amount (and type) of fuel used in cars that consumers are prepared to buy. Three major new technologies are being developed:[14]

- *Hybrid cars*: a combination of a conventional internal combustion engine and a battery which recharges from energy produced by the car.
- *Plug-in cars*: hybrid or pure electric cars which can be recharged using a plug.
- *Hydrogen fuel cells*: electric cars powered by hydrogen fuel cells.

Although all the major manufacturers are engaged in each of these areas, so far only hybrids have had a significant impact. The widespread use of purely electric-driven cars has been inhibited by the limited range of the batteries. However, a huge amount of research and investment is going into the development of more reliable and longer-range batteries by automobile and electronics manufacturers. Now, 'for the first time, all of the world's major manufacturers are embracing electric or hybrid models, suggesting that the industry is reaching a tipping point'.[15]

A rather different product focus is on small, cheap-to-make and cheap-to-run cars primarily, though not exclusively, for developing country markets. Some, like the Renault Dacia Logan, are produced by developed country manufacturers, though usually in a variety of developing countries. Others reflect the emergence of substantial local firms, especially in China and India. In China, the Chery QQ3 sold at less than $5000, but it is in India that the most ambitious project has been developed: the Nano produced by the Indian firm Tata. The Nano claimed to be the world's cheapest car, advertised as the 'one-lakh car' – half the cost of the cheapest car in India. Of course, the production of a cheap, mass market car is far from new: think of the Ford Model T or the VW Beetle and their many successors. But a combination of stagnating developed country markets and the attractions of tapping into the huge potential first-time buyer market in developing countries has intensified the pressures to do so.

THE ROLE OF THE STATE

Protection and stimulation

Throughout the history of the automobile industry the state has always played a key role, notably in two respects:

- determining the *degree of access* to its domestic market, including the terms under which foreign firms are permitted to establish production plants;
- establishing the kind of *support provided by the state* to its domestic firms and the extent to which the state *discriminates* against foreign firms.

Use of tariff and non-tariff barriers against automobile imports has been pervasive in virtually all countries at various times, although the level of tariffs has fallen enormously. Today, few developed market economies operate particularly high tariffs against automobiles. Tariffs are substantially higher, though unevenly so, in the developing markets. Far more prevalent has been the continued use of various NTBs, including import quotas.

The specific geographical configuration of the automobile industry is influenced not just by the *level* of tariffs or quotas, but also by frequently used *differential* tariffs and quotas between assembled vehicles and components. States may levy high tariffs on imported vehicles but lower tariffs on imported components in order to stimulate local production, especially where there is an insufficiently well-developed local components sector. *Local content* regulations have become particularly pervasive and have been especially influential in affecting automobile firms' policies towards their suppliers and in influencing the geographical configuration of the automobile component industries. The perceived importance of the automobile industry as a key developmental sector has meant that national governments have been extremely active in offering financial and other stimuli to producers to establish or maintain production within their territories. Indeed, the automobile industry is the paradigmatic example of competitive bidding and TNC–state bargaining (see Chapter 7).

The global financial crisis in 2008 dramatically changed the relationship between states and automobile firms. Outside the financial sector itself, the automobile industry became the highest-profile casualty of the drying up of credit and the collapse in consumer demand. The very scale and nature of the industry meant that states were virtually forced into massive intervention. Every major automobile producing country, but especially the USA and many in Europe, invested massive funds to try to save 'their' industries from extinction as the firms lobbied strenuously for support. The amount of money involved was astronomical: in the billions. Several governments, including the US, Germany, France and the UK governments, implemented a 'cash for clunkers' scheme, whereby consumers could receive a lump sum to trade in their older cars for new ones.

The auto assistance packages inevitably altered the relationship between governments and producers, at least temporarily. This was especially so in the USA where, in order to receive government aid, General Motors and Chrysler were forced to agree to draconian restructuring measures. As one headline put it, the US auto industry was forced to opt for the 'unthinkable': supervision by the government. But because of the transnationally integrated nature of automobile production, and the fact that the major producers have operations in many countries, action (or inaction) by one government has massive implications for other governments. The most egregious example involved the attempts by General Motors to restructure its European operations by selling a controlling interest to another firm. Because General Motors' major European plants were in its Opel division, based in Germany, the German government offered a huge amount of financial assistance. This immediately raised concerns among other European governments that General Motors' German plants (and jobs) would be favoured at the expense of those in the UK, Belgium and Spain.

As it turned out, General Motors ultimately decided against selling its European operations but still bargained with EU governments for state aid. At the same time, Renault was under pressure from the French government to retain production of the Clio in France instead of moving it to Turkey. Other EU governments argued that such pressure could contravene EU regulations on state aid.[16]

Environmental regulation

The state is also heavily involved through environmental and vehicle safety policies, each of which has profound implications for the design, technology and materials used in cars and, therefore, in their cost. Complying with changes in legislation can be especially problematical where it involves fundamental design changes. Legislation to control noxious emissions from automobile engines has become increasingly stringent. But such measures vary enormously from country to country. The EU has introduced legislation that will cut carbon emissions by 40 per cent by 2020 (compared with 2007) by insisting on tight controls on engine efficiency. In the USA, the Obama administration announced national limits on car exhaust emissions aimed at cutting CO_2 by 30 per cent by 2016. At the same time, the US government made billions of dollars available in cheap loans to auto manufacturers to build a new generation of fuel-efficient vehicles.

A more recent development within the EU is policy towards 'end-of-life' vehicles. The EU has issued a directive under which automobile manufacturers would have to cover the cost of recycling the vehicles they have manufactured. It is estimated that the annual cost of this operation in Europe will be around 2.1 billion euros. Manufacturers will have to ensure that recyclable components account for 85 per cent of each vehicle's weight.

CORPORATE STRATEGIES IN THE AUTOMOBILE INDUSTRY

Concentration and consolidation

From being an industry in which virtually every major producing country had large numbers of nationally based firms, the automobile industry is now dominated by a small number of huge transnational producers (Table 15.1). The seemingly permanent dominance of the US 'Big Three' has been destroyed by the rise, in particular, of Japanese and European (notably German) firms and more recently by the Korean firm Hyundai.

The consolidation of large numbers of automobile producers into a much smaller number of large TNCs is primarily the result of successive waves of merger and acquisition. For example,

> GM and Volkswagen bought their way to scale. GM snapped up companies in Europe, Britain, Australia and South Korea. VW swallowed Audi, Seat, Skoda, Lamborghini, Bentley and Porsche to build the most complete portfolio.[17]

During the 1990s, both General Motors and Ford acquired firms in the luxury market segments: Saab in the case of General Motors, Jaguar, Land Rover and Volvo in the case of Ford. In 1999, Renault acquired 44 per cent of the equity in the Japanese firm Nissan and also bought the South Korean firm Samsung. But the biggest acquisition, by far, was of the US firm Chrysler by the German-owned Daimler-Benz in 1998. In 2000, DaimlerChrysler acquired 34 per cent of

Table 15.1 The world league table of automobile manufacturers, 2012

Rank	Company	Headquarters country	No. of passenger cars produced
1	Volkswagen	Germany	8,576,964
2	Toyota	Japan	8,381,968
3	Hyundai	South Korea	6,761,074
4	General Motors	USA	6,608,567
5	Honda	Japan	4,078,376
6	Nissan	Japan	3,830,954
7	Ford	USA	3,123,340
8	PSA	France	2,554,059
9	Suzuki	Japan	2,483,721
10	Renault	France	2,302,769

Source: based on OICA statistics

Mitsubishi Motors. In 2002, General Motors acquired the Korean assets of the bankrupt Korean firm Daewoo.

Some of these consolidations were relatively short-lived. Most dramatic, though not unexpected, was the break-up of the DaimlerChrysler marriage in 2007. But the 2008 crisis resulted in even bigger changes. General Motors sold its Swedish luxury brand, Saab, and also its Hummer brand. Ford sold its Jaguar Land Rover business to the Indian company Tata in 2008 and also sold Volvo to the Chinese firm Geely. Chrysler was fully acquired by the Italian firm Fiat in 2014. However, not all growth has been through acquisition and merger. Toyota, for example, has grown entirely organically: 'Apart from scooping up Daihatsu to get small-car engineering and engines … Toyota has … pursued a relentless focus on efficiency, cost-cutting and a flood of new variations of successful models brought to market at an increasingly rapid rate.'[18]

In addition to these changes in ownership and control, all the world's automobile manufacturers are deeply embedded in *collaborative agreements* with other manufacturers.[19] In some cases, a joint venture agreement with a local firm is the only means of entry to a particular market (as in the case of China). In fact, the automobile industry is a veritable spider's web of short- and long-term technical and marketing *alliances* in a continuous state of flux. Technology joint ventures are especially important for all automobile manufacturers because of the huge cost of producing new cars and components:

> Every one of the world's biggest carmakers by sales operates some form of alliance or joint venture with another large carmaker. Some work with as many as 10 of their rivals, while many own chunks of each other's shares … The logic for carmakers is simple. The cost of developing a new platform, a new engine family or building a factory can run to several billion dollars. Sharing that with another carmaker halves the investment while maintaining the benefits … [for example] Renault engines are used by Mercedes. Peugeot and Citroën's electric-powered car is built by Mitsubishi. Fiat builds engines for Suzuki. Ford engines power Jaguars and Aston Martins. Dacia cars sell around the world with Renault or Nissan badges on them. General Motors and Peugeot's forthcoming MPV will be the same car under the skin.[20]

New alliances are announced every year while others are terminated. A recent example is the 2012 global alliance between General Motors and PSA (although primarily focused on Europe), which is to 'share vehicle platforms, components and modules and create a global purchasing joint venture'.[21]

However, the long-term viability of such alliances is always in doubt. In late 2013, for example, General Motors announced that it was reviewing its alliance with PSA while, at the same time, PSA was negotiating a new alliance with the Chinese firm Dongfeng.

Changing relationships between automobile assemblers and component manufacturers

Similar consolidation and concentration trends have occurred in the component industries as leading companies – such as Bosch, Delphi, Valeo, Denso and others – have developed into global suppliers. As with the assemblers, much of the continuing consolidation among suppliers is being driven by mergers and acquisitions. The fundamental driving force behind consolidation among component manufacturers is the increasing pressure being exerted by assemblers to deliver quickly (just-in-time), to deliver at lower cost on a continuous basis, and to raise the quality of components. Such pressures are manifested in two important ways. One is the pressure on suppliers to take on more of the design, research and risk of developing component modules and systems. The second is the pressure on suppliers to locate geographically close to assembly plants.[22]

Such pressures have resulted in a massive decline in the number of suppliers. For example, in 1990 there were some 30,000 suppliers in North America, 10,000 by the year 2000, and a predicted further decline to between 3000 and 4000 by the year 2010. The effects of the 2008 financial crisis accelerated this trend, creating what one headline termed 'the "living dead" among supply chains'.[23] Meanwhile, the incessant pressure on suppliers to reduce their prices to the assemblers continues unabated. But there are risks, as the disastrous experience of Toyota demonstrated, when it had to recall several million cars in early 2010 because of faulty components involving a number of its models. Such safety recalls have become more common as auto manufacturers come to rely more heavily on a small number of suppliers of highly complex components.

Structurally, the auto supply system is becoming more *functionally segmented* (Figures 15.5 and 15.6). In place of the myriad specialist raw materials and component suppliers, four major strategies seem to be evolving as Figure 15.5 shows. The raw materials and component specialist strategies are, of course, not new. What is new is the emergence of other categories of supplier, notably the standardizers and the integrators, both of which have significantly greater design and manufacturing responsibilities and have a different kind of relationship both with assemblers and with their own suppliers. This latter characteristic is especially significant in the case of the integrators.

The relatively simple tiered supply hierarchy has metamorphosed into a structure in which the connection between Tier 1 suppliers and the assemblers is being mediated by a new layer of module and system integrators – what some analysts term a 'Tier 0.5' to signify its closer relationship with the assemblers (Figure 15.6). These system integrators are more powerful because 'carmakers can no longer design certain modules by themselves ... There has been a spectacular rise in suppliers' production and research capacities.'[24] At the same time, the major suppliers have been drastically redrawing their own production map. For example, 'between

	Raw materials supplier	Component specialist	Standardizer	Integrator
Focus	A company that supplies raw materials to the OEM or its suppliers	A company that designs and manufactures a component tailored to a platform or vehicle	A company that sets the standard on a global basis for a specific component or system	A company that designs and assembles a whole module or system for a car
Market presence	• Local • Regional • Global	• Global for Tier 1 • Regional or local for Tiers 2 and 3	• Global	• Global
Critical capabilities	• Material science • Process engineering	• Research, design and process engineering • Manufacturing capabilities in varied technologies • Brand image	• Research, design and engineering • Assembly and supply chain management capabilities	• Product design and engineering • Assembly and supply chain management capabilities
Types of components or systems	• Steel blanks • Aluminium ingots • Polymer pellets	• Stampings • Injection moulding • Engine components	• Tyres • ABS • ECU	• Interiors • Doors • Chassis

Figure 15.5   **Supplier strategies in the automobile industry**

Source: based on Veloso and Kumar, 2002: Table 1

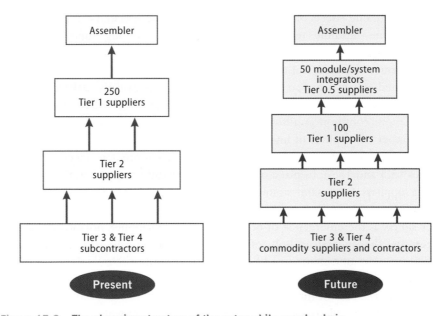

Figure 15.6   **The changing structure of the automobile supply chain**

Source: based on ABN-AMRO, 2000: p. 10

2001 and 2006, the French supplier Valeo closed 59 sites, opened 29 new sites, sold 26 locations and acquired 13 units.[25]

This is a very typical pattern among leading suppliers as they have to respond, both organizationally and geographically, to the demands of the major assemblers.

Organizationally 'distant' relationships have been replaced by much 'closer' relationships. Much greater degrees of organizational interdependence between automobile manufacturers and component suppliers have developed. Relationships with key suppliers have become longer term. At the same time, the need for suppliers – especially Tier 1 and Tier 0.5 suppliers of complex modules and systems – to locate geographically close to their customers has intensified: JIT supply has become the norm. Even so, enormous diversity persists in the geography of supplier–assembler relationships: a mixture of long- and short-distance arrangements, reflecting the path dependency of present patterns on those that evolved in earlier periods. This is especially the case for second- and third-tier component suppliers. Geographical change tends to be incremental rather than radical.

For first-tier suppliers, especially modular suppliers, the most developed situation involves their co-location in so-called *industrial condominiums*:

> a small group of the automaker's direct suppliers … are physically installed within the walls of the automaker's plant and participate in a share of the plant's infrastructure costs. These suppliers generally supply the automaker with systems (usually more complex systems with difficult logistics or that facilitate postponing diversification of the product and increase its customization potential) on a just-in-time … basis right next to the assembly line, but do not participate in the vehicle's final assembly line. The final assembly is done by the automaker.[26]

Whether or not these 'assembly lines of the future' become accepted practice is a matter for conjecture. Certainly it is much harder to introduce such revolutionary practices in the old-established manufacturing heartlands of the automobile industry. It is significant that most of the existing cases are located well away from traditional automobile manufacturing areas (Brazil has been a favoured location). A diluted version of the industrial condominium, more common in Europe, is the *supplier park*: 'complexes that bring suppliers together in close proximity to one another, contiguous to the assembly site – a contiguity that is sometimes materialized through the overhead tunnels that connect the various plants'.[27]

Clearly, profound changes are occurring in the nature of the assembler–supplier relationship, driven primarily by the time, price and technology/design pressures exerted by the assemblers on suppliers. Suppliers have been driven to consolidate and to take on enhanced roles. That, in turn, changes the balance of power between assemblers and the mega-suppliers upon which the assemblers now depend for a much larger part of their business. So, although, in general, assemblers have more bargaining power than suppliers, there are clear exceptions: those mega-suppliers which have developed particularly valuable capabilities and which are able to provide a global supply service to their geographically dispersed customers.

Contrasting transnationalization strategies of the major automobile producers

In view of the technological and competitive pressures facing all automobile producers, it is not surprising that their strategies have some similarities. However, the big producers remain creatures of their specific histories. As we noted in Chapter 5, firms tend to develop a 'strategic predisposition', built up over time, which leads them to favour some kinds of approaches rather than others. They also remain creatures of their particular geographies. Where they come from, where they are still headquartered, matters a lot in terms of the precise ways in which they pursue their objectives.

Figures 15.7 to 15.10 summarize the transnational profiles of the leading US, Japanese, European and Korean producers in terms of two sets of measures:

- Changes between 2007 and 2012 in the companies' *Transnationality Index* (TNI). This is an average of three ratios: foreign assets to total assets; foreign sales to total sales; foreign employment to total employment.
- The proportion of production located in each firm's home country, in its broader region (including the home country) and in its largest other production base.

The US big two

General Motors and Ford (Figure 15.7) dominated the world automobile industry for decades. They were the first automobile firms to transnationalize their production, initially (and logically) in Canada and then in Europe. Ford built its first European manufacturing plant in Manchester in 1911 (subsequently replaced in 1931 by the massive integrated plant at Dagenham, near London), and spread into France and Germany. General Motors expanded transnationally through acquiring existing companies in both Canada and Europe (Opel in Germany, Vauxhall in the UK).

These early transnational ventures were triggered by the existence of protective barriers around major national markets as well as by the high cost of transporting assembled automobiles from the USA. Subsequently, both Ford's and General Motors' transnational strategies were concerned, first, with expanding and integrating, and then rationalizing their operations globally. Since 2008 both General Motors and Ford have been forced to close large numbers of plants in the USA and are struggling to restructure their European operations. General Motors has become significantly more transnational in recent years. In fact, the biggest single difference between General Motors' and Ford's global operations is General Motors' massive involvement in China, where Ford is weak. This largely explains the big increase in General Motors' TNI between 2007 and 2012 and also the fact that North American production is relatively a much smaller share of the total than Ford's. However, Ford is investing massively ($760 million) in new production

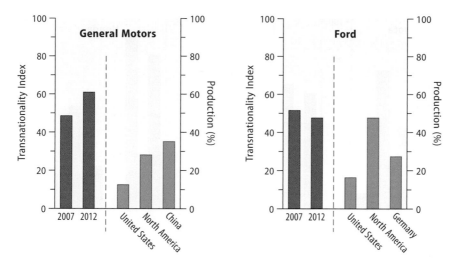

Figure 15.7   Transnational profiles of the US big two

Source: based on data in UNCTAD, 2009: Table A.1.9; UNCTAD, 2013a: Web Table 28; OICA statistics, 2013

facilities in Eastern China to double its production capacity[28] and, at the same time, like General Motors, ending its long-standing operations in Australia.

Japanese producers

Whereas both Ford and General Motors have had international operations for many decades, the spectacular rise of the leading Japanese companies was achieved almost entirely without any actual overseas production, apart from small-scale, local assembly operations, using imported kits. Beyond such operations, Toyota had no overseas production facilities for cars before the early 1980s, while less than 3 per cent of Nissan's total production was located outside Japan. The biggest Japanese producer, Toyota, was, in fact, the slowest to transnationalize. Toyota did not build its first European plant until 1992, six years after Nissan. Paradoxically, it was one of the smaller Japanese automobile manufacturers, Honda, which was the first to build production facilities outside Asia (in Ohio in 1982).

However, the transnationality of the Japanese producers changed dramatically during the 1980s, because of a combination of political pressures in the USA and Europe and the increased need to be inside major markets. By 1989, 28 per cent of Honda's output was produced outside Japan; today the proportion is 76 per cent. Toyota vastly increased its overseas production share (from 8 per cent to 56 per cent); Nissan now produces 72 per cent of its cars outside Japan compared with 14 per cent in 1989. As Figure 15.8 shows, the three leading Japanese producers are now far more transnationalized than either Ford or GM.

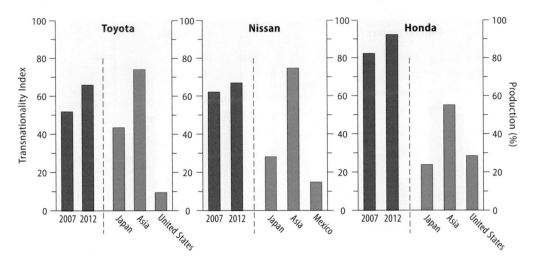

Figure 15.8   **Transnational profiles of Japanese producers**

Source: based on data in UNCTAD, 2009: Table A.1.9; UNCTAD, 2013a: Web Table 28; OICA statistics, 2013

European producers

Until recently, the major European automobile producers (Figure 15.9) were over-whelmingly Eurocentric. For example, while the Japanese were busy building large manufacturing plants in the USA during the 1980s, both VW and Renault pulled out of their earlier involvement there. Subsequently, VW has pursued by far the most extensive and systematic transnational strategy of all the European producers. Today, 56 per cent of its car production is located in Europe, with an increasing emphasis on Eastern Europe (especially the Czech Republic and Slovakia). Outside Europe, VW's biggest production base is in China.

While VW was expanding its European production base to incorporate Spain in the 1980s, the Italian automobile firm Fiat initially moved in the opposite direction and reconcentrated production in its home market. But that has changed radically. Only 27 per cent of Fiat's production is now in Italy. Outside Europe, Brazil is Fiat's major production focus. In 2008, Fiat made a failed attempt to buy General Motors' European operations which, together with its acquisition of Chrysler, would have made it a truly major global player.

The two French automobile companies, Renault and PSA, were both tradition-ally strongly home-country oriented in their production. Renault has been, for more than 40 years, the French government's national champion, supported by massive state aid, which served to constrain its activities. State control has been reduced to 15 per cent and Renault has been involved in major restructuring, including its major coup in acquiring a large equity stake in Nissan. For Renault, Europe remains the dominant production location with 70 per cent of its total

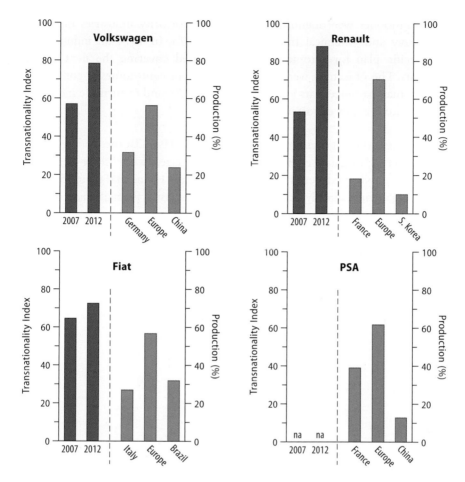

Figure 15.9 Transnational profiles of European producers

Source: based on data in UNCTAD, 2009: Table A.1.9; UNCTAD, 2013a: Web Table 28; OICA statistics, 2013

world production, although it now has a substantial presence in South Korea through its acquisition of Samsung and a new joint venture with Dongfeng Motor in China. PSA, formed through a state-induced merger in 1975, has recently become far more transnational in its operations. Although 62 per cent of its production is in Europe, it has a growing presence in China.

Korean, Indian and Chinese producers

The US, Japanese and European automobile companies have exerted such market dominance that there have been virtually no new entrants to the industry in the past 30 years. The major exception is in South Korea and, more recently, India. In the case of Korea, automobiles were identified as one of the priority industries in the Heavy and Chemical Industry Plan of 1973. In 1974 an industry-specific plan for automobiles was published covering the next ten years. The objectives were to achieve a 90 per cent domestic content for small passenger cars by the end of the 1970s and to turn the industry into a major exporter by the early 1980s.[29]

Although the Korean government effectively made Hyundai the leading producer in the industry, giving it an enormous relative advantage, in 1997 there were still five Korean automobile producers. Today, there is just one – Hyundai (Figure 15.10) – the others being victims, directly or indirectly, of the East Asian financial crisis of 1997.

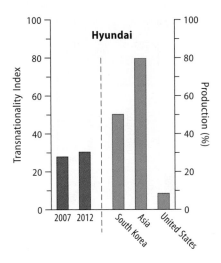

Figure 15.10   Transnational profile of Hyundai

Source: based on data in UNCTAD, 2009: Table A.1.9; UNCTAD, 2013a: Web Table 28; OICA statistics, 2013

Hyundai depended for its early development on close technological and marketing relationships with US and Japanese firms. Its strategy was to compete with the Japanese in a very narrow product range and entirely on price. Its initial export success was remarkable. On the strength of this success, Hyundai built a plant in Canada, with the capacity to produce 120,000 cars and to employ 1200 workers directly, but this plant was closed in 1991 because of quality problems.

As a result of the 1997 crisis, Hyundai was forced to undertake major restructuring and refocusing of its operations. First, it acquired Kia, one of the smaller Korean automobile firms. Second, in 2000, it separated from its parent company, the Hyundai *chaebol*. Third, it began to move away from being merely a low-price regional producer of cars primarily for the Asian market to one with much wider ambitions. Hyundai sees itself as a major global producer of high-quality vehicles (operating a two-brand strategy, with Kia providing the lower-cost cars). It is shedding its cheap-car image focusing, like Toyota, on high-quality control. It has rapidly expanded geographically to operate plants in China, India, Turkey, the USA (a new plant in Alabama opened in 2005), the Czech Republic and, in 2012, Brazil. As a result, almost 50 per cent of its production is now located outside Korea. It is a remarkable record of rapid growth to become the world's third-largest automobile producer (see Table 15.1).

The Indian company Tata is in a smaller league, but has huge ambitions to become a global automobile producer. Having acquired Jaguar Land Rover (JLR) from Ford in 2008, Tata now produces more cars outside India than domestically. Its introduction of the Nano small car will undoubtedly help to expand its international operations at the low end of the market. At the high end, Tata is having huge international success with JLR and has invested heavily in R&D and design in the UK as well as building new plants in China and Brazil.

So far, Chinese firms have made relatively little impact outside China. But this is changing. SAIC (Shanghai Automotive Industrial Corporation) acquired the Ssangyong plants in South Korea and the British MG brand via its subsidiary, the Nanjing Automobile Corporation, BAIC (Beijing Automotive Industrial Corporation) bought some of Saab's assets from General Motors, and Geely acquired Volvo from Ford.

REGIONALIZING PRODUCTION NETWORKS IN THE AUTOMOBILE INDUSTRY

Although, in one sense, the automobile industry is one of the most globalized of industries, it is also an industry in which the *regionalization* of production and distribution is especially marked.[30] Geographically, rather than attempting to organize (and reorganize) operations on a truly global scale, the tendency of most of the leading automobile producers is towards the creation of distinctive production and marketing networks within each of the three major world regions. Figure 15.11 shows that this is especially the case in both North America and Europe, where almost three-quarters of automobile trade is intra-regional, compared with less than one-third in Asia.

Europe

Three major events in the past 30 years have dramatically reshaped the region's automobile industry:

- the completion of the EU single market in 1992;
- the opening up – and subsequent political integration – of Eastern Europe;
- the financial crisis of 2008.

The actual geographical configuration of automobile production within Europe (Figure 15.12) still bears the very strong imprint of each firm's national origins

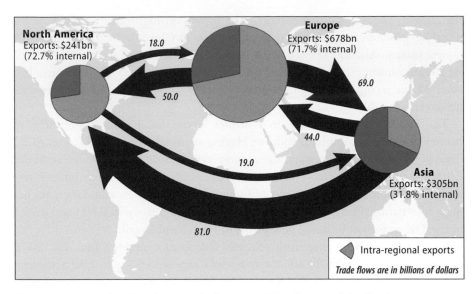

North America
Exports: $241bn
(72.7% internal)

Europe
Exports: $678bn
(71.7% internal)

Asia
Exports: $305bn
(31.8% internal)

18.0

50.0

69.0

44.0

19.0

81.0

Intra-regional exports

Trade flows are in billions of dollars

Figure 15.11   **Regional trade networks in automobiles: Europe, Asia, North America**

Source: calculated from WTO, 2013: Table II.57

and the history of their development. For example, Ford and General Motors have been in Europe for almost 100 years, building up multilocational, initially nationally oriented, production networks. Both have drastically rationalized their European operations in recent years. General Motors, in particular, aims to cut its European production capacity by one-fifth, which will involve the closure of its Opel plant in Antwerp, Belgium, and a loss of more than 8000 jobs within Europe. Opel will close its Bochum plant in Germany after 2016.

In contrast, the position of the Japanese producers is very different. With no history of European car production and no inherited structure, the Japanese were able to treat Europe as a 'clean sheet'. Beginning in the early 1980s, Japanese firms established production facilities in Europe. All three leading Japanese firms – Toyota, Nissan, Honda – initially built their plants in the UK. This led to political friction within the EU during the 1980s and 1990s. Significantly, Toyota's second European plant was built in northern France. Japanese auto production in Europe, and especially in the UK (where Nissan continues to invest heavily), has continued to grow.

The geographical configuration of the indigenous European automobile producers is, of course, much more embedded in their national contexts. Only VW has anything approaching a pan-European production network, focused around the three nodes of Germany, Spain and its acquired Eastern European plants in the Czech Republic and Slovakia. Prior to the opening up of Eastern Europe, VW

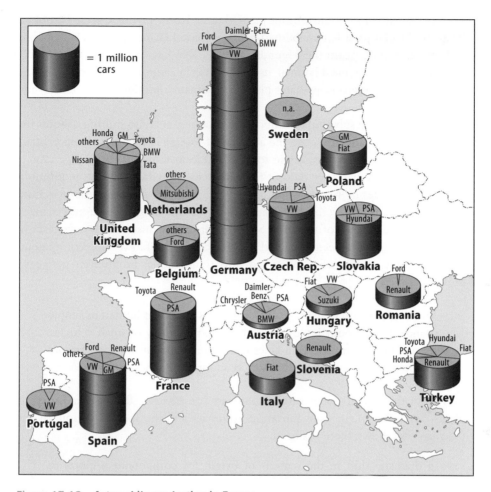

Figure 15.12 **Automobile production in Europe**

Source: calculated from OICA statistics

had developed a clear strategy of geographical segmentation. High-value, technologically advanced cars were produced in the former West Germany; low-cost,
small cars were produced in Spain. After 1990, VW moved very rapidly to establish
production of small cars in eastern Germany and to take a controlling stake in the
Czech firm Skoda. VW now has operations in the Czech Republic, Hungary,
Poland and Slovakia.

Indeed, Eastern Europe is now the primary focus of change in European automobile production networks.[31] In addition to joining with (or taking over) existing local automobile firms, automobile producers have built new plants in Eastern
Europe. For example, General Motors established operations in Poland and Russia;
Toyota has established a joint venture with Peugeot Citroën (PSA), to develop and

assemble small cars for the European market at Kolin in the Czech Republic; Peugeot Citroën itself has established plants in Slovakia and the Czech Republic and closed its UK plant; the Hyundai affiliate, Kia, has established an assembly plant in Slovakia, while Hyundai itself has built a large assembly plant in the Czech Republic; Renault operates plants in Romania (producing the Dacia) and in Slovenia.

At the same time, substantial components production is also shifting towards the east. On the one hand, there are the affiliates of foreign companies set up primarily to follow the assemblers. While some of these investments may be genuinely 'new' (in the sense that they did not formerly exist elsewhere), or are acquisitions of local companies by foreign firms, others are, in effect, locational transfers from elsewhere in Europe. On the other hand, there are the indigenous suppliers, many of them the successors of formerly SOEs prior to the onset of privatization. In many cases, these have been restricted to the production of low-value components and are rather peripherally connected into transnational production networks. However,

> the specialization of many ECE countries is no longer limited to simple standard and labour intensive products and assembly of small vehicles. A significant value creation takes place due to manufacturing of more complex, high-value-added products and growing local sourcing.[32]

Inevitably, the shift in focus towards the east has adverse effects on automobile plants (and jobs) in the core European countries and the Iberian region. As the German case shows, there has been

> a dramatic shift in the regions of origin for component imports to Germany. The share of ECE in German automotive component imports rose from 9 per cent to 37 per cent between 1995 and 2005. Rather than displacing manufacturing in Germany, component imports from ECE countries seem to have supplanted imports from Western Europe and the Iberian peninsula. In the case of Spain and Portugal, the share of German imports was not only halved: their absolute value was reduced.[33]

However, there has recently been a resurgence of investment in Spain's auto industry:

> A €1.5bn expansion of Ford's flagship plant … saw the US group install an additional two assembly lines, build a massive paint shop, buy 262 industrial robots and – most importantly for the people of this recession-plagued region – hire 1,420 new workers … [M]akers such as Renault, General Motors and Volkswagen have followed, upgrading their plants in Spain and transferring production from countries such as Belgium and South Korea.[34]

North America

Although political–economic integration in North America is much shallower than in the EU, in the case of the automobile industry political agreements have had profound repercussions on its geographical structure. By the early 1970s, the US–Canadian automobile industry was fully integrated as a result of the 1965 Automobile Pact. The 1988 Canada–US Free Trade Agreement (CUSFTA) redefined the level of 'North American content' necessary for a firm to be able to claim duty-free movement within the North American market. The 1994 North American Free Trade Agreement (NAFTA) had even more far-reaching implications for the automobile industry because it incorporated the vastly lower-production-cost Mexican auto industry.

Figure 15.13 shows the broad geographical structure of the North American production system. Prior to the 1980s, it was totally dominated by US producers. But from the mid-1980s onwards the position changed dramatically. Three major waves of foreign involvement have occurred.

First, each of the major Japanese firms established large-scale production facilities in the USA and Canada during the 1980s. The pioneer was Honda, which established a manufacturing plant at Marysville in Ohio in 1982. This was followed, in 1983, by the Nissan plant at Smyrna, Tennessee. In contrast, Toyota entered North America very cautiously in 1984, through a joint venture (NUMMI) based at General Motors' Fremont, California, plant. Since then, each of the major Japanese firms has continued to increase its capacity and to make major investments in engine, transmission and component plants. As the Japanese plants progressively increased their North American content they were followed by a wave of Japanese component manufacturers. In other words, during the period of less than a decade an entirely new Japanese-controlled automobile industry was created in North America in fierce, direct competition with domestic manufacturers. This 'new' automobile industry had a very different geography from that of the traditional one, simply because the Japanese had no existing plants or allegiance to specific areas. With few exceptions, the old-established automobile industry centres were not favoured.

The second, very much smaller, wave of foreign investment in the North American automobile industry began in the mid-1990s in the form of German luxury car manufacturers Daimler-Benz and BMW. Daimler-Benz built a new plant at Tuscaloosa, Alabama, in 1993; BMW built a plant at Spartanburg, South Carolina, in 1994. Subsequently, of course, Daimler-Benz created a major shake-up of the North American automobile industry when it acquired Chrysler in the late 1990s (sold to Fiat in 2007). These incursions by the two upmarket German producers were the first major European involvements in North America after the failed ventures of Volkswagen and Renault in the 1970s. In 2005, the Korean firm Hyundai opened a major plant in Montgomery, Alabama, and its subsidiary, Kia, has built a new plant in Georgia.

The third development has been the large-scale investment by foreign automobile producers in Mexico.[35] Prior to the Mexican economic reforms of the 1980s and, later, the NAFTA in 1994, most of the automobile investment in Mexico was

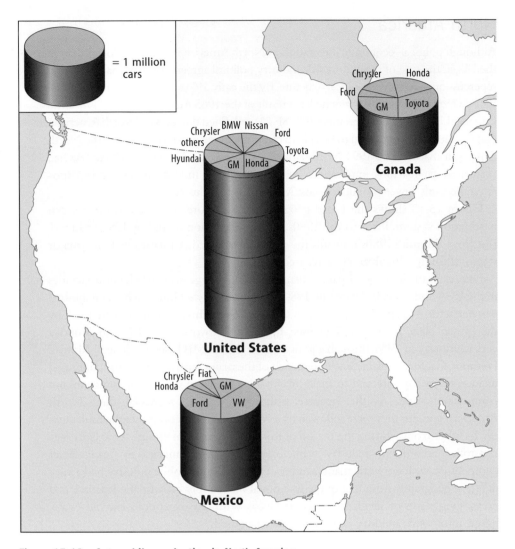

Figure 15.13   **Automobile production in North America**

Source: calculated from OICA statistics

domestic market oriented. Subsequently, these investments were replaced by 'strategic asset-seeking and cost-reducing FDI',[36] with rather different locational characteristics. The plants oriented to the Mexican domestic market were concentrated in the central region, around Mexico City. The newer investments, oriented to the North American market as a whole, are located nearer the border with the USA. The major exception is VW's large integrated facility in Puebla. At the same time, rationalization of some of the former core-region plants has occurred.

By the early 2000s, then, a very different regional production network had evolved in North America compared with that existing before the 1980s, which

Knocked Down) plants in different parts of the region for many years, while General Motors and Ford have had significant equity involvement in Japanese firms. Today, virtually all the major Western automobile companies are in the process of establishing operations in the region, particularly in China.

The restrictive nature of trade policy within ASEAN has made the development of a genuinely regionally integrated automobile industry difficult to achieve, although significant regulatory changes have been introduced to facilitate cross-border flows of vehicles and components. Within South East Asia, Thailand has become the preferred production focus for many major automobile assemblers and component manufacturers, a deliberate outcome of state policy. Thailand has set out to be the 'car capital' of South East Asia and with some considerable success. Virtually all the major foreign producers have a presence there. Not only does it have a major concentration of Japanese automobile and components production, but also it is the favoured point of entry of Western car manufacturers, notably General Motors and Ford through Japanese partners. BMW established an assembly plant for its 3-Series model in Thailand. However, Thailand was hit hard by the 2008 crisis as exports (and, therefore, production) fell sharply. More than half of Thai automobile production is exported so it is very vulnerable to the global slowdown.

Whereas Western automobile firms see Thailand as, potentially, a base for serving the whole of South East Asia, their reasons for wishing to establish operations in China are rather different: access to the world's biggest automobile market. Because *all* the major automobile manufacturers are extremely anxious to establish themselves in China, the Chinese government has been able to retain the bargaining power to impose specific entry restrictions (see Chapter 7).[39]

The Chinese automobile industry consists of a large number of state corporation groups together with a number of joint ventures between members of these groups and foreign firms.[40] VW was one of the earliest Western automobile firms to establish a joint venture in China, first with SAIC in 1985, and then with First Auto Works (FAW). For more than 10 years, VW was virtually unchallenged in the Chinese market and it still has a major market share, although its position has been heavily eroded by new entrants. In fact, US firms have found entry to China rather more difficult. Like VW, General Motors established a joint venture with SAIC in Shanghai. Ford took considerably longer and only agreed a joint venture with the CAIC (China Automotive Industry International Corporation) Group in 2001. Japanese firms continue to strengthen their presence in China: Toyota has established a new joint venture with Guangzhou Automotive. However, Japanese firms, other than Nissan, have been relatively unsuccessful in China.[41] Hyundai is expanding in China through its Kia affiliate, which already had Chinese operations before its acquisition by Hyundai.

The prospect of gaining access to what is seen as the world's largest and fastest-growing consumer market has led to a scramble by automobile producers to enter China. But the Chinese government has exerted virtually complete control over such entry and has adopted a policy of limited access for foreign firms, including the form that their involvement can take. Here, therefore, we have the obverse of the usual situation. Whereas, in many cases, TNCs are able to play off one country against another to achieve the best deal, in the Chinese case it is the state whose unique bargaining position has enabled it to play off one TNC against another.[42]

NOTES

1   Drucker (1946: 149).
2   ABN-AMRO (2000: 11); Freyssenet and Lung (2000: 83).
3   UNIDO (2003: 22).
4   Liu and Yeung (2008).
5   *Financial Times* (11 July 2013).
6   *Financial Times* (8 March 2013).
7   Veloso and Kumar (2002: 3).
8   Delphi Automotive Systems, quoted in EIU (2000: 1).
9   *Financial Times* (20 May 2013).
10   EIU (2000: 7).
11   *Financial Times* (16 June 2004).
12   *Financial Times* (9 May 2008).
13   *Financial Times* (9 May 2008).
14   *Financial Times* (7 August 2008).
15   *Financial Times* (12 September 2013).
16   *Financial Times* (18 January 2010).
17   Foy (2013).
18   *The Economist* (10 September 2005: 73).
19   Foy (2013).
20   Foy (2013).
21   *Financial Times* (1 March 2012).
22   Frigant and Layan (2009), Frigant and Lung (2002).
23   *Financial Times* (25 February 2009).
24   Frigant and Layan (2009: 13).
25   Frigant and Layan (2009: 13).
26   Pires and Neto (2008: 329).
27   Frigant and Lung (2002: 746).
28   *Financial Times* (20 April 2012).
29   Wade (1990: 310).
30   See Dicken (2003a), Freyssenet and Lung (2000), Rugman and Collinson (2004), Sturgeon et al. (2008), UNIDO (2003: 9–16).
31   See Domanski and Lung (2009), Frigant and Layan (2009), Jürgens and Krzywdzinski (2009), Pavlinek et al. (2009).
32   Domanski and Lung (2009: 9).
33   Jürgens and Krzywdzinski (2009: 32).
34   *Financial Times* (4 November 2013).
35   Carrillo (2004), Contreras et al. (2012), Mortimore (1998), UNCTAD (2000).

36 Mortimore (1998: 417).
37 Rutherford and Holmes (2008), Sturgeon and Florida (2004), Sturgeon et al. (2008).
38 Horaguchi and Shimokawa (2002).
39 Liu and Dicken (2006).
40 Liu and Dicken (2006), Liu and Yeung (2008).
41 *Financial Times* (22 November 2013).
42 Liu and Dicken (2006).

Want to know more about this chapter? Visit the companion website at **www.guilford.com/dickenGS7** for free access to author videos, suggested reading and practice questions to further enhance your study.

Sixteen

'MAKING THE WORLD GO ROUND': ADVANCED BUSINESS SERVICES

THE CENTRALITY OF ADVANCED BUSINESS SERVICES

Advanced business services (ABS) – notably banking, accountancy, insurance, logistics, law, advertising, business consultancy, high-level personnel recruitment – are absolutely central to the operation of the economy. They are the 'lubricants' to all production circuits and increasingly dominant in all economies. For example, financial services are both *circulation* services and *commodities* or *products* produced and traded in the same way as more tangible manufactured goods are traded. ABS are, in other words, GPNs in their own right.

Money counts

Every economic activity (whether a material product or a service) has to be financed at all stages of its production. Without the parallel development of systems of money- and credit-based exchange there could have been no development of economies beyond the most primitive organizational forms and the most geographically restricted scales:

> The geographical circuits of money and finance are the 'wiring' of the socio-economy ... along which the 'currents' of wealth creation, consumption and economic power are transmitted ... money allows for the deferment of payment over time-space that is the essence of credit. Equally, money allows propinquity without the need for proximity in conducting transactions over space. These complex time-space webs of monetary flows and obligations underpin our daily social existence.[1]

Financialization, as we have seen, is now an endemic feature of contemporary economic life (see Chapter 3). Finance is also one of the most controversial of all economic activities because of its historical relationship with state 'sovereignty'. Ever since the earliest states emerged, the creation and control of money have been regarded as central to their legitimacy and survival. Today, in the context of a globalizing world economy rocked by the 2008 crisis, this tension has become acute (see Chapter 11).

A global casino

Almost 30 years ago, Susan Strange coined the graphic term 'casino capitalism' to describe the international financial system:

> every day games are played in this casino that involve sums of money so large that they cannot be imagined. At night the games go on at the other side of the world ... [the players] are just like the gamblers in casinos watching the clicking spin of a silver ball on a roulette wheel and putting their chips on red or black, odd numbers or even ones.[2]

Twelve years later, she used the term 'mad money' to reflect the increased volatility of the financial system and the uncertainty it generates throughout the world economy. How perceptive she was; these labels are even more appropriate today in light of the 2008 crisis.

International financial flows and foreign currency transactions have reached unprecedented levels, totally dwarfing the value of international trade in manufactured goods and in other services (Figure 16.1). In 1973, daily foreign exchange transactions were roughly twice that of world trade; in 2007, they were 100 times greater! Only a very small percentage of those transactions are directly related to international trade. The overwhelming majority are, essentially, *speculative* dealings – aimed at making short- or long-term profits as ends in themselves – through a bewildering variety of financial instruments. Of course, in practice it is often difficult to draw a clear line between speculative and productively essential financial transactions.

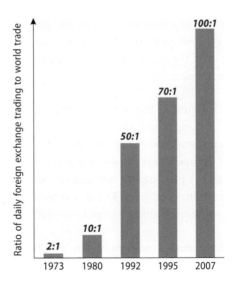

Figure 16.1   **The growing disparity between foreign exchange trading and world trade, 1973–2007**

Source: based on Dore, 2008: 3; Eatwell and Taylor, 2000: pp. 3–4

THE STRUCTURE OF ADVANCED BUSINESS SERVICES

Figure 16.2 distinguishes between financial and professional business service firms. They are all basically providers of highly specialized knowledge which facilitates the increasingly complex configuration and operation of GPNs. All are, in some sense, *intermediaries* in the processes of production, distribution and consumption. In the case of banking, the key function is

> the pooling of financial resources among those with surplus funds to be lent out to those who choose to be in deficit, that is to borrow … With financial intermediation, investors in new productive activities do not themselves have to generate a surplus to finance their projects; instead the projects can be financed by surpluses generated elsewhere within the economy.[3]

Financial services

Type	Primary functions
Commercial bank	Administers financial transactions for clients (e.g. making payments, clearing cheques). Takes in deposits and makes commercial loans, acting as intermediary between lender and borrower.
Investment bank/ securities house	Buys and sells securities (i.e. stocks, bonds) on behalf of corporate or individual investors. Arranges flotation of new securities issues.
Credit card company	Operates international network of credit card facilities in conjunction with banks and other financial institutions.
Insurance company	Indemnifies a whole range of risks, on payment of a premium, in association with other insurers/reinsurers.
Accountancy firm	Certifies the accuracy of financial accounts, particularly via the corporate audit.

Professional business services

Type	Primary functions
Legal firm	Provides legal advice on regulatory requirements in specific territorial and international jurisdictions.
Business consultancy firm	Provides advice in diverse aspects of business organization, including strategic issues, corporate re-organization, etc.
Advertising agency	Designs and implements commercial campaigns across the media to promote branded products and/or corporate identity.
Executive recruitment ('head-hunting') firm	Searches for and recruits high-level executive personnel.

Figure 16.2 **Major types of ABS**

The process of intermediation has constituted the basic function of banks from the very beginning (Figure 16.3). The first two stages of credit provision to borrowers depend greatly upon the nature of geographically specific knowledge to legitimize lending and borrowing. The geographical scope of knowledge and trust grows through such developments as inter-bank lending (i.e. lending outside the local area) in stage 4 and, eventually, of a central bank that ultimately acts as the lender of last resort to the banking system as a whole (stage 5). Subsequent developments, especially in securitization, create a totally different scale and complexity of financial activity. Such increased complexity of the financial system involves a huge variety of different types of financial institution, each of which has a specific set of core functions (Figure 16.2). In fact, the boundaries between these individual activities and institutions have become increasingly blurred.

The stages of banking development	Banks and space	Credit and space
Stage 1: Pure financial intermediation Banks lend out savings. Payment in commodity money. No bank multiplier. Saving precedes investment.	Serving local communities. Wealth-based, providing foundation for future financial centres.	Intermediation only.
Stage 2: Bank deposits used as money Convenient to use paper money as means of payment. Reduced drain on bank reserves. Multiplier process possible. Bank credit creation with fractional reserves. Investment can now precede saving.	Market dependent on extent of confidence held in banker.	Credit creation focused on local community because total credit constrained by redeposit ratio.
Stage 3: Inter-bank lending Credit creation still constrained by reserves. Risk of reserves loss offset by development of inter-bank lending. Multiplier process works more quickly. Multiplier larger because banks can hold lower reserves.	Banking system develops at national level.	Redeposit constraint relaxed somewhat, so can lend wider afield.
Stage 4: Lender-of-last-resort facility Central bank perceives need to promote confidence in banking system. Lender-of-last-resort facility provided if inter-bank lending inadequate. Reserves now respond to demand. Credit creation freed from reserves constraint.	Central bank oversees national system, but limited power to constrain credit.	Banks freer to respond to credit demand as reserves constraint not binding and they can determine volume and distribution of credit within national economy.
Stage 5: Liability management Competition from non-bank financial inter-mediaries drives struggle for market share. Banks actively supply credit and seek deposits. Credit expansion diverges from real economic activity.	Banks compete at national level with non-bank financial institutions.	Credit creation determined by struggle over market share and opportunities in speculative markets. Total credit uncontrolled.
Stage 6: Securitization Capital adequacy ratios introduced to curtail credit. Banks have an increasing proportion of bad loans because of over-lending in Stage 5. Securitization of bank assets. Increase in off-balance-sheet activity. Drive to liquidity.	Deregulation opens up international competition, eventually causing concentration in financial centres.	Shift to liquidity by emphasis being put on services rather than credit; credit decisions concentrated in financial centres; total credit determined by availability of capital, i.e. by central capital markets.
?	?	?
Stage 7: Response to 2008 crisis Potential for redrawing of boundaries between different banking functions.	Possible re-regulation at national and/or international scales.	Possible re-focus on lending to domestic borrowers.

Figure 16.3   **The sequence of development of the banking system**

Source: based, in part, on Dow, 1999: Tables 1 and 2

DYNAMICS OF THE MARKETS FOR ADVANCED BUSINESS SERVICES

Demand for ABS is primarily driven by the increasing complexity and speciali-zation of functions within economies in general and in production networks in particular. ABS providers are both the beneficiaries of such developments and, in turn, contributors to that increased complexity, thus helping to create their own growing markets. This is especially the case as production networks have become increasingly global, creating more and more market opportunities for firms to follow their clients abroad. Very often the relationships established between ABS firms and their customers in a domestic context are transferred to an international context because of the build-up of trust. Alternatively, the geographical differentiation of rules and regulations between different national territories creates opportunities for ABS firms to construct more complex and geographically diverse operations and to build extensive networks.

The increased diversity (and volatility) of the market for financial services

From being fairly simple and predictable, the markets for financial services have become increasingly diverse and far less predictable. The intensity of competition for consumers (whether corporate or individual) has increased enormously. Four processes have been especially important:

- *Market saturation*: by the late 1970s, traditional financial services markets were reaching saturation, particularly in the commercial banking sector but also in the retail sector in the more affluent economies.
- *Disintermediation*: corporate borrowers have increasingly sought capital from non-bank institutions, for example through securities, investment trusts and mutual funds. However, new forms of supplier–customer relationship are emerging (reintermediation), for example through the Internet.[4]
- *Deregulation of financial markets*: has facilitated the opening of new geographical markets, the provision of new financial products, and changes in how prices of financial services are set.
- *Internationalization of financial markets*: demand for financial services is no longer restricted to the domestic context; financial markets have become increasingly global.

Each of these forces for change in the demand for financial services is interrelated; together they created a *new competitive environment*. But, of course, such developments rarely proceed smoothly: the inherent volatility of financial markets creates periodic large-scale upheavals. The history of the twentieth century provides clear evidence of such a succession of 'financial disasters':[5] the bankers' panic in the USA in 1907; the Wall Street Crash in 1929; 'Black Monday' in 1987; the Asian financial crisis in 1997; and, most recently, the global financial crisis of 2008. Such market volatility has profound implications for the ABS sector in general. Some ABS firms prosper – notably those concerned with corporate bankruptcies and restructuring – while others experience difficulties as demand for their services contracts.

TECHNOLOGICAL INNOVATION AND ADVANCED BUSINESS SERVICES

Centrality of information and communications technology

ICT is absolutely central to all ABS. Information – about markets, risks, currency exchange rates, returns on investment, creditworthiness – is both their process and their product. In the words of one financial services executive:

> We don't have warehouses full of cash. We have *information* about cash – *that* is our product.[6]

Indeed, money itself

> is primarily an item of information governed by rules. Money is there-fore shaped by the development and adoption of information and communication technologies ... (how the information is managed, and to a degree the very nature of the information) and regulation (how information is ruled).[7]

It is, of course, the *speed* with which financial service firms can perform transactions and the *global extent* over which they can be made that are especially important:

> Travelling at the speed of light, as nothing but assemblages of zeros and ones, global money dances through the world's fiber-optic networks in astonishing volumes ... National boundaries mean little in this context: it is much easier to move $41 billion from London to New York than a truckload of grapes from California to Nevada.[8]

From a technological viewpoint, global trading 24 hours a day – 'following the sun' – whether this is in securities, foreign exchange, financial and commodities futures or any other financial service – is perfectly feasible.[9] As Figure 16.4 shows, the trading hours of the world's major financial centres overlap. In reality, pure 24-hour trading is currently limited to certain kinds of transaction partly because, although the technology is available, either the organizational structure or the national regulatory environment creates an obstacle (see next section).

To the extent that electronic transactions do not require direct physical proxim-ity between seller and buyer, they are a form of 'invisible' international trade. In that sense, therefore, financial services are one kind of ABS that is *tradable*. The global integration of financial markets brings many benefits to its participants: in speed and accuracy of information flows and rapidity and directness of transac-tions, even though the participants may be separated by many thousands of miles and by several time zones. But such global integration and instantaneous financial trading also create costs. 'Shocks' occurring in one geographical market now

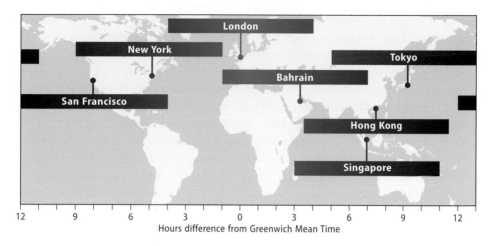

Figure 16.4 The potential for 24-hour financial trading

Source: based on Wart, 1989: Figure 5

spread instantaneously around the globe, creating the potential for global financial instability. Financial 'contagion' is endemic in the structure and operation of the contemporary financial system. It is nothing new – just more extreme.

An epidemic of new financial products

Innovations in ICT and in process technologies have helped not only to transform the operations of financial services firms, but also to facilitate the creation of new financial products. Many of these bypass the commercial banks and contribute towards the greater *securitization* of financial transactions: the conversion of all kinds of loans and borrowings into 'paper' securities which can be bought and sold on the market. Such transactions may be performed directly by buyers and sellers without necessarily going through the intermediary channels of the commercial banks. A virtual epidemic of new financial instruments (product innovations) appeared on the scene with increasing frequency, notably:

- those providing new methods of lending and borrowing;
- those facilitating greater spreading of risk.

An especially important product innovation since the mid–1980s has been the phenomenal growth of the *derivatives* markets. Derivatives are

> financial tools derived from other financial products, such as equities and currencies. The most common of these are futures, swaps, and options … The derivatives market aims to enable participants to manage their exposure to the risk of movements in interest rates, equities, and currencies.[10]

Figure 16.5 gives examples of the confusing variety of such 'structured financial products'. Their underlying logic is the spreading of risk. However, as the 2008 crisis showed, with such great force, the nature of such risks was simply not understood: 'risk has become *delocalized* and outsourced'.[11] It was the packaging, repackaging and selling on (and on and on) of mortgage-based securities (MBS) derived from loans in the US sub-prime mortgage market (loans to individuals without the means to repay them) that triggered the crisis when borrowers began to default. Nobody, not even the financial institutions themselves, really knew either where the risks lay or how large they were. When it is realized that 'the notional value of the derivatives market was almost eleven times the value of the world's financial assets'[12] then the dangers of such risk-taking become apparent. No wonder the US investor Warren Buffett called derivatives 'time bombs' or 'financial weapons of mass destruction', or that Gillian Tett talked about 'destructive creation' – a neat reversal of Schumpeter's notion of 'creative destruction' (see Chapter 4).

In effect:

> The modern financial services industry is a casino attached to a utility. The utility is the payments system, which enables individuals and companies to manage their daily affairs. It allows them to borrow and lend in line with the fundamental value of business activities. In the casino, traders make profits from arbitrage – differences in the prices of related assets – and from short-term price movements. The users of the utility look to fundamental values. The players in the casino are preoccupied with the mind of the market.[13]

Without question, therefore, developments in both ICT and products have transformed the ABS industries. The global integration of financial markets has collapsed space and time and created the potential for virtually instantaneous financial transactions in loans, securities and a whole variety of financial instruments. However, completely borderless financial trading does not actually exist, for the simple reason

Type of financial instrument	Basic characteristics
Asset-backed Securities (ABS)	Debt parcelled up and sold as securities backed by the repayment from those loans.
e.g. Mortgage-backed Securities (MBS)	Securities based on the selling-on of mortgages in packages.
Credit Default Swaps (CDS)	Insurance against corporate default.
Collateralized Debt Obligations (CDOs)	Structured financial products that pool different kinds of loans and bonds, funding themselves by issuing new bonds whose price depends upon the risk level.
Constant Proportion Debt Obligations (CPDOs)	Leveraged bets on a group of high-quality US and European companies. These vehicles issued securities to generate to pay out by selling protection on credit default swaps.

Figure 16.5   **Examples of recent product innovations in financial markets**

Source: based on material in the *Financial Times*, 13 October 2009: p. 33

that most financial services remain very heavily supervised and regulated by individual national governments. Let us now see how the regulatory system works – or does not work – and how it has changed.

THE ROLE OF THE STATE: REGULATION, DEREGULATION, REREGULATION

Although some ABS are 'tradable', most depend on having a direct physical presence within their markets. This is especially true of legal and accounting services because both are subject to tight regulation at the national scale. Even within the EU, national regulatory structures still operate. But it is in finance that regulatory systems are especially significant. The history of the past six decades is one of a dramatic shift from tight to looser regulation to deregulation – that is, until the 2008 financial crisis and reregulation returned to the agenda.

A tightly regulated financial system

Before the 1960s there was no such thing as a 'world' financial market. The IMF, together with the leading industrialized nations, operated a broadly efficient global mechanism for monetary management based, initially, on the post-war Bretton Woods agreement (see Chapter 11). At the national level, financial markets and institutions were very closely supervised, primarily because of concerns over the vulnerability of the financial system to periodic crises and because of the centrality of finance to the operation of a country's economy.

Two types of financial regulation are especially important:

- Those governing the *relationships* between different types of financial activity. National financial services markets have generally been *segmented* by regulation: banks performed specified activities; securities houses performed other activities. Neither was allowed to perform the functions of the other.
- Those governing the *entry* of firms (whether domestic or foreign) into the financial sector. Restricted entry into the financial services markets has been virtually universal. Governments have been especially wary of the expansion of *branches* of foreign banks and insurance companies. This is because branches, unlike separately incorporated subsidiaries, are far more difficult to supervise. They form an integral part of a foreign company's activities. In almost every case, there are limits on the degree of foreign ownership permitted in financial services.

'The crumbling of the walls'

Although many of these restrictions continued to exist, the regulatory walls crumbled – even collapsed altogether in some cases. The process was relatively slow at first but accelerated rapidly after the late 1980s. Pressures for deregulation came from several sources, most notably the increasing abilities of transnational financial firms to take advantage of 'gaps' in the regulatory system and to operate outside national regulatory boundaries:

> Money has a habit of seeking out geographical discontinuities and gaps in ... regulatory spaces, escaping to places where the movement of financial assets is less constrained, where official scrutiny into financial dealing and affairs is minimal, where taxes are lower and potential profits higher.[14]

The starting point was the emergence of the Eurodollar (i.e. offshore) markets in the 1960s. Initially, Eurodollars were simply dollars held outside the US banking system, largely by countries anxious to prevent their dollar holdings being subject to US political control. The rapid growth of this market was reinforced by pressure from banks and other financial services firms to operate in a less constrained and segmented manner, both domestically and internationally. In fact, the *internationalization* of financial services and the *deregulation* of national financial services markets are essentially two sides of the same coin: each reinforces the other.

Major deregulation occurred in all the major developed economies. In the USA, a series of changes from the 1970s both eased the entry of foreign banks into the domestic market and facilitated the expansion of US banks overseas, as well as allowing banks to become involved in a whole variety of financial services and to operate nationwide branching networks. In 1999, the Glass–Steagall Act, which prohibited the joint ownership of commercial and investment banking, was abolished. In the UK, the so-called 'Big Bang' of October 1986 removed the traditional barriers between banks and securities houses and allowed the entry of foreign firms into the London Stock Exchange. In France, the 'Little Bang' of 1987 gradually opened up the French Stock Exchange to outsiders and to foreign and domestic banks. In Germany, foreign-owned banks were allowed to lead-manage foreign issues, subject to reciprocity agreements.

Financial deregulation also occurred in East Asia. In Japan the restrictions on the entry of foreign securities houses were relaxed (though not removed) and Japanese banks could open international banking facilities. But the Japanese financial system remained more tightly regulated than elsewhere until, in 1996, the Japanese government announced its intention to undertake a wide-ranging deregulation. Even the highly paternalistic Singaporean government progressively loosened the restrictions on the financial sector in order to maintain the country's position as a major Asian, potentially global, financial centre. Most recently, China has allowed foreign participation in big state-owned banks and has listed them on overseas stock exchanges.

Reintervention of the state

The 2008 financial crisis halted this apparently unstoppable deregulatory trend in its tracks. The collapse of major banks and investment firms, initially in the USA and the UK, was a shock of unprecedented magnitude, at least since the Wall Street Crash of 1929. The IMF estimated that financial institutions faced losses of $4.1 trillion.[15] Governments ploughed billions of their currencies into propping up their collapsing banking systems. Some institutions were allowed to fail but, in the main, governments stepped in with massive financial support. Rescuing their banks became the preoccupation of national governments, simply because credit is so absolutely essential for an economy to operate. The banks were regarded as being too big to fail. But the cost of such short-term fixes to the taxpayer has been immense. In the longer run, a new *global* financial architecture is clearly needed (see Chapter 11).

CORPORATE STRATEGIES IN ADVANCED BUSINESS SERVICES

Concentration and consolidation

The history of most ABS is of a powerful trend towards greater concentration into a smaller number of bigger companies. Much of this consolidation has occurred through merger and acquisition. In some ABS, like accounting, advertising, law and executive recruitment, the development of alliances and networks has become especially apparent. As a result, virtually all ABS sectors are dominated by a small number of very large firms or networks of firms (Figure 16.6) although smaller 'boutique' firms continue to find profitable niches and new, starter firms are continuously being formed. In each of the ABS sectors shown in Figure 16.6 there has been a huge amount of 'churning'. Advertising has long been transformed by a stream of mergers and acquisitions.[16]

The changes in banking have been especially dramatic. In 1989, seven of the top ten banks were Japanese; in 2013, there was only one – Mitsubishi UFJ – which evolved from a whole series of mergers. First, the Bank of Tokyo, Mitsubishi Bank and Mitsubishi Trust merged to form MTFG. Then, Sanwa Bank and Tokai Bank merged in 2002 to form the UFJ Bank. Finally, MTFG merged with UFJ in 2005. Five of the top ten banks in 2013 were from the USA and the UK and these, too, reflect a history of mergers. In the USA, Chase Manhattan Bank merged with JP Morgan to form JP Morgan Chase. Citigroup grew aggressively through acquiring a whole series of banks and financial services firms, including Travelers Group. In the UK, the major banks have all grown through merger and acquisition: for example, Bank of Scotland and Halifax combined to form HBOS.

In the aftermath of the 2008 financial crisis, however, many of these deals involving commercial and investment banks have unravelled. For example, Bank

Top 10 banks, 2013		Tier 1 capital (US$bn)
1. Industrial & Commercial Bank of China	China	160.65
2. JPMorgan Chase	US	160.00
3. Bank of America	US	155.46
4. HSBC Holdings	UK	151.05
5. China Construction Bank	China	137.60
6. Citigroup	US	136.53
7. Mitsubishi UFJ	Japan	129.58
8. Wells Fargo & Co	US	126.61
9. Bank of China	China	121.50
10. Agricultural Bank of China	China	111.49

Top 10 law companies, 2013		Revenue (US$m)
1. Baker & McKenzie	US	2,104
2. Skadden, Arps, Slate, Meagher & Flom	US	2,100
3. Clifford Chance	UK	1,874
4. Linklaters	UK	1,852
5. Latham & Watkins	US	1,821
6. Freshfields Bruckhaus Deringer	UK	1,787
7. Allen & Overy	UK	1,644
8. Jones Day	US	1,520
9. Kirkland & Ellis	US	1,428
10. Sidley Austin	US	1,357

Top 10 global executive search firms, 2012		Number of offices
1. Cornerstone International	US	87
2. Amrop	Belgium	85
3. Stanton Chase	UK	70
4. Koru/Ferry International	US	64
5. Egon Zehnder	Switzerland	64
6. Boyden	US	64
7. Heidrick & Struggles	US	56
8. Transearch	France	55
9. IIC Partners Worldwide	Canada	54
10. Spencer Stuart	US	53

Top 10 global advertising agencies, 2012		Revenue (US$m)
1. Dentsu	Japan	22,000
2. Omnicom	US	13,900
3. WPP	UK	10,022
4. Publicis	France	7,500
5. Interpublic	US	7,010
6. Hakuhodo	Japan	2,045
7. Havas	France	2,036
8. Aegis	UK	1,775
9. Asatsu–DK	Japan	444
10. MDC Partners	US	443

Figure 16.6   Dominant firms in ABS

Source: based on data in *The Banker*; *The Lawyer*; Beaverstock et al. 2014: Table 2.8; press and company reports

of America acquired Merrill Lynch; in the UK, HBOS was acquired by Lloyds which, in turn, had to be rescued by the British government, as did the largest bank of all, RBS. Not part of these banks' corporate plan! In investment banking, JP Morgan Chase acquired Bear Stearns; the Japanese firm Nomura acquired the Asian and European operations of Lehman Brothers; the UK bank, Barclays, acquired some of Lehman's core US assets.

However, the most spectacular shift involves Chinese banks: 'The tectonic plates of global banking have been shifting noticeably ever since the financial crisis began in 2008 … For the first time ever, a Chinese bank, ICBC, sits atop the rankings.'[17] In fact, four of the top ten global banks in 2013 were Chinese. A seismic shift indeed.

Product diversification

It is a short, and supposedly logical, step from this pursuit of bigness to the notion that ABS firms should supply a *complete package of related services* to their clients. The services conglomerate or the services supermarket arrived, greatly stimulated, in the case of financial services, by increasing deregulation. As we saw earlier, it became increasingly possible for banks to act as securities houses, for securities houses to act as banks, and for both to offer a bewildering array of financial services way beyond their original operations. A typical leading bank's portfolio of offerings came to include: clearing banking, corporate finance, insurance broking, commercial lending, life assurance, mortgages, unit trusts, travellers' cheques, treasury services, credit cards, stockbroking, fund management, development capital, personal pensions and merchant banking. At the same time, entirely new non-bank financial services companies emerged. In non-financial ABS sectors a similar trend developed. For example, companies offering accountancy, consulting and other services under a single umbrella became common.

The rationale for such product diversification was the familiar one of economies of scale and scope and to give reassurance to potential customers that they would receive the highest-quality service wherever they were located. However, there is little evidence that such diversifying mergers lead to significant improvements in efficiency. In the case of financial services, the problem is the nature of financial services products themselves:

> Mergers between car manufacturers or consumer goods companies allow production to be centralized because the products are essentially the same … The same is not true for many financial services … 'A bottle of beer is a real thing but financial products are intangible constructs of regulation, culture and behaviour. A current account is a different product in every country, while life insurance policies are tax-driven products and tax systems are not harmonised. Where will the synergies come from?'[18]

Transnationalization

The provision of ABS to customers depends, more than in any other sector, on *geographical proximity*. Although some services can be supplied at a distance – including, of course, many financial services – the need for face-to-face contact is hugely important. As their major customers have expanded their overseas operations, ABS firms have been under intense pressure to follow. Not surprisingly, then, all the leading ABS firms have become increasingly *transnational*.[19]

Financial services
Although banks have long engaged in international business – for example, through foreign exchange dealing or providing credit for trade – historically, this kind of business was carried out from their domestic bases. Any business that could not be carried out by mail or using telecommunications was handled by local correspondent banks; there was no need for a direct physical presence abroad. A small number of banks certainly set up a few overseas operations towards the end of the nineteenth century. But even in the early part of the twentieth century, the international banking network was very limited indeed. Almost all international banking operations at that time were 'colonial' – part of the imperial spread of

British, Dutch, French and German business activities. In 1913 the four major
US banks had only six overseas branches between them. By 1920 the number of
branches had grown to roughly a hundred but there was little further change until
the 1960s.

As with TNCs in manufacturing industries, the most spectacular expansion of
transnational banking occurred in the 1960s and 1970s. In both cases, US firms
led the initial surge, following their major clients overseas. The number of foreign
affiliates of banks increased from 202 in 1960 to 1928 in 1985. At the same time,
the *geographical composition* of the international banking network changed. US
banks became less dominant while European and Japanese banks increased the
size of their international branch network. The trend towards greater deregulation of national financial markets from the late 1980s and through the 1990s gave
a fresh impetus to transnationalization, especially to transnational mergers and
acquisitions.

Such broad developments also pulled more and more securities firms into
international operations:

> Up to 1979/80, the US multinational investment bank had little more
> than a large office in London and perhaps some much smaller ones in
> other European countries, perhaps an Arab country and possibly
> (though less likely) Japan. From 1980 onward, the development of the
> US investment bank as a multinational changed qualitatively.[20]

As a result, all of the transnational financial services firms have based their strategy
on a direct presence in each of the major geographical markets and on providing a
local service based on global resources. They are, in fact, selling a *global brand image*,
with the clear message that a global company can cope most easily and effectively
with every possible financial problem that can possibly face any customer wherever they are located. This may, or may not, be what actually happens.

Today, the extent of transnationalization among financial services firms is considerable, but variable, as Table 16.1 shows. Although size and transnationality are
related, it is not necessarily the biggest firms that are the most transnationalized. It
is notable that only 2 US firms are among the 20 most transnational financial
services firms. Although the 2008 crisis brought transnational expansion to a halt,
some firms actually increased their transnational presence. Nomura's takeover of
the Asian and European operations of Lehman, for example, 'turned Nomura
from a bank serving Japanese clients globally to a bank serving local clients in
global markets'.[21] Chinese banks also began to pursue active transnationalization
strategies.

Legal services

The provision of legal services to companies requires a direct contact with clients
in each of the territories in which they operate because of the following:

Table 16.1 The transnational scope of leading financial services firms, 2012

Rank by Geographical Spread Index	Company	Headquarters	No. of foreign affiliates	No. of host countries
1	Allianz	Germany	585	65
2	Citigroup	USA	595	74
3	BNP Paribas	France	723	69
4	Assicurazioni Generali SpA	Italy	436	53
5	HSBC	UK	746	65
6	Deutsche Bank	Germany	1031	56
7	Société Générale	France	386	61
8	Unicredit SpA	Italy	861	44
9	AXA	France	515	40
10	Standard Chartered	UK	153	45
11	Credit Suisse	Switzerland	231	36
12	Zurich Insurance Group	Switzerland	318	31
13	UBS	Switzerland	279	50
14	Munich Reinsurance Group	Germany	272	54
15	ING	Netherlands	327	44
16	Bank of Nova Scotia	Canada	108	30
17	Morgan Stanley	USA	163	32
18	Credit Agricole	France	229	43
19	Royal Bank of Canada	Canada	129	26
20	Nomura Holdings	Japan	114	27

Source: based on UNCTAD, 2013a: Web Table 30

- Legal regulations differ from country to country; a lawyer qualified and registered in one country may not be able to operate in another country. It is impossible to offer legal services at a distance.
- The nature of the information being transmitted and the high level of trust involved necessitate a high level of face-to-face interaction.

As a result, the leading law firms have developed increasingly extensive and complex transnational operations:[22]

> The *raison d'être* of transnational law firms … is the development of competitive advantage by providing a *globally aligned, seamless and consistent service* worldwide to all clients … As such, transnational law firms have sought to reproduce faithfully their home country best practices … when establishing offices in overseas jurisdictions.
>
> The rationale for this 'one-firm' strategy … is twofold. First, the firms' most profitable clients originate from their home jurisdictions, namely England and the USA. Transnational law firms were primarily born to service the global needs of home country TNCs which, as they expand their international operations, require consistent and predictable advisory services. Second, the dominance of English and US law in the structuring of cross-border commercial activities has further encouraged English and US firms to export their home country norms to overseas offices.[23]

However, the jurisdictional constraints within which legal firms have to work have a major effect on the kind of organizational structures that transnational legal firms employ and make the implementation of a 'one-firm' strategy difficult. Legal firms are primarily organized as *partnerships*, in which the top individuals/partners own the company. A direct presence in individual markets may be achieved by establishing an office staffed by local and/or expatriate lawyers. An indirect presence is usually organized through membership of a 'legal network, such as Interlex or through the establishment of a "best friends" arrangement with "local" law firms in overseas jurisdictions'.[24] An increasingly common way of operating transnationally is through

> 'temporary teams' that are formed to fulfil a client's requirements and then disbanded … The main strategy transnational law firms have used to manage this need for team-work is the practice group. As worldwide groupings practice groups act as an umbrella under which all lawyers with the same legal speciality sit … the aim of firms is to make practice groups cohesive and based on a common set of values.[25]

However, perhaps more than many other kinds of TNC, legal firms face an especially strong tension between creating a global way of working and local integration.[26] Table 16.2 lists the leading legal services firms, all of which are from either the USA or the UK. These leading firms tend to use their own direct operations rather than work within a network.[27]

Executive recruitment

The global executive search ('headhunting') industry has a rather brief history, originating in the USA in the 1950s, but growing very rapidly from the 1970s.[28]

Table 16.2   The transnational scope of leading legal services firms, 2009

Company	Headquarters	No. of lawyers	No. of global offices
Skadden Arps Slate Meagher & Flom	USA	2100	22
Baker & McKenzie	USA	3627	70
DLA Piper	USA/UK	2267	59
Linklaters	UK	2367	30
Freshfields Bruckhaus Deringer	UK	2263	28
Clifford Chance	UK	2904	28
Latham & Watkins	USA	2150	22
Allen & Overy	UK	2122	25
Sidley Austin	USA	1892	16
Jones Day	USA	2516	29

Source: based on Faulconbridge et al. 2012: Table 1

It developed primarily out of the management consultancy sector. Headhunting exemplifies one of the key attributes of contemporary global business: the perceived importance of business leaders with transnational experience. Headhunters search out suitable senior managerial or board executives on behalf of corporate clients; it is an elite labour market function. As a rule, the target individuals are already employed in another firm, so the term 'headhunting' is rather appropriate.

It is the very largest headhunting firms that have expanded the most rapidly and aggressively. The top 15 firms had increased their number of offices to 850 by 2012 (Table 16.3); in 1992 the top 15 had 461 offices:

> Five of the consistently ranked global top-six headhunters had increased their regional office networks by 173%, from 100 offices to 273, between 1987 and 2005.[29]

Executive search firms are hired by clients for a fee (based upon a candidate's salary) to fill a vacant senior position (either actual or potential):

> Whilst they are fundamentally offering the same service … different firms have their own unique executive search cultures and styles … Distinctions can be made between specialist boutiques that concentrate on headhunting in a limited number of sectors … and integrated 'complete service' corporations that offer executive search in any major industry … As with other producer services, a long 'tail' exists with firms that have some form of 'international operation' – circa 5000 firms.[30]

Table 16.3   The transnational scope of leading executive search firms, 2012

Company	Headquarters	No. of countries	No. of offices
Cornerstone	USA	41	87
Amrop	Belgium	52	85
Stanton Chase	UK	46	70
Korn/Ferry International	USA	37	64
Egon Zehnder	Switzerland	38	64
Boyden	USA	40	64
Heidrick & Struggles	USA	31	46
Transearch	France	38	55
IIC Partners Worldwide	UK	38	54
Spencer Stuart	USA	29	53
Odgers Bernstson	UK	28	42
Signium International	USA	27	41
Russell Reynolds	USA	21	40
Horton Group International	UK	24	38
Alexander Hughes	France	31	37

Source: based on Beaverstock et al. 2014: Table 2.8

As in other business service sectors, headhunters use a variety of organizational forms to operate transnationally:[31]

- *Wholly-owned firm.* A firm that operates a tightly organized set of offices across the world, all of which work within the parent firm's brand identity, control and work practices.
- *Networked firm.* A strategic alliance between several independent firms: 'architectures linking single country firms together into a global network … that can perform labour searches across many nations when needed'.
- *Hybrid firm.* '[I]nvolves tighter integration than in a network which has only one office in each country and shared standards and approaches existing across the alliance'.
- *Combined structures.* Some of the biggest headhunting firms may adopt different approaches at the same time to meet specific circumstances.

Advertising

Just as the transnationalization of banking was largely stimulated by the need to follow major client TNCs overseas, so, too, has advertising followed a similar trajectory.[32] As in the case of banking, it was US agencies (such as McCann Erickson) and, subsequently, UK agencies (such as Saatchi & Saatchi) that led the way. Initially, the relationship between client and agency was relatively simple: agencies were intimately tied to specific clients. But as the consumer landscape changed – as markets became global in some senses but intensely local in others, as consumers became more aware and discriminating and, ultimately, increasingly consuming through the Internet and the social media – the challenges facing advertising firms became vastly more complex:

> Global agencies had to develop the ability to create demand for a product in multiple geographically dispersed and heterogeneous markets in which consumer behaviours and relationships to products differed ... Place-specific product variations tend to prohibit global adverts.[33]

Organizationally, the response has been to create *global holding groups* – developed over a relatively short time through mergers and acquisitions – within which individual advertising agencies are embedded. The purpose of such holding groups is to get around the constraints imposed by the traditional long-term, one-client-per industry relationship:

> Thus the umbrella of the holding group was born to allow 'Chinese walls' to be created between agencies whereby clients in competition can be serviced within the same group but by different agencies ... In their current guise, the leading global agencies ... have grown within their holding groups to become, alongside accountants ... and management consultants ... perhaps some of the most geographically dispersed knowledge-intensive business service organizations ... 'the global land grab' by agencies is now almost complete with all of the ten largest global agencies having offices on every continent including Africa.[34]

Figure 16.7 illustrates the structure of some of the world's leading communications holding groups and their major global advertising agencies.

Holding group	Main global agencies	No. of global offices, 2009
Omnicom	BBDO Worldwide DDB Worldwide Communications TBWA Worldwide	287 200 233
WPP	J. Walter Thomson Ogilvy & Mather Worldwide Young & Rubican Grey	227 450 304 –
Publicis	Publicis Worldwide Saatchi & Saatchi Leo Burnett Worldwide	170 150 –
Interpublic	Draft Foote Cone & Belding Worldwide McCann Erickson Worldwide Lowe Worldwide	106 417 –

Figure 16.7　Major communications holding groups and their advertising agencies

Source: based on Faulconbridge et al., 2011: Tables 2.1, 2.2

GEOGRAPHIES OF ADVANCED BUSINESS SERVICES

At first sight, ICT developments would appear to release ABS, especially financial services, from geographical constraints. Such firms might seem to be especially footloose: they are not tied to specific raw materials locations, and at least some of their transactions can be carried out electronically over vast geographical distances. Such considerations have led many to write geography and distance out of the script as far as financial services, in particular, are concerned.[35]

Certainly, revolutionary developments in ICT permit information (including financial transactions) to whizz around the world while deregulation has reduced the resistance of national boundaries to financial flows. But, far from heralding the 'end of geography', this has, in fact, made geography *more* – not less – important. Indeed, we find that, at global, national and local scales, ABS continue to be extremely *strongly concentrated geographically.* They are, in fact, more highly concentrated than virtually any other kind of economic activity, except those based on highly localized raw materials.

Cities as the 'natural habitat' for advanced business services

Above all, the geographies of ABS are enmeshed and embedded in *cities*: cities of all kinds but, especially, the biggest cities whose top tier consists of the so-called *global* or *world cities.* The geographies of ABS, then, are synonymous with the geographies of big cities in which the leading financial, legal, accounting, consultancy, headhunting, advertising and other ABS and their corporate clients cluster. Such cities are their 'natural habitat' constituting an *ecology* of ABS, in which each component feeds upon the others. From a global perspective, what matters, however, is not just the 'local' ecology, but also the intensity of *connectivity* between cities: the position of individual cities in the world city network.

Figure 16.8 shows two dimensions of the world city network (WCN):

- An index of global network connectivity (GNC), based upon an analysis of 175 office networks in accountancy, advertising, financial services, legal services and management consultancy across 525 cities. The inset shows the top 20 most highly connected cities in 2008.
- A measure of the visibility of individual cities, based upon an analysis of the number of 'mentions' in business advertisements in *The Economist.*

A comparison of changes in GNC between 2000 and 2008 shows three significant features:[36]

- *Changes in the rank of cities.* 'Among cities with the largest global network connectivity (GNC) in 2000 and 2008 … the most notable feature is the

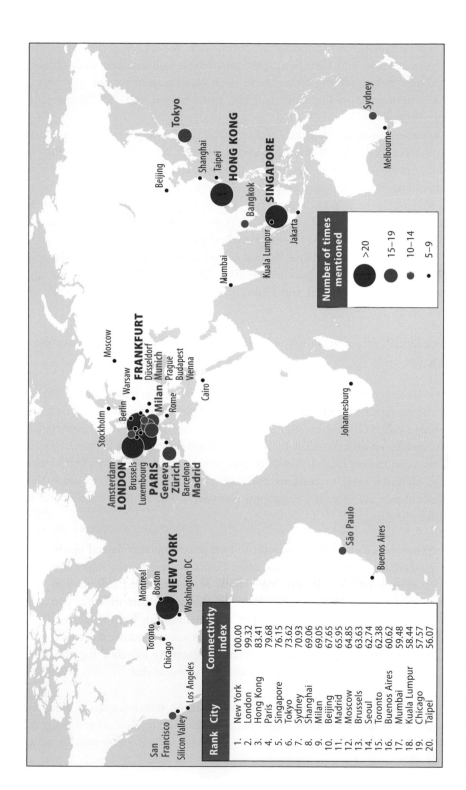

Figure 16.8   **Key cities in the global economy**

Source: based on Taylor, 2001: Figure 2; Taylor, 2004: Table 3.5; Derudder et al., 2010: Table 2

stability at the apex of the world city network: London, New York and Hong Kong remain the most connected cities, with NY-LON as the undisputed dominant dyad; and Paris, Singapore and Tokyo follow, albeit with different rankings. Below the top 6 there have been some major changes ... [notably] the plummeting of US cities and the concomitant rise of Chinese cities' (pp. 1866–868).

- *Changes in the overall connectivity of cities.* 'Overall, 179 out of 307 cities are more connected to the WCN at large than they were in 2000. This indicates that the globalisation of services has been a dynamic and growing economic sector, expanding offices in many cities and extending office networks to new cities ... Although the NY-LON dyad still dominates the network, its structure has become more horizontal between 2000 and 2008 ... The result has been an increasingly integrated world-city network' (p. 1869).

- *The rise of cities in Pacific Asia.* 'Shanghai and Beijing have witnessed the most substantial connectivity gains in the 2000–2008 period ... although *all* cities in Pacific Asia in general and China in particular have become more connected' (p. 1871).

The locational attractions of major world cities for ABS firms reflect four interlocking processes:[37]

- The characteristics of the *business organizations* involved in such centres: (a) much of the production of ABS occurs at the boundaries of firms and there is a strong reliance on repeat business; (b) the firms tend to be 'flattened and non-hierarchical' and based around 'small teams of relationship and product specialists'; (c) firms need to cooperate as well as to compete, as in the case of syndicated lending; (d) firms need to compare themselves with one another to judge their performance; (e) there is a need for a constant search for new business and for rapid response.

  > These shared characteristics point to two important correlates. First, in general, these firms must be sociable. Contacts are crucially important in generating and maintaining a flow of business and information about business. 'Who you know is, in this sense, part of what you know ...; 'relationship management' is a vital task for both employees and firms. Second, this hunger for contacts is easier to satisfy if contacts are concentrated, are proximate. When contacts are bunched together they are easier to gain access to, and swift access at that.[38]

In the case of industries like advertising, for example, which involve a great deal of project work, the presence of 'agglomerations both of freelancers and firms that can be drawn on as and when needed to provide particular expertise' is vital.[39] Face-to-face contact is overwhelmingly important in ABS.

- The *diversity of markets* in international centres: (a) their large size which makes them both flexible in terms of entry and exit and also socially differentiated: 'more likely to consist of social "micro-networks" of buyers and sellers, whose effect on price-setting can sometimes be marked'; (b) their basis in rapid dissemination of information which may lead to major market movements; (c) their speculative and highly volatile nature. 'Again, as with the case of organizations, there are the two obvious corollaries to these characteristics: the twin needs for sociability and proximity.'

- The *culture* of international cities: (a) they receive, send and interpret increasing amounts of information; (b) they are the focus of increasing amounts of expertise which arise from a complex division of labour involving workforce skills and machinery; (c) they depend on contacts and such contacts have become increasingly reflexive because of their basis in trust founded on relationships. Such cultural aspects are increasingly important.

- The *dynamic external economies of scale* which arise from the sheer size and concentration of ABS firms in such centres. Such economies include: (a) the sharing of the fixed costs of operating financial markets (e.g. settlement systems, document transport systems) between a large number of firms; (b) the attraction of greater information turnover and liquidity; (c) the enhanced probability of product innovations in such clusters (the 'sparking of mind against mind'); (d) the increased probability of making contacts, which rises with the number of possible contacts; (e) the attraction of linked services such as accounting, legal, computer services, which reduces the cost to the firm of acquiring such services; (f) the development of a pool of skilled labour; (g) the enhanced reputation of a centre which, in a cumulative way, increases that reputation and attracts new firms. In other words, the constellation of traded and untraded interdependencies, 'buzz' and creative dynamism, described in Chapters 3 and 4, reach their maximum development in leading world cities.

High-level *financial* services, in particular, tend to concentrate in a small number of cities which control almost all the world's financial transactions (Figure 16.9). It is a remarkable level of geographical concentration. Of course, such cities are more than just financial centres. For example, there is clearly a close relationship with the distribution of the corporate and regional headquarters of transnational corporations (see Chapter 5). These global financial centres may, indeed, be regarded as the geographical *control points of the global economic system*: what Cassis calls 'the capitals of capital'.[40]

But not all global financial centres – even those at the top of the hierarchy – are identical: each tends to have distinctive characteristics reflecting its specific history and geography. On criteria measuring both the breadth and depth of global financial activity, New York and London stand at the apex of the global financial hierarchy. London is the more broadly based international financial centre,

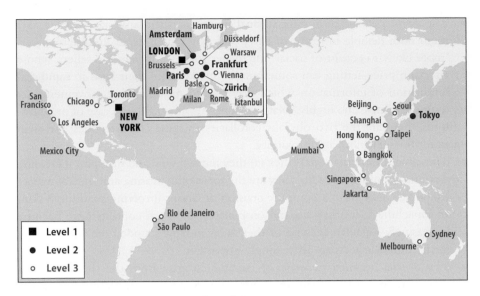

Figure 16.9   **The global network of financial centres**

Source: based on Reid, 1989: Figure 1; data in Taylor, 2004

particularly in terms of its strengths in foreign exchange, international equities and derivatives. The daily turnover on the London foreign exchange market is almost as large as the turnover in New York and Tokyo put together.

London's significance as a global financial centre is attributable to several factors:[41]

- The historical evolution of the City as a world centre has created both a large pool of relevant skills and an almost unparalleled concentration of linked institutions within a very small geographical area.
- Its geographical position located in a time zone between Asia and New York.
- The regulatory environment has encouraged the growth of transnational banking. Foreign banks in London can operate as 'universal' banks.
- Its key role as a 'capital switching centre' – 'the London market brings together in one place great diversity of market participants and, consequently, great diversity of risk preferences and profiles'.[42]

London still has the largest concentration of foreign banks in the world: its strength as a financial centre is based primarily on the scale of its foreign exchange business and its deregulated securities markets. New York is the world's largest securities market in addition to a huge concentration of transnational banks and other financial activities. London and New York stand apart from Tokyo as truly global financial centres. The international significance of Tokyo has rested primarily on the strength of the Japanese economy itself. London also maintains its lead over such key European cities as Frankfurt and Paris, even though both of these cities have strengthened their financial centres. In addition, London has made strong efforts to become a global centre of Islamic finance.

Although this global financial network has certain stable features it is by no means static. New centres emerge, as shown by the increasing status of East Asian financial centres, particularly Singapore, Hong Kong and Shanghai. The two latter cities are also locked in competition as the leading financial centres of China.[43] But these are long-term processes. It takes time for real, sustained change to become apparent, which is why it is impossible to predict, with any certainty, the effect of the 2008 crisis on London's or New York's standing. On the one hand, there are anecdotal stories of financial firms planning to move out of London because of the fear of increased regulation or higher taxation. On the other hand, a 2012 Global Financial Centres Index report[44] showed London retaining its first place among the world's leading financial centres, closely followed by New York.

Geographical decentralization and offshoring of business services

All of the discussion of global financial centres suggests that the potential for other cities, outside the favoured few shown in Figure 16.9, to develop as significant centres of finance and related activities is very limited. In the UK, for example, the sheer overwhelming dominance of London makes it extremely difficult for provincial cities to develop more than a very restricted financial and ABS function.

It is, of course, the 'higher-order' financial and ABS functions which are especially heavily concentrated in the major global financial centres. However, as we have seen, the essence of ABS activities is the transformation of massive volumes of *information*. Much of that activity is routine data processing performed by clerical workers. Such 'back-office' activity can be separated from the front-office functions and performed in different locations. The early adoption of large-scale computing by banks, insurance companies and the like from the late 1950s led many of them to set up huge *centralized* data processing units. To escape the high costs (both land and labour) in the major financial centres such units were often relocated to less expensive centres or in the suburbs. Access to large pools of appropriate (often female) labour was a key requirement.

The introduction of dispersed computer networks made such centralized processing units unnecessary and the trend shifted to *decentralizing* back-office functions. At the same time, the distinction between back-office and front-office functions became less clear. In fact, it is not just routine back-office activities that have been decentralized. It has become increasingly common for some of the higher-skilled functions to be relocated away from head office into dispersed locations, both nationally and, in some cases, transnationally. Within the UK, for example, several leading banks (notably Bank of America, JP Morgan and Deutsche Bank) recently announced plans to move around 3000 jobs out of the City of London to other UK centres.[45] However, such shifts still tend to be rather limited (both in number of jobs and the level of functions involved) when set against the continuing concentration of financial services in London.

Beyond the continued tendency to retain their major presence in key centres, ABS firms have become increasingly involved in offshoring some of their functions:

> In 2006, over 75 per cent of major financial institutions had offshore activities, compared with less than 10 per cent in 2001 … The main activities offshored are those involving the use of IT, lower value-added activities (such as payroll) and lower value-added contact with customers (such as scripted outbound sales calls). But offshoring has spread across nearly all business functions, with significant growth in transaction processing, finance and various aspects of human resources activity. Even activities requiring specific skills, such as financial research and modelling, have the potential to be ultimately offshored as well.[46]

As the extent of ABS offshoring has increased, its organizational form has become more varied, as Figure 16.10 shows. Initially, most offshoring by financial services firms was *vendor direct outsourcing* to a foreign firm located overseas. As major financial services firms became increasingly involved in offshoring they began to establish systems of *captive direct offshoring*: setting up their own subsidiary operations in other countries. The third, most recent, arrangement, *vendor indirect offshoring*, reflects the tendency for specialist outsourcing companies to establish their own transnational networks to serve more diverse customers. So, for example, one of the leading Indian IT-outsourcing companies, Tata Consultancy Services (TCS), established its own operations in Hungary, as part of its increasingly global network:

	Vendor direct	**Captive direct**	**Vendor indirect**
	Place contract with specialist firm in specific country	Set up own directly-owned operation(s) overseas	Place contract with specialist firm with operations in several countries
Potential benefits	Cost reduction Use of specialist expertise Speed	Increased control Reduced risk Greater security	Lower costs Use of specialist expertise Vendor reputation
Potential costs	Loss of control Security risks	High cost of establishment and control	Control issues Security risks

Figure 16.10   **Alternative modes of offshoring**

Source: based, in part, on material in the *Financial Times*, 18 February 2004

TCS first opened a software centre in Hungary in 2001 ... it is now building a *global delivery network* so that projects can be completed closer to the customer where necessary ... TCS chose Hungary because, as well as English, many Hungarians can speak other European languages, including German, French, and Italian. 'We want to provide a European front and [point of contact] for our European customers' ... TCS preferred eastern Europe over western Europe because it was much cheaper ... Eastern Europe is where India was a decade ago.[47]

However, India itself remains by far the most popular ABS offshoring location

with around two-thirds of global offshored staff employed in the sub-continent. A number of other countries have also attracted offshoring activity. These include South Africa, Malaysia and the Philippines, where financial institutions can find the necessary skill and work quality. These countries have large pools of young, educated, technologically competent and English-speaking workers. There are a large number of graduates with finance, accounting or management and information technology backgrounds, who are ideally suited to off-shore work in the financial sector.[48]

Overall, however, the phenomenon of offshoring/onshoring in the ABS industries remain highly volatile, with trends and countertrends occurring all the time.

NOTES

1   Martin (1999: 6, 11).
2   Strange (1986: 1).
3   Dow (1999: 33).
4   French and Leyshon (2004).
5   *Financial Times* (18 March 2008).
6   *Financial Times* (16 March 1994).
7   O'Brien and Keith (2009: 245–6).
8   Warf and Purcell (2001: 227).
9   See Langdale (2000).
10 Kelly (1995: 229). See also Crotty (2009), Dore (2008), Mügge (2009), Tett (2009).
11 O'Brien and Keith (2009: 249).
12 O'Brien and Keith (2009: 249).
13 Kay (2009: 57).
14 Martin (1999: 8, 9).
15 *Financial Times* (22 April 2009).
16 Faulconbridge et al. (2011: 15).

17   *The Banker* (July 2013).

18   *Financial Times* (26 May 2000).

19   Jones (2005).

20   Scott–Quinn (1990: 281).

21   *Financial Times* (9 September 2009).

22   This section is based on Faulconbridge (2008), Faulconbridge et al. (2012), Jones (2007), Muzio and Faulconbridge (2013). See also Beaverstock (2004).

23   Faulconbridge et al. (2012: 51, 52).

24   Faulconbridge (2008: 502).

25   Faulconbridge (2008: 504).

26   Faulconbridge et al. (2008: 504), Faulconbridge et al. (2012), Muzio and Faulconbridge (2013).

27   Faulconbridge (2008: 502).

28   Beaverstock et al. (2014), Faulconbridge et al. (2008), Faulconbridge et al. (2009).

29   Faulconbridge et al. (2008: 222).

30   Faulconbridge et al. (2008: 214).

31   Faulconbridge et al. (2008: 226–7, 230).

32   See Faulconbridge et al. (2011) for an excellent discussion of the globalization of advertising and its geographies. This section relies heavily on that work.

33   Faulconbridge et al. (2011: 13–14).

34   Faulconbridge et al. (2011: 17).

35   O'Brien (1992). See also O'Brien and Keith (2009).

36   Derudder et al. (2010).

37   Thrift (1994).

38   Thrift (1994: 333).

39   Faulconbridge et al. (2011: 36).

40   Cassis (2006).

41   Lewis and Davis (1987).

42   Clark (2002: 448).

43   Karreman and van der Knaap (2009).

44   *Financial Times* (19 March 2012).

45   *Financial Times* (10 December 2012).

46   WTO (2008: 114).

47   *Financial Times* (3 August 2005; emphasis added).

48   WTO (2008: 114).

Seventeen

'MAKING THE CONNECTIONS, MOVING THE GOODS': LOGISTICS AND DISTRIBUTION SERVICES

TAKING LOGISTICS AND DISTRIBUTION FOR GRANTED

Whereas there is a huge literature and a continuous, often frenzied, debate on the role of financial services in the processes of globalization, logistics and distribution rarely make an appearance on the stage. They remain hidden, mainly confined to the specialist fields of supply chain management and transportation. The logistics and distribution processes get taken for granted.[1] It is more or less assumed that, as transportation and communication systems have allegedly shrunk geographical distance, the problems of getting products from points of production to points of consumption have been solved.

In fact, the very opposite is the case. The *circulation processes* that *connect* together all the different components of the production network are absolutely fundamental (see Chapter 3). The logistics industries themselves are huge:

> As an area of economic activity, logistics were worth an estimated US$3.6 trillion in 2009 – and predicted to reach US$3.9 trillion by 2013 … Logistics costs account, on average, for 10–15 per cent of the final cost of finished products in the developed world, including transport costs (7–9 per cent), warehousing costs (1–2 per cent) and inventory holdings (3–5 per cent).[2]

They have become especially significant in light of the broader forces of change discussed in earlier chapters, notably:

- new production methods, involving increased flexibility;
- changing relationships between customers and suppliers;
- increasing use of JIT procurement and delivery systems;
- increasing geographical complexity and extent of production networks;
- changing consumer preferences.

In particular, *time* has come to be seen as the essential basis of successful competition.[3] In such a context, the nature and efficiency of distribution systems become central:

> Time- and quality-based competition depends on eliminating waste in the form of time, effort, defective units, and inventory in manufacturing-distribution systems … [requiring] firms to practice such logistical strategies as just-in-time management, lean logistics, vendor-managed inventory, direct delivery, and outsourcing of logistics services so that they become more flexible and fast, to better satisfy customer requirements.[4]

THE STRUCTURE OF LOGISTICS AND DISTRIBUTION SERVICES

The essential function of the logistics and distribution services – which should be regarded as GPNs in their own right – is to *intermediate* between buyers and sellers at all stages of a production circuit (Figure 17.1). This involves not only the *physical movement* of materials and goods, but also the transmission and manipulation of *information* relating to such movements. They involve, above all, the organization and coordination of complex flows across increasingly extended geographical distances. In that respect, these services have been revolutionized by the technological developments in transportation and communication discussed in Chapter 4. They have also been transformed by the increased outsourcing of logistics and distribution services by manufacturing firms, by the intensifying pressures from the big retailers and by the emergence of new forms of logistics service providers.

In Figure 17.1 there are no political or other obstacles to complicate the basic system. In reality, of course, such obstacles greatly affect the structure and operation of logistics and distribution processes. Two kinds of 'barrier' to movement are especially significant:

- Physical conditions that necessitate the transfer from one transportation mode to another – for example, land/water interfaces.
- Political boundaries that create complications of customs clearance, tariffs, duties, administration, and the like. Such barriers have become increasingly significant as economic activity has become more globalized.

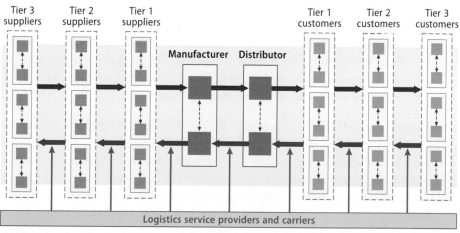

Figure 17.1   **Logistics and distribution in the production circuit**

Source: based, in part, on Schary and Skjøtt Larsen, 2001: Figure 1.6

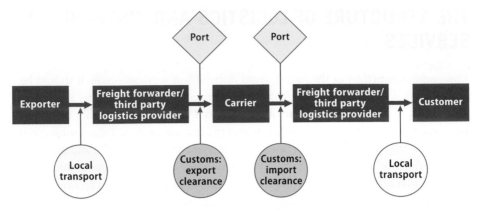

Figure 17.2   **Logistics processes in a transnational context**

Source: adapted from Schary and Skjøtt-Larsen, 2001: Figure 11.7

Hence, as Figure 17.2 shows, there are many stages in the process of getting products to their final market:

> A typical door-to-door journey for containerised international shipments involves the interaction of approximately 25 different stakeholders, generates 30–40 documents, uses two to three different transport modes and is handled in 12–15 physical locations.[5]

However, the more extended a production circuit becomes – both organizationally and geographically – the greater the potential problems. For example:

> Companies deciding to source in China rather than producing in-house may think they are adding a single link to their supply chain … In fact, they are probably adding at least five: the production agent in China, a logistics company in China, China customs, the freight shipper, customs and transport in the domestic market.[6]

The logistics and distribution processes shown in Figures 17.1 and 17.2 can be performed in a variety of ways and by a variety of organizational forms. At one extreme, each individual transaction may be performed by a separate firm; at the other extreme, the entire process may be carried out by a single integrated firm or related group of firms. Between these two ends of the spectrum there is, of course, a shifting of positions as circumstances change. However, there is a very clear trend towards greater outsourcing of logistics functions.[7]

The major types of organization involved in logistics and distribution include:

- transportation companies
- logistics service providers (LSPs)

- wholesalers
- trading companies
- retailers
- e-tailers.

Transportation companies (rail, road, shipping, airlines), wholesalers and retailers perform fairly clearly defined and restricted roles in the production circuit. On the other hand, trading companies and the more recent specialist logistics service providers perform a far broader range of activities. Not only are the boundaries between these types of organization often blurred, but also one form of organization may mutate into another, as we will see later in this chapter. At the same time, the significance of some types of intermediary has changed.

For example, traditionally, the wholesaler played a major role in collecting materials or products from a range of individual producers and then distributing them to the next stage of the production process, or to the retailer in the case of final demand. However, the importance of the wholesaler as the key intermediary has changed substantially as the major retailers have bypassed wholesalers to deal directly with the manufacturer, or as other forms of logistics and distribution services have developed. In a similar way, the development of e-commerce makes it possible to bypass the traditional retailer as the key intermediary between producer and final consumer and to create a new type of retailer: the *e-tailer*. Figure 17.3 shows just one way in which the production/supply circuit may be organized.

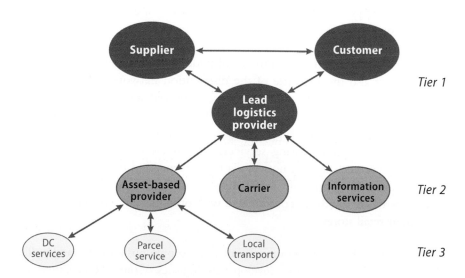

Figure 17.3 A potential way of organizing logistics services

Source: adapted from Schary and Skjøtt-Larsen, 2001: Figure 7.4

THE DYNAMICS OF THE MARKET FOR LOGISTICS SERVICES

In aggregate terms, the growth of the market for logistics and distribution services is closely related to growth in the economy as a whole. Hence, the 2008 economic recession had a huge impact, reducing demand for transportation and logistics services and putting on hold some major infrastructural projects in ports and other transportation and communications hubs and routes. But beyond this cyclical variation in demand, the market for logistics and distribution services is highly heterogeneous. Demand for some kinds of distribution services has grown more rapidly than others.

Ultimately, as Figure 17.1 shows, the system is driven by the demands of the final consumer, although this influence becomes increasingly indirect the further back up the production circuit we go. Although the primary driver of final consumer demand is the level of disposable income, consumption, as we have discussed at various points in this book, is an immensely complex socio-cultural process. The intensely competitive retail markets have major repercussions on the demand for distribution and logistics services further up the production circuit. As we saw in the agro-food (Chapter 13) and clothing (Chapter 14) industries, the major retailers and buyers exert intense pressure on their suppliers to deliver more rapidly, more cheaply and in greater variety. This, in turn, creates opportunities (and challenges) for the suppliers of logistics and distribution services to provide a faster and more integrated supply system between the different components of the production circuit.

The enhanced power of the major retailers greatly affects the logistics firms responsible for getting the products to the retail stores:

> A shifting power structure in the retail trade not only changes market shares but also the structure of the distribution network. The major international retail customers ask for customized logistics solutions across borders. Apart from negotiating frame orders with significant price advantages with suppliers, the most powerful retailers also require information sharing services, such as electronic data interchange, advance shipping notices via the Internet and track and trace capabilities. They typically prefer delivery to their own distribution centers where goods are consolidated with other products for delivery to their retail stores.[8]

In effect, there has been a pronounced shift from 'supply push' to 'demand pull', a shift which generates pressure to develop new logistics systems. Hence, there is a link between the changing demand pressures on the suppliers of logistics and distribution services and changing technologies. Let us now look at these technologies.

TECHNOLOGICAL INNOVATION AND LOGISTICS AND DISTRIBUTION SERVICES

Three criteria dominate the logistics and distribution services:

- speed
- flexibility
- reliability.

Technological innovations have revolutionized all three. At a general level, techno-logical developments in transportation and communication have been immensely important in transforming the basic time–space infrastructure of the logistics and distribution industries. Likewise, these industries have also been revolutionized by the shift in process technologies from mass production to more flexible and cus-tomized production systems. The mass production systems of the late nineteenth and first two-thirds of the twentieth century were facilitated by mass distribution systems, based on rapidly developing rail, road and ocean shipping networks (see Chapter 4).

Such mass distribution systems depended heavily on the use of large ware-houses to store components and products and from which deliveries were made to customers on an infrequent basis. This was an immensely expensive system in terms of the capital tied up in large inventories. It was also, very often, a source of waste in terms of faulty products that were not discovered until they were actually used. Together with a major shift towards lean, JIT, systems of production, there has also been a parallel shift towards *lean systems of distribution*, whose purpose is to minimize the time and cost involved in moving products between suppliers and customers, including the holding of inventory.

Three key elements form the core of such lean distribution systems:[9]

- *Electronic data interchange (EDI)*. This enables the rapid transmission of large quantities of data electronically (rather than using paper documents). Such data can encompass all aspects of the logistics and distribution system throughout the production circuit, including the retailer. Information on product specifi-cations, purchase orders, invoices, status of the transaction, location of the ship-ments, delivery schedules, and so on can be exchanged instantly. EDI requires a common software platform to enable data to be read by all participants in the chain.
- *Bar code systems and radio frequency identification technology*. Bar codes were first developed in the 1970s by grocery manufacturers and food chain stores to enable each item to be given a unique, electronically readable identity. They are now ubiquitous throughout the production circuit: 'Bar codes permit organizations to handle effectively the kind of vast product differentiation that

would have been prohibitively expensive in an earlier era. They also facilitate instantaneous information at the point of sale, with significant effects on inventory management and logistics.'[10] Radio frequency identification (RFID) technology greatly increases the sophistication and flexibility of the bar code principle. Bar codes can be difficult to read (they require a clear line of sight). RFID technology gets around this by using small radio tags that allow goods to be tracked continuously throughout their progression through a production circuit. By combining the tag with a unique electronic product code (EPC) it becomes possible to incorporate a large quantity of information about each object. One observer (admittedly with a vested interest in RFID technology) described it as 'a bar code on steroids'.[11]

- *Distribution centres.* Modern distribution centres hold inventory for much shorter periods of time and turn it over very rapidly: 'Four technologies have made the modern distribution centre possible: (1) bar codes and associated software systems; (2) high-speed conveyers with advanced routing and switching controls; (3) increased reliability and accuracy of laser scanning of incoming containers; and (4) increased computing capacities.'[12] In the most advanced distribution centres – such as the system used by the US retailer Wal-Mart – a method known as 'cross-docking' is used. This is a 'largely invisible logistics technique … [in which] … goods are continuously delivered to Wal-Mart's warehouses, where they are selected, repacked, and then dispatched to stores, often without ever sitting in inventory. Instead of spending valuable time in the warehouse, goods just cross from one loading dock to another in 48 hours or less. Cross-docking enables Wal-Mart to achieve economies that come with purchasing full truckloads of goods while avoiding the usual inventory and handling costs.'[13]

Computer-based electronic information systems are at the heart of all three of these technological developments in logistics and distribution systems. They have evolved over a period of 30 years, often incrementally rather than as a spectacular 'revolution'. Now, however,

> [l]iterally every item in motion in the physical flows of the global economy can be (and often is) tagged with detailed digital information about its origin, contents and destination and is already deeply integrated into factory production schedules or retail sales.[14]

E-commerce: a logistics revolution

The later 1990s brought into existence an entirely new set of distribution methods based upon the Internet: *e-commerce*. In essence, e-commerce has developed out of the convergence of several technological strands: EDI, the Internet, e-mail and

Types of e-commerce

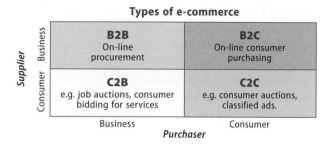

The major components of e-commerce organization

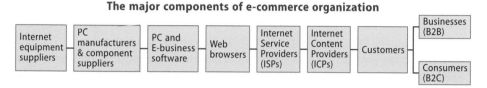

Figure 17.4 **Types of e-commerce**

Source: based, in part, on Gereffi, 2001: Figure 2

the medium of the World Wide Web (WWW).[15] The e-commerce revolution has changed the world of distribution and the main reason, once again, is *speed*.

Although four types of e-commerce are shown in Figure 17.4, two dominate:

- *B2B (business-to-business).* This encompasses potentially the whole range of transactions between businesses, notably procurement of products and services and logistics. B2B websites are electronic 'marketplaces' where firms come together to buy or sell products and services. They may be 'vertical': that is, industry specific. One example is the B2B procurement system, Covisint, established in 2000 by General Motors and Ford, together with some other automobile manufacturers, to increase the efficiency of component purchasing. Covisint is now a diversified cloud computing company involved in a wide range of sectors. Alternatively, B2B websites may be 'horizontal', organized around the products and services provided rather than the industry. Connecting together large numbers of buyers and sellers through electronically automated transactions has a number of potential benefits, notably vastly increasing choice to both sellers and buyers, saving costs on transactions, and increasing the transparency of the entire supply chain.
- *B2C (business-to-consumer).* B2C business is the selling of consumer products and services directly over the Internet by a Web-based firm. The pioneers included Amazon, eBay and Dell but, of course, the dotcom revolution created millions of 'e-tailers', some with a very short life. E-tailing has also been adopted by the traditional retailers. Indeed, contrary to predictions that traditional retailers would be adversely affected by Internet shopping, the opposite has occurred, especially with the development of comparison sites which allow customers to

compare products and prices and read reviews. The potential benefits of B2C transactions are, to the consumer, greater choice, ease of comparison of prices, instant (or very fast) delivery to the home or on a click-and-collect basis from a local store, and, to the seller, direct access to a massive potential market without the need for physical space in the form of retail outlets and the associated inventory and staffing costs. As a result, online shopping has grown extremely rapidly. One estimate is that in the UK it accounted for 12.7 per cent of total retail sales in 2012; in the USA for around 9 per cent.[16]

E-commerce (both B2B and B2C) has enormous potential implications for the traditional intermediaries of business and retail transactions. Early predictions were that many would disappear as their functions were displaced by direct online transactions. In fact, this has not happened to anything like the extent predicted. On the contrary, e-commerce has actually enhanced opportunities for such roles and created entirely new Internet-based service companies. Some traditional intermediaries have adapted and found new ways of adding value as providers of logistics, information and financial services; new intermediaries have emerged.[17] Some of these are what are sometimes termed *infomediaries*, notably the Internet service and content providers shown in Figure 17.4. Figure 17.5 shows that in the case of both physical goods and electronic goods and services, either old intermediaries transform themselves or new ones appear. As in financial services (Chapter 16), both disintermediation and reintermediation occur simultaneously.

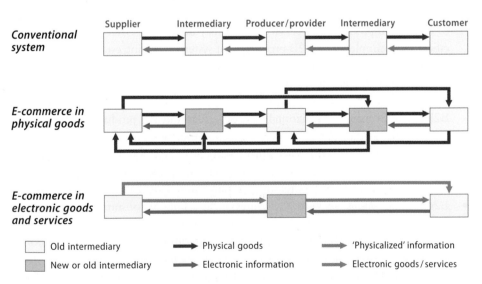

Figure 17.5   **The continuing role of intermediaries in an e-commerce world**

Source: based on Kenney and Curry, 2001: Figure 3.2

Related to the perception that e-commerce spells the end for the traditional inter-mediary organization is the idea that traditional physical infrastructures will also be displaced. Again, this is an illusion. As Figure 17.6 shows, there are several ways of fulfilling e-commerce orders:[18]

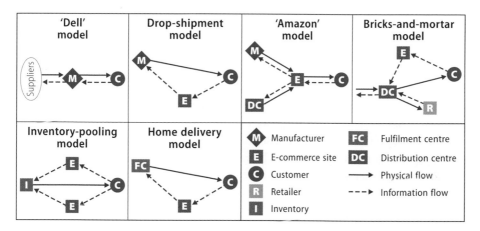

Figure 17.6   **Methods of fulfilling e-commerce orders**

Source: based, in part, on Schary and Skjott-Larsen, 2001: Figure 4.5

- *'Dell' model.* The supplier receives orders for specific products, which are then integrated directly into production: 'The customer order activates the supply chain. Customers can "design" their products from a list of options to be incorporated into a production schedule. The order then initiates a flow of component parts from suppliers to be assembled into a final product, turned over to a logistics service provider, merged with a monitor from another source and delivered to a final customer. The system avoids holding finished product inventory, providing both lower cost and more product variety.'[19]
- *Drop shipment model.* The e-commerce firm receives an order and passes on the order to a manufacturer for production and delivery direct to the customer from the manufacturer.
- *'Amazon' model.* This is the electronic version of an old mode of direct retailing where a 'catalogue' of products is held electronically and accessed via the Internet. Customer orders are either fulfilled by the seller from its own distri-bution centre or 'drop-shipped' direct from the manufacturer or other provider.
- *Bricks-and-mortar model.* This combines both conventional retail stores, fed by distribution centres, with an Internet website that channels orders to the same distribution centres. A problem with this system is that whereas retail orders generally require large orders, individual Internet-based orders require indi-vidual units.

- *Inventory-pooling model.* This enables customers in a specific industry to acquire common components from an inventory pool controlled by a Web-based provider.
- *Home delivery model.* Customers requiring regular deliveries of, say, groceries, can place their order with a Web-based service which will deliver on a routine basis to the customer's home address.

Thus, a whole variety of technological developments has transformed the nature and operations of the logistics and distribution industries. Initially, in the early twentieth century, they were the technologies that enabled mass distribution systems to facilitate the output of the mass production systems of the day. By the last two decades of the twentieth century, the technologies had become predominantly electronic. Such technologies facilitate the operations of more flexible production systems through their ability to transmit and process vast quantities of information on all aspects of the supply circuit. Increasingly, these processes take place in the 'cloud' (see Chapter 4).

THE ROLE OF THE STATE: REGULATION AND DEREGULATION OF LOGISTICS AND DISTRIBUTION SERVICES

There is a significant obstacle to the smooth, seamless operation of the kinds of logistics and distribution systems made possible by these technological innovations: the existence of state *regulatory* regimes. By definition, transnational production and distribution involve crossing political boundaries. All national governments regulate, in various ways, the cross-border movement of goods and services. We have discussed one aspect of this in Chapter 6 and in the other case study chapters: the variety of trade measures (both tariff and non-tariff barriers, including customs requirements and procedures) that states use. The existence of such regulations creates major discontinuities in the geographical surface over which distribution services operate (see Figure 17.2).

In this section, we are concerned with the regulatory structures affecting the basic functions of the logistics and distribution services themselves, especially transportation and communication systems. Such regulations are implemented at various political–geographical scales: international, regional and national. In the past three decades, in particular, there have been major waves of deregulation.

Regulation and deregulation of transportation and communication systems

Regulation of transportation and of communications has a very long history.[20] It has involved a varying mix of national and international level systems in the public sphere, as well as private organizations in the form of the operators themselves. Much of the regulatory system in air and sea transportation relates to issues of safety and security, while in communications a key issue is harmonization of standards to enable communications originating in one place to be received and understood in other places. International bodies such as the IMO (International Maritime Organization), the ICAO (International Civil Aviation Organization), and the ITU (International Telecommunication Union) are the primary players.

Within such international frameworks, individual national states have also regulated telecommunications and air transportation. These are both sectors in which states believe (or have believed until recently) that 'natural monopolies' exist. For example,

> telecommunications' regulation contains one of the earliest examples of international regulatory cooperation between states, with the creation of the International Telegraphic Union (ITgU) in 1865. But in other respects the regulation of telecommunications is a story of territorial containment. Much of the early regulatory development in the first half of the twentieth century was influenced by the economic view that telecommunications is a 'natural monopoly'. But no state thinks that there should be one world monopolist. Instead, the contours of this natural monopoly correspond with state boundaries.[21]

In most cases this involved state ownership, although in the USA it was a private monopoly, AT&T.

Similarly in the air transportation industry,

> just as almost every nation ha[d] its telecommunications carrier (and rarely more than one), almost every nation ha[d] a flagship airline (and rarely more than one). The state controls landing rights (just as it tends to control the telecommunications infrastructure) and rations those rights, usually in ways that favour the national flag-carrier.[22]

In both cases, the operation of the regulatory framework has involved a tension between

- the desire on the part of most states for control over their own national spaces and;
- the drive (primarily by business organizations) for the least possible regulation consistent with safety and efficiency.

As globalizing processes have intensified, however, the balance has shifted decisively towards greater deregulation of the nationally based systems and the privatization of state-owned companies. In the case of telecommunications, the initial moves came in the USA, with the enforced break-up of the AT&T monopoly in the early 1980s. The US example stimulated a wave of European deregulation in telecommunications during the 1980s, led by the UK's Thatcher government.

The air transportation industry has experienced a similar wave of deregulation. Again, the early moves began in the USA. In the late 1970s, a US–UK bilateral agreement was signed which helped to undermine the cartelization of the airline industry within IATA. In 1978, the US domestic airline industry was deregulated. Subsequently,

> both the US and the UK then set about reshaping their bilateral agreements towards more liberal policies. For example, France has been the most vigorous opponent of liberalization, so the US worked at isolating France by negotiating open-skies agreements with Belgium and other countries around France ... In short, the process in the 1990s is US-led liberalization that is seeing the world become gradually and chaotically more competitive. The process is chaotic because even the most liberal states, such as the US and UK ... are 'liberal mercantilists' ... Another chaotic element is that many European, African, and South American states support liberalization within their continents but want protection from competition outside the continent (especially from the US).[23]

The continuing tensions between states in terms of their own air spaces (and often their 'national' airlines) has important implications for logistics and distribution services. Two examples illustrate this. First, the continuing disagreement between the USA and the UK over mutual access over the North Atlantic route means that, on the one hand, US airlines have restricted access to London Heathrow while, on the other, British airlines are not allowed to fly routes onwards within the USA beyond their initial point of entry. This also means that the US company FedEx has been unable to operate a fully fledged operation from its UK base at Stansted; it is allowed to fly from the USA to Stansted but only to a small number of destinations from there. Instead, it has to charter planes to fly from the UK to Paris to connect with its European hub.[24]

A second example is the now resolved dispute between the USA and Hong Kong, which was especially important for the large express couriers (FedEx, DHL and UPS). The US company FedEx was allowed only five flights a week from Hong Kong to destinations outside the USA. This was because Hong Kong wanted its airline, Cathay Pacific, to be able to fly within, as well as to, the USA (which it refused to allow). The agreement signed in 2002 increased the daily flights for all-cargo carriers from 8 to 64, phased in over three years, although Cathay Pacific insisted that the agreement over-benefited US carriers.[25]

Some of the biggest changes in the regulatory environment affecting the logistics industries have resulted from the emergence of regional economic blocs, such as the EU and the NAFTA. The completion of the Single European Market in 1992 removed virtually all obstacles to internal movement of goods and services within the EU. Liberalization of trucking within and between the USA, Canada and Mexico was also a part of the NAFTA. Under this 1994 agreement, the US and Mexican border states were to be opened to international trucking by the end of 1995. By January 1997, Mexican trucking companies would be allowed to operate as domestic carriers in the border states and for international cargo in the rest of the USA and, by January 2000, they would be able to file to operate in the entire USA. In fact this did not happen. Not until 2004 did the US Supreme Court overthrow the opposition of the House of Representatives to Mexican and US truckers operating in each other's domestic markets. In fact, it still did not happen. In 2009, Mexico retaliated with tariffs against US products because of the continued failure to implement the NAFTA. Finally, in 2011, some 16 years late, an agreement was reached, though not without huge opposition from some groups in the USA.

Regulating transportation and communication systems is not easy, given the number of conflicting interests involved. But it is far easier than regulating the Internet. As a medium that 'knows no boundaries' and that is allegedly (although, as we have seen, not actually) 'placeless', it involves some intractable issues as to who regulates it. The answer is far from clear, not least because of the very newness of the Internet and e-commerce and its phenomenally rapid growth. The key issue is 'whose laws apply?' when e-commerce transactions transcend different national jurisdictions.

CORPORATE STRATEGIES IN LOGISTICS AND DISTRIBUTION SERVICES

Logistics and distribution services cover an immensely wide range of activities and encompass a mix of traditional shipping and carriage of goods through to the highly complex and sophisticated *logistics service providers* (LSPs), from trading companies to large transnational retail chains. In this section we outline the major trends in corporate strategies as firms have responded to market, technological and regulatory forces. Although there are many niche areas within the distribution sector, there is a broad tendency in most activities for the size of firms to be increasing and for higher degrees of concentration into a smaller number of large firms. Growth through merger and acquisition, and through network alliances, has been especially prominent in this sector as firms strive to provide *global* logistics services. This has meant that the names and identities of many firms are continuously changing. Table 17.1 lists the world's 10 largest logistics firms.

Global logistics: from transportation companies to integrated logistics service providers

As customer demands have become more complex (and more global), the providers of logistics and distribution services have responded in a number of ways. Some

Table 17.1   Leading global logistics firms (ranked by revenue)

Company	Country	Revenue, 2011 ($m)	Employment	Number of offices	Number of countries
DHL Logistics	Germany	37,780	>280,000	c.18,000	>220
Kuehne & Nagel	Switzerland	22,104	>63,000	>1,000	>100
DB Schenker Logistics	Germany	19,685	94,600	>2,000	c.120
CEVA Logistics	Netherlands	9,593	>51,000	n.d.	>130
C H Robinson Worldwide	USA	8,741	>15,000	>235 ex. N. America	21
DSV	Denmark	8,162	22,000	n.d.	>70
Panalpina	Switzerland	7,331	15,000	500	>90
SNCF Geodis	France	6,200	>20,000	n.d.	>50
Expeditors International	USA	6,150	>13,000	>250	n.d.
UPS Supply Chain Solutions	USA	6,058	n.d.	n.d.	>150

n.d. – no data.

Source: based on material in www.supplychaindigital.com; company reports and websites

have diversified into complete 'one-stop shops'; others have remained more narrowly focused on providing a limited range of functions. In both cases, the trend has been towards greater consolidation and concentration through acquisition and merger. Some examples illustrate this trend.

In the shipping sector, Maersk acquired Nedlloyd in 2005 to become the largest container operator in the world. In the logistics field, acquisitions and mergers have accelerated. For example, in 2000 Exel was formed from a merger of a shipping company, Ocean, and a contract logistics supplier, NFC. In 2004, Exel purchased the second-largest UK logistics company, Tibbett and Britton, to become the sector leader with 111,000 employees in more than 135 countries. In turn, in 2005, Deutsche Post World Net (owner of DHL, which it had acquired in 2003) acquired Exel. This created by far the world's largest logistics service company, providing air freight, ocean freight and contract logistics services. The new group, DHL Logistics, employs over 280,000 people worldwide.

As a result of such developments, together with the movement of other service companies into logistics provision, we can identify four major types of logistics service firm (Figure 17.7), according to the kinds of physical and management services they provide:[26]

- *Traditional transportation and forwarding companies* provide the simplest functions and are the longest established.

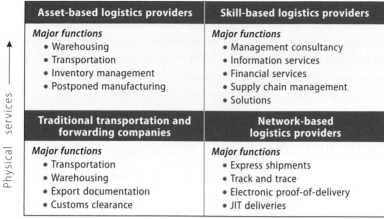

Figure 17.7 **Types of LSPs**

Source: based, in part, on Schary and Skjott-Larsen, 2001: Figure 7.3

- *Asset-based logistics providers* first emerged during the 1980s, developing primarily from the diversification of some traditional transportation companies into more complex LSPs. Several of the world's leading container-shipping companies, such as Maersk-Sealand and Nedlloyd/P&O, moved in this direction. For example, in 1992 Nedlloyd took on responsibility for all of IBM's distribution activities as part of its strategy to become a worldwide logistics provider.
- *Network-based logistics providers* such as DHL, FedEx, UPS and TNT appeared on the international scene during the early 1990s:

  These third-party logistics providers started as couriers and express parcel companies and built up global transportation and communication networks to be able to expedite express shipments fast and reliably. Supplemental information services typically include electronic proof-of-delivery and track-and-trace options from sender to receiver … Recently, these players have moved into the time-sensitive and high-value-density third-party logistics market, such as electronics, spare parts, fashion goods and pharmaceuticals, and are competing with the traditional asset-based logistics providers in these high margin markets.[27]

The nature of these logistics services demands geographically extensive, and tightly integrated, networks of operations. All the leading firms, therefore, have a global presence, each company operating global hub-and-spoke transportation networks, either owned by themselves or with partners.

- *Skill-based logistics providers* became increasingly significant in the later 1990s. These are firms that do not own any major physical logistics assets but provide a range of primarily information-based logistics services. These encompass consultancy services (including supply chain configuration), financial services, IT services and a range of management expertise. Examples include GeoLogistics, a firm created in 1996 through the merger of three existing logistics companies (Bekins, LEP, Matrix) and recently rebranded as Agility, now the 12th-largest logistics company in the world.

Global trading companies

Trading companies have a history going back many hundreds of years. From the earliest days of long-distance trade they played an especially important role in facilitating trade in materials and products. Here we look at two important contemporary examples, both taken from East Asia.

The first example is the Japanese *sogo shosha*. The common translation of the term *sogo shosha* is 'general trading companies', but they are very much more than this, having been central to the development of the Japanese economy since the late nineteenth century.[28] This was the true Japanese general trading oligopoly, each member of which had a major coordinating role within one of the Japanese *keiretsu* (see Figure 5.10). The five leading *sogo shosha* – Mitsubishi, Mitsui, Itochu, Marubeni, Sumitomo – operate a massive network of subsidiaries and thousands of related companies across the globe (Figure 17.8) and handle tens of thousands of different products.

Historically, the *sogo shosha* developed to organize exchange and distribution within the Japanese domestic market. Subsequently, they became the first Japanese companies to invest on a large scale outside Japan. These foreign investments were primarily designed to organize the flow of imports of much needed primary materials for the resource-poor Japanese economy and to channel Japanese exports of manufactures to overseas markets. It was the particular demands of these Japanese-focused trading activities that necessitated the development of the globally extensive networks of the *sogo shosha*. In other words, they were to set up a global marketing and economic intelligence network. Once in place, this network, with all its supporting facilities, not only facilitated the growth of Japanese trade, but also enabled a whole range of Japanese firms to venture overseas. Indeed, a good deal of the early overseas investment by Japanese manufacturing firms was organized by the *sogo shosha*.

Their four primary functions are:

- *trading and transactional intermediation*: matching buyers and sellers in a long-term contractual relationship;
- *financial intermediation*: serving as a risk buffer between suppliers and purchasers;
- *information gathering*: collecting and collating information on market conditions throughout the world;
- *organization and coordination of complex business systems*: for example, major infrastructural projects.

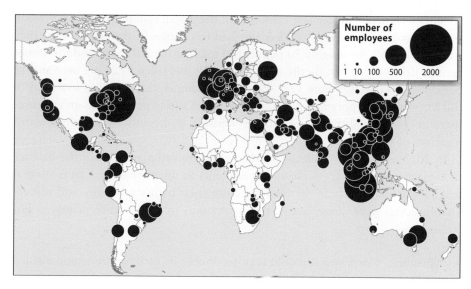

Figure 17.8 **The global distribution of Japanese *sogo shosha* offices**

Source: company reports

(a) Past business model

Major function: to act as intermediary in commercial transactions

(b) Present business model

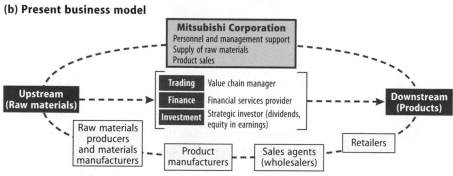

Major function: to participate in entire value chain

Figure 17.9 **Mitsubishi Corporation's strategic shift**

Source: Mitsubishi Corporation

As the position of the Japanese economy in the global system has changed, however, the role of the *sogo shosha* has also had to change. In the early 1990s, they were responsible for roughly 70 per cent of total Japanese imports and for 40 per cent of Japanese exports. By the early 2000s, this had fallen to 22 per cent and 12 per cent respectively. Figure 17.9 shows one example: the changing strategies of the Mitsubishi Corporation as it has moved from acting primarily as an intermediary in commercial transactions to participating in the entire value chain across a variety of sectors.

In 2013, each of the leading *sogo shosha* announced plans to shift the balance of their activities by accelerating 'investments in unconventional areas such as food, retail and healthcare, as earnings from their mainstay energy and minerals businesses suffer from across-the-board falls in commodity prices'.[29] For example:

- Mitsubishi Corp. said it would seek to double its earnings from non-natural resources businesses by about 2020 and aim at a 50:50 balance between resource and non-resource assets.
- Marubeni Corp. announced a new medium-term strategy involving allocating 60 per cent of its budget over three years to non-resource assets, such as infrastructure, transportation, machinery and food.

The second example of a trading company, also taken from East Asia, is the Hong-Kong-based firm *Li & Fung*. This firm is not only the biggest export trading company in Hong Kong, but also – and more importantly – a sophisticated logistics company, with offices spread across over 40 countries (see Figure 17.10), employing more than 28,000 people. Established in Canton in 1906, Li & Fung was originally a simple commodity broker, connecting buyers and sellers for a fee. Today, although still a Chinese family firm, it has been transformed from the simple brokerage to an immensely sophisticated organizer of geographically dispersed manufacturing and distribution operations, still with a strong specialization in garments (see Chapter 14) but increasingly in a whole variety of other consumer goods:

> Li & Fung provides sophisticated, one-stop-shop supply chain solutions to meet customers' specific needs. From product design, raw material sourcing and production management to quality control, logistics, shipping and other important functions, its spectrum of services covers the entire supply chain end-to-end.[30]

These two examples show that traditional trading companies have carved out new roles for themselves, both responding to and creating new demands for distribution and logistics services.

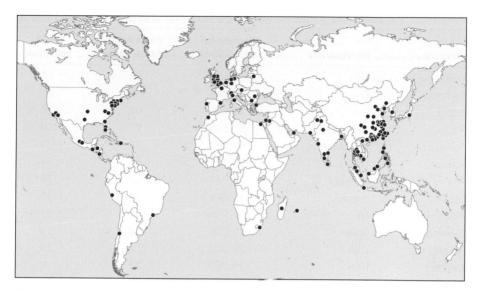

Figure 17.10 The global spread of the offices of Li & Fung

Source: Li & Fung

Globalizing retailers

Retailing is the final link in the production circuit. As such, it is extremely sensitive to the specific characteristics of the consumer markets it serves. Consumer markets continue to have a high degree of individuality, despite the apparent universalization of some types of consumer preference. Consequently, retailing has always had – and continues to have – a strong local orientation, although retailers invariably source their products from a much broader spectrum of geographical locations. A few retailers moved into foreign markets at a relatively early stage in their development. One of the pioneers was the US company F.W. Woolworth, which opened stores in Canada in 1897, in the UK in 1909 and in Germany in 1926. Indeed, so familiar did Woolworths become in most big cities in the UK that few of its customers realized it was a foreign firm. But this was an exceptional case. For the most part, retailers were very reluctant entrants into foreign markets. Where they did so, it was usually into geographically and/or culturally proximate locations.

But there has been a marked acceleration in the transnational activities of major retailers in recent years.[31] Table 17.2 lists the world's leading transnational retailers ranked by their international sales volume. The list includes the big food retailers discussed in Chapter 13 (see Figures 13.8 and 13.9). It is significant that only five of the top twenty transnational retailers are from the USA; many very large US retailers remain entirely domestically oriented.

Table 17.2   **The world's leading transnational retailers, 2012 (ranked by international sales volume)**

Company	Headquarters	International sales (US$m)	Percentage of total sales	No. of countries
Wal-Mart	USA	121,456	28	14
Carrefour	France	62,715	55	26
Metro	Germany	53,856	61	33
Ahold	Netherlands	51,590	77	10
Schwartz	Germany	42,872	52	23
Auchan	France	41,254	60	11
Aldi	Germany	37,847	52	16
IKEA	Sweden	35,314	94	33
Tesco	UK	33,930	35	11
Seven & I	Japan	31,036	30	16
Amazon	USA	26,602	54	29
Costco	USA	24,010	27	9
Casino	France	20,185	45	11
Rewe	Germany	17,824	28	11
H & M	Sweden	16,419	94	28
Delhaize	Belgium	16,274	77	11
Apple	USA	14,065	44	19
Inditex	Spain	13,685	73	40
Best Buy	USA	11,535	25	6
Kering	France	10,637	94	102

Source: data supplied by Neil Coe

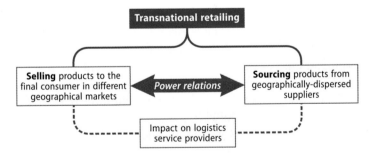

Figure 17.11   **Two dimensions of transnational retailing**

Transnational retailing has two main dimensions: *selling* products and *sourcing* products (Figure 17.11).

Selling products in transnational markets involves setting up a new store, merging with or acquiring an existing retailer in a target market, or setting up a joint venture with a local firm. The latter two modes have been by far the most prevalent. In some cases, this is because local regulations restricted direct entry. The major retail chains have shown a particular propensity to invest heavily in the emerging markets of East and South Asia, Latin America and Eastern Europe.

The core of this process involves four major types of transfer into a new market:[32]

- *Transfer of the total culture and business model of the firm*: 'All aspects of the culture and business model of the retailer are transferred to the host retail economy when retailers decide that they are international firms with internationalization integrated into their strategy. Within Tesco, for example, this has become known as "Tesco in a Box"' (p. 389).

- *Transfer of the capability to adapt to the market*: 'Retailing is a response to culture. An international retailer, in order to be successful, has to adapt to the consumer culture in the market ... Adaptation involves not only the understanding of the difference between home and host country but also the differences in consumer culture within the host country ... The absence of this capability either in the firm generally (Boots, Marks and Spencer) or in the transfers to a particular country (Ahold in China, Carrefour in Japan and in the USA, IKEA's original entry to Japan, Wal-Mart in Germany) is one of the reasons for "failed" international retailing' (p. 390).

- *Transfer of operational techniques of retailing*: 'The operations of an international retailer (the formula of the retailer) interact with and become part of the structure of the total retail system ... A firm may use different entry and growth mechanisms with acquisitions, joint ventures, agents and merchandising agreements with consequential different types of transfer of operations in each case' (p. 391).

- *Transfer of consumer values and expectations*: 'Retailers create consumption in addition to responding to consumer needs. In a foreign market international retailing often brings to a country new consumer values and expectations. These in turn change the ways that consumers behave ... The retailer helps to create the consumer culture and in doing this delivers changes in lifestyle ... In countries where consumption cultures have been weak for an extended period, for example in Central and Eastern Europe, and in cultures where there is rapid change in consumption culture, for example, East Asia, then the foreign retailer, with a clearly defined formula, generates a substantial impact on consumer values and expectations' (pp. 391, 392).

Sourcing of products is the second dimension of transnational retailing shown in Figure 17.11. We referred to this process in the case of food retailing and clothing in Chapters 13 and 14. But there has been a general trend across virtually all retail sectors for firms to increase the geographical extent of their sourcing systems as well as to extend their power and influence over their suppliers. As a result retail supply and logistics networks have been transformed in the following ways:[33]

- *Centralization*: the establishment of centralized distribution centres, distribution systems and buying activities.
- *Upgrading of logistics systems*: adoption of sophisticated logistics technologies and management systems, including electronic data exchange, vendor management inventory, etc.
- *A shift from traditional to specialized/dedicated procurement agents*: switch away from use of wholesalers to specialized procurement agents, often involving contractual-type relationships with suppliers.
- *A shift towards preferred supplier systems*: the use of a smaller number of suppliers willing/able to meet the stringent standards of quality, price and speed and flexibility of delivery.
- *Increased use of quasi-formal and formal contracts*: to increase control and ensure on-time delivery.
- *Imposition of private standards*: adoption of private, rather than public, standards of quality and/or safety.

LOGISTICS 'PLACES': KEY GEOGRAPHICAL NODES ON THE GLOBAL LOGISTICS MAP

These developments in the global logistics industries have highly distinctive geographies, which help to shape their activities and are also shaped by them. For example, among the thousands of seaports and airports across the world, a few key nodes have become increasingly important. They reflect three sets of forces:

- Their position in the twenty-first-century global economy, especially in light of the global shifts in economic activities we have been discussing throughout this book.
- The strategies of states in investing in port, airport and IT facilities: for example, the highly focused investment strategies of the Singaporean government to create a 'globally-integrated logistics hub':

   an integrated IT platform that manages the flow of trade-related information ... will enable exchange of information between shippers, freight forwarders, carriers and financial institutions to facilitate the flow of goods within, through and out of Singapore ... The government will invest up to S$50 million over five years to develop the platform.[34]

Other states are pursuing broadly similar strategies to develop their logistics capabilities.[35]

- The strategies of the major *logistics firms* in creating their own globally-dispersed operations and choosing certain key places as their 'hubs'.

Figures 17.12 and 17.13 show two examples of these trends. The emergence of East Asia as the most dynamic economic region in the world is clearly reflected in Figure 17.12. No fewer than 14 of the 20 leading container ports are located in East Asia, 8 of them in China (excluding Hong Kong). None of

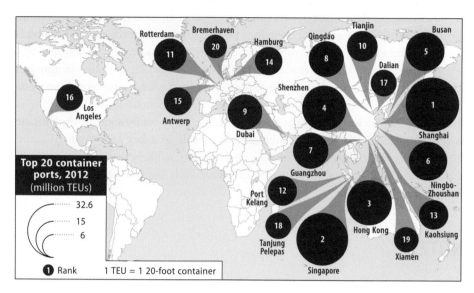

Figure 17.12 **The leading world container hubs**

Source: based on World Shipping Council data

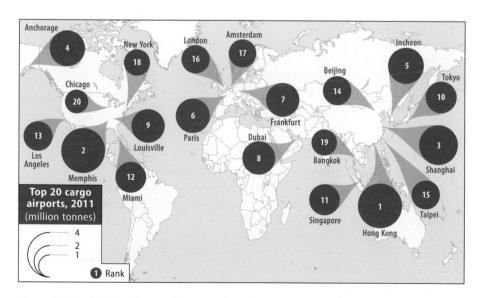

Figure 17.13 **The leading world cargo airports**

Source: based on Airports Council International data

them was in the top ten in 1995; now six of them are. Conversely, the leading European container ports – Rotterdam and Hamburg – have fallen down the rankings.

The global map of leading cargo airports (Figure 17.13) has some features in common with the container ports map. Certain key cities, for example Hong Kong, Shanghai, Tokyo, Singapore, Los Angeles, Dubai, have developed as leading air cargo hubs as well as major container ports. They are, indeed, key geographical nodes on the global logistics map. But there are other leading cargo airports that are quite different. They are the strategic hubs of the leading specialist freight and logistics firms themselves. The place of Memphis, Tennessee, as the world's second-biggest cargo airport is entirely due to its role as FedEx's main hub. In similar vein, Louisville, Kentucky, is the main hub of UPS. The importance of Anchorage Airport in Alaska, likewise, is attributable to its role as a key hub for FedEx and UPS in their links with China. Leipzig, in Germany, is likely to join this group in the future: DHL opened its principal European hub there in 2008, replacing its former hub in Brussels.

NOTES

1   Coe (2014) provides an excellent review of the logistics industries in the context of GPNs. See also Wrigley (2000).
2   Coe (2014: 225).
3   Schoenberger (2000).
4   Min and Keebler (2001: 265).
5   OECD (2004: 178).
6   *Financial Times* (25 August 2005).
7   Coe (2014: 228).
8   Schary and Skjøtt-Larsen (2001: 129).
9   Abernathy et al. (1999: chapter 4).
10   Abernathy et al. (1999: 61).
11   Quoted in the *Financial Times* (20 April 2005).
12   Abernathy et al. (1999: 66).
13   Stalk et al. (1998: 58).
14   Zook and Shelton (2012: 43).
15   Leinbach (2001: 15).
16   Centre for Retail Research (2013), www.retailresearch.org/onlineretailing.php.
17   US Department of Commerce (2000: 18).
18   Schary and Skjøtt-Larsen (2001: 132–6).
19   Schary and Skjøtt-Larsen (2001: 132). See also Fields (2004).
20   See Braithwaite and Drahos (2000).
21   Braithwaite and Drahos (2000: 322).
22   Braithwaite and Drahos (2000: 454).
23   Braithwaite and Drahos (2000: 456–7).

24 *The Sunday Times* (23 January 2005).

25 *Commercial Aviation Today* (21 October 2002).

26 This section is based primarily on Schary and Skjøtt-Larsen (2001: 230–41).

27 Schary and Skjøtt-Larsen (2001: 231).

28 See Dicken and Miyamachi (1998).

29 *Financial Times* (9 May 2013).

30 Company website, www.lifung.com/eng/company.

31 Coe and Wrigley (2009), Dawson (2007).

32 Dawson (2007: 388–92). Numbers in parentheses refer to pages in this work.

33 Coe and Wrigley (2009).

34 Singapore Economic Development Board, June 2004.

35 Wang and Cheng (2010) provide a detailed analysis of the transition of the port of Hong Kong from a hub port city to a 'global supply chain management centre'.

Want to know more about this chapter? Visit the companion website at **www.guilford.com/dickenGS7** for free access to author videos, suggested reading and practice questions to further enhance your study.

BIBLIOGRAPHY

Abernathy, F., Dunlop, J., Hammond, J.H. and Weil, D. (1999) *A Stitch in Time: Lean Retailing and the Transformation of Manufacturing: Lessons from the Apparel and Textile Industry*. New York: Oxford University Press.

Abernathy, F.H., Dunlop, J.T., Hammond, J.H. and Weil, D. (2004) Globalization in the apparel and textile industries: what is new and what is not? In M. Kenney and R. Florida (eds) *Locating Global Advantage: Industry Dynamics in the International Economy*. Stanford, CA: Stanford University Press. Chapter 2.

ABN-AMRO (2000) *European Auto Components: Driven by Technology*. London: ABN-AMRO.

Abo, T. (2000) Spontaneous integration in Japan and East Asia: development, crisis, and beyond. In G.L. Clark, M.P. Feldman and M.S. Gertler (eds) *The Oxford Handbook of Economic Geography*. Oxford: Oxford University Press. Chapter 31.

Agnew, J. and Corbridge, S. (1995) *Mastering Space*. London: Routledge.

Alderson, A.S. and Beckfield, J. (2004) Power and position in the world city system. *American Journal of Sociology*, 109: 811–51.

Alkire, S., Roche, J.M. and Seth, S. (2013) Multidimensional Poverty Index 2013. Oxford Poverty and Human Development Initiative (www.ophi.org.uk).

Amin, A. (2000) The European Union as more than a triad market for national economic spaces. In G.L. Clark, M.P. Feldman and M.S. Gertler (eds) *The Oxford Handbook of Economic Geography*. Oxford: Oxford University Press. Chapter 33.

Amin, A. (2002) Spatialities of globalization. *Environment and Planning A*, 34: 385-99.

Amin, A. (2004) Regulating economic globalization. *Transactions of the Institute of British Geographers*, 29: 217–33.

Amin, A. and Thrift, N.J. (1992) Neo-Marshallian nodes in global networks. *International Journal of Urban and Regional Research*, 16: 571–87.

Amsden, A. (1989) *Asia's Next Giant: South Korea and Late Industrialization*. Oxford: Oxford University Press.

Andersen, P.H. and Christensen, P.R. (2004) Bridges over troubled water: suppliers as connective nodes in global supply networks. *Journal of Business Research*, 58: 1261–73.

Anderson, M. (1995) The role of collaborative integration in industrial organization: observations from the Canadian aerospace industry. *Economic Geography*, 71: 55–78.

Anderson, S. and Cavanagh, J. (2000) *Top 200: The Rise of Corporate Global Power*. Washington, DC: Institute for Policy Studies.

Appelbaum, R.P. (2008) Giant transnational contractors in East Asia: emergent trends in global supply chains. *Competition & Change*, 12: 69–87.

Archibugi, D. and Michie, J. (eds) (1997) *Technology, Globalization, and Economic Performance*. Cambridge: Cambridge University Press.

Archibugi, D., Howells, J. and Michie, J. (eds) (1999) *Innovation Policy in a Global Economy*. Cambridge: Cambridge University Press.

Asheim, B. (2007) Differentiated knowledge bases and varieties of regional innovation systems. *Innovation: The European Journal of Social Science Research*, 20: 223–41.

Asheim, B. and Gertler, M. (2005) The geography of innovation: regional innovation systems. In J. Fagerberg, D.C. Mowery and R.R. Nelson (eds) *The Oxford Handbook of Innovation*. Oxford: Oxford University Press. pp. 291–317.

Baaij, M., van den Bosch, F. and Volberda, H. (2004) The international relocation of corporate centres: are corporate centres sticky? *European Management Journal*, 22: 141–9.

Badaracco, J.L. Jr (1991) The boundaries of the firm. In A. Etzioni and P.R. Lawrence (eds) *Socio-Economics: Towards a New Synthesis*. Armonk, NY: M.E. Sharpe. pp. 293–327.

Bair, J. (2002) Beyond the maquila model: NAFTA and the Mexican apparel industry. *Industry and Innovation*, 9: 203–25.

Bair, J. (2006) Regional trade and production blocs in a global industry: towards a comparative framework for research. *Environment and Planning A*, 38: 2233–52.

Bair, J. (2008) Surveying the post-MFA landscape: what prospects for the Global South post-quota? *Competition & Change*, 12: 3–10.

Bair, J. (ed.) (2009) *Frontiers of Commodity Chain Research*. Stanford, CA: Stanford University Press.

Bair, J. and Gereffi, G. (2001) Local clusters in global chains: the causes and consequences of export dynamism in Torreón's blue jeans industry. *World Development*, 29: 1885–1903.

Bair, J. and Gereffi, G. (2003) Upgrading, uneven development, and jobs in the North American apparel industry. *Global Networks*, 3: 143–96.

Barham, B.L. and Coomes, O.T. (2005) Sunk costs, resource extractive industries, and development outcomes. In P.S. Ciccantell, D.A. Smith and G. Seidman (eds) *Nature, Raw Materials, and Political Economy*. Amsterdam: Elsevier. pp. 159–86.

Barrientos, S. (2008) Contract labour: the 'Achilles Heel' of corporate codes in commercial value chains. *Development and Change*, 39: 977–90.

Barrientos, S., Gereffi, G. and Rossi, A. (2011) Economic and social upgrading in global production chains: a new paradigm for a changing world. *International Labour Review*, 150: 319–40.

Bartlett, C.A. and Ghoshal, S. (1998) *Managing Across Borders: The Transnational Solution*, 2nd edn. New York: Random House.

Bartlett, D. and Seleny, A. (1998) The political enforcement of liberalism: bargaining, institutions, and auto multinationals in Hungary. *International Studies Quarterly*, 42: 319–38.

Bathelt, H. and Gertler, M.S. (2005) The German variety of capitalism: forces and dynamics of evolutionary change. *Economic Geography*, 81: 1–9.

Bathelt, H., Malmberg, A. and Maskell, P. (2004) Clusters and knowledge: local buzz, global pipelines and the process of knowledge creation. *Progress in Human Geography*, 28: 31–56.

Bayly, C.A. (2004) *The Birth of the Modern World, 1780–1914*. Oxford: Blackwell.

BBC World Service (2008) Widespread unease about economy and globalization – global poll (www.bbc.co.uk/pressoffice/pressreleases/stories/2008/02_february/07/poll.shtml).

Beath, J. (2002) UK industrial policy: old tunes on new instruments? *Oxford Review of Economic Policy*, 18: 221–39.

Beaverstock, J.V. (2004) 'Managing across borders': knowledge management and expatriation in professional service legal firms. *Journal of Economic Geography*, 4: 157–79.

Beaverstock, J.V., Faulconbridge, J.R. and Hall, S. (2014) *The Globalization of the Executive Search Industry: Professional Services Strategy and Dynamics in the Contemporary World*. London: Routledge.

Beck, U. (2005) *Power in the Global Age: A New Global Political Economy*. Cambridge: Polity Press.

Begg, B., Pickles, J. and Smith, A. (2003) Cutting it: European integration, trade regimes, and the configuration of East-Central European apparel production. *Environment and Planning A*, 35: 2191–207.

Belderbos, R. and Capannelli, G. (2001) Backward vertical linkages of foreign manufacturing affiliates: evidence from Japanese multinationals. *World Development*, 29: 189–208.

Belderbos, R., Leten, B. and Suzuki, S. (2013) How global is R & D? Firm-level determinants of home-country bias in R & D. *Journal of International Business Studies*, 44: 765–86.

Bello, W. and Rosenfeld, S. (1990) *Dragons in Distress: Asian Miracle Economies in Crisis*. San Francisco: Institute for Food and Development Policy.

Benewick, R. and Wingrove, P. (eds) (1995) *China in the 1990s*. London: Macmillan.

Bennett, E.A. (2013) Global social movements in global governance. *Globalizations*, 9: 799–813.

Berger, S. (2005) *How We Compete: What Companies Around The World Are Doing To Make It In Today's Global Economy*. New York: Doubleday.

Berger, S. and Dore, R. (eds) (1996) *National Diversity and Global Capitalism*. Ithaca, NY: Cornell University Press.

Berggren, C. and Bengtsson, L. (2004) Rethinking outsourcing in manufacturing: a tale of two telecom firms. *European Management Journal*, 22: 211–23.

Berndt, C. and Boeckler, M. (2009) Geographies of circulation and exchange: construction of markets. *Progress in Human Geography*, 33: 535–51.

Beukering, P.J.H. van (2001) *Recycling, International Trade and Environment: An Empirical Analysis*. Amsterdam: Kluwer.

Beukering, P.J.H. van and Bouman, M.N. (2001) Empirical evidence on recycling and trade of paper and lead in developed and developing countries. *World Development*, 29: 1717–37.

Bhagwati, J. (2004) *In Defense of Globalization*. New York: Oxford University Press.

Bieler, A., Hilary, J. and Lindberg, I. (2014) Trade unions, 'free trade' and the problem of transnational solidarity: an introduction. *Globalizations*, 11: 1–9.

Birkinshaw, J. (2001) Strategy and management in MNE subsidiaries. In A.M. Rugman and T.L. Brewer (eds) *The Oxford Handbook of International Business*. Oxford: Oxford University Press. pp. 380–401.

Birkinshaw, J. and Morrison, A.J. (1995) Configurations of strategy and structure in subsidiaries of multinational corporations. *Journal of International Business Studies*, 26: 729–55.

Blanc, H. and Sierra, C. (1999) The internationalisation of R&D by multinationals: a trade-off between external and internal proximity. *Cambridge Journal of Economics*, 23: 187–206.

Blois, K. (2006) The boundaries of the firm – a question of interpretation? *Industry and Innovation*, 13: 135–49.

Blonigen, B.A. (2006) Foreign direct investment behavior of multinational corporations. *NBER Reporter: Research Summary*, Winter.

Blowfield, M. (1999) Ethical trade: a review of developments and issues. *Third World Quarterly*, 20: 753–70.

Blythman, J. (2004) *Shopped: The Shocking Power of British Supermarkets*. London: HarperCollins.

Bonanno, A., Busch, L., Friedland, W. and Mingione, E. (eds) (1994) *From Columbus to ConAgra: The Globalization of Agriculture and Food*. Lawrence, KS: University Press of Kansas.

Borrus, M., Ernst, D. and Haggard, S. (eds) (2000) *International Production Networks in Asia: Rivalry or Riches?* London: Routledge.

Bowles, P. (2002) Asia's post-crisis regionalism: bringing the state back in, keeping the (United) States out. *Review of International Political Economy*, 9: 230–56.

Boyd, W. and Watts, M.J. (1997) Agro-industrial just-in-time: the chicken industry and post-war American capitalism. In D. Goodman and M.J. Watts (eds) *Globalizing Food: Agrarian Questions and Global Restructuring.* London: Routledge. Chapter 8.

Braithwaite, J. and Drahos, P. (2000) *Global Business Regulation.* Cambridge: Cambridge University Press.

Brenner, N., Peck, J.A. and Theodore, N. (2010) Variegated neoliberalization: geographies, modalities, pathways. *Global Networks,* 10: 182–222.

Bridge, G. (2004) Mapping the bonanza: geographies of mining investment in an era of neoliberal reform. *Professional Geographer,* 56: 406–21.

Bridge, G. (2008a) Environmental economic geography: a sympathetic critique. *Geoforum,* 39: 76–81.

Bridge, G. (2008b) Global production networks and the extractive sector: governing resource-based development. *Journal of Economic Geography,* 8: 389–419.

Bridge, G. (2009) Material worlds: natural resources, resource geography and the material economy. *Geography Compass,* 3 (www.geography-compass.com).

Brohman, J. (1996) Postwar development in the Asian NICs: does the neoliberal model fit reality? *Economic Geography,* 72: 107–31.

Brooks, A. (2013) Stretching global production networks: the international second-hand clothing trade. *Geoforum,* 44: 10–22.

Brown, T.J., Shaw, R.A., Bide, T., Petavratzi, E., Raycraft, E.R. and Walters, A.S. (2013) *World Mineral Production 2007–2011.* Nottingham: British Geological Survey.

Brunn, S.D. and Leinbach, T.R. (1991) *Collapsing Space and Time: Geographic Aspects of Communication and Information.* New York: HarperCollins.

Buck, T. and Shahrim, A. (2005) The translation of corporate governance changes across national cultures: the case of Germany. *Journal of International Business Studies,* 36: 42–61.

Buckley, P.J. and Casson, M. (1976) *The Future of the Multinational Enterprise.* London: Macmillan.

Bunker, S. and Ciccantell, P. (2005) *Globalization and the Race for Resources.* Baltimore, MA: Johns Hopkins University Press.

Bunnell, T.G. and Coe, N.M. (2001) Spaces and scales of innovation. *Progress in Human Geography,* 25: 569–89.

Burgoon, B. (2009) Globalization and backlash: Polanyi's revenge? *Review of International Political Economy,* 16: 145–77.

Cable, V. (1999) *Globalization and Global Governance.* London: Royal Institute of International Affairs.

Cameron, A. and Palan, R. (2004) *The Imagined Economies of Globalization.* London: Sage.

Campbell-Lendrum, D. and Corvalán, C. (2007) Climate change and developing-country cities: implications for environmental health and equity. *Journal of Urban Health,* 84 (Suppl. 1): 109–17.

Cantwell, J. (1997) The globalization of technology: what remains of the product cycle model? In D. Archibugi and J. Michie (eds) *Technology, Globalization, and Economic Performance.* Cambridge: Cambridge University Press. Chapter 8.

Cantwell, J. and Iammarino, S. (2000) Multinational corporations and the location of technological innovation in the UK regions. *Regional Studies,* 34: 317–32.

Carr, N. (2008a) A revolution is taking shape. *Financial Times,* 30 January 2008.

Carr, N. (2008b) *The Big Switch: Rewiring the World, From Edison to Google.* New York: W.W. Norton.

Carrillo, J. (2004) Transnational strategies and regional development: the case of GM and Delphi in Mexico. *Industry and Innovation,* 11: 127–53.

Carroll, W.K. (2007) Global cities in the global corporate network. *Environment and Planning A,* 39: 2297–323.

Carroll, W.K. and Carson, C. (2003) Forging a new hegemony? The role of transnational policy groups in the network and discourses of global corporate governance. *Journal of World-Systems Research*, IX: 67–102.

Carswell, G. and De Neve, G. (2013) Labouring for global markets: conceptualising labour agency in global production networks. *Geoforum*, 44: 62–70.

Cassis, Y. (2006) *Capitals of Capital: A History of International Financial Centres, 1780–2005*. Cambridge: Cambridge University Press.

Castells, M. (1996) *The Information Age: Economy, Society and Culture*, 3 vols. Oxford: Blackwell.

Castells, M. (2008) *Communication Power*. Oxford: Oxford University Press.

Castells, M. (2013) The impact of the Internet on society: a global perspective. In F. González (ed.) *Ch@nge: 19 Key Essays on How the Internet is Changing Our Lives*. Madrid: BBVA. pp.127–48.

Castells, M., Fernández-Ardèvol, M., Qiu, J.L. and Sey, A. (2007) *Mobile Communication and Society: A Global Perspective*. Cambridge, MA: MIT Press.

Castles, S. and Miller, M.J. (2009) *The Age of Migration: International Population Movements in the Modern World*, 4th edn. New York: Guilford.

Castree, N., Coe, N.M., Ward, K. and Samers, M. (2004) *Spaces of Work: Global Capitalism and Geographies of Labour*. London: Sage.

Cerny, P.G. (1991) The limits of deregulation: transnational interpenetrations and policy change. *European Journal of Political Research*, 19: 173–96.

Cerny, P.G. (1997) Paradoxes of the competition state: the dynamics of political globalization. *Government and Opposition*, 32: 251–74.

Cerrato, D. (2006) The multinational enterprise as an internal market system. *International Business Review*, 15: 253–77.

Chang, H.-J. (1998a) South Korea: the misunderstood crisis. In K.S. Jomo (ed.) *Tigers in Trouble: Financial Governance, Liberalization and Crises in East Asia*. London: Zed Books. Chapter 10.

Chang, H.-J. (1998b) Transnational corporations and strategic industrial policy. In R. Kozul-Wright and R. Rowthorn (eds) *Transnational Corporations and the Global Economy*. London: Macmillan. Chapter 7.

Chang, H.-J. (2007) *Bad Samaritans: Rich Nations, Poor Policies, and the Threat to the Developing World*. London: Random House.

Chang, H.-J. (2011) *23 Things They Don't Tell You About Capitalism*. London: Penguin.

Chase-Dunn, C., Kawano, Y. and Brewer, B.D. (2000) Trade globalization since 1795: waves of integration in the world-system. *American Sociological Review*, 65: 77–95.

Chorev, N. (2007) A fluid divide: domestic and international factors in US trade policy formation. *Review of International Political Economy*, 14: 653–89.

Clark, G.L. (2002) London in the European financial services industries: locational advantages and product complementarities. *Journal of Economic Geography*, 2: 433-53.

Clarke, D. (2007) *The Battle for Barrels: Peak Oil Myths and World Oil Futures*. London: Profile Business.

Coe, N.M. (2003a) Globalization, regionalization and 'scales of integration': US IT industry investment in South East Asia. In M. Miozzo and I. Miles (eds) *Internationalization, Technology and Services*. Cheltenham: Edward Elgar. pp.117–36.

Coe, N.M. (2003b) Information highways and digital divides: the evolving ICT landscapes of Southeast Asia. In L.S. Chia (ed.) *SouthEast Asia Transformed: A Geography of Change*. Singapore: ISEAS. Chapter 9.

Coe, N.M. (2011) Geographies of production II: a global production network A–Z. *Progress in Human Geography*, 36: 389–402.

Coe, N.M. (2014) Missing links: logistics, governance and upgrading in a shifting global economy. *Review of International Political Economy*, 21: 224–56.

Coe, N.M. and Hess, M. (2005) The internationalization of retailing: implications for supply network restructuring in East Asia and Eastern Europe. *Journal of Economic Geography*, 5: 449–73.

Coe, N.M. and Hess, M. (eds) (2013) Global production networks, labour and development. *Geoforum*, 44: 4–9 (Themed Issue).

Coe, N.M. and Lee, Y.-S. (2006) The strategic localization of transnational retailers: the case of Samsung-Tesco in South Korea. *Economic Geography*, 82: 61–88.

Coe, N.M. and Wrigley, N. (eds) (2009) *The Globalization of Retailing*, 2 vols. Cheltenham: Edward Elgar.

Coe, N.M. and Yeung, H.W.-c. (2015) *Global Production Networks: Theorising Economic Development in an Interconnected World*. Oxford: Oxford University Press.

Coe, N.M., Kelly, P.F. and Olds, K. (2003) Globalization, transnationalism and the Asia-Pacific. In J. Peck and H.W.-c. Yeung (eds) *Remaking the Global Economy: Economic–Geographical Perspectives*. London: Sage. Chapter 3.

Coe, N.M., Hess, M., Yeung, H.W.-c, Dicken, P. and Henderson, J. (2004) 'Globalizing' regional development: a global production networks perspective. *Transactions of the Institute of British Geographers*, 29: 468–84.

Coe, N.M., Dicken, P. and Hess, M. (2008a) Global production networks: realizing the potential. *Journal of Economic Geography*, 8: 271–95.

Coe, N.M., Johns, J. and Ward, K. (2008b) Flexibility in action: the temporary staffing industry in the Czech Republic and Poland. *Environment and Planning A*, 40: 1391–415.

Cohen, B. (2004) Urban growth in developing countries: a review of current trends and a caution regarding existing forecasts. *World Development*, 32: 23–51.

Cohen, B.J. (2012) The future of the euro: let's get real. *Review of International Political Economy*, 19: 689–700.

Cohen, D. (1998) *The Wealth of the World and the Poverty of Nations*. Cambridge, MA: MIT Press.

Cohen, S.S. and Zysman, J. (1987) *Manufacturing Matters: The Myth of the Post-Industrial Economy*. New York: Basic Books.

Collis, D., Young, D. and Goold, M. (2007) The size, structure, and performance of corporate headquarters. *Strategic Management Journal*, 28: 383–405.

Comer, J.C. and Wikle, T.A. (2008) Worldwide diffusion of the cellular telephone, 1995–2005. *Professional Geographer*, 60: 252–69.

Commission on Global Governance (1995) *Our Global Neighbourhood*. New York: Oxford University Press.

Contreras, O.F., Carrillo, J. and Alonso, J. (2012) Local entrepreneurship within global value chains: a case study in the Mexican automotive industry. *World Development*, 40: 1013–23.

Corbett, J., Winebrake, J.J., Green, E.H., Kasibhatla, P., Eyring, V. and Lauer, A. (2007) Mortality from ship emissions: a global assessment. *Environmental Science & Technology*, 41: 8512–18.

Council of Economic Advisers (2012) *Economic Report of the President*. Washington, DC: USGPO.

Crane, G.T. (1990) *The Political Economy of China's Special Economic Zones*. Armonk, NY: M.E. Sharpe.

Crang, M., Hughes, A., Gregson, N., Norris, L. and Ahamed, F. (2012) Rethinking governance and value in commodity chains through global recycling networks. *Transactions of the Institute of British Geographers*, 38: 12–24.

Crook, C. (2001) Globalization and its critics: a survey of globalization. *The Economist*, 29 September.

Crotty, J. (2009) Structural causes of the global financial crisis: a critical assessment of the 'new financial architecture'. *Cambridge Journal of Economics*, 33: 563–80.

Cudahy, B.J. (2010) Evolution of freight transportation. In L.A. Hoel, G. Giuliano and M.D. Meyer (eds) *Intermodal Freight Transportation: Moving Freight in a Global Economy*. Washington, DC: Eno Transportation Foundation. Chapter 3.

Cumbers, A. and Routledge, P. (2010) The entangled geographies of transnational labour solidarity. In A.C. Bergene, S.B. Endresen and H.M. Knutsen (eds) *Missing Links in Labour Geography*. Aldershot: Ashgate. pp. 43–55.

Cumbers, A., Nativel, C. and Routledge, P. (2008) Labour agency and union positionalities in global production networks. *Journal of Economic Geography*, 8: 369–87.

Daniels, P.W. and Bryson, J.R. (2002) Manufacturing services and servicing manufacturing: knowledge-based cities and changing forms of production. *Urban Studies*, 39: 977–91.

D'Aveni, R.A. (1994) *Hypercompetition: Managing the Dynamics of Strategic Maneuvering*. New York: Free Press.

Dawson, J.A. (2007) Scoping and conceptualizing retailer transnationalization. *Journal of Economic Geography*, 7: 373–97.

Dean, M. and Sebastia-Barriel, M. (2004) Why has world trade grown faster than world output? *Bank of England Quarterly Review*, Autumn: 310–20.

Dedrick, J., Kraemer, K.L. and Linden, G. (2010) Who profits from innovation in global value chains? A study of the iPod and notebook PCs. *Industrial and Corporate Change*, 19: 81–116.

Deese, D.A. (2008) *World Trade Politics: Power, Principles and Leadership*. Abingdon: Routledge.

De Marchi, V. and Grandinetti, R. (2014) Industrial districts and the collapse of the Marshallian model: looking at the Italian experience. *Competition and Change*, 18: 70–87.

Department of International Development (2000) *Eliminating World Poverty: Making Globalization Work for the Poor*. London: DoID.

Derudder, B., Taylor, P.J., Ni, P., De Vos, A., Hoyler, M., Hassens, H., Bassens, D., Witlox, F. and Yang, X. (2010) Pathways of change: shifting connectivities in the world city network, 2000–2008. *Urban Studies*, 47: 1861–77.

Dicken, P. (2000) Places and flows: situating international investment. In G.L. Clark, M.P. Feldman and M.S. Gertler (eds) *The Oxford Handbook of Economic Geography*. Oxford: Oxford University Press. Chapter 14.

Dicken, P. (2003a) Global production networks in Europe and East Asia: the automobile components industries. *University of Manchester, GPN Working Paper*, 7 (www.sed.manchester.ac.uk/geography/research/gpn/gpnwp.htm).

Dicken, P. (2003b) 'Placing' firms: grounding the debate on the 'global' corporation. In J. Peck and H.W.-c. Yeung (eds) *Remaking the Global Economy: Economic–Geographical Perspectives*. London: Sage. Chapter 2.

Dicken, P. (2004) Geographers and 'globalization': (yet) another missed boat? *Transactions of the Institute of British Geographers*, 29: 5–26.

Dicken, P. and Malmberg, A. (2001) Firms in territories: a relational perspective. *Economic Geography*, 77: 345–63.

Dicken, P. and Miyamachi, Y. (1998) 'From noodles to satellites': the changing geography of the Japanese *sogo shosha*. *Transactions of the Institute of British Geographers*, 23: 55–78.

Dicken, P. and Yeung, H.W.-c. (1999) Investing in the future: East and Southeast Asian firms in the global economy. In K. Olds, P. Dicken, P.F. Kelly, L. Kong and H.W.-c. Yeung (eds) *Globalization and the Asia-Pacific: Contested Territories*. London: Routledge. Chapter 7.

Dicken, P., Kelly, P.F., Olds, K. and Yeung, H.W.-c. (2001) Chains and networks, territories and scales. *Global Networks*, 1: 89–112.

Dieter, H. and Higgott, R. (2003) Exploring alternative theories of economic regionalism: from trade to finance in Asian cooperation. *Review of International Political Economy*, 10: 430–54.

Dodge, M. and Kitchin, R. (2001) *Atlas of Cyberspace*. Reading, MA: Addison-Wesley.

Dolan, C. and Humphrey, J. (2002) Changing governance patterns in the trade in fresh vegetables between Africa and the United Kingdom. *Environment and Planning A*, 36: 491–509.

Domanski, B. and Lung, Y. (2009) The changing face of the European periphery in the automotive industry. *European Urban and Regional Studies*, 16: 5–10.

Donaghu, M.T. and Barff, R. (1990) Nike just did it: international subcontracting and flexibility in athletic footwear production. *Regional Studies*, 24: 537–52.

Dore, R. (1986) *Flexible Rigidities: Industrial Policy and Structural Adjustment in the Japanese Economy, 1970–1980*. Stanford, CA: Stanford University Press.

Dore, R. (2008) Financialization of the global economy. *Industrial and Corporate Change*, 17: 1097–113.

Dorling, D. (2012) The case for austerity among the rich. IPPR Discussion Paper, London.

Dosi, G., Freeman, C., Nelson, R., Silverberg, G. and Soete, L. (eds) (1988) *Technical Change and Economic Theory*. London: Pinter.

Douglass, M. (1994) The 'developmental state' and the newly industrialized economies of Asia. *Environment and Planning A*, 26: 543–66.

Dow, S.C. (1999) The stages of banking development and the spatial evolution of financial systems. In R. Martin (ed.) *Money and the Space-Economy*. Chichester: Wiley. Chapter 2.

Doz, Y. (1986a) Government polices and global industries. In M.E. Porter (ed.) *Competition in Global Industries*. Boston, MA: Harvard Business School. Chapter 7.

Doz, Y. (1986b) *Strategic Management in Multinational Companies*. Oxford: Pergamon.

Drogendijk, R. and Slangen, A. (2006) Hofstede, Schwartz, or managerial perceptions? The effects of different cultural distance measures on establishment mode choices by multinational enterprises. *International Business Review*, 15: 361–80.

Drucker, P. (1946) *The Concept of the Corporation*. New York: John Day.

Dunford, M. (2006) Industrial districts, magic circles, and the restructuring of the Italian textiles and clothing chain. *Economic Geography*, 82: 27–59.

Dunning, J.H. (1992) The competitive advantages of countries and the activities of transnational corporations. *Transnational Corporations*, 1: 135–68.

Dunning, J.H. (2000) The eclectic paradigm as an envelope for economic and business theories of MNE activity. *International Business Review*, 9: 163–90.

Dunning, J.H. and Lundan, S.M. (2008) *Multinational Enterprises and the Global Economy*, 2nd edn. Reading, MA: Addison-Wesley.

Durand, C. (2007) Externalities from foreign direct investment in the Mexican retailing sector. *Cambridge Journal of Economics*, 31: 393–411.

Dustmann, C. and Glitz, A. (2005) *Immigration, Jobs and Wages: Theory, Evidence and Opinion*. London: CEPR.

Eatwell, J. and Taylor, L. (2000) *Global Finance at Risk: The Case for International Regulation*. Cambridge: Polity Press.

Eden, L. and Monteils, A. (2002) Regional integration: NAFTA and the reconfiguration of North American industry. In J.H. Dunning (ed.) *Regions, Globalization and the Knowledge-Based Economy*. Oxford: Oxford University Press. Chapter 7.

Edgerton, D. (2007) *The Shock of the Old*. London: Profile Books.

Edgington, D.W. and Hayter, R. (2013) 'Glocalization' and regional headquarters: Japanese electronics firms in the ASEAN region. *Annals of the Association of American Geographers*, 103: 647–68.

EIU (2000) *World Automotive Components: Market Prospects to 2005*. London: The Economist Intelligence Unit.

Elango, B. (2004) Geographic scope of operations by multinational companies: an exploratory study of regional and global strategies. *European Management Journal*, 22: 431–41.

Elliott, L. (2000) Free trade, no choice. In B. Gunnell and D. Timms (eds) *After Seattle: Globalization and its Discontents*. London: Catalyst. Chapter 2.

Elliott, L. (2002) Morals of the brothel. *Guardian*, 15 April.

Emel, J., Bridge, G. and Krueger, R. (2002) The earth as input: resources. In R.J. Johnston, P.J. Taylor and M.J. Watts (eds) *Geographies of Global Change: Remapping the World*. Oxford: Blackwell. Chapter 24.

Epstein, G.A. (ed.) (2005) *Financialization and the World Economy*. Cheltenham: Edward Elgar.

Ericsson, M. (2008) Global mining: new actors! *Nordic Steel and Mining Review*, 2008/03: 112–18.

Ernst, D. and Kim, L. (2002) Global production networks, knowledge diffusion, and local capability formation. *Research Policy*, 1419: 1–13.

ETC Group (2008) *Who Owns Nature? Corporate Power and the Final Frontier in the Commodification of Life*. Toronto: ETC Group.

Eurofound (2012) *Born Global: The Potential of Job Creation in New International Businesses*. Luxembourg: Publications Office of the European Union.

Evans, P. (2010) Is it labor's turn to globalize? Twenty-first century opportunities and strategic responses. *Global Labour Journal*, 1: 352–79.

FAO (2009) *Statistical Yearbook, 2009*. New York: United Nations.

Farole, T. and Akinci, G. (eds) (2011) *Special Economic Zones: Progress, Emerging Challenges and Future Directions*. Washington, DC: World Bank.

Farooki, M. and Kaplinsky, R. (2012) *The Impact of China on Global Commodity Prices – The Global Reshaping of the Resource Sector*. London: Routledge.

Faulconbridge, J.R. (2008) Negotiating cultures of work in transnational law firms. *Journal of Economic Geography*, 8: 497–517.

Faulconbridge, J.R., Hall, S.J.E. and Beaverstock, J.V. (2008) New insights into the internationalization of producer services: organizational strategies and spatial economies for global headhunting firms. *Environment and Planning A*, 40: 210-34.

Faulconbridge, J.R., Beaverstock, J.V., Hall, S.J.E. and Hewitson, A. (2009) The 'war for talent': the gatekeeper role of executive search firms in elite labour markets. *Geoforum*, 40: 800-8.

Faulconbridge, J.R., Beaverstock, J.V., Nativel, C. and Taylor, P.J. (2011) *The Globalization of Advertising: Agencies, Cities and Spaces of Creativity*. London: Routledge.

Faulconbridge, J.R., Muzio, D and Cook, A. (2012) Institutional legacies in TNCs and their management through training academies: the case of transnational law firms in Italy. *Global Networks*, 12: 48–70.

Faux, J. and Mishel, L. (2000) Inequality and the global economy. In W. Hutton and A. Giddens (eds) *On the Edge: Living with Global Capitalism*. London: Jonathan Cape. pp. 93–111.

Feenstra, R.C. (1998) Integration of trade and disintegration of production in the global economy. *Journal of Economic Perspectives*, 12: 31–50.

Fichter, M., Helfen, M. and Sydow, J. (2011) Employment relations in global production networks: initiating transfer of practices via union involvement. *Human Relations*, 64: 599–622.

Fields, G. (2004) *Territories of Profit: Communications, Capitalist Development, and the Innovative Enterprises of G. F. Swift and Dell Computers*. Stanford, CA: Stanford Business Books.

Flecker, J., Haidinger, B. and Schönauer, A. (2013) Divide and serve: the labour process in service value chains and networks. *Competition and Change*, 17: 6–23.

Florida, R. (2005) The world is spiky. *Atlantic Monthly*, October: 48–51.

Forsgren, M., Holm, U. and Johanson, J. (2005) *Managing the Embedded Multinational: A Business Network View*. Cheltenham: Edward Elgar.

Foy, H. (2013) Hybrid carmakers. *Financial Times*, 11 December: 12.

Frank, A.G. (1998) *ReORIENT: Global Economy in the Asian Age*. Berkeley, CA: University of California Press.

Freeman, C. (1982) *The Economics of Industrial Innovation*. London: Pinter.

Freeman, C. (1987) The challenge of new technologies. In *Interdependence and Co-operation in Tomorrow's World*. Paris: OECD. pp. 123–56.

Freeman, C. (1988) Introduction. In G. Dosi, C. Freeman, R. Nelson, G. Silverberg and L. Soete (eds) *Technical Change and Economic Theory*. London: Pinter. Chapter 1.

Freeman, C. (1997) The 'national system of innovation' in historical perspective. In D. Archibugi and J. Michie (eds) *Technology, Globalization and Economic Performance*. Cambridge: Cambridge University Press. Chapter 2.

Freeman, C. and Louçã, F. (2001) *As Time Goes By: From the Industrial Revolutions to the Information Revolution*. Oxford: Oxford University Press.

Freeman, C. and Perez, C. (1988) Structural crises of adjustment, business cycles and investment behaviour. In G. Dosi, C. Freeman, R. Nelson, G. Silverberg and L. Soete (eds) *Technical Change and Economic Theory*. London: Pinter.

Freeman, C., Clark, J. and Soete, L. (1982) *Unemployment and Technical Change*. London: Pinter.

French, S. and Leyshon, A. (2004) The new, new financial system? Towards a reconceptualization of financial reintermediation. *Review of International Political Economy*, 11: 263–88.

Freyssenet, M. and Lung, Y. (2000) Between globalisation and regionalisation: what is the future of the motor industry? In J. Humphrey, Y. Lecler and M.S. Salerno (eds) *Global Strategies and Local Realities: The Auto Industry in Emerging Markets*. London: Macmillan. Chapter 4.

Friedland, W. (1994) The new globalization: the case of fresh produce. In A. Bonanno, L. Busch, W. Friedland, and E. Mingione (eds) *From Columbus to ConAgra: The Globalization of Agriculture and Food*. Lawrence, KS: University Press of Kansas: Chapter 10.

Friedman, T.L. (1999) *The Lexus and the Olive Tree*. New York: HarperCollins.

Friedman, T.L. (2005) *The World is Flat: The Globalized World in the Twenty-First Century*. London: Penguin.

Friedmann, J. (1986) The world city hypothesis. *Development and Change*, 17: 69–83.

Frigant, V. and Layan, J.-B. (2009) Modular production and the new division of labour within Europe. *European Urban and Regional Studies*, 16: 11–25.

Frigant, V. and Lung, Y. (2002) Geographical proximity and supplying relationships in modular production. *International Journal of Urban and Regional Research*, 26: 742–55.

Fröbel, F., Heinrichs, J. and Kreye, O. (1980) *The New International Division of Labour*. Cambridge: Cambridge University Press.

Fruin, W.M. (1992) *The Japanese Enterprise System*. Oxford: Clarendon Press.

Frynas, J.G. and Paulo, M. (2006) A new scramble for African oil? Historical, political, and business perspectives. *African Affairs*, 106: 229–51.

Gabrielsson, M. and Kirpalani, V.H.M. (2004) Born globals: how to reach new business space rapidly. *International Business Review*, 13: 555–71.

Gallagher, K.P., Moreno-Brid, J.C. and Porzecanski, R. (2008) The dynamism of Mexican exports: lost in (Chinese) translation? *World Development*, 36: 1365–80.

Gamberoni, E. and Newfarmer, R. (2009) Trade protection: incipient but worrisome trends. *Trade Notes*, International Trade Department, World Bank.

Gereffi, G. (1990) Paths of industrialization: an overview. In G. Gereffi and D.L. Wyman (eds) *Manufacturing Miracles: Paths of Industrialization in Latin America and East Asia*. Princeton, NJ: Princeton University Press. Chapter 1.

Gereffi, G. (1994) The organization of buyer-driven global commodity chains: how US retailers shape overseas production networks. In G. Gereffi and M. Korzeniewicz (eds) *Commodity Chains and Global Capitalism*. Westport, CT: Praeger. Chapter 5.

Gereffi, G. (1996) Commodity chains and regional divisions of labor in East Asia. *Journal of Asian Business,* 12: 75–112.

Gereffi, G. (1999) International trade and industrial upgrading in the apparel commodity chain. *Journal of International Economics,* 48: 37–70.

Gereffi, G. (2001) Shifting governance structures in global commodity chains, with special reference to the Internet. *American Behavioral Scientist,* 44: 1616–37.

Gereffi, G. (2005) The global economy: organization, governance and development. In N. Smelser and R. Swedberg (eds) *The Handbook of Economic Sociology,* 2nd edn. Princeton, NJ: Princeton University Press. Chapter 8.

Gereffi, G. (2014) Global value chains in a post-Washington Consensus world. *Review of International Political Economy,* 21: 9–37.

Gereffi, G. and Memedovic, O. (2004) The global apparel value chain: what prospects for upgrading by developing countries? In J. O'Loughlin, L. Staeheli and E. Greenberg (eds) *Globalization and its Outcomes.* New York: Guilford. Chapter 4.

Gereffi, G., Garcia-Johnson, R. and Sasser, E. (2001) The NGO-industrial complex. *Foreign Policy,* July–August: 56–65.

Gereffi, G., Spener, D. and Bair, J. (eds) (2002) *Free Trade and Uneven Development: The North American Apparel Industry after NAFTA.* Philadelphia, PA: Temple University Press.

Gereffi, G., Humphrey, J. and Sturgeon, T. (2005) The governance of global value chains. *Review of International Political Economy,* 12: 78–104.

Gerlach, M. (1992) *Alliance Capitalism: The Social Organization of Japanese Business.* Berkeley, CA: University of California Press.

Gertler, M.S. (1995) 'Being there': proximity, organization and culture in the development and adoption of advanced manufacturing technologies. *Economic Geography,* 71: 1–26.

Gertler, M.S. (2003) Tacit knowledge and the economic geography of context, or the undefinable tacitness of being there. *Journal of Economic Geography,* 3: 75–99.

Gertler, M.S., Wolfe, D.A. and Garkut, D. (2000) No place like home? The embeddedness of innovation in a regional economy. *Review of International Political Economy,* 7: 688–718.

Ghose, A.K., Majid, N. and Ernst, C. (2009) *The Global Employment Challenge.* Geneva: ILO.

Gibbon, P. (2002) At the cutting edge? Financialisation and UK clothing retailers' global sourcing patterns and practices. *Competition and Change,* 6: 289–308.

Gibson-Graham, J.K. (2006) *Post-Capitalist Politics.* Minneapolis, MN: Minnesota University Press.

Gilpin, R. (1987) *The Political Economy of International Relations.* Princeton, NJ: Princeton University Press.

Gilpin, R. (2000) *The Challenge of Global Capitalism: The World Economy in the 21st Century.* Princeton, NJ: Princeton University Press.

Gilpin, R. (2001) *Global Political Economy: Understanding the International Economic Order.* Princeton, NJ: Princeton University Press.

Giroud, A. and Mirza, H. (2006) Factors determining supply linkages between transnational corporations and local suppliers in ASEAN. *Transnational Corporations,* 15: 1–32.

Glasius, M., Kaldor, M. and Anheier, H. (eds) (2002) *Global Civil Society, 2002.* Oxford: Oxford University Press.

Glassner, M.I. (1993) *Political Geography.* New York: Wiley.

Gleick, J. (2012) *The Information: A History, A Theory, A Flood.* London: Fourth Estate.

Goerzen, A., Asmussen, C.G. and Nielsen, B.B. (2013) Global cities and multinational enterprise location strategy. *Journal of International Business Studies,* 44: 427–50.

Goldstein, J. (2007) China's international recycling trade. USC US–China Institute (http://china.usc.edu).

Gomes-Casseres, B. (1996) *The Alliance Revolution: The New Shape of Business Rivalry.* Cambridge, MA: Harvard University Press.

Goodhart, D. (2013) *The British Dream.* London: Atlantic Books.

Gordon, D.M. (1988) The global economy: new edifice or crumbling foundations? *New Left Review,* 168: 24–64.

Graham, M. (2009) Known unknowns. *Technology Guardian,* 3 December: 3.

Graham, M. (2010) Neogeography and the palimpsest of place: Web 2.0 and the construction of a virtual earth. *Tijdschrift voor Economische en Sociale Geografie,* 101: 422–36.

Graham, M. (2012) The knowledge based economy and digital divisions of labour. In V. Desai and R. Potter (eds) *Companion to Development Studies.* London: Hodder.

Graham, M. (2014) Internet geographies: data shadows and the digital divisions of labour. In Graham, M. and Dutton, W.H. (eds) *Society and the Internet: How Networks of Information and Communication Are Changing Our Lives.* Oxford: Oxford University Press.

Graham, M., Hale, S.A. and Stephens, M. (2011) *Geographies of the World's Knowledge.* London: Convoco Edition.

Graham, M., Hale, S.A. and Stephens, M. (2012) Digital divide: the geography of Internet access. *Environment and Planning A,* 44: 1009–10.

Graham, S. and Marvin, S. (1996) *Telecommunications and the City: Electronic Spaces, Urban Places.* London: Routledge.

Granovetter, M. (1985) Economic action and social structure: the problem of embeddedness. *American Journal of Sociology,* 91: 481–510.

Granovetter, M. and Swedberg, R. (eds) (1992) *The Sociology of Economic Life.* Boulder, CO: Westview Press.

Grant, C. (2012) A three-tier Europe puts the single market at risk. *Financial Times,* 26 October.

Greider, W. (1997) *One World, Ready or Not: The Manic Logic of Global Capitalism.* London: Penguin.

Gretschmann, K. (1994) Germany in the global economy of the 1990s: from player to pawn? In R. Stubbs and G.R.D. Underhill (eds) *Political Economy and the Changing Global Order.* London: Macmillan. Chapter 29.

Griffiths, I. (2012) How one word changed so Amazon pays less tax on its UK activities. *Guardian,* 5 April.

Gritsch, M. (2005) The nation-state and economic globalization: soft geo-politics and increased state autonomy? *Review of International Political Economy,* 12: 1–25.

Grugel, J. (1996) Latin America and the remaking of the Americas. In A. Gamble and A. Payne (eds) *Regionalism and World Order.* London: Macmillan. Chapter 5.

Guan, D., Peters, G.P., Weber, C.L. and Hubacek, K. (2009) Journey to world top emitter: an analysis of the driving forces of China's recent CO_2 emissions surge. *Geophysical Research Letters,* 36 (4).

Gwynne, R. (1994) Regional integration in Latin America: the revival of a concept? In R. Gibb and W. Michalak (eds) *Continental trading Blocs: The Growth of Regionalism in the World Economy.* Chichester: Wiley. Chapter 7.

Haggard, S. (1995) *Developing Nations and the Politics of Global Integration.* Washington, DC: Brookings Institution.

Haig, R.M. (1926) Toward an understanding of the metropolis. *Quarterly Journal of Economics,* 40: 421–33.

Hale, A. and Wills, J. (eds) (2005) *Threads of Labour: Garment Industry Supply Chains from the Workers' Perspective.* Oxford: Blackwell.

Hall, P. and Preston, P. (1988) *The Carrier Wave: New Information Technology and the Geography of Innovation, 1846–2003.* London: Unwin Hyman.

Hall, P.A. and Soskice, D. (2001) *Varieties of Capitalism: The Institutional Foundations of Comparative Advantage*. Oxford: Oxford University Press.

Hamilton, G.G. and Feenstra, R.C. (1998) Varieties of hierarchies and markets: an introduction. In G. Dosi, D.J. Teece and J. Chytry (eds) *Technology, Organization and Competitiveness*. Oxford: Oxford University Press. pp. 105–46.

Hamilton-Hart, N. (2003) Asia's new regionalism: government capacity and cooperation in the Western Pacific. *Review of International Political Economy*, 10: 222–45.

Harvey, D. (2011) *The Enigma of Capital and the Crises of Capitalism*. London: Profile Books.

Harzing, A.-W. (2000) An empirical analysis and extension of the Bartlett and Ghoshal typology of multinational companies. *Journal of International Business Studies*, 31: 101–20.

Hawkins, R.G. (1972) Job displacement and the multinational firm: a methodological review. *Center for Multinational Studies Occasional Paper 3*. Washington, DC.

Hedlund, G. (1986) The hypermodern MNC – a heterarchy. *Human Resource Management*, 25: 9–35.

Heenan, D.A. and Perlmutter, H. (1979) *Multinational Organizational Development: A Social Architecture Perspective*. Reading, MA: Addison-Wesley.

Held, D. and McGrew, A. (2007) *Globalization/Anti-Globalization: Beyond the Great Divide*, 2nd edn. Cambridge: Polity Press.

Helm, D. (2009) Environmental challenges in a warming world: consumption, costs and responsibilities. Tanner Lecture, New College Oxford (www.dieterhelm.co.uk).

Helman, C. (2012) The world's biggest oil companies. *Forbes*, 16 July.

Henderson, J. (1998) Danger and opportunity in the Asia-Pacific. In G. Thompson (ed.) *Economic Dynamism in the Asia-Pacific*. London: Routledge. Chapter 14.

Henderson, J. (2011) *East Asian Transformation: On the Political Economy of Dynamism, Governance and Crisis*. London: Routledge.

Henderson, J. and Castells, M. (eds) (1987) *Global Restructuring and Territorial Development*. London: Sage.

Henderson, J., Dicken, P., Hess, M., Coe, N. and Yeung, H.W.-c. (2002) Global production networks and the analysis of economic development. *Review of International Political Economy*, 9: 436–64.

Herod, A. (1997) From a geography of labor to a labor geography: rethinking conceptions of labor in economic geography. *Antipode*, 29: 1–31.

Herod, A. (2001) *Labor Geographies: Workers and the Landscape of Capitalism*. New York: Guilford.

Hess, M. (2004) 'Spatial' relationships? Towards a re-conceptualization of embeddedness. *Progress in Human Geography*, 28: 165–86.

Hess, M. (2009) Investigating the archipelago economy: chains, networks and the study of uneven development. *Journal für Entwicklungspolitik*, 2009/2: 20–37.

Higgott, R. (1999) The political economy of globalization in East Asia: the salience of 'region building'. In K. Olds, P. Dicken, P.F. Kelly, L. Kong and H.W.-c. Yeung (eds) *Globalization and the Asia-Pacific: Contested Territories*. London: Routledge. Chapter 6.

Hirsch, F. (1977) *Social Limits to Growth*. London: Routledge & Kegan Paul.

Hirst, P. and Thompson, G. (1992) The problem of 'globalization': international economic relations, national economic management and the formation of trading blocs. *Economy and Society*, 21: 357–96.

Hirst, P., Thompson, G. and Bromley, S. (2009) *Globalization in Question*, 3rd edn. Cambridge: Polity Press.

Hoekman, B. and Kostecki, M. (1995) *The Political Economy of the World Trading System: From GATT to WTO*. Oxford: Oxford University Press.

Hofstede, G. (1980) *Culture's Consequences*. London: Sage.

Hollingsworth, J.R. and Boyer, R. (eds) (1997) *Contemporary Capitalism: The Embeddedness of Institutions.* Cambridge: Cambridge University Press.

Holmes, J. (2000) Regional economic integration in North America. In G.L. Clark, M.P. Feldman and M.S. Gertler (eds) *The Oxford Handbook of Economic Geography.* Oxford: Oxford University Press. Chapter 32.

Hood, N. and Young, S. (2000) Globalization, corporate strategies and business services. In N. Hood and S. Young (eds) *The Globalization of Multinational Enterprise Activity and Economic Development.* London: Macmillan. Chapter 4.

Horaguchi, H. and Shimokawa, K. (eds) (2002) *Japanese Foreign Direct Investment and the East Asia Industrial System.* Berlin: Springer.

Hosman, L. (2009) Dynamic bargaining and the prospects for learning in the petroleum industry: the case of Kazakhstan. *Perspectives on Global Development & Technology*, 8: 1–25.

Hotz-Hart, B. (2000) Innovation networks, regions and globalization. In G.L. Clark, M.P. Feldman and M.S. Gertler (eds) *The Oxford Handbook of Economic Geography.* Oxford: Oxford University Press. Chapter 22.

Howells, J. (2000) Knowledge, innovation and location. In J.R. Bryson, P.W. Daniels, N. Henry and J. Pollard (eds) *Knowledge, Space, Economy.* London: Routledge. Chapter 4.

Howells, J. (2012a) The geography of knowledge: never so close but never so far apart. *Journal of Economic Geography*, 12: 1003–20.

Howells, J. (2012b) Introductions: innovation and economic geography: a review and analysis. *Journal of Economic Geography*, 12: 929–42.

Huang, S.W. (2004) Global trade patterns in fruits and vegetables. *US Department of Agriculture, Agriculture and Trade Report WRS-04-06.*

Hudson, R. (2001) *Producing Places.* New York: Guilford.

Hudson, R. (2005) *Economic Geographies: Circuits, Flows and Spaces.* London: Sage.

Hughes, A., Wrigley, N. and Buttle, M. (2008) Global production networks, ethical campaigning and the embeddedness of responsible governance. *Journal of Economic Geography*, 8: 345–67.

Hulme, D. and Arun, T. (eds) (2009) *Microfinance: A Reader.* Abingdon: Routledge.

Hulme, M. (2004) A change in the weather? Coming to terms with climate change. In F. Harris (ed.) *Global Environmental Issues.* Chichester: Wiley. Chapter 2.

Humbert, M. (1994) Strategic industrial policies in a global industrial system. *Review of International Political Economy*, 1: 445–64.

Humphrey, J. and Schmitz, H. (2002) How does insertion in global value chains affect upgrading in industrial clusters? *Regional Studies*, 36: 1017–27.

Hurley, J. (2005) Unravelling the web: supply chains and workers' lives in the garment industry. In A. Hale and J. Wills (eds) *Threads of Labour: Garment Industry Supply Chains from the Workers' Perspective.* Oxford: Blackwell. Chapter 5.

Hymer, S.H. (1976) *The International Operations of National Firms: A Study of Direct Foreign Investment.* Cambridge, MA: MIT Press.

Iles, A. (2004) Mapping environmental justice in technology flows: computer waste impacts in Asia. *Global Environmental Politics*, 4: 76–107.

ILO (1996) *Globalization of the Footwear, Textiles, and Clothing Industries.* Geneva: ILO.

ILO (1997) *World Employment, 1996/97: National Policies in a Global Context.* Geneva: ILO.

ILO (2001) *World Employment Report 2001: Life at Work in the Information Economy.* Geneva: ILO.

ILO (2003) *Employment and Social Policy in Respect of Export-Processing Zones (EPZs).* Geneva: ILO.

ILO (2004a) *Economic Security for a Better World.* Geneva: ILO.

ILO (2004b) *A Fair Globalization: Creating Opportunities for All.* Geneva: ILO.

ILO (2005) *Promoting Fair Globalization in Textiles and Clothing in a Post-MFA Environment*. Geneva: ILO.

ILO (2006) *Global Employment Trends Brief, January 2006*. Geneva: ILO.

ILO (2007a) ILO database on export processing zones. *ILO Sectoral Activities Working Paper*, 251.

ILO (2007b) *Visions for Asia's Decent Work Decade: Sustainable Growth and Jobs to 2015*. Geneva: ILO.

ILO (2012) *Global Wage Report 2012/2013*. Geneva: ILO.

ILO (2013a) *Global Employment Trends 2013*. Geneva: ILO.

ILO (2013b) *Global Employment Trends for Youth 2013*. Geneva: ILO.

ILO (2014) *Global Employment Trends 2014. Risk of a Jobless Recovery?* Geneva: ILO.

International Energy Agency (2012) *World Energy Outlook 2012*. Paris: IEA.

IPCC (Intergovernmental Panel on Climate Change) (2007) *Climate Change 2007: The Physical Science Basis*. Paris: IPCC.

IPCC (Intergovernmental Panel on Climate Change) (2013) *Climate Change 2013: The Physical Science Basis*. Paris: IPCC.

Ito, T. (2001) Growth, crisis, and the future of economic recovery in East Asia. In J.E. Stiglitz and S. Yusuf (eds) *Rethinking the East Asia Miracle*. New York: Oxford University Press. Chapter 2.

Jackson, T. (2009) *Prosperity Without Growth: Economics for a Finite Planet*. London: Earthscan.

Jacques, M. (2012) *When China Rules the World*, 2nd edn. London: Penguin.

James, O. (2007) *Affluenza*. London: Vermillion.

Jessop, B. (1994) Post-Fordism and the State. In A. Amin (ed.) *Post-Fordism: A Reader*. Oxford: Blackwell. Chapter 8.

Jessop, R. (2002) *The Future of the Capitalist State*. Cambridge: Polity Press.

Johnson, C. (1985) The institutional foundations of Japanese industrial policy. *California Management Review*, XXVII: 59–69.

Jones, A. (2005) Truly global corporations? Theorizing 'organizational globalization' in advanced business service. *Journal of Economic Geography*, 5: 177–200.

Jones, A. (2007) More than 'managing across borders'? The complex role of face-to-face interaction in globalizing law firms. *Journal of Economic Geography*, 7: 223–46.

Jones, A. (2008) The rise of global work. *Transactions of the Institute of British Geographers*, 33: 12–26.

Jones, A. (2010) *Globalization: Key Thinkers*. Cambridge: Polity Press.

Jones, H.R. (1990) *A Population Geography*, 2nd edn. London: Paul Chapman.

Jordaan, J.A. (2011) FDI, local sourcing and supporting linkages with domestic suppliers: the case of Monterrey, Mexico. *World Development*, 39: 620–32.

Jürgens, U. and Krzywdzinski, M. (2009) Changing east-west division of labour in the European automotive industry. *European Urban and Regional Studies*, 16: 27–42.

Kaldor, M. (2003) *Global Civil Society: An Answer to War*. Cambridge: Polity Press.

Kaltenthaler, K. and Mora, F.O. (2002) Explaining Latin American economic integration: the case of Mercosur. *Review of International Political Economy*, 9: 72–97.

Kang, N.-H. and Sakai, K. (2000) International strategic alliances: their role in industrial globalization, *OECD STI Working Paper, 2000/5*.

Kaplinsky, R. (2001) Is globalization all it is cracked up to be? *Review of International Political Economy*, 8: 45–65.

Kaplinsky, R. (2004) Spreading the gains from globalization: what can be learned from value chain analysis? *Problems of Economic Transition*, 47: 74–115.

Kapstein, E.B. (1999) *Sharing the Wealth: Workers and the World Economy*. New York: W.W. Norton.

Karreman, B. and van der Knaap, B. (2009) The financial centres of Shanghai and Hong Kong: competition or complementarity? *Environment and Planning A*, 41: 563–80.

Kay, J. (2009) Making banks boring again. *Prospect*, January: 54–8.

Kelly, P.F. (1999) The geographies and politics of globalization. *Progress in Human Geography*, 23: 379–400.

Kelly, P.F. (2013) Production networks, place and development: thinking through global production networks in Cavite, Philippines. *Geoforum*, 44: 82–92.

Kelly, R. (1995) Derivatives: a growing threat to the international financial system. In J. Michie and J. Grieve-Smith (eds) *Managing the Global Economy*. Oxford: Oxford University Press. Chapter 9.

Kennedy, P. (2002) Global challenges at the beginning of the twenty-first century. In P. Kennedy, D. Messner and F. Nuscheler (eds) *Global Trends and Global Governance*. London: Pluto Press. Chapter 1.

Kenney, M. and Curry, J. (2001) Beyond transaction costs: e-commerce and the power of the Internet dataspace. In T.R. Leinbach and S.D. Brunn (eds) *Worlds of E-Commerce: Economic, Geographical, and Social Dimensions*. Chichester: Wiley. Chapter 3.

Kessler, J.A. (1999) The North American Free Trade Agreement, emerging apparel production networks and industrial upgrading: the southern California/Mexico connection. *Review of International Political Economy*, 6: 565–608.

Keynes, J.M. (2007) *The General Theory of Employment, Interest and Money*. Basingstoke: Palgrave Macmillan.

Kiple, K.F. (2007) *A Movable Feast: Ten Millennia of Food Globalization*. New York: Cambridge University Press.

Klein, N. (2000) *No Logo*. London: Flamingo.

Kobrin, S.J. (1987) Testing the bargaining hypothesis in the manufacturing sector in developing countries. *International Organization*, 41: 609–38.

Koh, T. (1993) 10 values that help East Asia's economic progress and prosperity. *Singapore Straits Times*, 14 December.

Kolk, A. and van Tulder, R. (2005) Setting new global rules? TNCs and codes of conduct. *Transnational Corporations*, 14: 1–27.

Koo, H. and Kim, E.M. (1992) The developmental state and capital accumulation in South Korea. In R.P. Appelbaum and J. Henderson (eds) *States and Development in the Asian Pacific Rim*. London: Sage. Chapter 5.

Kozul-Wright, R. (1995) Transnational corporations and the nation-state. In J. Michie and J. Grieve-Smith (eds) *Managing the Global Economy*. Oxford: Oxford University Press. Chapter 6.

Kozul-Wright, R. and Rowthorn, R. (1998) Spoilt for choice? Multinational corporations and the geography of international production. *Oxford Review of Economic Policy*, 14: 74–92.

Krugman, P. (1998) What's new about the new economic geography? *Oxford Review of Economic Policy*, 14: 7–17.

Lall, S. (1994) Industrial policy: the role of government in promoting industrial and technological development. *UNCTAD Review*, pp. 65–90.

Langdale, J.V. (2000) Telecommunications and 24-hour trading in the international securities industry. In M.I. Wilson and K.E. Corey (eds) *Information Tectonics: Space, Place, and Technology in an Electronic Age*. Chichester: Wiley. Chapter 6.

Lasserre, P. (1996) Regional headquarters: the spearhead for Asia-Pacific markets. *Long Range Planning*, 29: 30–7.

Law, J. (1986) On the methods of long-distance control: vessels, navigation and the Portuguese route to India. *Sociological Review Monograph*, 32: 234–63.

Lawrence, R.Z. (1996) *Regionalism, Multilateralism, and Deeper Integration.* Washington, DC: Brookings Institution.

Layard, R. (2005) *Happiness: Lessons from a New Science.* London: Penguin Allen Lane.

League of Nations (1945) *Industrialization and Foreign Trade.* New York: League of Nations.

Leclair, M.S. (2002) Fighting the tide: alternative trade organizations in the era of global free trade. *World Development*, 30: 949–58.

Lee, R. (1996) Moral money? LETS and the social construction of local economic geographies in southeast England. *Environment and Planning A*, 28: 1377–94.

Lee, R. (2007) The ordinary economy: tangled up in values and geography. *Transactions of the Institute of British Geographers*, 31: 413–32.

Lee, R. (2009) Economic society/social geography. In S.J. Smith, R. Pain, S.A. Marston and J.P. Jones III (eds) *The Sage Handbook of Social Geographies.* London: Sage. Chapter 8.

Lee, R. and Smith, D.M. (eds) (2004) *Geographies and Moralities: International Perspectives on Development, Justice and Place.* Oxford: Blackwell.

Lee, R., Clark, G.L., Pollard, J. and Leyshon, L. (2009) The remit of financial geography – before and after the crisis. *Journal of Economic Geography*, 9: 723–47.

Leichenko, R.M. and O'Brien, K.L. (2008) *Environmental Change and Globalization: Double Exposures.* New York: Oxford University Press.

Leichenko, R.M., O'Brien, K.L. and Solecki, W.D. (2010) Climate change and the global financial crisis: a case of double exposure. *Annals of the Association of American Geographers*, 100: 963–72.

Leinbach, T.R. (2001) Emergence of the digital economy and e-commerce. In T.R. Leinbach and S.D. Brunn (eds) *Worlds of E-Commerce: Economic, Geographical and Social Dimensions.* Chichester: Wiley. Chapter 1.

Leonard, H.J. (1988) *Pollution and the Struggle for World Product: Multinational Corporations, Environment and International Comparative Advantage.* Cambridge: Cambridge University Press.

Lepawsky, J. and Mather, C. (2011) From beginnings and endings to boundaries and edges: rethinking circulation and exchange through electronic waste. *Area*, 43: 242–9.

Lepawsky, J. and McNabb, C. (2010) Mapping international flows of electronic waste. *Canadian Geographer*, 54: 177–95.

Levinson, M. (2006) *The Box: How the Shipping Container Made the World Smaller and the World Economy Bigger.* Princeton, NJ: Princeton University Press.

Levitt, T. (1983) The globalization of markets. *Harvard Business Review*, May–June: 92–102.

Levy, D.L. (2008) Political contestation in global production networks. *Academy of Management Review*, 33: 943–63.

Levy, D.L. and Prakash, A. (2003) Bargains old and new: multinational corporations in global governance. *Business and Politics*, 5: 131–20.

Levy, F. and Murname, R. (2004) *The New Division of Labour: How Computers Are Creating the Next Job Market.* Princeton, NJ: Princeton University Press.

Lewis, M.K. and Davis, J.T. (1987) *Domestic and International Banking.* Oxford: Philip Allan.

Liao, S. (1997) ASEAN model in international economic cooperation. In H. Soesastro (ed.) *One South East Asia in a New Regional and International Setting.* Jakarta: Centre for Strategic and International Studies.

Linden, G. (2000) Japan and the United States in the Malaysian electronics sector. In M. Borrus, D. Ernst and S. Haggard (eds) *International Production Networks in Asia: Rivalry or Riches?* London: Routledge. Chapter 8.

Lipsey, R.G., Carlaw, K.I. and Bekar, C.T. (2005) *Economic Transformations: General Purpose Technologies and Long-Term Economic Growth.* Oxford: Oxford University Press.

List, F. (1928) *The National System of Political Economy.* New York: Longman.

Liu, B.J. (2011) MNEs and local linkages: evidence from Taiwanese affiliates. *World Development*, 39: 633–47.

Liu, W. and Dicken, P. (2006) Transnational corporations and 'obligated embeddedness': foreign direct investment in China's automobile industry. *Environment and Planning A*, 38: 1229–47.

Liu, W. and Yeung, H.W.-c. (2008) China's dynamic industrial sector: the automobile industry. *Eurasian Geography and Economics*, 49: 523–48.

Luhmann, N. (1998) *Observations on Modernity*. Stanford, CA: Stanford University Press.

Lundvall, B.-Å. (2007) National innovations systems – analytical concept and development tool. *Industry and Innovation*, 14: 95–119.

Lundvall, B.-Å. and Maskell, P. (2000) Nation-states and economic development: from national systems of production to national systems of knowledge creation and learning. In G.L. Clark, M.P. Feldman and M.S. Gertler (eds) *The Oxford Handbook of Economic Geography*. Oxford: Oxford University Press. Chapter 18.

Lüthje, B.-Å. (2002) Electronics contract manufacturing: global production and the international division of labor in the age of the Internet. *Industry and Innovation*, 9: 227–47.

Lynn, B.C. (2005) *End of the Line: The Rise and Coming Fall of the Global Corporation*. New York: Doubleday.

Maddison, A. (2001) *The World Economy: A Millennial Perspective*. Paris: OECD.

Maignan, I. and Ralston, D.D. (2002) Corporate social responsibility in Europe and the US: insights from businesses' self-presentations. *Journal of International Business Studies*, 33: 497–514.

Malecki, E.J. (2002) The economic geography of the Internet's infrastructure. *Economic Geography*, 78: 399–424.

Malecki, E.J. (2010) Global knowledge and creativity: new challenges for firms and regions. *Regional Studies*, 44: 1033–52.

Malecki, E.J. and Hu, W. (2006) A wired world: the evolving geography of submarine cables and the shift to Asia. Paper presented at the Association of American Geographers Annual Conference, Chicago.

Malmberg, A. (1999) The elusive concept of agglomeration economies: theoretical principles and empirical paradoxes. Swedish Collegium for Advanced Study in the Social Sciences Seminar Paper.

Malnight, T.W. (1996) The transition from decentralized to network-based MNC structures: an evolutionary perspective. *Journal of International Business Studies*, 27: 43–63.

Manning, S. (2013) New Silicon Valleys or a new species? Commoditization of knowledge work and the rise of knowledge services clusters. *Research Policy*, 42: 379–90.

Mansfield, E. and Milner, H.V. (1999) The new wave of regionalism. *International Organization*, 53: 589–627.

Markusen, A. (1996) Sticky places in slippery space: a typology of industrial districts. *Economic Geography*, 72: 293–313.

Markusen, A. (1999) Fuzzy concepts, scanty evidence, policy distance: the case for rigor and policy relevance in critical regional studies. *Regional Studies*, 33: 869–94.

Marsh, P. (2012) Product developers enter a new dimension. *Financial Times*, 15 June: 21.

Martin, R. (1999) The new economic geography of money. In R. Martin (ed.) *Money and the Space-Economy*. Chichester: Wiley. Chapter 1.

Martin, R. (2000) Institutional approaches in economic geography. In E. Sheppard and T. Barnes (eds) *A Companion to Economic Geography*. Oxford: Blackwell. Chapter 6.

Martin, R. and Sunley, P. (2003) Deconstructing clusters: chaotic concept or policy panacea? *Journal of Economic Geography*, 3: 5–36.

Mason, M. (1994) Historical perspectives on Japanese direct investment in Europe. In M. Mason and D. Encarnation (eds) *Does Ownership Matter? Japanese Multinationals in Europe*. Oxford: Clarendon Press. Chapter 1.

Massey, D. (1994) A global sense of place. In D. Massey, *Space, Place and Gender*. Cambridge: Polity Press. Chapter 6.

Massey, D. (2000) The geography of power. In B. Gunnell and D. Timms (eds) *After Seattle: Globalization and its Discontents*. London: Catalyst.

Massey, D. (2005) *For Space*. London: Sage.

Mathews, J.A. (2006) Dragon multinationals: new players in 21st century globalization. *Asia Pacific Journal of Management*, 23: 5–27.

Mathews, J.A. (2009) China, India and Brazil: tiger technologies, dragon multinationals and the building of national systems of economic learning. *Asian Business and Management*, 8: 5–32.

Mathews, J.A. and Zander, I. (2007) The international entrepreneurial dynamics of accelerated internationalization. *Journal of International Business Studies*, 38: 387–403.

Mattsson, H. (2007) *Locating Biotech Innovation: Places, Flows and Unruly Processes*. Uppsala: Uppsala University.

Mazzucato, M. (2013) *The Entrepreneurial State: Debunking Public vs. Private Sector Myths*. London: Anthem Press.

McConnell, J. and MacPherson, A. (1994) The North American Free Trade Agreement: an overview of issues and prospects. In R. Gibb and W. Michalak (eds) *Continental Trading Blocs: The Growth of Regionalism in the World Economy*. Chichester: Wiley. Chapter 6.

McHale, J. (1969) *The Future of the Future*. New York: George Braziller.

McMichael, P. (2007) Globalization and the agrarian world. In G. Ritzer (ed.) *The Blackwell Companion to Globalization*. Malden, MA: Blackwell. Chapter 10.

McNeill, J. (2000) *Something New Under the Sun: An Environmental History of the Twentieth Century*. London: Allen Lane.

Melén, S. and Nordman, E.R. (2009) The internationalization modes of Born Globals: a longitudinal study. *European Management Journal*, 27: 243–54.

Merino, F. and Rodriguez, D.R. (2007) Business services outsourcing by manufacturing firms. *Industrial and Corporate Change*, 16: 1147–73.

Metcalfe, J.S. and Dilisio, N. (1996) Innovation, capabilities and knowledge: the epistemic connection. In J. de la Mothe and G. Paquet (eds) *Evolutionary Economics and the New International Political Economy*. London: Pinter. Chapter 3.

Micklethwait, J. and Wooldridge, A. (2000) *A Future Perfect: The Challenge and Hidden Promise of Globalization*. New York: Crown Business.

Milberg, W. (2008) Shifting sources and uses of profits: sustaining US financialization with global value chains. *Economy and Society*, 37: 420–51.

Milberg, W. and Winkler, D. (2010) Financialisation and the dynamics of offshoring in the USA. *Cambridge Journal of Economics*, 34: 275–93.

Miles, R. and Snow, C.C. (1986) Organizations: new concepts for new forms. *California Management Review*, XXVIII: 62–73.

Miles, R., Snow, C.C., Mathews, J.A. and Miles, G. (1999) Cellular-network organizations. In W.E. Halal and K.B. Taylor (eds) *Twenty-First Century Economics: Perspectives of Socioeconomics for a Changing World*. New York: St Martin's Press. Chapter 7.

Miller, D. (1995) Consumption as the vanguard of history. In D. Miller (ed.) *Acknowledging Consumption: A Review of New Studies*. London: Routledge. Chapter 1.

Millstone, E. and Lang, T. (2003) *The Atlas of Food*. London: Earthscan.

Min, S. and Keebler, J.S. (2001) The role of logistics in the supply chain. In J.T. Mentzer (ed.) *Supply Chain Management*. Thousand Oaks, CA: Sage. Chapter 10.

Mitchell, K. (2000) Networks of ethnicity. In E. Sheppard and T. Barnes (eds) *A Companion to Economic Geography*. Oxford: Blackwell. Chapter 24.

Mittelman, J.H. (2000) *The Globalization Syndrome: Transformation and Resistance*. Princeton, NJ: Princeton University Press.

Mockler, R.J. (2000) *Multinational Strategic Alliances*. Chichester: Wiley.

Mohan, G. (2013) Beyond the enclave: towards a critical political economy of China and Africa. *Development and Change*, 44: 1255–72.

Mohan, G. and Lampert, B. (2012) Negotiating China: reinserting African agency into China-Africa relations. *African Affairs*, 112: 92–110.

Mol, M.J., van Tulder, R.J.M. and Beije, P.R. (2005) Antecedents and performance consequences of international outsourcing. *International Business Review*, 14: 599–617.

Monbiot, G. (2012) We were wrong on peak oil. There's enough to fry us all. *Guardian*, 3 July.

Moran, T.H. (2011) Enhancing the contribution of FDI to development: a new agenda for the corporate responsibility community, international labour and civil society, aid donors and multilateral financial institutions. *Transnational Corporations*, 20: 69–102.

Morgan, G., Kristensen, P.H. and Whitley, R. (eds) (2004) *The Multinational Firm: Organizing Across Institutional and National Divides*. Oxford: Oxford University Press.

Morgan, K. (2004) The exaggerated death of geography: learning, proximity and territorial innovation systems. *Journal of Economic Geography*, 4: 3–21.

Morrison, A.J. and Roth, K. (1992) The regional solution: an alternative to globalization. *Transnational Corporations*, 1: 37–55.

Mortimore, M. (1998) Mexico's TNC-centric industrialization process. In R. Kozul-Wright and R. Rowthorn (eds) *Transnational Corporations and the Global Economy*. London: Macmillan. Chapter 13.

Mortimore, M. and Vergara, S. (2004) Targeting winners: can foreign direct investment policy help developing countries industrialise? *European Journal of Development Research*, 16: 499–530.

Mügge, D. (2009) Tales of tails and dogs: derivatives and financialization in contemporary capitalism. *Review of International Political Economy*, 16: 514–26.

Muller, A.R. (2004) *The Rise of Regionalism: Core Company Strategies Under the Second Wave of Integration*. Rotterdam: Erasmus University.

Munro, W.A. and Schurman, R.A. (2009) Chain (re)actions: comparing activist mobilization against biotechnology in Britain and the United States. In J. Bair (ed.) *Frontiers of Commodity Chain Research*. Stanford, CA: Stanford University Press. pp. 207–27.

Murray, S. (2007) *Moveable Feasts: The Incredible Journeys of the Things We Eat*. London: Autumn Press.

Muzio, D. and Faulconbridge, J.R. (2013) The global professional service firm: 'One firm' models versus (Italian) distant institutionalized practices. *Organization Studies*, 34: 897–925.

Myrdal, G. (1958) *Rich Lands and Poor*. New York: Harper & Row.

Mytelka, L.K. and Barclay, L.A. (2004) Using foreign investment strategically for innovation. *European Journal of Development Research*, 16: 531–60.

Narine, S. (2008) Forty years of ASEAN: a historical review. *Pacific Review*, 21: 411–29.

Neilson, J. and Pritchard, B. (2009) *Value Chain Struggles: Institutions and Governance in the Plantation Districts of South India*. Chichester: Wiley.

Neilson, J., Pritchard, B. and Yeung, H.W.-c. (2014) Global value chains and global production networks in the changing international political economy: an introduction. *Review of International Political Economy*, 21: 1–8.

New Economics Foundation (2009) *National Accounts of Well-Being: Bringing Real Wealth onto the Balance Sheet*. London: NEF.

Nixson, F. (1988) The political economy of bargaining with transnational corporations: some preliminary observations. *Manchester Papers in Development*, IV: 377–90.

Nolan, P. (2001) *China and the Global Business Revolution*. London: Palgrave.

Nölke, A., Heires, M. and Bieling, H.-J. (2013) Editorial: The politics of financialization. *Competition and Change*, 17: 209–18.

Nye, J.S. Jr (2002) *The Paradox of American Power: Why the World's Only Superpower Can't Go It Alone*. Oxford: Oxford University Press.

O'Brien, K.L. and Leichenko, R.M. (2000) Double exposure: assessing the impacts of climate change within the context of economic globalization. *Global Environmental Change*, 10: 221–32.

O'Brien, R. (1992) *Global Financial Integration: The End of Geography*. London: Royal Institute of International Affairs.

O'Brien, R. and Keith, A. (2009) The geography of finance: after the storm. *Cambridge Journal of Regions, Economy and Society*, 2: 245–65.

OECD (2004) *A New World Map in Textiles and Clothing: Adjusting to Change*. Paris: OECD.

OECD (2011) *Divided We Stand: Why Inequality Keeps Rising*. Paris: OECD.

OECD (2013) *Action Plan on Base Erosion and Profit Sharing*. Paris: OECD.

OECD-WTO (2013) *OECD-WTO Database on Trade in Value-Added*. Paris/Geneva: OECD-WTO.

O'Rourke, K.H. and Williamson, J.G. (1999) *Globalization and History: The Evolution of a Nineteenth-Century Atlantic Economy*. Cambridge, MA: MIT Press.

Oswald, A.J. (1997) Happiness and economic performance. *Economic Journal*, 107: 1815–31.

Oviatt, B.M. and McDougall, P.P. (2005) Toward a theory of international new ventures. *Journal of International Business Studies*, 36: 29–41.

Oxfam (2002) *Rigged Rules and Double Standards: Trade, Globalization, and the Fight Against Poverty*. London: Oxfam.

Oxfam (2004) *Like Machines in the Fields: Workers Without Rights in American Agriculture*. Boston, MA: Oxfam America.

Oxford Martin Commission (2013) *Now for the Long Term: The Report of the Oxford Martin Commission for Future Generations*. Oxford: Oxford Martin School.

Page, B. (2000) Agriculture. In E. Sheppard and T.J. Barnes (eds) *A Companion to Economic Geography*. Oxford: Blackwell. Chapter 15.

Palan, R. (2003) *The Offshore World: Sovereign Markets, Virtual Places, and Nomad Millionaires*. Ithaca, NY: Cornell University Press.

Palpacuer, F. (2008) Bringing the social context back in: governance and wealth distribution in global commodity chains. *Economy and Society*, 37: 393–419.

Palpacuer, F. and Parisotto, A. (2003) Global production and local jobs: can global enterprise networks be used as levers for local development? *Global Networks*, 3: 97–120.

Palpacuer, F. and Tozanli, S. (2008) Changing governance patterns in European food chains: the rise of a new divide between global players and regional producers. *Transnational Corporations*, 17: 69–97.

Palpacuer, F., Gibbon, P. and Thomsen, L. (2005) New challenges for developing country suppliers in global clothing chains: a comparative European perspective. *World Development*, 33: 409–30.

Patel, P. (1995) Localized production of technology for global markets. *Cambridge Journal of Economics*, 19: 141–53.

Patel, P. and Pavitt, K. (1998) Uneven (and divergent) technological accumulation among advanced countries: evidence and a framework of explanation. In G. Dosi, D.J. Teece and J. Chytry (eds) *Technology, Organization and Competitiveness*. Oxford: Oxford University Press. pp. 289–317.

Pauly, L.W. and Reich, S. (1997) National structures and multinational corporate behavior: enduring differences in the age of globalization. *International Organization*, 51: 1–30.

Pavlinek, P., Domanski, B. and Guzik, R. (2009) Industrial upgrading through foreign direct investment in central European automotive manufacturing. *European Urban and Regional Studies*, 16: 43–63.

Pearce, D.E. (1995) *Capturing Environmental Value*. London: Earthscan.

Peck, J.A. (1996) *Work-Place: The Social Regulation of Labour Markets*. New York: Guilford.

Peck, J.A. (2000) Places of work. In E. Sheppard and T. Barnes (eds) *A Companion to Economic Geography*. Oxford: Blackwell. Chapter 9.

Peck, J.A. (2001) *Workfare States*. New York: Guilford.

Peck, J.A. and Theodore, N. (2007) Variegated capitalism. *Progress in Human Geography*, 31: 731–72.

Peet, R. et al. (2003) *Unholy Trinity: The IMF, World Bank and WTO*. New York: Zed Books.

Perez, C. (1983) Structural change and the assimilation of new technologies in the economic and social systems. *Futures*, 15: 357–75.

Perez, C. (1985) Microelectronics, long waves and world structural change. *World Development*, 13: 441–63.

Perez, C. (2010) Technological revolutions and techno-economic paradigms. *Cambridge Journal of Economics*, 34: 185–202.

Phelps, N. and Fuller, C. (2000) Multinationals, intra-corporate competition and regional development. *Economic Geography*, 76: 224–43.

Phillips, N. (2009) Migration as development strategy? The new political economy of dispossession and inequality in the Americas. *Review of International Political Economy*, 16: 231–59.

Picciotto, S. (1991) The internationalisation of the state. *Capital & Class*, 43: 43–63.

Picciotto, S. (2012) Towards unitary taxation of transnational corporations. Tax Justice Network.

Piketty, T. (2014) *Capital in the Twenty-First Century*. Cambridge, MA: The Belknap Press.

Pires, S.R.I. and Neto, M.S. (2008) New configurations in supply chains: the case of a condominium in Brazil's automotive industry. *Supply Chain Management*, 13: 328–34.

Pirie, I. (2012) The new Korean political economy: beyond the models of capitalism debate. *Pacific Review*, 25: 365–86.

Pitelis, C. (1991) Beyond the nation-state? The transnational firm and the nation-state. *Capital and Class*, 43: 131–52.

Pollard, N., Latorre, M. and Sriskandarajah, D. (2008) *Floodgates Or Turnstiles? Post-EU Enlargement Migration To (And From) The UK*. London: IPPR.

Ponte, S. (2002) The 'Latte Revolution'? Regulation, markets and consumption in the global coffee chain. *World Development*, 30: 1099–122.

Population Reference Bureau (1999) *World Population Data Sheet*. Washington, DC: Population Reference Bureau.

Porter, M.E. (1990) *The Competitive Advantage of Nations*. London: Macmillan.

Porter, M.E. (1998) Clusters and the new economics of competition. *Harvard Business Review*, November–December: 77–90.

Porter, M.E. (2000) Locations, clusters and company strategy. In G.L. Clark, M.P. Feldman and M.S. Gertler (eds) *The Oxford Handbook of Economic Geography*. Oxford: Oxford University Press. Chapter 13.

Porter, M.E., Takeuchi, H., and Sakakibara, M. (2000) *Can Japan Compete?* London: Macmillan.

Power, M., Mohan, G. and Tan-Mullins, M. (2012) *China's Resource Diplomacy in Africa. Powering Development?* Basingstoke: Palgrave Macmillan.

Prahalad, C.K. and Doz, Y. (1987) *The Multinational Mission*. New York: Free Press.

Pritchard, B. (2000a) Geographies of the firm and transnational agro-food corporations in East Asia. *Singapore Journal of Tropical Geography*, 21: 246–62.

Pritchard, B. (2000b) The tangible and intangible spaces of agro-food capital. Paper presented at the International Rural Sociology Association World Congress, Rio de Janeiro.

Pritchard, B. (2000c) The transnational corporate networks of breakfast cereals in Asia. *Environment and Planning A*, 32: 789–804.

Rabach, E. and Kim, E.M. (1994) Where is the chain in commodity chains? The service sector nexus. In G. Gereffi and M. Korzeniewicz (eds) *Commodity Chains and Global Capitalism*. Westport, CT: Praeger. Chapter 6.

Ramesh, M. (1995) Economic globalization and policy choices: Singapore. *Governance: An International Journal of Policy and Administration*, 8: 243–60.

Ramesh, R. (2005) Chindia, where the world's workshop meets its office. *Guardian*, 30 September.

Ramirez, M.D. (2006) Is foreign direct investment beneficial for Mexico? An empirical analysis, 1960–2001. *World Development*, 34: 802–17.

Rasche, A. (2009) 'A necessary supplement': what the United Nations Global Compact is and is not. *Business & Society*, 48: 511–37.

Rasiah, R. (2004) Exports and technological capabilities: a study of foreign and local firms in the electronics industry in Malaysia, the Philippines and Thailand. *European Journal of Development Research*, 16: 587–623.

Raworth, K. and Kidder, T. (2009) Mimicking 'lean' in global value chains; it's the workers who get leaned on. In J. Bair (ed.) *Frontiers of Commodity Chain Research*. Stanford, CA: Stanford University Press. pp. 165–89.

Reardon, T., Henson, S. and Berdegué, J. (2007) 'Proactive fast-tracking' diffusion of supermarkets in developing countries: implications for market institutions and trade. *Journal of Economic Geography*, 7: 399–431.

Reich, S. (1989) Roads to follow: regulating direct foreign investment. *International Organization*, 43: 543–84.

Reid, H.C. (1989) Financial centre hegemony, interest rates, and the global political economy. In Y.S. Park and N. Essayyad (eds) *International Banking and Financial Centres*. Boston, MA: Kluwer. Chapter 16.

Rennstich, J. (2002) The new economy, the leadership long cycle and the nineteenth K-wave. *Review of International Political Economy*, 9: 150–82.

Rigby, D.L. and Breau, S. (2006) Impacts of trade on wage inequality in Los Angeles: analysis using matched employer-employee data. UCLA Center for Economic Studies Discussion Paper.

Rivoli, P. (2005) *The Travels of a T-Shirt in the Global Economy*. New York: Wiley.

Roberts, P. (2008) *The End of Food: The Coming Crisis in the World Food Industry*. London: Bloomsbury.

Roberts, S. (1994) Fictitious capital, fictitious spaces: the geography of offshore financial flows. In S. Corbridge, R. Martin and N.J. Thrift (eds) *Money, Power and Space*. Oxford: Blackwell. Chapter 5.

Rodan, G. (1991) *The Political Economy of Singapore's Industrialization*. Petalang Jaya: Forum Books.

Rodrik, D. (1999) *The New Global Economy and Developing Countries: Making Openness Work*. Washington, DC: Overseas Development Council.

Rodrik, D. (2011) *The Globalization Paradox: Why Global Markets, States, and Democracy Can't Coexist*. Oxford: Oxford University Press.

Ross, R.J.S. (2002) The new sweatshops in the United States: how new, how real, how many and why? In G. Gereffi, D. Spener and J. Bair (eds) *Free Trade and Uneven Development:*

The North American Apparel Industry after NAFTA. Philadelphia, PA: Temple University Press. Chapter 5.

Rossi, A. (2013) Does economic upgrading lead to social upgrading in global production networks? Evidence from Morocco. *World Development*, 46: 223–33.

Rothenberg-Aalami, J. (2004) Coming full circle? Forging missing links along Nike's integrated production network. *Global Networks*, 4: 335–54.

Rothkopf, D. (2012) Free-market evangelists face a sad and lonely fate. *Financial Times*, 1 February.

Rugman, A.M. and Brain, C. (2003) Multinational enterprises are regional, not global. *Multinational Business Review*, 11: 3–12.

Rugman, A.M. and Collinson, S. (2004) The regional nature of the world's automotive industry. *European Management Journal*, 22: 471–82.

Rugman, A.M. and Verbeke, A. (2004) Regional transnationals and Triad strategy. *Transnational Corporations*, 13: 1–20.

Rugman, A.M. and Verbeke, A. (2008) A regional solution to the strategy and structure of multinationals. *European Management Journal*, 26: 305–13.

Rutherford, T. and Holmes, J. (2008) 'The flea on the tail of the dog': power in global production networks and the restructuring of Canadian automotive clusters. *Journal of Economic Geography*, 8: 519–44.

Sachs, J.D. and Warner, A.M. (2001) The curse of natural resources. *European Economic Review*, 45: 827–38.

Saith, A. (2008) China and India: the institutional roots of differential performance. *Development and Change*, 39: 723–57.

Sampson, G.P. (ed.) (2001) *The Role of the World Trade Organization in Global Governance*. Tokyo: United Nations University Press.

Sandel, M.J. (2012) *What Money Can't Buy: The Moral Limits of Markets*. London: Penguin.

Sasi, V. and Arenius, P. (2008) International new ventures and social networks: advantage or liability? *European Management Journal*, 26: 400–11.

Sassen, S. (2001) *The Global City: New York. London, Tokyo*, 2nd edn. Princeton, NJ: Princeton University Press.

Saunders, C., Barber, A. and Taylor, G. (2006) Food miles – comparative energy/emissions performance of New Zealand's agricultural industry. *Research Report 285, Agribusiness & Economics Research Unit, Lincoln University, New Zealand*.

Saxenian, A. (2002) Transnational communities and the evolution of global production networks: the cases of Taiwan, China and India. *Industry and Innovation*, 9: 183–202.

Saxenian, A. (2006) *The New Argonauts: Regional Advantage in a Global Economy*. Cambridge, MA: Harvard University Press.

Sayer, A. (1986) New developments in manufacturing: the just-in-time system. *Capital & Class*, 30: 43–72.

Schary, P.B. and Skjøtt-Larsen, T. (2001) *Managing the Global Supply Chain*, 2nd edn. Copenhagen: Copenhagen Business School Press.

Scherer, A.G., Palazzo, G. and Matten, D. (2014) The business firm as a political actor: a new theory of the firm for a globalized world. *Business and Society*, 53: 143–56.

Scheve, K. and Slaughter, M.J. (2001) *Globalization and the Perceptions of American Workers*. Washington, DC: Institute for International Economics.

Scheve, K. and Slaughter, M.J. (2004) Economic insecurity and the globalization of production. *American Journal of Political Science*, 48: 662–74.

Schiff, M. and Winters, L.A. (2003) *Regional Integration and Development*. Washington, DC: World Bank.

Schoenberger, E. (1997) *The Cultural Crisis of the Firm*. Oxford: Blackwell.

Schoenberger, E. (1999) The firm in the region and the region in the firm. In T. Barnes and M. Gertler (eds) *The New Industrial Geography: Regions, Regulation and Institutions.* London: Routledge. Chapter 9.

Schoenberger, E. (2000) The management of time and space. In G.L. Clark, M.P. Feldman and M. Gertler (eds) *The Oxford Handbook of Economic Geography.* Oxford: Oxford University Press. Chapter 16.

Schoenberger, E. (2014) *Nature, Choice and Social Power.* London: Routledge.

Schumpeter, J. (1943) *Capitalism, Socialism and Democracy.* London: Allen & Unwin.

Schwartz, S.H. (1994) Beyond individualism/collectivism: new cultural dimensions of values. In U. Kim, H.C. Triandis, C. Kagitcibasi, S.C. Choi and G. Yoon (eds) *Individualism and Collectivism: Theory, Methods and Applications.* Thousand Oaks, CA: Sage. pp. 85–119.

Scott, A.J. (1998) *Regions and the World Economy: The Coming Shape of Global Production, Competition and Political Order.* Oxford: Oxford University Press.

Scott, A.J. (2008) Resurgent metropolis: economy, society and urbanization in an interconnected world. *International Journal of Urban and Regional Research,* 32: 548–64.

Scott-Quinn, B. (1990) US investment banks as multinationals. In G. Jones (ed.) *Banks as Multinationals.* London: Routledge. Chapter 5.

Seidler, E. (1976) *Let's Call it Fiesta.* London: Patrick Stephens.

Sen, A. (1999) *Development as Freedom.* Oxford: Oxford University Press.

Siegle, L. (2011) *To Die For: Is Fashion Wearing Out The World?* London: Fourth Estate.

Silva, J.A. and Leichenko, R.M. (2004) Regional income inequality and international trade, *Economic Geography,* 80: 261–86.

Simonis, U.D. and Brühl, T. (2002) World ecology – structures and trends. In P. Kennedy, D. Messner and F. Nuscheler (eds) *Global Trends and Global Governance.* London: Pluto Press. Chapter 4.

Singer, P. (2004) *One World: The Ethics of Globalization,* 2nd edn. New Haven, CT: Yale University Press.

Skidelsky, R. (2010) *Keynes: The Return of the Master.* London: Penguin.

Sklair, L. (2001) *The Transnational Capitalist Class.* Oxford: Blackwell.

Smarzynska, B.K. and Wei, S.-J. (2001) Pollution havens and foreign direct investment: dirty secret or popular myth? *NBER Working Paper 8465.*

Smelser, N. and Swedberg, R. (eds) (2005) *The Handbook of Economic Sociology,* 2nd edn. Princeton, NJ: Princeton University Press.

Smith, A. (2013) Europe and an inter-dependent world: uneven geo-economic and geo-political developments. *European Urban and Regional Studies,* 20: 3–13.

Smith, A. (2014) The state, institutional frameworks and the dynamics of capital in global production networks. *Progress in Human Geography,* 38: 1–26.

Smith, A., Pickles, J., Begg, B., Roukova, P. and Bucek, M. (2005) Outward processing, EU enlargement and regional relocation in the European textiles and clothing industry. *European Urban and Regional Studies,* 12: 83–91.

Smith, A., Pickles, J., Bucek, M., Begg, R. and Roukova, P. (2008) Reconfiguring 'post-socialist' regions: cross-border networks and regional competition in the Slovak and Ukrainian clothing industry. *Global Networks,* 8: 281–307.

Smith, D.A. (2005) Starting at the beginning: extractive economies as the unexamined origins of global commodity chains. In P.S. Ciccantell, D.A. Smith and G. Seidman (eds) *Nature, Raw Materials, and Political Economy.* Amsterdam: Elsevier. pp. 141–57.

Smith, D.M. (2000) *Moral Geographies: Ethics in a World of Difference.* Edinburgh: Edinburgh University Press.

Sonn, J.W. and Storper, M. (2008) The increasing importance of geographical proximity in knowledge production: an analysis of US patent citations, 1975–1997. *Environment and Planning A,* 40: 1020–39.

Sonnino, R. and Marsden, T. (2006) Beyond the divide: rethinking relationships between alternative and conventional food networks in Europe. *Journal of Economic Geography*, 6: 181–99.

Spence, J.D. (2013) *The Search for Modern China*, 3rd edn. New York: W. W. Norton.

Stalk, G., Evans, P. and Shulman, L.E. (1998) Competing on capabilities: the new rules of corporate strategy. *Harvard Business Review*, March–April: 57–69.

Stephens, P. (2008) Broken banks put the state back in the driving seat. *Financial Times*, 28 November: 24.

Stephens, P. (2013) Transatlantic free trade promises a bigger prize. *Financial Times*, 15 February.

Stiglitz, J.E. (2002) *Globalization and its Discontents*. London: Allen Lane.

Stiglitz, J.E. (2012) *The Price of Inequality*. London: Penguin.

Stiglitz, J.E. and Charlton, A. (2005) *Fair Trade for All: How Trade Can Promote Development*. Oxford: Oxford University Press.

Stiglitz, J.E. and Fitoussi, J.P. (2009) *Report of the Commission on the Measurement of Economic Performance and Social Progress*. Report submitted to the President of the French Republic.

Stopford, J.M. and Strange, S. (1991) *Rival States, Rival Firms: Competition for World Market Shares*. Cambridge: Cambridge University Press.

Storper, M. (1995) The resurgence of regional economies, ten years later: the region as a nexus of untraded interdependencies. *European Urban and Regional Studies*, 2: 191–221.

Storper, M. (1997) *The Regional World: Territorial Development in a Global Economy*. New York: Guilford.

Storper, M. and Venables, A.J. (2004) Buzz: face-to-face contact and the urban economy. *Journal of Economic Geography*, 4: 351–70.

Strahan, D. (2007) *The Last Oil Shock: A Survival Guide to the Imminent Extinction of Petroleum Man*. London: John Murray.

Strange, S. (1986) *Casino Capitalism*. Oxford: Blackwell.

Strange, S. (1995) The limits of politics. *Government and Opposition*, 30: 291–311.

Stross, R. (2008) *Planet Google: How One Company is Transforming Our Lives*. London: Atlantic Books.

Struna, J. (2013) Introduction: Global capitalism and transnational class formation. *Globalizations*, 10: 651–7.

Studland, J. (2013) *How Asia Works: Success and Failure in the World's Most Dynamic Region*. London: Profile.

Sturgeon, T.J. (2002) Modular production networks: a new American model of industrial organization. *Industrial and Corporate Change*, 11: 451–96.

Sturgeon, T.J. (2003) What really goes on in Silicon Valley? Spatial clustering and dispersal in modular production networks. *Journal of Economic Geography*, 3: 199–225.

Sturgeon, T.J. and Florida, R. (2004) Globalization, deverticalization, and employment in the motor vehicle industry. In M. Kenney and R. Florida (eds) *Locating Global Advantage: Industry Dynamics in the International Economy*. Stanford, CA: Stanford University Press. Chapter 3.

Sturgeon, T.J., Biesebroeck, J. van and Gereffi, G. (2008) Value chains, networks and clusters: reframing the global automotive industry. *Journal of Economic Geography*, 8: 297–321.

Subramanian, A. and Kessler, M. (2013) The hyperglobalization of trade and its future. *Global Citizen Foundation, Working Paper 3*.

Sutcliffe, B. (2009) The world distribution of gross national income, 2007. *Environment and Planning A*, 41: 764.

Swyngedouw, E. (2000) Elite power, global forces, and the political economy of 'glocal' development. In G.L. Clark, M.P. Feldman and M.S. Gertler (eds) *The Oxford Handbook of Economic Geography*. Oxford: Oxford University Press. Chapter 27.

Tavares, A.T. and Young, S. (2006) Sourcing patterns of foreign-owned multinational subsidiaries in Europe. *Regional Studies*, 40: 583–99.

Taylor, P.J. (1994) The state as container: territoriality in the modern world-system. *Progress in Human Geography*, 18: 151–62.

Taylor, P.J. (2001) Commentary: being economical with the geography. *Environment and Planning A*, 33: 949–54.

Taylor, P.J. (2004) *World City Network: A Global Urban Analysis*. London: Routledge.

Taylor, P.J., Watts, M.J. and Johnston, R.J. (2002) Geography/globalization. In R.J. Johnston, P.J. Taylor and M.J. Watts (eds) *Geographies of Global Change: Remapping the World*. Oxford: Blackwell. Chapter 1.

Taylor, R. and Morrissey, K. (2004) Coping with pollution: dealing with waste. In F. Harris (ed.) *Global Environmental Issues*. Chichester: Wiley. Chapter 9.

Terpstra, V. and David, K. (1991) *The Cultural Environment of International Business*. Cincinnati, OH: South-Western Publishing.

Tett, G. (2009) *Fool's Gold: How Unrestrained Greed Corrupted a Dream, Shattered Global Markets and Unleashed a Catastrophe*. London: Little Brown.

The Economist (2011) The surge in land deals: when others are grabbing their land. 5 May.

Thornhill, J. (2008) The nature of the beast. *Financial Times*, 28 June: 17.

Thrift, N.J. (1994) On the social and cultural determinants of international financial centres: the case of the City of London. In S. Corbridge, R. Martin and N.J. Thrift (eds) *Money, Power and Space*. Oxford: Blackwell. Chapter 14.

Thrift, N.J. (1996) *Spatial Formations*. London: Sage.

Tokatli, N. (2008) Global sourcing: insights from the global clothing industry – the case of Zara, a fast fashion retailer. *Journal of Economic Geography*, 8: 21–38.

Turner, R.K., Pearce, D. and Bateman, I. (1994) *Environmental Economics: An Elementary Introduction*. Hemel Hempstead: Harvester Wheatsheaf.

Turok, I. (1993) Inward investment and local linkages: how deeply embedded is 'Silicon Glen'? *Regional Studies*, 27: 401–17.

Ulset, S. (2008) The rise and fall of global network alliances. *Industrial and Corporate Change*, 17: 267–300.

UN (2013) *The Millennium Development Goals Report, 2013*. New York: United Nations.

UN Centre for Human Settlements (Habitat) (2001) *Global Report on Human Settlements, 2001*. New York: United Nations.

UN Centre for Human Settlements (Habitat) (2003) *Global Report on Human Settlements, 2003*. New York: United Nations.

UN-HABITAT (2008) *State of the World's Cities, 2008/2009*. Nairobi: United Nations.

UNCTAD (1994) *World Investment Report 1994*. New York: United Nations.

UNCTAD (1995) *World Investment Report 1995: Transnational Corporations and Competitiveness*. New York: United Nations.

UNCTAD (2000) *The Competitiveness Challenge: Transnational Corporations and Industrial Restructuring in Developing Countries*. New York: United Nations.

UNCTAD (2001) *World Investment Report 2001: Promoting Linkages*. New York: United Nations.

UNCTAD (2002) *Trade and Development Report 2002: Developing Countries in World Trade*. New York: United Nations.

UNCTAD (2004) *World Investment Report: The Shift Towards Services*. New York: United Nations.

UNCTAD (2005) *World Investment Report 2005: Transnational Corporations and the Internationalization of R&D*. New York: United Nations.

UNCTAD (2007) *World Investment Report 2007: Transnational Corporations, Extractive Industries and Development*. New York: United Nations.

UNCTAD (2008) *World Investment Report, 2008.* New York: United Nations.

UNCTAD (2009) *World Investment Report 2009: Transnational Corporations, Agricultural Production and Development.* New York: United Nations.

UNCTAD (2011) *World Investment Report: Non-Equity Modes of International Production and Development.* New York: United Nations.

UNCTAD (2012) *World Investment Report: Towards a New Generation of Investment Policies.* New York: United Nations.

UNCTAD (2013a) *World Investment Report: Global Value Chains: Investment and Trade for Development.* New York: United Nations.

UNCTAD (2013b) *Trade and Development Report, 2013: Adjusting to the Changing Dynamics of the World Economy.* New York: United Nations.

UNDP (1999) *Human Development Report 1999.* New York: United Nations.

UNDP (2005) *Human Development Report 2005.* New York: United Nations.

UNEP (2004) *Vital Waste Graphics.* Nairobi: United Nations.

UNIDO (2003) *The Global Automotive Industry Value Chain: What Prospects for Upgrading by Developing Countries?* Vienna: UNIDO.

UN Population Division (2001) *World Population Prospects: The 2000 Revision.* New York: United Nations.

UN Population Division (2009) *World Population Prospects: The 2008 Revision.* New York: United Nations.

UN Population Division (2012) *World Population Prospects, 2012.* New York: United Nations.

US Department of Commerce (2000) *Digital Economy 2000.* Washington, DC: US Department of Commerce.

US Senate Committee on Homeland Security and Governmental Affairs, Permanent Subcommittee on Investigations (2013) *Offshore Profit Shifting and the US Tax Code – Part 2 (Apple Inc.) Part III Apple Case Study.* Washington, DC: US Senate.

USEPA (2011) *Municipal Solid Waste (MSW) in the United States: Facts and Figures.* Washington, DC: USEPA.

USGS (2013) *Copper: Statistics and Information.* Washington, DC: US Geological Survey.

Van Grunsven, L., van Egeraat, C. and Meijsen, S. (1995) New manufacturing establishments and regional economy in Johor: production linkages, employment and labour fields. Department of Geography of Developing Countries, University of Utrecht Report Series.

Van Tulder, R. (2009) Chains for change. Max Havelaar Lecture.

Van Tulder, R. with van der Zwart, A. (2006) *International Business-Society Management: Linking Corporate Responsibility and Globalization.* London: Routledge.

Van Tulder, R., van Wijk, J. and Kolk, A. (2009) From chain liability to chain responsibility. *Journal of Business Ethics,* 85: 399–412.

Van Veen, K. and Marsman, I. (2008) How international are executive boards of European MNCs? National diversity in 15 European countries. *European Management Journal,* 26: 188–98.

Veloso, F. and Kumar, R. (2002) The automotive supply chain: global trends and Asian perspectives. *Asian Development Bank ERD Working Paper,* 3.

Veltz, P. (1996) *Mondialisation, Villes et Territoires: L'Économie d'Archipel.* Paris: Universitaires de France.

Vernon, R. (1966) International investment and international trade in the product cycle. *Quarterly Journal of Economics,* 80: 190–207.

Vernon, R. (1979) The product cycle hypothesis in a new international environment. *Oxford Bulletin of Economics and Statistics,* 41: 255–68.

Vernon, R. (1998) *In the Hurricane's Eye: The Troubled Prospects of Multinational Enterprises.* Cambridge, MA: Harvard University Press.

Vitols, S. (ed.) (2004) The transformation of the German model? *Competition and Change*, 8 (4) (Special Issue).

Voltaire (Arouet, F.-M.) (1947) *Candide*, trans. J. Butt. London: Penguin.

Wade, R. (1990) Industrial policy in East Asia: Does it lead or follow the market? In G. Gereffi and D.L. Wyman (eds) *Manufacturing Miracles: Paths of Industrialization in Latin America and East Asia*. Princeton, NJ: Princeton University Press. Chapter 9.

Wade, R.H. (1996) Globalization and its limits: reports of the death of the national economy are greatly exaggerated. In S. Berger and R. Dore (eds) *National Diversity and Global Capitalism*. Ithaca, NY: Cornell University Press. Chapter 2.

Wade, R.H. (2003) What strategies are viable for developing countries today? The World Trade Organization and the shrinking of 'development space'. *Review of International Political Economy*, 10: 621–44.

Wade, R.H. (2004) *Governing the Market: Economic Theory and the Role of Government in East Asian Industrialization*, 2nd edn. Princeton, NJ: Princeton University Press.

Wallerstein, I. (1979) *The Capitalist World-Economy*. Cambridge: Cambridge University Press.

Wang, J.J. and Cheng, M.C. (2010) From a hub port city to a global supply chain management centre: a case study of Hong Kong. *Journal of Transport Geography*, 18: 104–15.

Ward, N. and Almås, R. (1997) Explaining change in the international agro-food system. *Review of International Political Economy*, 4: 611-29.

Warf, B. (1989) Telecommunications and the globalization of financial services. *Professional Geographer*, 41: 257–71.

Warf, B. (2006) International competition between satellite and fiber optic carriers: a geographic perspective. *Professional Geographer*, 58: 1–11.

Warf, B. (2007) Geopolitics of the satellite industry. *Tijdschrift voor Economische en Sociale Geografie*, 98: 385–97.

Warf, B. (2013) Geographies of global telephony in the age of the Internet. *Geoforum*, 45: 219–29.

Warf, B. and Purcell, D. (2001) The currency of currency: speed, sovereignty, and electronic finance. In T.R. Leinbach and S.D. Brunn (eds) *Worlds of E-Commerce: Economic Geographical and Social Dimensions*. Chichester: Wiley. Chapter 12.

Watts, M.J. and Goodman, D. (1997) Agrarian questions: global appetite, local metabolism: nature culture and industry in fin-de-siècle agro-food systems. In D. Goodman and M.J. Watts (eds) *Globalizing Food: Agrarian Questions and Global Restructuring*. London: Routledge. Chapter 1.

Webber, M.J. and Rigby, D.L. (1996) *The Golden Age Illusion: Rethinking Postwar Capitalism*. New York: Guilford.

Weiss, A. (2007) *The Global Food Economy: The Battle for the Future of Farming*. London: Zed Books.

Weiss, L. (1998) *The Myth of the Powerless State: Governing the Economy in a Global Era*. Cambridge: Polity Press.

Weiss, L. (ed.) (2003) *States in the Global Economy: Bringing Domestic Institutions Back In*. Cambridge: Cambridge University Press.

Wells, L.T. Jr (ed.) (1972) *The Product Life Cycle and International Trade*. Boston, MA: Harvard Business School.

Whatmore, S. (2002) *Hybrid Geographies: Natures, Cultures, Spaces*. London: Sage.

Whatmore, S. and Thorne, L. (1997) Nourishing networks: alternative geographies of food. In D. Goodman and M.J. Watts (eds) *Globalizing Food: Agrarian Questions and Global Restructuring*. London: Routledge. Chapter 11.

Whatmore, S., Stassart, P. and Renting, H. (2003) What's alternative about alternative food networks? *Environment and Planning A*, 35: 389–91.

Whitley, R. (1999) *Divergent Capitalisms: The Social Structuring and Change of Business Systems.* Oxford: Oxford University Press.

Whitley, R. (2004) How and why are international firms different? The consequences of cross-border managerial coordination for firm characteristics and behaviour. In G. Morgan, P.H. Kristensen and R. Whitley (eds) *The Multinational Firm: Organizing Across Institutional and National Divides.* Oxford: Oxford University Press. Chapter 2.

Wilkinson, J. (2002) The final foods industry and the changing face of the global agro-food system. *Sociologia Ruralis*, 42: 329–46.

Wilkinson, R. (2009) Concluding the Doha Round. Development at Manchester, 2.

Wilkinson, R. and Pickett, K. (2009) *The Spirit Level: Why More Equal Societies Almost Always Do Better.* London: Allen Lane.

Wills, J. (1998) Taking on the CosmoCorps? Experiments in transnational labour organization. *Economic Geography*, 74: 111–30.

Wills, J. (2002) Bargaining for the space to organize in the global economy: a review of the Accor-IUF trade union rights agreement. *Review of International Political Economy*, 9: 675–700.

WIPO (2008) *World Patent Report – A Statistical Review, 2008.* Geneva: WIPO.

WIPO-INSEAD (2012) *Global Innovation Index, 2012.* Geneva: WIPO-INSEAD.

Wolf, M. (2004) *Why Globalization Works.* New Haven, CT: Yale University Press.

Wolf, M. (2007) The dilemma of global governance. *Financial Times*, 24 January.

Wolf, M. (2008) China changes the whole world. *Financial Times*, 23 January.

Wolf, M. (2013) Why the world faces climate chaos. *Financial Times*, 15 May: 13.

Wolford, W., Borras, S.M. Jr, Hall, R., Scoones, I. and White, B. (2013) Governing global land deals: the role of the state in the rush for land. *Development and Change*, 44: 189–210.

Womack, J.R., Jones, D.T. and Roos, D. (1990) *The Machine that Changed the World.* New York: Rawson Associates.

Wood, A. (1994) *North–South Trade, Employment, and Inequality.* Oxford: Oxford University Press.

World Bank (1995) *World Development Report 1995: Workers in an Integrating World.* Washington, DC: World Bank.

World Bank (2005) *World Development Report 2005: A Better Investment Climate for Everyone.* Washington, DC: World Bank.

World Bank (2008a) *World Development Indicators 2008.* Washington, DC: World Bank.

World Bank (2008b) *World Development Report 2008: Agriculture for Development.* Washington, DC: World Bank.

World Bank (2009a) *World Development Indicators, 2009.* Washington, DC: World Bank.

World Bank (2009b) *World Development Report 2009: Reshaping Economic Geography.* Washington, DC: World Bank.

World Bank (2012) *World Development Report: Gender Inequality and Development.* Washington, DC: World Bank.

World Bank (2013) *World Development Indicators, 2013.* Washington, DC: World Bank.

Wrigley, N. (2000) The globalization of retail capital: themes for economic geography. In G.L. Clark, M.P. Feldman and M.S. Gertler (eds) *The Oxford Handbook of Economic Geography.* Oxford: Oxford University Press. Chapter 15.

Wrigley, N. and Lowe, M. (eds) (2007) Transnational retail, supply networks, and the global economy. *Journal of Economic Geography*, 7 (Special Issue).

WTO (2008) *World Trade Report, 2008.* Geneva: WTO.

WTO (2012) *International Trade Statistics, 2012.* Geneva: WTO.

WTO (2013) *International Trade Statistics, 2013.* Geneva: WTO.

Wu, X. and Perloff, J.M. (2005) China's income distribution, 1985–2001. Institute for Research on Labor and Employment, Working Paper Series, University of California, Berkeley.

Yao, S. (1997) The romance of Asian capitalism: geography, desire and Chinese business. In M.T. Berger and D.A. Borer (eds) *The Rise of East Asia: Critical Visions of the Pacific Century*. London: Routledge. Chapter 9.

Yergin, D. (1991) *The Prize: The Epic Quest for Oil, Money, and Power*. New York: Simon & Schuster.

Yeung, H.W.-c. (1998) The political economy of transnational corporations: a study of the regionalization of Singaporean firms. *Political Geography*, 17: 389–416.

Yeung, H.W.-c. (1999) Regulating investment abroad: the political economy of the regionalization of Singaporean firms. *Antipode*, 31: 245–73.

Yeung, H.W.-c. (2000) The dynamics of Asian business systems in a globalizing era. *Review of International Political Economy*, 7: 399–433.

Yeung, H. W.-c. (2001) Organising regional production networks in South East Asia: implications for production fragmentation, trade and rules of origin. *Journal of Economic Geography*, 1: 299–321.

Yeung, H.W.-c. (2004) *Chinese Capitalism in a Global Era: Towards Hybrid Capitalism*. London: Routledge.

Yeung, H.W.-c. (2006a) Innovating for global competition: Singapore's pathway to high technology development. In B.-A. Lundvall, P. Intarakumnerd and J. Vang (eds) *Asian Innovation Systems in Transition*. Cheltenham: Edward Elgar. pp. 257–92.

Yeung, H.W.-c. (2006b) Understanding Singapore's global reach: outward investment trends, firm-specific motivations and government policies. *East Asian Economic Perspectives*, 17: 40–73.

Yeung, H.W.-c. (2006c) State intervention and neoliberalism in the globalizing world economy: lessons from Singapore's regionalization programme. *Pacific Review*, 13: 133–62.

Yeung, H.W.-c. (2014) Governing the market in a globalizing era: developmental states, global production networks and inter-firm dynamics in East Asia. *Review of International Political Economy*, 21: 70–101.

Yeung, H.W.-c., Poon, J. and Perry, M. (2001) Towards a regional strategy: the role of regional headquarters of foreign firms in Singapore. *Urban Studies*, 38: 157–83.

Yoffie, D.B. and Milner, H.V. (1989) An alternative to free trade or protectionism: why corporations seek strategic trade policy. *California Management Review*, 31: 111–31.

Young, D., Goold, M., Blanc, G., Bühner, R., Collis, D., Eppink, J., Kagono, T. and Seminario, G.J. (2000) *Corporate Headquarters: An International Analysis of their Roles and Staffing*. London: Pearson.

Zanfei, A. (2000) Transnational firms and the changing organization of innovative activities. *Cambridge Journal of Economics*, 24: 515–42.

Zheng, Y. (2004) *Globalization and State Transformation in China*. Cambridge: Cambridge University Press.

Zook, M.A. (2001) Old hierarchies or new networks of centrality: the global geography of the internet content market. *American Behavioral Scientist*, 44: 1679–96.

Zook, M.A. (2005) *The Geography of the Internet Industry*. Oxford: Blackwell.

Zook, M.A. (2007) The geographies of the Internet. *Annual Review of Information Science and Technology*, 40: 53–78.

Zook, M.A. and Shelton, T. (2012) The integration of virtual flows into material movements within the global economy. In P. Hall and M. Hesse (eds) *Cities, Regions and Flows*. London: Routledge. Chapter 3.

INDEX

Key words and terms are in **bold**

About the Author

Peter Dicken, PhD, is Emeritus Professor of Economic Geography in the School of Environment and Development at the University of Manchester, United Kingdom. He has held visiting academic appointments at universities and research institutes in Australia, Canada, China, Hong Kong, Mexico, Singapore, Sweden, and the United States, and lectured in many other countries throughout Europe and Asia. He is an Academician of the Social Sciences, is a recipient of the Victoria Medal of the Royal Geographical Society (with the Institute of British Geographers) and of the Centenary Medal of the Royal Scottish Geographical Society, and holds an Honorary Doctorate from the University of Uppsala, Sweden.